Encyclopedia of

AMERICAN JEWISH HISTORY

Encyclopedia of

AMERICAN JEWISH HISTORY

Volume 1

Stephen H. Norwood and
Eunice G. Pollack, Editors

A B C ☱ C L I O

Santa Barbara, California Denver, Colorado Oxford, United Kingdom

Library of Congress Cataloging-in-Publication Data

Encyclopedia of American Jewish history / Stephen H. Norwood and Eunice G. Pollack, editors.

   p. cm.

   Includes bibliographical references and index.

   ISBN-13: 978-1-85109-638-1 (hard copy : alk. paper)

   ISBN-13: 978-1-85109-643-5 (ebook)

   1. Jews—United States—History—Encyclopedias. 2. Jews—United States—History. I. Norwood, Stephen H. (Stephen Harlan), 1951– II. Pollack, Eunice G.

E184.35.E53   2008

973'.04924--dc22

2007013889

12 11 10 09 08   1 2 3 4 5 6 7 8 9 10

Production Editor: Anna A. Moore
Editorial Assistant: Sara Springer
Production Manager: Don Schmidt
Media Editor: Jason Kniser
Media Resources Coordinator: Ellen Brenna Dougherty
Media Resources Manager: Caroline Price
File Manager: Paula Gerard

ABC-CLIO, Inc.

130 Cremona Drive, P.O. Box 1911

Santa Barbara, California 93116–1911

This book is also available on the World Wide Web as an ebook. Visit http://www.abc-clio.com for details.

This book is printed on acid-free paper. ∞

Manufactured in the United States of America

To all our Bobbes *and* Zaydes

The Tenenbaum family, ca. 1917. Lower East Side. All but the son were born in Polish Galicia. From left to right: Jennie, Mendel, Sarah, Moshe. (Eunice G. Pollack)

Contents

VOLUME 2

18
American Jews in Sports

20
American Jewish Literary Critics

19
American Jewish Novelists, Essayists, Poets, and Playwrights

21
American Jews and Art

22
American Jews and Music

23
American Jews and the Social Sciences

24
American Jews in Science

25
American Jews and Education

26
Jewish History and American Jewish Historians

Preface

The *Encyclopedia of American Jewish History* records and analyzes the American Jewish experience from its beginnings in the mid-seventeenth century to the present. It examines the encounters with, and impact on, America of successive waves of Jewish immigrants and their descendants, including Sephardim, Ashkenazim, Holocaust survivors, Soviet Jews, and Mizrahim.

The *Encyclopedia* considers American Jews both as a religious and an ethnic group. Articles trace the continuity and the changes that Judaism underwent in America, covering all the major branches and religious movements: Orthodox, Reform, Conservative, Hasidic, Reconstructionist. Authors explore the identities Jews forged in America. Reflecting Jews' varying degrees and rates of acculturation and assimilation, these identities are arrayed along a wide continuum.

Several articles provide overviews of the transformation of the Jewish ethnic community in America. They analyze demographic patterns, occupational structures, and social and economic mobility, tracing changes over time. Authors assess what was unique about the American Jewish experience. Other articles analyze American Jews' voting behavior, political alignments, and general involvement in public affairs.

The *Encyclopedia* examines a multiplicity of Jewish communities in America. These range from small settlements in early colonial cities to large, heavily Jewish neighborhoods in major late nineteenth- and twentieth-century metropolises, to concentrations in post–World War II suburbia. Authors assess what was distinctive about Jewish life in regions such as the South and the West, as well as in small towns and agricultural communities.

Although American historians and textbooks have generally marginalized and even ignored the Jewish experience, Jews have profoundly influenced American society. The *Encyclopedia* demonstrates that, despite the numerous barriers confronting them, Jews significantly shaped American culture. Jews have had a major impact on American literature, theater, film, and television. For significant periods they dominated comedy, and were of critical importance in the comic strip and comic book industries. Superman, Batman, and Spider-Man were Jewish creations. There were periods when Jews were heavily overrepresented in important sports, notably boxing and basketball, and in sportswriting. Their imprint on American art and music has been far-reaching.

Although Jews long encountered severe restrictions in American academia, their impact on many disciplines is striking. The *Encyclopedia* explores the Jewish role in such fields as psychoanalysis and psychology; the physical sciences and economics, in which American Jewish Nobelists have figured prominently; anthropology and sociology, and even African American history. Articles consider such social scientists as Franz Boas and Horace

Kallen, who pioneered in configuring a multicultural American identity.

Jews have been especially prominent in the American labor movement and in some sectors of American business, including department stores. Many Jews, such as Jacob Schiff and Julius Rosenwald, ranked among the nation's leading philanthropists. Many articles explore how Jewish men and women built thriving trade unions from the ground up, sparked some of the most important strikes and organizing campaigns in American history, and led national labor bodies, like the American Federation of Labor and the National Women's Trade Union League.

Jews were critical in molding important American political and social movements. These ranged from various forms of socialism on the Left to neoconservatism on the Right, all of which the *Encyclopedia* details. Jews played very significant roles in the twentieth-century civil rights movement, as frontline activists, advisors, lawyers, and financial supporters. Martin Luther King Jr. credited Jews with a massive contribution to the struggle for black advancement. Jewish women played decisive parts in initiating and leading the American feminist movement that resurfaced in the 1960s and 1970s.

As a minority, Jews have had complex and extensive relations with other religious and ethnic groups in America. Articles assess the nature, extent, and limitations of intergroup cooperation. The *Encyclopedia* examines the Christian majority's attitudes toward Judaism and treatment of Jews from the colonial period to the present. American Jews have been at the center of efforts to expand religious and civil liberties and to strengthen and maintain the separation between church and state. The work traces the relations between Jewish and Muslim associations in the United States, a subject of increasing importance. Several articles chronicle Jews' extensive contacts with African Americans, illuminating the significant commonalities and differences in the groups' experiences. Authors address black–Jewish cooperation as well as tensions between the groups, including the Crown Heights riot. Other essays highlight American Jewish social scientists' pioneering work on cultural diversity, recognizing America as the dynamic product of multiple ethnic influences.

Although often overlooked, the contribution of Jews to America's military endeavors has been significant. Articles detail Jews' participation in wartime service, often at rates higher than their percentages in the American population. Authors address antisemitism in the U.S. armed forces and Jews' efforts to combat it. Particular attention is devoted to Jews' experience in the Civil War, Spanish-American War, World War I, the Spanish Civil War, World War II, and the Jewish veterans' organizations.

The *Encyclopedia* examines the wide range of Jewish women's activities in America, including their experience in, and impact on, religious life inside and outside the synagogue and temple. Several authors address the unprecedented expansion of Jewish women's roles in Judaism in recent decades. Significant attention is also given to Jewish women's very prominent role in the American labor movement, with articles profiling several leaders and activists. Essays explore the roles of Jewish women entertainers in Yiddish theater, on Broadway, in film, and on television. Authors discuss American Jewish women writers, poets, and artists. Articles assess Jewish women's major impact on the shaping of women's sport in America.

Antisemitism, while less virulent than in Europe and the Middle East, significantly constricted Jews' lives in America. Jews encountered Christian theological antisemitism and discrimination from the time of their first arrival in North America in 1654. Throughout the *Encyclopedia,* authors assess the changes in severity and the impact of antisemitic prejudice, examining the roles of churches, federal, state, and local government, corporate business, higher education, social organizations, and other institutions. One author underscores the antisemitism of many of America's eminent literary figures, a subject often accorded little attention in works about them.

Particularly intense outbreaks of antisemitism receive close scrutiny, such as the Leo Frank case, the waves of physical assaults on Jews during World War II in Boston and New York, and the 1991 Crown Heights riot. Attention is also given to such antisemitic episodes as General Ulysses S. Grant's General Order No. 11 during the Civil War. Several articles analyze twentieth-century antisemitic movements, including those stimulated by Henry Ford's concerted campaign against the Jews, Coughlinism and the Christian Front, and post-1960 right-wing extremist groups, like the Liberty Lobby, Holocaust deniers, and Christian Identity. Other articles focus on various strains of African American antisemitism, including that of the Nation of Islam, as well as Muslim antisemitism.

Authors explore the impact of the Holocaust on American society and on American Jews. One article analyzes the causes of the U.S. government's limited response to the Nazis' annihilation of Europe's Jews. Others concentrate on literary and artistic attempts to grapple with the horrors and implications of the Holocaust, a genocide unprecedented in history. The U.S. Holocaust Memorial Museum, embodying a commitment to educate about the Shoah and to preserve the memory of the lives destroyed, also receives attention. One author focuses on the responses to Holocaust survivors who settled in America and on the experiences of their children.

American Jews were significant in the development of Zionism. Articles examine the origin and growth of the American Zionist movement and its relations with European Zionism, exploring the debates and divisions over strategies and goals. Attention is given to prominent Zionist leaders and activists in America, such as Louis Brandeis, Golda Meir (Meyerson), and Marie Syrkin.

American Jews have established numerous national organizations that address and express the needs of the Jewish community, defending the rights of Jews and combating antisemitism and other forms of prejudice and discrimination. The *Encyclopedia* traces the formation and evolution of many of these groups, and assesses their impact on American society and Jewish life. The organizations considered include the American Jewish Committee, the American Jewish Congress, the Anti-Defamation League, the Simon Wiesenthal Center, the Jewish War Veterans, the Workmen's Circle, and the Jewish Labor Committee.

The efforts of the American Jewish community to shape and sustain American Jewish identity found expression in Jewish education and journalism. Articles assess all levels and forms of Jewish education, covering the great variety of Jewish schools, including yeshivas, Talmud Torahs, day schools, Sunday schools, summer camps, seminaries for the training of Jewish teachers, and Jewish studies in universities. Authors explore the rich and diverse heritage of Jewish journalism, examining the proliferation of both Yiddish- and English-language newspapers in America. Jews have established major archival collections in the United States to preserve the record of Jewish life and culture in both pre-Holocaust Europe and America. The *Encyclopedia* contains articles on major Jewish archives in this country and on the scholars who first established the field of American Jewish history.

In formulating this *Encyclopedia,* we sought to provide a resource readily accessible to many audiences: to scholars across the humanities, the arts, and social sciences; to students and faculty in colleges, universities, and high schools; and to the general public. Articles both chronicle and analyze the American Jewish experience. In addition to offering a wealth of information, essays develop themes that give shape to American Jewish history, culture, community, and individual lives. The *Encyclopedia* brings together in one place multiple perspectives on the American Jewish experience, presented by eminent scholars in a wide range of fields, from the United States, Israel, England, and Canada.

Eunice G. Pollack
Stephen H. Norwood

Maps

By Sir Martin Gilbert

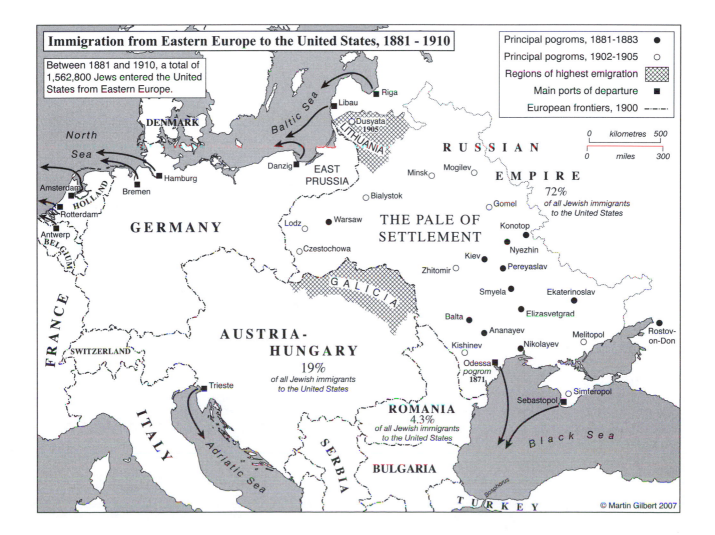

Immigration from Eastern Europe to the United States, 1881 - 1910

Between 1881 and 1910, a total of 1,562,800 Jews entered the United States from Eastern Europe.

Principal pogroms, 1881-1883 ●
Principal pogroms, 1902-1905 ○
Regions of highest emigration ▨
Main ports of departure ■
European frontiers, 1900 —·—·—

0 kilometres 500
0 miles 300

RUSSIAN EMPIRE

72% of all Jewish immigrants to the United States

THE PALE OF SETTLEMENT

DENMARK
North Sea
Baltic Sea
Riga
Libau
Dusyata 1905
LITHUANIA
Danzig
EAST PRUSSIA
Hamburg
Bremen
Amsterdam
HOLLAND
Rotterdam
Antwerp
BELGIUM
GERMANY
Minsk
Mogilev
Bialystok
Gomel
Lodz
Warsaw
Konotop
Czestochowa
Nyezhin
Kiev
Pereyaslav
Zhitomir
FRANCE
SWITZERLAND
GALICIA
Smyela
Ekaterinoslav
Balta
Elizasvetgrad
Ananayev
Melitopol
Rostov-on-Don
AUSTRIA-HUNGARY
19% of all Jewish immigrants to the United States
Kishinev
Nikolayev
Simferopol
Odessa pogrom 1871
Sebastopol
Trieste
ITALY
Adriatic Sea
ROMANIA
4.3% of all Jewish immigrants to the United States
SERBIA
Black Sea
BULGARIA
Bosphorus
TURKEY

© Martin Gilbert 2007

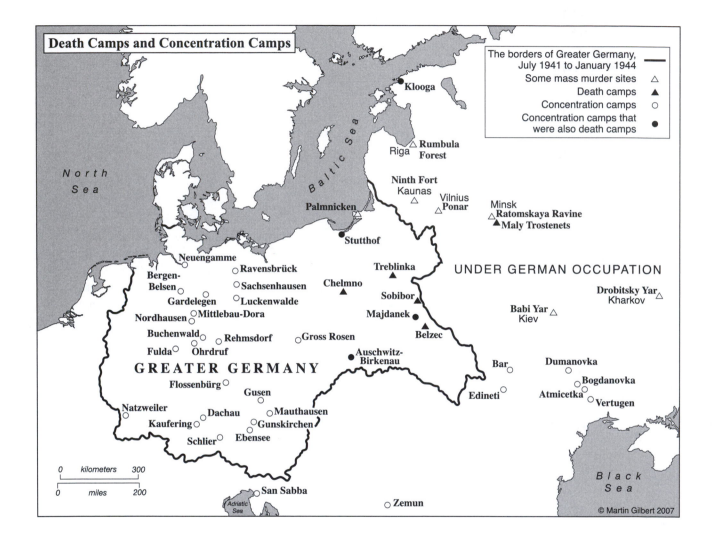

Death Camps and Concentration Camps

The borders of Greater Germany,
July 1941 to January 1944 ——
Some mass murder sites △
Death camps ▲
Concentration camps ○
Concentration camps that
were also death camps ●

North Sea

Baltic Sea

Klooga ●

Riga Rumbula △
Forest

Ninth Fort △
Kaunas
Vilnius △
Ponar

Minsk
△ Ratomskaya Ravine
▲ Maly Trostenets

Palmnicken △

Stutthof ●

UNDER GERMAN OCCUPATION

Neuengamme ○
Ravensbrück ○
Treblinka ▲

Bergen-
Belsen ○
Sachsenhausen ○
Chelmno ▲
Sobibor ▲

Drobitsky Yar △
Kharkov

Gardelegen ○
Luckenwalde ○
Majdanek ●

Babi Yar △
Kiev

Nordhausen ○
Mittlebau-Dora ○
Belzec ▲

Buchenwald ○
Rehmsdorf ○
Gross Rosen ○

Fulda ○
Ohrdruf ○
Auschwitz-
Birkenau ●

Bar ○
Dumanovka ○

GREATER GERMANY
Edineti ○
Bogdanovka ○
Atmicetka ○
Vertugen ○

Flossenbürg ○
Gusen ○

Natzweiler ○
Dachau ○
Mauthausen ○

Kaufering ○
Gunskirchen ○

Schlier ○
Ebensee ○

Black Sea

0 kilometers 300
0 miles 200

San Sabba ●

Adriatic Sea

Zemun ○

© Martin Gilbert 2007

Jews Murdered Between 1 September 1939 and 7 May 1945

The German Reich in 1937

International Frontiers in 1937 (Hungary in 1940)

line of furthest German advance 1942

FINLAND 11

NORWAY 728

SWEDEN *neutral*

ESTONIA 1,000

LATVIA 80,000

North Sea

Baltic Sea

Leningrad

WHITE RUSSIA (BYELORUSSIA)

WESTERN RUSSIA

DENMARK 77

MEMEL 8,000

LITHUANIA 135,000

BRITAIN

HOLLAND 106,000

EAST PRUSSIA

BELGIUM 24,387

FREE CITY OF DANZIG 1,000

POLAND 3,000,000

VOLHYNIA

SOVIET UNION 1,000,000

GERMANY 160,000

English Channel

PODOLIA

GALICIA

RUTHENIA

BUKOVINA 124,632

BESSARABIA 200,000

UKRAINE

LUXEMBOURG 700

CZECHOSLOVAKIA 217,000

60,000

FRANCE 83,000

AUSTRIA 65,000

HUNGARY 254,000

NORTHERN TRANSYLVANIA 105,000

CRIMEA

SWITZERLAND *neutral*

ROMANIA 40,000

Black Sea

VICHY FRANCE

YUGOSLAVIA 60,000

BULGARIA 4,221

7,122

T U R K E Y *neutral*

ITALY 8,000

Adriatic Sea

MACE-DONIA

THRACE

SPAIN *neutral*

Allied front line October 1943

ALBANIA 200

Aegean Sea

KOS 120

RHODES 1,700

Mediterranean Sea

GREECE 65,000

CRETE 260

0 kilometers 400

0 miles 250

The black rectangles show the estimated number of Jews murdered between the German invasion of Poland on 1 September 1939 and the unconditional surrender of Germany on 7 May 1945

LIBYA 562

ITALIAN NORTH AFRICA

© Martin Gilbert 2007

Encyclopedia of

AMERICAN JEWISH HISTORY

Immigration and Settlement

Sephardic Jews in America

The first Jewish settlers in what is today the United States were Sephardim of primarily Portuguese origin, many of them New Christian refugees of the Inquisition. Though Ashkenazim outnumbered them by the 1720s, Sephardim continued to exercise religious and institutional hegemony in the general Jewish community until the 1840s. Their dwindling population was replenished in the 1880s by primarily Ladino-speaking Sephardim from the crumbling Ottoman Empire, mostly (Judeo-)Arabic-speaking Mizrahim, and (Judeo-)Greek-speaking Romaniote Jews, numbering 30,000–60,000 in all. Tens of thousands of Jews from Arab and Muslim lands, speaking mostly (Judeo-)Arabic and (Judeo-)Farsi, arrived as refugees after the founding of the State of Israel. Since the 1980s, Catholic Hispanics of the American Southwest have emerged from hiding to assert their crypto-Jewish origins, and many have joined the organized Jewish community.

Currently representing some 3 percent of the U.S. Jewish population, Sephardi, Mizrahi, and Romaniote Jews attest to the diversity of the Jewish people, overlapping culturally and linguistically with other ethnic groups that do not commonly interact with American Jews. Mizrahi Jews are native to the Maghreb and western and central Asia, while the Romaniote are indigenous to Byzantium, or the eastern Roman Empire. Although, strictly speaking,

Sephardim are Jews who trace their ancestry to what are today Spain and Portugal—*Sefarad* was the medieval Hebrew word for the Iberian Peninsula—in modern times *Sephardic* has come to function as an umbrella term for all non-Ashkenazic Jews. Indeed, some attribute the relatively recent and now widespread adoption by Arab and Persian Jews of the term *Sephardi* to the "aristocratic cachet" of a Hispanic origin, "more desirable than a connection to Moslem culture" (Elkin 1988).

Spoken Judeo-Arabic varied widely depending on dialect and was sometimes unintelligible to gentile neighbors; the written language was completely unintelligible to most outsiders because it was written in Hebrew letters. Twentieth-century Judeo-Arabic, now declining as a spoken language as rapidly as Ladino, includes elements of classical Arabic, Hebrew, and Aramaic. Judeo-Greek (sometimes called Romaniote or Yevanic) increasingly lost its distinctiveness after the influx of Judeo-Iberian refugees in the late fifteenth century. Modern Judeo-Greek, which has almost completely disappeared, is somewhat distinct from the Greek spoken by Christians (including phonetic, intonational, and lexical differences); unlike Judeo-Arabic and Ladino, native speakers of Judeo-Greek did not consider their language distinct from that of their Christian neighbors. Judeo-Farsi dialects were formed from largely extinct local Persian dialects and are mutually unintelligible, with relatively few additions from

Hebrew and Aramaic (in comparison to European Jewish languages). Iranian Jews also cultivated a jargon, combining Persian or a local dialect with a large number of Hebrew and Aramaic loan words, that permitted them to secretly communicate in the presence of non-Jews.

As a distinct subethnic group in the United States, Jewish descendants of Spain and Portugal gained popular exposure in the early 1970s with the publication of Stephen Birmingham's best-selling book, *The Grandees*. This popular history, though laden with distortions and factual errors and criticized for its gossipy nature, succeeded "in making the public aware of the existence of Sephardim." As one reviewer remarked, *The Grandees* "created a stir not only among Jews in general but among many of those of the Christian community who perhaps had not even heard in all their lives the word Sephardic." Birmingham chronicles the history of a people who envisioned themselves "an elite, the nobility of Jewry, with the longest, richest, most romantic history" (Ben-Ur 1998).

The Grandees of Birmingham's account were descendants of Iberian Jews, many of them refugees of the Spanish and Portuguese Inquisitions, whose mass migration to North America via Western Europe, the Caribbean, and South America began in the mid-seventeenth century. The first among them—twenty-three men, women, and children who arrived by mishap in Nieuw Amsterdam (present-day New York) after the Portuguese recapture of Recife, Brazil, in 1654—are considered the first Jews to settle in what is today the United States. Among the illustrious successors of the seventeenth-century arrivals are Judah Touro (1775–1854), merchant and philanthropist, and his father, Isaac, for whom the Touro Synagogue in Newport, Rhode Island, is named; Mordecai Manuel Noah (1785–1851), politician, journalist, and playwright; Emma Lazarus (1849–1887), whose verses are inscribed on the Statue of Liberty; Annie Nathan Meyer (1867–1951), a founder of Barnard College; and U.S. Supreme Court justice Benjamin Nathan Cardozo (1870–1938). The public prominence of American Sephardim, their dramatic history of forced conversion to Christianity, Inquisitorial persecution, and subsequent return to professing Judaism, as well as their legendary noble descent (part of what Ismar Schorsch has called the "myth of Sephardi supremacy"), are what led Birmingham to nickname these acculturated Jews the Grandees.

As prominent as they eventually became in economic, literary, political, and civic affairs, Sephardic Jews also had a decisive and enduring impact on the development of the American Jewish community. Until 1802, all Jewish houses of worship were founded by Sephardim and followed the Judeo-Iberian rite, distinctive for its stately decorum, occasional use of Spanish and Portuguese, vernacular sermons, western Sephardi cantillation, and expurgation of kabbalistic liturgy. The most distinguished of these, New York's Congregation Shearith Israel (Remnant of Israel, 1655), was later joined by Savannah's Mikveh Israel (1735), Philadelphia's Mikveh Israel (Hope of Israel, 1740), Charleston's Beth Elohim (1750), Newport's Jeshuat Israel, today known as the Touro Synagogue (Salvation of Israel, 1763), and Richmond's Beth Shalome (House of Peace, 1789).

The synagogue-community developed by the Sephardic Jews, in effect the Jewish communal government responsible for maintaining local Jewish life, was the paradigm that shaped America's Jewish settlements. Thus, until the late eighteenth century, the only Jewish institution in a given community was the local Sephardic synagogue, which provided for the ritual needs of its members and withheld privileges, with varying degrees of success, from religious transgressors (Sarna 2004). The first Jewish school in New York, Yeshibat Minhat Areb, opened by Sephardim in 1731, was reorganized as the Polonies Talmud Torah after the American Revolution and retained its Sephardi rite in its "translation of the Hebrew and the instruction of the service of the synagogue" until at least 1821 (Ben-Ur 1998). The founders of New York's Jewish Theological Seminary of America, eventually associated with the Conservative movement, first met in the 1880s in the elegance of the Spanish and Portuguese synagogue (Congregation Shearith Israel) and counted among themselves a number of Sephardim. Well after the American Revolution and the proliferation of Judeo-Germanic synagogues, a number of Sephardi congregations and institutions were founded in various cities by Ashkenazim accustomed to the rite of their Hispanic coreligionists.

The western Sephardi tradition of the Grandees was also manifest in the language and collective historical memory of a crypto-Jewish past (the major forced conversions of Jews on the Iberian Peninsula occurred in 1391 and 1497). When Haim Isaac Carigal, a native of Hebron, Palestine, visited North American Jews in 1773, he chose to address his Newport audience in "Spanish," interspersed with Hebrew (Chyet 1966). Many Sephardim treasured heroic tales of escape from Iberia, among them Zipporah Nunes (1714–1799), great-grandmother of Mordecai Noah, who transmitted a harrowing account of her family's flight from the clutches of the Portuguese Inquisition in the early 1700s.

Travelers' descriptions, memoirs, letters, and genealogies suggest a community in an advanced stage of cultural integration with white Protestant society. Life in an environment that stressed consent over descent (i.e., an individual's choice over the constraints of tradition) and whose ruling class accepted Sephardim on some levels as equals facilitated this integration, as did the legacy of a former Christian existence. (The Catholicism of their ancestors, though at odds with Protestantism, gave Sephardim familiarity with Christian concepts and conditioned them for cultural adaptation.) Male members of the short-lived original Jewish community of Savannah, Georgia, first established in 1733, engaged in military service and were permitted to bear arms. A Protestant professor and promoter of conversion noted disdainfully in 1738, "The English, prominent and common alike, take the Jews for their equals. . . . They carouse, play, go for walks with them, and let them take part in all their fun. They even desecrate the Sunday with the Jews, which no Jew would do on his Sabbath to please a Christian" (Plaut 1939). The sons of Dr. Nunes, the community's heroic founding father, occasionally attended church. Malcolm Stern's thorough genealogical research of the 1950s revealed so many Christian branches grafted onto the trunks of colonial Jewish families (some 40,000 individuals) that it made sense to title the first edition of his book *Americans of Jewish Descent*. The acculturation of colonial Sephardim throughout the North American colonies paralleled similar patterns among contemporaneous Ashkenazim. Both groups, aspiring to middle-class status, quickly learned to emulate Christian ideals. To act respectably was to adopt the mores of Protestant, white, middle-class society.

The Sephardic population was always small relative to the gentile and was outnumbered by the burgeoning Central European Ashkenazi community by the third decade of the eighteenth century. New York City's Jewish population in 1810 numbered 300–400 Jews, 70–80 of those being unmarried male members of Congregation Shearith Israel. Acculturation and marriage with both gentiles and Ashkenazim weakened the distinctive traits of Sephardic Jews. By the close of the eighteenth century, Portuguese had com-

pletely disappeared as a spoken language and Spanish had nearly done so. Judge Benjamin N. Cardozo confessed in a 1937 letter that "[s]o far as my family is concerned it has no cultural traditions with reference to the survival of Spanish or with reference to its Spanish or Portuguese origin" (Benardete 1982).

Yet, largely due to its enduring religious institutions, the distinct Judeo-Iberian ethos (with its historical consciousness and sense of cultural refinement) was never completely abandoned. Mair José Benardete noted that, although Western Sephardim (also known as old Sephardim) may have lost their "Hispanic culture," they have "endeavored to maintain [their Sephardic] being through the substratum, that is, the Jewish religion" (Benardete 1982). Solomon Solis Cohen, addressing the congregation in 1903, with a derisive nod at the Reform movement noted that the remnant of Sefarad in America had "withstood the rising tide of innovation" by refusing to allow modernizing trends to infiltrate their religious ritual: Sephardim "have preserved in the synagogue the olden Jewish forms of worship and of thought" (Ben-Ur 1998).

During their roughly 250-year residence in America, the Grandees had defined what it meant to be a Sephardi in the United States. The influx of 30,000–60,000 Jews from the disintegrating Ottoman Empire between 1880 and 1924—representing the largest group of Sephardic Jews ever to immigrate to North America—portended a definitive transformation. The overwhelming majority of the new wave was Eastern Sephardic and spoke Ladino (not Spanish or Portuguese), a language based on early modern Castilian with admixtures of Portuguese, Italian, Hebrew, Greek, Arabic, Aramaic, and French and traditionally written in Hebrew letters. These Jews traced their ancestry to the expulsion of the Jews from Spain in 1492 and the subsequent home the exiles found in the Ottoman Empire, where they resided in relative calm for the next four hundred years.

Economically and educationally disadvantaged, speaking distinct languages, and exhibiting Middle Eastern dress and mores, the masses of Levantine Jews were, in Annie Nathan Meyer's words, "an altogether different sort" of Sephardi (Ben-Ur 1998). As newcomers, Levantine Jews had no American colonial or revolutionary history of which to boast. Not even their Sephardi rite easily united them with the Grandees, for it was distinctly "Oriental," a number of prayers were recited in Ladino, and the liturgical melodies reflected Levantine, not Western, musical traditions. History, too, was a dividing factor. While both Sephardic groups shared a common medieval ancestry on the Iberian Peninsula, their postexilic experiences differed radically. Levantine Jews, by and large, had existed under Muslim dominion in the Ottoman Empire, in contrast to old Sephardim, who generally hailed from Christian lands. Unlike old Sephardim, whose Western communities were founded primarily by former secret Jews, most new Sephardim proudly identified with ancestors who had chosen expulsion over forced conversion.

As the leading American institution to preserve old Sephardic identity and communal cohesiveness, Congregation Shearith Israel stepped forward in 1912 to assist in the reception and integration of the immigrants. The attitude of Western Sephardim toward the new arrivals was complex. On the one hand, the established community accepted the easterners as "our nearest kin," "whose ritual is our own, whose Hebrew accent is our own, whose traditions are our own, and whose ancestry and history are our own" (Ben-Ur 1998). Moreover, the congregation fretted over its dwindling numbers: "As we number the congregation to-day," spiritual leader David de Sola Pool noted, "how many can we count bearing the honored name of Judah, Gomez, Hart, Hays or Seixas—families once so numerous in this synagogue?" (Ben-Ur 1998). The newcomers were regarded as a replenishing and enriching force that gave "promise of an efflorescence of Sephardic life in the metropolis which shall be worthy of the finest pages in the annals of Sephardic Jewish life on this continent" (Ben-Ur 1998).

On the other hand, Congregation Shearith Israel recognized important cultural and ritual differences, such as Middle Eastern–style cantillation and the use of Ladino in liturgy, that it alternately respected and derided as "Oriental." The *Shearith Israel Bulletin* declared that "[t]he religious tradition that these descendants of medieval Spanish Jewry bring with them is of the finest; and our congregation must be foremost in every effort to preserve it" (Ben-Ur 1998). But outside observers and immigrants themselves quickly detected a class-based layer of condescension. *The World* noted that the congregation's volunteer social workers "think them [Eastern Sephardic immigrants] unrelated to the famous Spanish Jews of the Middle Ages, for these latest arrivals are not distinguished intellectually. . . . The women are garment makers in the

poorest shops and the men are most frequently bootblacks" (Ben-Ur 1998).

This haughtiness was also culturally motivated. In 1912, the congregation's sisterhood eagerly sought to Westernize Levantine immigrants by offering piano instruction and language classes to enable the immigrants to replace their Ladino with "the true Spanish-Castilian" (Ben-Ur 1998). Eastern Sephardim were ambivalent about the partnership. While in desperate need of philanthropy and guidance, they preferred to retain their "traditions, their various customs and their ways of conducting things [synagogue services]" (Ben-Ur 1998). On several occasions, their deep offense at the congregation's condescension led to boycotts of synagogue events or outright secession.

The conflicts between Western and Eastern Sephardim repeated earlier patterns within the broader Jewish community. Colonial Sephardim had initially been reluctant to intramarry with Central European Jews, regarding themselves as aristocratic and looking down upon Ashkenazim for their lack of refinement. Ashkenazim, in turn, looked askance at what they considered laxity in Sephardic religious observance. Still, the overriding pattern was Ashkenazic emulation of Sephardim and the unqualified acceptance of Ashkenazim into the Sephardic fold. A repeat performance occurred in the 1880s when Americanized Jews, predominantly of Germanic background, protested the influx of their Eastern coreligionists and regarded their Lower East Side enclave as an alarming mesh of medieval provincialism and political radicalism.

The two Sephardic subgroups, however, did not seriously endanger the reputation of American Jewry. Western Sephardim were a Jewish minority not commonly associated with mainstream Jewish America, in part because outsiders generally did not recognize the family names of both groups—Hendricks, Gomez, Nathan; and Soulam, Testa, Capouya—as Jewish. In addition, gentiles did not identify Levantine Jews physiognomically as Jewish but rather as Christian Greeks, Hispanics, and Italians. Thus, the conflict between Western and Eastern Sephardim was much more internal than the meeting of German Jews with *Ostjuden,* producing a subethnic conversation of which other American Jews were unaware. Western Sephardim did express concern for the image of Sephardim in the eyes of the American public but were more preoccupied with the achievement of public recognition as Jews by the Ashkenazic and non-Jewish communities in America. This concern provided a powerful impetus for the formation and preservation of a unified American Sephardic identity.

Levantine Jews, with their unfamiliar physiognomy, Middle Eastern and Mediterranean tongues, and distinct religious and social customs, baffled their Ashkenazic brethren. In the words of a satirist, "[H]ow could you be a Jew when you looked like an Italian, spoke Spanish, and never saw a matsah ball in your life?" (Ben-Ur 1998). A female contributor to the newspaper *La America* lamented, "[O]ur existence almost until the present day was not recognized even by our coreligionists, the Ashkenazim, some of them taking us for Greeks, others considering us Italians or Turks, but none taking us for Jews" (Ben-Ur 1998). The misunderstanding also came to the attention of the New York municipality. Sometime between 1909 and 1913, a number of Ashkenazic Jews of the Lower East Side protested the presence of the "Turks in our midst" and petitioned Mayor William Jay Gaynor for their removal. Upon learning that these "Turks" were fellow Jews, the Ashkenazim withdrew the petition (Ben-Ur 1998). "Co-ethnic recognition failure," defined as a co-ethnic's denial of a group member's common ethnicity, betrays the parochial self-awareness of Jews who assumed that only "Yiddish and its associated cultural symbols defined Jewish identity" (Ben-Ur 1998, Glazier 1985).

The reports of this experience from a variety of sources—contemporaneous and reminiscent, Jewish and gentile—make it clear that the experience was neither folkloric nor a case of snobbery. Forged of ignorance, it occurred everywhere Eastern Sephardim settled, including Seattle, Indianapolis, Chicago, Los Angeles, and New York. When Ladino newspapers were not available as evidence of Jewishness, an enlightened Ashkenazi leader, typically a rabbi, would undertake to enlighten his flock. Shortly after the arrival of Levantine immigrants, a Reform rabbi of Indianapolis began to visit various Ashkenazi communities and synagogues in the area, affirming that the new arrivals were "real Jews" (Glazier 2000). In Seattle, the spiritual leader of the city's Orthodox Jews took "great pains to explain to his members that the Sephardim were just as Jewish as those of the Ashkenazim . . . and that they too were sons of Israel" (Adatto 1939).

The denial of shared ethnicity and religion was perhaps the most painful and frustrating reaction Levantine Sephardim encountered in their dealings with Ashkenazim, especially when it impeded their employment.

Ladino newspaper editor Moise Gadol lamented that "many of our Turkinos, with tears in their eyes, tell us how, when they present themselves for employment, they are not believed by the Ashkenazim to be Jews, except with very great efforts and with all sorts of explanations" (Ben-Ur 1998).

The Ladino press was an important medium through which Sephardim struggled to achieve recognition as Jews by their fellow Ashkenazim. Between 1910 and 1948, as many as nineteen Judeo-Spanish periodicals appeared in the United States, all but two printed in New York. Moise Gadol's *La America*, dedicated to the adaptation of Levantine Sephardim to the United States, was the first enduring American Ladino tabloid, appearing from 1910 to 1925. In one of the earliest issues, Gadol observed that Turkinos seeking positions in Ashkenazic establishments were often able to convince incredulous employers of their Jewish identity "by showing our tabloid with [its] Hebrew letters," peppered with announcements from the Ashkenazic Jewish press (Ben-Ur 1998).

Addressing a rally of immigrant Sephardi strikers, Gadol proclaimed that, since the appearance of his journal and the 1912 establishment of the Hebrew Sheltering and Immigrant Aid Society's Oriental Bureau, responsible for receiving Eastern Jewish immigrants at Ellis Island, "all Ashkenazim are now clear that you are Jews of the same blood and faith" (Ben-Ur 1998). Other reports from that decade and later contradict his self-congratulatory affirmation. Ashkenazim did not refrain from referring to their coreligionists as gentiles (e.g., "Turks"), an image Eastern Sephardim sometimes internalized. "We used to speak about the Jewish guys, and the Sephardics were different," confessed American-born Ben Cohen, whose ancestors immigrated from Monastir, "really strange" (Glazier 1985 and 2000).

Where education campaigns failed, acculturation to mainstream America, intramarriage, and World War II, which effectively ended the isolation of Jewish subgroups, largely succeeded in breaking down barriers. Eventually, a number of Sephardic congregations accepted Ashkenazi rabbis as their leaders, there being few Eastern Sephardi rabbis. In 1972, Ashkenazi religious leaders headed Ladino-heritage congregations in Los Angeles, Seattle, and Cedarhurst (New York). Nearly all Sephardim who immigrated in the early twentieth century married fellow Sephardim; by the third generation, intramarriage "had become the rule, rather than the exception." Hayyim Cohen found in the early 1970s that 72 percent of second-generation Sephardim had married non-Sephardim, 87 percent of whom were Ashkenazim and 13 percent gentile. The figure jumped to 90 percent in the third and fourth generations (Angel 1973; Cohen 1971/1972).

Arabic-speaking Eastern Jews, generally with no ancestral or cultural bridge connecting them to Western culture, suffered particularly jarring encounters with Ashkenazi coreligionists and gentiles alike. Physiognomy, especially skin color, affected the experience of immigrants as well as their descendants. Dina Dahbany-Miraglia has examined the experiences of Yemeni Jewish immigrants and their children on street corners, in buses, and at social gatherings. When seeking housing in Jewish neighborhoods, these Jews dispatched the "lightest-skinned family member of a friend to do the necessaries." To avoid complicated explanations to passersby initiating fleeting contact, Yemenis often accepted "ascription as black, Hispanic, Italian, American Indian, and East Indian" (Dahbany-Miraglia 1988). Syrian Jews, who, like Balkan and Turkish immigrants, settled largely in New York, faced similar quandaries. "The Ashkenazi Jews . . . thought them 'queer,' and the amazed cry of '*Bist du a Yid?* [Are you a Jew?]' would often greet them as they appeared in a tallit, at a kosher butcher, or at the ritual bath. . . . This gulf of misunderstanding contributed to the Syrians' tendency to withdraw from the general Jewish community" (Sanua 1990).

Such negative experiences contributed to the clannishness of Brooklyn's Syrian American Jews, but fear of acculturation was likely more important. Unlike their Balkan and Turkish brethren, Syrians consistently established their own Jewish day schools and, when public education became mandatory, afterschool programs that maintained their children within the traditional cultural orbit (Sanua 1990, Sutton 1979). Demographers and community members have affirmed the resistance of Syrian Jews to extra-communal marriage with Ashkenazim or gentiles.

The central reason for this success was the presence of a strong rabbinical leadership representing Old Country values and, more importantly, the official acceptance of such values by all Syrian Jewish organizations. The relative rarity of intramarriage and almost nonexistent outmarriage can be traced back to a 1935 decree in Hebrew signed by Syrian rabbis in Bensonhurst (Brooklyn), ratified in 1942 and 1946 and reaffirmed in 1972 and 1984. Joseph

Sutton explained: "Such marriages would not be accepted under any circumstance, even when the non-Jewish partner had converted to Judaism; even if the conversion was not for the purpose of facilitating marriage." A male accepting a gentile or converted spouse would be effectively excommunicated, deprived of religious honors in the synagogue, and forbidden burial in the communal cemetery, his children barred from Syrian schools and rejected as legitimate marriage partners (Sutton 1979 and 1988).

The efficacy of the decree can also be attributed to the geographic ethnic enclaves Syrian Jews have largely maintained. As David Sitton observed in 1962:

> They generally live in one area, known as the Jewish neighbourhoods of Brooklyn, and they still preserve their ancient traditions and customs. This does not apply only to the elderly and the adult generation, for the youth are equally intent upon preserving their religious and cultural ties. Most of them receive a good grounding in religious values at home, learn to pray "*Arvit*" [evening prayers], and participate en masse in Shabbat and holiday services. Their synagogues are filled to capacity on the Sabbath, and the women's section is no less crowded. (Sitton 1985 [1962])

Affluent lay leaders have also been instrumental in shaping the community's ethnoreligious distinctiveness. The community's leader in 1962 was Yitzhak Shalom, a philanthropist who placed special emphasis on religious instruction. He headed the educational institution *Ozar Hatorah* [Torah treasury], which ran a network of schools and *Talmudei Torah* in New York, North Africa, and Iran. Fund-raising efforts among Jews from Arab lands covered the budgets of these schools, as did support from the Joint Distribution Committee. In the 1960s, 90 percent of New York Syrian Jews enrolled their children in *yeshivot* and Talmudei Torah, and by the next decade Syrian Jews were considered "the best organized Sephardi-Eastern Jewish community in the U.S.A." both spiritually and materially (Sitton 1985 [1962]).

The religious denominations that developed in Ashkenazi communities during the first half of the nineteenth century have no parallels in the Sephardi and Mizrahi worlds. This is because Jews outside of Europe were not affected by the challenges of Napoleon's Sanhedrin (which, in exchange for citizenship, challenged French leaders in 1806 to prove that their Jewishness was solely a religion, not an ethnicity or a peoplehood) and the various European emancipation movements. Once the descendants of Sephardi immigrants had become acculturated to American Ashkenazi society, however, a number of congregations adopted various denominations. Most Sephardi and Mizrahi congregations have found that their tenacity to religious traditions best coincides with the values of American Orthodox Judaism. New York's Congregation Shearith Israel, for example, belongs to the Orthodox Union, and its spiritual leader describes it as "a traditional, Orthodox congregation" (Angel 2004). Mizrahi synagogues, which constitute the majority of non-Ashkenazi congregations, are similarly affiliated with the Orthodox Union.

Subsequent waves of Jewish immigration from North Africa and the Middle East, tied directly to the founding of the State of Israel and the intensification of Arab anti-semitism, have further invigorated the Mizrahi community. About 10,000 Jews from Egypt, many of Syrian and Lebanese backgrounds, arrived in the United States after the 1956 and 1967 wars with Israel, most settling in the Syrian Jewish community of Brooklyn. Mizrahi *yordim* (a derogatory term for Israeli expatriates or, in this case, emigrés from Israel to the United States), numbering nearly 30,000 in the 1960s, have added diversity to New York's non-Ashkenazi population. The U.S. Yemeni community—which had nearly vanished—was replenished starting in 1959 with the immigration of 4,000–5,000 newcomers (Sitton 1985 [1962], Dahbany-Miraglia 1987).

Mashadi Jews are representative of the complexity of non-Ashkenazi communities. Mashadi Jews trace their ancestry to Iran, but their distinct history of forced conversion to Islam in the nineteenth century, subsequent return to Judaism, and current subgroup endogamy set them apart from the rest of the Persian Jewish community. Their principal organ, *Megillah* (published by the Mashadi Youth Committee of Great Neck, New York) appears in both English and Farsi, while their religious schools emphasize English, Hebrew, and Zionism. As a whole, Mizrahi Jews exhibit patterns of cultural retention (such as foodways, life-cycle rituals, and endogamy) not found in many far larger Ashkenazi communities and, particularly before the establishment of the State of Israel, nurtured ties to ethnic groups (such as Muslim and Christian Arabs) popularly considered inimical to world Jewry.

The crypto-Jewish phenomenon of the American Southwest gained national notoriety with the airing of a documentary on National Public Radio in 1987. In Santa Fe, New Mexico, Catholics of Hispanic background had come forth with tales of secret Jewish customs preserved through the generations. Some claimed to have been initiated into Judaism during young adulthood, when an older relative whispered, "*Somos Judíos* [We are Jews]." In the enthusiastic aftermath of the program, hundreds purchased recordings, and reports of secret Jews in New Mexico, Texas, Colorado, and Arizona proliferated in the domestic and international press.

The dean of the movement, Stanley Hordes, recorded some of the earliest claims to Hispano-Jewish descent while serving as New Mexico's state historian in the early 1980s. In 1990, he and Rabbi Joshua Stampfer of Portland, Oregon, founded the National Society for Crypto-Judaic Studies, self-described as "the major academic organization conducting and encouraging research on the Crypto-Jews." Struggling to delineate the boundary between the academic and the personal, the society recently resolved to make a clearer distinction between scholarly papers and reflections/life stories, and to professionalize its quarterly newsletter/journal, *Ha-Lapid: The Journal of the Society for Crypto-Judaic Studies* (Ferry and Nathan 2000; http://www.fiu.edu/~lavender/SCJS%20for%20adl%20website%201–13–04.htm).

The secret Jewish customs and oral traditions from the American Southwest have come under scrutiny by historians, folklorists, and journalists, who wonder if this is not a case of mistaken identity. Judith Neulander has discovered that many of the purportedly Jewish customs, such as a game with a spinning top akin to a dreidl, are at best of Ashkenazi (not Sephardi) origin and has called crypto-Jews an "imagined community." She and others suggest that the will to be Jewish stems from racism turned inward. Chicanos/Hispanos strive to disassociate themselves from their Native American ancestry by grasping Jewish identity "as a postmodern marker for ethnic purity" (Ferry and Nathan 2000).

Historian David Gitlitz points to the general extinction of hidden Judaism by the late eighteenth century. In a recent interview, he declared the assumption that Jewish ancestry renders one Jewish a "major misconception" (Ramirez 1999). Thus, Hordes's most recent project—to verify the Jewish ancestry of the claimants—would not prove crypto-Jewish authenticity. Seymour Drescher (2001) has noted that the Inquisition was largely successful in its goals. Even after the wars of independence, secret Jews of Iberian origin (if any survived) did not openly revert to Judaism. Roman Catholicism remained the dominant religion in Spanish- and Portuguese-speaking Latin America, and only in some isolated villages in Portugal and the Americas was crypto-Judaism "rediscovered or reinvented in the late twentieth century" (Drescher 2001). At the other end of the spectrum are academics who accept the self-proclaimed identity and do not seriously address the historicity of oral tradition or the controversy about invented heritage (Jacobs 2000).

Some doubts have sprung up in the organized Jewish community as well. Rabbi Marc Angel of Congregation Shearith Israel, while inspired by the romanticism of the phenomenon, has nonetheless issued a halakhic recommendation that such claimants formally convert to Judaism in order to eliminate all ambiguity (Angel 1994). Conversely, Daniel Bouskila of Sephardic Temple Tifereth Israel in Los Angeles believes that those who seem sincere and have authentic family traditions should be "welcomed back to the community" without conversion (Ramirez 1999). A parallel controversy rages among non-Jewish Hispanics themselves.

Historian Elmer Martínez, director of Albuquerque's Spanish History Museum, is dubious about the historicity of Southwest crypto-Judaism. He notes the absence of "solid documentation," and concluded in the early 1990s, "All we have is rumors and people reading between the lines to try and find it" (Almond 1991). Numerous families in the Southwest have been torn apart by members claiming Jewish descent. Some, echoing Judith Neulander, see this as a fantasy heritage that betrays shame of mestizo ancestry. On the other hand, Hispanos whose families have embraced civil rights activism as well as their own "non-white" phenotypes and ancestry reject Neulander's prestige claim as deeply offensive. With the increase in antisemitism, some ask rhetorically, what could they possibly gain by being Jews?

The secret Jewish revival has raised many legitimate questions that are often stifled beneath accusations that Jews are reluctant to admit descendants of Native Americans and Hispanics into their ranks or that they are Orthodox bigots who lack compassionate tolerance (Angel 1994). The historian cannot, however, dismiss the questions. Nagging inconsistencies include the intense identification with Spain, even as the overwhelming majority of

New Christians, whether Judaizing or not, who immigrated to the Americas were of Portuguese origin. Moreover, the word *judío* (Jew) was applied on the seventeenth- and eighteenth-century Iberian Peninsula to liberals, Freemasons, and others considered politically threatening. And the Southwestern disdain for Catholicism is strikingly similar to Native American hostility toward an imposed European religion. Self-proclaimed crypto-Jews who have been exposed as impostors motivated by eagerness for fame and financial gain have also stimulated scholarly caution. The survival of Jewish identity and heritage in the face of Inquisitorial persecution has been universally authenticated for converso descendants in Belmonte, Portugal (beginning in the first half of the twentieth century), but no study of a contemporary crypto-Jewish community can be complete without a consideration of the media's role in creating and shaping ethnic identity.

Since the early twentieth century, attempts to unite Sephardim in the United States have ranged from focusing on Ladino-speaking organizations to including all non-Ashkenazi Jews under the label *Oriental* or *Sephardic Jewish*. Today, under the umbrella of the American Sephardi Federation, non-Ashkenazim with origins as varied as Yemen, India, Iran, Ethiopia, Morocco, Sudan, and Turkey are organizationally united and collectively refer to themselves as Sephardim. Sephardim, Mizrahim, Romaniote Jews, and other non-Ashkenazi groups, some 3 percent of American Jewry, have at last fulfilled the communal aspiration to organize a minority within a minority. Although often their legacies and destinies never intersected before their arrival on American soil, the identities of different groups have now become tightly entwined.

The overwhelming majority of monographs describing the American Jewish past and present seem largely unaware of non-Ashkenazi communities. Narratives stretching back to colonial times typically include a perfunctory mention of Western Sephardim arriving in 1654 and their subsequent assimilation into majority cultures. Studies focusing on the late nineteenth and twentieth centuries rarely devote even one sentence to Eastern Sephardim. Like the failure of the Sephardim's twentieth-century co-ethnics to recognize them, the deep-seated assumption is that Ashkenazi heritage defines Jewishness. But the contemporary American Jewish community cannot be fully understood without considering its component parts, and the portrait of American Jewish history and society remains incomplete without the integration of non-Ashkenazi Jews.

Aviva Ben-Ur

References and Further Reading

Adatto, Albert. 1939. "Sephardim and the Seattle Sephardic Community." MA thesis, University of Washington.

Almond, Steven. 1991. "Hispanics Rediscover Jewish Identity." *New Mexico Magazine* (June): 26–31.

Angel, Hayyim J., ed. 1994. *Seeking Good, Speaking Peace: Collected Essays of Rabbi Marc D. Angel.* Hoboken, NJ: Ktav.

Angel, Marc Dwight. 1973. "Sephardim in the United States." *American Jewish Year Book* 73: 77–137.

Angel, Marc Dwight. 2004. *Remnant of Israel: A Portrait of America's First Jewish Congregation.* New York: Riverside Book Company.

Benardete, Mair José. 1982. *Hispanic Culture and Character of the Sephardic Jews.* New York: Sepher-Hermon Press.

Ben-Ur, Aviva. 1998. "Where Diasporas Met: Sephardi and Ashkenazi Jews in the City of New York—A Study in Intra-Ethnic Relations." PhD dissertation, Brandeis University.

Chyet, Stanley. 1966. *A Shavuot Sermon by Rabbi Haim Isaac Carigal, 1773.* Cincinnati, OH: American Jewish Archives.

Cohen, Hayyim. 1971/1972. "Sephardi Jews in the United States: Marriage with Ashkenazim and Non-Jews." *Dispersion and Unity: Journal on Zionism and the Jewish World* 13/14: 151–160.

Dahbany-Miraglia, Dina. 1987. "Yemenite Jewish Immigration and Adaptation to the United States, 1905–1941." In *Crossing the Waters: Arabic-speaking Immigrants to the United States before 1940,* edited by Eric J. Hooglund, 119–131. Washington, DC: Smithsonian Institution Press.

Dahbany-Miraglia, Dina. 1988. "American Yemenite Jews: Interethnic Strategies." In *Persistence and Flexibility: Anthropological Perspectives on the American Jewish Experience,* edited by Walter P. Zenner, 63–78. Albany: State University of New York Press.

Drescher, Seymour. 2001. "Jews and New Christians in the Atlantic Slave Trade." In *The Jews and the Expansion of Europe to the West,* edited by Paolo Bernardini and Norman Fiering, 439–470. New York and Oxford: Berghahn.

Elkin, Judith Laikin. 1988. "Review of Joseph M. Papo, *Sephardim in Twentieth Century America.*" *American Jewish History* 77 (March): 500–503.

Ferry, Barbara, and Debbie Nathan. 2000. "Mistaken Identity? The Case of New Mexico's 'Hidden Jews.'" *Atlantic Monthly* (December): 85–96.

Glazier, Jack. 1985. "The Indianapolis Sephardim: An Essay." *Shofar* 3 (Spring): 27–34.

Glazier, Jack. 2000. "American Sephardim, Memory, and the Representation of European Life." In *Charting Memory: Recalling Medieval Spain,* edited by Stacy N. Beckwith, 294–321. New York and London: Garland.

Jacobs, Janet Liebman. 2000. "The Spiritual Self-in-Relation: Empathy and the Construction of Spirituality among Modern Descendants of the Spanish Crypto-Jews." *Journal for the Scientific Study of Religion* 39 (March): 53–63.

Neulander, Judith. 1994. "Crypto-Jews of the Southwest: An Imagined Community." *Jewish Folklore and Ethnology Review* 16,1: 64–68.

Papo, Joseph M. 1987. *Sephardim in Twentieth-Century America: In Search of Unity.* San Jose, CA: Pelé Yoetz Books/Berkeley, CA: Judah L. Magnes Museum.

Plaut, W. Guenther. 1939. "Two Notes on the History of the Jews in America." *Hebrew Union College Annual* 14: 575–585.

Ramirez, Margaret. 1999. "Renewing a Jewish Heritage." *Los Angeles Times* (September 20): 1, A15.

Rosenberg, Mica. 2003. "Crypto Jews: New Mexican Hispanics Claim a Hidden Jewish Past." *New Voices: National Jewish Student Magazine* (March): 11–13.

Sanua, Marianne. 1990. "From the Pages of the Victory Bulletin: The Syrian Jews of Brooklyn during World War II." *YIVO Annual* 19: 283–330.

Sarna, Jonathan. 2004. *American Judaism: A History.* New Haven, CT, and London: Yale University Press.

Sitton, David. 1985 [1962]. *Sephardi Communities Today.* Jerusalem: Council of Sephardi and Oriental Communities, Jerusalem.

Sollors, Werner. 1986. *Beyond Ethnicity: Consent and Descent in American Culture.* New York: Oxford University Press.

Stern, Malcolm H. 1978. *First American Jewish Families: 600 Genealogies, 1654–1977.* Cincinnati, OH: American Jewish Archives/Waltham, MA: American Jewish Historical Society.

Sutton, Joseph A. D. 1979. *Magic Carpet: Aleppo-in-Flatbush—The Story of a Unique Ethnic Jewish Community.* New York: Thayer-Jacoby.

Sutton, Joseph A. D. 1988. *Aleppo Chronicles: The Story of the Unique Sephardeem of the Ancient Near East—in Their Own Words.* New York: Thayer-Jacoby.

American Jews in the Colonial Period

Few Jews lived in colonial British North America. Ten men, a *minyan,* are required for synagogue services, and for much of the time even the five communities that had emerged by the time of the Revolution failed to muster one. The first Jews arrived in New Amsterdam in the early 1650s, but no evidence of Shearith Israel, the first congregation, exists before the 1680s—although it still holds services today at an uptown location. Newport, Rhode Island, probably had a minyan by the third quarter of the seventeenth century, but by the mid-1790s, its beautiful new synagogue, built in the 1760s, was no longer in use. In Lancaster, Pennsylvania, a community related by blood and commerce to the town's leading merchant, Joseph Simon, had formed a minyan as early as the mid-1740s—before Philadelphia—but had gone out of existence when Simon died at age ninety-two in 1804. Philadelphia formed the still-functioning Mikveh Israel in 1771, whereas the congregation of the same name in Savannah, Georgia, begun in 1733 when forty-two Jews were among the town's earliest settlers, had to be founded three times before it achieved permanence in 1786. Jews lived in Charleston, South Carolina, in the late seventeenth century, but only in 1750 were enough men available to form Beth Elohim. Other Jews, usually merchants, peddlers, or frontier traders, were scattered throughout the colonies. In the Pennsylvania towns of Reading, Easton, Heidelberg, and Allentown, one Jewish family represented the faith in each location. Fewer than the 2,588—less than 0.1 percent of the population—counted in the first federal census of 1790 lived in the thirteen future states on the eve of the Revolution.

The fact that, for all the Jewish communities except Charleston and Savannah, it is unknown exactly when they began to hold religious services points to the precarious and, at first, obscure nature of Jewish collective existence in colonial America. Except for Savannah, the first Jews appear only occasionally in the surviving records. Most were males; yet if they were to remain true to the faith, they could only marry Jews. Consequently, more than 40 percent of traceable colonial Jews did not marry at all, and many of those who did, married and became Christians. Members of elite Jewish families, such as the Franks in New York and the DeLeons in Charleston, turned to England or the West Indies to find Jewish spouses. Indistinguishable in their portraits from gentiles, assimilated into an educated, cosmopolitan, and commercial world, and lacking knowledge of the Hebrew language and traditional literature—the United States only hosted visiting rabbis until the nineteenth century—those who wished to remain Jews clung tenaciously to their faith, insisting on the letter of the law when it came to observing the Sabbath, burying the dead, and defining who was Jewish.

Given the presence of so many single people and converts, Jews were exempt from the population explosion that characterized British North America. With so small a marriage pool of the appropriate religion and class, the mature, late colonial Jewish communities centered around a few extended families: the Franks, the Gratzes, and the Simons in New York, Philadelphia, and Lancaster; the Lopezes and the Riveras in Newport; the Minises and the Sheftalls in Savannah; and the DeLucenas and the DaCostas in Charleston. But when a comparatively large influx of newcomers—largely poor and from Eastern Europe—arrived in the 1760s and 1770s, American Jewry splintered. Although some of the earlier settlers had been ethnic Ashkenazim who hailed from Central Europe and spoke Yiddish, they had married into and followed the religious service of the Sephardim, whose roots lay in Portugal and Spain and who had emigrated to England, Holland, and their West Indies possessions to preserve their religion and their lives. The post–French and Indian War migrants, however, frequently wore beards and caftans and spoke English poorly or not at all, and a fair number proved to be economic burdens on the community. Class and ethnic tensions emerged in America's tiny Jewish communities on the eve of the Revolution, parallelling those in the larger society.

Colonial Jews clung tenaciously not only to their religion; principal characteristics of their communities represent continuities with the Jewish experience in the Netherlands and England. Colonial Jewish merchants were but one branch of worldwide trade networks developed by leading Jews in London and Amsterdam. For instance, Barnard Gratz of Philadelphia first sought his fortune in India. Gratz's Jewish relatives, including the Simons of Lancaster and their commercial agents in the Ohio Valley, represented London's Moses Franks, who supplied much of the British army's North American needs in the French and Indian War and the American Revolution. Franks's father, Jacob, and brother, David, ran the family business in North America. The family of Francis Salvador of South Carolina was among the largest stockholders in the British East India Company. Many New Amsterdam, Rhode Island, and South Carolina Jews came to the mainland from the West Indies.

Elite, wealthy Jews were valued by leaders in both Holland and Britain for their loyalty and large financial contributions to the wars against Catholic France, Spain, Portugal, and (after 1740) Austria. Ordinary folk, especially farmers, encountered Jews as peddlers, merchants, tax farmers, or estate managers (in Eastern Europe), reinforcing the traditional negative stereotype of the exploitative "wandering Jew." In colonial America, too, with few exceptions, imperial authorities and cosmopolitan elites protected Jews; their enemies were typically found among the ranks of the populist, Dissenting (Protestants who did not belong to the Church of England), and more locally oriented farmers and tradesmen. Elite Jews and gentiles mingled especially in the Masons, a worldwide society dedicated to Enlightenment ideals, within which distinctions of rank and religion disappeared as members referred to each other as "brother."

Also as in Europe, colonial Jews were perceived as both a religion and an ethnic group, which contemporary discourse referred to as a nation or race. Jews could change their religion; only with difficulty could they shed their ethnicity. Even people such as John Israel, western Pennsylvania's leading Democratic Republican printer in the early nineteenth century, was subjected to antisemitic attacks, although only one of his grandparents was Jewish. Jews could have changed their names, yet they did not. Even where marriage or conviction caused them to leave the faith, they remained loyal to their ethnic identification, inaugurating a trend still characteristic of many secular Jews.

Although not absent in colonial America, antisemitism was far less virulent than in Europe. With one possible exception, until the nineteenth century no Jew was a martyr to his faith in what became the United States. There were no ghettoes, and no riots occurred against Jews as in London and Barbados. Antisemitic violence instead took the form of desecration of Jewish cemeteries; by 1800, every Jewish cemetery had been attacked at least once. These were deliberate acts of vandalism, not the passing whims of groups of drunks, for, unlike Christian graveyards, which adjoined churches, Jewish cemeteries were located outside settlement boundaries to discourage such actions. Where Jews were attacked in print or in court or were forbidden the vote or the right to hold public office, they and their champions spoke up with at least equal vigor, eliciting attacks for being greedy and unpatriotic. Like every minority group seeking equality in America, Jews had to demonstrate exceptional virtue to obtain what white, Anglo-Saxon males claimed as a birthright. They would do so in the Revolution and the early republic.

In addition to these general patterns, the history of Jews in New Amsterdam/New York, Newport, Charleston, Savannah, and Philadelphia (in order of settlement) varied according to political and economic circumstances and the personalities of the relevant Jews and gentiles. In 1654, twenty-three Jewish refugees arrived in New Amsterdam from Dutch Brazil, having been forced to flee when the latter was reconquered by Portugal. Jews had constituted about a third of the colony's 1,450 white settlers. Although toleration varied in the Netherlands by jurisdiction—cosmopolitan Amsterdam was most liberal, the rural, Calvinist provinces least—the Dutch West India Company, a site of heavy Jewish investment, allowed Jews full religious freedom to develop the rich coastal territory.

Things were different in New Netherland, where Governor Peter Stuyvesant, backed by New Amsterdam's local authorities, was a staunch Calvinist who permitted only the Dutch Reformed church to worship publicly. Nevertheless, the twenty-three 1654 arrivals were not New Amsterdam's first Jews, and with the exception of Asser Levy, they left in short order. In addition to his personal antisemitism, Stuyvesant's main objections to their presence were that they would start a synagogue, thereby providing a precedent for toleration of more threatening groups such as Baptists and Quakers, and that they would be a drain on the colony's slender funds, as they were mostly destitute. Jewish merchants who preceded and followed them were allowed to practice their trades and, after petitioning the Dutch West India Company, to become burghers—fullfledged citizens of the city—and to serve in the militia, instead of being barred from service and at the same time forced to pay a fine.

When the English conquered New Amsterdam in 1664, the proprietor (the Duke of York and future King James II) supported toleration. Still, New York Jews lost almost all their privileges—including the right to engage in retail trade and the right to form a synagogue—with the so-called Charter of Liberties in 1683, coerced from the duke by the colony's Dutch and English merchants who competed with them. The Jews' status remained in flux for the next decade: Sir Edmund Andros's autocratic Dominion of New England, which was instituted in 1685 and included New York, protected them (though no Jews lived at the time in the intolerant Puritan colonies of Massachusetts and Connecticut); Jacob Leisler, who overthrew Andros in 1689, required all inhabitants to swear loyalty oaths to the Protestant religion and again confined the Jews to private worship. It is no wonder that in 1692 the Jews welcomed the new royal governor, who executed Leisler, and remained loyal to the Crown and its supporters into the eighteenth century.

Records list between twenty and thirty Jewish taxpayers in New York in the early eighteenth century. The Jews built their synagogue in the early 1690s on Mill Street and named their congregation Shearith (Remnant of) Israel. Increasing prosperity permitted its replacement in 1730. New York Jews, like those in South Carolina and Georgia and unlike those in Rhode Island and Pennsylvania, were routinely allowed to vote and hold office. Yet the Jewish community itself was severely divided between the Franks faction and the Levy faction, a split springing from animosity between Abigail Levy Franks and her young stepmother, Grace Mears Levy. Abigail had lost a good deal of her inheritance and considered her stepmother personally obnoxious. Abigail's husband, Jacob, was New York's wealthiest merchant; while they educated their children genteelly in the secular way of the upper class, they insisted the children marry within the Jewish faith. Their son, David, married outside the faith, thereby denying them Jewish grandchildren. Their daughter, Phila, defied them, secretly marrying wealthy merchant Oliver Delancey; her parents never spoke to her again. The parents were justly worried that their family line would disappear from the community.

Several instances of antisemitism in midcentury New York can be traced to Delancey. In 1737, the colony's Jews, who had voted and held political office without incident, were disfranchised in a narrow election contested between the Delancey and the Livingston factions. Although they were soon exercising their political rights again, and the credentials of several other groups of voters were questioned in the same election, the Reverend William Smith clinched the case for exclusion by raising the traditional deicide charge against the Jews. In the 1740s, Delancey, a young roustabout despite his family's high status, assaulted his wife's uncle, led a crowd that mocked a Jewish funeral procession by performing Christian rites as the corpse was interred, and broke the windows of a Jewish immigrant's house and threatened to rape his wife. He may also have been involved in the desecration of the Jewish cemetery that prompted Jacob Franks to offer a reward if the perpetrators could be found.

The Levy–Franks quarrels merged into another struggle, between the congregation's established rulers and Ashkenazi newcomers who arrived in the 1750s and 1760s.

Alignments were bewilderingly complicated, but people were expelled from the synagogue for quarreling and physically fighting, and enormous lawsuits were launched by Jews against other Jews for besmirching their reputations. The court cases meant that the Jews relied on Christian magistrates to arbitrate matters they could not resolve themselves. This was, however, exceptional; they resorted to the courts only twice in New York and never elsewhere.

On the eve of the American Revolution, the fifty-odd families of New York Jews were as severely divided among themselves as the province that probably produced the largest percentage of loyalists on the continent. Jewish revolutionary allegiances are maddeningly untraceable to colonial factional alignments, although the community split roughly in half. Paradoxically, the uniquely contentious colonial history of New York Jewry demonstrates just how well they had assimilated into the surrounding culture.

Philadelphia's Jewish community was an offshoot of New York's. In the late 1730s, representatives of the Franks and Levy families arrived (they seem to have worked much better together in the City of Brotherly Love), followed by the brothers Barnard and Michael Gratz from Silesia. The Gratzes intermarried with the family of Joseph Simon, the most prominent merchant in Lancaster. They all prospered during the French and Indian War, sending their agents to accompany the army and serve at frontier posts that included Pittsburgh and Detroit. Pennsylvania Germans, however, accused them of profiteering and of being as predatory as the Indians from whom the Quaker-led government had failed to protect them. By the late 1760s, two rival minyans—one Sephardic, dominated by the elite, and the other Ashkenazic, formed by poor Eastern European newcomers—existed within a community of some twenty-five families, although the division had been temporarily patched up by 1771 when Mikveh Israel built its first synagogue.

Nearly all Pennsylvania Jews were active in the resistance to Britain. Nine of twelve Philadelphia Jewish merchants protested the Stamp Act and supported nonimportation. The Jews were especially incensed because they had invested heavily in the frontier and lost £25,000 of the £86,000 claimed to have been lost by all traders in the French and Indian War and Pontiac's War. Their nearly unanimous support of the Revolution can be explained by the passage of the Quebec Act, which gave the

Ohio Valley to Canada and vanquished their hope of obtaining compensation in the form of frontier lands. Nevertheless, lower-class Philadelphians, along with the Scotch-Irish and German frontier settlers, identified the Jews with the wealthy elite who overthrew the provincial government and wrote the radical Constitution of 1776. There, Jews were still excluded from office, as during the colonial period. Still, Pennsylvania Jews supported the Revolution nearly unanimously in the hope of obtaining political equality, which they finally achieved in 1790.

Newport's Jewish community, like Philadelphia's, suddenly came to public attention in the mid-eighteenth century. But obscure Jews had lived in the tiny colony from its founding in 1636, thanks to the ideas of the founder, Roger Williams. While Williams was intensely antisemitic, in addition to despising most Christians as hypocrites, he believed it was necessary to allow freedom of religion. True Christians would always be a tiny minority, and it was important that the larger body of Christians not pollute the religious purity of that small remnant. A strict separation of church and state would prevent the former from threatening the latter. Thus, Rhode Island tolerated Jews from the beginning, although it did not allow them to vote or hold political office until the nineteenth century, by which time the Jewish community had dissolved.

Rhode Island's Jews are almost impossible to trace individually or communally before the 1750s. Most came from the West Indies, and as early as 1677 they had purchased a burial ground and, it seems, had enough men to hold services. But by 1700, the congregation no longer existed and would not be revived until 1754. From that year until the Revolution, Newport Jews emerged as one of the wealthiest, most cultivated, and most noticed groups in the fast-growing port city. The Jewish population grew from ten families in 1761 to twenty-five in 1773. Nearly all of Newport's Jews ranked among the town's top 10 percent of taxpayers; the wealthiest, Aaron Lopez, paid twice the tax of any other inhabitant. The Reverend Ezra Stiles, congregational minister and future president of Yale College, maintained close friendships with several leading Jews and the six rabbis who visited the town in the hope of securing funds for overseas charities.

Refugees from the Portuguese Inquisition, members of the Lopez family began arriving in the 1750s and intermarried with the established Rodrigues clan. Notable Jewish business ventures included the manufacture of snuff,

soap, potash, and candles and oil from spermaceti obtained from their whaling ships. Newport was also the slave trading capital of British North America, and Lopez and Rivera were two of the town's leading traders—they sent out a dozen voyages and imported about 3,000 slaves in the 1760s and 1770s. Slave trading was, however, only a small part of their business; the vast majority of slaves—about 90 percent—were imported by Newport Christians.

Newport Jews were also active in the cultural institutions Rhode Island built during its age of prosperity. They helped to found and purchased books for the Redwood Library, and Lopez and Rivera contributed the wood to build the college that became Brown University, because it welcomed students regardless of religious affiliation. Most prominently, Newport's Jews built what is now known as the Touro Synagogue between 1759 and 1763. The most architecturally attractive colonial synagogue, acknowledged as the most beautiful building in Newport, the edifice took four years to construct because the town's Jews not only wanted a place to worship but wished to demonstrate their wealth and culture. The synagogue's construction prompted the congregation to change its name from Nephutse Israel (the Scattered of Israel) to Yeshuat Israel (the Salvation of Israel).

Despite their wealth, social prominence, and contributions to the community—or perhaps because of them—Aaron Lopez and other Jews who sought naturalization were denied it by the Rhode Island legislature. Antisemitism was one factor; another was that they were wealthy Newport merchants allied to a political faction opposed by the colony's agricultural majority, for Jews who had served the colony well had been naturalized previously. Lopez was naturalized instead by the Massachusetts Superior Court, headed by Thomas Hutchinson.

Not all of Newport's Jews were among the privileged. Poor immigrants from the West Indies were sent back, and Lopez caught at least two men of color who were trying to pass themselves off as Jews to take advantage of the community's charity and connections. Among those who remained, lawsuits for damaged goods and reputations, although not as frequent as in New York, pointed to similar divisions between rich and poor, Ashkenazi newcomers and established Sephardim, on the eve of the Revolution.

The Revolution was a disaster for Newport Jews, as it was for the town itself. Although they were opposed to trade regulations and signed protests against the Stamp

Act, Newport merchants embarrassed their colleagues in the other port cities by refusing to honor the Non-Importation agreements of the late 1760s and early 1770s. Their exasperated colleagues imposed an embargo on trade with Newport itself to force it into line. Although several of Newport's Jews were patriots, and although Christian loyalists far outnumbered Jewish ones, Newport Jews were specifically blamed, by Bostonians especially and James Otis in particular, for their noncompliance, as they would be for identifying revolutionaries to the British troops who occupied the town from 1776 to 1779. Loyalist Jewish merchant Isaac Hart, who was brutally bayoneted and beaten to death after the British left, may have been the only Jew murdered for his faith as well as his politics in early America. About half of Newport's Jews were active loyalists; several of the rest, including the Lopez and Rivera clans, moved to Leicester, Massachusetts, after having traded with both sides. Lopez's accidental death by drowning when he attempted to return in 1782 symbolized the fate of a city whose Jewish community would soon disappear along with its commercial prosperity.

Written by philosopher John Locke, the Fundamental Constitutions of Carolina, promulgated in 1669, offered full freedom of religion to Jews in addition to heathens and Dissenters. In America's first law against hate speech, the document forbade verbal criticism of any religious group. Jews, who probably came from Barbados, may have lived in South Carolina as early as the 1670s; three merchants joined with sixty French Huguenots in successfully petitioning for citizenship in 1697. Jews served prominently as interpreters and frontier representatives of the royal government. Moses Lindo was chief inspector for indigo and dyes in the colonies. While the Dissenters who dominated the legislature once South Carolina became a royal province limited voting and holding office to Protestants, the law seems not to have been enforced. Francis Salvador, the only wealthy Jew who settled outside of Charleston—he developed lands in the Ninety-Six district on the frontier—was elected to the revolutionary provincial congress in 1775 and became the first Jew to die in combat the following year. South Carolina Jews were nearly all prorevolutionary.

Georgia Jews entered the colony at its very founding. Forty-two arrived in 1733, having evaded the trustees' careful efforts to limit settlers to Christian poor folk and prisoners who would live in a strictly regulated moral community. Constituting one-third of Savannah's population when they landed, the Jews were fortunate to arrive in the midst of an epidemic that their physician, Samuel Nunes Ribiero, ended by using homeopathic remedies he had employed before he was forced to flee Portugal. The helpful Jews were well liked at first, even by Lutheran minister Johann Boltzius and Methodist preacher John Wesley, but their friendliness was mistaken for a sign that they wished to convert to Christianity. When they failed to do so, Dissenting religious sentiment turned against them, although they continued to be favored by the trustees and later by the royal government.

Except for the Sheftall and Minis families, who are still prominent in Savannah today, Savannah's other Jews during the 1730s were Sephardim. The two groups quarreled and held separate services, but in 1740, when war with Spain broke out, all the Sephardim left Georgia, fearing the Spanish Inquisition would kill them. The Sheftalls and the Minises rose to the top of the colonial hierarchy. Abigail Minis (1701–1794) managed a tavern and a plantation, assisted by five daughters who did not marry. Dr. Nunes Ribiero's sons returned, moved to the frontier, and were active in Indian trade and diplomacy.

Latent antisemitism in Georgia came into the open with the arrival of the Reverend Samuel Frink, a militant Anglican from Massachusetts, in the late 1760s. He refused to bury Jews or Dissenters in the Savannah burial grounds, prompting the Sheftall family to open its private cemetery to the community. The provincial council took a leaf from Frink and refused to expand the public graveyard granted to the Jews by the colony's founder, James Oglethorpe. As a result, Mordecai Sheftall emerged as the leader of Savannah's revolutionary committee and joined with every Jew in Georgia except two in supporting the American Revolution.

Newport's Jews were mostly loyalists, and New York's were evenly divided, whereas those of Philadelphia, Charleston, and Savannah supported the American Revolution. In each case, the community's colonial experience explains its allegiance. Newport was an anglicized, prosperous port; the Jews were recent arrivals who had suffered discrimination at the hands of the democratic Rhode Island assembly after having recently left an England that offered them refuge from Portuguese tyranny. New York Jews' factionalism reflected the larger colony's. Pennsylvania Jews were especially aggrieved by the brusque denial of their frontier claims with the Quebec Act and also hoped to obtain full citizenship through fighting for the new nation. Charleston Jews joined that colony's united elite in overwhelmingly supporting the Revolution, whereas Georgia Jews, who might well have straddled the fence as did most of the colony's elite, were alienated by the Reverend Frink's and the provincial council's sudden challenge to their traditional privilege of burying their dead on equal terms with the general community. When tensions between rich and poor and Sephardim and Ashkenazim are added, it becomes clear that America's small Jewish communities endured the major divisions that plagued the midcentury colonies and shaped their revolutionary allegiances.

William Pencak

References and Further Reading

Brilliant, Richard. 1997. *Facing the New World: Jewish Portraits of the Colonial and Federal Era*. Munich, Germany: Prestel.

Chyet, Stanley F. 1970. *Lopez of Newport: Colonial American Merchant Prince*. Detroit: Wayne State University Press.

De Sola Pool, David and Tamara. 1955. *An Old Faith in the New World: Portrait of Shearith Israel, 1654–1954*. New York: Columbia University Press.

Faber, Eli. 1992. *A Time for Planting: The First Fruits 1654–1820*. Baltimore: Johns Hopkins University Press.

Hagy, James William. 1993. *This Happy Land: The Jews of Colonial and Ante-Bellum Charleston*. Tuscaloosa: University of Alabama Press.

Jaher, Frederic Cople. 1993. *A Scapegoat in the New Wilderness: The Origins and Rise of Anti-Semitism in America*. Cambridge, MA: Harvard University Press.

Jaher, Frederic Cople. 2002. *The Jews and the Nation: Revolution, Emancipation, State Formation, and the Liberal Paradigm in America and France*. Princeton, NJ: Princeton University Press.

Karp, Abraham, ed. 1969. *The Jewish Experience in America: I: The Colonial Period*. Waltham, MA: American Jewish Publication Society.

Marcus, Jacob R. 1959. *American Jewry: Documents, Eighteenth Century*. Cincinnati, OH: Hebrew Union College/American Jewish Archives.

Marcus, Jacob R. 1970. *The Colonial American Jew*. 3 vols. Detroit: Wayne State University Press.

Pencak, William. 2005. *Jews and Gentiles in Early America: 1654–1800*. Ann Arbor: University of Michigan Press.

Rubin, Samuel Jacob. 1983. *Third to None: The Saga of Savannah Jewry, 1733–1983*. Savannah, GA: Congregation Mickve Israel.

Snyder, Holly. 2005. *A Sense of Place: Jews, Identity, and Social Status in Colonial British America, 1654–1831*. Philadelphia: University of Pennsylvania Press.

Wolf, Edwin, and Maxwell Whiteman. 1956. *History of the Jews of Philadelphia from Colonial Times to the Age of Jackson*. Philadelphia: American Jewish Publication Society.

American Jews in the Revolutionary and Early National Periods

During the revolutionary and early national periods, American Jewry constituted a tiny proportion of the nation's population. In these years the number of Jews nearly tripled but remained fewer than 1 percent of the American population. Like their later coreligionists, the vast majority lived in the largest cities and proliferated in trade. Their relative acceptance there (compared to Europe) and the scarce religious resources, as well as their numbers, threatened the creedal solidarity of the Jewish enclaves, and this in turn promoted assimilation. Republican and multicultural impulses in the United States also undermined community cohesion. These forces fostered democratization of the synagogue, which weakened orthodoxy and traditional sources of authority. Another manifestation of American republicanism and cultural diversity, initiated during the Revolution and largely completed in the early republic, was the disestablishment of Christian sects and the removal of oaths attesting to the divinity of Christ as a prerequisite for public office. These elements of nation building, American style, enabled Jews to acquire civic equality and allowed Judaism to assume a place in the national civic religion. Nevertheless, antisemitism persisted. Sunday laws, resistance (though ultimately overcome) to political equality for Jews, and negative stereotyping continued to plague American Jewry but, unlike antisemitism in Europe, never seriously threatened to foreclose political rights or constrict economic activity.

Community Profile

In the revolutionary and early national eras, well over a century after its beginnings in New Amsterdam, American Jewry remained tangential, at least numerically. In 1776, fewer than 1,000 Jews—and in 1820, fewer than 2,750—resided in the United States, constituting .03–.04 percent of the total population. New York, Philadelphia, and Charleston, ranked by size of settlement, together contained two-thirds of the Jews in the nation. Unlike their gentile compatriots, who generally settled in rural areas, approximately 90 percent of the Jews were urbanites. Except in the South, the majority of America's Jews were foreign born; about three-quarters immigrated, in decreasing order, from England, Holland, and Germany. Here, too, Jews differed from other Americans, who were mostly native born. They did not resemble their European coreligionists or later generations of American Jews, who lived in ghettos. Jews were dispersed throughout American cities, although they concentrated in some neighborhoods. New York Jews were more concentrated than those in Philadelphia and Charleston. Proximity to the synagogue and occupational clustering motivated their residential convergence (Rosenwaike 1985).

American Jewry consisted of more males than females. About half the population was under twenty; less than one-fifth was over forty. Although the Jewish community was young, it was older than the gentile community. From colonial through early national times, the average number of children per Jewish marriage ranged from 5.1 to 6.4—a high fertility rate, though not as high as the total American birth rate of 7.0 in 1800 and 6.7 in 1820 (Rosenwaike 1985).

Contrary to myth, some of it antisemitic, Jews were not overrepresented among rich city dwellers. Although they appeared on lists of the wealthiest residents of New York, Baltimore, and Richmond, their numbers were in proportion to their percentage of each city's population. A survey of household heads indicated that most Jews in the workforce, whether well off or not, were in retail or wholesale trade, usually as shopkeepers. In New York and Philadelphia, the next most frequent occupation was manufacturing, but not in Charleston, a Southern city. Approximately one-eighth of the family heads were in the professions. This survey may undercount Jews in manual occupations because it derives from heads of households. Boarders (many of them transients or newcomers) and other family members were more likely to be in occupations of lower remuneration and status (Rosenwaike 1985).

Cohesion and Assimilation

Meager in resources as well as in numbers and influence, the Jewish community struggled to achieve minimal cohesion. An ordained rabbi did not serve an American congregation until the 1840s; not until 1814 was a Hebrew Bible printed here, and another nine years passed before a Jewish journal was published in the United States. Unlike Jews elsewhere, those in America usually did not belong to a synagogue and sent their children to non-Jewish schools. Most American congregations depended upon West Indian, British, and Dutch congregations for financial support and theological guidance.

Creedal ignorance and institutional weaknesses combined with demography to deter Judaic integration. Small numbers and the tendency of Jewish settlers to be young, single men—the type least tied to tradition, family, and community, the conventional forgers of religious solidarity—promoted assimilation. As early as 1736, the minutes of Shearith Israel in New York were kept in English, and the Constitution of 1805 directed that services be conducted in English. This reflected an uncertain knowledge of Hebrew in the congregation and its *hazzan* (spiritual leader), Gershom Seixas (Pool and Pool 1955; Elazar, Sarna, Monson 1992). In architecture, as in language, American culture made inroads. Synagogues built in Newport, Rhode Island (1763), and Charleston (1794) derived respectively from the neoclassical Palladian style fashionable in London and the colonies and from a Georgian church.

Cultural assimilation proceeded much faster than in France or Russia, nations with larger, more cohesive Jewish communities. Jews entered Yale's and West Point's first class (1802) long before they matriculated at English and European universities and military schools. They were among the founders of the New York City and Georgia medical societies, masters of Masonic lodges, and members and officers of prestigious professional organizations, social clubs, and cultural societies in Richmond, Philadelphia, Charleston, and other cities (Jaher 1994, Pool and Pool 1955).

American congregations sought to function like their forebears, Old World *kehillot* (local Jewish community organizations). Maintaining communal order and cohesion, however, was more tentative in the United States, where congregations were not corporations vested by civil law and government with disciplinary and other powers. Here, they were just another religious voluntary association, whose leverage came from the will of members. Since Jews in America moved more comfortably in the larger society and did not live and work in ghettos officially administered by kehillot, they did not need the organized

Jewish community for survival or as a buffer between them and the host society. They could, for example, obtain schooling and charity from their local government, whose services were available to residents independent of belief (Faber 1992). Thus, Shearith Israel tithed all Jews in the vicinity but collected only from those willing to pay. Refusers and remitters alike had alternative associations and other identities, which could be assumed without the grievous consequences they triggered in Europe (Elazar, Sarna, and Monson 1992). Choice was also furthered by the presence of more than one congregation—a trend begun in Philadelphia in 1795 (Sarna 1986).

Sectarian diversity and voluntary association, separation of church and state, and Enlightenment influence eroded traditional authority. Unlike its European counterparts, American Jewry had no central organization, grand rabbi, or government participation in appointment of lay or religious officials or in community functions. Democratization of the synagogue reflected the national values of individual liberty, voluntary association, and republicanism, further distancing American Jewry from the mode of authority in European Jewish communities. During the colonial era, the *parnas* (president) and other congregation officials were chosen by an executive board; after independence, by the entire congregation. New bylaws and constitutions provided for a small number of ordinary members to call meetings of the whole to bring up business of their choice. The language of congregational constitutions even echoed that of the country's foundation documents (Marcus 1959, Pool and Pool 1955).

Orthodoxy and religious authority were mutually dependent, and weakening one ensured erosion of the other. Before the Revolution, Shearith Israel ejected violators of dietary laws and the Sabbath from the congregation; afterward, these infractions drew fines or other minor penalties. Jacob Cohen, who defied the Talmudic ban on *Cohanim* (descendants of high priests of ancient Israel) marrying converted Jews, became a member of Mikveh Israel (Philadelphia) and in 1810, its president (Marcus 1951). In colonial times, Shearith Israel used the Hebrew calendar to date its records; in the 1770s, it used Western and Hebrew dates, but by 1800 the Hebrew calendar had been dropped (Grinstein 1945, Jick 1976).

Mikveh Israel's appeal in 1785 to Rabbi Saul Lowenstamm of Amsterdam over a marriage—between the daughter of a *Cohain* and a gentile that had been solemnized as Jewish—reveals the centrifugal forces that threatened American Judaism. The appeal was made to the more established Jewish community in Holland because American Jewry lacked the knowledge and solidarity to handle the disintegrative issue of marrying out. The Philadelphia congregation's plea displays an apprehension of communal endangerment through American assimilative individualism and an awareness of the lack of resources that bolstered cohesion in the Old World. The "matter touches the roots of our faith, particularly in this country where each acts according to his own desire," the petitioners told the Dutch rabbi. "The congregation has no power to discipline or punish anyone, except for the minor punishment of excluding them from the privileges of the synagogue." But "these evil people pay no heed and come to the synagogue, since it is impossible to restrain them for so doing because of the usage of the land" (Karp 1969).

Acculturation, as working on the Sabbath or violating dietary laws, also drew protests from Shearith Israel and Mikveh Israel (Marcus 1959). Some Jews had mixed feelings about adapting to America. "There is no *galut* [diasporic exile and rejection] here [Petersburg, Virginia]," gloated Rebecca Samuel in 1791. "Anyone can do what he wants. There is no rabbi in all of America to excommunicate anyone. This is a blessing here." Samuel subsequently bemoaned the new liberty and amity and the conditions in which it flourished: "Here they cannot become anything else [but gentile], Jewishness is pushed aside here," she now rued. "We have a shohet [ritual slaughterer] here who goes to market and buys *terefah* [nonkosher meat]. . . . We have no Torah scrolls and no *tallit* [prayer shawls] and no synagogue. We do not know what the Sabbath and the holidays are. On the Sabbath all the Jewish shops are open" (Marcus 1959).

Americanization was facilitated by the circumstances of Jewish existence in this country. Typically, and unlike many coreligionists in Europe, American Jews did not live in ghettos, wear traditional Jewish dress, or grow beards and sidelocks. From colonial times onward, gentile observers noted that Jews ate nonkosher food, dressed in European fashion, and shaved regularly (Kalm 1964, Goodman 1969). They anglicized their first and last names. Already marked in the colonial period, this practice considerably antedated French Jewry's adoption of French names, which did not become frequent until the 1860s (Marcus 1989).

Adaptation to America was also manifest in intermarriage, the most radical mode of assimilation. According to one survey, of 699 North American marriages uncovered between 1790 and 1840 involving Jews, 201 wedded gentiles. As exogamous unions were more likely to remain anonymous, such matches were probably undercounted. The non-Jewish spouse converted to Judaism in only 12 of these unions (Stern 1967). A 28.7 percent share of mixed marriages considerably exceeded that in France or Eastern Europe, or in later periods, in the United States (Jaher 2002). One study estimates the intermarriage rate in the first half of the nineteenth century at about 15 percent, with 8 percent of the gentile spouses converting to Judaism (Dimont 1978). The small numbers and dispersion of Jews in America expedited absorption. By the 1750s, the few isolated Jewish families in Connecticut had embraced Christianity. A German mercenary in 1777 reported: "Jews and Christians intermarry without scruple" (Goodman 1969).

Assimilation appeared theologically in a Judaic form of American civic religion. Civic Judaism quickened in the atmosphere of cultural diversity, inclusive nationalism, and freedom of thought—aspects of the national culture inscribed even before the United States became a nation. Unlike European venues for Jews, America had been settled after the religious strife of the Reformation and Counter-Reformation had waned, and no single established Church existed in either the provincial or the early national eras. Moreover, from its founding, the new land had needed settlers to be economically viable and thus was relatively reluctant to exclude religious or ethnic minorities or constrain them occupationally. Hence, American Jews never experienced the sectarian, residential, vocational, and other restrictions that plagued Old World Jewry.

Enlightenment values, revolutionary utopianism, and liberal republican sentiments coalesced with economic needs to foster a unique acceptance of Jews on this side of the Atlantic. In France, the emancipation of Jews in 1791 occasioned prolonged and impassioned debate and was reversed by the Vichy government (1940–1945). By contrast, the permanent conferral of citizenship by Article VI of the U.S. Constitution (" . . . no religious test shall ever be required as a Qualification to any office or public trust under the United States") provoked no such controversy in the Constitutional Convention of 1787, in state ratification conventions, or in the widespread debate over the Consti-

tution (Jaher 2002). Article VI passed after little discussion or dissent, with only North Carolina opposed and Maryland divided (Farrand 1966).

The few wary of excessive religious latitude in the Constitution were barely visible compared to the many who feared an insufficient support of freedom. New York, Massachusetts, Virginia, and several other states ratified the Constitution with recommendations for further protection of individual rights, among them liberty of conscience. Accordingly, Congress passed the Bill of Rights in 1789, and the states ratified these amendments in 1791. "Congress shall make no law respecting an establishment of religion, or prohibiting the free exercise thereof," stated the First Amendment. Once again, the congressional discussion was brief and dispassionate (Levy 1986).

Jews became full citizens of the United States at the time of its creation; political equality was immediate, absolute, and permanent. In the states, by contrast, political rights were only gradually acquired after colonial charters were replaced by state constitutions. Nevertheless, the trend toward religious equality was clear. Rhode Island, New Jersey, Pennsylvania, and Delaware never had an established church in the provincial age; during the Revolution, New York, Virginia, and North Carolina terminated public taxes for sectarian purposes. Disestablishment was completed in South Carolina (1790) and Georgia (1798) after the Northwest Ordinance (1787), the Constitution, and the Bill of Rights affirmed freedom of conscience. Other states (Vermont, 1807; Connecticut, 1818; New Hampshire, 1819; and Massachusetts, 1833) subsequently disestablished religion. No states formed after the United States became a nation funded any creed (Levy 1986).

The other state constitutional impingement on equality for Jews was swearing to belief in Christianity in order to hold government posts. This proviso reflected the historical Western tie between the state and Christianity. Membership in the body of Christ was deemed vital to the spiritual and social health of the commonwealth and therefore a necessary condition of membership in the body politic. While Article VI prohibited such oaths for federal service, many states initially required them for their own governments. This was true even for those with no religious establishments, as in the Pennsylvania, Delaware, and North Carolina Constitutions of 1776 (Thorpe 1909).

The influence of the Virginia Act for Religious Freedom (1786), the Federal Constitution, the Northwest

Ordinance, and the Bill of Rights helped ensure that new states did not require Christian oaths and that older states divested themselves of these tests. Within a decade of the Revolution, Delaware, Pennsylvania, South Carolina, and Vermont rescinded their abjurations, and Georgia did so in 1798. New York and New Jersey never required religious tests. Connecticut (1818), Massachusetts (1821), Maryland (1825), North Carolina (1868), and New Hampshire (1876) later discarded test oaths.

Many supporters of unconditional federal citizenship and, at the same time, religious qualifications for entering state government saw no incompatibility in these stances. Controls they regarded as an aggrandizement of national power were deemed appropriate for state and local governance. Sovereignty divided between state and federal governments was simply another aspect of an American pluralism that favored multiple attachments and tolerated variant institutions and beliefs. As citizens of the nation, Jews were equal to gentiles even when, as citizens of particular states, they may not have received equal rights. Still, equality on the national level accelerated a similar trend for civic parity for Jews in the states.

Unlike in France and the Soviet Union, Jewish emancipation in America occurred without a revolution. The French and Russian upheavals resulted not only in the sudden liberation of Jews—in 1791 and 1917–1918, respectively—but radically transformed the larger societies. The relatively moderate American rebellion, by contrast, generally led to gradual change. This was the case in relation to Jews as well.

The acquisition of *de jure* civic equality for American Jewry was incremental and prolonged (Jaher 1994). In this, America resembled its parent, Great Britain. Jewish political equality was also gradual there, although it started earlier and was completed later than in the United States. The experience of Jews in these countries was distinguished from those of continental Europe by historical contingencies. These nations had greater denominational variety and pluralism. For long periods, many in these nations deemed Catholics the most dangerous religious enemy. British and American Protestantism was also more philosemitic than French Catholicism, German Lutheranism, or the Russian Orthodox Church. America and Great Britain (since the Jews' return in the seventeenth century) enforced no ghettos or legally recognized communities, trade and vocational restrictions, or special tolls and taxes on Jews. And American and British Jews entered their respective national cultures earlier than did Jews on the Continent, with the possible exception of those in Holland. Perhaps more important, the United States and the United Kingdom have historically had weaker *völkish* urges and political tribulations than the other Western countries. Comparatively free of foreign invasions and conquests, insurrections, constitutional crises, and governmental turnovers, their stability is reflected in a sturdier, less threatened national identity (Jaher 2002).

Legal guarantee of Jewish political equality in America derived from the founding fathers' larger conviction about religious freedom and their unprecedented (compared to Western Europe) recognition of Jews. Benjamin Franklin "respected" all religions and opposed the test oath in the Pennsylvania constitution. Thomas Jefferson authored the Virginia Bill for Establishing Religious Freedom, an achievement he wanted etched on his tombstone, and James Madison maneuvered it through the legislature. Alexander Hamilton drafted an act to establish a state university in New York that forbade any religious qualification for its president and faculty; the charter he wrote for Columbia College forbade any creedal exclusion for its president.

America's first four presidents, Federalists and Republicans alike, included Jews in their avowals of religion, freedom, and equality, denounced prejudice against them, sympathized with their historical suffering, and praised their morality. No endorsement was more significant than that of George Washington. The substance and timing of his actions made him a paladin of creedal diversity and the legitimacy of American Jewry. Before various sectarian assemblies, he denounced "spiritual tyranny," proclaimed religious liberty and the moral and civic equality of all religious beliefs, and celebrated America for its dedication to freedom of conscience (Jaher 1994). Replying to encomiums from synagogues in Philadelphia, New York, Charleston, Richmond, Savannah, and Newport, Washington lauded freedom of worship and expressed respect for Jews (Blau and Baron 1963). These communications particularly reinforced the principles he pledged because they were voiced while he was president, and praised contemporary Jews instead of Old Testament Israelites. "[H]appily the government of the United States, which gives to bigotry no sanction, to persecution no assistance, requires only that they who live under its protection should demean themselves as good citizens," responded Washington to the head of the Newport congregation, who had thanked him for visiting the synagogue. Americans "possess alike liberty of conscience and immunities of citizenship." Washington conjoined what in France, Russia, and other nations were confrontations between loyalty to Judaism and to country. In his America, Judaism and patriotism were not contradictory. Believing that creedal communities could harmonize with the national community, the president asserted that "toleration" is no longer "spoken of as if it were the indulgence of one class of people that another enjoyed the exercise of their inherent natural rights." In propounding this higher standard of religious liberty, Washington linked interfaith equality with respect for Jews. "May the children of the stock of Abraham who dwell in this land," he told the Newport congregation, "continue to merit and enjoy the good will of the other inhabitants" (Marcus 1975).

Even more than his rhetoric, Washington's behavior enhanced esteem for Judaism. The president's visit to a synagogue was only the latest in a series of gestures that conveyed respect for Hebraic traditions. When the Continental Congress in 1776 considered designs for the nation's seal, Franklin proposed a representation of Moses dividing the Red Sea while Pharaoh's army drowned in its waters, and Jefferson suggested a portrayal of the Israelites in the wilderness following a cloud by day and a pillar of fire by night (Stokes 1950).

More pointed legitimizations, aimed at contemporary rather than Biblical Jews, occurred at the July 4, 1788, parade in Philadelphia and the presidential inauguration in New York City on April 30, 1789. At the Philadelphia parade, Rabbi Jacob Raphael of Mikveh Israel marched arm in arm with Christian clergymen. Two signers of the Declaration of Independence remarked approvingly that this display of interfaith amity affirmed the new nation's dedication to Article VI and religious freedom. After the parade, Jews ate a kosher meal at a separate table. The entire scene was emblematic of *e pluribus unum,* a core national value. Less than a year later, David S. Franks, scion of an eminent colonial Jewish family, was one of three marshals at the presidential inauguration. Hazzan Seixas walked in the procession beside twelve other clergymen. The early tendency toward civic parity for Judaism was reinforced in 1811 when New York mayor DeWitt Clinton drew up and sent to the state legislature a memorial for a charity school run by Shearith Is-

rael. The legislature granted the Polonies Talmud Torah privileges it previously had conferred upon Catholic and parochial institutions, and the city council made payments retroactive to the school's beginning (Blau and Baron 1963, Karp 1969, Pool and Pool 1955).

America's Jews responded to their acceptance by advancing claims of civic entitlement and incorporating a civic component into their creed. Civic entitlement on an individual or group basis took the form of demands for political equality. In 1776, Newport merchant Moses M. Hays was outraged that the General Assembly of the Province of Rhode Island doubted his commitment to the Continental cause and ordered him to sign a loyalty pledge. While proclaiming support for the war and love for America, Hays refused the oath: "[I] am an Israelite and am not allowed the liberty of a vote or voice in common with the rest of the voters," he told the assembly. "I ask of your House the rights and privileges due other free citizens" (Marcus 1975).

Civic assertiveness also moved the Philadelphia *Kahal* (the community organization of Philadelphia Jewry) in 1783 to protest to the Pennsylvania Council of Censors (an official committee of the state charged with safeguarding the rights of the people) against the Constitution of 1776, which prescribed that members of the general assembly acknowledge the divine inspiration of the New Testament. "[T]his religious test deprives the Jews of the most eminent right of freemen," asserted the "memorialists." As a "stigma on their religion," the petitioners "perceive that for their professed dissent to a doctrine which is inconsistent with their religious sentiments, they should be excluded from the most important and honourable part of the rights of a free citizen" (Marcus 1953).

Nearly a generation later, American Jews still vigorously protested infringements on their citizenship. Although the North Carolina Constitution (1776) required that only Protestants serve in the state government, Jacob Henry, a Jew, was elected to the House of Commons in 1808. His service there showed that, as in colonial times, informal arrangements and a rudimentary bureaucracy enabled Jews to defy legal and constitutional proscriptions. Henry was reelected in 1809, but this time his presence was contested on constitutional grounds. Henry argued that the state constitution guaranteed freedom of conscience in its Declaration of Rights. This "natural and unalienable right to worship Almightly God according to the dictates of their own Conscience" took precedence over the test oath clause (Schappes 1971).

The theological component of Judaic civil religion was expressed in a 1783 resolution of Shearith Israel to New York governor George Clinton. Here a religious voluntary association articulated its civic bond to the state. "[N]one has Manifested a more Zealous Attachment to the Sacred Cause of America, in the late war with Great Britain," the congregation told the governor. "[W]e now look forward with Pleasure to the happy days we expect to enjoy under a [New York] Constitution Wisely framed to preserve the inestimable Blessing of Civilization and Religious Liberty." Shearith Israel assured Clinton: "Taught by our Divine Legislator to Obey our Rulers, and prompted by the Dictates of our own Reason, it will be the Anxious endeavor of the Members of our Congregation to render themselves worthy of these Blessings, by Discharging the Duties of Good Citizens" (Lyons 1920).

Shearith Israel, the foremost congregation in the largest Jewish settlement in the country, was the citadel of civil Judaism. Its leader was the original personification of Judaism sanctified in the nation's civic cult, a process that currently mandates that a rabbi, a minister, and a priest bless important civic occasions. Seixas marched with other clergymen in the 1789 presidential inauguration procession, preached sermons on days officially designated for thanksgiving and prayer, and consulted with ministers of other faiths to plan such events. Thus he forged ties between Jewish and other religious communities, a role acknowledged by his being called "Reverend" and "minister." Seixas even occasionally preached in St. Paul's Episcopal Church and served as a Columbia College regent and trustee (1784–1815). The latter was unprecedented for a Jewish clergyman, and the former had not occurred since medieval disputations (Faber 1992, Jaher 1994, Karp 1975).

Civil Judaism was on display when President John Adams, alarmed at the prospect of conflict with Britain and France, on March 28, 1798, proclaimed a day of fasting, prayer, and national humiliation. Congregations flocked to their houses of worship to listen to sermons entreating God to rescue America. Shearith Israel's members listened intently and probably with pride as their hazzan preached. Many were successful in business and their professions, and among them was a former parnas who was president and a founder of the Anti-Federalist Democratic Society (Karp 1975). Their spiritual leader, Seixas, was respected by the genteel and gentile clergy and the urban elite in general and was the recipient of appropriate honors. He epitomized civil Judaism in a congregation that prided themselves on being citizens as well as Jews.

The leader of Shearith Israel, however, shied away from total assimilation. Although the event was national, his sermon remained Judaic: "Such are the works necessary to be done to procure redemption and salvation, that we may arrive at that glorious epoch, when we shall be taken from among the nations, and gathered out of all countries, and brought unto our own land." Messianic reservation against diaspora absorption surfaced still more starkly when Seixas contemplated the blessing of American citizenship: "It hath pleased God to have established us in this country where we possess every advantage that other citizens of these states enjoy, and which is as much as we could in reason expect in this captivity" (Karp 1975).

A more extreme commitment to the civil Judaism exemplified by Seixas and his congregation came from Charleston, home of the most Americanized antebellum Jewish community (Jaher 1994). On October 15, 1807, Myer Moses, a scion of the city's Jewish mercantile elite, addressed the Hebrew Orphan Society. Moses was its vice president; three years later, he would become a state legislator and, in 1823, commissioner of the city's public schools. The speech epitomizes American Jewry's exhilaration with equal rights. Moses began by saluting "that benign day [July 4, 1776], when man proclaimed and Heaven approved this our country, free and Independent!" He then substituted for the diaspora *mentalité* an American identity. "[F]rom that period must be dated that the Almighty gave to the Jews what had long been promised them, namely a second Jerusalem!" This epiphany prompted a plea to Jehovah to "collect together thy long scattered people of Israel, and let their gathering place be in this land of milk and honey" (Karp 1975). "Next year in Jerusalem" became this and every year in America. Loyalty to a new homeland supplanted hope of return to the Holy Land; the secular, not the sacred, now directed the Jewish mission. Israel was the beginning, but it was also the past; America meant fulfillment and the future.

For much of American Jewry, citizenship took priority over creed, modernity over history, and diaspora patriotism over Judaic messianism. Whether the messianic transpiration was to take place in America or Israel, eschatological expectations were stirred by discovery and settlement of the New World and further inspired by the Revolution and the emergence of the new nation. From the early sixteenth century, European Jewish commentators discerned in that earthly revelation and dispersion a sign of messianic redemption for the Jews. As Jonathan Sarna insightfully notes, many synagogues in the West Indies and North American mainland bore "messianic names:" *Mikveh* (Hope of) Israel; *Shearith* (Remnant of) Israel; *Nidhe* (Dispersed of) Israel; *Jeshuat* (Salvation of) Israel. Whether through religious calculation or natural signs, in 1768, 1769, and 1783 some Jews in North America and Europe believed that the Jewish Messiah was about to come (Bernardini and Fiering 2001).

Antisemitism

To many of America's Jews, the revolutionary and early national epochs were uplifting; to some, even exalting. But dispiriting countercurrents, more pronounced in subsequent eras, challenged these halcyon claims. Securing civic rights and religious parity and significant advances in social respectability, economic equality, and prosperity diminished, but did not dissipate, the specter of antisemitism. Although an ineffectual and unimportant minority, dissidents opposed to Article VI of the federal constitution argued that the moral and political indispensability of a "Christian commonwealth" and "uniformity of religion" necessitated the retention of test oaths. Madison told Jefferson, "One of the objections in New England was that the Constitution by prohibiting religious tests opened a door for Jews [*sic*] Turks and infidels." These arguments were used to retain test oaths—albeit temporarily—in several state constitutions (Jaher 2002).

Several prominent religious figures still harbored prejudices against Jews. Long a critic of Judaism, Massachusetts Baptist leader Isaac Backus applauded the state constitutional provision that kept Jews from becoming commonwealth officials. Another foe of Jews, Henry Melchior Muhlenberg, the most famous German Lutheran pastor of the era, defended the exclusion of Jews from public office in the Pennsylvania constitution as preventive of Christian degradation. John Carroll, the country's first Catholic bishop and archbishop, noted in the 1790s that Jews had "the shadow of Goodness, but [Christians] possess Truth itself. . . ." Liberal, as well as traditional, creeds voiced anti-

Jewish sentiments. The Unitarian Catechism of 1815 accused Jews of persecuting and killing Christ and being punished by God by the destruction of Jerusalem and the death, dispersion, and enslavement of the Hebrews (Jaher 1994).

Institutional disabilities were more important. The greatest controversy over granting Jews full citizenship occurred in Maryland, where the original state constitution (1776) required a pledge of Christian faith for state office holding. To no avail, Maryland Jews appealed to the legislature in 1797 and 1804 for repeal of the oath. A "Jew bill" was initially introduced in 1818 but failed to pass, as did similar legislation in 1822. The test oath was eliminated in 1825. In the election after the 1822 defeat, candidates running against the bill defeated sixteen incumbent supporters, including the main sponsor of repeal. The victor proclaimed that he was running on a "Christian ticket," while his opponent campaigned for a "Jew ticket" (Blau and Baron 1963, Jaher 1994).

Antisemites could be found in both major political parties in the early national period, although they were more influential among the Federalists. Eminent Federalist editors James Rivington and John Fenno identified Jews with Jacobins and Democratic-Republicans (Karp 1963, Jaher 1994). History's classic outsiders, Jews were now cast as America's current subversives.

Revolutionary turmoil and the tensions of founding the new nation intensified traditional Christological antisemitism. In 1784, a Georgia pamphleteer charged that Jews in that state were enemy aliens who entered politics to line their purses. In the same year, a Quaker lawyer argued for a charter for the Bank of Pennsylvania that would lower interest rates and protect Christians from Jewish brokers speculating in money and stocks.

Jews were also often aversive figures in popular culture, caricatured and lampooned as villains in many plays and novels. In the theater, as in *Slaves in Algiers* (1794) and *Trial without Jury* (1815), Jews were presented as sly, greedy Yiddish-speaking peddlers or as exotic, treacherous North African usurers. Novels featured similar characters. Capitalizing on the fascination with Barbary piracy, the anti-hero of *The Algerine Captive* (1797) was a sinister, avaricious, and duplicitous Levantine Jew. The immensely popular *Modern Chivalry* (1792–1815) ridiculed many types, but Jews were invariably presented as grasping, Yiddish-speaking clowns. It also quoted folk maxims, such as "Don't like to be as rich as a Jew" (Jaher 1994).

Political and religious attacks in popular culture led some observers to perceive widespread hostility, or at least contempt, for Jews. Rebecca Samuel Alexander, a Jewish convert to Episcopalianism, claimed in 1791 that respectable New Yorkers and Philadelphians of German stock disliked Jews. Renowned Unitarian minister and social reformer Samuel J. May recalled that "children of my generation were taught" in the early 1800s "to dread if not despise Jews" (Jaher 1994). M. Otto, the French minister to the United States, reported in 1786, "All Christian sects enjoy in America an entire liberty. The Jews have the exercise of their religion only." He concluded that "prejudices are still too strong to enable Jews to enjoy the privileges accorded to all their fellow citizens" (Stokes 1950).

In the next generation, these impressions did not change. A Maryland legislator told that state assembly, "Most of us have been taught from earliest infancy to look upon them [Jews] as a depraved and wicked people." New York's *German Correspondent* reached the same conclusion. In America, "Jews are not generally regarded with a favorable eye, and 'Jew' is an epithet that is frequently uttered in a tone bordering on contempt." The paper declared, "[P]rejudices against the Jews exist here and subject them to inconveniences from which other citizens of the United States are exempt" (Jaher 1994).

Historically, conflicting currents frequently coexist, and affirmations could counter the defamations of Jews. Nor need the condemnation result in hostile behavior, if the individuals also held the American values of diversity and liberty. Although the worst aspects of Jew-hatred never crossed the Atlantic, echoes of European antisemitism reverberated in the new land. Jews were not assaulted, eliminated, or massively boycotted, but they were insulted; they competed politically and commercially but faced obstacles not encountered by white Protestants. Lesser victims of bigotry than African Americans, Indians, and Catholics, Jews also suffered persecution.

Above all Western nations, the United States advanced Jewry's struggle for freedom. Colonial legacies, which facilitated the assumption of full citizenship and differentiated America from Europe, continued after independence. America was the first country that did not have a medieval past that demonized, segregated, banished, and massacred Jews. Here, the early modern denominational conflicts that tore Europe apart reverberated only relatively faintly.

In America, Jews confronted a unique promise and a related challenge. Incorporated for the first time into a national society, they experienced unsurpassed acceptance of their faith as a private belief and a constituent of the civic religion. Secularization and individualism helped Jews gain civic equality but presented adversity as well. Secularism undermined Christianity and Judaism alike, and individualism fragmented Jewry as it did other traditional communities. National consciousness might not be as ancestral or as committed to Christianity as in the Old World, but Anglo-American ethnicity and Protestantism enjoyed priority over the heritage and creeds of other citizens. Old preferences and bigotries still had the potential to marginalize America's Jews, and new liberties might lure them into complete absorption or disruptive individualism.

Frederic Cople Jaher

References and Further Reading

Bernardini, Paolo, and Norman Fiering, eds. 2001. *The Jews and the Expansion of Europe to the West, 1450–1800.* New York and Oxford: Berghahn Books.

Blau, Joseph L., and Salo W. Baron, eds. 1963. *The Jews in the United States, 1790–1840.* 3 vols. New York: Columbia University Press/Philadelphia: Jewish Publication Society of America.

Dimont, Max I. 1978. *The Jews in America: The Roots, History and Destiny of American Jews.* New York: Simon & Schuster.

Elazar, Daniel J., Jonathan D. Sarna, and Rela G. Monson, eds. 1992. *A Double Bond: The Constitutional Documents of American Jewry.* Lanham, MD: University Press of America.

Faber, Eli. 1992. *A Time for Planting: The First Migration 1654–1820.* Baltimore: Johns Hopkins University Press.

Farrand, Max, ed. 1966. *The Records of the Federal Convention of 1787.* New Haven, CT: Yale University Press.

Goodman, Abram Vossen. 1969. "A German Mercenary Observes American Jews During the Revolution." *American Jewish Historical Quarterly* 59 (December): 227.

Grinstein, Hyman. 1945. *The Rise of the Jewish Community of New York: 1654–1860.* Philadelphia: Jewish Publication Society of America.

Jaher, Frederic Cople. 1994. *A Scapegoat in the New Wilderness: The Origins and Rise of Anti-Semitism in America.* Cambridge, MA: Harvard University Press.

Jaher, Frederic Cople. 2002. *The Jews and the Nation: Revolution, Emancipation, State Formation, and the Liberal Paradigm in America and France.* Princeton, NJ: Princeton University Press.

Jick, Leon A. 1976. *The Americanization of the Synagogue, 1820–1870.* Hanover, NH: Brandeis University Press and the University Press of New England.

Kalm, Peter. 1964. *Travels in North America.* New York: Dover.

Karp, Abraham J., ed. 1969. *The Jewish Experience in America: Selected Studies from the Publications of the American Jewish Historical Society*. Waltham, MA: American Jewish Historical Society/New York: Ktav.

Karp, Abraham J., ed. 1975. *Beginnings, Early American Judaica: A Collection of Ten Publications in Facsimile*. Philadelphia: Jewish Publication Society of America.

Levy, Leonard. 1986. *The Establishment Clause: Religion and the First Amendment*. New York: Macmillan.

Lyons, Jacques J., ed. 1913. "The Earliest Extant Minute Book of the Spanish and Portuguese Congregation Shearith Israel in New York." *Publications of the American Jewish Historical Society* 21: 1–82.

Lyons, Jacques J., ed. 1920. "Items Relating to Congregation Shearith Israel, New York." *Publications of the American Jewish Historical Society* 27: 2-34.

Marcus, Jacob Rader. 1951, 1953. *Early American Jewry*. Philadelphia: Jewish Publication Society of America.

Marcus, Jacob Rader, ed. 1959. *American Jewry: Documents—Eighteenth Century*. Cincinnati, OH: Hebrew Union College.

Marcus, Jacob Rader. 1970. *The Colonial American Jew: 1492–1776*. Detroit, MI: Wayne State University Press.

Marcus, Jacob Rader, ed. 1975. *Jews and the American Revolution: A Bicentennial Documentary*. Cincinnati, OH: American Jewish Archives.

Marcus, Jacob Rader. 1989–1993. *United States Jewry: 1776–1985*. 4 vols. Detroit, MI: Wayne State University Press.

Pool, David de Sola, and Tamara de Sola Pool. 1955. *An Old Faith in the New World: Portrait of Shearith Israel 1654–1954*. New York: Columbia University Press.

Rosenwaike, Ira. 1985. *On the Edge of Greatness: A Portrait of American Jewry in the Early National Period*. Cincinnati, OH: American Jewish Archives.

Sarna, Jonathan D., ed. 1986. *The American Jewish Experience*. New York and London: Holmes & Meier.

Schappes, Morris U., ed. 1971. *A Documentary History of Jews in the United States: 1654–1875*. New York: Schocken Books.

Stern, Malcolm H. 1967. "Jewish Marriage and Intermarriage in the Federal Period (1776–1840)." *American Jewish Archives* 19 (November): 24–52.

Stokes, Anson Phelps. 1950. *Church and State in the United States*. 3 vols. New York: Harper.

Thorpe, Francis Newton, ed. 1909. *The Federal and State Constitutions, Colonial Charters, and Other Organic Laws of States, Territories, and Colonies Now or Heretofore Forming the United States of America*. Washington, DC: General Printing Office.

German Jews in America

There have been identifiably German Jews in America for about three hundred years, and Jews of German origin made up a majority of American Jews for nearly half of that time. Arriving during the early history of British North America, they later created the first large Jewish communities in the United States and were the first to bring a Jewish presence into most of the country. They kept coming right up into the second half of the twentieth century, and German Jewish immigrants or their children still make up a distinctive part of the American Jewish population. It can truly be said that German Jews shaped and reshaped in fundamental ways much of the culture and many of the institutions that characterize Jewish America.

Over many centuries, Yiddish-speaking Ashkenazi [i.e., German] Jews, their language based on medieval German, spread out from the Rhineland to the far reaches of Poland-Lithuania. Frequent persecutions and expulsions, as well as the opening of new areas of settlement or the re-opening of old ones, kept the Ashkenazi population mobile and prevented the hardening of regional divisions. Individuals from the remaining Jewish communities of the numerous sovereign German territories (there were more than 200 from 1648–1789 and 39 from 1815–1871) went East to study in the *yeshivas* of Poland-Lithuania, while Jews from the East moved West to fill rabbinical openings or to seek commercial and other opportunities as some German states slowly opened their territories to limited Jewish resettlement.

Only under the influence of the strongly pro-German and anti-Yiddish *Haskalah* (the Jewish Enlightenment) and the opening of German-language public education to Jews in the late eighteenth and early nineteenth centuries did increasing numbers of Jews abandon Yiddish for German and begin the creation of a new Jewish culture that was distinctively German in the modern sense. But even while many German Jews increasingly distinguished themselves from the Yiddish-speaking *Ostjuden* (Eastern Jews) in the nineteenth century, the influence of the Haskalah spread far to the East; "enlightened" Jews in Warsaw, Krakow, and even distant Lemberg (L'vov) in the Ukraine spoke German at home—as did Jews from the many predominantly German-speaking cities and towns across Central Europe, from Prague in Bohemia to Hermannstadt (Sibiu) in Romania—via Brünn (Brno) in Moravia, Pressburg (Bratislava) in Slovakia, and Klausenburg (Cluj) in Transylvania. In mid-nineteenth century Budapest German was so much the language of the Hungarian capital's

German Jews, ca. 1876. (Library of Congress)

Jews that the first Jewish newspaper designed to promote Hungarian nationalism had to be published in German rather than Hungarian. And some German rabbis who were epitomes of the new German Jewish culture went East to promote it in the Russian Empire—such as Bavarian-born Max Lilienthal, who was director of Jewish schools in Riga for several years before he left for America.

At the same time, many poor Jews living in rural areas of the southwestern and northeastern regions of the new German Empire of 1871 continued to speak Yiddish even into the twentieth century, as did their Western counterparts from French-ruled Alsace. Then, too, some Central European Jews Germanized by the Haskalah un-German-ized themselves in the late nineteenth and early twentieth centuries under the influence of rising anti-German nationalism in their homelands.

So the people who can be identified as German Jews cannot be limited to either the speakers of proper German or the boundaries of any particular collection of "German" states. Moreover, in determining whom to include under the rubric *German Jew*, we should not narrow the definition too precisely lest we exclude far too many Jews who need to be considered.

Thousands of Jews from German Central Europe moved west over the course of the seventeenth and eighteenth centuries to take advantage of economic opportunities opening for them in the Netherlands and Britain—and their overseas empires. Some followed Dutch trade links to Dutch and British North America, while others arrived by way of England. There was even a sponsored group migration in 1733, when wealthy Sephardic Jews in London raised money to send sixty-seven of the city's poorest Jews, mostly Germans, to the new British colony of Georgia. These colonists later removed themselves to Charlestown and New York when most of Georgia's residents fled the endangered colony in 1741. By the middle of the eighteenth century, many of the leading Jewish merchants of America were of German origin and corresponded in Yiddish, including the Gratz brothers of Philadelphia, who later outfitted privateers and provided supplies for George Washington's army.

The steady trickle of Ashkenazi migrants who arrived over the course of the eighteenth and early nineteenth centuries was readily absorbed into the existing Sephardic Jewish communities, and not until the nineteenth century would Ashkenazi synagogues be established. Most of these migrants became urban shopkeepers and artisans, although a few became wealthy merchants or plantation owners. But despite the continuing Sephardic ritual of the synagogues, the reality was that by 1750 the majority of American Jews were of German origin. So even though the number of German Jews who came to eighteenth-century America was small—there were only a couple of thousand Jews altogether in the United States at the end of the century (Rosenwaike 1985)—there is a sense in which the "German" era of American Jewish history began almost a century before its usually assigned starting date of 1830.

The thirty years following 1789 opened many opportunities for Jews in the German lands as victorious French revolutionary armies forced many states to demolish their ghetto walls and emancipate their Jews, but the extended warfare also virtually halted emigration from the European continent for a generation. The German nationalist reaction against defeat and French domination encouraged an increasingly strident sentiment directed against Jews, who were represented both as a foreign element and as one that had benefited from German defeat. So even though many German Jews volunteered in the war of liberation against France (seventy-one of whom were awarded Prussia's Iron Cross), most of the German states revoked, limited, or ignored their emancipation laws in the wake of France's defeat. Then came the Hep! Hep! riots of 1819, the worst outbreak of anti-Jewish violence in the German lands since the Middle Ages. While better-off German Jews often responded by redoubling their drive toward assimilation, others turned to migration to America—where the U.S. Constitution promised an equality denied in the German states.

In most of the German lands, strict limitations on the numbers of Jewish marriages combined with limited economic opportunities to provide an even greater incentive to emigrate than did the denial of political rights, and it was the young who led the way. The sons (and then the daughters) of petty traders joined young Jewish artisans denied the right to practice their trades and set off overseas. The retention or renewal of even the most limited political rights was generally accompanied by conscription, providing additional incentive for young men to emigrate—as did a second wave of Hep! Hep! riots in 1832. By the 1840s, a veritable "emigration fever" had set in, and so many young Jews left the villages and small towns of some regions that the viability of Jewish community life there was thrown into question.

Over the course of several decades after 1819, the renewed trickle of German Jewish migration to America increased to a steady flow that grew from the thousands of the 1830s to tens of thousands in the 1840s and 1850s. To some extent, this was part and parcel of the much larger, non-Jewish German migration to the United States, which totaled about 1.5 million by 1860. Not surprisingly, the influence of the German Jewish emigration quickly extended into adjacent areas of former Poland and even Russia, thereby laying the foundations for the massive Eastern European Jewish migration that characterized the end of the century. In some parts of the United States where their numbers were small, these Eastern Europeans were absorbed into the larger German Jewish communities. But where they were numerous enough, they rapidly established their own congregations and communities even before midcentury—an indication of the increasing cultural divisions growing between German-speaking Jews and their Eastern coreligionists.

Unlike the small numbers of their predecessors who lived mostly in a handful of Eastern cities—and also unlike the Eastern European Jews who followed them at the end of the century—the German Jews rapidly fanned out across the United States. By 1860 there were organized Jewish communities in 50 cities, and readers of Jewish publications lived in more than 1,200 different places (Glanz 1972). This dispersion was largely the consequence of the petty trader tradition that so many German Jews brought from their homelands to America and the way in which it met the needs of the rapidly expanding and commercially undeveloped United States.

The scattered residences of the American farming population created a need for retail services that did not require a long, difficult trip to a village or town that might take a full day of traveling. Yankee peddlers from New England provided some of these services early in the century, but they were not numerous enough to meet the rapidly growing demand, and that left a great area of opportunity for newcomers. The Jews of Alsace and southwestern Germany had long specialized in peddling and petty trading, so it was natural for them to continue this in the United States, especially as peddling was a business that required virtually no capital. Traveling peddlers identified promising locations in small towns and burgeoning Western cities, where they then opened stores that soon became the centers of small Jewish communities. Successful store owners brought in relatives from the Old Country or gave goods on credit to newly arrived fellow Jews, who then spread the peddling net even farther.

Joseph Seligman, from the village of Baiersdorf in Bavaria, was one of the earliest such immigrants when he arrived in 1837. He learned about American peddling from a Yankee peddler and soon started bringing over some of his many brothers as he developed his own trade network based on a store he opened in Lancaster, Pennsylvania; he ran the store and maintained the stock while his brothers set out on foot and wagon to peddle dry goods through the countryside. Eventually he relocated the central operation to New York City, the commercial capital of the United States, and his brothers spread out to regional trade centers across the country, where they set up their own trade networks of stores and peddlers. In 1844 Henry Lehman went from Rimpar, Bavaria, to Mobile, Alabama, where he began peddling in style with a wagon rather than a backpack. He, too, founded a family-based trading network built on a number of brothers, and the Lehmans, too, soon found they needed a New York base. After Henry's death, his brother Emanuel took over the family network and established the New York office in 1858. This sort of family-based network was widespread, and it is only the later successes of the Seligmans and Lehmans that made them stand out from their more ordinary contemporaries.

Cincinnati was the commercial center for the farming districts most favored by German immigrants in the first half of the nineteenth century, and it became a major center for the new family trading networks established by German Jews. Linking themselves to national wholesaling operations and credit sources created by other German Jews in New York, they set up regional wholesaling operations in their "Jerusalem on the Ohio" that supplied family and friends who peddled and ran small country stores throughout a wide swath of rural and small-town America between the Appalachian Mountains and the Mississippi, from the Gulf of Mexico to Canada—servicing both German- and English-speaking farmers and small townsfolk. Another such regional center developed out of St. Louis to supply a network of German Jewish traders across the trans-Mississippi and mountain West.

Women were often indispensable to the success, or even the survival, of these businesses. Wives tended the store while their husbands peddled or went for supplies, and sometimes they displayed far more business acumen than their husbands did. Peddlers often gained access to the credit needed to open a store by marrying the sisters or daughters of their suppliers, as when Samuel Rosenwald and his bride were given a store in Peoria as a wedding present from her parents. Marriageable shopkeepers moved to larger cities and even moved up into wholesaling using the same technique. And the owners of successful businesses assured their continued expansion and long-term success by encouraging their daughters to marry bright young men who had demonstrated a good head for business—a quality that might be lacking in their sons.

Most of these peddler and shopkeeper family networks provided the basis for a comfortable, middle-class family existence. Only a few grew rich off this trade, and some failed miserably, as Hasia Diner pointed out (Diner 1992). She attributed the great geographic mobility of German Jewish immigrants as much to business failures as to their successes and recounted the stories of a number of exemplary failures. One was Jacob Philipson, who died flat broke after having been the first successful Jewish merchant in St. Louis. Financially embarrassed Marcus Cohen, on the other hand, had never had any sort of success before he committed suicide in Brooklyn's Greenwood cemetery in 1849.

Some did indeed get rich as they built successful dry goods stores into large-scale wholesale and retail networks—while others turned their shops into department stores. Edward Filene of Boston, Adam Gimbel of New York, and the sons of Lazarus Straus (who parlayed their father's crockery business into the ownership of R. H. Macy & Co.) are just some of the most conspicuous examples of late nineteenth-century department-store magnates whose careers were rooted in their fathers' peddling careers—as was that of Sears, Roebuck & Co. co-owner Julius Rosenwald.

In some cases, retailing was only the first step toward a vastly more lucrative career in finance for some German Jewish peddlers-turned-shopkeepers. A few talented and lucky families were able to build great fortunes upon these small beginnings. Two of the Seligman brothers took a large inventory of goods to San Francisco in 1850 to open a store in the center of the California gold rush. The Seligmans not only sold their inventory at a great profit, they soon found themselves dealing in large quantities of gold with their New York–based brothers as agents. By the middle of the 1850s, the New York Seligmans were running a bank that financed the operations of many of the Jewish family trading networks across the country. From there they grew into one of the major investment banks in nineteenth-century America. The Southern–based Lehman brothers went from dry goods to cotton brokerage before they, too, became investment bankers. A few other German Jews, such as Joseph Sachs and Marcus Goldman, followed similar trajectories into investment banking.

By the last third of the nineteenth century, a small group of German Jewish families, mostly from Bavaria, was active in investment banking in New York and helping to finance America's industrial expansion. The children of these families soon intermarried, and promising young employees were also brought into the family network—just like their counterparts with retail trade networks. By the early twentieth century, they formed a close-knit financial elite. None of them was as wealthy or powerful as the German American ex-Jew August Belmont or the Anglo-Americans J. P. Morgan, Jay Gould, and John D. Rockefeller, but they were conspicuous, and their visibility helped create the image of German Jews as wealthy businessmen who were extremely successful in America.

Less conspicuous but far more numerous were the German Jewish dry-goods merchants who moved into manufacturing as well as selling clothing. The most famous of these was Levi Strauss from Bavaria, who extended his half brothers' dry-goods operation from New York to San Francisco in 1853 and moved into manufacturing work pants (Levi's) as well as selling them. But Strauss was only one of many shopkeepers who took their stock of cloth and paid tailors to sew it into ready-made clothing. The demand for army uniforms during the Civil War transformed the ready-made clothing business from a shopkeepers' sideline into a major industry. The Seligmans alone provided the army with more than a million dollars worth of uniforms, but most contracts were for $10,000–$20,000 worth at a time, and relatively small operators could compete for them. With this experience in mass production and the capital accumulated from very profitable wartime production, these manufacturers created a new, high-quality, ready-made clothing industry after the war—and German Jews dominated the business.

While peddler–shopkeeper–wholesaler networks dispersed large numbers of German Jews around the country, many also concentrated in major cities such as New York, Philadelphia, and Baltimore. By 1850, New York City alone was the home of about a third of the entire Jewish population of the United States, a proportion that would only increase as the century wore on. Even as the great wave of Eastern European Jews began to flood into the country in the 1880s, the New York City region's 85,000 German Jews (Nadel 1990) accounted for a full third of America's entire Jewish population. Indeed, in 1880 a majority of Jews lived in just half a dozen large cities (Lee Shai Weissbach in Gurock 1998), so any attempt to depict the experience of German Jews in America must take them into account. But the German Jews of New York and other large cities differed from the stereotype of German Jews as mostly peddlers, shopkeepers, merchants, and bankers. Not that these types were absent from the large cities; indeed, German Jewish bankers were hardly to be found anyplace else, while peddlers and shopkeepers were there in strength—but in most of the big urban centers they were vastly outnumbered by a very different population of German American Jews.

For much of the second half of the nineteenth century, these cities were home to a large German Jewish working class that more closely resembled the stereotypical Eastern European Jewish working class of the early twentieth century than it did the German Jewish elite of Stephen Birmingham's *Our Crowd*. New York's German Jews lived in Kleindeutschland (Little Germany)—the same Lower East Side inhabited later by their Eastern European successors—and they often labored in the same trades.

The needle trades employed German Jewish tailors early on, and when a group of striking German tailors was arrested for picketing in 1850, at least one of them was Jewish. By 1865 the city's tailors included large numbers of German Jews, and they belonged to a multiethnic union led by Jacob Morestadt, a German Jew. But while German Jews continued to predominate among the employers in this industry well past the end of the century, German Jewish tailors were driven from the trade in the late 1870s and 1880s by the willingness of more recently arrived "Polaks" to work for even lower wages. It was this wage competition that led the German Jewish tailor and union leader Charles L. Miller to get the citywide Central Labor Union and United German Trades to finance the creation of a United Hebrew Trades—to organize unions among Yiddish-speaking Eastern European Jews. The UHT would become an important factor in the creation of the Yiddish labor movement of the World of Our Fathers, but it was a product of German Jewish workers and labor activists.

Organized German Jewish workers also made hats and shoes. The capmakers' union did not have a Jewish president in 1874, just German Jews as vice president, secretary, and treasurer—while one section of the Knights of St. Crispin shoemakers' union was called the Purim Lodge. Other German Jews worked as butchers and bakers, but it was the cigarmakers who stood out as German Jewish workers, employers, and trade unionists par excellence. And not only in New York; it was the Chicago cigarmakers who sent the German American Jew Jacob Selig as their delegate to the 1867 meeting of the National Labor Union. But the cigarmaking industry centered in New York, and it

was there that Adolf Strasser, Louis Berliner, and Samuel Gompers rebuilt the Cigarmakers' International Union after the depression of the 1870s.

The English-born Gompers (of Dutch Jewish parentage) was a German Jew only by ancestry and association, having grown up among German Jews in New York, but he was also the most junior of the trio. The real leader was Gompers's mentor, Adolf Strasser, a Hungarian-born Jew who was a prominent Lassallean socialist first in Vienna and then New York. German-born Louis Berliner had been a leading member of a Marxist section of the International Workingmen's Association in America. All in all, these German Jewish workers, with their radical labor unions and socialist leaders, far more closely approximated our stereotype of the Eastern European Jew in America than that of the German.

German Jews in America also spawned a small criminal class. Jewish gangsters such as "Sheeny" Mike Kurtz, Little Freddy, and Johnny Irving led New York's "Dutch Mob" of the 1860s and 1870s. It was a minor gang by New York standards, but they provided a mid-nineteenth-century foreshadowing of later Jewish gangsters such as Monk Eastman and Dopey Benny—or even such later big-time organized crime figures as Arnold Rothstein, Dutch Schultz, and Meyer Lansky. Then there was Moses Ehrich, one of a number of German Jews in New York who followed the old tradition of mixing pawnbroker operations with fencing stolen goods—and they had their counterparts among some of the many German Jewish pawnbrokers who followed the peddlers and shopkeepers into small-town America.

Perhaps the most famous German Jewish criminal of the time was Fredrika "Marm" Mandelbaum of New York, who began her career peddling stolen goods door to door in the tenements of Kleindeutschland. Like many other peddlers, she moved up to keeping her own shop. But her shop was not only a front for selling stolen goods; it was also the headquarters of a gang of thieves who stole according to her instructions. At one point, before she retired to Montreal in 1884, she reputedly ran an academy of crime to train new associates, offering courses on everything from picking pockets to cracking safes. Mrs. Mandelbaum was also said to have been a generous supporter of her synagogue.

Like their later Eastern European counterparts, poor German Jewish women often worked hard to support their families. Many took up the needle along with their tailor husbands, as it often took the work of two to make a living as a tailor in the growing mass-production clothing industry. Widows, too, took up the needle and worked long hours for little pay—that their exploiters were fellow German Jews provided them with little comfort. Sewing paid badly, but it could be done at home and fit in around other household tasks. Taking in boarders fit in even better with household work, and it often paid a lot better than sewing. While this work was an often unreported but vital supplement to the incomes of the poorest German Jews, it was also an important aspect of the shopkeeper–peddler nexus, as the wives of some shopkeepers provided clean beds, laundry services, Jewish cooking, and some of the comforts of home to the peddlers whom their husbands supplied. Taking in boarders was also an area in which German Jewish women could develop their own businesses. Many married or widowed women did not just take in a boarder or two; they operated full-scale boardinghouses. Other German Jewish women, such as Amelia Dannenberg from the Rhineland, not only ran their own clothing shops but had their own manufacturing operations similar to those of their male counterparts (Diner 1992).

German Jews in America also engaged in professional activities from early on. Two German Jews practiced medicine as early as the 1740s, and the numbers of German Jewish doctors swelled rapidly with the mass migration of the nineteenth century. By the late 1850s, perhaps a third of the doctors in New York City were German, and a large proportion of these were Jewish. Some, such as Joseph Goldmark, Ernst Krakowitzer, and Abraham Jacobi, were well-known political figures from the revolutions of 1848–1850, while others were responding to the limited career possibilities at the time for Jewish doctors in Central Europe. Jacobi was the most successful of the lot. Landing in New York with a hero's reputation after his acquittal in the Cologne Communist trial of 1852, he went on to become the "father of pediatrics" in America and a founder of New York's Mt. Sinai Hospital before being elected president of the American Medical Association in 1912. While Michael Reese of Chicago was not a doctor but rather one of those Bavarian peddlers who got rich in trade and real estate, in 1881 he founded the Jewish hospital that bears his name, which engaged the services of many German Jewish doctors, including his fellow Bavarian, chief of medicine Dr. Ernst Schmidt. Indeed, most German Jewish settlements of any size had at least one German-trained doctor, and the larger communities usually had a German Jewish hospital as well by 1880.

Legal careers were far less portable that medical ones. Maurice Meyer was only one of a number of established German Jewish lawyers who found they could not practice law when they arrived in the United States. Meyer, a member of the revolutionary government of the Bavarian Palatinate in 1848, turned to the German Jewish fraternal movement for an alternative career and became general secretary of B'nai B'rith in 1863.

Nonetheless, some younger members of even this first immigrant generation became lawyers in the United States. Sigismund Kaufmann arrived in New York as a German radical 1848er like Dr. Jacobi, but, unlike Jacobi, he maintained his radicalism for decades after his arrival. He was a founder of the North American Socialist *Turnverein* [Gymnastics Union]; as editor of its newspaper in the 1850s, he published the writings of Karl Marx and other German socialists while he prepared for his legal career. He was a prominent abolitionist, an elector for Abraham Lincoln, a Republican candidate for lieutenant governor of New York in 1870, and a member of the State Board of Commissioners of Emigration that ran Castle Garden (the main immigrant landing depot before the opening of Ellis Island)—while also serving as a trustee for Temple Beth Elohim. Simon Wolf practiced law in Washington, D.C., and was the leading, albeit unofficial, Jewish lobbyist for decades. Like Kaufmann, he opposed slavery and supported Lincoln. He took the lead in protesting General Grant's 1862 order expelling "Jews as a class" from his military district and quickly got the order canceled; nonetheless, he was later closely associated with President Grant, who turned to him for advice on Jewish matters. Wolf also published *The American Jew as Patriot, Soldier and Citizen* (1895) to refute an influential *North American Review* article that had charged that Jews participated in the Civil War only as war profiteers. But it was the American-born generation of German Jews that produced the bevy of attorneys who led American Jewry for many decades into the twentieth century, one even reaching the U.S. Supreme Court. These included such luminaries as Max Kohler, Oscar Straus, Louis Marshall, and Louis Brandeis.

The most Jewish profession of all involved leading synagogues; German Jews provided innovative leaders who first influenced and then transformed the practice of

Judaism in America, which had never before attracted trained rabbis. Although Isaac Leeser from Westphalia had ended his formal religious training at age fourteen, it was still enough to make him stand out in 1830s America. At age twenty-four, he was invited to take over the religious leadership of Philadelphia's old Sephardic synagogue, Mikveh Israel, and he became one of the most prominent leaders of traditionalist Judaism in the country—especially after he founded a widely read monthly, the *Occident,* in 1843.

In 1845, as German Jewish migration grew, two German synagogues in New York recruited Leo Merzbacher to come from Bavaria to be the first fully trained rabbi in American history. But Merzbacher had already been influenced in Germany by a reform movement that wanted to "modernize" Judaism, and before the end of the year he left the Orthodox synagogues to become the founding rabbi of New York's Temple Emanu-El. This was one of the opening moves in the creation of Reform Judaism in America. In 1873 the Reformers formally organized the Union of American Hebrew Congregations, and they founded the Hebrew Union College in 1875 to train Reform rabbis.

By the end of the 1850s, the Reform movement was making rapid progress as more reform-oriented rabbis arrived from Germany. Isaac Leeser's *Occident* led a traditionalist attack on the reformers in 1856. The defense of Reform fell to Max Lilienthal of Cincinnati, another Bavarian rabbi who had been brought over to be Merzbacher's Orthodox successor, before he too defected to the Reform movement and became co-editor of the *Israelite* with the moderate Reform leader Isaac Mayer Wise from Bohemia. Although they were traditionalist opponents of Reform, Leeser and his Orthodox colleagues also adopted some innovations. Leeser moved the *bimah* from the center to the front of the synagogue and faced the congregation while leading prayers. He also gave full support to Rebecca Gratz as she led the formation of a Jewish Sunday school movement in the United States.

The argument between traditionalists and reformers played itself out again at a more intellectually sophisticated level a generation later in 1885, by which point Reform had become the dominant form of Judaism in the United States. The defense of Reform again fell to a Bavarian, the Berlin-trained rabbi Kaufmann Kohler, who had succeeded the radical German American reformer David Einhorn as rabbi of Temple Beth El in New York. This time the tradi-

tionalist attack came from the Hungarian-born but German-trained rabbi Alexander Kohut. As a traditionalist, Kohut was highly critical of Reform, but he, too, believed that Orthodox Judaism needed modification to prosper in America. The year after his influential attack on Reform, Kohut joined with a group of like-minded traditionalists to create their own Jewish Theological Seminary to provide training for more traditional rabbis in a "spirit . . . of Conservative Judaism" (Sorin 1992).

This set the foundation for the formation of a third denomination of American Judaism, one that prospered in the twentieth century with the financial support of a number of wealthy German American Reform Jews who had concluded that the Reform movement would not appeal to large numbers of Eastern European Jews. Eventually, Eastern European Jews and their descendants would take over the leadership of all three major Jewish denominations in the United States (though there would be a renewal of German leadership in the Reform movement in the latter part of the twentieth century), but in the nineteenth century it was German Jews who led all three and who had literally created both of the newer varieties of Judaism.

German Jews also created many other Jewish institutions and organizations in America. Leeser's *Occident* and Isaac Mayer Wise's *Israelite* (founded in 1854 and renamed the *American Israelite* in 1874) were major Jewish newspapers. Wise also published *die Deborah* in German for women who might not understand English. By 1861 there were nine German Jewish papers in German or English or both, and many more were added in later decades, including the *American Hebrew* (1878–1957). Some second-generation German American Jews such as Adolph Ochs, publisher of the *New York Times,* took to mainstream journalism and published major newspapers, while others such as pioneering scholar Dr. Cyrus Adler created the Jewish Publication Society (1888) and the American Jewish Historical Society (1892) to promote serious Jewish scholarship in America.

But publications were only part of the institutional framework created by German American Jews. Soon after large-scale migration began, they founded national fraternal–sororal orders such as the B'nai B'rith (Sons of the Covenant, 1843), the *Orden Treuer Schwestern* (Order of True Sisters, 1846), and the *B'nai Israel* (Free Sons of Israel, 1849), along with countless local organizations such as the Maimonides Library Association of New York City, the

Masthead for Deborah. *German-language supplement to the newspaper* Israelite, *written mainly for Jewish women in the United States.* *(New York Public Library)*

German Literary Association of Albany, and the Minerva Society of Louisville. In 1854 the Young Men's Hebrew Association was founded as a local group in Baltimore, but by 1880 there were about eighty such organizations in twenty-five cities.

Synagogues had always engaged in charitable activities, but with the arrival of large numbers of unaffiliated and secular German Jews, charitable organizations were created to serve the larger community without making religious distinctions. These included burial societies, orphanages, old age homes, medical clinics, and hospitals. In the decades after 1859, they moved to professionalize and centralize their activities, forming numerous citywide United Hebrew Relief Associations and United Hebrew Charities wherever there were substantial numbers of Jews. Just as with synagogue sisterhoods, women often took the lead in supporting these philanthropic organizations, and German American Jewish women such as Hannah Solomon formed a National Council of Jewish Women (NCJW) in 1893 to promote Jewish "religion, philanthropy and education" and "the work of social reform"—as well as opposing all religious persecution (Schappes 1965). The outbreak of World War I in Europe led to the internation-alizing of American Jewish philanthropy, as German American Jews took the lead in organizing the Joint Distribution Committee to assist the hundreds of thousands of Jewish refugees in their German and Austro-Hungarian ancestral homelands who had fled from marauding czarist armies and pogroms.

Indeed, it was Old World antisemitism that spurred several German Jewish moves to unify American Jewry. When the Jews of Damascus, Syria, were accused of murdering a Catholic priest so his blood could be used to bake matzah, Isaac Leeser and Rebecca Gratz organized a protest campaign and thanked President Van Buren for intervening with the Ottoman government. Jewish protests were less successful when the United States signed a trade treaty with Switzerland in 1850 that acknowledged a Swiss-claimed right to discriminate against American Jews. Despite a campaign sparked by Bavarian-born Sigismund Waterman and promoted by both the traditionalist Leeser and the Reformer Wise, the Senate ratified the treaty in 1855. Two years later, an American was ordered to leave a Swiss canton that prohibited Jewish entry, and protests resumed.

Then came the official kidnapping in Italy of six-year-old Edgardo Mortara after a nursemaid claimed that she had secretly baptized him. By this time, most American Jews were German born, and German Jews took the lead in calling on President Buchanan to follow the precedent of Van Buren and intervene with the Vatican. Buchanan expressed sympathy to two separate Jewish delegations but refused to act because that might legitimate foreign intervention over American slavery—not to mention that it might alienate Irish Catholic voters from the Democratic Party.

Responding to this double failure, the representatives of twenty-five German Jewish congregations met in 1859 and founded the Board of Delegates of American Congregations to defend Jewish rights, the first such national organization in U.S. history. Four years later, the Board of Delegates convinced Secretary of State Seward to ask Morocco to protect its Jews from attack after a series of pogroms.

The wave of antisemitism that spread across the United States in the late nineteenth century failed to generate any new defense organizations. It only splintered Jewish unity, as many assimilated German Jews blamed rising antisemitism on the visibility of newer arrivals from Eastern Europe. It was only the renewal of Russian pogroms in 1903 that stimulated the creation of a new organization. Seeking to create an organization that might effectively influence U.S. policy toward Russia, a group of prominent German American Jews led by Louis Marshall, Jacob Schiff, and Oscar Straus met to form the American Jewish Committee (AJC) in February 1906. Although some moves were later made to bring a few leading Eastern European Jews into the organization, it remained predominantly German for many years.

Nonetheless, the AJC took the lead in opposing immigration restriction proposals directed against Eastern European Jews. It also won the abrogation of an old commercial treaty with Russia that permitted discrimination against Jews, thereby both vindicating the rights of American Jews and punishing Russia for its persecution of Russian Jews—an achievement eased by the appointment of AJC leader Oscar Straus as Secretary of Commerce. The AJC also undertook the lead in defense of Jewish rights in the United States. In 1913 the AJC led the successful campaign for a New York state law against discriminatory advertisements by summer resorts, and then it helped win a gubernatorial commutation of Leo Frank's death sentence after he was unjustly convicted of murder in Georgia.

Most German Jews in America long opposed Zionism on the grounds that their Judaism was purely religious. As Jacob Schiff put it in 1904, "I am an American pure and simple and cannot possibly belong to two nations" (Sorin 1992). Nonetheless, American Zionism found its organizational leadership among German American Jews. Reform Rabbi Richard Gottheil broke with most of his colleagues when he founded the Federation of American Zionists in 1898 after attending the first World Zionist Congress in Basle, and he served as its president until 1904. Fellow Reformer Stephen Wise was an important early popularizer of the movement, and the recruitment of Louis Brandeis to the Zionist leadership in 1912 was crucial to the movement's later growth and influence. A number of German Jewish women were also important figures in the Zionist movement in America, including Henrietta Szold, the translator of Heinrich Graetz's *History of the Jews* from its German original. Szold was the main figure in the 1912 creation of the women's Zionist organization Hadassah, leading it to become the largest Jewish women's organization in the world.

The relationship between the German Jewish immigrants of the nineteenth century and the German America created by the contemporary migration of millions of non-Jewish Germans was complex. Some German Jews were highly integrated into their German American communities and, like Sigismund Kaufmann of New York and Simon Wolf of Washington, played important leadership roles in the broader communities even as they continued to identify strongly as Jews. German-educated rabbis promoted German *Kultur* in America, organized German cultural associations, and were often invited to address German American celebrations. In 1859 Rabbi Bernhard Felsenthal of Chicago coined the label "American-German Jews," and at the beginning of the twentieth century, he defined his identity by saying "Racially I am a Jew. . . . Politically I am an American. . . . Spiritually I am a German" (Felsenthal 1924). By the same token, as German Jewish communities developed, they became increasingly distinct, and as collectivities (though not as individuals), they tended to participate less and less in broader German American activities. But this could also be said about German American Catholics and Lutherans, so even here they fit into the variegated mold of German America.

Like their labor movement colleagues, numerous German Jewish radicals in America generally functioned as part of the large German American radical movement rather than in purely Jewish organizations—leading many Jewish historians to downplay or even deny their importance. But their importance often lay in the very fact that they led much larger and more influential organizations than would have been possible had they confined their activities to Jews. August Bondi was exceptional among German Jewish abolitionists in joining John Brown to fight against slavery in Kansas, but there were many German Jewish abolitionists—rabbis such as David Einhorn, Bernhard Felsenthal, and I. M. Wise but also radicals like Socialist Turnverein leader Sigismund Kaufmann and *Kommunist Klub* secretary Fritz Jacobi (First Lieutenant Fritz Jacoby died fighting slavery in 1862).

After the Civil War, German Jewish radicals continued to be active in the broader German American context. Augusta Lilienthal joined the Socialist Labor Party (SLP) and wrote on women's rights for its German-language paper, *die Neue Zeit,* while a generation later her daughter Meta "Hebe" Lilienthal did the same for the *New Yorker Volkszeitung* and served briefly on the Socialist Party's Women's National Committee before devoting most of her efforts to the fight for women's suffrage. Adolf Strasser and Louis Berliner were also important early socialist leaders in post–Civil War America, while Victor Berger started off in Kaufmann's Socialist Turnverein after he arrived in 1878. Berger soon moved on to the SLP and was a founding leader of the Socialist Party of America in 1901. As editor of the *Wisconsin Vorwärts,* he became the undisputed leader of the powerful Socialist movement of Milwaukee, where he was elected mayor before he became the first Socialist ever elected to the U.S. Congress. He was reelected five times, and by 1919 he was one of the leaders of the less radical wing when the Socialist Party splintered. Ludwig Lore, who arrived in the United States in 1903, joined the German Socialist movement in New York. By 1919 he was editor of the *New Yorker Volkszeitung* and executive secretary of the German Socialist Federation, which he led into the new Communist Party when the Socialist Party split apart. He led his followers out of the CP in 1925 and continued to be the most prominent leader of German American radicalism until he died in 1942. By then, another well-known socialist–pacifist German Jewish activist (part-time) had taken up residence in the United States: Albert Einstein. As these examples from nearly a century of radical activism suggest, German Jewish radicals were far more numerous in America than their better-known German Jewish banker contemporaries.

In some ways, the German Jews' relationship with the rest of the American Jewish community paralleled their relationship with German America. They were a part of the larger whole, but they remained a distinct and separate part. The distinction was relatively minor until the later part of the nineteenth century, when the term *Germans* took on the connotation of greater assimilation, wealth, and status—to be contrasted with the recently arrived, unassimilated, poorer, lower-status Russians, or *Ostjuden.* Indeed, successful and assimilated early arrivals among the Easterners staked their claims to higher status by redefining their origins as German. When the term *German* took on this class connotation, large numbers of working- and middle-class German Jews and their descendants were consigned to a sort of invisibility until, with the appearance of American-born descendants of Eastern European Jews, they merged into a generalized category of "American" Jews. Without the financial resources to maintain a status distinction, and with the ancestral homelands of both groups declining in importance, they intermarried with the more numerous descendants of the Easterners and ceased to exist as a separate group.

The relationship between the high-status "Germans" and the newly arrived Easterners was fraught with tension. Fearing that the Easterners' distinctive appearance would heighten antisemitism, German American Jews sponsored a series of programs to disperse the Eastern Europeans into rural settlements. By 1882 thousands had been sent off to nearly two hundred different places, and in 1890 a Jewish Alliance of America was formed to expedite the dispersal. A decade later the German Jewish–supported Baron de Hirsch Fund, Jewish Colonization Society, and Industrial Removal Office all poured large amounts of money and effort into the dispersion program, but their small successes in funding some 160 agricultural settlements and tens of thousands of removals had little real impact on the growing concentration of new arrivals in a few major cities.

After toying briefly with support for immigration restriction to keep down the numbers of Eastern European Jews, most German Jews and their organizations (including the B'nai B'rith, the Board of Delegates, and the AJC, as well as the major German Jewish papers) campaigned vigorously against immigration restriction proposals that would have prevented millions of Jews from fleeing persecution in Europe—until the combined effects of World War I and the Red Scare overwhelmed their opposition in 1921. In 1917, when they could no longer block a literacy requirement, German American Jews even got literacy in the long-despised "jargon" Yiddish included as grounds for admission—along with a total exemption for those fleeing religious persecution.

When mass immigration from Eastern Europe took off after 1880, the Jewish charities established by the Germans undertook the increasingly expensive task of aiding the new arrivals. Many German Jewish women, such as Hannah Solomon of the NCJW, took the lead in finding new ways to aid them. In 1896 Solomon founded the Bureau of Personal Service, staffed by German Jewish women, to channel aid to needy Jewish women, while other NCJW members helped create separate juvenile courts to deal with the rising level of Jewish juvenile delinquency in such cities as New York and Chicago. German Jewish men such as Isidor Straus, Jacob Schiff, and Julius Rosenwald funded the creation of settlement houses such as the Educational Alliance, the Jewish People's Institute, and Lillian Wald's famous Henry Street Settlement—along with orphanages, day nurseries, training schools, free medical clinics, hospitals, and old age homes, to aid the growing masses of poor Jews. These increasingly professionalized—and often patronizing—efforts of German American Jews were often resented by the Eastern Europeans as "cold charity and colder philanthropy" (Sorin 1992), but they provided important resources and created some degree of solidarity between the two groups.

The German Jewish migration of the nineteenth century did not end in 1880 but continued up to 1914, as another 40,000–50,000 German Jews made their way to America. It was overshadowed, however, by the much larger contemporary mass migration from Eastern Europe, and it is unclear what proportion was assimilated by the earlier German Jewish migrants and what was simply submerged among the Easterners. What is clear is that it had no special identity of its own.

The same cannot be said about the next wave of perhaps 150,000 German Jews who arrived as refugees and survivors of Nazi persecution in the 1930s and 1940s. There were so many scientists and intellectuals among them that the New School for Social Research set up the University in Exile to accommodate some of them. Columbia University took in Karl-August Wittfogel and encour-

aged Max Horkheimer, Erich Fromm, Herbert Marcuse, and Franz Neumann to re-create the Frankfurt School around Columbia's Institute of Social Research. Albert Einstein went to the Institute for Advanced Study in Princeton, and Leo Strauss went to the University of Chicago after a stint at the New School. These are just a few of the many famous figures who invigorated higher education and psychoanalysis in America. Other German Jewish academics, able to find work only on the margins of American academia, teaching at historically black colleges, helped inspire a younger generation of civil rights activists across the South. German-trained Jewish doctors also dispersed around the country, often ending up in medically underserved small cities such as Jamestown, New York.

But while this cohort of German Jewish immigrants is often dubbed the "Intellectual Migration," the vast majority were not intellectuals and had no university training. Irene Fürst had worked in a restaurant before she married the owner of a small shop in Salzburg, Austria, so when she fled the Nazis and found herself in Charleston with no money and unable to speak the language, she opened a restaurant. In her *Landjuden* (small-town Jew) origins, she was far more typical of this migration stream than were the famous academics and scientists, but most of the small-towners gravitated to the American Jewish capital, New York City.

Perhaps 40,000 of them congregated in Manhattan's Washington Heights–Inwood neighborhood, which became known as "the Fourth Reich" and "Frankfurt on the Hudson." There they created a closely knit ethnoreligious community, read their own newspaper *die Aufbau (The Building)*, and encouraged their children (such as Joseph Maier, Henry Huttenbach, and Henry Kissinger) to pursue higher education. By the 1980s, this community was aging rapidly, but many of their German-born children not only went on to great academic success but also reestablished German leadership of many Reform institutions and several Orthodox ones. But like their predecessors among nonelite German American Jews, the American-born children of these migrants have rapidly begun to merge with an undifferentiated American Jewish population of mostly Eastern European origin. And with the German lands virtually emptied of Jews, it is unlikely that there will ever again be a significant German Jewish population in America.

Stanley Nadel

References and Further Reading

Barkai, Avraham. 1994. *Branching Out: German-Jewish Immigration to the United States 1820–1914.* Teaneck, NJ: Holmes & Meier.

Birmingham, Stephen. 1967. *"Our Crowd": The Great Jewish Families of New York.* New York: Harper & Row.

Brinkmann, Tobias. 2003. "Exceptionalism and Normality: 'German Jews' in the United States, 1840–1880." In *Toward Normality? Acculturation and Modern German Jewry,* edited by Rainer Liedtke and David Rechter. Tübingen, Germany: Mohr Siebeck.

Cohen, Naomi W. 1984. *Encounter with Emancipation: The German Jews in the United States, 1830–1914.* Philadelphia: Jewish Publication Society of America.

Diner, Hasia. 1992. *A Time for Gathering: The Second Migration, 1820–1880.* Baltimore: Johns Hopkins University Press.

Felsenthal, Emma. 1924. *Bernhard Felsenthal, Teacher in Israel: Selections from His Writings, with Biographical Sketch and Bibliography.* New York: Oxford University Press.

Glanz, Rudolf. 1972. "Where the Jewish Press Was Distributed in Pre–Civil War America." *Western States Jewish Historical Quarterly* 5, 1.

Gurock, Jeffrey S., ed. 1998. *Central European Jews in America, 1840–1880: Migration and Advancement.* New York: Routledge.

Hirshler, Eric E., ed. 1955. *Jews from Germany in the United States.* New York: Farrar, Straus & Cudahay.

Lowenstein, Steven M. 1991. *Frankfurt on the Hudson: The German-Jewish Community on Washington Heights, 1933–1983.* Detroit, MI: Wayne State University Press.

Nadel, Stanley. 1990. *Little Germany: Ethnicity, Religion, and Class in New York City, 1845–1880.* Urbana: University of Illinois Press.

Peck, Abraham J., ed. 1989. *The German-Jewish Legacy in America, 1938–1988: From Bildung to the Bill of Rights.* Detroit, MI: Wayne State University Press.

Rosenwaike, Ira. 1985. *On the Edge of Greatness: A Portrait of American Jewry in the Early National Period.* Cincinnati, OH: American Jewish Archives.

Schappes, Morris U. 1965. *A Pictorial History of the Jews in the United States.* New York: Marzani & Munsell.

Sorin, Gerald. 1992. *A Time for Building: The Third Migration, 1880–1920.* Baltimore: Johns Hopkins University Press.

East European Jewish Immigration

Between 1881 and 1924, approximately 2.5 million Jews emigrated from the Russian empire (78 percent), Austria-Hungary (18 percent), and Romania (4 percent). This was not only one of the largest migrations in world history (one-third of East European Jewry permanently left the lands of their birth), but the vast majority, more than 2

American Jews welcoming Jews immigrating from Russia to the United States, ca. 1910. (Library of Congress)

million, went to the United States, eventually generating the largest, most vibrant Jewish community in the world.

The causes of this mass migration were many and complex. In 1880 close to 6 million of the world's 7.7 million Jews lived in Eastern Europe, more than 4 million confined to the Pale of Settlement, which consisted of the 15 western provinces of European Russia and the 10 provinces of Russian-held Poland. For Jews, life in Eastern Europe, and particularly in the Russian empire, had never been comfortable. Deeply rooted in popular legend and Russian official doctrine, including the teachings of the Russian Orthodox and Uniate churches, was the belief that Jews were guilty of deicide and constituted a pariah people standing in the way of the coming of the millennium. And the czars, though occasionally indifferent toward the Jews or even tolerant of them, were more often responsible for extended periods of severe oppression. The most zealous of them instituted coercive policies for the "conversion" of the Jews. Nicholas I (1825–1855), under a general program of "modernization," issued more than 600 anti-Jewish decrees, including expulsion from particular areas, censorship of Hebrew and Yiddish literature, and military conscription of young boys for periods of up to *25 years*.

Under Alexander II (1855–1881), there was some liberalization, but despite increases in the right of residence for "useful Jews" and the increasing enrollment of Jews in Russian secondary schools and universities, legal humiliation and economic harassment continued. Heavily dependent on petty trade and crafts, Jews were generally kept out of the economic centers. Large cities such as Kiev and Moscow were closed to Jews without special permission. And St. Petersburg was open only to the upper bourgeoisie and a handful of students.

The restructuring of the East European economy, along with antisemitism, had a negative effect on Jews and proved a powerful force for dislocation. In many areas of Eastern Europe in the late nineteenth century, peasant-based economies were slowly eroding. Railroads and peasant cooperatives changed the distributive role played by large numbers of Jews in the small market towns, virtually eliminating local fairs. In addition, the emancipation of the serfs (1861–1862) left nobles in need of fewer stewards and administrators and left the newly freed peasants heavily in debt, unable to afford the services of Jewish middlemen. The dynamics of modernization, particularly in the Pale, where Jews in the 1890s constituted approximately 70 percent of those engaged in commerce and 30 percent of those engaged in crafts, led to the displacement of petty merchants, peddlers, and artisans as well as teamsters and innkeepers.

In the context of general economic dislocation and spreading Russian discontent, the government, in an attempt to deflect resentment, encouraged antisemitism by focusing on the Jews' preeminence as middlemen. In addition, the government offered loans to a nascent indigenous class of commercial men waiting for businesses to be abandoned by Jews and encouraged native middlemen to organize boycotts of Jewish merchants. In Galicia (Austria-Hungary) in the 1880s, 60 percent of the Jews had to be supported by the community, and each year 5,000 died of starvation or of diseases brought on by malnutrition. Still, the death rate for Jews in most of Eastern Europe was relatively low, and the

Jewish population soared from 1.5 million in 1800 to 6.8 million in 1900, greatly exacerbating the decline of economic opportunity.

The pressures on Jews to seek livelihoods elsewhere mounted from year to year. In 1863, an unsuccessful Polish uprising, antisemitic in tone as well as extremely nationalistic, intensified those pressures. So did a famine in Lithuania (1867–1869) and a cholera epidemic in Poland in 1869. Galician Jews migrated toward eastern Hungary and Vienna; Polish Jews overflowed such cities as Lodz, Warsaw, and Vilna. Bialystock drew uprooted *shtetl* (small-town) dwellers, artisans, and laborers. By 1897, 41 percent of the urban population of the Russian empire was Jewish. But even the cities offered only a precarious existence. Jews, victims of Russian paranoia, patriotism at its most vulgar, and narrowly defined economic self-interest, were excluded from many branches of the economy.

Scapegoating became even more intense after terrorists assassinated Alexander II in 1881. Confusion reigned, and revolutionaries called on the people to rebel. The Russian press and the government, attempting to defend itself, stepped up the accusation that Jews were responsible for the misfortunes of the nation, and pogroms (anti-Jewish riots) broke out in numerous towns and hamlets of southern Russia. Between 1881 and 1882, there were pogroms in 225 communities, including Yelizavetgrad and Kiev. There was a massive pogrom in Warsaw in December 1881; 1,500 homes, shops, and synagogues were sacked before troops intervened. An even more bloody and destructive episode took place in the largely Jewish town of Balta in Podolia in late March 1882.

In the aftermath of violence, between 1881–1884 more than 70,000 Jews emigrated from Russia to the United States. This was more than double the number that had arrived in the United States in the entire decade of the 1870s. Russian commissions investigating the causes of the pogroms concluded that "Jewish exploitation" was at the root of the violence. Based on this finding, the government published the Temporary Laws (May Laws, 1882). These were designed to isolate the Jew from the peasant. They circumscribed movement within the Pale, prohibiting Jews from living in villages. This meant the expulsion of 500,000 Jews from rural areas. No business could be conducted by Jews in the larger towns, nor could any business be conducted on Sunday. Jews were forbidden to purchase real property or even to negotiate mortgages. And in 1886, reacting to the virtual flood of Jews seeking entry to secondary schools and universities, the government, as part of the administrative harassment of the Jews, limited the number of Jewish students to 10 percent of the student body in the Pale and 3.5 percent outside it.

In 1887, more than 23,000 Russian Jews immigrated to the United States—the highest total for a single year up to that point. By 1891, 700,000 Jews living east of the Pale were driven into the confined area, and previously privileged Jews were subject to wholesale expulsion from Russian cities; 20,000 were expelled from Moscow alone. The press continued a campaign of unbridled antisemitic propaganda; K. Pobedonostev, the head of the governing body of the Russian Orthodox Church, clarified the goals of the government when he predicted that "one-third of the Jews will convert, one-third will die, and one-third will flee the country." Between 1891 and 1892, 107,000 Jews left Russia for the United States.

After a short interregnum (1893–1898), the strict application of the discriminatory laws was continued under Nicholas II (1894–1918). His government subsidized close to 3,000 antisemitic publications, including the classic forgery *Protocols of the Elders of Zion*. Free reign was given to anti-Jewish agitation, particularly in reaction to the growth of the revolutionary movement, in which a disproportionate number of Jewish youth took part.

An explosion of pogroms filled the years from 1903 to 1906. In contrast to those that took place between 1881 and 1884, these involved a steep escalation of violence and mass murder. In the Kishinev pogrom of April 1903, 47 Jews were killed, and hundreds were severely beaten. In Zhitomer in April 1905, 29 were killed; 100 were murdered in Kiev in July; 60 in Bialystok in August, and 800 in Odessa in October. In 1906, pogroms became practically uncountable, with many hundreds dead, robbed, raped, and mutilated. As in the l880s, the pogroms in the beginning of the twentieth century were followed by a steep jump in the rate of emigration from Russia to the United States. In 1900, 37,000 Jews emigrated. In 1904, 77,500 left; 92,400 emigrated in 1905 and 125,200 in 1906. Another 200,000 left between 1907 and 1908.

While pogroms were clearly a factor in mass emigration, a case can be made that pogroms alone do not explain the extraordinary movement of the Jewish population between 1881 and 1924. The highest rate of emigration was experienced, after all, in Galicia, where there were economic hardship and some local repression but virtually no pogroms. The Ukraine, the heartland of pogroms in the Russian empire, produced a relatively low rate of emigration before World War I, and Lithuania, with relatively few pogroms, had a very high emigration rate. Also, concurrent with the acceleration of the Jewish emigration was an expanded emigration from the Russian empire of non-Jewish Poles, Lithuanians, Finns, and even Russians. Jewish emigration then can be seen as directly related to the economic strains and dislocations of Eastern Europe and particularly of prerevolutionary Russia. Persecution, however, was critical. Jews, constituting only about 5 percent of the population of the Russian empire, made up close to 50 percent of the Russian emigrant stream between 1881 and 1910. And from Romania, where Jews were treated oppressively and violently as aliens, more than 75,000 (30 percent of the Jewish population) came to the United States between 1881 and 1915.

Mass Jewish migration from Eastern Europe had been gathering momentum throughout the 1870s. After 1881, however, Jews had to face antisemitism not simply as a permanent inconvenience but as a threat to their very existence. The Russian government was encouraging pogroms as a matter of policy. This seemed a new and frightening matter, distinct from the government's mere indifference to Jewish victimization in the past. By the time of Alexander III and certainly by Nicholas II, the desire was no longer to Russify the Jews but to be rid of them. At a conference of Jewish notables in St. Petersburg in 1882, a majority continued to maintain that mass emigration would appear unpatriotic and might undermine the struggle for emancipation. But thoughts about emigration soon became pervasive. Some eminent Jews who had once been enthusiastic assimilationists, including M. L. Lilienblum, the Hebrew writer and political journalist, and Leon Pinsker, an Odessa physician and author of the pioneering Zionist tract *Autoemancipation* (1882), now saw antisemitism as deeply rooted—not a vestige but a disease incurable in the foreseeable future. After 1881, more and more believed that emancipation for Jews was not possible within the intolerable conditions of the Russian Empire.

Fear had become a central factor in Jewish life in Russia. But fear, intensified by new and more violent persecution, dislocation, and deepening poverty, does not by itself account for the stunning uprooting and transplantation of millions of East European Jews. It is necessary to include the ingredients of cultural ferment and renewal. East European Jewish life was based on deeply rooted tradition and for centuries had been relatively static. There was a reality, too, however, of internal conflict and change. The seventeenth century saw the false messianism of Sabbatai Zevi, which indicated a revulsion against passive waiting for redemption. In the late eighteenth and early nineteenth centuries, Hasidism, an enthusiastic, pietistic movement of religious renewal, challenged rabbinic authority. Later, from the West came the *Haskalah,* or Enlightenment, a secular expression of new intellectual styles and ethical concepts derived in part from Jewish religious tradition, which strove toward complete and equal citizenship for Jews.

This collective resurgence of Jews reached its height in the last three decades of the nineteenth century with the blossoming of a secular Yiddish literature and the self-education and increasing social awareness of the Jewish masses. Among city Jews and *shtetl* Jews, as they struggled to synthesize the forces of modernization with their tradition, was a widespread feeling that Jewish culture was experiencing a renaissance. The postliberal movements—Zionism and socialism and the various blends of the two—initially products of the failure of emancipation and the irresponsibility of radical Russia during the pogroms, also reflected the cultural renaissance. *Takhles,* or the aspiration "to become" all one was capable of being, was always central to Jewish culture. Modernization redirected and intensified that desire, and increasing East European antisemitism frustrated it. For large numbers, relocation seemed the only answer.

Without external assault and increasing poverty, this collective energetic resurgence, instead of leading to mass emigration, would more likely have produced a temporary culture of *Yiddishkeit* for the Jews as they moved toward assimilation. Persecution, pogroms, and poverty, without cultural renewal, would more likely have produced internal upheavals and perhaps new religious enthusiasms rather than an exodus. The combination, however, of spiritual hope and physical wretchedness proved explosive. Between 1881 and 1910, 1,562,800 Jews came to the United States from Eastern Europe—almost 72 percent from Russia, 19 percent from Austria-Hungary, and 4.3 percent from Romania. Another 435,000 would arrive between 1911 and 1914 and a quarter million more between 1915 and 1924.

In the 1880s, there was also the pervasive belief that overseas emigration was now finally a viable alternative. As early as 1817, there existed in Eastern Europe a Yiddish translation of *The Discovery of America,* a popular celebration of the United States. Between 1820 and 1870, there had already been a trickle of Jewish emigration (7,500) to America from Eastern Europe. Between 1870 and 1890, however, America became more clearly the "distant magnet," a place for potential collective renewal for Jews. In these years the American economy experienced a 28-percent growth in the number of industries and a net increase in the value of production of 168 percent. In addition, large-scale, regularly scheduled steamship transportation became more available; companies actually sent out agents to solicit travelers from the Old World. At the same time, published reports began to appear in Hebrew and Yiddish about the opportunities in the *goldene medine* (golden land). More than 3 million Jews would cross borders in Eastern Europe, seeking their fortunes elsewhere. Of these, 7 percent went to Western Europe, 10–13 percent to Canada, Australia, Argentina, South Africa, and Palestine, and more than 80 percent ended up in the United States.

Jews from the Ukraine and southern Russia crossed borders illegally, often to Brody in Galicia, traveled from there by train to Vienna or Berlin, and regrouped to go to Hamburg, Bremen, Rotterdam, Amsterdam, and Antwerp, where for $34 (by 1903) one could purchase a steamship ticket to the New World. Jews from western Russia came surreptitiously across the German borders, while the Austro-Hungarians could cross legally. And the Romanians arrived at the northern ports mainly through Vienna. Western Jewish organizations, at first reluctant and even ready to oppose emigration whenever hope arose that the position of Jews in Russia might be improved, began to face the reality of mass Jewish migration from Eastern Europe.

A group of German Jewish associations, the *Hilfsverein der Deutschen Juden,* organized to help their coreligionists and to avoid being overrun by the mass influx, set up information bureaus, negotiated special rates with railroad companies and steamship lines, and lobbied governments to ease the immigrants' journey and speed them on their way. Between 1905 and 1914, 700,000 East European Jews passed through Germany, and 210,000 were directly aided by the Hilfsverein. Baron de Hirsch, scion of financiers to the Bavarian Royal Court, who had made a fortune in banking and railway finance, contributed large amounts to improve the conditions of East European Jews. In the late 1880s, however, after the pogroms and mass expulsions, Baron de Hirsch encouraged emigration, and he set up the Jewish Colonization Association in 1891 with vast programs for international resettlement.

The several organized efforts, while important particularly in terms of making the idea of transplantation viable, directly helped move only a small number compared to the migration of individuals. The voyage of these individuals was filled with tribulation. In Europe they had to face rapacious peasants and smugglers and, often, brutal border guards. Even legal travelers had to deal with the bewildering confusion of various bureaucracies and the officious manner of German authorities, who, fearful of plague, among other things, conducted innumerable inspections. There were questions upon questions, disinfections, and the constant fear of being sent back or quarantined. Success meant facing a thirteen-to-twenty-day voyage in steerage in the most primitive conditions. The suffering endured by the travelers was real and persistent, exacerbated by swindlers and unscrupulous steamship agents. By the early 1900s, there was some improvement. Competition among steamship lines led to a modification of steerage into compartments on newer ships; the voyage was reduced to between six and ten days; and the Jewish organizations at various transit points now had more experience and were better able to serve and protect the emigrés.

Between 1899 and 1910, 86 percent of the Jews heading for the United States landed in the North Atlantic states, the vast majority in New York City. Here they faced a grueling ordeal at Castle Garden or, after 1891, Ellis Island. Immigration employees, always overworked (processing 4,000 immigrants a day at peak periods) and often insensitive, checked arrivals for "defects," tuberculosis, "dull-wittedness," eye problems, and "contagious and loathsome diseases." Piled into massive halls in dozens of lines, the immigrants underwent incessant pushing, prying, probing, and poking. There were some exceptional officials, including Philip Cowen and Alexander Harkavy, who helped ease the immigrants' predicament.

The Hebrew Emigrant Aid Society (HEAS), a makeshift organization (founded in 1880 by German Jews in America), despite fear of the consequences of the in-migration of large numbers of East European Jews and some contempt for the "wild Russians," cared for approximately 14,000 Russian immigrants. HEAS eventually evolved into the Hebrew Sheltering and Immigrant Aid Society, which by 1897 combined under one roof employment, training, housing, and legal aid for immigrants. From 1884 to 1892, the aid given Jewish arrivals was sporadic and unsystematic. In 1892, this changed when, with generous funding from Baron de Hirsch, several groups concerned with the welfare of the immigrants joined forces.

Aid was often necessary, for the average Jewish immigrant arrived with less money and more dependents than other immigrants. Between 1899 and 1910, 44 percent of the Jewish immigrants were female, and 25 percent were children under fourteen. For other groups in the same period, only 30.5 percent were females and 12.3 percent children under fourteen. The Jewish migration was much more a movement of families than that of other European nationalities and groups. More dependents meant more burdens but also more emotional sustenance in a relatively unfamiliar environment. Also sustaining the Jewish immigrants was the fact that they appear to have had better preparation for urban life than did most other immigrants from Eastern and Southern Europe. Before World War I, nearly two-thirds of Jewish male immigrants were classified as skilled laborers. There is little doubt that this is an exaggerated proportion, but many were craftsmen and artisans who had had at least some experience in living and working in semi-urban environments.

Of the skilled Jewish workers between 1899 and 1914, 60 percent were clothing workers. The American garment industry was undergoing a period of rapid expansion precisely at the time of the East European arrivals, and by 1910 New York City was producing 70 percent of the women's clothes and 40 percent of the men's clothes made in the United States. By the late 1880s German Jews owned more than 95 percent of the clothing factories and shops in the city, and their East European cousins believed that they would find familiarity in those shops and the possibility of not having to work on *Shabos* (the Sabbath).

When German Jews in the United States initially faced mass immigration of East European Jews, or *Ostjuden*, they had two responses. One was fear; the Germans were afraid that antisemitism, on the rise since the 1870s, would inevitably increase in the face of a Russian Jewish "tidal wave." The second reaction was arrogance—a condescending attitude toward the East Europeans based on the Germans' sense of class and cultural superiority. Leaders of the German Jewish community actually admitted in the 1880s that "immigration was not popular among our people," and claimed that the "mode of life" of the Russian Jew "has stamped upon them . . . marks of permanent pauperism." Nothing but "disgrace and a lowering of the opinion in which American Israelites are held . . . can result from the continued residence among us of these wretches." The widespread Russian pogroms (1881–1883) appeared to threaten the Germans with a significantly increased burden of impoverished Eastern newcomers, but even prior to the mass flight that the pogroms produced, many of the German philanthropic agencies cautioned against open immigration. Indeed, in 1880 the United Hebrew Charities of New York and the newspaper *American Hebrew* urged the passage of restrictive immigration laws.

A representative of the United Charities of Rochester in 1882 called the Yiddish-speaking Russian Jews "a bane to the country and a curse to all Jews," and warned that the "enviable reputation" German Jews had earned in the United States was being "undermined by the influx of thousands who are not ripe for enjoyment of liberty." He went on to say that all "who mean well for the Jewish name should prevent them as much as possible from coming here." From as early as the 1870s, when the Easterners were few in number, German Jews, though generous materially, shunned their less assimilated coreligionists. The unofficial slogan of the Harmony Club in New York, perhaps the most prestigious German Jewish social club in the United States, was "More polish and less Polish." Though there were very few visible reminders of their own peddler origins, the German Jews in the 1880s were apparently too insecure to feel comfortable with the poverty, the Yiddish, the Orthodoxy, and the socialism of the new arrivals from Eastern Europe.

German Jews eventually became champions of unrestricted immigration, but until the early 1890s, they remained ambivalent about the massive influx from the East. In June 1880, for example, the *American Hebrew* advocated tighter immigration laws and the diversion of immigrants to farms. But only eight months later, the editors demanded uninterrupted immigration: "Hither the tide of immigration should come," they wrote, "these shores . . . have room for all." In November 1881, however, there was another noticeable shift, the paper insisting that America was not the only haven for Russian immigrants. On June 30, 1882, the *Hebrew* went even further: "Jews of Europe!" the editors warned, referring to the European counterparts of HEAS, "Know that you are inviting a danger to us . . . !

You send us hither a multitude of men, women and children whom we cannot sustain."

This last was a somewhat frantic exaggeration; most needy immigrants received aid from previously arrived relatives and *landslayt* (people from the same shtetl, or community) as well as from their own mutual aid societies, and no more than 5 percent ever turned to the German Jewish philanthropic agencies for help. The worry of the German Jews was not so much over economic cost as over the prejudice that would be generated by masses of Eastern Jews— prejudice "dangerous to the Jews of refinement and culture in this country."

But things changed, especially after 1891, when the condition of Russian Jews under Nicholas II grew desperate. German Jews in America put aside considerations of comfort and even concern about the rise of antisemitism to support their Russian cousins. Indeed, at the same time that non-Jewish Americans generally inclined toward immigration restriction, leaders of the German Jewish community committed themselves to open immigration as well as to aiding the East Europeans materially. In 1891 the United Hebrew Charities, for example, began maintaining an agent at the old Barge office in New York City, and through March 1893 the Free Employment Bureau run by Boston's German Jews found jobs for more than a thousand applicants. In 1894, the editors of the *American Hebrew* not only applauded these and many other philanthropic efforts, they loudly proclaimed their fears for the Jews of Russia. And while occasionally warning against the possibility of millions of Eastern Jews pouring "pell-mell . . . into the country," the staff of the newspaper vehemently resisted all legislative efforts to curtail Jewish immigration.

If any uncertainty lingered on the part of German Jewish leadership regarding the mass arrival of Russian Jews, it disappeared in the face of the horrors of the pogroms in Russia between 1903 and 1906. The arrogance of the German Jews and their fear of antisemitism never fully dissipated. Likewise, the Eastern Europeans never quite put away their resentment over the condescension and what they called the "cold philanthropy" of the *Yahudim*. Despite the hostility and rivalry, however, the Germans and the Russians, everywhere in America in the late nineteenth and early twentieth centuries, entered into and sustained a relationship marked ultimately by cooperation, if not the cozy warmth of *gemutlikhkayt*. Even after the East

European Jews were able to sustain their own aid agencies, the foremost of which was the Hebrew Immigrant Aid Society (HIAS) founded in 1902, there were sporadic contributions from German Jews.

Ultimately, the Germans played an important role in the fight against immigration restriction and provided much philanthropy. In addition to fighting restriction directly, German Jewish leaders such as Simon Wolf, Jacob Schiff, and Louis Marshall involved themselves in relocation, agricultural colonization, and diversion of immigrants to ports of entry other than in the Northeast (e.g., Galveston, Texas). Dispersal, it was incorrectly believed, would ward off immigration restriction. There were several significant anti-immigration bills passed by Congress between 1875 and 1903, but anti-foreign sentiment did not seriously impede the flow of immigration until World War I, when in 1917 Congress passed a bill, over President Woodrow Wilson's veto, that required immigrant literacy. This affected the relatively more literate Jews less than other immigrant groups in this period. But in 1921 and 1924 stringent quotas were imposed for immigrants from Southern and Eastern Europe, which did radically restrict the Jewish influx.

Of the East European Jews who entered the United States in the period from 1881 to 1924, relatively few left. As many as 25 percent, however, did return to Eastern Europe prior to 1900 in response to variations in economic conditions in America and political conditions in Europe. But after 1903, the return rate dropped off radically, and between 1908 and 1914, only 7 percent of the number of entrants left. The rate of return migration for all other groups was higher, ranging from 9.5 percent to 57.5 percent and averaging 33 percent for the entire period of mass migration. Neither hardship upon arrival nor recurrent economic depression could drive the Jews back to Europe in significant numbers.

Jews voted with their feet for America and mainly for its urban centers. By 1920, 45 percent of the Jewish population of the United States lived in New York City. The next two largest Jewish cities, Chicago and Philadelphia, accounted for 13 percent, and seven other cities in the East and Midwest held another 14 percent. Between 1881 and 1920, the U.S. population experienced a general population increase of 112 percent, while the Jewish population rose 1,300 percent, mainly from the immigration of East European Jews. By 1928, of the 4.7 million Jews in the

United States, 3 million were of East European origin. Living on the West Side of Chicago, in Boston's North End, in Philadelphia's downtown, and especially on New York's Lower East Side (by 1925 one of every three New Yorkers was a Jew!), the Jews from Russia and other parts of Eastern Europe became a "conspicuous minority"—in factories and stores, on streets and in cafes, in *landsmanshaftn* (regional mutual-aid societies) and labor unions, in synagogues, in Yiddish theater and press, in philanthropic and self-help organizations.

Millions had left the *shtetlekh* (small towns) and Old World cities in which they had built their lives. Those who came were artisans, stewards, and peddlers faced with dislocation or obsolescence; socialist militants faced with repression and Jew-hatred; students and the religiously committed faced with grave uncertainties; and above all the innumerable *kleine yidn* (ordinary Jews) faced with impoverishment and persecution. They made the decision to leave Eastern Europe in the late nineteenth and early twentieth centuries. But they did not merely flee. With a strength born of cultural renewal, they yearned "to become." The United States, in a period of extensive industrial expansion and economic growth and with its reputation as a land of opportunity, provided the context for fulfillment.

Gerald Sorin

References and Further Reading

Bodnar, John. 1985. *The Transplanted.* Bloomington: Indiana University Press.

Frankel, Jonathan. 1981. *Prophecy and Politics: Socialism, Nationalism and the Russian Jew, 1862–1917.* Cambridge: Cambridge University Press.

Glazier, Jack. 1998. *Dispersing the Ghetto.* Ithaca, NY: Cornell University Press.

Hersch, Liebmann. 1931. "International Migration of the Jews." In *International Migrations*, Vol. 2, edited by Imre Ferenczi and Walter F. Wilcox, 471–520. New York: National Bureau of Economic Research.

Howe, Irving. 1976. *World of Our Fathers: The Journey of the East European Jews to America and the Life They Found and Made.* New York: Harcourt Brace Jovanovich.

Joseph, Samuel. 1969. *Jewish Immigration to the United States from 1881 to 1910.* New York: Arno Press.

Kuznets, Simon. 1975. "Immigration of Russian Jews to the United States: Background and Structure." *Perspectives in American History* 9: 35–124.

Lederhandler, Eli. 1983. "Jewish Immigration to America and Revisionist Historiography: A Decade of New Perspectives." *YIVO Annual* 18: 391–410.

Mendelsohn, Ezra. 1970. *Class Struggle in the Pale.* Cambridge: Cambridge University Press.

Nadell, Pamela. 1981. "The Journey to America by Steam: The Jews of Eastern Europe in Transition." *American Jewish History* 71 (December): 269–284.

Sarna, Jonathan. 1981. "The Myth of No Return: Jewish Return Migration to Eastern Europe, 1881–1914." *American Jewish History* 71 (December): 265–267.

Sorin, Gerald. 1992. *A Time for Building: The Third Migration.* Baltimore: Johns Hopkins University Press.

Sorin, Gerald. 1993. "Mutual Contempt, Mutual Benefit: The Strained Encounter between German and Eastern European Jews in America, 1880–1920." *American Jewish History* 81 (Autumn): 34–59.

Stanislawski, Michael. 1983. *Tsar Nicholas I and the Jews: The Transformation of Jewish Society in Russia, 1825–1855.* Philadelphia: Jewish Publication Society of America.

Taylor, Philip. 1971. *The Distant Magnet: European Emigration to the United States.* New York: Harper & Row.

Jewish Immigration to Galveston

Jewish immigration to Galveston began in 1814 and continued for more than a hundred years. From the Civil War to World War I, Jews were prominent in business, philanthropy, and municipal government in Galveston, one of the South's most important ports. Galveston Jews founded the first Reform congregation in Texas and established and helped administer several benevolent institutions. They assumed a significant role in the city's relief activities after the devastating storm of 1900. During the first decade of the twentieth century, some Jewish leaders, concerned that America's Jews were concentrated too heavily in New York City, developed a plan to distribute European Jewish immigrants across the country by making Galveston a major port of entry.

Before 1836, some 200 Jews came to Texas while it was under Mexican governance. Galveston served as a port of entry for most newcomers. One such immigrant was Jao de la Porta, a Portuguese Jew who arrived in Galveston in 1814. He sold land to the French pirate Jean Laffite who, with his crew, found shelter on the island between 1816 and 1821. Following Laffite's departure, Galveston was incorporated in 1839 with 1,000 residents and 250 dwellings.

After the Texas war for independence from Mexico in 1836, a full-scale campaign to attract settlers began. Broadsides printed in German newspapers, "*Geh mit uns Texas* [Go with us to Texas]," advertised the state as a haven for refugees. The first wave of Jewish immigrants came to Galveston and to Texas in the 1840s and 1850s mainly from the German states, and Central and Eastern Europe. In the years before the Civil War, Galveston became the principal port of entry for the state. The only deepwater port between New Orleans and Tampico, Mexico, the city relied on the harbor and shipping for its prosperity. Texas was an attractive destination for Jewish immigrants, who fled political persecutions, the revolutions of 1848 (particularly in Prague and Budapest), and the brutal conscription policies of Russian authorities. These immigrants sought political liberalism, economic opportunity, and religious freedom. By 1852 the tiny Jewish community of Galveston had established a Hebrew cemetery within the city cemetery. Another cemetery, Hebrew Rest, was added in 1868 in response to a yellow fever epidemic. The 1850 census indicates that, in a population of 6,000, there were 12 Jewish adults and 14 children living in Galveston. It was not until Yom Kippur 1856 that members of the faith held the first worship service.

Some of the first Jews known to settle in Galveston between 1838 and 1840 were Samuel Maas, Michael Seeligson, Joseph and Rosanna Dyer Osterman, and Isadore Dyer. Seeligson actively pursued politics, serving as alderman in 1840 and 1848 and mayor in 1853. Born in Dessau, Germany, Dyer was the younger brother of Major Leon Dyer, who fought for Texas independence, and Rosanna Dyer Osterman. It was in Dyer's home that the first worship service was conducted. Like Seeligson, Rosanna Dyer Osterman and her husband Joseph, who established a trading business with the interior of Texas, were civic-minded. During a yellow fever episode in 1853, Rosanna Osterman created a makeshift hospital on their property and cared for the sick and the dying. Outbreaks of the disease led to the founding of the Howard Association in Galveston to treat victims of the fever; Rosanna bequeathed $1,000 to this association in her will. During the Civil War, Rosanna Osterman, then a widow, chose to remain in the city and opened her home to the wounded of both the Union and the Confederate armies, as they occupied the city at different times. Soldiers from the Eighth Texas Infantry Regiment published a letter of thanks to her in the Galveston *News.*

Rosanna Osterman died in 1866 and bequeathed the major share of her estate, valued at more than $204,000, to charitable organizations, including the Osterman Widows and Orphans Home Fund. The fund supported three Galveston orphanages and a home for elderly women, the Letitia Rosenberg Women's Home, between 1905 and 1951. Her will provided $5,000 toward a synagogue in Galveston, which became Temple B'nai Israel, dedicated in 1871, the first Reform congregation in Texas; $2,500 toward Congregation Beth Israel in Houston; $1,000 each for Hebrew benevolent societies in Galveston and Houston (the Hebrew Benevolent Society of Galveston was founded in 1866); $1,000 to fund a school for poor Jewish children in Galveston and Houston; $1,000 for the expansion and upkeep of the Galveston Hebrew Cemetery; and $1,000 for a Galveston Sailor's Home. In one of the first instances of interfaith charity, Rosanna Osterman bequeathed fifty shares of stock in the Galveston Wharves to be used "for the support of indigent Israelites, if any there be, if not, of any other denomination residing in Galveston."

In 1868, Galveston Jewish women formed the Ladies Hebrew Benevolent Society (LHBS). Although intended to be an auxiliary to the men's society, it remained apart and aided mainly Jewish women. Some members of the LHBS acted as midwives or nursed indigent or infirm Jewish women and upon a death prepared the body for burial according to Jewish custom. They established an efficient organization with committees for visiting the sick, distributing clothing, finding employment, and donating funds to the poor. Thus, the earliest Jewish immigrants to Galveston quickly established the religious and charitable institutions necessary to sustain community life and to help future immigrants.

In 1870 Galveston, with 13,818 people, ranked as the largest city in Texas; more than 1,000 were Jews. By 1880 the city had grown to 22,248; the foreign born numbered 5,046, or 23 percent of the population—a decrease in the percentage of foreign born from an estimated 40 percent in 1855. After the Civil War, a new influx of Jewish immigrants came to Galveston; many traveled via New Orleans, while others followed the trails west and south, often peddling merchandise in rural counties before making their way to Galveston. Among these adventurers was Harris Kempner, who with his family established cotton brokering, banking, and sugar refining businesses, including the Imperial Sugar Company in Sugar Land, Texas. Others who came were Marks Marx, Kempner's first partner in a wholesale grocery business, and Morris Lasker, the even-

tual owner of the Texas Star Flour and Rice Mills, who became a Texas state legislator in 1895. Following the arrival of new Jewish residents, Galvestonians founded a chapter of B'nai B'rith in 1875. More land was needed for burial; thus, in 1897 and 1951 additional Jewish cemeteries were created. In 1890 the first Jewish house of worship, Temple B'nai Israel, was constructed. As Reform Jews, the congregation voted to become a charter member of the Union of American Hebrew Congregations in 1875; it also established a school, Temple B'nai Israel school, and Hebrew became a requirement in 1877.

As the Jews settled into community life, they conducted business with people of all faiths on the island; they socialized with gentiles after hours, belonged to the same clubs, and intermarried. By 1875, a coalition of Jews, Episcopalians, Presbyterians, and Lutherans, united by their class affiliation, established social societies and proto-welfare institutions. Jews and Christians belonged to Masonic orders, trade unions, political parties, city government, and cultural societies such as the German *Garten Verein*. In 1874, the Ladies German Benevolent Society was founded with about forty Jewish and Christian members. The Jews' early arrival, their small numbers relative to the gentile population, their non-Catholic status—Protestant leaders openly discriminated against Catholics socially—their rapid rise to wealth, and their goodwill toward the community brought about a high degree of acceptance and even assimilation.

Because wealthy Jewish families were an integral part of Galveston society, between 1878 and 1894 genteel Protestant and Jewish women founded or helped to found four permanent benevolent institutions: the Island City Protestant and Israelitish Orphans' Home (later the Galveston Orphans' Home, 1880), the Lasker Home for Children (1894), the Letitia Rosenberg Women's Home (1888), and the Johanna Runge Free Kindergarten (1893). Many Jewish women served on the boards of lady managers for these benevolent institutions and constituted between 6 and 25 percent of the boards' membership before 1920. Others joined social, literary, and culture clubs during the 1880s and 1890s. Galveston Jewish women enjoyed a high degree of assimilation with others of their economic station. One such person was Isabella Dyer Kopperl, the niece of Rosanna Dyer Osterman and wife of successful merchant, city councilman, and Texas legislator Moritz Kopperl. She served on the interfaith Board of Lady Managers of the

Galveston Orphans' Home from 1885 until her death in 1902 and presided over the board as first director from 1885 to 1887. The Kopperls bequeathed $4,000 to establish the orphanage infirmary and kindergarten. Isabella Kopperl's uncle, Isadore Dyer, bequeathed $5,000, half of his estate, to the orphanage in 1888. Thus, the Ostermans, the Dyers, and the Kopperls significantly underwrote charitable endeavors before the turn of the century, providing a model for Jewish philanthropy. In honor of their beneficence, the Women's Health Protective Association established the Isabella Kopperl Memorial Park after her death. In 1912 Morris Lasker donated $15,000 for the expansion and renovation of the Home for Homeless Children, subsequently renamed the Lasker Home for Children. Later, the philanthropy of the Harris Kempner family would be made available to the city and the state through the Harris and Eliza Kempner Fund, which exists today.

The wave of new immigrants to the United States between 1880 and 1924 brought East European Jews to Galveston. As these Jews began to arrive, they formed the Hebrew Orthodox Benevolent Society in 1897, which associated with Congregation Ahavas Israel, first listed in the Galveston city directory in 1898. In 1930, Congregation Beth Jacob was founded, merging two Orthodox congregations into one. Earlier Jewish immigrants came to the aid of the Russian and East European Jews, although attitudes toward the newest arrivals ranged from benevolent altruism to outright resentment. Island City Jewish women, responding to the influx of newcomers, in 1910 formed a branch of the Jewish Council of Women. This organization, with a gift from Eliza Kempner and a donation from the Ladies Hebrew Benevolent Society, established the Jewish Free Kindergarten in 1913 to help Americanize the newcomers. The kindergarten opened in the rooms and yard of Temple B'nai Israel with eight children but soon grew to forty. Mothers, who suffered the greatest isolation due to language and custom barriers, were invited to form Mothers' Clubs. Teachers and administrators planned programs around child welfare work, in which they taught the fundamentals of hygiene.

The Storm of 1900, which swept through Galveston on September 8, was North America's worst recorded natural disaster. It destroyed one-third of the city, damaged the remaining buildings at an estimated cost of $30 million, and took at least 6,000 lives. On September 9, survivors formed a Central Relief Committee for Galveston Storm Sufferers (CRC), an emergency body that directed relief and recovery. Jewish civic leaders participated fully on the CRC and in the island's recovery. Rabbi Henry Cohen (1863–1952), English immigrant and beloved spiritual leader of Temple B'nai Israel from 1888 to 1949, served on the hospital committee and helped to maintain a tent city, which acted as a refuge for several hundred homeless. Isaac H. Kempner, son of Harris Kempner, served as financier and member of the finance committee. Ben Levy, a city alderman, chaired the burial committee. Morris Lasker chaired the correspondence committee and raised funds for the rebuilding committee. One long-term result of this disaster was the creation of a five-man city commission government, a model for Progressive municipal reform. Isaac H. Kempner was elected city treasurer from 1901 to 1915 and mayor from 1917 to 1919. He rescued the city from financial disaster and secured it an A1 financial rating. This resulted in Galveston's seawall construction and grade raising, a process that protected the island against future hurricanes and elevated the habited east end of the island to seventeen feet above sea level on the island's south side. By 1907, the city had largely recovered from the storm. It ranked fifth among U.S. ports and first among Gulf Coast ports in the number of immigrants arriving each year. In 1912 the county and city finished building across the bay a causeway that allowed for improved connections to the mainland via car, train, and interurban.

The new wave of Jewish immigration to the United States reached a peak of 100,000 arrivals a year before World War I. In 1914, 3 million Jews lived in the United States. Most of the recent arrivals came from Eastern Europe and from Russia, in part because of persecution. More than 300 pogroms between 1901 and 1906 alone resulted in the migration flow of Jews to the United States and areas such as Palestine.

As a result of this influx of humanity, in 1905 close to a million Jews lived in New York City, where many experienced crowded tenements, poor working conditions, and barriers related to language and antisemitism. Plans to divert immigrants were endorsed by national labor leader Terrence Powderly and by President Theodore Roosevelt, who believed the labor needs of the South and the Midwest could be supplied by the newly arrived immigrants. To relieve the congestion and give immigrants more opportunities in America's heartland, New York financier and philanthropist Jacob Schiff devised a plan for routing through Galveston the flow of East European Jews to the South and the Midwest. The sponsoring organization for this migration, also known as the Galveston Movement, was the Jewish Immigrant Information Bureau (JIIB), financed with a gift of $500,000 from Jacob Schiff. To expedite the migration, Schiff induced the Jewish Territorial Organization (JTO) in London to set in motion the plan for the redirection of Jews from Europe straight to Galveston. The JTO contacted the Jewish Emigration Society in Kiev to advertise the prospect of settling in the American West. Selected families were provided train tickets to Bremen, accommodations in Bremen, boat tickets to Galveston, and letters of introduction in English for their future employers. Rabbi Henry Cohen in Galveston became the local agent for this enterprise.

Galveston was chosen as the site of immigration for four reasons: the port's location away from New York City was ideal for redirecting immigrants to another part of the country; the steamship company North German Lloyd had direct routes from Bremen to Galveston; the city's size was such that it would not be able to absorb the immigrants, thus implementing the plan to populate the Midwest; and train connections to the cities of Texas and the Midwest facilitated migration to the nation's hinterland.

Between 1907 and 1914, approximately 10,000 Jews entered the port of Galveston, whence they traveled inland. The majority of these sojourners settled in Texas, Iowa, Missouri, Nebraska, and Minnesota. The JIIB acted as a traveler's aid society. Often Rabbi Cohen met these wayfarers at the dock, took them through customs, and escorted them to the bureau office, where they could eat, bathe, write home, and prepare for the journey inland. The JIIB had contacts with local representatives in towns and cities across the Midwest; their tasks were to help the immigrants find jobs and housing and obtain English language instruction. The JIIB provided train fare to selected cities and money to settle before employment began. The Galveston newspapers reported the arrival of each ship laden with Jewish immigrants with genuine enthusiasm, but at the same time, the U.S. Department of Commerce and Labor began to interfere with the movement and turned away more immigrants from Galveston than from any other port. The government agency found violations of the 1907 Immigration Law that forbade agents to pay for the immigrants' passage; others were turned away for

medical reasons, namely hernias and eye problems; others were deemed too poor and were likely, officials claimed, to become public charges. Single females were often excluded for fear of prostitution, white slavery, and organized crime.

In 1914, with the outbreak of World War I, the flow of Jews from Europe slowed to a trickle, severely limiting the number of Jewish immigrants to Texas through Galveston. Ironically, after years of planning and waiting for federal funds, Galvestonians opened an immigrant receiving station on Pelican Island in the middle of Galveston Bay. It lasted only three years, from 1913 to 1916; it was underused after 1914 and badly damaged in the 1915 hurricane. Once the war ended, Americans turned against the flood of immigrants entering the United States, and Congress imposed immigrant quota systems in 1921 and 1924. These acts effectively cut off the unfettered Jewish migration from Europe to Galveston and Texas.

After a century of immigration, first from Central Europe and then from East European nations and Russia, the tide of humanity flowing into Galveston slowed. Houston's port, built in 1914, competed with Galveston's smaller one, and the advantages of a larger city with oil refining prospects attracted future immigrants, including arrivals from Latin America. The 1900 and the 1915 hurricanes drove leading merchants inland to the Bayou City. Although only 300 of the 10,000 Jews who came through Galveston stayed in Texas, their presence and that of other immigrants, Catholics, and African Americans contributed to the rise of the Ku Klux Klan in the 1920s. Galveston was not immune from Klan recruiting efforts, but Father James Kirwin of St. Mary's Cathedral and Rabbi Henry Cohen, who were great friends, publicly opposed the Klan. It was never able to establish a lasting tenure on the island. Notably, in 1905, when the five-man City Commission voted to segregate Galveston's streetcars, one of only two votes opposed was that of Isaac Kempner.

Galveston's Jewish population would not grow in proportion to the advance of other groups on the island or the Jewish population in other Texas cities. The number of Jews in the state, mainly in the larger cities, doubled from approximately 15,000 to 30,000 between 1910 and 1920, and from an estimated 50,000 in 1945 to 92,000 in 1988. Even so, Jewish contributions to the well-being of the commercial aspects of Galveston, accompanied by humanitarianism and the strong sense of social justice manifest in their continued philanthropy, persist into the twenty-first century.

Elizabeth Hayes Turner

References and Further Reading

Bixel, Patricia Bellis, and Elizabeth Hayes Turner. 2000. *Galveston and the 1900 Storm: Catastrophe and Catalyst.* Austin: University of Texas Press.

Cohen, Anne Nathan. 1941. *The Man Who Stayed in Texas: The Life of Rabbi Henry Cohen.* New York: McGraw-Hill.

Fornell, Earl Wesley. 1961. *The Galveston Era: The Texas Crescent on the Eve of Secession.* Austin: University of Texas Press.

Hardwicke, Susan Wiley. 2002. *Mythic Galveston: Reinventing America's Third Coast.* Baltimore: Johns Hopkins University Press.

Hyman, Harold M. 1990. *Oleander Odyssey: The Kempners of Galveston, Texas, 1854–1980s.* College Station: Texas A & M University Press.

Marinbach, Bernard. 1983. *Galveston: Ellis Island of the West.* Albany: State University of New York Press.

McComb, David G. 1986. *Galveston: A History.* Austin: University of Texas Press.

Osterman Widows and Orphans Home Fund of Galveston Records. Rosenberg Library, Galveston.

Rosanna Dyer Osterman Will, Galveston Will Book. Vol. 2., Filed March 26, 1866, pp. 229–244. Galveston County Courthouse, Galveston.

Rozek, Barbara J. 2003. *Come to Texas: Enticing Immigrants, 1865–1915.* College Station: Texas A & M University Press.

Turner, Elizabeth Hayes. 1997. *Women, Culture, and Community: Religion and Reform in Galveston, 1880–1920.* New York: Oxford University Press.

Winegarten, Ruthe, and Cathy Schechter. 1990. *Deep in the Heart: The Lives and Legends of Texas Jews.* Austin, TX: Eakin Press.

Soviet Jewish Immigration

Soviet Jewish emigrés began to arrive in the United States during the early 1970s. From that time to the early twenty-first century, nearly three-quarters of a million Jews left the Soviet Union (USSR) and the nations that succeeded it and settled in the United States. They have arrived in two major waves. The first wave was allowed to leave the USSR in response to years of pressure both from dissident Jews within the Communist bloc and from Jewish activists in Western Europe and the United States. Soviet authorities during this period granted exit visas to Jewish emigrés only if they had received invitations from relatives in Israel.

The Hebrew Immigrant Aid Society (HIAS) and other immigrant aid organizations met emigrés in Vienna and Rome to assist them in gaining required entrance visas to Israel. By the mid-1970s, an increasing number of emigrés wanted to emigrate not to Israel but to the United States. In response to pressure from American Jewish organizations, and over the objections of the State of Israel, HIAS and other immigrant aid organizations decided, in 1976, to help Soviet Jews who wished to emigrate to the United States. This wave of Jewish immigration from Europe to the United States lasted until the early 1980s, when Soviet authorities shut the door to further emigration. In total, it brought about 200,000 emigrés to the United States.

The exodus of Soviet Jews began again in the late 1980s, as the government of Mikhail Gorbachev began loosening restrictions of all kinds. This time, Soviet Jews could apply for exit visas to emigrate directly to the United States if they had family already living there. This emigration grew dramatically after the collapse of the Soviet Union, driven by the desire for family reunification but also by economic hardship, rising crime, ethnic violence, and the contamination of southwestern portions of the former USSR after the accident at the Chernobyl nuclear energy plant in 1986. This migration continues into the twenty-first century.

By far the largest number of Soviet Jewish emigrés settled in New York City and surrounding suburban areas. By the late 1990s, they numbered more than 300,000. Other cities with sizable populations of Soviet Jewish emigrés include Los Angeles, Chicago, San Francisco, and Boston. In each of these cities, this diverse and well-educated immigrant population has left a mark on commerce, culture, and Jewish community life—opening the food stores, restaurants, Russian language bookstores, and small businesses that characterize visible ethnic enclaves but also creating high-technology companies, medical practices, design firms, and international trading companies as well as distinctive art, theater, and music.

The most famous enclave created by Soviet emigrés is a tiny Brooklyn neighborhood called Brighton Beach. This crowded strip of Atlantic seashore soon became known as Little Odessa in recognition of the Ukrainian origins of most of its residents. By 1980, it was the largest Soviet emigré outpost in the world—home to more than 30,000

Soviet Jews. But by 1991, when the collapse of the Soviet Union sparked a new wave of Jewish out-migration, Brighton had lost much of its allure for new arrivals. Class condescension and regional snobbery among well-educated emigrés from Moscow and Leningrad had long generated cracks about "the Odessan riffraff" washing up on Brooklyn's shores. The image of a rough-and-ready gangster ghetto was reinforced by sensational media coverage of "the Russian mob" and semiregular stories in both the local and national press about the neighborhood's "exotic, foreign flavor." Brighton's ghetto image repelled many new immigrants. To them it had become what the Lower East Side was to an earlier generation of American Jews and their immigrant forebears: an ambivalent symbol of the immigration's early years, a place to shop, to gather for family parties, to visit one's elderly parents, and maybe to indulge in a bit of nostalgia for home, but not a place for ambitious new Americans to live. Whenever they could, the 1990s emigrés settled elsewhere.

Still, Jewish immigrant aid agencies, such as the venerable Hebrew Immigrant Aid Society and the New York Association for New Americans, tended to settle newly arrived Soviet emigrés in neighborhoods with long-established Jewish communities. In New York, new arrivals were settled in Williamsburg and Brighton Beach. In Chicago, new arrivals were sent to West Rogers Park. In Los Angeles, Soviet emigrés were first settled in Fairfax and West Hollywood.

Settling emigrés in large groups in densely populated areas made it easier for Jewish social service agencies to provide adjustment counseling to help immigrants deal with the traumas of uprooting and resettlement, loneliness, generational conflicts, and marital tensions. Emigrés in the 1970s had more publicly funded services available to them because they were granted federal refugee status—entitling them to housing aid, health care, and a fast track to citizenship. Automatic refugee status for Soviet emigrés ended in 1988, and since that time new arrivals have had to depend more heavily on private resettlement agencies, usually funded by the American Jewish community.

In many cities, local Jewish agencies created "host family" or "one on one" programs, which paired immigrants with American Jewish families who had children of similar ages as well as matching professional and social interests. In these cities, Soviet emigrés have established bonds with American Jewish families. In cities such as New York and Los Angeles with huge Soviet emigré populations, immigrants and their children have remained relatively insular, socializing with and often marrying within the Soviet emigré community.

In every city with a large Soviet Jewish population, the move to the suburbs and to less ghettolike urban communities began quickly. Suburban ethnic enclaves are now as common as urban ethnic islands. In Southern California, Soviet emigré communities now dot the San Fernando and Simi valleys. In the Bay Area, Soviet Jews have poured into the high-technology sector, settling in San Mateo, Hayward, and Berkeley as well as Silicon Valley. In Fairlawn, New Jersey, and Newton, Massachusetts, well-heeled towns near New York and Boston, Soviet Jewish emigrés have transformed the landscape. Like most suburbanites, they take comfort both in their closeness to urban centers and in their self-imposed distance.

The Soviet immigrant population in all of these major metropolitan areas is large enough that there can be no single Soviet Jewish community. There are pockets and subsets of immigrants, divided as they were in the former Soviet Union by economic and political differences as well as by region of origin. One can find more than a few neighborhoods or suburban streets where emigrés from Kishinev or Minsk, Moscow or Odessa gather together in mini-communities.

One of the most distinctive is the Central Asian emigré community in New York's Forest Hills, Queens. Since the 1970s, more than 35,000 Jewish emigrés from Uzbekistan, Tajikistan, Kazakhstan, and Armenia have created a bustling ethnic enclave there. Culturally, linguistically, and religiously distinct from their Western Soviet counterparts, Bukharan emigrés identify with the Middle East rather than Europe. They have never spoken Yiddish; rather, they speak a dialect of Persian written in Hebrew characters. They believe themselves to be descendants of an ancient Persian Jewish community and trace their origins in Uzbekistan back to the fifth century. Bukharan Jews have faced prejudice from other Soviet emigrés as well as from American-born Jews. If Soviet emigrés have bristled at charges by American-born Jews that they were not "real Jews," Bukharans are angered by those who say that they are not "real Russians."

Soviet emigrés are divided as well by class, gender, generation, and culture. Even in the "worker's state," those with university degrees experienced a far higher standard of living than those who did not finish high school. While Boston and San Francisco are home to emigrés with an almost uniformly high level of education, one-third of emigrés to New York did not have high school degrees when they arrived. Many of these are elderly. Older and less educated emigrés have had a harder transition to American life than younger emigrés, especially those with university degrees from Moscow, St. Petersburg, Minsk, and Kiev.

Elderly Soviet Jewish emigrés—those over sixty make up about one-third of the immigration—have had the benefit of access to Social Security benefits and Medicare upon arrival in the United States. Settled in urban communities with large populations of World War I– and World War II–era Jewish immigrants, many were able to communicate immediately, having Yiddish as a common language. The oldest, like the youngest among the emigrés, have been able to forge bonds outside the emigré community, joining synagogues and senior centers and moving into senior citizen housing projects, where they come into contact with elderly Jewish immigrants from pre-Soviet Russia, Poland, Hungary, and Germany. Still, this elderly population is vulnerable economically. Federal legislation mandating cuts in social services to noncitizens has left thousands on the brink of hunger and homelessness. These cuts generated fear and panic among a population traumatized by two world wars and Nazi and Soviet repression.

Middle-aged and elderly professionals have had their own problems. Many say that they have experienced an intellectual catastrophe in the United States that has forced physicians and lawyers, PhDs and classical musicians to take jobs as store clerks, taxi drivers, and garment workers—at least for a while. *Science* magazine estimates that 15 percent of Soviet immigrants arriving in the United States between 1987 and 1990 had PhDs or equivalent degrees in science and engineering. Only a handful were able to pick up their careers in the United States. Many have found it difficult even to break into lower-level jobs in the sciences because they are considered overqualified. "In Russia," one engineer commented, "we had to hide that we are Jews. Here, to get a job, we have to hide that we have a Ph.D." (Orleck 1999).

The job market has been much harder for older women. According to a 1995 Office of Refugee Resettlement statistic, Soviet Jews have the largest gender-based wage gap of any recent immigrant group. Almost all Soviet Jewish women worked outside the home before emigra-

tion. And they were just as likely as men to have earned college degrees and to have achieved professional success. Of Soviet Jewish emigré women in the United States, 60 percent reported having held academic, scientific, professional, or technical jobs prior to emigration. Only 31 percent of these, mostly the young, have found employment in those fields in the United States. At the time of the survey, more than 55 percent of Soviet emigré women were working in clerical or service jobs in the United States.

By contrast, most young adults with strong educational backgrounds have been able to find work and move into the middle class. By the 1990s, Soviet emigrés had made their presence felt in New York, Boston, Chicago, Los Angeles, and scores of suburban communities as physicians, entrepreneurs, stock analysts, industrial researchers, accountants, and computer specialists. Those who emigrated as children have begun to appear in large numbers in both public and private institutions of higher learning. By one estimate, one-third of students enrolled in Boston-area community colleges in the late 1990s were Soviet emigrés. They are also well represented in more selective institutions, Brandeis University having perhaps the highest percentage (Orleck 1999).

Despite complaints by some in the American Jewish community that Soviet emigrés are less strongly Jewish identified than American-born Jews, national surveys suggest otherwise. Although half a century of Soviet suppression of Jewish religious life and Yiddish culture has caused lapses in Jewish education as well as ambivalence about Jewish identity, Soviet Jewish emigrés strongly identify as Jews. Indeed, middle-aged and elderly emigrés, who have survived Cossack pogroms, Stalinist purges, and the Nazi *Einsatzgruppe* death squads, are outraged when Jews who have lived comfortably in the United States during all of those years dare to say that Soviet Jews are "not really Jews."

Surveys done in the mid-1990s show that, in fact, Soviet emigrés relate to their Judaism in the same ways as other American Jews. They attend synagogue regularly, celebrate Jewish holidays in their homes, and send their children to Hebrew school in about the same percentages as American Jews (approximately 35 percent). But they are more likely than American Jews to say that being Jewish is central to their identity, a fact interviewees attribute to persecution at the hands of the Nazis and the Soviet authorities. And a staggering number of adult men have sought circumcisions upon arrival in the United States, more than 10,000 in New York City alone (Orleck 2001).

Increasingly, there are signs that Soviet emigrés are reaching accord with American Jewish leaders. Emigrés have founded a Russian division of the Federation of Jewish Philanthropies and have become active in a wide range of American Jewish charitable organizations. As for relations between Soviet emigrés and American Jews more generally, time is healing resentments and misunderstandings, just as it did between East European emigrés and German Jews in the United States earlier in the twentieth century. There never has been a monolithic American Jewish community. The Soviet emigrations of the 1970s and the 1990s have further complicated the demographics, culture, and politics of American Jewry. From New York to Seattle, Soviet Jewish emigrés are rapidly becoming American Jews, but what that means to each emigré and in each community is as varied as the immigration itself.

Annelise Orleck

References and Further Reading

Gold, Steven. 1995. *From the Workers' State to the Golden State.* Boston: Allyn & Bacon.

Markowitz, Fran. 1993. *A Community in Spite of Itself: Soviet Jewish Emigres in New York.* Washington, DC: Smithsonian Press.

Orleck, Annelise. 1999. *Soviet Jewish Americans.* Westport, CT: Greenwood Press.

Orleck, Annelise. 2001. "Soviet Jews." In *New Immigrants in New York,* edited by Nancy Foner, 111–140. New York: Columbia University Press.

Jewish Identity in America

In his 1782 book *Letters from an American Farmer,* the Frenchman J. Hector St. John de Crèvecoeur asked the most important question in American history: "What, then, is the American, this new man?" This question of identity has been of particular concern to American Jews, and it is not too much to say that identity has been the grand theme of American Jewish history. In America, Crèvecoeur wrote, the European discards "all his ancient prejudices and manners, [and] receives new ones from the new mode of life he has embraced, the new government he obeys, and the new rank he holds." And just as Crèvecoeur emphasized the newness of America, so have America's

Jews, who were never more American than when they were inventing and then reinventing their Jewishness. America's Jews have been particularly adept at leaving behind ancient prejudices and manners and receiving new ones compatible with this new way of life. Their combining of "the immediate and the transcendent, the quirky and the hallowed," the historian Jenna W. Joselit wrote, "was virtually without parallel in modern Jewish history." American Jewish identity, Joselit continued, was "a malleable and protean social construct." Little troubled by inconsistencies, contradictions, or the burdens of the past, Jews "fashioned a home-grown American Jewishness" (Joselit 1994).

If the social and economic conditions of America were new to European immigrants, this was especially true for Jewish immigrants. Antisemitism in America was relatively mild, citizenship was a matter of right and not of sufferance, barriers to economic and social advancement were comparatively low, and assimilation was not difficult. In 1783, Mordecai Sheftall, a Jew living in Georgia, emphasized to his son that "an entire new scene" had opened itself before America's Jews, "and we have the world to begin again" (Lipset and Raab 1995). But this new scene presented unique challenges to Jewish identity and continuity.

If America was not the promised land, it certainly was the land of promise. "God Bless America," wrote Irving Berlin, who had been born in a Polish ghetto. Here, the state did not reinforce any particular definition of Jewish identity, nor did it bolster the power of any Jewish religious establishment. The American Jew could be any kind of Jew (or non-Jew) he or she wished. It is not surprising, then, that American Jews brought forth novel definitions of what it meant to be a Jew or that Jewish intellectuals should be so concerned with analyzing and defining the nature of American and of American Jewish identity. Of America's major ethnic groups prior to the late twentieth century, only the Jews were both an ethnic minority and a religious one. Other ethnic groups were at least Christian. Jews from Europe, North Africa, and the Middle East had been the most isolated and communally organized of groups and had to make the most radical adaptation to the individualistic ethos of American society. The compatibility of Jewish and American identity could not be taken for granted but had to be continually asserted and defended.

The historian Paul Buhle noted that the word *identity* was at one time "a virtual monopoly of Jewish writers," and this was true whether the topic was American identity in general or American Jewish identity in particular (Buhle 2004). It is not coincidental, as Marxists were fond of saying, that no American novel has probed more deeply the process of immigrant acculturation than Abraham Cahan's *The Rise of David Levinsky.* Nor was it coincidental that the three major paradigms of American identity—Anglo-conformity, the melting pot, and cultural pluralism—were most famously enunciated by Jews who had the condition of America's Jews uppermost in their minds.

Anglo-conformity, the belief that immigrants should conform to preexisting cultural and social patterns and values dating from the eighteenth century, was best expressed by Emma Lazarus, America's first Jewish poet of note. Lazarus, a member of a distinguished and largely assimilated Sephardic New York family, had her Jewish consciousness awakened in the 1880s when she encountered East European Jewish immigrants who were settling in New York City. Lazarus defended the immigrants against their detractors and was, in the words of the historian John Higham, "the first modern American laureate of their history and culture" (Higham 1975). Lazarus is best known for her sonnet "The New Colossus," which was inscribed on the base of the Statue of Liberty. When Frederic Auguste Bartholdi's statue, which he titled "Liberty Enlightening the World," was placed in New York harbor in 1886, it was supposed to denote America as the land of liberty. Soon, though, and largely because of Lazarus's poem, the statue came to symbolize the openness of America to oppressed immigrants. "Give me your tired, your poor/Your huddled masses yearning to breathe free," it read.

The next line in the sonnet—"The wretched refuse of your teeming shore"—has puzzled historians. The immigrants hardly considered themselves the flotsam of Europe, and it was incongruous that Lazarus would describe them as garbage. In the 1880s, however, *wretched* often was used as a synonym for *distressed,* and *refuse* frequently referred to objects that were valueless as well as worthless. Whatever meaning Lazarus had in mind, "wretched refuse" was easily assimilated into the ideology of Anglo-conformity, and "The New Colossus" strengthened the optimistic assumption that the beneficent environment of America could transform even the "wretched refuse" of European immigrants into productive citizens.

Israel Zangwill, the most famous exponent of the "melting pot," had a different view of American identity and of its Jews. Born in 1864 in London's Jewish ghetto of

Whitechapel to impoverished Russian Jewish immigrants, Zangwill would become the most prominent English-speaking Jewish writer of his generation. He wrote nostalgic novels of the ghetto, and yet in his own life he was a militant assimilationist. An ardent Zionist, he argued that Jews who decided to remain in the Diaspora should follow his example and relinquish all Jewish peculiarities. He believed intermarriage to be the answer to antisemitism, and he himself married an English Christian. The couple's first son was neither baptized nor circumcised.

Zangwill's 1908 play, *The Melting Pot,* which was the sensation of that year's Broadway season, reflected Zangwill's universalistic ideology as well as his exalted image of America as a land in which all ethnic identities, including that of Anglo Americans, were being melted down to create a new American. The plot of *The Melting Pot* revolves around the romance of David Quixano, a Jewish immigrant in America, and Vera Revendal, a Christian settlement house worker. After they decide to marry, David discovers that Vera's father had been responsible for the pogrom in Russia in which his family had been murdered. The drama of the play revolves around whether David would remain faithful to his image of America as a land in which the nationalities of Europe were being fused into a new American nationality or would reject marriage with Vera as quixotic and return to the insular Jewish loyalties of his youth.

As might be expected, love wins out. The play's melodramatic conclusion has David and Vera standing on the roof of a settlement in lower Manhattan. David pleads with Vera to "cling to me till all these ghosts are exorcised, cling to me till our love triumphs over death." He then looks toward the harbor where the Statue of Liberty gazes benignly on the ships bringing the immigrants to America. He is inspired by the view and confirms his vision of an American national character being shaped in the crucible of New York City's harbor. "It is the fires of God round his Crucible. There she lies, the great Melting-Pot—listen! Can't you hear the roaring and the bubbling? . . . Ah, what a stirring and a seething! Celt and Latin, Slav and Teuton, Greek and Syrian—black and yellow. . . . Yes, East and West, and North and South, the palm and the pine, the pole and the equator, the crescent and the cross—how the great Alchemist melts and fuses them with his purging flame! Here shall they all unite to build the Republic of Man and the Kingdom of God."

Theatergoers, including President Theodore Roosevelt, were rhapsodic over Zangwill's vision of a new American identity free of the ethnic animosities of Europe. It is doubtful, however, that those such as Roosevelt, who traced their American lineage back to the colonial period, agreed with Zangwill that they, too, were obliged to jump into the melting pot alongside the immigrants. Jewish spokesmen also criticized the message of *The Melting Pot* for suggesting that Jewish identity had no future in America. An editorial in the *American Hebrew* called the play's thesis a "counsel of despair" (Gleason 1992). Zangwill believed that antisemitism and continued immigration from Europe might slow down but would not fundamentally impede the inevitable melting pot process. He suggested to those American Jews committed to remaining Jewish to settle in Palestine where they could help create a new Jewish society. Jews who chose to stay in America would inevitably be amalgamated within a couple of generations.

For Zangwill, American identity was all about ethnicity. His evolving American identity was a blending of the most desirable elements of the various ethnic groups being cooked in the melting pot. But American Jewish identity had a religious as well as an ethnic component, and Zangwill's metaphor did not speak to those American Jews who were committed to Judaism. A group such as the Jews, who were in part a community of faith, had no place in Zangwill's schema.

Zangwill's great opponent was another Zionist, Horace Kallen. Kallen, the son of an Orthodox rabbi in Boston, had rejected traditional Judaism as a youth, but, in contrast to Zangwill, he was optimistic regarding the Jewish future in America. While a student at Harvard, Kallen was influenced by Barrett Wendell, a professor of literature. Wendell believed that Hebraic ideals and the Bible had played an important role in the development of America. Wendell and William James, Kallen's dissertation mentor, encouraged Kallen to think of American culture as diverse rather than monistic. Kallen became even more convinced of the "*pluribus*" rather than the "*unum*" of American identity when he taught at the University of Wisconsin prior to World War I. He was impressed by the extent to which the various ethnic groups of Wisconsin were seemingly maintaining their separate identities, and he concluded that America was developing into a federation of nationalities similar to Switzerland. Kallen was a poor prophet. Most American immigrants did not live in isolated rural communities in the Midwest, where the maintenance of ethnic traditions was easier. And the attacks on German culture during World War I and the immigrant restriction legislation of the 1920s were more revealing of the attitudes of most Americans toward the cultural balkanization of their country than was Kallen's paean to ethnic diversity.

Kallen argued that ethnic identity was the most important and permanent part of a person's being, "the center at which he stands, the point of his most intimate social relations, therefore of his intensest emotional life." (One would think that the family and not the ethnic group was the setting of a person's most intimate social relations and his intensest emotional life.) The one thing a person could not change, Kallen said, was his grandfather. But neither could this grandfather predict the identity of his grandchildren. For example, America recently had a secretary of defense named Cohen who does not identify as a Jew and who is married to a black person. It is hardly likely that this was anticipated by his grandparents.

In 1915 Kallen published a seminal essay in the *Nation* titled "Democracy versus the Melting Pot: A Study of American Nationality." This is the seminal document of what would come to be known as cultural pluralism. Democracy, Kallen argued, required that the choices of groups as well as those of individuals be respected. Zangwill's melting pot concept was inherently antidemocratic because it called for the disappearance of group identity. Kallen replaced the metaphor of the melting pot with that of an orchestra. Just as every instrument in an orchestra makes a distinctive contribution to the music, so every ethnic group makes a singular contribution to America. "In the life and culture of a nation," he said, ethnic, religious, and occupational groups "compound their different activities to make up the national spirit. The national spirit is constituted by this union of the different."

Kallen's vision of a pluralistic America was influenced by his own Jewish identity. Although alienated from Judaism, he was not estranged from his people. Kallen was an ardent Zionist and an advocate of Hebrew culture, and he described himself as a Hebraist. For Kallen, Jewishness was a modern, secular, ethnic identity shorn of any supernaturalism and compatible with advanced thinking. In his 1932 book, *Judaism at Bay: Essays Toward the Adjustment of Judaism to Modernity,* a revealing title, he rejected the conflating of Jewishness with religion. Rather, it was "the Jewish way of life become necessarily secular, humanist, scientific, conditioned on the industrial economy, without having ceased to be livingly Jewish."

Sidney Hook, a philosopher at New York University from 1927 to 1973, also developed a theory of American Jewish identity compatible with modernity. While he was an agnostic and had no interest in Zionism or Hebrew culture, Hook nevertheless had a lifelong interest in Jewish matters and wrote intermittently on Jewish topics. In his writings, he equated Jewishness with the American democratic way of life. For Hook, a socialist, this involved three items in particular: economic justice, the recognition of group differences, and the pragmatic scientific method of John Dewey. "As I interpret Jewish culture," Hook said in "Promise without Dogma: A Social Philosophy for Jews," a 1937 *Menorah Journal* essay, "its noblest feature is the characteristic way in which its traditions have fused passion for social justice with respect for scientific method and knowledge. When Jews forsake this method, they forsake a precious part of their tradition." The logic of Jewish identity, Hook claimed, led inexorably to socialism. Socialism, more so than liberalism or conservatism, joined "the ideals of the good life in the good society to the methods of intelligent analysis and action."

In conflating Jewishness with Dewey's instrumentalism and neo-Marxism, Hook presented his own ideological choices as a model for other Jews. But his definition of Jewish identity had no room for anything that was distinctively Jewish, whether it be language, religious ritual, or love of Zion. In the 1940s and 1950s, Hook warned American Jews that taking too much comfort in Israel's economic and social development and military victories could lead to ethnic chauvinism. "A people that has . . . been rational and pacific," he said, now seek to show that "they are like everyone else—inconsistent, fanatical, atavistic." Hook admitted that the social philosophy he recommended to Jews was equally valid for gentiles as well. Jews did not have a monopoly on social justice, the scientific method, and pluralism. In fact, Hook's model was not Moses Maimonides, the medieval Jewish philosopher, or even Moses Mendelssohn, the nineteenth-century founder of Reform Judaism, but John Dewey, a naturalistic philosopher (Shapiro 1990).

Alan Dershowitz, the Harvard Law School professor, grew up in a far more religious environment than Hook. During the 1930s and 1940s, his pious family lived in Boro Park, the center of Orthodoxy in Brooklyn. Early in his life,

Dershowitz rebelled against religious restrictions. He remained, however, deeply Jewish. His 1991 book, *Chutzpah,* attempted to ground American Jewish identity not in religious rituals but in political activism. If anything could drive him back to observance, he said, it would not be religious conviction but "a political desire to fight those who want to see Judaism and Jews relegated to interesting museum exhibits and poignant memorials." For his generation, "political Judaism is not only possible, it may well be the most logical prototype" (Dershowitz 1991).

Dershowitz acknowledged that there was no specific content to his political Judaism. It was broad enough to encompass the entire spectrum of politics, and it included items with which he was in fundamental disagreement. But if Jewish politics encompassed everything, then it really stood for nothing in particular. And if it encompassed everything, then what was specifically Jewish about it? If some Jews believed that liberal politics was the essence of Jewish identity, others believed liberalism to be hostile to Jewish interests. If some Jews were pro-life, others were pro-choice. If some Jews believed that Jewish interests required that Israel take a hard-line attitude toward the Palestinians, others favored a more conciliatory approach. In espousing a political Judaism, Dershowitz seemed to be clutching at straws, determined to find something that would guarantee Jewish survival at a time when only a small minority of American Jews were attracted to traditional Judaism. And even he was skeptical that a Jewish identity revolving around politics could be passed on to children and grandchildren whose political experiences and memories were not his.

Despite these caveats, *Chutzpah* was enthusiastically received by American Jews. This reception indicated the extent to which American Jewry was evolving from a religio-ethnic community to an interest group. This metamorphosis was manifested in the frequent use by Jewish leaders of the word *agenda* when describing their objectives and activities. Philanthropic organizations, interest groups, and lobbyists have agendas and do things, while religions and ethnic groups have beliefs, rituals, and culture, and simply are.

The two major items on Dershowitz's agenda were defending the state of Israel and attacking antisemitism. But how relevant were these concerns to most American Jews? Undoubtedly support for Israel was the lowest common denominator of Jewish identity during the 1960s and

1970s. But it is likely that this Israelism has receded as American Jewry's economic importance to Israel has diminished and as a generation of American Jews has emerged that does not have personal memories of the heroic days of the late 1940s when the State of Israel was created, or of the Mideast wars of 1967 and 1973. While older Jews view Israel against the backdrop of Jewish powerlessness and the Holocaust, younger Jews view Israel against the backdrop of its vast military power, its domination of more than a million restive Arabs, and its often sordid politics, particularly concerning religion. Surveys of Jewish attitudes toward Israel have noted a decline in emotional attachment to Israel among younger Jews. Critics also questioned the relevance of the second item on Dershowitz's political agenda—fighting antisemitism—in shaping American Jewish identity. By the late twentieth century, domestic antisemitism had ceased to be a serious problem, although antisemitism remained important in the Middle East and Europe.

Walt Whitman, in his *Democratic Vistas,* said that American identity would never be secure until "it founds and luxuriantly grows its own forms of art, poems, schools, theology, displacing all that exists, or as has been produced anywhere in the past under opposite influences." Unhampered by restrictions on religious expression imposed by the state or by an established church, American Jews have been free to develop fresh forms of religious expression and theology. This was particularly true after World War II, when Judaism became the major context within which Jewish identity was expressed, supplanting competing forms of Jewishness such as left-wing politics and Yiddish secular culture. This was a creative period for American Judaism, and each of its major branches—Orthodoxy, Conservative Judaism, and Reform—spawned new movements offering novel alternatives of Jewish religious identity.

Out of Orthodoxy came Modern Orthodoxy, which sought to integrate American cultural and social norms with traditional Judaism. Conservative Judaism gave birth to Mordecai Kaplan's Reconstructionist movement, which emphasized Jewish peoplehood and was skeptical of many of the traditional supernatural tenets of Judaism. Reform Judaism produced the anti-theistic Humanistic Judaism. These new religious options reflected the openness of American life and the difficulty of imposing imported religious norms and practices in the new world, conditions that had existed for centuries.

In 1785, for example, the leadership of Congregation Mikveh Israel of Philadelphia complained to the chief rabbi of Amsterdam, Holland, about the spread of heretical practices within its membership. "In this country . . . everybody does as he pleases," it lamented. "They consult so-called 'scholars,' thoroughly corrupt individuals, who flagrantly profane the name of Heaven and who contrive erroneous legalistic loopholes." These "vicious people," the leadership protested, continued to attend synagogue services "because under the laws of the country it is impossible to enjoin them from so doing." Within a couple of decades, however, even Mikveh Israel was doing as it pleased. Thus, it rejected the advice of London's rabbinical authorities and accepted as a member a *mamzer,* a person born from a forbidden sexual union. In defending its decision, the congregation claimed that the ruling of London's rabbinate was "utterly uncongenial to the liberal spirit of the constitutions and laws of this enlightened age and country" (Sarna 2004). For Mikveh Israel's leaders and for American Jews, individualism and voluntarism trumped Jewish law and tradition. A century later, an enterprising rabbi on New York's Lower East Side advertised himself as the chief Hungarian rabbi of New York City. When asked what religious body had appointed him to this position, he replied, "the sign painter."

There seemed no universally acceptable answer to the question of Jewish identity. As one joke noted, the only thing that two Jews could agree on was what a third should contribute. The lowest common denominator of American Jewish identity had little to do with religion. A Jew apparently was anyone who wanted to be viewed as such, and the motivation was usually social rather than religious. Jewish fraternal organizations such as B'nai B'rith and the National Council of Jewish Women, Jewish charities such as Jewish hospitals and Jewish federations, and Jewish political organizations such as the American Jewish Committee and the American Jewish Congress provided secular and voluntary options for Jews to act Jewishly, however they might define Jewish identity.

American Jews remained after 350 years what they had been when they first settled in New York in 1654: a choosing people. Some social scientists asserted that the most decisive determinant in American Jewish identity was the sociological choices that Jews made and not the causes they espoused or the religious rituals they practiced. These sociologists believed that it was far more important that Jews belonged to Jewish organizations, that their friends were Jews, and that they lived among other Jews, rather than whether they kept kosher, read books on the Holocaust, and supported liberal causes. By the end of the twentieth century, however, most Jews were no longer living in neighborhoods in which the majority of people were Jews, nor were they confined to occupations in which most of their fellow workers were Jews. Critics of the social scientists wondered whether Jews would continue to relate to other Jews on a social basis if their religious and ideological ties to Jewish life atrophied.

In a nation that strongly values individual autonomy, the survival of a passionate Jewish identity among a large number of Jews is problematic. America's Jews have gone from being a chosen people to being a choosing people, and the choices they have made are troubling to Jewish survivalists. The 1990 National Jewish Population Survey estimated that there were 1.1 million Jews who practiced no religion and another 1.3 million born Jews who practiced a religion other than Judaism. There were also 185,000 converts to Judaism and more than 1.3 million gentiles living with Jews (Heilman 1995). For Jews, America has been, as is stated on the country's Great Seal, a *novus ordo seclorum*—a new order of the ages, something new under the sun.

Edward S. Shapiro

References and Further Reading

Buhle, Paul. 2004. *From the Lower East Side to Hollywood: Jews in American Popular Culture.* London: Verso.

Dershowitz, Alan M. 1991. *Chutzpah.* Boston: Little, Brown.

Gleason, Philip. 1992. *Speaking of Diversity: Language and Ethnicity in Twentieth-Century America.* Baltimore: Johns Hopkins University Press.

Gordon, Milton M. 1964. *Assimilation in American Life: The Role of Race, Religion, and National Origins.* New York: Oxford University Press.

Heilman, Samuel C. 1995. *Portrait of American Jews: The Last Half of the Twentieth Century.* Seattle: University of Washington Press.

Higham, John. 1975. *Send These to Me: Jews and Other Immigrants in Urban America.* New York: Atheneum.

Joselit, Jenna Weissman. 1994. *The Wonders of America: Reinventing Jewish Culture, 1880–1950.* New York: Hill and Wang.

Lipset, Seymour Martin, and Earl Raab. 1995. *Jews and the New American Scene.* Cambridge, MA: Harvard University Press.

Sarna, Jonathan. 2004. *American Judaism: A History.* New Haven, CT: Yale University Press.

Selengut, Charles, ed. 1999. *Jewish Identity in the Postmodern Age: Scholarly and Personal Reflections.* St. Paul, MN: Paragon House.

Seltzer, Robert M., and Norman J. Cohen. 1995. *The Americanization of the Jews.* New York: New York University Press.

Shapiro, Edward S. 1990. "The Jewishness of the New York Intellectuals: Sidney Hook, a Case Study." In *American Pluralism and the Jewish Community,* edited by Seymour Martin Lipset, 153–171. New Brunswick, NJ: Transaction Press.

Shapiro, Edward S. 1992. *A Time for Healing: American Jewry since World War II.* Baltimore: Johns Hopkins University Press.

Shapiro, Edward S. 2003. "Will Herberg's Protestant-Catholic-Jew: A Critique." In *Key Texts in American Jewish Culture,* edited by Jack Kugelmass, 258–274. New Brunswick, NJ: Rutgers University Press.

Sollors, Werner. 1986. *Beyond Ethnicity: Consent and Descent in American Culture.* New York: Oxford University Press.

Sorin, Gerald. 1997. *Tradition Transformed: The Jewish Experience in America.* Baltimore: Johns Hopkins University Press.

Wertheimer, Jack. 1993. *A People Divided: Judaism in Contemporary America.* New York: Basic Books.

Demographic and Economic Profiles of Twentieth-Century American Jewry

The Demography of Jews in Twentieth-Century America

The Jewish population of the United States increased almost fourfold during the twentieth century, from an estimated 1.5 million in 1900 to between 5.5 and 6 million a century later. Population growth has not been evenly spread over this period. Rapid increase in population size due to immigration at the turn of the twentieth century was followed by small and steady increases through the 1970s and relative stability during the last three decades of the century. These changes in the size of the Jewish population have been accompanied by dramatic shifts in the level and sources of Jewish immigration, reductions in the size of Jewish families, significant changes in the timing of marriage and family formation, increases in life expectancy, and alterations in migration and the regional distribution of the Jewish population within the United States.

Population gains and losses through intermarriage are difficult to gauge, but by the end of the twentieth century, intermarriage had replaced immigration as the critical element of American Jewish demography. Increases in the level of intermarriages over the last century have resulted in Jewish population declines, with some compensating gains due to formal conversions and the identification of those not born Jewish with the Jewish community. The ethnic–religious identification of the adult children of mixed marriages of Jews and non-Jews remains unclear and has become an important issue at the beginning of the twenty-first century.

The American Jewish population has always been a small proportion of the total American population. Starting in the middle of the nineteenth century with a base population of around 15,000 in 1840, the American Jewish population increased to around 50,000 at mid-nineteenth century, largely due to the influx of German Jews, and increased substantially to almost 250,000 by 1880. The large increase reflected the beginning of the mass immigration of Jews from Eastern Europe, where there was the largest concentration of world Jewry. By the beginning of the twentieth century, the American Jewish population had increased to just over 1 million, representing about 1.4 percent of the total U.S. population (Goldstein 1971).

In 1907 the estimated Jewish population in the United States was 1.8 million, and by 1917 it had almost doubled to 3.4 million, or 3.3 percent of the total U.S. population. Another 1 million was added in the next decade and another 500,000 by 1937, when the Jewish population was estimated at 4.7 million, representing 3.7 percent of the total U.S. population. Smaller increases in population size characterized the U.S. Jewish population through the 1950s and 1960s. From an estimated 5 million Jews in 1950, the size of the American Jewish population has hovered between 5 million and 6 million during the

1990s. Jews represent around 2.2 percent of the total U.S. population (Goldscheider 2004).

Due to the problems of data collection and the absence of data by religion in official government documents, a demographic description of the American Jewish community can only be estimated. A general portrait and trends can be pieced together from a combination of government data sources, sample surveys on specific topics that include a relatively small number of Jewish respondents, and local Jewish community surveys. National Jewish population surveys sponsored by Jewish organizations and conducted around 1970, 1990, and in 2000 are important sources of information on the demography of American Jews, but these have also been limited in coverage and accuracy. In the absence of other national data sources, national Jewish population surveys represent the best available information on American Jews.

By the end of the twentieth century, it had become unclear how American Jews were to be defined for demographic purposes—by religion, by ethnicity, by self-definition, or by some combination. Much of the uncertainty about the size of the Jewish population reflects the limited data available and the changing definitions of who is Jewish. Nevertheless, it is generally agreed that Jewish population size has remained relatively stable over the last two decades of the twentieth century. The influx of Jews from the former Soviet Union starting in the 1970s, and to a lesser extent from the State of Israel, has contributed to the general stability despite the below-population-replacement fertility rate and the increasing rate of outmarriages. How adult Jews of intermarried parents are counted represents a major unknown factor in estimating American Jewish population size.

The internal movement of Jews within the United States over the twentieth century has resulted in the changing distribution of Jewish population by region, state, and metropolitan area. Increases in Jewish population in the southern and western regions of the United States balance the decline in the proportion of Jews in the Northeast. Along with regional shifts have come changes in the reconcentration of Jews in particular metropolitan areas, away from the large cities on the East Coast to cities on the West Coast and in the South. By the end of the twentieth century, an estimated 45 percent of America's Jews lived in the Northeast, 20 percent lived in the South, and 20 percent lived in the West (*American Jewish Year Book* 2005).

Since the 1920s, the Jewish fertility rate has been rather low, fluctuating on average around two children per family through the 1970s. Starting in the 1980s and 1990s, average completed Jewish family size dipped slightly below two children. The family size of the younger generation of American Jews hovers at below the level needed for population replacement. At the end of the twentieth century, later ages at marriage and the delay in the birth of the first child until women are in their late twenties, combined with higher educational levels and professional work commitments of women, characterized American Jews as well as other middle-class, urban, professional, educated whites. Low fertility over the twentieth century reflected the very careful family planning and contraceptive efficiency characteristic of American Jews in the context of their upward social mobility, high educational attainment, and professional life styles. The key family changes in the two decades before the twenty-first century have been delayed marriage and postponed childbearing, higher levels of divorce and remarriage, increased cohabitation, and greater gender equality in relationships.

Mortality rates are the least well documented of the components of American Jewish demography. There is little evidence that Jewish mortality levels are unique beyond the social class, urban, and age composition of the Jewish population compared to the total population. Certainly the decline in mortality and the improvement of health had an impact, particularly on the aging of the Jewish population and the changing size of the Jewish population in particular places within the United States. The trend toward high life expectancy over the twentieth century, the greater mortality rate of men compared to that of women, and the general tendency of changes in the specific causes of death toward cancer and heart disease have characterized the Jewish population as well as the general population.

The story of American Jewish demography can be told by focusing on two major themes: immigration to America and Jewish intermarriage. Immigration was the source of population expansion and development in the beginning of the twentieth century, and intermarriage was the story a hundred years later.

Immigration to America and Origins

The immigration to the United States from the countries of Eastern Europe that began in the 1870s and continued through the 1920s became the demographic foundation of the contemporary American Jewish community. Drawing on significant proportions of Jewish communities of origin, immigration to America involved 2.5 million Jews, mostly from towns and urban areas. Social and ideological changes had already characterized immigrants and their communities before they left, resulting in the greater receptivity of immigrants to the range of opportunities in America.

The volume of immigration and the distribution of immigrants converted the scattered local American Jewish communities into a national ethnic group, from a population size of 200,000 in 1870 to more than 4 million in the mid-1920s (Goldscheider and Zuckerman 1984). The guiding ideology of this immigration was secular–socialist, not religious. An ethnic Jewish identity in the broadest sense, not a narrowly defined Judaism, characterized the immigrant community. The economic motives underlying the immigration were dominant (an escape from economic discrimination and oppression, not only the fear of pogroms); the capitalist goal of the immigrants was to take advantage of the economic opportunities (grounded in political freedoms) that were available in America. Socialism was their politics; capitalism was their economics; Jewishness was their social and family life and their culture.

The heaviest volume of Jewish immigration from Eastern Europe occurred between 1904 and 1908, when 650,000 Jews arrived, and in 1913 and 1914, when an additional 250,000 arrived. In no year was Jewish immigration more than 14 percent of general immigration, and more often than not it was less than 10 percent (Goldscheider 2004). Aided by local and national Jewish American organizations, informed by extended family members and persons from their towns of origin, the overwhelming majority of Jews remained in America, arriving with family members or bringing them in subsequent years. The permanent, family- and community-based immigration of Jews made it reasonable for them to invest in learning English, to form new families, and to finance the education of their children. With little or no incentive to return to places of origin, with economic opportunities available in America, and with financial assistance from earlier Jewish immigrants from Germany, Jews from Eastern Europe became citizens in their new homeland. They competed well with the millions of other immigrants who were less well prepared because of their more rural origins and lower levels of commitment to remaining in America.

As in other migrations, younger adults were more likely to move, as were skilled laborers. Many of the immigrants were already freed from the constraints of family and tradition and had experienced some social and economic mobility before migrating. Through immigration, Jews were becoming more independent of their families; yet, ironically, families were developing bonds of assistance for immigrants and supporting assimilation to America. Independence did not mean the rejection of family ties but the establishment of new forms of kinship bonds and family support.

Most of the religious leaders and their closest followers remained in Eastern Europe. They correctly viewed America as threatening to their authority and their religious traditions. As they defined America as the *trayfa medina,* the "unfit country," the socialists and secularists, who represented a disproportionate share of the immigrants, viewed America as the "golden land" and often as the "Promised Land." The immigrants brought with them the cultural societies, unions, and political parties of Eastern European Jewry, leaving behind most of the religious institutions, including the religious educational institutions.

Most Jewish immigrants did not sever their ties to their places of origin, even as they became American. Kinship and friendship ties were the bases of further immigration from communities of origin. Chain migration, not return migration, was a dominant feature of Eastern European Jewish immigration to America. Settlement and organizational patterns in America reinforced ties to communities of origin. Building religious and welfare institutions, coming from the same region, living close together in neighborhoods, immigrants conveyed to their children the sense of community and culture of places of origins, including the depths of their Jewish identification. By the first and second decades of the twentieth century, thousands of independent *landsmanshaftn* and local immigrant organizations existed in American cities where Jews were concentrated.

The immigrant generation was concentrated in particular neighborhoods in a few large cities. By 1920 almost half the Jews in the United States lived in New York, and almost two-thirds lived in only three states. Almost 85 percent were concentrated in cities of 100,000 or more population, compared to less than 30 percent of the total population; only 3 percent lived in rural areas, compared to 46 percent of the total (Goldstein 1971). The economic activities of Jewish immigrants distinguished them from those they left behind in places of origin and from other immigrants. The overwhelming concentration of immigrant Jews in skilled labor and shopkeeping provided them with enormous structural advantages over other immigrants in the pursuit of social mobility. A distinct overlap of ethnicity and occupation emerged among Jewish immigrants, and powerful economic networks and occupational concentration developed.

Their common social and economic background, residential and occupational concentration, and family characteristics allowed immigrant Jews to take advantage of the expanding educational opportunities in America. Working in more skilled and stable occupations, Jews earned more money than did other immigrant groups. This facilitated their investment in the education of their children. Over time, the direction of the links between occupations and educational levels reversed, allowing those with better educations to obtain better jobs. But the mobility away from neighborhoods of initial settlement and to new jobs and higher levels of education was a group process. Most who attended college, for example, commuted from home, and even as they moved away from their families, they created new communities of Jews. By 1920 more than 80 percent of the students enrolled in City College and Hunter College in New York were Jewish. Before Columbia University instituted restrictive quotas after World War I, 40 percent of its student body was Jewish (Steinberg 1974).

The Jews of the immigrant generation could not shed their Jewishness, but they changed it. Their foreignness and their characteristics constrained their full assimilation, as did the discrimination they encountered. Residential, educational, and occupational networks joined family and organizational networks to reinforce a cohesive community. The bases of cohesion would inevitably change as the children of immigrants moved to new neighborhoods, attended different schools for longer periods of time, obtained better jobs, and faced the economic depression of the 1930s and war in the 1940s. Yet the children of immigrants were raised in families where an ethnic language was distinctive, where cultural closeness to origins was undeniable, where families were cohesive and supportive, and where networks and institutions were ethnically based. Combined, these powerful elements made the second generation Jewish by both religion and ethnicity. But their ethnicity (in the sense of national origin) was fading, and their Jewishness was becoming Americanized. Although sharply different from the Jewishness of their parents' generation, the children's Jewishness was clear and distinctive by American standards. The continuation of integration into the third and fourth generations, distant from cultural origins, raised directly the question of the changing quality of American Jewish life.

In the pre–World War II period, immigrant Jews and their children interacted with other Jews at work, in neighborhoods, in schools, and in religious, political, and social activities. Yiddish and socialist schools and newspapers competed with public and religious schools. Credit associations, *landsmanshaftn,* and local fraternal and communal institutions appeared and expanded. While learning English, Yiddish remained the language of business and social life among Jewish immigrants. Even when their children rejected Yiddish, it was still the cultural environment of their upbringing. And Jewish families and communities rejected those who rejected their community through intermarriage or by their behavior. The overlap of occupation, residence, and ethnicity was as high in America as anywhere in urban Europe. Jews left the Old World behind—but not all of it—to become American. Their Jewishness was conspicuous by their background, culture, and community.

Intermarriage and Jewish Population Changes

In contrast to the first half of the twentieth century, when intermarriage rates were low and inconsequential demographically, the critical question of the last third of the twentieth century has been the impact of intermarriage rates on the quality of Jewish life and on American Jewish population growth. Estimates of the impact of intermarriages on Jewish population size have been made, but the identity of the children of the intermarried remains unclear.

During most of the twentieth century, when Jewish intermarriage rates were low, those who intermarried repudiated their religion, their families, and their communities. And their religion, their families, and their communities abandoned them. Intermarriage thus resulted in a loss of the intermarried to the Jewish community. Most Jewish parents at the end of the twentieth century grew up in communities where intermarriage was low, where the intermarried were largely Jewish men married to non-Jewish-born women, where conversions to Judaism were not encouraged and were often seriously discouraged, and where the intermarried couple and their children were not accepted members of the Jewish community.

In the last decades of the twentieth century, as a result of increasing social contacts between Jews and others, intermarriage has become less idiosyncratic and less symbolic of alternative religious discovery or of political or economic necessity (as it had often been in the past in America and in Europe). Rather, Jewish intermarriages are now a reflection of the routine interaction among individuals, an integral part of the daily lives of American Jews. Marrying someone of a different ethnic or religious background has become consistent with the way Jewish parents and their children live and has become embedded in American Jewish culture.

The demographic issue of American Jewish continuity is not intermarriage per se but the Jewishness that characterizes families and households. Most American Jews are Jewish because they were born to Jewish parents. But an increasing number of Jews become Jewish through commitments to their newly formed families and their identification with the Jewish community. Becoming Jewish through having a Jewish home and identifying with the Jewish community, as well as formal conversion to Judaism, varies through the life course. Jewish identification often increases as families are formed and children need to be educated.

The rates of intermarriage between Jews and non-Jews in the United States vary nationally between 40 and 50 percent of those who married in the period 1990–2000 (Goldscheider 2004). There is a considerable range among communities in the level of intermarriage. In the past, Jewish men married out more than Jewish women did, but gender differences in intermarriages have diminished considerably. Because women tend to take a more active role in the home, the gender difference was the basis for more concern in the past, for the non-Jewish-born spouse would be more likely to define the ethnoreligious orientation of the home. The changing gender pattern of intermarriage may have a more positive effect on the Jewishness of the home. The relative rates of generational continuity of the intermarried within the Jewish community have increased during the last decades of the twentieth century (i.e., the

number of children raised in households where at least one parent was not born Jewish who remain Jewish as they form their own families). This new pattern is connected with the increased levels of intermarriage and conversions and the increased acceptance of the intermarried within the Jewish community.

High intermarriage rates may result in population stability when conversions occur or when the non-Jewish-born partner identifies with the Jewish community. More importantly, Jewish demographic stability with high rates of intermarriage occurs when many children are raised as Jews. The impact of Jewish intermarriages on American Jewish population size will reflect the extent to which Jewishness is an integral part of the homes and families of the intermarried.

Equal proportions (40 percent) of intermarried Jewish parents identify their children as Jewish and as non-Jewish. The rest (20 percent) are noncommitted (Goldscheider 2004). How they will identify themselves Jewishly as they grow up to have families of their own is open to speculation. Many non-Jewish-born persons identify themselves as Jews and are so identified by their family, friends, and the Jewish community without formal religious conversions. Many engage in family, communal, and organizational activities that are Jewish. The failure to have a Jewish marriage ceremony does not preclude subsequent Jewish commitments.

Unlike in the past, in most intermarriages the Jewish partner remains attached in some ways to the Jewish community. Often the non-Jewish-born partner becomes attached to the Jewish community in some ways, and many of the children of the intermarried identify Jewishly through family, friends, neighborhood, and Jewish organizational ties. Many of their friends are Jewish, support Israel, and identify themselves as Jews, and most have important relationships with Jewish relatives. Some proportion of spouses and their children formally convert to Judaism.

Thus, the increasing rate of intermarriage does not necessarily mean the demographic erosion of the Jewish community. Intermarriage rates unambiguously mean that vast networks of Jews are now affected and linked to the intermarriage issue. There is hardly a Jewish household in America that has not experienced the intermarriage of a family member, neighbor, or friend. The extension of intermarriage to encompass most of the Jewish community has been the critical family transformation among American Jews over the last decades of the twentieth century.

Calvin Goldscheider

References and Further Reading

American Jewish Year Book. Annual publication of American Jewish demographic population statistics.

Cohen, Steven M., and Arnold Eisen. 2000. *The Jew Within: Self, Family, and Community in America.* Bloomington: Indiana University Press.

Goldscheider, Calvin. 1986. *Jewish Continuity and Change: Emerging Patterns in America.* Bloomington: Indiana University Press.

Goldscheider, Calvin. 2004. *Studying the Jewish Future.* Seattle: University of Washington Press.

Goldscheider, Calvin, and Alan Zuckerman. 1984. *The Transformation of the Jews.* Chicago: University of Chicago Press.

Goldstein, Sidney. 1971. "American Jewry, 1970: A Demographic Profile." *American Jewish Year Book.*

Steinberg, Stephen. 1974. *The Academic Melting Pot.* New York: Carnegie Foundation.

The Economic Status of American Jews in the Twentieth Century

The twentieth century was a period of rapid and profound change in the economic circumstances of American Jewry. It is best understood as a transitional period, from a community of struggling Eastern European and Russian immigrants centered in inner-city slums at the beginning of the century to a predominantly highly educated, thoroughly assimilated American group centered in upper-middle-class urban and suburban neighborhoods. As individuals and families pursued their private goals, the Jewish community developed institutions to support their needs and help them adjust to these new circumstances. Like much of American economic history in general, however, the upward socioeconomic mobility of American Jewry was both rapid and unplanned, a grassroots phenomenon whose leaders sometimes seemed to be struggling to keep up with their followers.

To begin to appreciate the magnitude of this change, consider the contrast between American Jewry in 1900 and in 2000. Although the United States already had a well-established Jewish community before 1880, one primarily of German origin, the immigrants arriving between 1880 and 1920 from czarist Russia and Eastern Europe were far more

numerous, and by 1900 their experience was already shaping the future of American Jewry. The immigrants earned their living primarily as machine operators, craftsmen, and shopkeepers. By the year 2000, their descendants would be primarily highly educated white-collar workers in professional and managerial occupations. The immigrant Jews in 1900 lived primarily in slum tenements or crowded, low-income neighborhoods, but by 2000 most of the Jewish community would be financially secure and living in upper-middle-class urban or suburban neighborhoods. In 1900 Jewish immigrants were familiar with antisemitism as a constant presence, and many families had direct experience with antisemitic violence (especially in the Old Country) and/or workplace discrimination, even in the United States. By 2000 the Jewish community would be well assimilated into the American mainstream, its identity and interests would be profoundly affected by the existence of a vibrant Jewish state in Israel, few American Jews would feel vulnerable to antisemitism, and even fewer would have experienced antisemitism directly.

In 1900 American Jewish religious institutions were in turmoil as Reform, Conservative, and Orthodox synagogue movements organized themselves to find "American" adaptations of Jewish observance appropriate for a socioeconomic environment of religious pluralism, personal freedom, and economic opportunity largely unprecedented in Jewish history. In 2000 American synagogues were again adapting, as the three dominant movements responded to challenges posed by changes in the interests of their members, by new offshoots and unaffiliated movements, including the growth of independent "post-denominational" congregations, and by an increasing number of members with non-Jewish spouses and other relatives.

In 1900 the primary communal issue facing American Jewry was how to Americanize the poor, non-English-speaking immigrants from Russia and Eastern Europe, and socioeconomic advancement was its goal. By 2000 the focus would be on third- and fourth-generation American Jews who were so well assimilated that their attachment to Judaism and to Jewish continuity, as well as to the Jewish community, would be the primary concern.

The Early Twentieth Century

In 1880 the small American Jewish community, which numbered about 200,000 persons or 0.5 percent of the U.S.

population, was comprised mainly of immigrants arriving from Germany since the 1840s and their descendants. By 1917, after a large wave of Jewish immigration primarily from Eastern Europe and the Russian Empire, American Jews numbered approximately 3.4 million, about 3.3 percent of the U.S. population. These new immigrants were culturally quite different from the earlier German Jewish immigrants. They came from a part of Europe that was much less developed economically, they spoke Yiddish rather than German, and they were more traditional in their religious practices. Unlike the German American Jews, who could be found scattered across the country, the Russian and East European Jews were intensely concentrated in the major industrial centers of the Northeast and Midwest, especially New York City.

Equally dramatic was the occupational disparity between the East European Jewish immigrant men, German Jewish men, and men in the non-Jewish population. Men in the German Jewish community worked primarily in sales occupations ranging from peddler to merchant and in clerical jobs. In 1910 Yiddish-speaking, male Jewish immigrants were also much more likely to be in sales occupations (27 percent) than either other white immigrant men (7 percent) or white native-born men (10 percent). Yiddish-speaking, Jewish immigrant men were concentrated in blue-collar jobs in light manufacturing, with 32 percent in craft occupations and 22 percent working in "operative" jobs (i.e., as unskilled or semiskilled machine operators). Many of these jobs were in the expanding garment industry, in which many of the immigrant Jews had worked in Europe. In contrast, 25 percent of non-Jewish, white male immigrants (most of whom had arrived at the same time as the Russian Jews) were in craft occupations, and 18 percent were in operative jobs; and among non-Jewish, native-born white males, these occupations accounted for only 18 and 15 percent, respectively. Farmers and laborers were major occupations both for non-Jewish immigrants (37 percent) and for white native-born men (also 37 percent) but accounted for only about 4 percent of the Jewish men.

Even by 1910, there was substantial evidence of upward occupational mobility among the immigrant generation as well as their American-born children. With time in the United States, the Jewish immigrants learned about the American labor market, adjusted their skills to the new economic environment, and improved their English language proficiency. Some continued as blue-collar workers,

no longer as the lowest-skilled workers but moving upward in craft and operative jobs, while others moved into sales and managerial occupations. Their sons, Yiddish-origin Jewish men born in America, were proficient in English and educated in the United States. As a result, by 1910 some 32 percent—nearly one-third—were in sales and another 20 percent in clerical occupations, while only 13 percent and 15 percent, respectively, were in craft and operative jobs.

Self-employment was important among the Jews, accounting for 38 percent of Yiddish-origin immigrant men in 1910, in contrast to only 22 percent of non-Jewish immigrant men. The self-employed accounted for 36 percent of the native-born white men, but most of these were farmers. By 1920, with more time in the United States, self-employment among the Yiddish-speaking Jewish immigrants had increased to 46 percent, while for non-Jews the proportions had remained constant over the decade. Self-employment also appealed to the second generation, the U.S.-born children of Yiddish-speaking immigrants. Although only 16 percent were self-employed in 1910, at that time they were still quite young. By 1920 about 33 percent—one-third—were self-employed in nonfarm activities.

During this period, young Jewish women typically worked for wages in the years after the completion of schooling, while others worked in small family businesses with their parents or husbands. Although early on they engaged in factory work (the garment industry being most important), later they would find jobs as clerical workers, secretaries, and bookkeepers. Once they married and became mothers, however, Jewish women were more likely to stay home to care for children. In this respect they differed from the women in most other European immigrant groups at the time, who were more likely to continue working and to have their older daughters care for the young children.

Two interrelated features of the Jewish immigration differentiated them from other immigrants and facilitated their investments in skills relevant to the U.S. economy. The Jews were more likely than other groups to immigrate as families—husbands, wives, and children—even if they did not all arrive at the same time. They also came with the intention of making the United States their permanent home; the proportion who expected to return or who actually returned to their country of origin was far smaller than in other immigrant groups. America was the land of freedom as well as economic opportunity, and the Jews came not only for work but also to escape the antisemitism pervasive in the societies of Eastern Europe and Russia.

American Jewry at Midcentury

There was relatively little immigration, including Jewish immigration, during and after World War I because of severe immigration restrictions that began in 1921 (and lasted until the mid-1960s) and the Great Depression of the 1930s. By 1940 there were about 4.8 million Jews in the United States, constituting about 3.7 percent of the population. By that time, it was evident that there had been dramatic changes in the occupational structure of American Jewry.

Among foreign-born Jewish men, 43 percent were still in craft and operative occupations in 1940, but 17 percent were in white-collar, sales, and clerical jobs, another 28 percent were in managerial occupations, and 6 percent were in the professions. In all, 41 percent of these men were self-employed. Non-Jewish white men also experienced upward occupational mobility during this period but at a more modest rate. By 1940 only 11 percent of non-Jewish white men, whether foreign born or natives of the United States, were in managerial jobs, with only 4 percent and 6 percent, respectively, in professional occupations.

Second-generation American Jews with Yiddish-speaking origins showed an even greater movement out of blue-collar jobs. By 1940 only 23 percent were in craft and operative jobs, 35 percent were in sales and clerical jobs, and 22 percent were in managerial occupations. Perhaps most dramatic was their disproportionate presence in the professions, despite discrimination against Jews in access to higher education and professional schooling. By 1940 professional occupations accounted for 6 percent of non-Jewish white males, 4 percent of non-Jewish immigrant men, 6 percent of Jewish immigrant men, and an impressive 15 percent of the American-born sons of Jewish immigrants.

Even more dramatic were the occupational differences within the professions. Among Jewish immigrant men, 2.1 percent were doctors, dentists, or lawyers; among the second generation, 6.4 percent were in these occupations. Among non-Jewish white men, immigrant or native, these occupations employed only 0.5 percent and 1.3 percent, re-

spectively. Jewish professionals were thus predominantly in medicine and law, two occupations in which self-employment was then the norm. In other professions, such as accounting, Jews were also much more likely to be self-employed. This helped Jews avoid discrimination in access to professional employment in large corporate firms, heavy manufacturing, and the banking and insurance sectors.

Self-employment remained high among Jews even as it was falling in the general population with the decline in farming. In 1940, 41 percent of the Jewish immigrant men (an older group) were self-employed, and 27 percent of the second generation of Yiddish origin were self-employed. In contrast, 21 percent of foreign-born, non-Jewish white men were self-employed, as were 27 percent of native-born white men, again primarily in agriculture.

The rapid increase in occupational attainment from the immigrant generation to their American-born children, especially dramatic in comparison with other immigrant groups at the same time and even in comparison with nonimmigrant Americans, can be attributed to their similarly rapid increase in schooling level. Jews valued education for its own sake, but also—perhaps primarily for many immigrants—as a means to improve economic opportunities in the United States for themselves and their children. Although sons often acquired more schooling than daughters, Jewish women were encouraged to stay in school much longer than young women in other groups, and many entered the professions, especially as teachers and social workers. The wife of a relatively well-educated, second-generation Jewish man was also typically well educated, and the home environment of their Jewish children was one that encouraged educational achievement.

The Late Twentieth Century

In the second half of the twentieth century, the Jewish population increased from about 5 million shortly after World War II to about 5.9 million in the 1970s and then declined to about 5.2 million in 2000. As the non-Jewish population grew more rapidly from higher rates of fertility and immigration, the Jewish proportion of the population declined from a peak of about 3.7 percent to slightly less than 2.0 percent in 2000.

Throughout the second half of the twentieth century, both Jewish and non-Jewish men experienced increases in their occupational status, but again the increase was more dramatic for Jewish men. The proportion of Jewish men in professional occupations increased from 14 percent in the early post–World War II period to 20 percent in 1957 and 44 percent by 2000, about the same as its peak at 47 percent in 1990. In contrast, while professional employment increased dramatically among non-Jewish white men, it was still only 19 percent by 1990. Blue-collar employment also continued to decline during this period, leaving only 13 percent of Jewish men in crafts or low-skilled jobs by 2000. Managerial occupations comprised 23 percent of the Jewish male labor force in 2000, still a substantial fraction but far less than the 45 percent seen during the early post–World War II years.

Self-employment among Jewish men peaked at 56 percent in the early post–World War II period and has since declined to 27 percent in 1990, remaining substantially greater than the 14 percent for non-Jewish men, among whom agriculture still accounts for an important fraction of the self-employed. Jewish employment has thus shifted dramatically in recent decades, first from self-employed managers to self-employed professionals and then from self-employed professionals to salaried professionals. This is partly a consequence of the rapid increase in the educational attainment of Jewish men. It is also due to enhanced professional career opportunities in corporations, government, and universities previously closed to Jews or limited by antisemitism.

During the second half of the twentieth century, American women in all groups were more likely than ever before to enter the labor market in paid occupations, accelerating a trend begun in the century's early decades. This was due in part to a decline in fertility that greatly reduced the child-rearing responsibilities of married women. It was also due to the appearance of safe, inexpensive prepared foods (cans and packages) and newly affordable consumer durables—timesaving household appliances such as washing machines, vacuum cleaners, refrigerators, and freezers. Thus, the same technological changes that increased women's productivity in the labor market and raised wage rates for all women, including those working as domestic servants, also reduced the amount of time needed for household chores.

Jewish women participated in this movement, but their labor force patterns differed from those of other groups. Before the birth of the first child, married Jewish women were more likely than their non-Jewish counterparts to work in the labor market, but Jewish women were less likely than non-Jews to stay in the labor market when they had children of preschool age. Once their children were older, however, Jewish women would reenter the labor market, often in part-time or part-year jobs, and they were more likely than non-Jewish women to work full time after their children had graduated from high school. Jewish children had the advantages of better-educated mothers, more maternal time devoted to them during their early years, and higher parental income during their adolescence and youth.

This pattern of work among Jewish women undoubtedly contributed to the high educational attainment of both sons and daughters in the following generation. By the year 2000, fully 82 percent of married Jewish men of working age had wives who were also in the labor force, and only 12 percent had wives who were full-time homemakers. More than two-thirds of those in the labor force, whether men or women, were in high-level careers, with professional occupations alone accounting for 51 percent of the men and 46 percent of the women. Two-career couples had become the norm in the American Jewish community, and in a striking 28 percent of these couples, both husband and wife had professional careers.

Prospects for the Future

At the turn of the twenty-first century, America's Jewish children tend to come from homes with few siblings and with highly educated, professionally employed parents. All the ingredients necessary for the next generation of Jewish children to become equally successful adults are present, yet there are also questions as to whether the high level of occupational attainment (and hence also earnings) of the American Jewish community can be sustained. If parents have high-powered careers, child care becomes an issue not only for the parents but also for the community as a whole. High-quality, early childhood day-care services are prized by working couples and have become common in the Jewish community; such services are often located in the local Jewish Community Center or a nearby synagogue.

After-school care and activities for older children (including attendance at Hebrew school) are also important. These may require some coordination that is complex for parents with demanding careers, especially if there are several children in the family. The growing popularity of Jewish day schools—private schools that combine a high-quality general curriculum with education in Jewish subjects—is testimony to Jewish parents' commitment to the future of their children with respect to both economic achievement and Jewish knowledge. The expansion of Jewish day schools, to more Jewish communities as well as from kindergarten through high school, also requires a refocusing of Jewish communal institutions and resources and is thus a measure of the community's ability to adapt to new economic circumstances.

Another question facing the Jewish community at the turn of the twenty-first century is whether the motivation to succeed economically that was so evident among the immigrants and their children will persist into the fourth and fifth generation of American Jews. Immigrants are typically a self-selected group that is adventurous, adaptable, and willing to work hard to achieve its ambitions. Some of this is passed on to their children, but their grandchildren and great-grandchildren are not self-selected for these qualities, and they grow up in high-income homes without the urgency of economic need. If the story of immigrant families includes many examples of "shirtsleeves to suits in two generations," the phenomenon of "shirtsleeves to shirtsleeves in three generations" is not uncommon.

With socioeconomic assimilation into the American mainstream, Jews have become much more likely to marry non-Jewish partners. Rates of religious intermarriage were very low for Jews in 1900, rising slowly during much of the twentieth century and sharply in its last three decades, until at its end about half of all Jews marrying for the first time chose non-Jewish spouses. The non-Jewish spouses of Jews are similar to Jewish spouses of Jews with respect to education, occupation, and other economic characteristics, but intermarried couples are much less likely to raise their children with close attachments to Judaism and the Jewish people. The adult children of intermarriage are an increasingly large component of the American Jewish community,

raising questions about the very nature of its boundaries as well as the statistical definition of American Jewry. It also raises questions for Jewish economic success, as to whether families of mixed Jewish parentage will make the same financial and time commitments to the development of their children's skills as those of families with two Jewish parents. These questions are still unresolved and will undoubtedly continue to occupy the Jewish community for decades.

At present it appears that Jewish families continue their commitment to high levels of education, although perhaps commitment is not quite so high as in the previous generation. In the meantime, the education levels of other immigrant groups and of native-born American youth are rising as they adopt some of the same paths followed earlier by American Jews. Thus, even if American Jews continue their record of high economic achievement well into the twenty-first century, this will no longer be as exceptional as it was in the twentieth. Already by the year 2000, the economic experiences of Jews and non-Jews are converging, and it may be a matter of only a few decades before the two groups converge and the economic assimilation of American Jewry is complete.

Barry R. Chiswick and Carmel U. Chiswick

References and Further Reading

Chiswick, Barry R. 1988. "Labor Supply and Investment in Child Quality: A Study of Jewish and Non-Jewish Women." *Contemporary Jewry* 9,2: 35–53.

Chiswick, Barry R. 1999. "The Occupational Attainment and Earnings of American Jewry, 1890–1990." *Contemporary Jewry* 20: 68–98.

Chiswick, Carmel U. 2001. "The Economics of Jewish Immigrants and Judaism in the United States." *Papers in Jewish Demography 1997*: 331–344.

Glenn, Susan A. 1990. *Daughters of the Shtetl: Life and Labor in the Immigrant Generation*. Ithaca, NY: Cornell University Press.

Godley, Andrew. 2001. *Jewish Immigrant Entrepreneurship in New York and London, 1880–1914: Enterprise and Culture*. New York: Palgrave.

National Jewish Population Survey 2000.

Judaism in America

Orthodox Judaism

The freedom and opportunities that America has granted to its Jews have posed daunting challenges to the perpetuation of Orthodox Jewish life in this country. The openness of American society and culture, and the desire of American Jews to advance and to live harmoniously with those around them, has led most Jews to ignore or to oppose traditional laws and regulations (*halacha*) that might retard their integration or mobility. And, given the legal separation of church and state and the religious voluntarism that has shaped the American way of life, Orthodox religious leaders and institutions have had few available means to prevent the masses of Jews from choosing to disconnect from the faith and practices of their ancestors. Moreover, since the mid-nineteenth century, American Jews who wished to maintain a religious identity but cared little for Orthodoxy's strictures have had the option to affiliate with other Jewish religious expressions, most notably Reform or Conservatism.

In response to these challenges, Orthodox officials and their institutions have exhibited two basic modalities of behavior. Despite the pressures of the host culture, *resisting* rabbis and lay leaders have made every effort to avoid changing the teachings and practices of the faith. At the expense of losing many potential adherents, they have often rejected making even sociological modifications in Ortho-

doxy's ways. These preservers of past policies and procedures have generally displayed a palpable lack of tolerance toward their coreligionists who responded very differently to the American challenges.

It is the *accommodationist* Orthodox leaders—sometimes even more than their Reform and Conservative counterparts—who have been the object of the resisters' ire and critique. The accommodationists, the more flexible cohort, have maintained that Orthodoxy can and must make sociological modifications—in both secular and sacred precincts—if this most traditional Jewish religious expression is to have a chance to attract and maintain the allegiance of the large numbers of acculturated American Jews. Far less disturbed than resisters by the ideas and activities of the more modern Jewish expressions, accommodationist rabbis and lay spokespeople have, on occasion, joined with Conservatives and Reformers in fighting against assimilation.

Still, despite the clear divide within Orthodox Judaism between the proponents of resistance and the advocates of accommodation to America, each side was far from monolithic. Not every rabbi who opposed acculturation was equally insistent on blocking modern ways from the lives of his followers. And not all who preached the viability of reconciling traditional strictures with American mores accepted the same extent of change. The various approaches of the rabbis could often be traced to where and how they were trained. American-educated Orthodox rabbis usually were more lenient than those ordained in Europe. Strictness was also a function of where the rabbi was located in the United States. Generally, rabbis in large, Eastern, urban centers were more dogmatic than colleagues who served smaller Jewish communities. The responses of Orthodox lay leaders to the challenges of America have been even more variegated.

From the beginnings of Jewish settlement in America in the seventeenth century until the mid-1820s, whenever Jews attended a synagogue, they prayed and socialized in an Orthodox synagogue—most of which adhered to the Sephardic (descendant of Spanish Judaism) rite. (Liberal Jewish denominational life began in earnest only in the 1830s, with the arrival and Americanization of Central European Jews.) The reach of these traditional congregations was limited, however, and most Jews did not adhere to halachic strictures outside of the sanctuary. The unavailability of the basics for maintaining religious life—kosher meats or wines or Passover matzos or sacred books and objects—often made observance very difficult in this frontier Jewish society. American Jews' desire to prosper also led many to work on Saturday at the expense of Sabbath observance. In addition, the minuscule population pool made finding a Jewish spouse problematic. Moreover, there were few trained religious functionaries who could have helped those who wanted to maintain ancestral traditions. The first ordained rabbi, Abraham Rice from Gochsheim, Germany, did not arrive in the United States until 1840. Before that, itinerant—and in larger towns, permanent—all-purpose Jewish functionaries served their communities as cantors and ritual slaughterers, performed circumcisions, and officiated at weddings.

In response to religious nonconformity, the lay leaders who controlled American Jewish congregational life vacillated between inclusionary and exclusionary policies. Hard-line protocols called for the denial of synagogue rights and honors to—or at least the fining of—those known to be less observant than those who set the rules. Accommodationists, on the other hand, chose to overlook the activities of religious miscreants. Over time, synagogues often oscillated between the two positions. For example, in 1798, in coping with one of this country's earliest and more enduring communal problems—intermarriage—Philadelphia's Mikveh Israel denied "religious rights and privileges" to any Jew who intermarried. But twenty-eight years later, it voted down a similar motion to withhold "all synagogue honors and privileges" from the exogamous.

Accommodationists introduced only a few changes in the conduct of the Orthodox service in an effort to make worship more attractive to potential communicants. In the mid-eighteenth century, for example, open galleries were created for women worshippers, who had chafed at their inability to see activities at the altar. This architectural departure—which was well within the boundaries of halacha—also satisfied the Jews' need to conduct themselves, and build their religious edifices, in an American way to garner the approbation of their non-Jewish neighbors.

Beginning in the 1830s, Orthodox Jewish leaders faced not only the ongoing dilemma of nonobservance but also the challenges posed by liberal Judaism, as incipient Reform and Conservative congregations were established. Ironically, most of the liberal congregations stemmed from immigrant Orthodox roots. These congregations, some with outspoken rabbis at their helms, proffered and preached forms of religious life that found wide acceptance among acculturated Jews, since they conformed to American styles of public prayer. Many who affiliated with these modern congregations liked their new synagogue's family pew seating arrangements, as well as the shorter, English-based service, which often included instrumental music and a mixed-voice choir. Moreover, these liberal expressions of the faith were popular because they tacitly or explicitly countenanced personal Jewish religious lifestyles that deviated from Orthodox practice. Reform Judaism ideologically supported a Jew's nonadherence to the traditional understanding of Sabbath rest and failure to follow the strictures of the kosher laws.

In attempting to forestall the fundamental transformation of their synagogues, some prescient Orthodox groups made social adjustments in their services. Seeking to project themselves, too, as American congregations, accommodationist elements added English prayers and discourses to the traditional devotions, emphasized the need for decorum during the prayers, and in most places curtailed or abolished the sale of synagogue honors. More combative Orthodox forces, however, rested their hopes for institutional survival on exclusionary control of synagogue governance—such as restricting who could vote on ritual policies. The most resistant cohorts placed their faith in even stricter exclusionary policies, such as denying membership to Jews known to be Sabbath violators. And when Orthodox efforts failed within congregational ranks, some turned to the civil courts for relief. There they argued that the reforms violated publicly filed articles of incorporation that specified that services be run along Orthodox lines. Out-of-court agreements often provided the traditionalist plaintiffs with financial assistance to establish new institutions.

The survival rate of these breakaway synagogues was not particularly high, however, as over time many nominally Orthodox *shul*-goers became increasingly comfortable with the religious values that their more liberal coreligionist espoused. Few of these congregations remained Orthodox through the end of the 1870s. Some were drawn into the Reform or Conservative orbit. Others chose a hybrid ceremonial. They called themselves Orthodox but, despite halachic constraints, permitted men and women to sit together during prayers, even as they disdained other, liturgical changes. Indeed, when the Union of Orthodox Jewish Congregations of America (OU)—Orthodoxy's first national organization—was created in 1898, a number of its constituent groups had family pews.

The leading accommodationist Orthodox rabbis of this period, Morris J. Raphall and Samuel Isaacs, and one uncommonly important *hazzan*/communal leader, Isaac Leeser, attempted to do more than just hold sway within their congregations. They battled against the tide of assimilation that threatened all religious efforts and opposed the most radical ideological deviations from traditional religious teachings. Thus, in 1855 Leeser joined with compromising Reform Rabbi Isaac Mayer Wise and others to develop national religious unity schemes. The resultant Cleveland Conference tried to formulate a universally acceptable American ritual and also directly addressed the radicalism advanced by the inflexible Reform Rabbi David Einhorn.

Thirty-one years later, in 1886, Rabbi Sabato Morais brought together a more important coalition. To combat the antinationalist and antitraditional ritual postures that the Reform movement adopted in its 1885 Pittsburgh Platform, Morais led rabbis Henry W. Schneeberger, Henry P. Mendes, Bernard Drachman, and other Orthodox spokesmen into an alliance with Conservative leaders. Together they formed an institutional bulwark against the unfettered growth of Reform in America. Together they created

Isaac Leeser. (Library of Congress)

the Jewish Theological Seminary of America (JTSA), a school that at its inception—and long thereafter—trained rabbis who would occupy both Americanized Orthodox and Conservative pulpits.

With the arrival of East European immigrants en masse that began in the early 1880s, the calculus of Jewish denominational strength in America changed dramatically. By 1890 the hundreds of immigrant Orthodox synagogues that served the spiritual and social needs of the newcomers outnumbered the existing Americanized synagogues of all denominations. But even as transplanted Orthodox piety was on display on a large scale daily and on the Sabbath within the sacred precincts of downtown neighborhoods, most Jewish immigrants also demonstrated a definite lack of commitment to Orthodox regulations. Thus, when Jews in the areas of first settlement attended services, they would go only to an Orthodox shul, in the East European mold. As the new immigrants strove to advance, however, the frequency with which they attended their *shtibls* (storefront synagogues) steadily declined. Many did not have time for the long Sabbath services, since they worked on the Sabbath day.

The world of transplanted Orthodoxy, embodied in the *landsmanshaft* shtibls (synagogues built to re-create the spirit and culture of ancestral hometowns), held almost no attraction for the children of the immigrants. Introduced to new values in the public schools and settlement houses, the young became rapidly Americanized, becoming estranged from Old World social mores and languages—Hebrew and Yiddish—that resounded through their parents' synagogues. And as second-generation Americans anxious to succeed, they had even less patience than their elders for Orthodox religious obligations that would retard their progress.

Organized in 1887 and composed of representatives of fifteen of the largest congregations on New York's Lower East Side, the Association of Orthodox Hebrew Congregations sought only to restore the religious patterns of the Old World. Its plan focused on the selection of a Chief Rabbi, who would inspire a religious revival among both the immigrants and their children. Indeed, that same year they recruited Rabbi Jacob Joseph from Vilna, Lithuania, assigning him the mission of engendering mass commitment to Old World religious values. Specifically, he was to motivate adults and young people to be more scrupulous in observance of the Sabbath. He was to convince parents to send their sons to the Yeshiva Etz Chaim, the small *heder* (Jewish school) established just a year earlier in the downtown immigrant neighborhood. In this highly parochial Jewish educational environment, youngsters would be spared the assimilationist pressures of American public education. Rabbi Joseph was also told to bring order to the rarely monitored and often corrupt kosher meat industry.

Despite his best efforts, this country's culture proved too powerful to overcome. Even downtown rabbinical families often acted just like the immigrant masses. Caught up in the lures of the promises of public education, even they refused to remove their children from those temples of Americanization. Nor could the Chief Rabbi control the lay leaders, who impeded his efforts. The rabbi wanted to control the kosher meat markets without passing the costs on to consumers. The Association's leaders, however, demanded the imposition of a surcharge on the meat, a move that infuriated many downtowners and further weakened Rabbi Joseph's appeal to potential followers.

In the days immediately following Rabbi Joseph's death in 1902, another, more enduring effort to inculcate an Old World religious way of life in America took root.

Made up initially of fifty-nine East European–trained rabbis, the Agudath ha-Rabbanim (Union of Orthodox Rabbis of the United States and Canada, or UOR) recognized that it would take a continent-wide organization and considerable pooled resources and energies to defeat the forces of Americanization. They also understood from the outset that, if the masses did not heed their voices, they had to raise at least an elite group of young people who would fully commit themselves to the ways of the Jewish religious past. In one of its first acts, the UOR designated the Yeshiva Rabbi Isaac Elchanan—also known as the Rabbi Isaac Elchanan Theological Seminary (RIETS)—as its central American-based institution. Founded in 1897, this extension of Yeshiva Etz Chaim—the forerunner of the rabbinical school of Yeshiva University—trained rabbis as they were then being educated in the great Lithuanian *yeshivas*. It proffered Torah and Talmudic studies exclusively, rejecting the modern, professional, ministerial training—such as courses in sermonics—that obtained at an institution like the JTSA. Indeed, the UOR also looked askance at the mission and products of the Seminary, declaring its "unlearned" graduates, who had studied Jewish history and philosophy and modern Hebrew literature almost as much as the Bible and rabbinics, unqualified for the Orthodox rabbinate.

For all its difficulties, however, over time the UOR made some compromises with the realities of Jewish life in America. The Association maintained its support for the Yeshiva even as, between the turn of the twentieth century and 1915, the school gradually introduced the practical sides of modern rabbinical training, such as homiletics and pedagogy, into its curriculum. In acquiescing to the changes brought to the school by Dr. Bernard Revel, the Yeshiva's first permanent president, the UOR tacitly acknowledged that for Orthodox ordainees to meet the challenge of assimilation and compete with graduates of the seminary, the Yeshiva must Americanize its operation.

Arguably, the UOR showed some flexibility, however slight, because its members were a somewhat idiosyncratic group, different in an essential way from the wider world of Orthodoxy in East Europe. The day these American-based rabbis (among the foremost of whom were Philip Hillel Klein, Moses Sebulun Margolis, and Bernard Levinthal) decided to ignore the view, widely held among the religious in Russia, that the United States was an unkosher land, hopelessly inimical to the survival of traditional life, they evinced a potential willingness to respond pragmatically to Judaism's conditions in the New World. These UOR members accepted the minority opinion of the Yeshiva's eponymous Rabbi Isaac Elchanan Spektor that rabbis should migrate to America to assist that floundering community to create an enduring Orthodox life.

UOR members also differed from most of their East European counterparts in their attitudes toward the nascent Zionist movement. The majority of Old World Orthodox rabbis strongly opposed the modern national movement that aspired to return Jews to their ancestral land before the coming of the Messiah. The Agudath ha-Rabbanim's rank and file, however, lined up with the Mizrachi movement that was founded in Poland in 1902, the same year that the UOR was created in America. This Religious Zionist organization contended that Orthodox Jews must play an active role in directing the Zionist organizations to adhere to traditional religious values as they moved forward to develop their modern statehood plans.

If the Agudath ha-Rabbanim grudgingly acknowledged that some American realities had to be accepted, the Union of Orthodox Jewish Congregations of America openly admitted that, to survive, Orthodoxy had to work with and within the country's larger culture. Formed from among the American Orthodox lay and rabbinical founders of the JTSA, this accommodationist organization developed new congregational, political, and educational initiatives to suit the lifestyles of its potential Americanized, second-generation constituents. As early as 1900, its youth wing began organizing "model" modern Orthodox services under the auspices of the Jewish Endeavor Society (JES). Conducting its devotions on Shabbat afternoons—after the American workweek ended—it opened its doors to the young who labored while Saturday morning prayers droned on in the half-filled immigrant synagogues.

The Endeavorers demonstrated their fidelity to Orthodoxy through their gender separation during prayers, use of the traditional *siddur* (prayer book), and maintenance of an unabridged service, complete with the Saturday afternoon Torah reading. Their modernity was evidenced through their weekly English-language sermons, the recitation of some prayers in that vernacular, and the introduction of numerous ancillary congregational activities, such as synagogue suppers and Saturday night dances. The wide range of tasks and events offered by the Endeavorers provided essential training for a generation of JTSA

students who would become both American Orthodox and Conservative rabbis. Such future national leaders as Mordecai M. Kaplan, Herman Abramowitz, Charles Kauvar, and Elias L. Solomon all worked under the JES banner. Beginning in 1913, JTSA students also organized the (more enduring) Young Israel movement, which would continue the Society's work within and beyond immigrant Jewish neighborhoods for generations.

Even while the JES opened its doors to those who had to work on the Jewish holy day, OU's political wing lobbied hard in Albany, New York, to overturn the onerous Blue Laws, which undercut the opportunity to observe the Jewish Sabbath by requiring businesses to close on Sundays. Ever the activists, the accommodating organization also supported a Sabbath Observers Association and called upon those who rested from their labors on Saturday to hire their own.

On the educational front, the Orthodox Union accepted the incontrovertible fact that immigrant Jews wanted their children to receive a public school education. (As of 1900, at most 150 boys attended Yeshiva Etz Chaim.) Therefore, the OU developed modern *talmud torahs* to draw youths back to Jewish life. Operating after public school hours, these institutions offered boys—and girls—educational, social, and recreational activities designed to make them feel comfortable with a new American Jewish identity rooted in traditional teachings.

The years between the world wars witnessed the emergence of new challenges for both Orthodoxy's resisting and accommodating groups in America. The contingent that continued to embrace the model of Old World Judaism now confronted the fact that many of its transplanted rabbis and much of its base of lay followers would pass away during the 1920–1940 period. And, the strict immigration quotas that the U.S. Congress passed in 1924 limited the number of first-generation Jews whom the Agudath ha-Rabbanim might hope to reach. Those resisters who harbored any optimism about the future placed their faith in an idiosyncratic group of second-generation Jews who resided primarily in interwar Brooklyn, New York. Somehow the families of these young people had not succumbed to most of the lures of Americanization that had so transformed other Jews, and they supported the establishment of yeshivas such as Williamsburg's Mesifta Torah Vodaath—or its distaff counterpart Bais Yaakov—or Yeshiva Chaim Berlin of Brownsville. A few like-minded schools could be found elsewhere in New York, Baltimore, and New Haven. These institutions sought to renew the effort that had earlier energized the Etz Chaim-RIETS crowd: to reconstitute the religious civilization of the past on American soil. As hard-core resisters, they looked contemptuously at Bernard Revel's compromises in educating well-integrated American Orthodox rabbis and laypeople. Although they comprised only several thousand families—including some strictly Orthodox newcomers who entered this country despite the quotas—these communities formed a base for efforts at even greater separatism in the post–World War II period.

Concomitantly, accommodating rabbis—mostly RIETS men—continued their struggle to engage the majority of generally disinterested American Jews with the values of religious life. These efforts of Orthodox leaders often paralleled those of their Conservative counterparts outside the sanctuary. Within their own synagogue centers, they promoted a broad range of ancillary activities, from dances to sports to theater productions—all predicated on the hope that those who came to play might be convinced to stay to pray. Some of these rabbis moved even closer to what Conservatives did, modifying synagogue practice to conform to potential congregants' lifestyles. Many Orthodox Union affiliates allowed men and women to sit together during services, particularly during the High Holidays, when many Jews appeared for their annual visit to the house of worship and wanted to have their entire families around them. These and other self-defined Orthodox synagogues often conducted late Friday night services to attract those who would not leave work at early sundown during the winter months. Indeed, by the early 1940s, such accommodations that violated halachic strictures were so commonplace that the lines between American Orthodoxy and Conservatism were effectively blurred. This lack of distinctiveness was particularly true in midwestern and southern Jewish communities. Such commonalities could also be found, however, within Orthodoxy's New York epicenter, though not in the heart of the resistant Brooklyn neighborhoods.

After World War II, accommodationist Orthodoxy followed American Jewry to new, suburban locales, where it began to battle Conservatives and, to a lesser extent, Reformers for the allegiance of the next generation of Jews. This robust competition among Americanized Jewish movements took place in an era of religious revival, when it was an important national value to affiliate with the reli-

gion of your choice. Founded in 1937 and consisting primarily of RIETS graduates, the Rabbinical Council of America (RCA) sought to make their version of the faith a viable option by admitting all Jews who approached their synagogues' portals, regardless of personal levels of observance. In keeping with their traditions from the interwar years, these rabbis continued to approximate what liberal Judaism's leaders did outside sacred spaces. Work with youth groups was particularly important, as Orthodox synagogues attempted to capitalize on parental apprehensions that, in an increasingly accepting host society, their children might marry non-Jews.

Postwar modern Orthodox rabbis differed from their immediate predecessors in their lack of tolerance for congregations and religious leaders who called themselves Orthodox but deviated from the halacha in their synagogue practices. This insistence on more precise standards was an outgrowth, in part, of the many disputes that raged between accommodationist Orthodox and Conservative forces over control of long-standing synagogues that in the late 1940s–1960s moved from inner cities to suburban locales. There, far-reaching debates were held over whether it was appropriate for a so-called "modern Orthodox" synagogue to seat men and women together or to have Sabbath services without regard for when sundown occurred. The decisions that were made helped put an end to the period of endemic fluidity among Jewish movements.

Much of the confidence that this new breed of RIETS rabbi effused is attributable to the presence of Rabbi Joseph Soloveitchik, a towering and charismatic figure. From his perch as the most distinguished *Rosh Yeshiva* (Talmudic sage) at RIETS, for hundreds of disciples he set authoritative parameters for what constituted an acceptable Orthodox approximation of what the Conservative movement was doing. Although accommodationist Orthodox rabbis and their lay supporters won only a minority of the campaigns for Jewish allegiance on the suburban frontiers, they were proud of, and secure in, their minority status.

The early postwar years, however, also saw a new beginning for strident, resistant Orthodoxy. Some refugees from, and survivors of, the Holocaust added members and vitality to the old-line forces. These newcomers were among those who had implicitly harkened to the advice of those East European sages who had warned believers against settling in the *treif* (unkosher) America. Now in this country because antisemitism had destroyed their communities, these so-called Yeshiva World or Hasidic sects went about re-creating European Jewish conditions on American soil with emphatic zeal.

Whether they affiliated with the Agudath Israel, a European-based, Orthodox anti-Zionist organization (the American branch was founded in 1913 but rose to prominence after World War II), or with the long-standing UOR, which they effectively took over after 1945, or with independent Hasidic entities, their spokesmen had little positive to say about accommodationist Orthodoxy. And they were completely opposed to cooperation with or even recognition of more liberal forms of Judaism. Moreover, they were against the RCA's and the OU's long-standing advocacy of Religious Zionism and its strong support for the modern, secular State of Israel. In 1956, the UOR's Council of Torah Sages demanded that the OU and RCA cease their work with the interdenominational Synagogue Council of America, an umbrella organization that studiously avoided divisive religious issues. The accession by some RIETS faculty and RCA members to the demand marked the beginning of the resisters' impact on accommodationist values.

In the most recent period, the 1970s to the present, accommodating rabbis have ministered to a different type of Americanized constituency. During these decades, as the number of Jews who identified with the movement declined, a winnowing of Orthodoxy took place. Many of the less observant who had affiliated out of filial piety or nostalgia found that they were more comfortable in Conservative and Reform settings. The nonreligious lost interest in any form of Jewish religious expression and more easily assimilated into an increasingly open and often secular American society. Those who remained in most modern Orthodox synagogues—particularly in the largest Jewish urban centers—tended to be punctilious in their observances, notwithstanding their high degree of acculturation to American society in other ways. In smaller American towns and cities, however, many of the less devoted could still be found in Orthodox precincts.

The modern followers of halacha were usually products of the proliferating Orthodox Jewish day schools, founded by a movement that began in the 1920s and 1930s, but which had expanded exponentially in the postwar period. In these schools, the young were taught how to live harmoniously with both Jewish religious and American secular cultures. Although not all the graduates remained within the

fold, many of the alumni, Orthodox "baby boomers"—people who were in their late forties and early fifties at century's end—were in community leadership positions. When these men and women speak to their rabbis about accommodations, their talk is of such ancillary features as *eruvim* (enclosures permitting carrying on the Sabbath), which allow the parents to wheel baby carriages to services, enabling the Orthodox family to stay together while praying, albeit on opposite sides of a *mechitza* (partition separating the genders). For them, the modern Orthodox synagogue is not a center for the inculcation or intensification of Jewish identity. It is a place where the already committed assemble, worship, and learn, and familiarize themselves with tradition beyond what they were taught in school.

As the new millennium began, the growing camp of resisters—with a fertility rate much higher than any other cohort of contemporary Jews—became increasingly resolute in its mission. The social values and way of life of the resisters—from their way of dress and speech, to their strict rules on gender separation, to their undervaluing the importance of secular education—deeply permeated the behavior and consciousness of observant, modern Orthodox Jews.

Still, Orthodox resisters and accommodators are far from fully united on all social policy and religious issues. Their attitudes toward female roles in their communities' congregational and social life serve as a demarcation both between and within factions. Generally, resisters do not countenance the active participation of women within their synagogues. Indeed, these men and women have loudly opposed what they perceive as the deleterious impact of feminism on American Jewish life. They have censured liberal Jewish leaders for their broad redefinition of women's roles and have criticized those Orthodox accommodators who have stretched the halacha to allow women greater participation in public ritual and to hold religious leadership positions.

At the same time, those who have altered the architecture of synagogues to make women more comfortable in Orthodox precincts, or who have elected women as presidents of their synagogue boards, or who, beginning in the 1970s, have supported the creation of women's *tefilla* (Orthodox prayer) groups, have acted in accord with their long-standing belief that, for traditional Judaism to survive here, it must and can adjust to the American environment. Withal, these accommodationists have not always agreed on the extent of female participation permissible in religious life. While the most progressive have even appointed women to quasi-clerical positions in their synagogues and have predicted that women will eventually be ordained and recognized as Orthodox rabbis, others have focused their efforts on providing girls and women with ever-increasing Jewish educational opportunities comparable to those available to males.

Jeffrey S. Gurock

References and Further Reading

Goldman, Karla. 2000. *Beyond the Synagogue Gallery: Finding a Place for Women in American Judaism.* Cambridge, MA: Harvard University Press.

Grinstein, Hyman B. 1945. *The Rise of the Jewish Community of New York.* Philadelphia: Jewish Publication Society.

Gurock, Jeffrey S. 1988. *The Men and Women of Yeshiva: Orthodoxy, Higher Education and American Judaism.* New York: Columbia University Press.

Gurock, Jeffrey S. 1996. *American Jewish Orthodoxy in Historical Perspective.* Hoboken, NJ: KTAV Publishing House.

Helmreich, William B. 1983. *The World of the Yeshiva: An Intimate Portrait of Orthodox Jewry.* New York: The Free Press.

Joselit, Jenna Weissman. 1990. *New York's Jewish Jews: The Orthodox Community in the Interwar Years.* Bloomington: Indiana University Press.

Liebman, Charles. 1965. "Orthodoxy in American Jewish Life." *American Jewish Year Book* 65: 21–97.

Mintz, Jerome R. 1992. *Hasidic People: A Place in the New World.* Cambridge, MA: Harvard University Press.

Rakeffet-Rothkoff, Aaron. 1972. *Bernard Revel: Builder of American Jewish Orthodoxy.* Philadelphia: Jewish Publication Society.

Rakeffet-Rothkoff, Aaron. 1981. *The Silver Era in American Jewish Orthodoxy: Rabbi Eliezer Silver and His Generation.* New York: P. Feldheim.

Sarna, Jonathan D. 1987. "The Debate over Mixed Seating in the American Synagogue." In *The American Synagogue: A Sanctuary Transformed,* edited by Jack Wertheimer, pp. 363–394. Cambridge: Cambridge University Press.

Sussman, Lance. 1995. *Isaac Leeser and the Making of American Judaism.* Detroit, MI: Wayne State University Press.

Reform Judaism

Reform Judaism, also known as Liberal or Progressive Judaism, was the first branch of American Judaism to be for-

mally organized into a denomination. In the last quarter of the twentieth century, it became the largest Jewish denomination in the United States with respect to the number of formally affiliated members. Reform Judaism is also the largest and oldest "liberal" religious tradition in the world, far exceeding Unitarian-Universalism, Ethical Culture, and Reconstructionist Judaism. Beginning in Germany early in the nineteenth century, the Reform movement quickly spread to the United States, where it has enjoyed its greatest institutional success. Still, the Reform movement in America has faced numerous challenges, including religious laxity, lack of ideological clarity, and severe criticism from external sources. Nevertheless, the Reform movement continues to demonstrate vitality, particularly among its core adherents and leaders, and an ability to retain members on a multigenerational basis.

Highly adaptive to its cultural environment, American Reform Judaism passed through several stages of ideological and religious development and at any one time often encompassed a spectrum of beliefs and practices. The polity of the Reform movement has been essentially congregationalist since its inception and generally views Halachah (rabbinic law) as advisory. The American Reform movement also spawned a strong, well-organized rabbinate, which has played a major role both in articulating the movement's ideology and in shaping its liturgical traditions. The movement established three major national organizations: a union of congregations, Union for Reform Judaism; a seminary system, Hebrew Union College–Jewish Institute of Religion (HUC-JIR); and an independent association of rabbis, the Central Conference of American Rabbis (CCAR). A "work in progress," the Reform movement is currently being reshaped by gender egalitarianism, inclusion of gays and lesbians, outreach, folk-rock music, and neotraditionalism in its ritual life.

Constructing a history of Reform Judaism in America is complicated by a number of historiographical factors. Most studies of American Reform Judaism focus on the institutions and the elite of the movement, even though it may be as much a "bottom up" movement as a "top down" tradition. Second, despite its Central European origins, American Reform Judaism is both a transplantation of ideas and practices and a set of adaptations to a distinctly American environment. Thus, understanding American Reform Judaism requires knowledge of general American religious history as well as the broader American Jewish experience. And, as noted by Michael A. Meyer, the movement's premier historian, the question of continuity versus discontinuity in American Reform Judaism is pronounced. "It is not possible," Meyer concluded, "to isolate a doctrinal essence of the Reform movement . . . it is perhaps more helpful to understand the movement in terms of dynamic tensions created by specific sets of polarities" (1988). Identifying what is normative in Reform is difficult, if not impossible.

Traditionally, scholars have focused on the reorientation of the Reform movement during the interwar years, when a broad shift from a rational universalism to a more ethnic Jewish particularism occurred. This reorientation did not result in a permanent schism within the Reform movement or a rejection of its fundamental religious liberalism. By contrast, by the end of the twentieth century many features of the movement's essential modernism had been called into question, including the divine origins of the Torah and the authoritative nature of Halachah. In many ways then, both ideological and ritual discontinuities within the Reform movement are potentially more profound today than during the movement's debate over Zionism in the 1930s and 1940s. Still, despite the intense debates about the movement's deepest spiritual foundations and religious practices, the institutional integrity of the Reform movement does not seem to be threatened.

Beginnings, 1824–1865

Although muffled calls for religious reform in the American synagogue were heard in the eighteenth century, only in 1824 was there an overt call for significant changes. Led by a Jew of North African origin, Isaac Harby (1788–1828), a small group of young members of K. K. Beth Elohim in Charleston, South Carolina, petitioned the synagogue's *junta* (governing council), seeking numerous reforms in the worship, educational, and business practices of the congregation. Harby and his followers were probably moved to act after reading articles in the local paper about the Reform congregation in Hamburg, Germany. When the junta refused to consider their requests, the dissidents formed themselves into the Reformed Society of Israelites (1825–1833), producing a handwritten prayer book and other religious materials for themselves. Following Harby's untimely death, Abraham Moise, a young attorney,

emerged as the new leader. After a fire destroyed the city's synagogue, Moise and the Society gained the support of the congregation's *hazzan,* Gustavus Poznanski (1805–1879), who agreed to have an organ installed in the new structure. The traditional faction rejected the introduction of instrumental music in the Shabbat service and ultimately withdrew from the congregation, forming their own synagogue, Shearith Israel.

Although the first group of Reformers was largely Sephardic, the vast majority of Reform Jews in America are of Ashkenazic origin. With the end of the War of 1812 and improved transatlantic transportation, Jewish emigration from Germany soared from 1815 to 1855. Numbering only 2,700 to 3,000 in 1820, the American Jewish community reached 150,000 on the eve of the Civil War (Meyer 1988). Embedded in their ranks were Reform Jews and Reform rabbis, who would lay the foundation for a Reform movement during the 1840s and 1850s.

Lay German reformers organized nascent congregations in Baltimore (Har Sinai) in 1842 and New York (Congregation Emanuel) in 1845. Emanuel grew rapidly and recruited Leo Merzbacher (1809–1856) as its religious leader. Rabbi Dr. Max Lilienthal (1815–1882) arrived in New York in 1845 and established a Jewish boarding school. Four years later, he became the Chief Rabbi of several of New York's orthodox German immigrant congregations. After settling in Cincinnati years later, Lilienthal embraced Reform as the rabbi of the city's Bene Israel congregation.

Cincinnati, a gateway to the American interior, also attracted the indefatigable Isaac Mayer Wise (1819–1900) to one of its pulpits, Bene Yeshurun. Wise, more than anyone else, was responsible for creating the national organizations of the Reform movement and making Cincinnati its principal spiritual home for nearly eighty years. Born in Bohemia, Wise had limited Jewish religious training and minimal formal credentials. Energetic and resourceful, he came to America in 1846 and presented himself to Lilienthal. Lilienthal directed him to Albany, New York, where Wise proclaimed himself Chief Rabbi. There, Wise's soaring ambition put him at odds with his congregation's lay leadership, and following a physical scuffle with its president in the synagogue on Rosh Hashanah, 1850, he left the Beth El pulpit. After briefly serving a second, independent congregation, in 1854 Wise moved to Cincinnati, which became his home for the rest of his life.

Isaac Mayer Wise. (Bettman/Corbis)

In Cincinnati, Wise launched his own newspaper, the *American Israelite,* and published his own prayer book, *Minhag America,* which he believed could serve as a common text for American Jews of all religious persuasions. Wise's dream was to unite the increasingly factionalized American Jewish community of his time under a single banner and to become its leader. Wise had two principal opponents. Isaac Leeser (1806–1868), the religious leader of Philadelphia's Mikveh Israel congregation for twenty years and the editor-publisher of *The Occident and American Jewish Advocate,* relentlessly promoted his Americanized, modern, Sephardic-style Judaism in opposition to Wise's vision of moderate Reform as the religious common ground for American Jews. After years of public disagreement, the two men agreed to meet at a conference in Cleveland in 1855 to work out a common platform. However, the Cleveland Conference ended in failure, largely because of the fierce attacks of a newly arrived, radical reform rabbi from Germany, Dr. David Einhorn (1809–1879).

Although Isaac M. Wise was the principal institution builder of the national Reform movement in America,

Rabbi Dr. Einhorn was its leading ideologue and liturgist. Brilliant, uncompromising, and steeped in both rabbinics and German culture, Einhorn arrived in the United States in 1855 at the invitation of Baltimore's Har Sinai congregation. Ordained at the Fuerth Yeshiva and intellectually reshaped by his doctoral studies at several German universities, Einhorn was a veteran both of the Reform rabbinic conferences and of the Reform–Orthodox controversies in Germany. Shortly after arriving in Baltimore, Einhorn published his prayer book, *Olat Tamid* (*The Eternal Sacrifice*), in German and Hebrew, as an alternative to Wise's book. Nearly forty years later, an English-language version of Einhorn's prayer book became the basis of the first denominational, Reform prayer book, the *Union Prayer Book,* published by the CCAR in 1892.

Although Einhorn developed his own systematic philosophy of Judaism, which he referred to as Mosaism, the three basic tenets of classical or radical Reform Judaism are all present in his work. First, he understood Judaism to be an "ethical monotheism." As a religious doctrine, ethical monotheism valued morals over ritual and universalism over ethnic particularism. Second, Einhorn maintained a belief in "progressive revelation," which mandated Reform's fundamental commitment to adapting to ongoing cultural change. Lastly, he strongly believed in the "mission of Israel," the principal idea that explained why Jews needed to stay Jewish and thereby serve the larger interests of humanity as they led the way to universal salvation. Notably, "the mission of Israel" or "the chosen People" concept provided Einhorn with a powerful argument against mixed marriage and rabbinic officiation at interfaith weddings.

Einhorn was also the most outspoken of the rabbinic abolitionists in the United States. Indeed, he was compelled to leave Baltimore and resettle in Philadelphia because of his staunchly antislavery views, which he published in his German-language journal, *Sinai.* By contrast, Wise was a Copperhead Democrat, while the majority of Reform religious leaders remained neutral on the great issue of human enslavement. A few, however, such as James Gutheim (1817–1886), were openly proslavery and Confederate patriots. The war ended on the evening of the first *seder* in April 1865. Shortly thereafter, Wise and Leeser went together to Richmond, Virginia, as an act of unity and healing. Einhorn and many other rabbis joined together to eulogize Abraham Lincoln following his assassination.

A Modern American Denomination, 1865–1900

Before the Civil War, despite the intense debates about and within the Reform movement, Reform Judaism in the United States was still very small and seriously divided into pro-Wise and pro-Einhorn camps. It was only after the war that the Reform movement began to grow. In part, its growth was a reaction to the war itself and the search for a deeper spirituality. An increasing number of American Jewish families of German origin were second generation, and they sought a more Americanized expression of Judaism. In addition, in the years following the war, religious modernism was on the rise in mainstream Protestant denominations in America. Religious modernism's rationality and proscientific worldview further strengthened Reform as an attractive religious ideology for upwardly mobile American Jews.

The first step toward galvanizing a Reform movement took place in Philadelphia in November 1869. David Einhorn convened a small group of like-minded, German-speaking, Reform rabbis to discuss "Principles of Divine Worship," "Marriage Laws," and "Circumcision." In each instance, the rabbis looked for ways to liberalize Reform practice and, in general, to help shape the direction of the movement in its "classical" phase. Soon, however, the German language, to which Einhorn was particularly devoted, lost its sway over the majority of Reform Jews in the United States.

By contrast, Isaac M. Wise advocated the use of the English vernacular as the principal language of Jewish worship and discourse in the United States and rallied a group of lay leaders, who founded the Union of American Hebrew Congregations (UAHC) in 1873. The Union was to act as an umbrella organization for American Jews in general and to serve as the patron of a new American rabbinic school, the Hebrew Union College (HUC). Two years later, HUC opened; like the UAHC, it was located in Cincinnati. Wise's dream of uniting American Jewry under his theological banner seemed to be coming true. In 1883, at the graduation dinner for HUC's first class of rabbis, nonkosher food was served at the so-called Trefa Banquet, scandalizing Wise's more traditional supporters. Although

the culinary faux pas was probably more a case of insensitivity than a purposeful baiting of the kosher guests, the fallout was enormous and contributed directly to the founding of the Jewish Theological Seminary in New York as a traditional alternative to HUC.

Assailed by the religious right, Wise also came under fire from his left. The Ethical Culture Society, founded by Felix Adler in 1876, rejected both Jewish ethnicity and Reform Judaism's inherent theism. The Society's philosophy proved attractive to an increasing number of Reform Jewish laity. To counter their views and reposition Reform between Ethical Culture and traditional Judaism, a second group of rabbis met in Pittsburgh to work out a centrist platform. The principal architect of the Pittsburgh Platform was Kaufmann Kohler, son-in-law of Einhorn and subsequently president of HUC.

The Platform declared, "Judaism presents the highest conception of the God-idea" and affirmed a "mission of Israel" theology. On the other hand, the Pittsburgh Platform (1885) supported Philadelphia's conference, the first meeting of Reform rabbis in America, in rejecting all vestiges of Jewish nationalism and historicizing a broad range of Jewish ritual practices—that is, the practice was appropriate for Biblical times but was no longer relevant. Opposed to some of the Platform's views and its endorsement of Einhornian principles, Isaac Mayer Wise declared it to be a "Declaration of Independence" from Judaism. In time, however, the Platform became the ideological banner of Classical Reform Judaism in America.

Not to be outdone, Wise turned to his rabbinic supporters, and in 1889 a national meeting of the UAHC founded the Central Conference of American Rabbis, the third leg of the national Reform movement. Within three years, the CCAR issued the first *Union Prayer-book,* which was widely (but not universally) adopted by Reform congregations across the country. A second volume for the High Holy Days was authorized a few years later and, in 1897, the CCAR issued the first *Union Hymnal.* A complete annual liturgy was now available to the Reform movement. By the time Isaac M. Wise died on March 24, 1900, the Reform movement had been transformed into an American denomination.

Uptown Progressivism, 1900–1920

With the dawn of the new century, new forces began to reshape Reform Jewish life in America. Most important, a rising tide of Jewish immigration from East Europe redefined the subethnic character of the Jewish community. As early as 1720, Jews of German origin had predominated in American Jewish life. By 1900, however, immigration had radically redrawn the demographic map. Unlike in Germany, where Emancipation in the nineteenth century had resulted in a denationalization of Jewish identity, Jews in czarist Russia and the eastern provinces of the Hapsburg Empire continued to understand themselves as part of a Jewish people. Moreover, despite the rise of revolutionary doctrines among Russian Jews, a widespread traditionalism, as well as *yeshiva* and Hasidic communities, persisted among East European Jews. East European Jews were often poor, and government policies in Europe were designed to further impoverish them. For a huge portion of the population in the Pale of Settlement, hope was to be found in immigration to America.

The traditionalism, sense of peoplehood, and poverty that the East European Jews brought with them to America presented the established Reform community with challenges that even the physical separation of uptown and downtown Jews could not resolve. Because the German Jews employed thousands of East European Jews, the two communities quickly became economically intertwined. Moreover, the larger society saw uptown and downtown Jews as a single community. Unable to divorce themselves from their Eastern cousins, the German Jews, often with disdain, were compelled to work with them, to promote their Americanization, and—in the case of the Conservative movement, sponsored in part by Reform Jewish elites—to reshape their Jewishness and mode of Judaism.

To accomplish these tasks, Reform Judaism in America adopted the broader strategies of uptown progressivism, including its rationalism, its quest for justice, and its belief in cultural conformity. Still, the traditionalism of East European Jewry also affected and reshaped the culture of the uptown German Jews. Thus, in 1902, the Central Conference voted to retain the traditional Jewish Sabbath on the seventh day and not reconfigure it on Sunday. In 1906 the Conference rejected the idea of establishing a synod, with its greater claim of ecclesiastical power, and instead formed the advisory Responsa Committee, thereby maintaining its ongoing advisory role in the Reform movement. On the progressive side of the equation, the Conference passed its first resolution on social justice in 1908 and spoke out against child labor, thereby invoking a long-dormant plank

of the Pittsburgh Platform. In 1913, the National Federation of Temple Sisterhoods (NFTS) was formed, signaling the changing place of women in the Reform movement. However, typical of the more conservative side of progressivism, the CCAR did not vote in favor of women's suffrage until 1917.

Reorientation, 1920–1945

The years following World War I again witnessed major changes in American Jewish life that would reshape the American Reform movement. Early in the 1920s, Congress restricted immigration to the United States. Anti-Jewish quotas in universities and restrictions in housing and employment also signaled the growing xenophobia and antisemitism of the period. Without a fresh supply of immigrants, the pace of Americanization among naturalized Jews quickened, and by 1940, for the first time in more than a century, the majority of American Jews were native born. Reaction to the horrors of war contributed not only to American isolationism but to a renewed commitment to pacifism in the Reform movement itself, which would put many Reform Jews on an ideological collision course with Zionism. Although by 1930 the UAHC could claim 285 affiliated synagogues, the combined membership was only 60,000.

The most significant change in Reform Judaism during the interwar years was in its attitude toward Zionism and, more broadly, toward Jewish peoplehood. Abroad, the issuance of the Balfour Declaration in 1917 and the growth of the *yishuv* in British Palestine greatly bolstered world Zionism. Internally, a new class of Reform leaders emerged who advocated reorienting Reform Judaism away from universal ethical monotheism to a more particularistic view of Jewish life. Stephen S. Wise (1874–1949), no relation to Isaac M. Wise, not only spoke for Zionism and social justice within the broader Reform movement but also became the principal voice of Jewish nationalism in America up to the early years of World War II. Parallel to Wise's founding of his pandenominational Jewish Institute of Religion (JIR) in New York in 1922 (later merged with HUC) were the appointments of a Zionist, Emanuel Gamoran (1895–1952), as the head of the education program of the UAHC and of Jane Evans (1907–2004) as executive director of the NFTS. In 1922, the CCAR even introduced the Hebrew text of "Hatikvah," the national anthem of the

Zionist movement, into a revised addition of the *Union Hymnal.*

The main debate over Zionism and the nature of Jewish culture, however, focused on the writing of a new platform for the Reform movement. Reacting to the rise of Nazism in Central Europe, the increase in domestic anti-semitism, and the intellectual challenge posed by Mordecai Kaplan in his massive book *Judaism as a Civilization* (1934), a new generation of Reform rabbis was eager to reevaluate Reform's ethical monotheism and move it in the direction of a monotheistic ethnicity. In 1935, the CCAR took up the challenge and, led by Professor Samuel S. Cohon (1888–1959), drafted a new set of principles that was traditionally theistic and embraced Zionism.

The new "Guiding Principles of Reform Judaism" passed by the CCAR in Columbus, Ohio, in 1937 recognized "in the rehabilitation of Palestine, the land hallowed by memories and hopes . . . the promise of renewed life for many of our brethren. We affirm," the Principles continued, "the obligation of all Jewry to aid in its up-building as a Jewish homeland." The same year, the UAHC passed a resolution calling for "the establishment of a Jewish homeland in Palestine." However, the new platform did not end opposition to Zionism within the Reform movement. In 1942, the American Council for Judaism was formed by Reform anti-Zionists resisting the call to raise a Jewish army in Palestine and for immediate statehood for the yishuv. News of the destruction of European Jewry and the establishment of the State of Israel in 1948 rendered the council largely ineffective.

A reoriented Reform Judaism was in need of a new prayer book. The CCAR turned to the distinguished scholar of Halachah and leading pulpit rabbi Solomon B. Freehof (1892–1990) to revise the *Union Prayer-book* (UPB) so it would reflect the new religious reality of the Reform movement, including the practices of Saturday morning worship and *bar mitzvah,* previously discarded by the Reform movement. A masterpiece of prose, the 1940 UPB initially met with stiff resistance from the classical camp. Ironically, neo-reformers criticized it as insufficiently traditional. A prayer book issued by the Jewish Welfare Board for American Jewish soldiers included many selections from the UPB, thereby introducing Reform-style worship to tens of thousands of American Jews. By the end of the war, a reoriented neo-Reform Judaism was poised for a period of remarkable expansion.

Suburban Reform Judaism, 1945–1965

The mass movement of Americans to the suburbs after World War II transformed the Reform movement. Suburbanization, combined with the Cold War campaign against "atheistic" Communism, created an unprecedented boom in the building of new churches and synagogues across the country. Synagogue architecture took on a distinctly suburban look, with lawns, parking lots, and a movable wall between the sanctuary and social hall to accommodate uneven patterns in worship attendance.

New leadership guided the Reform movement through the unknown landscape of American suburbia. Rabbi Maurice N. Eisendrath (1902–1973), UAHC president, and Nelson Glueck (1900–1971), a world-renowned archeologist and president of the HUC-JIR, were the most important leaders. In 1943, Eisendrath was named executive director of the Union and, three years later, president. Intent on revitalizing and expanding the Reform movement, Eisendrath moved UAHC headquarters from Cincinnati to New York, resituating it in the capital of American Jewish life. After succeeding Julian Morgenstern as president of HUC in 1947, Glueck led a successful effort to merge Cincinnati's HUC with Stephen Wise's New York–based JIR. The new institution, the HUC-JIR, opened a third branch in Los Angeles (1954) and a fourth in Jerusalem (1963).

Driving this institutional expansion was exceptional growth in membership in both the United States and Canada. By 1955, the Union had 520 congregations with 255,000 affiliated families. Within ten years, another 140 congregations had joined the Union, and the number of Jews affiliated with Reform reached a million. Expansion also affected the CCAR, which hired its first executive director, Rabbi Sidney Regner, in 1954. The Conference started publishing the *Journal of Reform Judaism* and began regulating rabbinic placement, a process previously controlled largely by powerful faculty members at HUC-JIR.

In the years after World War II, the Reform movement expanded its youth activities. Founded in 1939 for people in their twenties, the National Federation of Temple Youth (NFTY) refocused on teenagers and grew rapidly. In 1947, the UAHC opened its first summer camp, Camp Swig, in California. Thereafter, nearly a dozen more camps were opened, and camping emerged as a critical program in the development of future Reform leadership.

During the 1950s and early 1960s, the central focus of the Reform movement was social justice, particularly the civil rights movement. In 1961, with financial help from Kivie Kaplan, a Reform Jew and civil rights activist, the UAHC opened the Religious Action Center (RAC) in Washington, D.C., and established itself as part of the broader liberal political coalition in the nation's capital. In 1964, Eisendrath actively began to oppose the growing American military involvement in Vietnam. Although most Reform Jews supported the liberal agenda, some, particularly in the South, were unhappy with the new activism. With the breakup of the civil rights movement and the withdrawal of American forces from Vietnam, the Reform movement lost its political focus. Malaise set in, sparking a period of self-reflection and uncertainty about the future direction of Reform Judaism in America.

The "Big Tent" Years, 1972–1995

Despite considerable internal controversy, the Reform movement regained its institutional footing and began to expand again. During the last quarter of the twentieth century, it overtook the Conservative movement as the largest Jewish denominational body. In part, Reform benefited from the surge in American Jewish pride after the 1967 Arab-Israeli war and from the continued upward mobility of American Jews. But it also took positive steps of its own, redefining and broadening its ideology and creating a new set of prayer books.

The outstanding Reform leader of the period and perhaps the most widely recognized since Isaac M. Wise had reshaped Reform into an American denomination was the German-born Rabbi Alexander M. Schindler (1925–2000). Energetic and daring, Schindler helped launch Reform's massive Outreach Program to meet the religious needs of the rising proportion of intermarried Jews and was the major force behind the 1983 CCAR decision to embrace patrilineal descent—the idea that any child with at least one Jewish parent could be presumed to be a Jew. Patrilineality played a major role in the global Jewish debate over the sensitive question, Who is a Jew? It sparked protests around the world and quickly presented the Association of Reform Zionists of America (ARZA, est. 1977) with a major challenge. ARZA attempted to balance the new Reform position with remaining part of the larger Jewish community.

German-born Rabbi Alfred Gottschalk (b. 1930), a scholar of the work of the cultural Zionist Ahad Ha-am, was another important leader of the movement in these years. An exceptional fund-raiser, under his tutelage the Jerusalem and Los Angeles campuses of the HUC-JIR became major cultural centers in their communities. Responding to vast social changes, Gottschalk helped usher in a new era in 1972 when he ordained Sally Priesand, the first woman institutionally ordained in the history of the Jewish people. By 1980, as the number of female ordainees of HUC-JIR grew, they established the first association of women rabbis, the Women's Rabbinic Network (WRN).

New prayer books and the "Centenary Perspective" reflected the broadening of the Reform movement. In 1975, at the urging of Rabbi Joseph B. Glaser (1925–1994), the new executive director of the CCAR, the Central Conference published a new, massive prayer book, the *Gates of Prayer*. With multiple Shabbat services, it reflected the religious diversity of the movement, although it did not anticipate the development of gender-sensitive language.

Religious diversity also became the organizing theme of the movement's new platform, drafted by Rabbi Eugene Borowitz, a professor of Jewish education and theology at the New York school of HUC-JIR. As adopted, the 1976 statement reflected the movement's "big tent" philosophy.

Although the broadly inclusive approach helped Reform Judaism expand, it also created problems for the movement, especially with respect to what became known as "border" issues. Most acute was the question of rabbinic officiation at interfaith weddings. In 1973, to reassert itself and anchor Reform Judaism in the historic tradition of classical rabbinic Judaism, the CCAR boldly declared its official opposition to rabbis participating in mixed marriage ceremonies. Despite the subsequent controversy and the establishment of marriage referral agencies outside the boundaries of the Reform movement, the rabbinate held firm and maintained its authority as the principal interpreter of the tradition. It used this to launch a reevaluation of the "big tent" philosophy, a reassessment that has become the hallmark of Reform Judaism in America at the beginning of the twenty-first century.

Post-Modern Reform, 1995–Present

Currently, affiliation rates in many mainstream religious groups have declined, while right-wing religious activity has increased. The Reform movement is no exception, and membership is flat at best. Still, interest in the spiritual in the United States is on the rise, although many observers of religion at this time point to a tendency toward postdenominationalism. The founding of nondenominational rabbinic seminaries, private ordinations, and a sweeping generational shift could all combine to produce unforeseen consequences for Reform Judaism in the next decade.

Equally complex are the seemingly contradictory trends in the religious life of the Reform movement. At the same time that Reform is reclaiming traditional rites and increasing the use of Hebrew, it is also forging bold new social policies, including the normalization of homosexuality and lesbianism. Although not unique to Reform, this elite bidirectionality, an expression of religious postmodernism, may present a significant challenge to the movement's rank and file. Notably, older members, as well as members of the some of the older, larger, and southern congregations, have sought to slow the rate of the revolution in Reform worship.

These tensions became evident and were heightened in the debate over the Central Conference's adoption of a new set of principles in Pittsburgh in 1999. Spearheaded by CCAR president and Hillel regional administrator Richard N. Levy (b. 1937), the text of the principles was rewritten six times before being brought to a vote before the rabbinic organization. A picture of Rabbi Levy wearing a *tallit* (prayer shawl) on the front cover of the 1998 winter edition of *Reform Judaism,* the official magazine of the UAHC, created a firestorm across the American Reform movement. The final version of the principles was decidedly more centrist than what Levy had originally proposed but clearly indicated the neotraditionalist trend within the Reform movement. A similar pattern of rewriting and repositioning has delayed publication by the CCAR of the proposed new Reform prayer book *Mishkan Tefillah* (*Sanctuary of Prayer*) for several years. By contrast, the CCAR took decisive action in passing the "Resolution on Same-Gender Officiation" at its 2000 Conference in Greensboro, North Carolina, at the urging of both the Ad Hoc Committee on Human Sexuality and the WRN.

The top leadership of both the UAHC and HUC-JIR also changed in the late 1990s. In June 1996, Rabbi Eric H. Yoffie, formerly a vice president of the Union and executive director of ARZA, was installed as president of the UAHC. He quickly established a neotraditional agenda, emphasizing increased adult study, and called for a "revolution" in Reform worship that would combine classical liturgical texts and practices with folk-rock music. For budgetary reasons, early in 2003 Yoffie ordered the elimination of regional outreach offices and, later that year, triumphed in his efforts to change the name of the Union of American Hebrew Congregations to the Union for Reform Judaism. For nostalgic reasons, the term *union* was deemed nonnegotiable, *Reform* was introduced as a denominational marker, and *Hebrew* was removed as anachronistic. The removal of the term *congregation* may reflect a redefinition of the Union away from the prevailing congregationalism of the Reform movement toward its own corporate activism.

In recent years, HUC-JIR appointed two new presidents. In 1996, Rabbi Sheldon Zimmerman, a nonacademic, charismatic, pulpit rabbi with strong fund-raising abilities, was installed as the head of the Reform seminary system. Compelled to resign because of misconduct, Zimmerman was succeeded in 2001 as president of the College–Institute by Rabbi David Ellenson. A respected and energetic scholar of Jewish thought and law, Ellenson served as a healer and brought a sense of vitality to HUC-JIR. Married to Rabbi Jacqueline Koch Ellenson, Rabbi David Ellenson fully embodies the bidirectionality of postmodern American Reform Judaism.

Speculations on the future of the Reform movement have generally been split between those who have confidence in the movement's ability to adapt to changing circumstances and those who see the corrosive effects of modernity as irrepressible. At present, Reform Judaism faces a number of significant problems, including the decline of liberalism in American society as well as in religion. Often tagged a "religion of convenience," the movement continues to struggle to define itself, its organizational boundaries, the extent of personal autonomy it assigns to its members, and its basic paradigms of worship, prayer, and sacred music. The Reform movement continues to attract and hold the attention of the socioeconomic elite in the American Jewish community. But it has a large, aging infrastructure to support at a time of declining membership and the aging of the American Jewish population. A shift toward nonsynagogue organizations (NSOs) presents yet another challenge to Reform's essential congregationalism.

Despite these challenges, Reform Judaism continues to offer a religious program that responds meaningfully to the deepest spiritual needs of its members and continues to attract a solid core of lay and religious leaders. If the past is prologue, it is more than possible that an adaptive and daring Reform Judaism will not only endure but thrive in America for the foreseeable future.

Lance J. Sussman

References and Further Reading

Greenstein, Howard R. 1981. *Turning Point: Zionism and Reform Judaism.* [*Brown Judaic Studies* 12.] Ann Arbor, MI: Scholars Press.

Jacob, Walter, ed. 1983. *American Reform Responsa: Collected Responsa of the Central Conference of American Rabbis, 1889–1983.* New York: CCAR.

Kaplan, Dana Evan. 2001. *Contemporary Debates in American Reform Judaism: Conflicting Visions.* New York: Routledge.

Kaplan, Dana Evan. 2003. *American Reform Judaism: An Introduction.* New Brunswick, NJ: Rutgers University Press.

Karff, Samuel, ed. 1976. *Hebrew Union College–Jewish Institute of Religion at One Hundred Years.* Cincinnati, OH: HUC Press.

Korn, Bertram Wallace, ed. 1965. *Retrospect and Prospect: Essays in Commemoration of the Seventy-Fifth Anniversary of the Founding of the Central Conference of American Rabbis.* New York: CCAR.

Meyer, Michael A. 1988. *Response to Modernity: A History of the Reform Movement in Judaism.* New York: Oxford University Press.

Meyer, Michael A., and W. Gunther Plaut. 2001. *The Reform Judaism Reader: North American Documents.* New York: UAHC Press.

Nadell, Pamela S. 1998. *Women Who Would Be Rabbis: A History of Women's Ordination, 1889–1985.* Boston: Beacon Press.

Olitzky, Kerry M., Lance J. Sussman, and Malcolm H. Stern. 1993. *Reform Judaism in America: A Biographical Dictionary and Sourcebook.* Westport, CT: Greenwood Press.

Plaut, W. Gunther. 1965. *The Growth of Reform Judaism: American and European Sources to 1948.* New York: World Union for Progressive Judaism.

Plaut, W. Gunther. 1981. *The Torah: A Modern Commentary.* New York: UAHC Press.

Temkin, Sefton D. 1992. *Isaac Mayer Wise, Shaping American Judaism.* Oxford: Oxford University Press.

Washofsky, Mark. 2001. *Jewish Living: A Guide to Contemporary Reform Practice.* New York: UAHC Press.

Conservative Judaism

Conservative Judaism, until recently the largest stream of American Judaism, occupies the center of the Jewish religious spectrum, standing for the maintenance of tradition while at the same time allowing for change.

In contrast to Reform, situated to its theological left, Conservative Judaism upholds the binding nature of Halakhah, traditional Jewish law. But unlike Orthodoxy, which stands to its right, Conservative Judaism teaches that Halakhah can be interpreted flexibly to fit new conditions. Conservatism's middle-of-the-road orientation has tended to discourage emphasis on ideology, nurturing instead a healthy respect for the folkways of middle-class American Jews—a strategy that proved highly successful in the middle decades of the twentieth century. Beginning in the late 1960s, however, changes in American society and in the Jewish religious landscape raised serious problems for the movement, which have since accelerated, leaving great uncertainty over whether Conservative Judaism can regain its earlier strength and self-confidence.

Conservatism was not launched as a self-conscious movement, but rather evolved gradually over the nineteenth and early twentieth centuries, as an informal coalition of Jews, both rabbinic and lay, slowly carved out a moderate middle ground between Orthodox and Reform Judaism.

This process began in Central Europe after 1815, when Reform first challenged the religious status quo through changes in liturgy, synagogue practice, and theology, aimed at removing medieval vestiges and modernizing Judaism. There were considerable differences of opinion among the Reformers over how much of the tradition had to be jettisoned, and one of the rabbinic moderates, Zechariah Frankel, who parted ways with his Reform colleagues in 1845 when they voted to abrogate the need for praying in the Hebrew language, is often cited as the ideological father of Conservatism. The rabbinical seminary Frankel headed in Breslau, Germany, beginning in 1854, the Juedisch-Theologisches Seminar, is similarly viewed as the prototype for later Conservative rabbinical training, as it emphasized a critical approach to texts along with a positive evaluation of Jewish ritual practice.

Whether there was a de facto Conservative Judaism in early and mid-nineteenth-century America is a matter of scholarly controversy, largely hinging on how one defines "Conservative" in the period preceding the emergence of a self-conscious movement. Historian Moshe Davis, in *The Emergence of Conservative Judaism* (1963), argues that vir-

Zechariah Frankel. (American Jewish Archives)

tually all the traditionalist leaders who opposed the surging Reform movement were in fact proto-Conservative, constituting a "historical school" of Judaism. Davis's thesis has been criticized by other scholars, who categorize some of these men as modern Orthodox. This dispute highlights the indistinct boundary between the two religious camps that would only be clarified after World War II.

Conservative Judaism's first institutional embodiment, the Jewish Theological Seminary of America (JTSA), did not emerge until the 1880s, and even then without any sectarian "Conservative" identification. Two developments within American Reform, both indicating radical breaks with tradition, induced traditionalists to form their own seminary. The first, in 1883, was the serving of nonkosher seafood at the first graduation from Hebrew Union College (HUC), the Reform seminary in Cincinnati, and the second, in 1885, was the promulgation of the so-called Pittsburgh Platform, whereby Reform flatly declared that only the ethical principles of the Hebrew Bible were binding, not the rituals. The traditionalist response came the next year, as a small group of rabbis and laymen launched JTSA. It opened in 1887 in New York City with eight students,

under the leadership of Rabbi Sabato Morais, the Italian-born rabbi of Mikveh Israel, the old Sephardic congregation in Philadelphia. The school's aim, according to its charter, was not to service a new movement but, more broadly, to train rabbis and teachers dedicated to "the preservation in America of the knowledge and practice of historical Judaism as ordained in the law of Moses expounded by the prophets and sages of Israel in Biblical and Talmudic writings."

The new seminary was not a success. Not only was its faculty lackluster, its students few, and its finances shaky, but it had no real constituency. The existing Jewish community, to the extent that it identified religiously, was overwhelmingly Reform, and the newly arriving immigrants from Eastern Europe, whether or not they observed Jewish law, could only envision rabbis as they had been back home—bearded, Yiddish speaking, and lacking secular education.

In 1902 JTSA, on the verge of bankruptcy, was reorganized under the leadership of prominent and wealthy American Jews who themselves identified with Reform. Their purpose was to ease the acculturation of the children of the new immigrants by providing them rabbis who combined traditional Judaism with modern culture. To head the school, they hired a well-known Judaic scholar then on the staff of Cambridge University, the Romanian-born Solomon Schechter. Eager to make the seminary a center of modern, scientific Jewish scholarship, Schechter built a distinguished faculty.

Schechter was the first to spell out an ideological platform for what would become known as Conservative Judaism. It was based on the concept of "Catholic Israel." This meant that Jews were to be guided in their daily lives neither by every detail recorded in the Code of Jewish Law (as were the Orthodox) nor by the dictates of universal ethics and reason (as was Reform), but by the practices honored by the mainstream of the Jewish people through the ages. Thus, the Jewish lifestyle that had evolved over the course of Jewish history was determinative. Schechter, however, was vague about which Jews constituted "Catholic Israel" whose practice would be considered normative—all nominal Jews, or only the observant ones—and who was authorized to determine the Jewish validity of deviations from precedent. These unresolved questions would later generate different schools of thought within the movement.

In the early twentieth century, however, few were interested in spelling out a hard-and-fast ideological platform. A distinct Conservative Judaism was taking shape not through the force of ideas but by the rise of rabbinic and congregational organizations allied with and devoted to the Seminary. The school's alumni association adopted the name Rabbinical Assembly in 1918 and broadened its membership to include rabbis who had not attended JTSA but were servicing congregations sympathetic with its approach.

Even earlier, in 1913, representatives of twenty-two of those congregations had met to organize the United Synagogue of America. Like JTSA itself and the Rabbinical Assembly, the United Synagogue avoided any explicit sectarian label, hoping to appeal to the broadest possible spectrum of American Jewry (it was not until the 1990s that the organization acknowledged that its appeal was confined to one sector of the community by changing its name to United Synagogue of Conservative Judaism). The new union's platform affirmed "the maintenance of Jewish tradition in its historical continuity," specifically mentioning Sabbath observance, the dietary laws, "the traditional character of the liturgy," and "the hopes of Israel's restoration." At the same time, "while not endorsing the innovations introduced by any of its constituent bodies," the United Synagogue was open to "all elements essentially loyal to traditional Judaism." Among the innovations in many of the synagogues were the mixed seating of men and women, recitation of certain prayers in English, and having the rabbi and cantor turn to face the congregation rather than forward to the ark; a few also incorporated organ music into the service.

Although their motives were to serve the religious needs of all Jews who were not Reform, by replicating the tripartite structure that Reform Judaism had pioneered—a seminary, a congregational body, and a rabbinical association—Schechter and his backers had, willy-nilly, created the Conservative movement. The fact that it was the JTSA that gave rise to the United Synagogue and the Rabbinical Assembly ensured the central role of the seminary within Conservative Judaism ever after. This was in contrast to Reform, in which the congregational organization created the seminary and its rabbinic group, and the lay leaders have always maintained control.

Upon Schechter's death in 1915, Cyrus Adler succeeded him as president of the Seminary, first on an acting basis and, beginning in 1924, in a permanent capacity. A traditional Jew who had served as professor of Semitics at Johns Hopkins University and librarian of the Smithsonian Institution, Adler played a leadership role in virtually every national Jewish communal endeavor of his time. During Adler's tenure, which lasted until his death in 1940, the latent tensions in Conservatism between those viewing it as an organic continuation of traditional Judaism and those eager to mark it off as a denomination separate from Orthodoxy came to the surface at the Seminary.

Most of the faculty were comfortable with traditionalism and saw no need to sanction innovations, even those being practiced in Conservative congregations. In fact, these academicians rarely used the word *Conservative* to describe their orientation. But there was another, generally younger group, led by Mordecai Kaplan, that urged explicit renunciation of such doctrines as a supernatural God, the chosen people, revelation, and any divine sanction for the performance of ritual.

Kaplan, the son of an East European Orthodox rabbi, had himself started out in an Orthodox pulpit, but the intellectual impact of the philosophic pragmatism associated with John Dewey and the prevalent theories of the time in anthropology and sociology made it impossible for Kaplan to maintain the traditional beliefs. His book *Judaism as a Civilization,* published in 1934, suggested recasting Judaism as "a religious civilization" and its practices as "folkways." Ultimately, this school of thought, which Kaplan called Reconstructionism, would break away from the Conservative movement and constitute a separate branch of American Judaism, but in the fourth and fifth decades of the twentieth century it profoundly influenced the religious views of many Conservative rabbis. One of Kaplan's innovations, the *bat mitzvah* ceremony for girls upon reaching the age of twelve—the first was that of his daughter, Judith, in 1922—was adopted by a growing number of Conservative synagogues in succeeding decades. By the 1970s, it had become almost universal for young women in the movement and today is practiced in many Reform and Orthodox congregations as well.

More important for the future of the movement than the debates at the Seminary were far-reaching structural changes occurring in American Jewish life. A massive new constituency was entering Conservative Judaism, attracted not by ideas but by social needs. These new members would enable the movement to surpass Reform and become, by the 1950s at the latest, the largest Jewish denomination. The process has been masterfully analyzed by sociologist Marshall Sklare in his 1955 book, *Conservative Judaism: An American Religious Movement,* a classic of American Jewish social science.

Sklare noted that Conservative synagogues tended to sprout in areas of "third settlement"—the suburbs—among the children and grandchildren of immigrants. Unlike the situation in the older, urban neighborhoods they came from, Jews moving into the suburbs constituted a small minority in a gentile area; furthermore, these gentiles were not the familiar Italian and Irish Catholics but Protestants, many of old American stock. The Jews, although possibly just as affluent as their new neighbors, felt uneasy about their social status and acted in such a way as to "pass" as true Americans—they stopped speaking Yiddish, for example, and minimized the hours of religious education so as to provide their children, like the other children in the neighborhood, time for sports and extracurricular activities. Ritual observance became less consistent and increasingly confined to the home and the synagogue, since public display of Judaism would mark these newcomers as different from the Christian families.

And yet these Jews, still not accepted socially by the gentiles, felt the need to associate with other Jews. This was an ethnic need, not a religious one, but since Judaism was understood, in the suburban American mind, as a religious grouping, "the local synagogue becomes the Jewish badge of identification to the neighborhood at large."

But what kind of synagogue? An Orthodox one "bears the stigma of the 'ghetto.'" A Reform temple, for most, was too jarring a departure from Jewish tradition. The Conservative synagogue fit perfectly. Its service was recognizable enough for comfort, and yet the unaccented English spoken by the rabbi, and his sermon topics—often issues of general social concern or cultural interest rather than homilies explicating Jewish texts—signaled the community's acculturation. "Conservatism," explained Sklare, "mediates between the demands of the Jewish tradition . . . and the norms of middle-class worship." And, as an ethnic institution in the guise of a religious congregation, the suburban Conservative synagogue developed social programs for every age group, with special emphasis on the young, in the hope that "sports, entertainments, dances, social clubs, and similar activities" under Jewish auspices would ensure generational continuity (Sklare 1955).

Sklare surveyed the ways in which the typical Conservative synagogue managed to find just the right balance between tradition and innovation. By eliminating the separate seating of women characteristic of Orthodoxy and replacing it with "family pews," it made women feel emancipated from second-class religious status and ensured their attendance at services in large numbers. Insistence on synagogue decorum and elimination of the traditional practices of auctioning off honors and publicly announcing monetary contributions marked "the adoption of middle-class norms of convention and aesthetics." The rabbi, along with a corps of ushers, choreographed the services, just as was done at the Protestant church. The services remained traditional, but the synagogue was full only on the High Holy Days. Attendance was meager during weekday services and even on Sabbath mornings unless there was a bar mitzvah. Conservative congregations pioneered a new service, held on Friday evening after everyone had had time to eat dinner at home. This innovative service, noted Sklare, provided "some type of Sabbath observance" that was "free of the rigor and legalistic approach to observance characteristic of Orthodoxy," typifying "the new norms assimilated by the Conservative group" (Sklare 1955).

As for the religious opinions and practices of Conservative Jews, Sklare found that most understood their Conservative affiliation as a means of preserving Jewish identity while allowing themselves a wide degree of latitude in the area of ritual observance. Not one of Sklare's respondents suggested a theological reason for subscribing to the Conservative version of Judaism. Sklare warned that the movement's lack of "a substantial ideological or theological superstructure" (Sklare 1955) might pose a danger for its future, but the Conservative laity did not share his concern. The October 15, 1951, issue of *Time* featured a picture of Louis Finkelstein, president of the Jewish Theological Seminary, on its cover, and the article that went with it presented Conservative Judaism as *the* form of traditional Judaism that would thrive in America.

Finkelstein, who assumed the presidency in 1940, sought to continue along the path of his predecessors in avoiding any open break with Orthodox Jewish law and theology, while retaining Mordecai Kaplan on the faculty and ignoring complaints by Kaplan's colleagues about his deviations from tradition. But in the post–World War II years, as the growth of the movement accelerated—the number of Conservative synagogues jumped from 350 to

800 between 1945 and 1960—pressure mounted within the rabbinate and the laity for changes.

In 1946, the movement produced its first officially authorized prayer book. Although the traditional structure and almost all of the content were retained, two significant alterations were designed to eliminate conceptions deemed jarring to modern sensibilities: the ancient prayer in which a man thanked God for not making him a woman was dropped, and the stated hopes for the restoration of the sacrificial system in a rebuilt Jerusalem temple were recast into the past tense as historical reminiscences.

Another innovation sought to address a long-standing problem in Jewish life, that of the *agunah,* the "chained" woman whose estranged husband will not grant her a Jewish divorce. In the late 1940s, the movement began to insert a clause in the traditional Jewish marriage contract by which the groom obligated himself to give his wife the document should a rabbinic court so direct him. Many halakhic experts considered such a clause legitimate from the standpoint of Jewish law, but the reaction from Orthodox rabbis was universally hostile.

Far more significant than the prayer book and the marriage clause was the 1950 decision explicitly sanctioning driving to the synagogue on the Sabbath (use of any kind of electricity was barred by Orthodox interpretation of Jewish law). For one thing, it was the work of the movement's Committee on Jewish Law and Standards, a body mandated to decide on questions of religious practice, which had existed under different names for years but only now, with this ruling, signaled its emergence as a powerful force within Conservative Judaism. Second, the rationale for the ruling—that in the neighborhoods where new Conservative synagogues were being built, it was unrealistic to expect people to walk to services—marked a recognition that Conservative Judaism was fast becoming a predominantly suburban phenomenon. Third, those who supported the change expressed the hope that enabling Jews in good conscience to drive to services would lead, in the end, to an enhanced Sabbath experience. The argument that leniencies could induce people to be *better* Jews would subsequently be used to justify other deviations from tradition as well. And fourth, the authorization to drive on the Sabbath marked an irrevocable break with Orthodox Judaism. To be sure, many Orthodox Jews drove to synagogue, but the practice was never given a stamp of approval. The distinction between the movements was now

clear: both contained sinners, but only one was prepared to change the rules to ease their consciences. The other held out hope for changing its members' behavior or at least that of their children.

This decision was followed by two others enhancing the role of women that widened the gap with the Orthodox. In 1954, synagogues were given the option of calling women up to the Torah; in 1968 the agunah problem was solved by simply giving rabbis the power to annul a marriage if the husband would not give a religious divorce, a power that contemporary Orthodoxy did not recognize.

At midcentury, enjoying the allegiance of almost half of American Jews (according to a number of surveys), the Conservative movement expanded its institutional reach. In 1948 it founded a network of summer camps, Ramah, whose success was proven by the number of young people it interested in Judaism, some of whom rose to leadership positions in the movement. The Conservatives also started their own day schools in several cities, called Solomon Schechter schools (there were fifteen by 1965), but the great majority of Conservative families continued to send their children to public schools. The Jewish Theological Seminary opened a West Coast branch in Los Angeles in 1947 called the University of Judaism (fifty years later it would sever its ties with the Seminary and become independent), and a world council of Conservative synagogues was announced in 1957, followed shortly thereafter by the formation of a rabbinical seminary in Argentina to serve the needs of Latin American Jewry. In Israel the movement sponsored several synagogues (although the government, under the influence of the Orthodox establishment, refused to recognize the credentials of its rabbis) and, in 1963, set up an academic center in Jerusalem. A sign of the movement's maturation was the entry into the rabbinate of young men who had grown up Conservative; until the 1950s, rabbis in Conservative pulpits generally came from Orthodox backgrounds.

Although Conservative Judaism continued to ride high in the early 1960s, the tumultuous events of that decade bore seeds of the movement's decline. There were manifold assaults on the suburban American middle-class values that underpinned the Conservative enterprise: the counterculture spawned by the civil rights and antiwar movements, as well as the incipient wave of feminism, deeply affected young Jews, turning many of them against what they viewed as the culturally stifling, patriarchal, materialistic, cold, and unspiritual synagogues of their parents. Many of the early activists of Jewish feminism came from Conservative homes, where their religious impulses were often frustrated by the virtual male monopoly on synagogue ritual (in Orthodoxy, gender distinctions were considered religiously mandated, while in Reform ritual was far less important for either sex). Almost all the young people who set up Havurat Shalom, the first Jewish countercultural community, had been brought up in the Conservative movement. And *The Jewish Catalogue* series, the core text of the Jewish counterculture, was put together by people who were products of the Conservative youth movement.

Conservative Judaism faced a challenge on another front as well: Orthodoxy, long assumed to be on its way to irrelevance if not disappearance, was showing vibrancy and attracting some of the more seriously religious young people in the Conservative movement. Indeed, as much of the Jewish community turned inward, in the wake of the 1967 Six Day War and a much-delayed reckoning with the meaning of the Nazi Holocaust, to focus on such "Jewish" issues as Israel and Soviet Jewry, Orthodoxy's more intensive preoccupation with matters Jewish contrasted favorably, for many, with the seemingly pallid, middle-of-the-road Judaism that had been the secret of Conservative success just a few years earlier.

Once again, it was sociologist Marshall Sklare who provided the most clear-sighted diagnosis of the movement. In a new epilogue he wrote for a second, augmented edition of *Conservative Judaism* that appeared in 1972, Sklare noted several trends: a drastic decline in the morale of Conservative rabbis; a dawning realization that Jewish observance, far from being strengthened by Conservative liberalization of the strictures of the law, was in rapid decline; the growing incidence of intermarriage among children of Conservative Jews (far more prevalent among the sons than among the daughters); and the movement's inability to retain the allegiance of those attracted to the "Woodstock nation."

A study of the movement released at the 1979 biennial convention of the United Synagogue confirmed that Conservative Judaism was in trouble. Conducted by Charles Liebman, a noted social scientist who was then a visiting professor at JTSA, and Saul Shapiro, a Conservative lay leader, the survey found a massive hemorrhaging of young people who had been reared as Conservative

Jews. Many were choosing to avoid any congregational affiliation, while those most serious about religion defected to Orthodoxy. Conservative leaders did not allow public distribution of the report's recommendations, which included "greater affirmation of traditional Judaism" so as to maintain the allegiance of the movement's observant constituency.

The reason for their sensitivity was that strong forces within Conservatism were pushing in quite another direction: ordination of women was on the agenda. A movement that prided itself on the harmonious balance of tradition and change was about to make a fateful choice between them.

The first indication of feminism's impact on Conservative policy came in 1973, when the Committee on Jewish Law and Standards gave rabbis the option of counting women in a *minyan,* the ten-person quorum necessary for communal prayer. The following year, the committee took up the issue of female rabbis and cantors (Reform's seminary, HUC, had begun admitting women to rabbinic and cantorial programs in the late 1960s and ordained its first female rabbi in 1972).

Battle lines were quickly drawn within the movement, as opponents of the change sensed that Conservative adherence to Schechter's concept of "Catholic Israel," maintaining mainstream Jewish tradition, was at stake. The decisive factor proved to be Gerson Cohen, chancellor of JTSA, who was at first wary of the innovation but then took the side of the innovators. Cohen appointed a special commission, whose 1979 majority report recommended the ordination of women and gave four reasons: that many of the responsibilities of the contemporary rabbi could be performed, according to Jewish law, even by women; that "ethical considerations" mandated equal career access for men and women; that a male-only rabbinate stood in contradiction to the gender equality prevailing in the Judaism practiced by Conservative Jews; and that evidence showed wide support within the movement for the ordination of women.

The JTSA faculty, the body that granted ordination and therefore would have to authorize the change, was bitterly divided and put the matter off. In 1983 a woman ordained by HUC applied for membership in the Rabbinical Assembly; her application was supported by a majority of the rabbis present at the group's convention but not by the necessary three-quarters. That year Chancellor Cohen brought the issue before the faculty, which since 1979 had lost a number of its traditionalist members through death and retirement. Women's ordination passed by a vote of thirty-four to eight, as several of the remaining opponents, knowing the numbers were against them, boycotted the vote in protest. By the fall of 1984, nineteen women had enrolled in the rabbinical school. Female cantors were accepted a few years later.

As soon as the Seminary faculty voted to ordain women, some opponents of the decision organized themselves as the Union for Traditional Conservative Judaism (UTCJ), ostensibly as an internal lobby to stave off further deviations from tradition. But its creation of a Panel of Halakhic Inquiry to rule on issues of Jewish law gave clear indication of secessionist tendencies, and in 1990 the Union deleted the word *Conservative* from its name and established its own rabbinical seminary.

Clearly, the Conservative ordination of women constituted a shift away from the movement's old preference for a "big tent" encompassing the right and the left. Conservative Judaism was hitching its future to feminism and to what was coming to be called egalitarianism. This sea change was evident, as well, in the pages of a new Conservative prayer book, *Sim Shalom,* published in 1985; its elimination of many traditional gender distinctions was a major reason for the UTCJ's Panel of Halakhic Inquiry to rule that it should not be used for prayer.

Having broken the logjam in Jewish practice by ordaining women, Conservative Judaism sought to do the same for Jewish theology in 1988 with the release of *Emet Ve-Emunah,* a statement of the movement's beliefs and principles. Although questions of ideology had been of little importance to the middle-class suburban Jews Marshall Sklare had studied in the 1950s, thirty years later such questions were high on the agenda of college-educated Jews, who could not find, in the fuzzy rhetoric of the movement, any clear description of what Conservative Judaism stood for and how it differed from the other denominations. *Emet Ve-Emunah,* however, drafted by a committee, could not escape the "on-the-one-hand-and-on-the-other-hand" approach that had bedeviled the movement from the start. The document's opening section, on God, is typical: after flatly stating that God is at the very core of Conservative Judaism, it goes on to discuss the "doubts," "complexities," and "confusions" this belief entailed.

The decade of the 1990s brought a new divisive issue that had the potential to divide the movement even more seriously than had women's ordination: the religious status of homosexuals. In 1990 the Rabbinical Assembly came out against all civil discrimination against gays and lesbians and welcomed Jews of whatever sexual orientation into Conservative congregations. The next year the Committee on Jewish Law and Standards, taking up the question of whether homosexuals might be appointed as rabbis or to other positions of religious influence, produced two diametrically opposed opinions: one that Jewish tradition can countenance no validation of homosexuality, and the other that negative references to homosexuality in ancient Jewish sources were directed at coercive and exploitative relations and did not apply to "mutually exclusive, committed" relationships.

The debate, still unresolved, has since heated up, with rabbinic officiation at homosexual commitment ceremonies also coming up for consideration. In 2002 the president of the United Synagogue came out in favor of liberalizing the movement's position on homosexual rights, and JTSA students have been especially vociferous in support of the admission of openly homosexual rabbinical students. However, the school's chancellor, Ismar Schorsch, emerged as a staunch opponent of any change, warning that it could very well trigger a schism.

Should Conservative Judaism manage to weather the storm over homosexuality, an even tougher issue lurks on the horizon—intermarriage. In contrast to Reform Judaism, many of whose rabbis perform intermarriages and which can recognize as a Jew someone with either parent Jewish, the Conservative movement has so far hewn to the traditional line: its rabbis may not participate in weddings between Jews and non-Jews, and only children of Jewish mothers (or converts) are considered Jews. Not only has this placed Conservative rabbis under great pressure from families incensed that "their" rabbi will not marry their children, but it has undoubtedly contributed to the transfer of allegiances of many families from Conservative to Reform. Surveys of the Conservative laity have consistently shown a majority in favor of adopting the Reform patrilineal definition of Jewishness, which grants Jewish status to the children of Jewish men and non-Jewish women.

As the twenty-first century dawned, the Conservative movement was plagued by declining numbers and low morale. The 2000–2001 National Jewish Population Study indicated that only 33 percent of Jewish households affiliated with a synagogue were Conservative, a drop of ten points since 1990. Reform, with 39 percent of affiliated households, was now the largest stream of American Judaism. A demographic survey of Jews in New York City, by far the nation's largest Jewish community, showed a similar trend: 26 percent of Jews self-identified as Conservative in 2002, a drop of eight points since 1991 (Reform declined in the city as well, though it still led the Conservatives). Furthermore, a sophisticated longitudinal study of young Conservative Jews, which tracked some 1,000 individuals from their bar/bat mitzvahs in 1994–1995 through college in 2004, gave little cause for optimism. Conducted by the Ratner Center at the JTSA, it found that the young people expressed continued positive feelings about being Jewish as they grew older, but their ritual practices steadily declined. In 2004, only 12 percent of the sample said that they had recently read a Jewish-themed book, and just 18 percent reported that they dated only fellow Jews.

The evident malaise in the movement has elicited several reactions. Some hope that ambitious new initiatives of "synagogue revitalization" will renew Conservative Judaism; others point to the impressive growth of Conservative schools as a foundation stone for resurgence; and yet another perspective cites the need for the movement's leadership to demonstrate greater vision. For his part, Chancellor Schorsch, Conservative Judaism's most visible leader, shocked the biennial convention of the United Synagogue in 2003 by going all the way back to 1950 to find what had led to the current state of decline. The decision that year to allow driving on the Sabbath, Schorsch argued, was a "mistake" because it "gave up on the desirability of living close to the synagogue and creating a *Shabbos* community."

Toward the end of 2004, American Jews learned that the Jewish Theological Seminary, the venerable institution from which Conservative Judaism grew, was in serious financial difficulty. What the future held for the movement it had spawned, now in decline, was anyone's guess.

Lawrence Grossman

References and Further Reading

Davis, Moshe. 1963. *The Emergence of Conservative Judaism.* Philadelphia: Jewish Publication Society.

Elazar, Daniel J., and Rella Mintz Geffen. 2000. *The Conservative Movement in Judaism: Dilemmas and Opportunities.* Albany: State University of New York Press.

Emet Ve-Emunah: Statement of Principles of Conservative Judaism. 1988. New York: Jewish Theological Seminary, Rabbinical Assembly, and United Synagogue of America.

Fierstien, Robert E., ed. 2000. *A Century of Commitment: One Hundred Years of the Rabbinical Assembly.* New York: Rabbinical Assembly.

Gillman, Neil. 1993. *Conservative Judaism: The New Century.* New York: Behrman House.

Karp, Abraham J. 1964. *A History of the United Synagogue of America, 1913–1963.* New York: United Synagogue of America.

Karp, Abraham J. 1985. "The Conservative Rabbi—'Dissatisfied But Not Unhappy.'" In *The American Rabbinate: A Century of Continuity and Change, 1883–1983,* edited by Jacob Rader Marcus and Abraham J. Peck, pp. 98–172. Hoboken, NJ: Ktav Publishing House.

Karp, Abraham J. 1986. "A Century of Conservative Judaism in the United States." In *American Jewish Year Book,* edited by David Singer and Ruth Seldin, pp. 3–61. New York: The American Jewish Committee.

Nadell, Pamela S. 1988. *Conservative Judaism in America: A Biographical Dictionary and Sourcebook.* Westport, CT : Greenwood Press.

Nadell, Pamela S. 1998. *Women Who Would Be Rabbis: A History of Women's Ordination, 1889–1985.* Boston: Beacon Press.

Schechter, Solomon. 1896. *Studies in Judaism.* Philadelphia: Jewish Publication Society.

Scult, Mel. 1993. *Judaism Faces the Twentieth Century: A Biography of Mordecai M. Kaplan.* Detroit, MI: Wayne State University Press.

Sklare, Marshall. 1955, 1972. *Conservative Judaism: An American Religious Movement.* Glencoe, IL: The Free Press. (1955)/New, augmented ed. (1972). New York: Schocken.

Waxman, Mordecai, ed. 1958. *Tradition and Change: The Development of Conservative Judaism.* New York: Burning Bush Press.

Wertheimer, Jack. 1993. *A People Divided: Judaism in Contemporary America.* New York: Basic Books.

Wertheimer, Jack. 1997. *Tradition Renewed: A History of the Jewish Theological Seminary.* 2 Vols. New York: Jewish Theological Seminary.

Wertheimer, Jack, ed. 2000. *Jews in the Center: Conservative Synagogues and Their Members.* New Brunswick, NJ: Rutgers University Press.

Reconstructionist Judaism

Reconstructionist Judaism, the youngest and smallest of the four denominations of American Judaism, was founded as an ideology by Rabbi Mordecai M. Kaplan in the first decades of the twentieth century as a response to the unprecedented challenges posed to Judaism in America. It developed denominational institutions after World War II—the Jewish Reconstructionist Federation in 1955, the Reconstructionist Rabbinical College in 1968, and the Reconstructionist Rabbinical Association in 1974. It defines Judaism as the evolving religious civilization of the Jewish people. Initially, the movement was known for its bold stands in favor of gender equality, a nonsupernatural definition of God, and revisions of the words of the traditional liturgy, and for its repudiation of the belief that the Jews are the "chosen people." As it grew rapidly in the last two decades of the twentieth century, to more than 100 affiliated congregations and *havurot* (smaller, lay-led groups that meet for worship, study, and/or celebration), it also became identified with participatory decision-making communities, liberal Jewish spirituality, the inclusion of gay and lesbian Jews, Jewish ethical decision making, Jewishly grounded social action, and progressive Zionism.

Reconstructionist Judaism began in 1922, when Mordecai Kaplan founded the Society for the Advancement of Judaism (SAJ) in New York City. The son of Rabbi Israel Kaplan, he immigrated from Lithuania with his family in 1889 when he was eight years old. His father was a product of the Lithuanian *yeshiva* world of Kovno and Volozhin and was a follower of the *Musar* movement, which emphasized the cultivation of ethics, and *Mizrachi*, the Orthodox Zionist movement; his mentor, Rabbi Isaac Jacob Reines, was distinctive for his advocacy of secular learning and reform in yeshiva education.

Mordecai Kaplan was an early graduate of the Jewish Theological Seminary in 1902 (where he served on the faculty for fifty-four years, 1909–1963) who also received Orthodox *semikhah* (rabbinic ordination) in Lithuania from Reines (1908). He studied at City College in New York and did his graduate work in the Columbia University Department of Philosophy. His intellectual influences included William James, the Biblical scholar Arnold B. Ehrlich, the sociologist Franklin Giddings, the philosopher Henry Sidgwick, Matthew Arnold, and the Zionist thinker Ahad Ha-am. While serving in New York at Kehilath Jeshurun and as the founding rabbi of the Jewish Center, both Orthodox congregations, Kaplan was often attacked in the Orthodox world for his controversial sermons and articles: he spoke in English from the pulpit, he condemned economic injustice, and he demanded that Orthodoxy liberalize its inter-

Mordecai Kaplan, founder of Reconstructionist Judaism. (American Jewish Archives)

pretation of ritual and theology. His experience in those pulpits put him at odds with traditionalists as he sought to formulate ways of addressing second-generation American Jews of Eastern European descent. In 1922 he finally left the Jewish Center and founded the SAJ with a group of his followers that included half of the Jewish Center's members.

The SAJ became a laboratory for his efforts to reconstruct the institutions, beliefs, and practices of the Jewish community in order to address the unprecedented social and political circumstances facing American Jewry. The congregation experimented with revisions of the traditional liturgy, with "revaluation" of ritual, with the inclusion of women—including the introduction of the first *bat mitzvah* ceremony in Jewish history in 1922—and with the application of Jewish values to current social and political issues in the greater society, including support of Palestine (which at the time was not the majority position in the Jewish community) and sensitivity to Arab-Jewish relations there; creation of a "seven-day synagogue" that would be the center of members' social lives; support of labor unions, the five-day workweek, and socialism; integration of the arts into Jewish life; exhortation of members to study and practice Jewish ethics; and the establishment of a Board of Arbitrators that mediated disputes between members. Kaplan began to publish his emerging program for the reconstruction of Jewish life in the *Menorah Journal* and the *SAJ Review* (1922–1929), thereby reaching a wider group of Jewish intellectuals.

In 1934, Kaplan published his first book, *Judaism as a Civilization*, a critical analysis of the challenges posed by modernity to the Jewish community and a fully developed proposal for the reconstruction of Jewish life based on current social scientific theory. Understanding religion as an outgrowth of the life of an organic community, Kaplan traced the crisis of Jewish life to the breakdown of autonomous, self-governing Jewish communities as the result of political emancipation, which granted Jews individual citizenship and eliminated their need for the Jewish community. He criticized Reform and Orthodox definitions of Judaism as a religion, maintaining that religious belief and practice could not survive without organic communities that nurtured them. His proposed reconstruction of Jewish life consisted of renewed emphasis on Judaism as a civilization that encompassed all aspects of a Jew's life and on proposals to create organic communities that would function effectively in the new political environment of Western democracy.

The book was unique in its application of the viewpoint of the university to an analysis of Jewish life and its bold criticism of supernaturalistic theology and *halakhic* (Jewish legal) authority. In addition, several of Kaplan's ideas—including his definition of Judaism as a civilization and his recognition that religion is only one aspect of Jewish peoplehood, his demand that Jewish leaders adapt to unprecedented circumstances, and his assertion of the importance of such values as democracy, citizenship, and equality for women—exerted a powerful impact on the American Jewish world, influencing several generations of leaders in the Conservative and Reform movements. Kaplan's book remains a classic of modern Jewish thought.

Building on that impact, he began publishing the *Reconstructionist* magazine in 1935 to promote his approach. Edited first by Kaplan and then by Rabbi Ira Eisenstein, the *Reconstructionist* served as a forum for progressive ideas across denominations in the Jewish community and significantly influenced its development.

In 1940, Kaplan and Eisenstein founded the Jewish Reconstructionist Foundation and began to publish a series of prayer books, including *The New Haggadah* (1941) and *The Sabbath Prayer Book* (1945), in which contemporary readings were added and the traditional Hebrew text was altered—most controversially, eliminating references to the chosenness of Israel and to the resurrection of the dead. In 1945 several members of the Union of Orthodox Rabbis burned *The Sabbath Prayer Book* in a public ceremony of *herem* (excommunication), providing publicity that led to the growth of the SAJ.

Kaplan had not been interested in establishing a fourth denomination, but beginning in the 1950s, Eisenstein and others gave up on Kaplan's hope to remain a school of thought that influenced the entire Jewish community. In 1955, four congregations joined to form the Federation of Reconstructionist Congregations, now called the Jewish Reconstructionist Federation (JRF). The Reconstructionist Rabbinical College (RRC) opened in Philadelphia in 1968, and the Reconstructionist Rabbinical Association (RRA) was founded in 1974. All three bodies developed into established institutions that are recognized participants in the larger Jewish world. They are represented on such organizations as the Conference of Presidents of Major Jewish Organizations, United Jewish Communities, the National Council of Synagogues, the World Union for Progressive Judaism, and the Religious Coalition for Reproductive Choice and have led in the formation of others, such as the Academic Coalition for Jewish Bioethics. The movement cooperates with the Reform and Conservative movements in such areas as rabbinic placement and social action and with all other denominations in the Conference on Rabbinic Education.

Although originally based in the New York area, the movement has spread across North America, with additional concentrations in Philadelphia, Washington, D.C., Chicago, and Southern California. It also has affiliates outside the United States in Canada, Curaçao, and Prague. Its members tend to be well-educated professionals and academics attracted by its emphases on participatory decision making for laypeople, intellectual inquiry, social justice, creative liturgy and ritual, and spirituality.

Major Beliefs

Reconstructionists define Judaism as the evolving religious *civilization* of the Jewish people. The focus on Judaism as a civilization pointedly resists the American

Students davvening during Sukkot at Reconstructionist Rabbinical College. (Reconstructionist Rabbinical College)

impulse to understand Judaism as fitting neatly into a Protestant-influenced paradigm that assumes a dichotomy between sacred and secular, church and state. Until the modern era, Jews lived in self-governing communities in which Jewish law was the law and in which the culture, social services, languages, and so forth, were Jewish. When political emancipation granted Jews individual (rather than corporate) citizenship in the greater society, the Jewish community was ruptured beyond recognition. Reconstructionists believe that long-term Jewish survival depends on a reconstruction of Jewish communities that are essential to all aspects of their members' lives. They maintain that it is futile to identify Judaism with a particular set of religious beliefs, both because Jewish beliefs have always been diverse and because beliefs always develop within the context of the specific community in which individuals are raised. Thus, Reconstructionists have included study, language, literature, music, customs, and community services as primary components of Judaism alongside belief and ritual practice.

Evolution

Seen through the Reconstructionist lens, Jewish civilization has *evolved* perpetually through the centuries in response to ever-changing historical circumstances. Rabbis-in-training at the RRC study the changes in Jewish practice, belief, and institutional structure in successive eras of Jewish history so that, when they are rabbis, they will be able to continue the reconstruction in response to changing circumstances in the future.

The Reconstructionist Hermeneutic

The focus on change as one of the constants in Jewish history leads to a distinctive Reconstructionist hermeneutic. In contrast both to traditionalists, who assume that the Torah is divinely revealed and the interpretations of halakhic (legal) authorities divinely authorized, and to other liberals, who argue that their innovations are authentic elaborations of essential Jewish values, Reconstructionists do not begin with the assumption that there has ever been an unchanging corpus of teachings, practices, or values. Based on the evolutionary perspective, Reconstructionists view innovation itself as a traditional Jewish approach. Tradition is given a vote but not a veto.

Reconstructionists value and study seriously the wisdom embedded in the teachings and practices of the Jewish heritage, but there is no assumption that the values of preceding generations should command allegiance when they conflict with contemporary values. To the contrary, it is a Reconstructionist principle that every generation has the *obligation* to continue to reconstruct in order to adapt to ever-emerging new circumstances. For example, the assumption of early generations of Reconstructionists that religious naturalism led to rationalism and trust in science has been replaced in recent decades by an embrace of the spiritual practices of more mystical strains in the tradition and by an appreciation of the mythic, poetic power of prayer to express mystery and nonrational truth. Similarly, the early inclusion of women has been expanded to pioneer outreach to interfaith couples and to the inclusion of gay and lesbian Jews. In all such cases, innovations are grounded in the Reconstructionist "tradition" of ongoing evolution in response to an ever-changing world.

Peoplehood, Community, and Israel

Reconstructionists view the Jewish people as the unchanging constant through a history in which beliefs, practices, and institutions have continuously evolved. Jewish civilization has developed in the context of Jewish communities, so that belonging is prior to behavior and belief, both of which emerge as community members learn its language, symbols, customs, and values. Identification with the Jewish people in general and with a particular Jewish community is thus the common denominator of Reconstructionists; therefore, Reconstructionist communities embrace a wide diversity of belief and practice among their members. Members are expected—sometimes formally through congregational bylaws—to be active participants in communal life: on committees that study traditional sources together to formulate communal policies; as teachers and service leaders; in synagogue support networks in which members' talent, time, energy, and expertise are shared with others; and in a host of other areas of communal life.

In this way, members of Reconstructionist communities, many of whom are highly educated and qualified in

their fields of expertise, are encouraged to continue their Jewish study and increase their Jewish knowledge and practice by way of contributing to their communities—thereby subjecting their own personal decision making to the influence of their fellow members. This communitarian approach neither requires nor desires conformity of belief, values, or practice; it seeks to construct the opportunity for members to see the world through "Jewish-colored lenses." New members often describe the attractiveness of Reconstructionist congregations as the *heimish* (homelike) atmosphere created by those who are invested in creating communities that embody Jewish values.

Kaplan was among the early fervent advocates of the Zionist movement. He viewed the *yishuv* (Jewish settlement) in Palestine as an extraordinary opportunity to reconstruct Jewish civilization as a "religion of ethical nationhood" and counted himself among the cultural Zionists led by Ahad Ha'am. The logo of *The Reconstructionist* became a wheel with Zion at its center and with spokes radiating outward to diaspora communities that would derive their spiritual sustenance from the society in which Jewish civilization was primary and being rejuvenated on Jewish soil. After the establishment of the State of Israel in 1948, Kaplan and *The Reconstructionist* sought to hold Israel up to the measure of ethical Jewish values, urging the state to embody a "religion of ethical nationhood." Reconstructionists today remain fervently committed to the Zionist enterprise but tend to identify and ally with the Israeli peace movement, a position that follows directly from the notion of "ethical nationhood" and from the movement's earlier identification with the Israeli Labor Party.

Living in Two Civilizations and Democratic Values

The development of vital, participatory communities seeks to address the chief challenge posed by the modern political emancipation of the Jews—the fact that Western Jews live primarily in the secular and not the Jewish civilization. Reconstructionists thus speak about "living in two civilizations." This is not a circumstance to be deplored but rather an opportunity for Jews to contribute to the larger culture and to enrich Jewish civilization by incorporating the noblest and most elevated values of Western culture. Kaplan was unambivalent in his enthusiastic embrace of American democracy as a value system that built upon Judaism's prophetic strand and that Jews ought to incorporate into their communal life. Freedom, equality, inclusion of those who have previously been excluded, social justice, and the participation of *all* members with rabbis in communal policymaking—these are among the values that Reconstructionists celebrate as they continue the ongoing evolution of Jewish civilization.

Those who have joined the Reconstructionist movement since the 1970s often cite its commitment to "American" values as one of its attractions. Prominent among those values is a commitment to interreligious understanding and social justice. Many Reconstructionist synagogues are known in their communities for their members' commitment—following from living in two civilizations—to reaching out as Jews to address racism, sexism, poverty, and injustice. Among the many Reconstructionists who lead in this area are Rabbi Sid Schwarz (founder and president, Panim: Institute for Jewish Leadership and Values), Rabbi Steve Gutow (executive director, Jewish Council for Public Affairs), Rabbi Rebecca Alpert (board member of Faith and Public Life, The Family Planning Council, and the Women's Law Project), Rabbi Joy Levitt (board member, Americans for Peace Now), Rabbi Brian Walt (executive director, Rabbis for Human Rights North America), Ruth Messinger (president, American Jewish World Service), Jeffrey Dekro (president, Shefa Fund), Rabbi Fred Dobb (leader at Coalition on the Environment and Jewish Life), and Rabbi Arnold Rachlis (board member, Mazon).

Theology

Kaplan sought to address the disparity between traditional, supernatural Jewish beliefs about God and contemporary scientific and social scientific understandings of the world. He understood this as a major cause of Jews' alienation from their heritage. In the first half of the twentieth century, many Jews regarded the miraculous stories in the Torah and the images of God in the prayer book as antiquated and irrelevant.

Given his view that beliefs about the nature of God had varied widely throughout the evolution of Jewish civilization, Kaplan saw no problem with the construction of new descriptions of God. He offered his theology as one option. He neither wanted nor expected all Reconstructionists to share it. For him, it was essential for Jews to be-

lieve in God but not to believe in any particular conception, as long as their beliefs were grounded in Jewish tradition and study.

Kaplan spoke about God as the Power That Makes for Salvation, in general, and for Freedom, for Truth, for Altruism, for Love, and so forth, in particular. He was influenced by Process Philosophy and by Pragmatism. He saw God as the name we give to those forces in the universe that make for human virtue and that call to us to transcend self-interest and to work for the greater good. God, for him, was not a person and did not intervene supernaturally to effect the divine will in human affairs. Ever the pragmatist, he measured the "quality" of a particular belief in God by the way the believer behaves in the world. Rabbi Harold Schulweis built on Kaplan's theology in the 1970s in developing Predicate Theology. According to Schulweis, we cannot know what God is as a subject; we can only know when God is manifest in our experience. Thus, we cannot know that God is just, for example, but we can know that justice is godly.

The movement published a series of new prayer books called *Kol Haneshamah (The Whole Soul)* beginning in 1989. The series embodies Reconstructionist principles in a number of noteworthy ways: all passages to be recited or sung communally are accompanied by English transliteration on the same page so that those who are not yet skilled in reading Hebrew can participate. English translations, by renowned poet Joel Rosenberg, are placed on the left, aligned with the original Hebrew, to facilitate comprehension of the Hebrew for those in the process of learning it. English translations are gender neutral. Alternative gender-neutral and nonhierarchical Hebrew blessing forms are offered. There are explanatory and contemplative commentaries on each page from a variety of perspectives, so that worshippers can enrich their prayer experience. The *Kol Haneshamah* series has sold widely beyond affiliated congregations and has come to represent the movement's commitment to inclusiveness and feminism.

Reconstructionists have been accused of being atheists because of their rejection of a personal God who hears and responds to prayer. Kaplan, however, was an excellent model of an intensely religious man of faith with a life of serious prayer and ritual observance. Once the RRC began training rabbis in 1968, it attracted students who were enthusiastic about *davvening* (traditional Jewish praying) and eager to adapt the traditional prayer and ritual forms to express contemporary values, most notably feminist values. This trend has continued as the RRC and the Reconstructionist movement have led in the recent return of liberal Jews to spirituality—leading in the 1980s and 1990s in the development of Jewish meditation and chanting, and founding in 1998 the first program in Jewish Spiritual Direction that emphasizes cultivating an awareness of God at every moment.

Although the movement has a reputation for rationalism among its detractors, it is not surprising that it developed a spiritual emphasis. Beginning with Kaplan, Reconstructionists' discomfort with inherited theologies has derived less from secular skepticism than from a yearning for a spiritual practice that they can embrace fully. Reconstructionists believe, for example, that the Torah is a record of the Israelites' experience of their encounters with God but that the record reveals more about the values and cultural conditioning of the fallible human beings who encountered God than it does about a literal transcript of what God said. This is hardly a denial of those encounters. Rather, it is an assertion that all human reports of divine revelation are necessarily filtered through the imperfect vessel of the human reporters, who are inevitably shaped by their historical context.

Ritual Practice

The definition of Judaism as a civilization has also led Reconstructionists to emphasize the centrality of ritual observance. They seek to live in Jewish time and Jewish space, and they believe that ritual forms are vehicles for moving us toward a Jewish way of seeing the world, understanding reality, and living a sanctified Jewish life. Belonging to the community comes first; behaving in ways that constantly reinforce the community's beliefs and values follows directly. Reconstructionist liturgy is largely in Hebrew. Heads are covered, and *tallitot* (prayer shawls) are worn—by both men and women—at services. Traditional *nusakh* (liturgical chant) is followed. Communal kitchens are kosher. And a 1996 study of Reconstructionists found that Reconstructionists with a wide range of backgrounds maintain a significantly higher level of ritual observance than their parents (Rappeport 1996). Jews join Reconstructionist communities when they are interested in increasing the traditional component of their lives.

The guiding principle of ritual observance is that traditional practice is maintained and revalued. That is, the underlying values expressed in the ritual are determined, and the ritual then becomes the form through which those values are expressed or reinterpreted in a contemporary idiom. Reconstructionists contrast this *conscious* "revaluation" with the *unconscious* "transvaluation" that occurred in the premodern era, when Jews, lacking a historical consciousness, reinterpreted beliefs and practices but assumed that their interpretations were the original meaning (Kaplan 1936). Thus, the form of the Passover seder, for example, is maintained while participants reflect on contemporary political and personal issues of bondage and liberation.

Revaluation is abandoned and the ritual changed only when the values expressed by the traditional practice are determined to be objectionable, and only a change of form can address the concern. The best-known such change is the elimination of all liturgical references to the Jews as the chosen people. *The Sabbath Prayer Book* (Kaplan 1945) revised the traditional wording of the Torah blessing from "Who has chosen us from among all the nations" to "Who has brought us near to God's service." It also deleted the phrase "Who has not made us like the nations of the Earth" from the concluding *Alenu* prayer. Kaplan and the other prayer book editors believed that there had been nothing objectionable about these words when they were recited by Jews who believed literally in the divinely revealed nature of the Torah and the *mitzvot* (the 613 commandments of Jewish law). In that context, the Jews are chosen to observe the Torah. When recited by Jews who do not believe literally that the Torah is God's word and that the commandments are binding, however, the words become an assertion of the supremacy of the Jewish people rather than of the Torah and are thus ethically objectionable and dangerous, insofar as they cultivate a chauvinistic sense of privilege and superiority.

Although not all Reconstructionists recite the revised words, the bold revision of the liturgy precisely at the moment when a person ascends to the *bimah* (the raised platform at the front of the synagogue from which worship is conducted), in a reenactment of the Sinaitic revelation, to recite the blessing over the reading from the Torah scroll, signals the basic Reconstructionist principle: that Judaism is not superior to other religions. Each people and culture has its own path to God, and all paths, like Judaism, are in a state of ongoing evolution, so that each group has the responsibility to reconstruct its practices and values into ever more divine forms. Jews are Jewish not because Judaism is superior but rather because it is our path and contains the sum total of the wisdom inherited from the quests of preceding generations.

Feminism and the Creation of an Inclusive Community

Reconstructionist Judaism has led the Jewish community with regard to the principle of gender equality since the SAJ instituted the first bat mitzvah ceremony in the first year (1922) of the congregation's existence. The principle has been straightforward: given the change in the social, political, educational, and economic status of women in the modern era, the reconstruction of gender differentiation in ritual and leadership follows directly. The SAJ began counting women in the *minyan* (prayer quorum) in 1950, the community voting to do so after a long, extended series of discussions. The RRC admitted women to study for the rabbinate from the moment of its founding in 1968. The RRA developed an egalitarian *get* (divorce document) in 1983. Movement milestones include the first woman president of a synagogue movement (1984), the first woman president of a rabbinical association (1987), and the first woman to serve as academic dean of a rabbinical seminary (2004).

Beyond gender equality, however, Reconstructionists have pioneered in the feminist transformation of Jewish culture—introducing gender-neutral language about God, including women's voices in the liturgy, developing rituals to mark previously ignored stages in women's lives. Kolot, RRC's Center for Jewish Women's and Gender Studies, continues to do groundbreaking work in rereading texts and traditions to bring issues to the surface and address them.

In line with its historic inclusion of women, the movement has sought to welcome other groups who had been excluded by the Jewish community. In 1979 the RRA affirmed a 1968 JRF resolution on patrilineal descent, recognizing as Jews those who have a Jewish father and non-Jewish mother and have been raised as Jews. In 1982, the RRA's Guidelines on Intermarriage publicly acknowledged the soaring rate of intermarriage and welcomed intermarried couples into Reconstructionist communities,

developing strategies to increase the likelihood that their children would be raised as Jews. In 1983, the RRC faculty passed a nondiscriminatory policy for admission to the rabbinical program based on sexual orientation. This was followed in 1989 by a movement-wide commission report that encouraged all affiliates to welcome gay and lesbian Jews and advocated the development of same-sex commitment ceremonies. Since then, lesbian and gay Jews have been fully integrated into all levels of the movement's lay and rabbinic leadership.

Ethical Decision Making

The ongoing work of the RRC's Center for Jewish Ethics illustrates the Reconstructionist method of balancing traditional and contemporary values called values-based decision making. Directed by David Teutsch, former president of RRC, the Center has published materials on Jewish approaches to speech ethics, a volume on bioethics, and the first sections of a guide to Jewish practice. The method involves the study of inherited Jewish values and contemporary values and the resolution of issues in which there are conflicts between them. Its goals are to enable the voice of traditional teaching to be heard and taken seriously without being absolutely authoritative. For example, study of traditional texts has led to the conclusion that what passes through the feeding tube is medicine, not food, and so the tube can be disconnected when the patient is no longer alive, and that stem cells may be used for research as long as new embryos are not created solely for that purpose.

Jacob J. Staub

References and Further Reading

Alpert, Rebecca T., and Jacob J. Staub. 2000. *Exploring Judaism: A Reconstructionist Approach.* Elkins Park, PA: Reconstructionist Press.

Eisenstein, Ira. 1986. *Reconstructing Judaism: An Autobiography.* New York: Reconstructionist Press.

Kaplan, Mordecai M. 1934. *Judaism as a Civilization: Toward a Reconstruction of American-Jewish Life.* New York: Schocken Books.

Kaplan, Mordecai M. 1936. *The Meaning of God in Modern Jewish Religion.* New York: Reconstructionist Press.

Kaplan, Mordecai M., ed. 1945. *Sabbath Prayer Book.* New York: Reconstructionist Jewish Foundation.

Kaplan, Mordecai M., Eugene Kohn, and Ira Eisenstein. 1941. *The New Haggadah.* New York: Behrman House.

Levitt, Joy, and Michael Strassfeld. 2000. *A Night of Questions: A Passover Haggadah.* Elkins Park, PA: Reconstructionist Press.

Rappeport, Michael. 1996. *1996 Demographic Study of the Reconstructionist Movement.* Elkins Park, PA: Jewish Reconstructionist Federation.

Scult, Mel. 1993. *Judaism Faces the Twentieth Century: A Biography of Mordecai M. Kaplan.* Detroit, MI: Wayne State University Press.

Teutsch, David A., editor. 1994. *Kol Haneshamah: Shabbat Vehagim.* Wyncote, PA: Reconstructionist Press.

Teutsch, David A. 2001a. *A Guide to Jewish Practice.* Wyncote, PA: RRC Press.

Teutsch, David A. 2001b. "Values-Based Decisionmaking." *The Reconstructionist* 65,2: 22–28.

Hasidic Judaism

Hasidism is a populist, mystical, Jewish religious movement that originated in the Polish province of Podolia with the disciples of the charismatic teacher and faith-healer R. Israel ben Eliezer Baal Shem Tov of Medzibozh (ca. 1698–1760), popularly known by his acronym, Besht. The disciples of the Besht, most notably the *Magid* (preacher) Dov Ber of Mezeritch (d. 1772) and his many students, spread Hasidism's revolutionary, optimistic, mystical teachings that celebrated the immanence of God and His closeness to even the simplest, most uneducated Jews, throughout Eastern Europe during the last half of the eighteenth century. R. Dov Ber's disciples became charismatic Hasidic masters (known as *tsadikim,* or *rebbes*) who established courts throughout Eastern Europe from the Russian Pale of Settlement to Austria-Hungary.

Hasidic life centers on the joyful worship of God through ecstatic prayer, song, dance, and feasting, all performed in the ambience of the rebbe's court. Unlike conventional rabbis, who are essentially teachers and adjudicators of Jewish law, the Hasidic rebbes are personal spiritual guides to whom are attributed great, even supernatural powers to intercede with God.

The emergence of Hasidism provoked a strenuous, organized opposition from the established Jewish communities and their rabbis, who became known as the *Mitnagdim* (opponents). The Mitnagdim, whose power base was in Lithuania, believed that the Hasidim's emphasis on prayer and religious ecstasy was a threat to traditional rabbinic Judaism, which placed Torah study at the pinnacle of the hierarchy of religious values, so they excommunicated the Hasidim and banned the rebbes' courts.

Despite this opposition, Hasidism spread very rapidly, largely because of its popularization of Jewish mysticism's most optimistic and joyful doctrines and its celebratory approach to religious life. Hasidic courts, where the rebbes held forth royally, sprouted all across Eastern Europe, serving as community centers where the Hasidim gathered, especially on Sabbaths and Jewish holidays, to worship and celebrate in the presence of their revered masters.

By the end of the nineteenth century, the Hasidim accounted for a majority of Eastern Europe's fervently Orthodox Jews. Though suffering some attrition to the rapid modernization and urbanization of Jewish life in Eastern Europe since the mid-nineteenth century, dozens of Hasidic sects flourished until World War II. On the eve of the war, Hasidic life was concentrated almost exclusively in Eastern Europe, which was home to more than 90 percent of the world's Hasidic population.

The Hasidic world was devastated by the Holocaust. Although a few of the most prominent Hasidic rebbes managed to escape the Nazis, approximately 95 percent of Europe's Hasidim were murdered during the war. Because of their distinctive appearance and general ignorance of European languages and customs, hiding from the Nazis or escape from war-torn Europe, while never easy, was more difficult for the Hasidim than for more assimilated European Jews. The Holocaust decimated hundreds of Hasidic communities across Europe, not one of which remained intact.

Most Hasidic Holocaust survivors emigrated to Palestine or America, where they tried to regroup, when possible, in accordance with their prewar Hasidic court affiliation. The largest Hasidic sects to reestablish themselves after the war were Ger, Vizhnitz, and Belz in Israel, and Lubavitch, Satmar, and Bobov in the United States. Significant Hasidic communities were also established in London, Antwerp, and Montreal. The large majority of Hasidim who found refuge in the United States settled in New York City. The first major Hasidic communities there emerged in the Williamsburg and Crown Heights sections of Brooklyn.

In the 1960s, as living conditions in those neighborhoods rapidly deteriorated, many Hasidim fled to the middle-class Boro Park section of Brooklyn. Nonetheless, at the insistence of their rebbe, the Lubavitcher Hasidim remained in Crown Heights. Similarly, the Satmar rebbe

Hasidic Rebbe Menachem Mendel Schneerson. (Corbis)

and most of his Hasidim stayed in Williamsburg. In the 1970s, Boro Park had the largest Hasidic population in the country, numbering approximately 40,000 (Mayer 1979). Currently, about 12,000 Hasidim, mostly Lubavitchers, remain in Crown Heights (Fishkoff 2003), and some 50,000 Hasidim, mostly Satmar, live in Williamsburg (Rubin 1997). There are also some sizable suburban Hasidic enclaves, including Kiryas Joel, New Square, and Monsey, all about 30 miles northwest of New York City. Smaller Hasidic communities exist in Boston, Chicago, Detroit, Los Angeles, and Milwaukee.

Hasidism in America before the Holocaust

Prior to the Holocaust, there were only three bona fide rebbes with Hasidic congregations in the United States. The Boyaner Rebbe, Mordechai Shlomo Friedman (d. 1971), emigrated from Eastern Europe in 1927 and settled in Manhattan's Lower East Side. The Stoliner Rebbe, Jacob Perlow (d. 1945), arrived there in 1929, as did the Kapitshinitzer Rebbe, Abraham Joshua Heschel (d. 1967), in 1939. All three maintained only minor congregations in lower Manhattan.

The Kapitshinitzer Rebbe was succeeded by his son, Rabbi Moshe Heschel, while the Boyaner Rebbe was succeeded by his son, Rabbi Israel Friedman. Neither of these prewar American Hasidic sects has maintained a viable community. Kapitshinitzer Hasidism is today all but extinct, while the majority of Boyaner Hasidim live in Israel. A few dozen Boyaner families remain in New York, scattered in various neighborhoods from Manhattan's Upper West Side to Boro Park. While there remains a Stoliner synagogue in Boro Park, the current rebbe and most of his followers are today in Israel.

Habad-Lubavitch in America

Since its founding by R. Shneur Zalman of Lyadi (1745–1813), two characteristics have set Habad (also known as Lubavitch, after the town in Byelorussia where R. Shneur Zalman's son, R. Dov Ber, established the Habad court in 1815) apart from other Hasidic sects. The first is its unusual combination of radical mysticism with intense intellectualism. Hence the acronym for the movement—Habad—which stands for *Hokhma, Binah, Daat,* Hebrew for knowledge, understanding, and wisdom. The other distinction of Habad Hasidism is its evangelism and commitment to spreading Hasidic doctrine to Jews the world over, no matter what their Jewish education or level of religious observance.

At the beginning of the Nazi occupation of Poland, the sixth Lubavitcher Rebbe, Joseph Isaac Schneerson (1880–1950), fled the Warsaw ghetto to Riga, Latvia, from which he finally managed to escape to America in 1940 with help from the U.S. State Department. Before the war, R. Joseph Isaac had been the most prominent Orthodox leader of beleaguered Soviet Jewry. Upon arriving in America, he immediately established a synagogue at 770 Eastern Parkway in the Crown Heights section of Brooklyn, which remains the world headquarters of the Lubavitch movement today.

R. Joseph Isaac died in 1950 and was succeeded a year later by his son-in-law, R. Menachem Mendel Schneerson (1902–1994) who, after an unprecedented career of almost half a century, passed away, leaving no successor. R. Menachem Mendel raised Habad evangelism to new heights, transforming Lubavitch from a small, rather insular, Brooklyn-based sect into a powerful, well-endowed, and well-oiled international religious movement with branches in almost every city, town, and hamlet in the world in which there are Jews. It is estimated that Habad-sponsored programs currently reach more than a quarter of a million Jews worldwide (Fishkoff 2003; Feldman 2003).

Schneerson's success in expanding Habad Hasidism was largely due to his willingness to enlist modern technology and social theory in the service of a premodern mystical theology, as well as his refusal to exclude any Jews—no matter how geographically or religiously distant—from his vision. Unlike most other Hasidic leaders, who have insisted on sealing their adherents off from every aspect of American life to ensure their piety, Schneerson was never intimidated by modernity. Unique among Hasidic leaders in having received a higher secular education—in philosophy at the University of Berlin and mechanical engineering at the Université de Paris—before being appointed Rebbe, Schneerson directed his followers to establish a major presence on all the major American university campuses through the creation of Habad Houses. These campus outposts offer courses in basic Judaism and Hasidism in addition to providing college students with kosher meals and a variety of religious, social, and psychological services.

Schneerson's pragmatism and his activist approach have inspired the Lubavitchers to develop an effective network of *shluchim* (emissaries), dispatched from the sect's Brooklyn headquarters to disseminate Habad doctrine throughout America. The shluchim are today a highly visible presence in dozens of cities, spreading Hasidism from their "mitzvah-mobiles," Habad's trademark Winnebago synagogues-on-wheels, on hundreds of America's main streets.

Long before Schneerson died in 1994, the majority of his followers had become possessed by the belief that he was the Jews' long-awaited Messiah. When he passed away without having groomed an heir, and after many years of Messianic preaching followed by a four-year, stroke-induced silence, many observers predicted that the Lubavitch community would either be torn asunder between majority *Moshiakhists* (messianists) and the small number of more rational Lubavitchers who accepted the rebbe's death, or that the Moshiakhists' faith would not be able to survive the trauma of their "savior's" death.

Despite these dire predictions and a clear ideological split within the community, and despite the absence of a new Rebbe, Habad/Lubavitch has continued to flourish during the decade since Schneerson's death. More than one hundred new Habad synagogues and campus Habad Houses have been established, including multimillion-dollar facilities in Bal Harbor (Florida), Las Vegas, Pittsburgh, San Diego, Washington D.C., and Tenafly. During this same period, more modest Habad centers have been established in such far-flung Jewish communities as Anchorage, Des Moines, El Paso, and Little Rock. The Habad population continues to grow, thanks to its high birthrate and the continued attraction of *"ba'alei teshuva"* ("returnees") responding to Habad's outreach work across the land.

The spread of Habad influence is not entirely unproblematic, as it has created many religious and political challenges to the American Jewish establishment. Perhaps the most conspicuous example is the Jewish First Amendment debate triggered by the array of Hannukah *menorahs* that the Lubavitchers annually erect in prominent public places throughout America, including the White House lawn. Though these religious displays have been challenged by many established Jewish organizations, such as the American Jewish Committee and the American Jewish Congress, and by prominent Jewish communal leaders and scholars as a breach of the constitutional "wall of separation" between religion and state, this has not deterred the Lubavitchers. Additionally, Habad's support of the far right in Israel, rooted in Schneerson's long-standing opposition to ceding so much as an inch of Israel's territory to the Palestinians, has created significant tensions with the American Jewish establishment as well as successive Israeli governments.

As the menorah campaign and other Habad initiatives (such as the Lubavitchers' vocal advocacy of prayer in public schools and their opposition to the legalization of abortion in America) indicate, the Lubavitchers have no regard for secular American values, but at the same time do not shy away from using any contemporary political device at their disposal to help advance their evangelical, politically rightist agenda.

In 1986, the Lubavitchers' evangelical passion and desire to make American society more religious reached unprecedented levels, as the Rebbe initiated a campaign of religious proselytizing to the gentiles to ensure their observance of the seven Noahide laws, which are binding upon all gentiles. This new religious universalism, unheard of in traditional Judaism since biblical times, largely explains Habad's use of such non-Jewish venues as public access cable television, highway billboards, and full-page ads in the *New York Times* to promote its agenda.

Habad's apparent modernity, its high-profile evangelism, its striking messianic claims about Rabbi Schneerson, and its outspoken support of the political far right in Israel have all been the source of contempt for the group on the part of America's more conservative Hasidic communities, most notably the largest and most religiously extreme sect, Satmar.

Satmar

Unlike Habad, with its long history and distinctive mystical teachings, Satmar Hasidism—notorious for its open hostility to Zionism and the State of Israel—is a relatively new movement forged largely by one man, Rabbi Joel Moshe Teitelbaum (1888–1979). Satmar Hasidism was established only in 1928, when Teitelbaum left his native town of Sighet in Carpathian Ruthenia to become the rabbi of the small Romanian city of Satu Mare (Satmar). The rapid rise, catastrophic destruction, and spectacular postwar growth of the Satmar sect are all the result of Teitelbaum's personal charisma, political leadership, and strong survivalist instincts in the face of the most tumultuous and tragic era of Hasidism's history.

While the majority of Hungarian Hasidim were killed during the Holocaust, a larger percentage of them survived than did the Polish, Belorussian, and Galician Hasidim, for the deportations of Hungarian Jewry to the concentration camps did not begin until May 1944, almost five years after the deadly persecutions had begun against the Jews of Poland. In December 1944, while his Hasidim were being rounded up by the Nazis, mostly for deportation to Auschwitz, the Satmar Rebbe escaped from the Bergen-Belsen concentration camp to Palestine, ironically enough on the transport arranged by the Zionist leader Rudolf Kastner.

In 1947 Teitelbaum left Jerusalem, where he had become one of the leaders of the radically anti-Zionist Neturei Karta sect, and settled in the Williamsburg section of Brooklyn. There he found a tiny Hasidic community of fewer than a hundred families. Most were Hungarian and Czechoslovakian survivors from a variety of prewar sects whose rebbes had perished in the camps. Teitelbaum immediately filled the vacuum of religious leadership to become the spiritual leader of these orphaned Hasidim. He was single-minded in his determination that Hasidic life would flourish in America exactly as it had in pre-Holocaust Europe, and he quickly established a Satmar synagogue, *yeshiva, mikvah* (ritual bath), kosher slaughterhouse, and *matzah* bakery, as well as a large charitable foundation devoted to helping Jewish refugees settle in his community.

Teitelbaum's success in re-creating Satmar Hasidism in the new land exceeded all expectations. From the few hundred Hasidic families that Teitelbaum found in 1947, the Satmar community of Williamsburg today numbers almost 40,000 (Mintz 1992). In 1974 the Satmars established a satellite suburban center adjacent to the town of Monroe in Rockland County, New York, named Kiryas Joel in honor of the Rebbe. Although it began with just a few dozen families, Kiryas Joel today has a population rapidly approaching 20,000 (Mintz 1992) and is the location of Satmar's central yeshiva. There are also smaller but not insignificant Satmar communities in Boro Park, Los Angeles, Montreal, London, and Antwerp.

Beyond his energy and talent for leadership, the key to Teitelbaum's success was his zealous resistance to any innovations or changes in the traditional way of life of his Hasidim. Satmar remains the most segregationist and ultraconservative of Hasidic sects, having remained hermetically sealed from all aspects of modern society other than those necessary for financial support.

The Satmar Rebbe was most notorious for his fierce struggle against Zionism, the inheritance of pre-Holocaust Hungarian Jewish ultra-Orthodoxy. The extent of the Satmar Rebbe's impermeability to the cataclysmic events of Jewish history in recent decades was remarkable. The eradication of Hasidic life in Eastern Europe and the subsequent rise of the State of Israel had a devastating, transformative effect on many religious leaders who had previously opposed any secular political solution to the "Jewish problem," that is, Zionism. But the trauma of the Holocaust and emergence of Israel, while converting most of these prewar Orthodox opponents of Zionism, had absolutely no effect on Joel Teitelbaum. He remained steadfast in his commitment to the old passive political posture of East European Jewry. Moreover, with each of Zionism's successes, his opposition to it became fiercer. In response to Israel's dramatic victory in the June 1967 Six Day War, Teitelbaum wrote an angry polemical tract entitled *Al ha-Geulah ve-al ha-Temurah (On the Redemption and Its Displacement)*, in which he argued that the Israeli military victory was a cosmic catastrophe engineered by Satan himself. The Satmar Rebbe's insistence on maintaining the prewar strategy of isolation from the outside world and his demonization of Zionism have not, however, hampered the growth of Satmar Hasidism, which today has far more adherents than before the Holocaust.

Thanks to the prominent role of charitable giving in the Satmar community, it is exceptionally well organized, boasting myriad institutions that see to the welfare of each and every member. These include a very effective refugee assistance board, a fund for those in need of food for the Sabbath, a highly subsidized kosher meat market, and a medical fund providing full health coverage for the needy.

The United Jewish Organizations (UJO) of Williamsburg, established as an intercommunal institution in 1966 by the Satmar Rebbe's right-hand man, Rabbi Lipa Friedman, today assists many other Hasidic sects while remaining firmly under Satmar control. The UJO is concerned with the community's economic and social well-being and has succeeded in attracting federal funding for increased housing subsidies for the Hasidic community. It negotiates the very tense relations with Williamsburg's majority Latino community, with whom the Hasidim are in fierce competition for the neighborhood's scarce housing and social services.

The Satmar community is also remarkable in the way it safeguards the physical needs of its members. The *Hatzoloh* ambulance network, while today serving Jews and gentiles in all five boroughs of New York City, was originally established by Satmar in Williamsburg to serve the needs of ultra-Orthodox who spoke little English. The *Shomrim* is an all-Hasidic security patrol that has developed a reputation for swift and tough justice.

Despite its deep isolationism, the one realm in which Satmar has maintained a high and aggressive public profile is its opposition to Zionism and the State of Israel. To the dismay of most American Jews, the Satmar Hasidim regularly engage in public protests against Israel, issue press releases, and take out prominent advertisements denouncing Zionism. The Satmar Hasidim also frequently battle the other major Hasidic sects, most notably Lubavitch and Belz, both of whom R. Joel Teitelbaum accused of modernist tendencies and Zionist sympathies.

The Satmar Rebbe died in August 1979 and was succeeded by his nephew, Rabbi Moshe Teitelbaum (b. 1915), who had previously served as the Sigheter Rebbe in Boro Park. He possessed neither the scholarship nor the personal charisma of his uncle, and the Satmar community began to experience numerous dissensions, which would have been unimaginable during the iron-fisted reign of R. Joel. A number of Satmar Hasidim refused to accept the new rebbe and pledged their allegiance instead to the late rebbe's widow, Feiga Shapiro, who resides in Kiryas Joel. Due to R. Moshe Teitelbaum's recent failing health, the Satmar community has become bitterly divided between the followers of his two sons, R. Aharon of Kiryas Joel and his younger brother, R. Zalman Leib of Williamsburg. Over the past decade, there have been numerous theological and civic disputes between the two brothers' followers, occasionally resulting in violence. There are even two competing Satmar Yiddish weekly newspapers, both published in Brooklyn: *Der Yid,* which supports R. Zalman Leib, and *Der Blatt,* which endorses R. Aharon's leadership. Despite these divisions, the Satmar community continues to thrive in apparently blissful isolation from the rest of American Jewry.

Boro Park and the Bobover Hasidim

The third-largest American Hasidic sect after Satmar and Lubavitch is Bobov, based in Boro Park, Brooklyn. As with Satmar, the Bobover sect is considerably larger today than it was before the Holocaust. Bobover Hasidism was founded by R. Shlomo (b. Meir Nathan) Halberstam (1847–1905), who established a major Hasidic Court and Yeshiva in the Galician town of Bobowa. His son, R. Bentzion Halberstam (1874–1944), was a popular Hasidic leader who continued to oversee the growth of Bobover Hasidism in Galicia until he and almost all his followers perished in the Holocaust. R. Bentzion's son, R. Shlomo Halberstam (1908–2000), was the sole survivor of the family and was appointed Rebbe after the war. In the early 1950s, together with the very few other survivors of prewar Bobov, he took on the daunting task of establishing the first sect of Polish Hasidim in America. The Bobovers were initially based in Crown Heights, but in 1966, responding to deteriorating urban conditions, the Bobover community relocated to Boro Park. R. Shlomo Halberstam was succeeded by his son, R. Naftali Halberstam, who passed away in 2005. His succession is being contested by his son R. Benzion Halberstam and his two nephews, R. Mordechai Unger and R. Yehoshua Rubin.

From fewer than 100 families in the early 1950s, the sect has grown to include some 10,000 adherents (Mintz 1992). Hundreds of Jews continue to gravitate to Bobov each year. Two key factors explain the rapid growth of Bobover Hasidism: the charismatic personality of the late Rebbe, R. Shlomo, and the impressive Bobover educational system he created. In rather sharp contrast to the Satmar Rebbe, whose religious extremism and isolationist vigilance kept his community intact, the source of Rabbi Shlomo Halberstam's wide appeal was his friendly, open, and relaxed demeanor, as well as his religious moderation and studious avoidance of partisan religious politics. The

Bobover attitude to Zionism and the State of Israel is a case in point. Although he was no Zionist, the Bobover Rebbe was careful never to attack Israel publicly. He was equally cautious in his attitude toward other Hasidic sects. For example, while the Bobover Rebbe disapproved of the Lubavitchers' crowning of Rabbi Menachem Schneerson as the Messiah, he refused to comment publicly on the subject, again in contrast to the open Satmar hostility to Lubavitch messianism. For many ultra-Orthodox Jews, tired of the intrigues and dissension that have plagued Hasidic life in America, the temperate Rabbi Halberstam proved to be a highly attractive leader. They therefore chose to affiliate with his court and send their children to Bobover educational institutions.

The Bobover educational network is another major factor in the growth of Bobov. The network Yeshivas and girls' schools operated by the sect quickly earned a reputation for high educational standards, leading hundreds of Hasidim from other sects, as well as many non-Hasidic Jews, to enroll their children. Very often, the children's educational experiences forged a family connection to the school's sponsoring institution and ultimately to the Bobover Rebbe himself. A major attraction of the Bobover educational philosophy to non-Hasidic parents is that, unlike other Hasidic sects, which categorically prohibit college education for their yeshiva graduates, the Bobover Rebbe tended to allow his followers to attend university in pursuit of practical disciplines that would enhance their financial security. Far from leading to assimilation and attrition as many stricter Hasidic leaders feared, this openness has actually strengthened and enriched the Bobover community. For, unlike more obscurantist Hasidic sects, the Bobovers today have their own homegrown lawyers, doctors, dentists, and architects who contribute significantly to raising the community's economic standards.

In addition to Bobov, there are about thirty smaller Hasidic groups active in Boro Park, most with their own Rebbes, synagogues, and Yeshivot. They include Amshinover, Belzer, Bostoner, Boyaner, Bialer, Gerer, Klauzenberger, Munkatcher, Rizhiner, Sigheter, Spinker, Stoliner-Karliner, and Vishnitzer Hasidim. The Council of Jewish Organizations of Boro Park (COJO), founded in 1972, represents almost two hundred religious, educational, and social institutions—the majority of which are under Hasidic auspices.

The Skverer Hasidim and Squaretown

One of the important disciples of the Magid of Mezeritch was R. Nahum Twersky of Tchernobil (1730–1798). His paternal descendants all became Hasidic Rebbes in a number of Ukrainian towns, the two most important being Talne and Skvira. The Talner and Skverer Hasidic sects were almost completely wiped out by the Nazis. But the Talner Rebbe, Meshulam Zushe Twersky (d. 1972), left Europe before the rise of Nazism and settled in the Boston neighborhood of Roxbury, where he established a small *shtiebel* (private prayer-house). After his death, his son, Professor Isadore Twersky (1930–1997) of Harvard University's Jewish Studies Program, officiated at the Talner shtiebel, which had been relocated to the suburb of Brookline. Isadore Twersky's son, R. Meir, currently serves as the Talner Rebbe of Boston. But the members of Boston's small "Talner shtiebel" are more likely to be Modern Orthodox philosophers and mathematicians than Hasidim.

One of Meshulam Zushe Twersky's cousins, Rabbi Yaakov Yosef Twersky, the Skverer Rebbe, came to New York after the war along with a handful of Hasidic survivors. The Skverer Rebbe was disheartened by the urban profanities and material temptations of New York City and yearned to re-create in America a rural, *shtetl*-like setting reminiscent of Skvira and more conducive to a life of piety. His Hasidim purchased several acres of farmland near Ramapo, New York, in 1954. The first sixty Hasidic families moved to the new settlement in 1958, and three years later—after numerous feuds over zoning and school board regulations with both the Jewish and gentile residents of neighboring Ramapo—the state Supreme Court ruled in favor of the Hasidim's request to incorporate the Hasidic village of New Square.

Despite its deep poverty (since the late 1960s, New Square has consistently had the lowest per capita income of any township in New York State), zoning conflicts that have hindered its development, and the death of the charismatic Skverer Rebbe in 1968, the community has grown impressively under the leadership of R. Yaakov Yosef's son, R. Dovid Twersky. It has a large yeshiva and girls' school, and an impressive Kolel (advanced yeshiva for married students). Today there are close to 600 families, with an average of eight children per family: in other words, a community of almost 6,000 (www.city-data.com/city/New-Square-New-York.html). New Square, New York, today has more Skverer Hasidim than ever lived in Skvira, Ukraine.

What is truly unique about New Square is the remarkable extent to which the dream of the old Skverer Rebbe has been realized: namely, to re-create the ambience of the prewar European Hasidic shtetl (Jewish village) in America. Unlike Satmar, the Hasidim of New Square are not politicized and do not publish in (or, for the most part, even read) the press. Radios, televisions, video recorders, and the Internet are absolutely banned from the town. A visit to New Square is the closest one can come to fathoming the vanished world of prewar European Hasidic life.

Hasidic Congregations outside New York City

Although New York was and remains the center of Hasidism in the United States, several Hasidic rabbis are functioning in other American cities. Though some are rabbis of sizable congregations, none of them has a genuinely Hasidic following of any significance. Moreover, over the past fifty years many small Hasidic synagogues around the country—in such cities as Detroit, Philadelphia, and Pittsburgh—have closed, and the few followers of these Rebbes have tended to assimilate into the local non-Hasidic community or have gravitated to New York's Hasidic centers. The main reason for the decline of Hasidism outside New York has been the inability of these small enclaves to maintain Hasidic schools and other essential religious institutions.

Despite the disappearance of most of these smaller Hasidic communities, there remain several interesting congregations led by American Hasidic rabbis. Unlike the highly autonomous New York Hasidic world, the rabbis of these smaller congregations are, as a rule, far more integrated into the local mainstream Jewish community and tend to participate more actively in public Jewish affairs. They have little choice, since, possessing little more than a modest synagogue, they depend on the broader Jewish community for almost all of their religious and social services.

The Bostoner Rebbe

The oldest and most significant of these Hasidic congregations outside New York, both numerically and in terms of its impact on the broader Jewish community, is Congregation Beth Pinchas in Brookline, Massachusetts. The congregation, which is also known as the New England

Hasidic Center, was originally founded in 1916 in Boston's West End (today, Government Center) by Rabbi Pinchas Horowitz, who immigrated to Boston from Palestine in 1914 and soon became known as the Bostoner Rebbe. Pinchas Horowitz was the first Hasidic Rebbe whose jurisdiction began in and was named after an American city. While in the West End, it was always a very modest congregation, with no more than fifty members. As the prospects for maintaining Hasidic life in Boston's inner city continued to diminish, Rabbi Horowitz left for New York in 1940 with his family and followers, where he died two years later. Although his elder son, Rabbi Moshe Horowitz, assumed the role of Bostoner Rebbe in Brooklyn, the few remaining, elderly Hasidim in Boston appointed his younger brother, Levi Yitzchok, to be their spiritual leader.

Rabbi Levi Yitzchok Horowitz returned to Boston in 1945 and pioneered a rejuvenation of Hasidic life there. In 1961, he moved his congregation from the declining neighborhood of Dorchester to larger quarters in the heavily Jewish suburb of Brookline and began to attract more members. The Boston-born Levi Yitzchok quickly earned a very positive reputation as a charming, genuinely spiritual, and deeply caring rabbi, and the majority of his Brookline congregation soon consisted of *ba'alei teshuva* (returnees) to Hasidism from the non-Orthodox and modern Orthodox communities.

The Bostoner Rebbe has made good spiritual use of Boston's two greatest human resources: students and doctors. Throughout the 1960s and 1970s, the Bostoner Rebbe attracted hundreds of students from the Boston area's many colleges and universities. Special weekend *shabbaton* programs were aimed specifically at the city's unusually large Jewish student population. One of the most important communal services of the New England Hasidic Center is a medical referral and assistance agency known as ROFEH (Hebrew for "doctor"; English acronym for "Reaching Out Furnishing Emergency Healthcare"). Through this agency, the Bostoner Rebbe helps needy Jews who require specialized medical attention at one of Boston's famous hospitals, with referrals, hospitality, kosher meals, and financial assistance.

Despite the Bostoner Rebbe's impressive achievements as a religious and communal leader, his core community remains quite small. There are fewer than one hundred families in the Beth Pinchas congregation. Moreover, despite its official Hasidic affiliation, the majority of these members are not true Hasidim but mainstream Orthodox Jews who identify to varying degrees with the Hasidic warmth of the Bostoner Rebbe's congregation.

The Hornosteipler Rebbes of Milwaukee and Denver

The Orthodox Jewish community of Milwaukee was for many years led by the Hornosteipler Rebbe, Yaakov Israel Twerski, a cousin of the Skverer Rebbe. With his death in 1973, his son, Rabbi Michel Twerski, inherited the Hornosteipler community's leadership and has overseen its gradual growth. R. Michel Twerski's educational background and personal style have enabled him to retain the allegiance of the entire Orthodox Jewish community of Milwaukee, which consists mostly of non-Hasidim. From 1956 to 1961, he studied at the famous *mitnagdic* Yeshiva, Beth Midrash Gevohah, in Lakewood, New Jersey, where he was ordained by R. Aaron Kotler. In his own style of religious leadership and in fashioning Milwaukee's Orthodox community, he has retained elements of both the Hasidic and mitnagdic worlds.

Twerski is one of the founders of the city's most important educational institutions: the Yeshiva Elementary School, the Mesivta Yeshiva Gedolah of Milwaukee (a high school), and the Milwaukee Kolel (for advanced Talmudic studies). His own congregation, Beth Jehudah, also known as the Hornosteipler Shul, has about two hundred members. As is the case with the Bostoner Rebbe, very few of his congregants lead fully Hasidic lives. Another, slightly smaller Hornostiepler Hasidic community in Denver, Colorado, is led by his cousin, Rabbi Mordechai Twerski, another "modern Hasidic" rebbe who is deeply involved in general Jewish community affairs. As in Milwaukee, the vast majority of Hornosteipler Hasidim in Denver do not lead fully Hasidic lives. The nature of the Hasidic communities of these two cities serves as a reminder of the extent to which authentic Hasidic life in America today is almost entirely restricted to New York.

Women in Hasidic Communities

The role of women in Hasidic communities is almost entirely limited to their domestic duties as wives, mothers, and homemakers. Given the Hasidim's unusually high fertility rate and their ultraconservatism regarding the Jewish laws of sexual modesty that require the strict public separation of men and women, this could hardly be otherwise. The most important public rituals of Hasidic religious life all take place in the rebbe's court, where only males congregate during the Sabbath and holiday prayers and communal meals. In fact, according to the eminent Jewish social historian Jacob Katz in his classic work *Tradition and Crisis,* the emergence of Hasidism in the mid-eighteenth century originally had a seriously disruptive effect on traditional Jewish family life in Eastern Europe, as thousands of Hasidic men, along with their mature (post–bar mitzvah age) sons, began to journey what were often great distances to spend the Sabbath and Jewish holidays with their rebbes, leaving the women and girls at home.

The only time Hasidic women have any direct contact with the rebbe is during specially arranged, individual meetings, which are typically scheduled for Saturday night after the end of the Jewish Sabbath. A notable exception to this pattern was the innovative practice of the previous Lubavitcher Rebbe, Menachem Mendel Schneerson, of meeting periodically in the central Habad synagogue in Brooklyn with hundreds of members of the women's organization N'shai U-Neshot Habad (the Wives and Women of Habad) during its quarterly conferences. The Lubavitcher Rebbe also approved of greater Torah study for women, for which he was roundly criticized by the late Satmar Rebbe, Joel Teitelbaum, and the Belzer Rebbe, Yissachar Dov Rokeach.

Education

Today, the curriculum at most Hasidic Yeshivot is largely indistinguishable from that of traditional non-Hasidic Orthodox, or mitnagdic, Yeshivot, where the focus is almost exclusively on Torah (with the classical rabbinic commentaries), Mishnah, and Talmud. There is very little formal instruction in the classical, esoteric Hasidic mystical texts, which are mainly studied by adults or by yeshiva students under careful adult supervision, during the Sabbath and holiday afternoons. Hasidic girls' schools offer a more limited curriculum of religious studies in which only those aspects of Jewish law (*halakha*) relevant to women (e.g., the laws of *kashrut,* child-rearing, and ritual purity) are taught. A notable exception is the curriculum in the Habad network of Yeshivot, known as Tomchei Temimim (Supporters of the Pure), where there is a strong emphasis on the study of *Likkutei Amarim: Tanya,* the work of Hasidism by the Habad founder, R. Shneur Zalman of Lyadi, and where girls are taught classical Jewish texts such as Torah and Mishnah. For the purposes of governmental accreditation by the states' departments of education, the minimally mandated curriculum of general studies is offered at all Hasidic schools but is usually treated perfunctorily.

Occupations

Because university education is generally proscribed in Hasidic society, very few Hasidim work in the legal, medical, or scientific professions. A notable exception is to be found among adult *ba'alei teshuva* (returnees) to Hasidism, many of whom are professionals and academics. Also, there are a significant number of university-trained members of the Bobover Hasidic community due to the Bobover Rebbe's more lenient attitude toward university education. Most Hasidic men work in a variety of retail businesses, and a large number are shop proprietors in Hasidic neighborhoods. The Hasidim are very highly represented in the diamond and clothing industries in New York City. However, since the high-tech revolution, many Hasidim have entered almost all aspects of the computer industry, and quite a few have made significant fortunes in computer programming as well as hardware and software manufacturing and retailing.

Conclusion

By all social, demographic, and religious indicators, the Hasidim in America constitute a secure and growing community in a country that only a generation ago was considered completely inhospitable to traditional Judaism. Unlike the mainstream American Jewish community, the Hasidim are not confronted with the specter of diminishing numbers in their ranks due to increasing levels of assimilation and intermarriage. To the contrary: attrition from the Hasidic community is far less common today than it was just twenty years ago.

Although the exact number of Hasidim—who are notoriously mistrustful of polls and who generally refuse to count their own numbers in accordance with a halakhic prohibition against "counting the heads of the children of Israel"—is very difficult to ascertain with any measure of precision, it is generally estimated that there are today more than 200,000 Hasidic Jews in the United States, the large majority residing in the New York tri-state area. The remarkable growth of the American Hasidic Jewish community since the end of World War II has defied the expectations of almost all Jewish historians, sociologists, and demographers. Given the unusually high Hasidic fertility rate, the young age of Hasidic marriages, and the very low rate of attrition from the Hasidic community—all contrasted with the diminishing general American Jewish population—the proportion of Hasidim in American Jewry will grow exponentially for the foreseeable future, as the Hasidim remain its fastest-growing sector.

Allan Nadler

References and Further Reading

Ben Amos, D., and Jerome R. Mintz, trans. and eds. 1970. *In Praise of the Baal Shem Tov.* Bloomington: Indiana University Press.

Dresner, Samuel. 1960. *The Zaddik.* New York: Abelard-Schuman.

Elior, Rachel. 1993. *The Paradoxical Ascent to God: The Kabbalistic Theosophy of Habad Hasidism.* Albany: State University of New York Press.

Etkes, Immanuel. 2005. *The Besht: Magician, Mystic and Leader.* Waltham, MA: Brandeis University Press.

Feldman, Jan. 2003. *Lubavitchers as Citizens: A Paradox of Liberal Democracy.* Ithaca, NY: Cornell University Press.

Fishkoff, Sue. 2003. *The Rebbe's Army: Inside the World of Chabad-Lubavitch.* New York: Schocken.

Foxbrunner, Roman A. 1992. *Habad: The Hasidism of R. Shneur Zalman of Lyady.* Tuscaloosa: University of Alabama Press.

Harris, Lis. 1985. *Holy Days: The World of a Hasidic Family.* New York: Summit Books.

Hundert, Gershon. 1991. *Essential Papers on Hasidism.* New York: New York University Press.

Idel, Moshe. 1995. *Hasidism: Between Ecstasy and Magic.* Albany: State University of New York Press.

Jacobs, Louis. 1976. *Hasidic Thought.* New York: Behrman House.

Jacobson, Yoram. 1998. *Hasidic Thought.* Tel Aviv: MOD Press.

Kranzler, George. 1995. *Hasidic Williamsburg: A Contemporary American Hasidic Community.* Northvale, NJ: Jason Aronson.

Loewenthal, Naftali. 1991. *Communicating the Infinite: The Emergence of the Habad School.* Chicago: University of Chicago Press.

Mayer, Egon. 1979. *From Suburb to Shtetl: The Jews of Boro Park.* Philadelphia: Temple University Press.

Mintz, Jerome R. 1992. *Hasidic People: A Place in the New World.* Cambridge, MA: Harvard University Press.

Nadler, Allan. 1982. "Piety and Politics: The Case of the Satmar Rebbe." *Judaism* 31(Spring): 135–152.

Poll, Solomon. 1962. *The Hasidic Community of Williamsburg.* New York: Free Press of Glencoe.

Rubin, Israel. 1997. *Satmar: Two Generations of an Urban Island.* New York: P. Lang.

Weiss, Joseph G. 1985. *Studies in Eastern European Jewish Mysticism.* Oxford: Littman Library.

Women in the Development of American Judaism

In the years since the ordination of the first American woman rabbi in 1972, female access to religious leadership has brought far-reaching change to American Jewish religious and cultural life. Opening the male club of the rabbinate brought forth a revolution of increased participation, the impact of which extends well beyond the relatively small number of women who have become rabbis or cantors. Changing ideas and expectations for women have opened new possibilities in every American Jewish denomination. Women have found a place in the once male-dominated arena of public Jewish worship through the creation of new ceremonies (such as baby naming), the adaptation of existing ceremonies (such as adult *bat mitzvah*), and the revival of traditional female ceremonies that had fallen into disuse (such as celebrating the new moon). Moreover, when women rabbis broke open men's control of Jewish spiritual leadership, they expanded access to Jewish leadership and learning for both men and women. As striking as these changes have been, they do not represent a new pattern in American Judaism. In fact, much of the growth and development of the American Jewish community over the last two hundred years has been keyed to women's evolving religious roles.

Historically, female Jewish religiosity has been most actively identified with home observance. Myriad rituals and practices that are critical to traditional Jewish life—from marital purity, to the laws of *kashruth*, to preparing holiday meals—fell within the purview of women. Overall, although a minority of American Jews have always maintained strict standards of personal observance, American Jewish life has been marked by laxity in religious observance, with mainly symbolic attention accorded Jewish law and life. In every era, however, women's choices, particularly among immigrants, have greatly influenced the varied levels of personal observance maintained by Jewish families; but that impact is difficult to isolate and evaluate.

Although public Jewish worship has not traditionally been associated with female religiosity, careful study reveals that many key transitions that defined a distinctly American Judaism have been related to women's changing roles within the synagogue. Change came early. Colonial American churches did not have to be bastions of gender equality to frame a critical perspective on women's place in colonial American synagogues. In a society that emphasized the centrality of piety and a religious nature to respectable female identity, American Jews quickly came to understand that perceptions of women's place in public worship would greatly influence how others would judge their religious tradition. Accordingly, transformations in women's place within the synagogue emerged early on in American Jewish experience.

In traditional European synagogues, women sat in balconies, separated from the male-led service by latticed, curtained, or grilled barriers. Unmarried women hardly ever attended regular worship services, and married women generally did so only on Saturday mornings. A shift in this pattern and in religious identity for American Jewish women found physical expression as early as 1763 with the dedication of the second synagogue built in what later became the United States. In the Newport, Rhode Island, synagogue, women sat behind a low balustrade, free of the opaque barriers of the European sanctuaries. This innovation was replicated in subsequent early American synagogues in Charleston (1794), New York (1818), and Philadelphia (1824).

This shift in gallery design combines with other evidence to suggest that, by the mid-eighteenth century, synagogue attendance had become important to both married and unmarried American Jewish women, and that male synagogue leaders were conscious of the need to reframe women's status in public worship. By the nineteenth century, expectations of women's presence within the synagogue had become an established pattern, as women began to incorporate a sense of themselves as synagogue-goers into their self-identity. Eventually, continuing adjustments to the gallery were no longer sufficient to address women's growing attendance or societal expectations that a woman's religious nature should be evident through her presence in the church as well as through her piety in the home. Ultimately, the American synagogue had to be re-configured in order to address the changing ways in which women were expressing their Jewish identity.

In 1851 a breakaway Albany congregation, led by reformer Isaac Mayer Wise, introduced family synagogue pews. The congregation chose not to add balconies when they moved into a former church building but simply adopted the existing design. Three years later, the Emanu-El Congregation in New York also adopted the existing family pews of the church building that they were converting to synagogue use. These pews were one component of a wide range of revisions to traditional practices introduced at Temple Emanu-El, which quickly became an influential national model of a reformed and Americanized Judaism. Significantly, all the Emanu-El reforms in 1854 replicated the efforts of German Jewish reformers except the introduction of mixed seating, which remained an exclusively American innovation until well into the twentieth century.

By the late 1860s and the 1870s, family pews became requisite features both in the Reform temples that were emerging as the dominant religious institution of America's acculturated Jewish population and in the more traditional synagogues that are now seen as the pioneers of the Conservative movement. Even those (Sephardic) synagogues that saw themselves as Americanized guardians of Jewish orthodoxy had to withstand internal campaigns to seat women next to men. In resisting this pressure, these synagogues established that one of the defining divisions between American Orthodox Judaism and more liberal movements would be measured by women's place in the synagogue.

Although family pews seemed to imply a new equality between male and female congregants, they did not actually confer any additional religious agency upon women. As weakly educated male congregants became less participatory in synagogue ritual, and their role as worshippers was greatly devalued, women gained a sort of equality with men. Still, offered a place in the sanctuary, women, in a departure from the traditional pattern of synagogue worship, quickly came to dominate attendance at weekly Sabbath services. It took the arrival during the 1880s and 1890s of the first wave of what would be more than 2 million Russian and Eastern European Jewish immigrants, however, to spark a public activism among these acculturated women that would once again enable them to redefine their communities.

Immigrant aid work opened new public roles for acculturated Jewish women of all religious tendencies. Many soon turned their newly established public identities to the needs of their own synagogue communities. Congregations led by male rabbis and male boards began to draw upon women's groups to attend to the physical, charitable, and social needs of the community. The activation of female energy for the benefit of the congregation was a critical component of an effort to extend the synagogue sphere beyond the elegant and formal worship service. This expansion led to another wave of synagogue building in the 1890s and the early twentieth century. These large synagogue complexes were intended not only to frame respectable Jewish worship but also to house the variegated institutional life that women's activism made possible.

As existing synagogues expanded, new immigrants established communities of their own. Chief among the adjustments many faced was the need to resolve the tensions between accustomed ritual observance and a setting that undermined traditional practice. Many women in the immigrant communities continued to take quite seriously their responsibilities for seeing to the ritual observance of their families. This was evidenced by a series of sometimes violent kosher meat boycotts in several cities, in which women, in their role as household managers, rebelled against steep increases in the price of kosher meat. In general, mothers' choices about household observance helped to determine which of the many available religious paths were taken by other family members.

The earliest worship settings created by Jewish immigrants in this era were notable for their exclusion of women. Storefront *shuls* gathered men connected by kinship and region of origin for the purposes of worship, sociability, and mutual aid, and generally excluded women. As soon as some of these smaller assemblies gathered together for the purpose of creating larger synagogue edifices, however, organizers understood that, to attract more members, they would have to incorporate women and children. Their grand immigrant synagogues boasted large women's galleries, preserving the traditional separation of men and women but conveying an understanding that, in America, women were expected to be present and seen in the synagogue.

As Jews began to move beyond their initial immigrant neighborhoods, many sought Americanized synagogues that no longer reflected regional European differences. This usually meant joining the emerging Conservative movement, which attempted to serve a traditionally inclined community that lacked extensive Hebraic knowledge and preferred rabbis without thick European accents. These synagogues adopted mixed seating as a key marker separating them both from the Old World and the immigrant ghetto. One key aspect of Americanized synagogues, whether Reform, Conservative, or Orthodox, was the role of women's groups in shaping and facilitating sociability within their congregations. The Conservative movement's National Women's League, under the leadership of Mathilda Schechter, was created in 1918, five years (to the day) after the creation of the Reform movement's National Federation of Temple Sisterhoods. An Orthodox counterpart was created in 1926. These organizations coordinated the work of local groups that were fundamental to shaping their communities and defining Jewish women's public roles. Sisterhoods chose synagogue decor, created communal events, and by teaching, organizing, and fund-raising supported Jewish education both locally and nationally. Conservative and Orthodox sisterhood efforts also focused on encouraging and training women to preserve traditional Jewish ritual within their homes.

During World War II, as in many communities during World War I, sisterhoods helped Jewish women formalize their contributions to the war efforts—through knitting, baking cookies, organizing blood banks, selling bonds, and resettling Jewish refugees, among other activities. In the postwar years, women's work facilitated a period of great energy in synagogue organizational life, both in older urban settings and in creating new frameworks for community in the suburbs. Moreover, sisterhoods played a major role in shaping the child-centered focus of many of these congregations during the 1950s and 1960s.

Thus, for decades, twentieth-century sisterhood women sustained much of the communal, social, and practical aspects of American Jewish congregational life. This tradition of intense involvement and support led to calls for recognition of women's religious voice, participation, and leadership. Sisterhood Sabbaths, for instance, introduced by the Reform movement in the early 1920s, created an annual venue where, in many communities, women created and conducted liturgy and delivered sermons. The growth of religious education for girls did even more to raise questions about the religious involvement of the women they would become. The bat mitzvah, a counterpart to the coming-of-age ritual for boys, was first introduced in 1922 when Jewish Reconstructionism founder Mordecai Kaplan asked his twelve-year-old daughter to read from (a printed text of) the Torah during Shabbat services. Bat mitzvah ceremonies—usually Friday-night variants of the Torah service led by *bar mitzvah* boys on Saturday morning—had taken hold in one-third of Conservative congregations by 1948 and grew more common through the 1950s (Schwartz 1997). Reform temples remained committed to the gender equality supposedly implicit in the group confirmation ceremony, but as bar mitzvah celebrations became more prevalent in Reform communities, confirmation seemed to become a girls' ritual. By the 1960s, however, bat mitzvah rituals had become more common in Reform congregations. After World War II, the growing Conservative and Reform camp movements also reinforced the importance of the participation of girls as well as boys. Orthodox communities, too, placed an increased emphasis on female education, symbolized by the inauguration of Stern College as a women's college within Orthodoxy's Yeshiva University in 1954, indicating a meaningful commitment to giving women access to serious Jewish study.

As the presumption of equality in religious education became more common and as American society became more attuned to issues of gender equality, questions began to arise about Judaism's complete denial of female access to formal religious leadership. With the rise of the feminist movement, the idea of distinctive rituals marking the religious obligations of boys and girls, or men and women, became increasingly untenable within the liberal movements. By the mid-1970s, a Saturday morning bat mitzvah service, identical in its requirements with the ceremony held for boys, was in place in many Reform and Conservative congregations.

Progress toward equality for women in the Reform and Conservative movements moved in fits and starts through the 1950s and 1960s, as the larger society became more engaged in questions of women's equality. Conservative leaders in the early 1950s attempted to mitigate the destructive impact of traditional Jewish divorce laws, which could leave women deserted by their husbands unable to remarry. In 1955, they voted to allow women the honor of being called to bless the Torah (*aliyot*), although this practice found expression in very few synagogues. In the Reform movement, the 1950s saw efforts to affirm women's

religious leadership, and in a few communities qualified women took on the role of spiritual leader. Sally Priesand came to Cincinnati's Hebrew Union College–Jewish Institute of Religion (HUC-JIR) in 1964 with every intention of becoming a rabbi. Finding support from the school's president, Nelson Glueck, she persevered in her studies and was ordained as the first American woman rabbi in 1972. The Reconstructionist Rabbinical College ordained its first woman rabbi, Sandy Sasso, in 1974. Barbara Ostfeld Horowitz became the first seminary-trained woman invested as a cantor by HUC-JIR in 1975.

The Conservative movement also felt the impact of societal feminism. In 1972, an activist group of young Conservative women calling themselves Ezrat Nashim challenged the Conservative rabbinate to bring true gender equity to the Conservative community. Change did occur: between 1972 and 1976, the percentage of Conservative congregations offering women aliyot went from 7 percent to 50 percent (Schwartz 1997). Questions of women's rabbinic leadership, however, brought forth intense internal conflict as some struggled to find a Jewish legal argument that would sanction women's religious leadership and others battled the great symbolic departure from traditional Judaism that women rabbis would represent. Following community-wide discussion, the faculty of the movement's Jewish Theological Seminary approved the ordination of women in 1983. Amy Eilberg became the first Conservative woman rabbi in 1985.

These pioneering steps in allowing women to take on the most prominent roles of Jewish religious leadership have had profound symbolic and practical implications for every variety of Judaism, reconfiguring expectations of what women should be allowed and encouraged to do. The last thirty years have brought a transformation across the religious spectrum of observance and belief, keyed, as so often in the nineteenth century, to accommodating changed notions of women as religious actors. The introduction of female religious leadership in the liberal denominations has led to significant changes in style, tone, organization, and experience of congregational life. Sally Priesand's ordination has been followed by more than seven hundred female ordinations in the mainstream movements. The leadership of these women has influenced tendencies ranging from a deepening emphasis on spirituality, a turn to the healing possibilities of Jewish tradition, challenges to continued exclusions within Jewish tradition and life such as those against gays and lesbians, and a general democratization of access to ritual participation, education, and religious authority.

Orthodox congregations continue to exclude the mixed seating of men and women and women rabbis, but some of the most dynamic and creative expressions of Jewish feminism can currently be found within certain sectors of the Orthodox community. Recent decades have brought a transformative expansion of institutional resources directed toward the education of traditional girls and young women. Unprecedented female engagement in advanced textual study has intensified challenges to what remains the largely male domain of Orthodox public worship. The first International Conference on Feminism and Orthodoxy, held in New York City in 1997, led to the creation of the Jewish Orthodox Feminist Alliance, which has sponsored biennial conferences on feminism and orthodoxy. Each conference has brought together more than 1,000 women committed to using traditional Jewish legal processes to advance Jewish women's leadership and participation. These challenges, as well as regular women's *tefillah* (prayer) groups that have been organized in many communities, face strong opposition from within Orthodoxy; nevertheless, they have done much to shift possibilities and realities for Orthodox Jewish women.

In the first decade of the twenty-first century, all aspects of American Judaism are marked by women's expanding involvement in worship and study alongside continuing tensions over their religious roles. Liberal denominations consider gender equity an established principle, yet rhetorical commitments to equality have not always been matched by institutional realities. There remain large pay inequities for men and women within similar rabbinic positions and high underrepresentation of women in the most influential rabbinical and denominational posts. Many women who have attained positions of status and authority previously occupied exclusively by men still must struggle to obtain respect and job security.

At the beginning of the twenty-first century, American responses to women's traditional exclusions from Jewish practice and leadership are finding echoes in Jewish communities around the world. Historical perspective reveals that current transformations have grown out of a long American Jewish tradition of engagement with the broader society's often confusing expectations for proper gender roles. The achievement of full gender equality

within American Jewish culture, as within American society, may always remain elusive. The recognition, however, that a vibrant and relevant Judaism must respond to the challenges raised by the position of women in contemporary life derives from the earliest days and concerns of American Judaism.

Karla Goldman

References and Further Reading
Goldman, Karla. 2000. *Beyond the Synagogue Gallery: Finding a Place for Women in American Judaism.* Cambridge, MA: Harvard University Press.
Goldman, Karla, Jeffrey Gurock, and Shuly Rubin Schwartz. 1997. "Reform Judaism," "Orthodox Judaism," "Conservative Judaism." In *Jewish Women in America: An Historical Encyclopedia,* edited by Paula E. Hyman and Deborah Dash Moore, pp. 1136–1140, 1009–1016, 275–278. New York: Routledge.
Lefton, Deborah Levine. 2001. "Women's Equality in the Synagogue: The National Federation of Temple Sisterhoods' Search for Autonomy, 1913–1930." Rabbinic thesis, Hebrew Union College–Jewish Institute of Religion, Cincinnati, OH.
Nadell, Pamela S. 1998. *Women Who Would Be Rabbis: A History of Women's Ordination, 1889–1985.* Boston: Beacon.
Sarna, Jonathan D. 1987. "The Debate over Mixed Seating in the American Synagogue." In *The American Synagogue: A Sanctuary Transformed,* edited by Jack Wertheimer, pp. 363–394. Cambridge: Cambridge University Press.
Stein, Regina. 1998. "The Boundaries of Gender: The Role of Gender Issues in Forming American Jewish Denominational Identity, 1913–1963." Ph.D. diss., Jewish Theological Seminary of America.

Isaac Leeser (1806–1868)

Religious Leader and Educator

Religious leader, educator, translator, and editor, Isaac Leeser was the major architect of American Judaism during the decades prior to the Civil War and an outspoken champion of an Americanized expression of orthodox Sephardic Judaism. Originally from Germany and not specifically trained for his remarkable career in religious leadership, Leeser advocated unity in American Jewish life and fiercely opposed the emerging Reform movement. Traditional in practice, he was a Biblical literalist and upheld rabbinic doctrines while urging decorum and Protestant-style preaching in the American synagogue. A person of his time, Leeser quietly rejected abolitionist interpretations of the Bible and urged American Jews to remain apolitical on the great issues of the day. Many scholars have characterized Leeser as a proto-Conservative Jew. Leeser also supported the development of modern Jewish agricultural projects in the land of Israel.

Born in the Westphalian village of Neunkirchen but orphaned at an early age, Leeser was raised by his paternal grandmother. He received a traditional elementary Jewish education in nearby Dulmen. Typical of that time and place in Germany, he then studied in a Jesuit gymnasium in Muenster and received private instruction from the district rabbi, Abraham Sutro, a well-known preacher and opponent of Reform Judaism. Although Leeser wanted to be a pharmacist, since there were few prospects for advanced training or gainful employment for young Jews in Germany, he accepted the invitation of Zalma Rehine, a maternal uncle, to immigrate to America.

Leeser arrived in the United States in 1824 and initially lived with his uncle's family in Richmond, Virginia. He became active in the local synagogue and quickly learned the Sephardic rite practiced there. In 1828 Leeser published two letters in Richmond's *Constitutional Whig* defending Judaism against charges made by Joseph Wolff, an apostate missionary. Word of his intellectual and religious abilities quickly spread throughout the small, highly interconnected American Jewish community, and, despite his misgivings, Leeser accepted an invitation to become the hazzan of Philadelphia's prestigious Mikveh Israel Congregation.

Leeser arrived in Philadelphia in 1829 and surprised the congregation with his personal energy and industriousness. Friction with the congregation's leadership remained a constant, ultimately leading to an ugly public dispute and his departure from that pulpit in 1850. Nearly blinded and badly scarred by smallpox in 1833, Leeser never married but poured himself into his work. His indefatigable efforts on behalf of Judaism in America over the next thirty years permanently changed the landscape of American Jewish religious life and demonstrated the immense cultural potential of the Jewish community in North America.

From the inception of his work in Mikveh Israel's pulpit, Leeser was a productive though not always original writer. In 1830 he published a catechism, *Instruction in the Mosaic Law,* followed by an antideistic work, *The Jews and the Mosaic Law,* four years later. He produced a second catechism "for younger children" (1839) in support of Rebecca Gratz's newly founded Hebrew Sunday school. Beginning in 1837, he published his sermons, which eventually included ten volumes of *Discourses* (1837, 1841, 1867) and a six-volume Hebrew-English *Form of Prayers According to the Custom of the Spanish and Portuguese Jews* (1837–1838).

In response to a medieval-style blood libel in Damascus, Syria, orchestrated by French imperial interests and spread by the Vatican, Leeser organized a multifaith response in Philadelphia in 1840 and encouraged similar protests in other American cities. The following year, he proposed the Plan for Union to unite all American Jews under a single religious banner. Essentially modeled on the centralized, government-sponsored French consistory system, the plan failed, exposing many of the heretofore unrevealed tensions in Jewish life.

Undeterred by his failure to create a religious union for American Jews, in 1843 Leeser launched the first sustained national Jewish periodical publication in the United States. Leeser served as the publisher, editor, and leading writer for *The Occident and American Jewish Advocate* for twenty-five years. Through its pages, he became even more widely known within the American Jewish community, linked American Jews with other Jewish communities throughout the Diaspora, and created a journal of record that remains essential reading to historians of the American Jewish experience to this day. Two years later, in 1845, Leeser published his English translation of the Pentateuch, a vocalized text of the entire Hebrew Bible, and organized the first American Jewish Publication Society.

Leeser's remarkable productivity was not disrupted by his bitter public dispute with Mikveh Israel in 1850. Following his departure from the synagogue, he turned his attention to an English translation of the complete Hebrew Bible, which began to appear in 1853. To promote the newly translated Bible, Leeser took a railway tour of the United States, which brought him into contact with numerous Jewish communities in the South and Midwest.

Still committed to the idea of national religious unity, Leeser, a theological traditionalist, attended a conference of a broad spectrum of American rabbis held in Cleveland, Ohio, and organized by his ideological opponent, Isaac M. Wise. The purpose of the conference was to create a common theological platform for all American Jews. Last-minute objections raised by a recently arrived radical Reform rabbi, Dr. David Einhorn, resulted in the collapse of the conference but not of the idea of religious unity. Wise revived the idea in 1873 with the founding of the Union of American Hebrew Congregations. However, instead of becoming the umbrella organization of all American synagogues, it quickly evolved into the synagogue arm of the emerging Reform movement.

By contrast, Leeser discovered more fertile ground for unity in nonreligious Jewish organizations. In 1859 he was elected a vice president of the Board of Delegates of American Israelites, the first Jewish defense organization in the United States. Although initially opposed to B'nai B'rith (founded in 1843), Leeser eventually joined the men's organization and with its support helped found the Jewish Hospital of Philadelphia during the Civil War.

Four years before the Civil War, Leeser found himself back in the pulpit at Philadelphia's Congregation Beth El Emeth, but he carefully steered clear of political controversy. During the war, he worked to preserve Jewish civil rights and to establish a Jewish chaplaincy corps in the Union army. Immediately following Lee's surrender (which occurred on the first night of Passover, 1865), Leeser worked to bring relief to southern Jewish communities devastated by the fighting.

Leeser's final achievement was the founding of Maimonides College in 1867 in Philadelphia. Although short-lived, Maimonides was the first rabbinic school in the United States to ordain rabbis. It failed shortly after Leeser's death on February 1, 1868. Leeser's funeral was the most attended Jewish event in the United States up to that time, and friend and foe alike eulogized him.

Although largely forgotten today, Leeser played a major role in shaping Judaism in America from 1830 to the period of Reconstruction. Although his hope for Jewish religious unity in the United States remains unrealized, his belief in the possibility of creating a vital center of Jewish life in America continues to inform new visions for the American Jewish community.

Lance J. Sussman

References and Further Reading

Korn, Bertram W. 1967. "Isaac Leeser: Centennial Reflections." *American Jewish Archives* 19 (November): 127–141.

Sussman, Lance J. 1995. *Isaac Leeser and the Making of American Judaism.* Detroit, MI: Wayne State University Press.

David Einhorn (1809–1879)

Radical Reform Rabbi, Liturgist, and Abolitionist

Erudite, principled, and uncompromising, Rabbi Dr. David Einhorn was a leading architect of Reform Judaism in the middle decades of the nineteenth century. Although in Germany Einhorn was one of the main voices calling for a systematic expression of Reform Judaism, it was principally in the United States, through his original prayer book and journalistic activities, that he helped shape Judaism's most liberal modern movement. Ironically, Einhorn resisted linguistic assimilation, advocating the preservation of the German language as the essential vehicle of Jewish religious reform in America.

Born in the village of Dispeck in Bavaria and raised by his strong, widowed mother, Einhorn was enrolled in a traditional *yeshiva* in nearby Fuerth under the tutelage of Rabbi Wolf Hamburger. Ordained at age seventeen, Einhorn sought out private lessons in mathematics prior to his studies at several local universities, where he became deeply influenced by contemporary German philosophy, particularly that of Friedrich W. J. Schelling. Einhorn was transformed by his advanced secular training, and for ten years his earlier mentors repeatedly blocked him from assuming a rabbinic post.

Perhaps embittered by his trials, Einhorn finally received an appointment in 1842 as "Chief Rabbi" of Birkenfeld, where he remained for the next five years, married Julie Henrietta Ochs, and quickly became embroiled in religious controversy. On the one hand, Einhorn defended his colleague Abraham Geiger against charges of antirabbinic heresy, but he also attacked radical and antirabbinic lay reformers in Frankfurt am Main. Although widely remembered as a radical himself, throughout his life Einhorn continued to support what was a middle position in the context of nineteenth-century Reform Judaism.

Einhorn, whose religious philosophy was already formed in the 1840s, generally referred to Judaism as

"Mosaism." He believed that Judaism had an infinite capacity "for continuous development both as to its form and its spirit," as he wrote in a letter in 1844. "Its essence," according to Einhorn, "is truth uniting all men." However, until the messianic "mission of Israel" is fully achieved, the Jews need to retain select elements of "the priestly garb of Israel among the nations" (Kohler 1909). In short, Einhorn believed in the necessity of Judaic particularism as a means to an ultimate, divinely sanctioned universalism.

The great Reform rabbinic conferences in Germany during the 1840s helped Einhorn sharpen his views on Reform Jewish practice, particularly on questions of ritual and the expanded role of women in the synagogue, which he openly championed. Einhorn also openly argued that dietary restrictions, Biblical and rabbinic, were contingent on the existence of a priestly cult and were therefore abrogated in contemporary Jewish life. After becoming Chief Rabbi of Mecklenburg-Schwerin, Einhorn became engaged in a highly nuanced controversy over circumcision—he believed that circumcision was necessary for adult converts but not for children of Jewish mothers—that spread beyond the Jewish community.

In 1849 he proposed writing a prayer book based on the principles of the rabbinic conferences but was unable to complete the task because of continual opposition to his views in the community. Two years later, he moved to Pest, Hungary, to head the Reform congregation there. However, after he had been there only two months, the government closed the synagogue. Compelled to give up the active rabbinate, Einhorn determined to write a systematic account of his philosophy of Judaism. He completed two volumes of his *Das Prinzip des Mosaismus (The Principle of Mosaism)* but suspended the project when he accepted an invitation in 1855 to serve a newly formed congregation, Har Sinai, in Baltimore, Maryland.

At age forty-six, Einhorn and his family resettled in the United States, a country whose democratic ideals he passionately supported but whose culture remained essentially alien to him for the rest of his life. True to form, Einhorn quickly became engaged in controversy in his new domicile, and in November 1855 publicly condemned the attempt of Isaac Mayer Wise and other reformers to construct a hybrid religious platform for all American Jews at a conference in Cleveland, Ohio. Ever the champion of Reform Judaism, early in 1856 Einhorn

began publishing a German monthly journal, *Sinai.* Over the nearly seven years it appeared, the journal not only gave Einhorn a critical platform but attracted the intellectual support of Samuel Holdheim and other elite leaders of the Reform movement in Europe. Moreover, to help frame his view of Reform Judaism in America and to provide his congregation with an authentic Reform liturgy, Einhorn prepared his own prayer book, *Olat Tamid.* Ironically, although it sold few copies, it became the model for the immensely popular *Union Prayer Book* nearly half a century later.

Einhorn's stay in Baltimore was complicated by his openly proabolitionist views. He was smuggled out of the city in 1862 to protect him from potential mob action and relocated in Philadelphia at Keneseth Israel Congregation. Einhorn helped consolidate Reform Judaism in his new synagogue, which grew rapidly under his tutelage and was able to build its first major sanctuary. While in Philadelphia, he also prepared a catechism for home and school, the *Ner Tamid (Eternal Light).*

Increasingly recognized as a first-class preacher, Einhorn accepted a call to serve New York's Adas Jeshurun congregation in 1869, which merged with Anshe Chesed in 1874 to form Temple Beth El. In New York, Einhorn began to advocate the establishment of an American rabbinic school. Unwilling to support the efforts of Samuel Adler at New York's Congregation Emanu-El, Einhorn later helped strengthen Isaac M. Wise's Cincinnati-based school, the Hebrew Union College, despite his tremendous cultural, liturgical, and theological differences with Wise. He also supported Wise's efforts to create the Union of American Hebrew Congregations, the first national umbrella organization of synagogues in the United States.

Shortly after leaving Philadelphia, Einhorn returned briefly to help lead the first conference of Reform rabbis in the United States. Widely viewed as the most radical of all the American Reform platforms, the Philadelphia document restated Einhorn's split view on ritual circumcision and offered a highly universalistic account of the mission of Israel. Still, Einhorn later publicly disagreed with his successor at Keneseth Israel, Rabbi Samuel Hirsch, and continued to argue against rabbinic officiation at mixed marriages. He also took exception to the theory of evolution and early expressions of Zionism in America. Einhorn died in New York in 1879. Out of respect for his relentless advocacy for Judaism, and despite their own philosophical differences with him, a broad spectrum of Jewish leaders attended the funeral of Einhorn, the principal nineteenth-century architect of American Reform Judaism.

Lance J. Sussman

References and Further Reading

Kohler, Kaufmann. 1909. "David Einhorn, The Uncompromising Champion of Reform: A Biographical Essay." *Yearbook of the Central Conference of American Rabbis:* 215–270.

Meyer, Michael A. 1988. *Response to Modernity: A History of the Reform Movement in Judaism.* New York: Oxford University Press.

Jewish Communities

The Lower East Side

During the 1880s and into the first decades of the twentieth century, the Lower East Side of Manhattan, a neighborhood that runs from Fourteenth Street south to Fulton Street and from Broadway east to the East River, became home to more than half a million immigrant Jews from Eastern Europe. These residents produced a culture of *Yiddishkeit* more intense and more pervasive than any other in the world up to that time. Not only did they build a vast network of religious, cultural, political, and social institutions for their own use, but many of those institutions, including the Yiddish press, the mutual aid societies, the labor movement, and the Yiddish theater, produced cultural styles and texts that flowed from the Lower East Side (LES) to much of American Jewry elsewhere as well as to the larger non-Jewish community beyond. The site of the densest and most animated mass of immigrants in the nation's history, the LES remained an emotional point of reference, a collective memory and a common heritage for Jews in the United States regardless of where they or their forbears lived.

Of the 23 million immigrants to the United States between 1880 and 1920, 17 million came through the port of New York. Although some newcomers dispersed to other places, great numbers collected in immigrant enclaves on the island of Manhattan. No group outdid the Jews in this regard. Practically all East European Jewish immigrants arriving after 1870 initially found their way to the Lower East Side, and the vast majority stayed within that nucleus. By 1892, 75 percent of the city's Jews lived on the Lower East Side. The percentage declined—to 50 percent in 1903 and to 23 percent by 1916. But the absolute number of Jews,

Lower East Side, New York, ca. 1907. (Library of Congress)

augmented by newcomers crowding into the district, continued to climb until it reached its peak of 542,000 in 1910. The Lower East Side literally bristled with Jews. Jacob Riis, the acerbic and energetic journalist interested in "how the other half lives," observed in the 1890s that "nowhere in the world are so many people crowded together in a square mile" as in the Jewish quarter. The Tenth Ward averaged 730 people per acre by the turn of the century, while some other areas of the Lower East Side approached the astounding rate of 1,000 per acre. Only Bombay and Calcutta had higher densities.

The great Jewish influx pushed the district's middle-class Germans and Irish, as well as the remnant of the German Jewish community north of Houston Street, to less crowded quarters. Their places were taken by five major varieties of Jews in an area described by one young immigrant as "a miniature federation of semi-independent allied states." Hungarian Jews were clustered in the northwest section just above Houston Street; the Galicians lived to the south between Houston and Broome. From Chrystie to Allen Streets in the west lay the Rumanian quarter, within which, after 1907, the Sephardic Jews (mainly from Syria, Greece, Turkey, and Spain) settled. The remainder of the Jewish quarter, from Grand Street south to Monroe, was the territory of the Russians—the most numerous and most heterogeneous of the Jewries of Eastern Europe.

In every Jewish section, there were streets like Suffolk Street, where, as Abe Cahan wrote, one "had to pick and nudge his way through dense swarms of bedraggled half-washed humanity, past garbage barrels rearing their overflowing contents," and "underneath tiers and tiers of fire escapes barricaded and festooned with mattresses, pillows and feather beds not yet gathered in for the night." The streets were crowded, but the congestion there was often preferable to the constriction experienced in the tiny flats. One immigrant boarding with the family of a cantor remembered that his two-room apartment on Allen Street contained parents, six children, and five other boarders. Two daughters took in dresses to sew at home, and one boarder plied his shoemaking craft in the apartment as well. "[The] cantor rehearses, a train passes, the shoemaker bangs, ten brats run around like goats, the wife putters in her 'kosher restaurant.' At night we all try to get some sleep in the stifling roach-infested two rooms."

Only a small number of flats had hot running water, and there was often only one hallway toilet for every ten people. These conditions persisted even in the face of remedial legislation in 1884 and 1887 regarding water closets, light, air, and fire safety. Despite these circumstances, new immigrant Jews continued to pour into the Lower East Side and, to a lesser degree, into Chicago's West End and other population centers in Philadelphia and Boston. This was so because few of the smaller cities and towns of the American interior offered so great a possibility of Jewish communalism and Yiddish-based culture as the major cities. Equally important, the ghettos, particularly the largest one on New York's Lower East Side, offered the possibility of employment for Jews.

At the time the masses of East European Jews were coming to America, the garment industry was undergoing rapid expansion, and New York City was central to this development. By 1910 the city was producing 70 percent of the nation's women's clothing and 40 percent of the men's clothing. As early as 1890, almost 80 percent of New York's garment industry was located below Fourteenth Street, and more than 90 percent of the clothing factories there were owned by German Jews. Lower New York, therefore, remained a powerful magnet for the East Europeans throughout the period of mass immigration. The immigrants were attracted by jobs and by Jewish employers who could provide a familiar milieu, as well as the opportunity to observe the Sabbath. By 1897 approximately 60 percent of the New York Jewish labor force was employed in the apparel field, and 75 percent of the workers in the industry were Jewish.

Newly arrived immigrants found advantages even in the sweatshops in lofts, storefronts, and apartments, where the worst conditions of the factory and the tenement came together in one place. The workers could communicate in their own language. The work, however arduous, did not prevent the performance of religious duties, the observance of the Sabbath, or the celebration of religious festivals. Moreover, by working together in small units, the immigrants thought they could preserve the integrity of their families.

Jews on the LES were also drawn to innumerable other crafts outside the garment industry, including bookbinding, watchmaking, cigarmaking, and tinsmithing, all of which became part of a growing ethnic economy. It has been estimated that only about one-third of heads of LES families retained their original East European vocations, but almost 24 percent of Jewish breadwinners moved out of factory work and into self-employment in small businesses at the earliest opportunity. In the virtually all-Jewish Eighth Assembly District, there were 144 groceries, 131 butcher shops, 62 candy stores, 36 bakeries, and 2,440 peddlers and pushcart vendors, many selling such traditional foodstuffs of Eastern Europe as blintzes, bagels, bialys, and herring. And in the late 1890s, Jews in relatively large numbers began moving into the building trades. Most were employed in the alteration and remodeling of old tenements on the Lower East Side as ironworkers, masons, plumbers, electricians, carpenters, and painters.

The remodeling business, the garment industry, and the general ethnic economy of the Lower East Side provided wide opportunities for Jews seeking employment. Nevertheless, most immigrants were poor, and with poverty came the full measure of its attendant ills: prostitution, juvenile delinquency, adult crime, and relatively high rates of desertion and divorce. Concerned discussion about East Side delinquency and vice filled many columns in the Yiddish papers. Accounts from Jewish and non-Jewish sources, including the respected and extensive Lexow and Mazet investigations of the 1890s, indicated that prostitution, gambling, and extortion rackets thrived in the Jewish district, as in every poor district in the city. As Michael Gold correctly pointed out in *Jews without Money* (1930), it was hard not to trip over the prostitutes who "sprawled indolently" on Allen Street, "their legs taking up half the pavement." And the names of Jewish gangsters such as "Dopey Benny" (Benjamin Fein), "Gyp the Blood" (Harry Horowitz), and "Kid Dropper" (Nathan Kaplan) were well known in the community. Racketeer Arnold Rothstein, who by 1906 had acquired, through a variety of illegitimate means, a $12 million bankroll, had become something of a minor folk hero on the Lower East Side. Crime was a marginal phenomenon confined to a relatively small proportion of the ghetto dwellers, but that it had roots in the Jewish community and that it befouled the life of the East Side was undeniable.

No one was more disturbed by the revelations of Jewish crime in the "downtown" ghetto than the established, "uptown" German Jews. Already distressed by the religious Orthodoxy and what they perceived as the political radicalism of their cousins from Eastern Europe, and repelled by their "strange ways and speech," the Germans saw the "immorality" and vice of the new immigrants as a great threat to themselves. By the twentieth century, the Germans, who had initially resisted massive Eastern European immigration, had become the champions of unrestricted entry, but they remained anxious over increasing anti-semitism among the general population. Spurred by this anxiety and by insecurity over their own status, the German Jews sponsored a series of programs to transform their coreligionists as quickly as possible.

One of the major social and educational vehicles for "remaking" the East Europeans was the Educational Alliance, a curious mixture of night school, recreational center, and settlement house quartered in a five-story building on East Broadway and Jefferson Street. It was for several decades an important source of help to the East European immigrants as well as a major source of friction and hostility between uptown and downtown Jews. The hostility diminished somewhat after 1898, when the directorship of the Alliance was assumed by David Blaustein, an acculturated East European immigrant who had made his way through Harvard and was sensitive to the immigrants' desire to retain the cultural supports of their language and folkways and their religious rites and rituals. While the formal, stated objective of the Alliance remained rapid Americanization, the daily programs, increasingly bilingual, became more responsive to immigrants' needs.

Many other institutions were created by the Jewish establishment in the 1890s to serve the needs of the LES ghetto, including the Hebrew Orphan Asylum, the Hebrew Technical Institute for boys, and a school to teach domestic arts to girls, the last two sponsored by the Baron de Hirsch Fund. In addition, the National Council of Jewish Women, an important philanthropic and protective organization, helped female arrivals avoid the "white slave" traders who circulated at ports of entry. And the Clara de Hirsch Home, endowed by the baroness in 1897 to provide recreational facilities and vocational training for immigrant girls, soon took on the task of "uprooting the evil" of prostitution by providing young women, Jews and non-Jews, with decent living arrangements and opportunities for employment, and occasionally by matchmaking.

One of the most notable German Jewish benefactors in the neighborhood was the Cincinnati-born settlement house social worker Lillian Wald (1867–1940). A nurse who, with the help of Jacob Schiff, founded the Henry Street Settlement, Wald grew into a woman of legend, acclaimed and adored on every street of the Lower East Side. As her work proved successful, Wald's reputation and influence grew, and she used them to persuade the city to start a program of public nursing and to put nurses into the public schools. In addition, she actively opposed child labor, supported the playground movement, lined up with the striking cloakmakers in 1910, and was a committed pacifist during World War I. Even as she became a figure of wide renown, Lillian Wald remained dedicated to her East Side neighbors. One of the most respected and genuine liberals of the Progressive Era, Wald, within the narrower Jewish world, was expert at creating links between the uptown Germans and the East Europeans, and she continued to work at gaining the confidence of the former on behalf of the latter.

Some of the attempts by the German Jews to bring order to the ghetto, however, fell short. This was especially true of the *Kehillah,* a comprehensive communal structure designed in 1908 to unite New York City's multifarious Jewish population. It did useful work in philanthropy and Jewish education, but the experiment was severely strained by ethnic, ideological, and class tensions. The Kehillah never matched its Eastern European namesake in reach or power and was defunct by 1922.

But from the start, East European Jews created their own web of voluntary organizations and improvised a viable, decentralized, collective existence. In spite of the disturbing new influences and internal stresses, the Jewish immigrants sustained general tranquility and relative order in the ghetto. The family, the *shul,* the *landsmanshaft,* the club, the mutual aid society, the cafe, the union, and even many workplaces were arenas of genuine interaction and psychological sustenance. Informal social networks, including the people of the block, those gathering on the rooftop, and the group at the candy store, provided similar kinds of contact and mutual support. Within these immigrant enclaves, protected from some of the chaos and brutality of the outside world, Jews in association with one another could borrow supports from the Old World and the New. Here they could achieve a sense of stability and remake their identities at their own, less bewildering pace.

Religion clearly played a role. Although the spiritual life of observant Jews did not show many signs of vitality on the Lower East Side before 1910, the ghetto's six hundred religious congregations testified to the "authenticity of the Jewish religious imperative to worship." Most of the congregations operated out of storefronts, but in addition to these smaller *shuln* there were also imposing and archi-

tecturally impressive houses of worship on the Lower East Side, including Beth Hamidrash Hagadol on Norfolk Street, Anshe Poland on Forsyth Street, and the Eldridge Street Synagogue.

Many of the congregations on the Lower East Side developed around *landslayt,* groups of Jews from the same East European towns, and they often operated as mutual aid societies, reflecting the Old World tradition of *tsedakah* (sometimes meaning "charity," but more often meaning "social justice") and communal responsibility. Landslayt groups frequently went on to form officially registered *landsmanshaftn.* As early as 1892, there were 87 East European landsmanshaftn, and by 1910 there were more than 2,000, representing more than 900 European cities and towns and embracing virtually every Jewish family in New York City. Some were independent, but most were connected to synagogues, unions, extended family circles, or fraternal orders. And all landsmanshaftn maintained some link to the Old Country location, particularly in times of crisis when the *shtetlekh* from which they sprang were in need of material relief. All continued to maintain important communal services, such as burial arrangements and poor relief, as well as a context for a shared and collective expression of nostalgia.

Equally important, the landsmanshaft was a context for reconciling American Jewish and East European identity. It served as a sanctuary from the excessive strains of acculturation, ambition, and even ideology, and it gave the immigrants a breathing space, a place to be themselves, to continue the tradition of communal self-help but also to settle into a game of pinochle. At the same time, it resembled an American fraternal order with its rites and constitutions, its camaraderie, and its opportunity for "doing a little business."

The strong ethnic and religious ties and the need for mutual aid that gave birth to the landsmanshaftn also promoted the creation of other institutions on the LES. Many hospitals, orphanages, and nursing homes that observed dietary laws and had Yiddish-speaking doctors were founded by the East Europeans in New York City, including Beth Israel Hospital (in 1890) located on East Broadway. This medical facility was specifically designed "to meet the peculiar needs of . . . sick poor among the Jewish immigrant population." In addition, there were so many political organizations, labor union locals, philanthropic organizations, loan societies, credit unions, and educational institutions that, by the second decade of the twentieth century, the East European Jews of the LES possessed a more elaborate organizational structure than any other ethnic group in America.

Many of the institutions created by the East European Jews became vital elements in the new transitional culture. Outstanding in this respect was the Jewish labor movement, which included the International Ladies' Garment Workers, the Amalgamated Clothing Workers, the United Hebrew Trades, the Workmen's Circle, the International Workers Order, and the Socialist and Communist press, all centered on the Lower East Side. This left-leaning Jewish labor movement combined socialist principles with day-to-day practical experience to build a power base for East European Jews in America. Without jettisoning their idealism, labor activists and propagandists used that power to establish an enduring union movement, to institutionalize labor–management cooperation, and to improve the conditions of life and labor for the Jews of the LES as well as for Jewish and non-Jewish workers in other U.S. cities. In the process, by bringing the Jewish workers into the American socioeconomic and political arena, the radical labor movement served the East European immigrants as a powerful agent of acculturation.

The Yiddish theater, too, served as a vehicle of Americanization. It had its origins in the Old World, but Yiddish theater arrived in New York City in its infancy. And it was nurtured on the LES at the turn of the century by its greatest audience, the largest, most heterogeneous aggregation of Jews in the world. By 1900 there were three major theater troupes in New York City (twenty by 1918) and numerous smaller endeavors in other Jewish population centers. But it was on the Lower East Side that the theater came to enjoy an unrivaled position as a major cultural institution in which all the problems, hopes, and dreams of the immigrant Jews were dramatized. By combining aspects of Old World culture, American culture, and the transitional culture of the ghetto, and by dealing with many of the immigrant dilemmas of that transitional culture, the Yiddish theater of the LES held up a mirror to its audiences. How to be an American *and* a Jew? How to protect the family from destabilization and religious values from disintegration in a secular, seemingly normless society? How to enjoy the opportunities for material success in America without giving up the spiritual values of Judaism? By posing these dilemmas, the Yiddish stage helped Jews

gain a better understanding of their role in the historical process of relocation, and even as it helped revitalize Yiddish, the theater gave the immigrants greater insight into the problems of creating new identities in the new world.

Intellectuals and political radicals also had an important role to play in the creation of a revitalized Yiddish language in New York. As in Eastern Europe, so on the LES, many intellectuals and political activists at first viewed Yiddish as merely a useful tool for "enlightening" the masses, but they soon helped develop the language into a compelling means of discourse. Yiddish, partly by promoting reading about American events, and partly by incorporating English words—*that'll do, politzman,* and *alle right,* for example—eventually became a vehicle for Americanization, and ultimately and ironically, for its own demise. But the continuing mass immigration, the momentum of Yiddish literary activity, and the involvement of Yiddish in the progressive social and political movements of the early twentieth century invigorated the language beyond all expectation.

In New York City, and especially on the LES, the hub of the Yiddish American universe, more than 150 Yiddish dailies, weeklies, monthlies, quarterlies, festival journals, and yearbooks appeared between 1885 and 1914. Some 20 dailies came into existence during that period, and for a time at the turn of the century, as many as 6 competed simultaneously for readers. The *Tageblatt,* founded in 1885, represented the Orthodox religious point of view. The *Morgen Journal,* also Orthodox, was the first (1901) truly successful Yiddish morning paper. The 1890s saw the beginning of the *Forvarts (Jewish Daily Forward),* a socialist paper that, under the guiding hand of Abraham Cahan, became the largest Yiddish newspaper in the world. In the same decade, the *Freie Arbeiter Shtime* (*Free Voice of Labor*) was born, representing the anarchists. Even the weekly *La America* (1910–1925), a Ladino paper for Sephardic readers, printed a Yiddish column to attract advertisers in the greater East European community. And in 1922 the *Morgen Freiheit,* the newspaper of the Jewish branch of the American Communist Party, launched its first issue from Chrystie Street. As Abraham Cahan pointed out, "the five million Jews living under the czar had not a single Yiddish daily paper even when the government allowed such publication, while [Russian Jews] in America publish six dailies . . . countless Yiddish weeklies and monthlies, and [enough] books [to make] New York the largest Yiddish book market in the world."

Producers and disseminators of the vibrant Yiddish culture of the ghetto often met in small restaurants and cafes to eat, talk, and argue. The staff of the *Jewish Daily Forward* were daytime regulars at the Garden Cafe on East Broadway. In the evenings, writers and poets left their factories and shops to gather in the Cafe Royale on Second Avenue or at the basement cafe Zum Essex on Rutgers Square, as well as in Sachs' Cafe on Norfolk Street.

"At most hours of the day and night," the sensitive gentile journalist Hutchins Hapgood reported, "these places are filled with men who have come here to sip Russian tea out of tumblers, meet their friends, and discuss everything under heaven. . . . It is Bohemia." Hapgood also correctly sensed the dominant "socialistic feeling . . . in these cafes," but as writer Harry Roskolenko, who sold papers to the tea-sipping patrons, astutely observed about his customers, they were not ideological purists: "Ideas about God, the synagogue, the union, intermeshed. It was difficult, then, for me to see how men could be two things—like Zionist-anarchists; or Zionists who were also atheists; or socialists who were Zionists and atheists. It was like a chess game—with no rules. . . . Who was not at least two or three separate spiritual and physical entities on the Lower East Side? My father managed socialism, Orthodoxy and Zionism, quite easily, and so did the kibitzers and the serious."

To most immigrants, the cafes probably seemed exotic, perhaps even frivolous, appropriate for free thinkers who "had nothing to do during the day" and who could stay up late into the night, but not for workers who had to rise early to earn a living. What many workers did take seriously, however, was the endless stream of lectures and public meetings sponsored by the Socialists, the Zionists, the unions, the Board of Education, the People's Institute at Cooper Union, and the Educational Alliance. A "certain grandeur of aspiration" was to be found in those men and women who toiled long hours in the shops and then somehow mustered the energy to drag themselves to evening lectures in pursuit of learning. On the Lower East Side, learning for its own sake or for the sake of future generations and learning for the social revolution all merged into one explosion of self-discovery.

Those who mastered at least the rudiments of English often attended the public night schools. In 1906 Jews constituted a majority of the 100,000 students enrolled in New York City evening classes. Almost 40 percent of the stu-

dents were women. "I admit that I cannot be satisfied to be just a wife and mother," one woman wrote to the *Forward*. "I am still young and I want to learn and enjoy life. My children and my home are not neglected, but I go to evening high school twice a week."

The virtual craze among Jewish adults of the LES for secular education appears to have been part of a general release of energy that for generations had been suppressed in the Old World. And the same passion for learning that adults displayed was instilled in the children. According to immigrant writer Mary Antin and repeated in nearly every immigrant autobiography, Jewish parents brought their boys and girls to the first day of school "as if it were an act of consecration," and parental encouragement was sustained throughout the child's school career.

This respect and drive for education partly explains Jewish economic and occupational mobility and helps us understand why a disproportionate number of immigrants achieved professional status relatively early. There was no large-scale social ascent to the professions in the immigrant generation or even in the second generation; but by 1907 the number of Jewish doctors making a living on the Lower East Side had doubled to 200 since the 1880s, and the number of lawyers increased almost as fast. There were also 115 Jewish pharmacists and 175 Jewish dentists serving the neighborhood.

Success in small business actually played a more important role than education in the relatively rapid mobility of the Jewish immigrant generation. Thousands of East Siders were involved in the pushcart trade and in subcontracting, and hundreds more had groceries, butcher shops, candy stores, and bakeries. Many of these businesses remained marginal in character, but some entrepreneurs advanced enough to constitute the beginning of a middle class.

As early as the 1890s, the apparel trade and the real estate business also became arenas for immigrant energy and aspiration. By 1905 German Jewish manufacturers and landlords had been virtually replaced by East European Jews. It is the "Russian-Jewish employer" now who hires the "Russian-Jewish laborer," wrote immigrant economist and statistician I. M. Rubinow in 1905; and it is the "Russian-Jewish landlord" now who collects "his exorbitant rent" from the "Russian-Jewish tenement dweller." The vast majority of gainfully employed Jews on the Lower East Side did not become manufacturers or property owners;

they remained proletarians for at least one generation, but the Jewish middle class was clearly growing. Consumption patterns on the Lower East Side reflected the growing affluence of the immigrant generation as well as the desire of Jews to Americanize. Significant numbers of families, pursuing both the "sanctification" of the home and the American ideal of social equality, installed gas ovens, turned bedrooms into "parlors" for daytime use, and bought pianos on the installment plan.

A much smaller number of immigrants grew rich. Harry Fischel, who arrived penniless in New York, became a millionaire in the building industry. Israel Lebowitz, who started as a peddler, graduated to a men's apparel shop on Orchard Street and by 1907 was among the largest shirt manufacturers in New York City. This was impressive, but the very thin crust of East European wealth remained unimportant in comparison to the wealth of the German Jews or the American elite. The East Europeans were not at the centers of American economic power. The major heavy industries, Wall Street, banking, and insurance remained closed to them. They were primarily confined to economic mobility in the fields of real estate, merchandising, and light manufacturing.

A considerable proportion of Jewish immigrants on the LES continued, of course, to be petty tradesmen, and a large majority stayed in the shops and factories throughout their working lives, about half of them in the garment industry. Life remained hard during these years, especially during the depression of 1893–1895, but working and living conditions, general amenities, and incomes did improve slowly for many immigrants. Real earnings of immigrant Jews on the LES rose at an average annual rate of 1.3 percent between 1890 and 1914. This enabled these workers to sustain a modest increase in standard of living and to underwrite education and economic mobility for their children.

Economic mobility often meant geographic mobility. For more than thirty years, immigrant Jews from Eastern Europe had sustained, in the Lower East Side ghetto and in its satellites in Brooklyn, the Bronx, and upper Manhattan, a vibrant transitional culture laced with elaborate institutional arrangements. But neither the Lower East Side Jewish community nor its spinoffs were destined to be permanent communities, and after 1910 mobility meant lower population density, declining attendance at the Yiddish theater, declining circulation of the Yiddish press, and declining membership in the United Hebrew Trades.

Yet it was only well after the Jewish crowds had dwindled, after the Yiddish language and the dietary habits of Eastern Europe had given way to the accents and foodways of China and the Caribbean, and well after the synagogues had become churches that the story of the LES was made to dovetail with American legend and became virtually archetypical of the story of Jewish life in the United States: a people fleeing religious persecution and political oppression in Eastern Europe came to New York, created an intimate, all-Jewish world, and suffered materially, but through moral discipline and hard work ultimately rose out of the neighborhood to become educated, middle-class Jewish Americans.

As the focal point of Jewish American memory, the LES was canonized to the level of myth. But the mythic dimensions of the story are challenged by a variety of facts: non-Jews also lived in the neighborhood; many Jews not from Eastern Europe lived on East Side streets, and many did so well before the 1880s when the tale of the LES is thought to have begun; the emigrés from Eastern Europe came to the United States for economic reasons as much as for political or religious ones. Moreover, in its heyday as an immigrant Jewish neighborhood, the LES did not have a fixed name. Visitors, writers, and reformers called it variously the Jewish quarter, the downtown Russian quarter, the Hebrew quarter, and most often, the ghetto. And there is little persuasive evidence that the Jews who inhabited what we now consider the LES ever thought of themselves as living in a unified neighborhood with fixed boundaries.

Indeed, for the first half of the twentieth century the Lower East Side held no special significance for American Jews and may even have been an embarrassing reminder of their unacculturated past. But after World War II and especially after the 1960s, the status of the Lower East Side was raised in Jewish American consciousness and memory. As they confronted the European Holocaust and a sense that their own Jewishness was eroding, and as ethnic identity became de rigueur in the age of "black is beautiful" and "the rise of the unmeltable ethnics," American Jews, as part of their culture of memory, reconstructed a venerated Lower East Side and transformed mundane urban real estate into something approaching sacred space.

Gerald Sorin

References and Further Reading

Diner, Hasia. 2000. *Lower East Side Memories*. Princeton, NJ: Princeton University Press.

Diner, Hasia, Jeffrey Schandler, and Beth Wenger, eds. 2000. *Remembering the Lower East Side*. Bloomington: Indiana University Press.

Glazier, Jack. 1998. *Dispersing the Ghetto*. Ithaca, NY: Cornell University Press.

Gold, Michael. 1984. *Jews without Money*. New York: Carroll and Graf Publishers.

Goren, Arthur. 1970. *New York Jews and the Quest for Community*. New York: Columbia University Press.

Hapgood, Hutchins. 1967. *The Spirit of the Ghetto*. Cambridge, MA: Belknap Press.

Heinze, Andrew. 1990. *Adapting to Abundance: Jewish Immigrants, Mass Consumption and the Search for American Identity*. New York: Columbia University Press.

Hindus, Milton, ed. 1996. *The Jewish East Side: 1881–1924*. New Brunswick, NJ: Transaction Press.

Howe, Irving. 1976. *World of Our Fathers: The Journey of the East European Jews to America and the Life They Found and Made*. New York: Harcourt Brace Jovanovich.

Moore, Deborah Dash. 1981. *At Home in America: Second Generation New York Jews*. New York: Columbia University Press.

Rischin, Moses. 1962. *The Promised City*. Cambridge, MA: Harvard University Press.

Roskolenko, Harry. 1971. *The Time That Was Then*. New York: Dial Press.

Sanders, Ronald. 1987. *The Downtown Jews*. New York: Dover.

Sorin, Gerald. 1985. *The Prophetic Minority: American Jewish Immigrant Radicals, 1880–1920*. Bloomington: Indiana University Press.

Sorin, Gerald. 1989. "Tradition and Change: American Jewish Socialists as Agents of Acculturation." *American Jewish History* 79, 1: 37–54.

Sorin, Gerald. 1992. *A Time for Building: The Third Migration, 1880–1920*. Baltimore: Johns Hopkins University Press.

Sorin, Gerald. 1993. "Mutual Contempt, Mutual Benefit: The Strained Encounter between German and Eastern European Jews in America, 1880–1920." *American Jewish History* 81 (Autumn): 34–59.

Brownsville

Brownsville, a poor, working-class district in East Brooklyn, was by the middle decades of the twentieth century home to one of the largest concentrations of Jews in the United States. Jewish social and religious institutions, including eighty-three synagogues in less than two square miles and dozens of Hebrew and Yiddish schools in the area stretching from Saratoga Avenue east to Sackman Street and from Pitkin Avenue south to Riverdale, helped define the Jewish character of the neighborhood that had come to be known as the "Jerusalem of America." Except for the high holy days, when *shuln* were packed to overflowing, most residents failed to attend religious services with any regularity; but virtual ethnic homogeneity in the neighborhood, visible Jewish fraternal and mutual aid institutions, and the Yiddish language of the street, home, and business allowed Brownsville Jews to develop a sense of Jewish identity independent of religious organizations. In this way, the area played an important role for Jewish immigrants to America, helping to ease transplantation and acculturation for tens of thousands. And although many residents agreed with writer Alfred Kazin, who called Brownsville "a place that measured all success by our skill in getting away from it" (Kazin 1951), just as many Jewish inhabitants looked back on their former "nurturing neighborhood" with nostalgia for the feeling of community and the opportunities it provided. By 1965, however, deteriorating infrastructure, worsening economic conditions, rising rates of crime and juvenile delinquency, and the shortsighted segregationist housing policies of the City of New York, along with Jewish social mobility and African American in-migration, had reduced the Jewish population of Brownsville to negligible proportions.

In the mid-nineteenth century, Brownsville was primarily farmland, with low-lying marshes prone to flooding. The area was also the site of the city's largest waste dump and home to significant numbers of stone and building material suppliers. Although aesthetically less appealing than other parts of Brooklyn, the neighborhood of open spaces attracted a diverse population of English and Irish families, Jewish immigrants, and a small number of black farmers. Then, in 1861, Charles Brown, a real estate speculator, purchased a vast swath of what was then called New Lots, renamed the area Brown's Village, and set out to market it to the working classes of congested Manhattan.

By 1883 the village had 250 frame houses occupied in the main by Jews. In the 1890s, Jewish residency grew even more significantly. Immigrants eager to escape Manhattan's increasingly crowded and industrialized Lower East Side moved to Brownsville, from which they could now commute by trolley over the newly constructed Brooklyn Bridge to work in factories back in their old neighborhood.

Brownsville, Brooklyn. (Library of Congress)

Brooklyn land was also purchased by New York clothing manufacturers, wholesale garment merchants, and contractors, who, in the hope of producing goods at lower cost, established "outside" shops in Brownsville. The increased possibility of jobs, as well as the promise of less dense living conditions, further stimulated migration, and by the end of the nineteenth century a sizable "Jewish town," pronounced "Brahnzvil" or "Brunzvil" by its mainly Yiddish-speaking inhabitants, had taken shape.

By moving to Brownsville, some Jewish manufacturers, including Elias Kaplan, who built an industrial unit on Watkins Street in 1882, sought not only to reduce costs but also to avoid the union organizers active on the Lower East Side. Kaplan, who employed more than one hundred Jewish men and women, was not, however, entirely unconcerned about his workers. He built relatively low-cost

housing for them and located Brownsville's very first synagogue, Ohev Shalom, in his factory.

As the neighborhood's Jewish population multiplied, more synagogues were built, including Eitz Chaim Machzikei Horov (1883), Beth Hamedrosh Hagadol (1889), and Thilim Keshet Israel (1891). These were relatively large congregations housed in impressive buildings and were still operating as late as the 1950s. But at the beginning of the twentieth century, most shuls were to be found in storefronts or converted residences and were generally short-lived.

The growing number of Jews in Brownsville led to ethnic tensions and even anti-Jewish violence, perpetrated mainly by English and Irish residents of neighboring East Flatbush and East New York. In 1890, the attacks moved Brownsville Jews to create the Hebrew Protection League, a self-defense organization. Antisemitism also included the refusal of many landowners in outlying districts to sell to Jews, and this helped push Brownsville's development upward rather than outward, leading to increased congestion in rows of multistoried buildings of railroad flats. Congestion was exacerbated by the construction of entrance ramps to the Williamsburg Bridge (1903) and the Manhattan Bridge (1909), which dislocated thousands of East Siders and helped relocate them and others to several Brooklyn neighborhoods, including Brownsville.

By 1904, Brownsville had nearly 25,000 people and the feel and look of an urban settlement. In the next decade, population skyrocketed, fed by steady streams from Europe, the Lower East Side, and Williamsburg. The expansion of the IRT and BMT subways to Brownsville continued to push the population upward even as World War I and legislation restricting immigration reduced the flow from Europe. By 1910, with nearly 90,000 inhabitants, the neighborhood was 85 percent Jewish, and it remained overwhelmingly so as it grew through 1940 to nearly 110,000 people.

With a higher population than many American cities, Brownsville included several clusters of small-scale manufacturing enterprises and a variety of shopping districts. Brownsville-born writer William Poster remembered "seven blocks of furniture stores on Rockaway Avenue . . . ; five teeming, pungent blocks of pushcarts, groceries and 'appetizing' stores on Belmont Avenue," and "a huge six-block square of junkshops, tinsmithies, stables, and garages and miscellaneous small enterprises" (Poster 1950). Brownsville's commercial section was the largest in Brooklyn, and Pitkin Avenue was at its center. The palatial Loew's Pitkin Movie Theatre with 3,600 seats, which opened in 1929 at the corner of East New York Avenue, was the showpiece of this shopping street and entertained Brownsville residents with "talkies" as well as Yiddish theater pieces.

By 1942, 372 stores lined Pitkin Avenue from Stone to Ralph. As many as 8 banks, 43 men's clothing establishments, dozens of stores for women's apparel, several restaurants, florists, furniture dealers, and liquor stores, and scores of other enterprises employed 1,000 people and did $90 million of business annually. A number of Brownsville businesses, including Abe Stark's Pitkin Avenue outlet for men's suits and Fortunoff's Jewelry on Livonia Avenue, grew from small shops to large stores that served all of Brooklyn. Still, few Brownsville families

achieved economic success or middle-class status. Large numbers of residents were employed in the garment and construction industries, and Brownsville remained a working-class neighborhood, one that the Great Depression hit especially hard. In the 1930s and 1940s, almost everyone, even owners of small businesses, barely scraped along.

Density provided the critical mass necessary to sustain Brownsville's commercial life, but it also meant a variety of unhealthy conditions, including overcrowding, and hastened the departure of the more upwardly mobile from the neighborhood. Between 1925 and 1940, Brownsville's population declined by 9,000, even as Brooklyn's increased by more than half a million. Still, Brownsville was the most heavily populated neighborhood in the borough (140 per residential acre) and was marked by considerable tenement deterioration and congestion, as well as overextended water and sewage facilities, crumbling schools, and many of the pathologies associated with widespread poverty: poor health, crime, and juvenile delinquency (Pritchett 2002, Sorin 1990).

In 1939 the New York City Department of Health reported that infant and maternal mortality rates for Brownsville were somewhat higher than for Brooklyn generally, and the morbidity rates for venereal disease, tuberculosis, and diphtheria were considerably higher. Similar rates were reported through 1942. Civic activists, including the writer, lawyer, and leftist social reformer Milton Goell and the liberal-minded Rabbi Alter Landesman of the Hebrew Educational Society (HES), were concerned about these "unwholesome" effects of impoverished living conditions. Areas with poor health and those with inadequate housing, it was argued, tended to coincide. Reformers drew an even stronger link between bad housing and lack of recreational facilities on the one hand and crime, gang fights, and juvenile delinquency on the other.

When Brownsville teacher and novelist Arthur Granit wrote that in Jewish "Brownsville, decaying even in those days . . . it was nothing unusual to have a body shot up and thrown in some side alleyway," he surely exaggerated (Granit 1985). But by the late 1920s, serious crime, mostly the activities of "murder-for-money" gangsters in Brownsville, had put the neighborhood on the national map. In 1940 William O'Dwyer, the new district attorney for Brooklyn, announced that crime in the Brownsville section had been getting worse for some time. Twenty murders had been committed in the district in 1939, mostly by the gang of Brooklyn hit men dubbed "Murder, Inc."

At its modest headquarters at Midnight Rose's candy store in Brownsville at the corner of Livonia and Saratoga avenues, the gang, including Lepke Buchalter, Abe ("Kid Twist") Reles, Motl ("Bugsy") Goldstein, and Philip ("Little Farfel") Cohen, met to sip egg creams as well as to plan assassinations. With men such as Joey Adonis, Lucky Luciano, and Albert Anastasia at or near the top of the organization, Murder, Inc., was certainly not a Jewish monopoly. And although Jewish criminals would be fewer in the postwar period and much less tied to a Jewish environment, adult crime in the 1930s and 1940s was clearly part of the Jewish ethnic milieu of Brownsville. As was juvenile delinquency: Henry Roth's novel *Call It Sleep* (1934) and Arthur Granit's *The Time of the Peaches* (1959) drew attention to the problem of poverty and youth crime in Brownsville. So did Irving Shulman's *The Amboy Dukes* (1947), a startlingly graphic picture of Brownsville Jewish youngsters involved with gangs, guns, rape, and murder. The Amboy Dukes were hardly meant to be representative of pervasive behavior patterns, but the novel, a fusion of the sociologist's analysis and the writer's art, proclaimed that Jews, like other groups in modern urban America, had the problem of juvenile delinquency.

Brownsville was clearly a squalid and dangerous neighborhood—indeed, a slum—looked upon with contempt by the "better classes" of Brooklyn and the rest of New York City. But it was also a vibrant Jewish community with supportive social and religious institutions. There were educational, charitable, and mutual aid institutions visible every few blocks. The largest library in Brooklyn (until 1940), with signs in Yiddish and an annual circulation of 330,000, sat on Glenmore and Watkins in the heart of the immigrant Jewish community (Tenenbaum 1949). And the first children's library in New York City, a Tudor-style brick building perhaps more at home in the English midlands than in Brownsville, was built on Stone Avenue in 1914. Also on Stone Avenue were the Brooklyn District office of the Jewish Board of Guardians and the New York Free Loan Society. The Ladies' Free Loan Society, the Hebrew Ladies' Day Nursery, and the HES were on Hopkinson Avenue. The Pride of Judea Children's Home on Dumont Avenue, the Hebrew Free Loan Society on Pitkin Avenue, and dozens of other organizations, such as the Daughters of Israel, which distributed food and medical aid to the poor, also did social service work in the neighborhood.

Brownsville also had a significant history of left–liberal activism. In 1915, the neighborhood sent Abraham Shiplacoff to the New York State Assembly, the very first Socialist to hold a seat in that legislative body. And in 1916, on Amboy Street, Brownsville witnessed the opening of the nation's first birth control clinic by the progressive pioneer Margaret Sanger. Jewish immigrant radicalism in Brownsville persisted into the 1920s and through the 1930s, when Jewish women of the neighborhood continued to be well represented in meat and rent strikes and in mobilizing voters, and when disproportionate numbers of Brownsville Communists were active in a variety of protest movements.

Brownsville had long been home to Workmen's Circle and Industrial Worker's Order clubs (Socialist and Communist mutual aid societies, respectively) as well as to local headquarters of militant unions such as the United Hebrew Trades and the International Ladies' Garment Workers, and on Sackman Street to the Labor Lyceum, which was often an arena for political mobilization and a forum for radical speakers. By 1942, the left-leaning Congress of Industrial Organizations (CIO) had also set up its own community councils in Brownsville.

Earlier, a confederation of neighborhood organizations created in 1938, the Brownsville Neighborhood Council (BNC), aimed to stimulate effective citizen participation in public affairs, to secure neighborhood improvements, and to cooperate with public and private agencies to promote the welfare of the Brownsville community. The BNC, whose public leaders included left–liberal activists Milton Goell and Alter Landesman, also worked to prevent juvenile delinquency by focusing on housing needs, health care, and education, and in the 1940s it was successful in securing public housing, child-care centers, and a new health center for Brownsville.

Also very much involved in the struggles for social welfare was the Brownsville Boys Club (BBC), which grew from an informal association of teenagers in 1940 fighting for access to gyms, playing fields, and increased recreational facilities generally into an agency of mutual aid, dedicated to social justice. The BBC was run for years by the youngsters themselves; through sports and various social and educational programs, it helped ameliorate youth violence and cooperated with the BNC in the struggle for racial integration and improved housing.

Public housing came to Brownsville just as the black population there was exploding and the general population, including the Jewish majority, was declining. Despite the facts that the Brownsville Houses were integrated in 1948 (a notable exception in NYC public housing) and that liberal Jewish Brownsville was more receptive to black neighbors than any other white neighborhood in Brooklyn, Brownsville would become, over the course of the next decade and a half, an African American and Latino ghetto.

Activist groups, including the Brownsville–East New York Jewish Community Council (formed in 1943), the BBC, and the BNC, joined now by such black leaders as the Reverend Boise Dent, tried to revitalize Brownsville and keep it a viable, multiethnic community. But, in the face of Cold War antileftism, government intransigence, entrenched racism, and a generally segregationist New York City housing policy, they failed to achieve the necessary reforms. Over time, this failure led to the departure of mobile, white, mostly Jewish residents, who, with the help of the GI Bill and Veteran's Administration loans, pursued comfortable quarters, safety, good schools, and modernized infrastructure.

With the Jewish exodus, Brownsville's synagogues declined in number from seventy-three in 1939 to fifty in 1951; many of these, without measurable congregations, were synagogues in name only. In the mid-1960s, with membership dwindling to a precious few, two of Brownsville's most distinguished synagogues, Chevra Torah Anshei Radishowitz and Beth Israel of Brownsville, sold their architecturally impressive buildings. The Hebrew Educational Society became virtually the last vestige of the Jewish community that had been founded in Brownsville in the late 1800s; and when the organization moved to new quarters in Canarsie in 1965, there were no significant Jewish institutions left in the neighborhood.

Jews continued to play a role, however, even as African Americans and Puerto Ricans came to constitute more than 90 percent of the population of Brownsville (Pritchett 2002). In 1962, for example, during the battle at Beth-El hospital (the largest employer in Brownsville) for union recognition and higher wages, African American and Latino activists (as independents and members of the National Association for the Advancement of Colored People and the Urban League) and strikers led by Local 1199 of the Hospital Workers Union were joined by white, mostly Jewish liberals. These included representatives of the Jewish Labor Committee, the Anti-Defamation League, the American Jewish Congress, and the *Jewish Daily Forward*, who argued that Jews (all thirty-six of the hospital's trustees were Jewish) had a special obligation to be fair to workers. Victory reinforced the notion that interracial cooperation could go a long way toward solving problems in changing neighborhoods such as Brownsville.

In 1968, the bitter struggle over community control of schools in Ocean Hill–Brownsville between the fledgling United Federation of Teachers, predominantly white and Jewish, and the largely black and Latino Brownsville Community Council led many to a less optimistic outlook. But from the 1940s to the 1960s, Jews, blacks, and Latinos in the Brooklyn neighborhood, though hindered by obstacles at the local, regional, and national levels, had, in the long tradition of their progressive community, worked together well in attempts to secure resources and rights for the beleaguered residents of Brownsville.

Gerald Sorin

References and Further Reading

Adamson, Florence. 1941. *A Study of the Recreational Facilities of the Brownsville Section of Brooklyn.* New York: Brownsville Neighborhood Council.

Brooklyn Communities. 1959. *Population Characteristics and Neighborhood Resources.* New York: Community Council of Greater New York.

Connolly, Harold X. 1977. *A Ghetto Grows in Brooklyn.* New York: New York University Press.

Donaldson, Greg. 1993. *The Ville.* New York: Ticknor and Fields.

Ford, Carole. 2000. *The Girls: Jewish Women of Brownsville, Brooklyn, 1940–1995.* Albany: State University of New York Press.

Granit, Arthur. 1985. *I Am from Brownsville.* New York: Philosophical Library.

Joselit, Jenna W. 1983. *Our Gang: Jewish Crime and the New York Jewish Community, 1900–1940.* Bloomington: Indiana University Press.

Kazin, Alfred. 1951. *A Walker in the City.* New York: Harcourt Brace.

Landesman, Alter. 1971. *Brownsville: The Birth, Development, and Passing of a Jewish Community in New York.* New York: Bloch.

Poster, William. 1950. "'Twas a Dark Night in Brownsville': Pitkin Avenue's Self-Made Generation." *Commentary* (May): 458–467.

Pritchett, Wendell. 2002. *Brownsville, Brooklyn: Blacks, Jews, and the Changing Face of the Ghetto.* Chicago: University of Chicago Press.

Savitch, Harold V. 1972. "Powerlessness in an Urban Ghetto: The Case of Political Biases and Differential Access in New York City." *Polity* (Fall): 19–56.

Sorin, Gerald. 1990. *The Nurturing Neighborhood: The Brownsville Boys Club and Jewish Community in Urban America.* New York: New York University Press.

Suher, David. 1948. *The Brownsville Neighborhood Council.* New York: New York School of Social Work.

Tenenbaum, Samuel. 1949. "Brownsville's Age of Learning: When the Library Stayed Open All Week." *Commentary* 8 (August): 173–178.

South Florida

During the 1970s, there was a popular television show, *All in the Family.* One day, a friend asked Archie Bunker, the star, about another friend, "the Hebe," whom he had not seen for a while. Archie answered, "He's gone to the 'Promised Land.'" "Oh," the friend replied, "the Hebe's gone to Israel." "No," Archie snapped back, "the Hebe's gone to Miami Beach." Between 1960 and 1972, the Jewish population in Florida grew three times faster than the general population. In Southeast Florida (Palm Beach, Broward, and Miami–Dade counties), the Jewish population grew from 50,000 in 1950 to close to 500,000 by 1980. The greater Miami Jewish population comprised nearly half of that total (230,000) and close to 20 percent of the total county population. Miami Beach, a small island off the mainland, was more than half Jewish (Sheskin 2005, Millon 1989). For those smitten with colonialism, "The Beach" was endearingly referred to as "New York South." South Florida, a peninsula encroached upon by malaria swamps (the Everglades) and bounded by water on three sides (the Atlantic, the Caribbean, and the Gulf of Mexico) and Lake Okeechobee on the north, had been transformed in three generations: from an absence of Jews in 1900 to the third most populated area for Jewry in the Americas.

By the 1970s, South Florida Jewry was engaged in every type of local industry and professional undertaking—finance, tourism, real estate, retail and wholesale merchandising, and manufacturing. They thrived on the high-rise condominium boom and took advantage of regional, national, and international expanding markets. As a result, those living in South Florida—particularly in greater Miami—built one of the foremost Jewish economic infrastructures in North America while erecting scores of synagogues, Jewish schools, and community centers.

Jews were politically active, committed voters, and Democrats. In the 1970s, the mayor of Miami Beach was Jewish, as were members of the city commission. Democratic Jewish state legislators were visible and influential. In 1974 Richard Stone of Miami Beach became the first Jew since David Levy Yulee, the "architect" of Florida statehood in 1845, to be elected to the U.S. Senate from Florida. On voting days, Miami Beach Jewish seniors were sighted marching to the polls en masse, organized by voting captains.

For many South Florida Jewish residents, Israel was a surrogate for Judaism and influenced their voting patterns. Political candidates who shared their pro-Israel ideology and liberal agendas were well received. South Florida Jews were frequent visitors to Israel and witnessed firsthand the uncanny similarity between Tel Aviv and Miami Beach. Both were around 26 degrees north latitude and had real estate on the water's edge. Both were modern cities founded in the early twentieth century, with international style (Bauhaus and Art Deco) architectural districts. Both had a significant concentration of Holocaust survivors. Just as Tel Aviv had blossomed into a Jewish tourist haven for American Jewry, so had Miami Beach become the American Jewish tourist capital for Israelis. Jokingly, Israeli fund-raisers visiting Miami would comment to their close friends that they had chosen the "wrong Promised Land."

Yet, three decades earlier (1940), fewer than 10,000 Jews lived between Palm Beach (on the eastern side of the peninsula), Sarasota (on the western side of the peninsula), and Key West, the southeasternmost tip of the United States (Sheskin 2005). Moreover, two decades earlier, in the 1950s, "Gentlemen's Agreements" still restricted Jews from purchasing land in South Florida. Yet South Florida, an invisible oasis with a handful of Jews on the eve of World War II, became paradise in one generation.

From Statehood (1845) through World War II (1945)

Sephardim were the early Jewish frontiersmen of Florida. They traveled as conversos (forced converts) with Columbus when he sailed to the Americas in the late fifteenth century and may have accompanied Ponce de León when he landed near St. Augustine, Florida, in 1513. Some scholars argue that Pedro Menendez Marques, the third Spanish governor of Florida (1577–1589), was a converso. The introduction of a Spanish Inquisition tribunal in Mexico in 1528, followed by others in Colombia and Peru, acutely reminded Sephardim of the consequences of visibly practicing their Judaism in the face of Catholic colonialism. The project MOSAIC: Jewish Life in Florida has hypothesized that Sephardim and conversos in the mercantile trade, escaping these tribunals in the sixteenth and seventeenth centuries, may have passed through South Florida. The twenty-three Jews who arrived in New Amsterdam in 1654, celebrated as the "founders" of American Jewry, were also Sephardim evading Catholic persecutors.

On March 3, 1845, Florida became the twenty-seventh state of the Union. There were a few dozen Jews in North Florida but no visible Jewish community. None lived in South Florida. Senator David Levy Yulee was a northern Floridian, a Southerner, and a Sephardic Jew. Levy County and the town of Yulee in Nassau County honor him. Levy Yulee, who married a Christian and agreed to raise his children as Christians, supported the Southern plantation system. Yulee was the first Jew to serve in the U.S. Senate, chosen seven years before his Louisiana cousin, Judah P. Benjamin. The Yulee family saga paralleled that of Sephardic Jewry following expulsion from Spain in 1492. They were "wandering Jews." In three centuries, they had migrated from Morocco to Gibraltar, to St. Thomas, to Cuba, and eventually to Spanish Florida.

The new twin engines of transportation—railroads and steamships—opened up north and central Florida in the post–Civil War era, but it was only in the 1890s, when Henry Flagler's Florida East Coast Railway pushed into Palm Beach and Miami, that they affected the development of South Florida. The few Jews who had migrated previously were lone pioneers who arrived by ship or on the Bay Stage Line that linked Lake Worth (Palm Beach) to Lemon City (Miami), a two-day stagecoach trip. Flagler, John D. Rockefeller's partner in the Standard Oil Company, can be considered the "father" of South Florida. Flagler appreciated that Americans, especially northern Protestants, would be attracted to his concept of an integrated hospitality (hotels) and transportation (train) system and to the land he made available for sale. Fiercely determined to exclude Jews, Flagler instituted the practice of restricted hotels and covenants. After Miami Beach was founded as a city in 1917, Carl Fisher, the owner of Prest-O-Lite (automobile lights) and the Indianapolis Speedway, followed

Flagler's precedent and offered "places in the sun" to non-Jewish clients on the beach. Miami's Chamber of Commerce slogan, "It's Always June in Miami," was parodied as "It's Always Jew'n in Miami" by the Ku Klux Klan, even though only a few hundred Jews lived there on the cusp of the Roaring Twenties.

The Jewish communities in South Florida grew slowly. Jews migrated especially from Key West (an American island that served as a commercial port for the Caribbean until the railroad arrived) and from Jewish communities in Georgia and the Northeast. Mitchell Wolfson arrived in Miami from Key West in 1915. Cofounder of WOMETCO (Wolfson Meyer Theater Company), Wolfson opened the first television station in Florida, WTVJ, and built the Miami Seaquarium. In 1943 he became the first Jewish mayor of Miami Beach. Joseph and Jennie Weiss, a New York couple, founded Joe's Stone Crab Restaurant at the tip of Miami Beach. Ninety years later, the family-run business is thriving and caters to American presidents and the Miami Dolphins football team. Max Lehrman and Rose Seitlin married in Miami in 1913 and moved to Ft. Lauderdale after their second daughter, Anne, was born in 1916. They opened a dry-goods store.

Some Jews immigrated directly from Russia and Romania, escaping pogroms. The Hebrew Immigrant Aid Society (HIAS) sent a few. Among them were Zionists Henry and Louis Zeitlin, Romanians, who tried to establish a proto-kibbutz (collective farm) in Homestead. The experiment attracted no Jews, and they moved on to Miami, the growing hub of South Florida. David Sokolow, a Russian immigrant, came with his bride, Gussie Rubinstein, to Dania; with their relative, Louis Brown, the couple started three stores in the county (Dania, Pompano, and Hollywood). Only a trickle of Jews settled on the gulf side of southern Florida during this period. The maintenance of Jewish identity and ritual was a challenge. When Isidor and Ida Cohen of Miami, early leaders in the Miami Jewish community, needed a *mohel* (ritual circumciser), they called on Rabbi Julian Shapo from Key West. The circumcision was front-page news in the *Miami Metropolis* (July 17, 1907). Little changed until after World War I.

The land boom of the 1920s, an expanding automobile transportation system (Dixie Highway), and commercial aviation (Pan American), packaged with appealing advertising campaigns, drew thousands to South Florida. Up and down the east and west coasts, land fever became an epidemic. Even the Jewish Agricultural Society sent Jewish immigrants from New York. Miami had special assets. Many northerners viewed Miami as a pleasure site with ample opportunity for gambling and access to illegal alcohol.

However, most of the development was short-lived. The boom went bust, and the hurricanes of 1926 and 1928 devastated South Florida. With the stock market crash, headlines screamed, "Miami Is Wiped Out." However, one change was immediately noticeable once the Depression rolled in: the center of gravity for the Jewish Floridian community had migrated from northern to southern Florida (Jacksonville to Miami). By 1939, a dozen Jewish-owned hotels took out ads in the Yiddish *Jewish Daily Forward* to spur Jewish tourism from New York.

By the 1930s, greater Miami's Jewish community in many ways resembled the Jewish community in New York institutionally, albeit with fewer organizational spin-offs. National philanthropic, social, and cultural institutions had offices in greater Miami: the United Jewish Aid Committee/the Jewish Welfare Bureau/Jewish Family Services (1920), the Zionist Organization of America (ZOA, 1926), Jewish newspapers (*Jewish Unity*, 1927; the *Jewish Floridian,* 1928), the Anti-Defamation League (ADL, 1933), the Jewish War Veterans (1937), the Greater Miami Jewish Federation (1938), and the American Jewish Congress (1939). There were local chapters of B'nai Brith, Hadassah, Young Judea, the Workmen's Circle, and the National Council of Jewish Women. Cemeteries (the earliest in 1913), synagogues (the earliest of the major denominations were Conservative, B'nai Zion/Beth David, 1912; Reform, Temple Israel, 1922; and Orthodox, Beth Jacob, 1927), congregational schools, community centers, and kosher hotels (the earliest, Nemo, in 1921) provided ample opportunity to live a Jewish life.

The onset of World War II dramatically changed South Florida. Tourist facilities, including restricted hotels, were converted to accommodate troops. The art deco hotels, designed by architects such as Henry Hohauser with his streamlined and nautical modern style, also came under this edict. One-fourth of all Army Air Forces officer candidates and one-fifth of its enlisted men trained at Miami Beach. Many were Jewish. Frequently, their families traveled to South Florida to be close by. They got "sand in their shoes" and vowed to return when the war was over.

The Golden Years: 1945–1980

After World War II, Jews increasingly migrated to the Sun Belt to live or vacation. South Florida's Jewish population grew from 10,000 in 1940, to 50,000 in 1950, and to 134,000 in 1960. A decade later, it nearly doubled again, and then again a decade later to 500,000 (Sheskin 2005). Although much of the growth was within greater Miami, Jews became more and more visible in every city up and down the peninsula, from Naples and Sanibel Island on the west side to Boca Raton and Bal Harbor on the east. In each case, a Jewish microcommunity developed institutionally and organizationally. Temple Sinai of Hollywood was founded in 1956; Temple Beth El, the first congregation in Boca Raton, was established in 1967, the year of the Israeli Six Day War.

With the transfer of aviation technology from the military to civilians in the postwar years and the development of air conditioning to cool homes and hotel rooms in the early 1950s, greater Miami became the number one destination for Jews migrating to the South. Ad firms sold Miami Beach to northern Jewry as a winter Catskills. With the opening of the Fontainebleau Hotel in 1954, Miami Beach became the easily accessible winter playground for American Jewry. A decade later, condominiums began competing with hotels for the tourist dollar, and condominium owners began identifying themselves as "snowbirds."

With tourism came entertainment, especially in Miami Beach. In 1960, the Miss USA and Miss Universe pageants became annual events. In 1963 the Jackie Gleason television show was launched. In 1964 Cassius Clay (Muhammad Ali) won the world heavyweight boxing championship in Miami. Judy Garland, Frank Sinatra, Ed Sullivan, and Louis Armstrong are only a few of the celebrities who drew audiences night after night during "the season." Jewish hotel owners lured superstars who had converted to Judaism—Marilyn Monroe, Sammy Davis Jr., and Elizabeth Taylor—to the Beach, where they were photographed with their Jewish clientele. Isaac Bashevis Singer lived in Surfside. Elie Wiesel and Meyer Lansky had condos on the Beach. Throughout the 1960s and 1970s, Miami Beach was in a "league of its own."

After Castro's revolution in Cuba in 1959, about 3,500 Cuban Jews arrived in Miami. In subsequent years, Central and South American Hispanics escaping political persecution and seeking social justice and human rights flooded the gates of greater Miami. A significant number were Jews. Over time, they reestablished their institutions (the Cuban-Hebrew Social Circle; the Cuban Sephardic Hebrew Congregation; the Cuban-Hebrew Congregation of Miami).

Because South Florida was antisemitic, racist, and segregated, liberal Jews migrating from the North built partnerships with African Americans to weaken discriminatory practices and change laws. The ADL played a vital role in this process, prodding private educational institutions, golf clubs, and other organizations to open their doors. Following the U.S. Supreme Court ruling in *Brown v. Board of Education of Topeka, Kansas* in 1954, African Americans began to be admitted to formerly segregated public schools and universities in the South. After the decision, Senator Richard Stone's father, Alfred, hosted an African American Baptist convention at his Blackstone Hotel in Miami Beach. He had to send his son, Richard, and the family off the island because of death threats during the convention. In the following decade, rabbis throughout South Florida advocated for civil rights. Congregations were bombed. The Ku Klux Klan snarled. Slowly, desegregation occurred. Ironically, some of the liberal parents who strongly supported civil rights and integration were not in favor of busing their white children to black schools or busing blacks to white schools. Miami Beach High School, with 90 percent Jewish students, required a Florida Supreme Court decision (1970) before African Americans on the mainland (Overtown) could be bused across the causeway to Miami Beach. Miami Beach white children were not bused to black schools on the mainland.

Among the many rabbis in South Florida who supported civil rights and built nationally prominent institutions in this period, three stand out: Joseph Narot (Temple Israel), Irving Lehrman (Temple Emanu-El), and Leon Kronish (Temple Beth Sholom). Among the three, Leon Kronish of Miami Beach was critical in bringing an Israeli presence to South Florida, Diaspora Jewry, and Reform Judaism. Under his direction, El Al began flights to Miami, and an Israeli consulate was established. Kronish led the effort to establish the American Israel Histadrut (labor union) Foundation. In addition, he was instrumental in shaping the policy that called for entering rabbinical students in the Reform movement to spend their first year of study in Israel. In short, Kronish was committed to "Israelization"—transforming Zionism to strengthen the bond between American Jewry and Israelis (Green 1995).

Many in South Florida shared Kronish's passion for Israel. Zionists such as Shepard Broad (a member of the Sonneborn Institute) and Ed Kaufmann (president, ZOA) led the clandestine effort to procure arms, boats, and planes from South Florida's World War II surplus to be shipped to Palestine/Israel in the late 1940s. Max Orovitz, Sam Blank, Dan Ruskin, and Samuel Friedland, affectionately known as the "Miami Group," were instrumental in raising capital and in developing the Israeli Dan Hotels. On the other hand, Israeli politicians (Golda Meir, Yitzhak Rabin, Menachem Begin, Abba Eban) made frequent trips to South Florida to inspire the flock and meet with local and national leadership. For Israelis, Miami was the "winter campaign capital of American Jewry."

These three decades, the 1950s, 1960s, and 1970s, were the golden years for greater Miami and South Florida Jewry. One snowbird summarized the significance for North American Jewry: "What we have here is a cumulative 800 million years of Jewish experience walking around. Everywhere is the 'world of our fathers and mothers'" (Green 1995). Soon, however, this would all change. The generation that had escaped pogroms and European persecution, experienced the Holocaust and empathized with social justice issues, and had strong Zionist sentiments with an ample dosage of *Yiddishkeit* would be part of history.

Reshaping Jewish Identity 1980–2007

In the early twenty-first century, about 10 percent of the American Jewish population lives in South Florida (600,000). Only New York and Southern California have larger concentrations of Jews. Yet, books on American Jewry, such as Jonathan Sarna's *American Judaism* (2004), a tribute to 350 years of Judaism in American life, still ignore Miami and South Florida. The Jewish population of greater Miami, once the jewel of South Florida Jewry, has shrunk to less than half its size a generation ago (113,000) due to mortality and the preference of many northerners, especially retirees, for other South Florida locations, such as Marco Island, Naples, Venice, Sarasota, and Ft. Myers on the west coast. All have substantial Jewish populations with a vibrant organizational life. On the east coast, Jews choose Broward County first (234,000: Hollywood, Hallandale, Ft. Lauderdale, Coral Springs, Deerfield, Margate, Pembroke Pines, and Plantation), with Palm Beach County a close second (218,000: Boca Raton, Delray Beach, West Palm Beach, Boynton Beach, and Jupiter) (Sheskin 2005). The center of gravity of the Jewish South Floridian community has moved forty miles north to Boca Raton, a suburban, upscale, gated *shtetl* (community).

In contrast to the Golden Years, twenty-first century South Florida Jewry is disproportionately a retiree population. Compared to 18 percent nationally, 50 percent of the Jews are age sixty-five and over. Hundreds of millions of dollars have been expended on developing Jewish institutions; yet South Florida Jewry's commitment to their Jewishness (measured by synagogue and community center membership and Jewish Federation participation) remains well below the national median. Moreover, it is unclear whether South Florida's Jewish population will be replenished in the next generation. The challenges facing Jewish organizations are overwhelming.

Natural forces have also played a role in reshaping South Florida Jewry. In August 1992, Hurricane Andrew smashed into South Miami and destroyed much of the Jewish community. It was the costliest disaster in American history until Hurricane Katrina traumatized New Orleans in 2005.

Today, South Florida's Jewish community is being transformed by the changing ethnic American landscape: the Hispanization of America. In 1960 the Hispanic population of Miami was 5 percent; today it pushes 60 percent. One-fifth of South Florida is Hispanic (Beacon Council 2002). This has changed the composition of Miami Jewry. Jews from Colombia, Venezuela, Brazil, and Argentina have joined "Jewbans" (Jewish Cubans) to strengthen their ethnic (Hispanic) voice. In 1989, South Floridian Hispanic Jews made the difference in sending a Catholic Cuban to Congress rather than a Jew. Ethnicity, not religious identification, was the deciding factor.

The Hispanization of greater Miami has led to "white flight." The non-Hispanic white population of greater Miami has decreased from 80 percent in 1960 to 20 percent in 2000. Consequently, the "winter Catskills" have evaporated, and a significant number of non-Hispanic Jews have left Miami and migrated to other parts of South Florida. The ensuing migration to Boca and its environs bred many unanticipated outcomes. Synagogues, day schools (Donna Klein, Solomon Schechter, and Yeshiva High School), and communal agencies were opened. Jews are now well represented politically throughout South Florida in municipal,

county, state, and federal councils and legislatures. Many representatives are women (Nan Rich, Debbie Wasserman-Schultz, and Gwen Margolis). Jewish federations and institutions reach out to the Jewish Hispanic population and cater to their specific needs, often under the guidance of organizations such as the Miami chapter of the Federation of Latin American Sephardim (FeSeLa). Jewish Hispanics have served as a bridge into the non-Jewish Hispanic community and have repeatedly used their political capital to gain support for Israel and American Jewish causes (Holocaust curriculums, hate crime legislation, and Jewish History Month).

In addition to Hispanic Jews, South Florida has welcomed Israelis, Soviet Jews and, more recently, Jews from France evading Islamization. In Aventura, one hears Hebrew; in Sunny Isles, Russian; in Hollywood, French. These are often combined with other languages such as Yiddish, Ladino, Spanish, and Portuguese. Yet despite language differences, generation gaps, and variances in year of immigration, the integration of these communities is reflected in a number of projects (e.g., The March of the Living). Educational institutions such as the University of Miami seed many: the Sue and Len Miller Center for Contemporary Judaic Studies, Sephardic Studies, MOSAIC: Jewish Life in Florida, the Jewish Museum of Florida, and the Miami Beach Holocaust Memorial.

The multiculturalism of South Florida Jewry has created a unique "New South." The climate, cruise ships, and real estate continue to draw Jews—the East European retiree, the Hispanic refugee, and the dual-citizen Israeli, all seeking the "Promised Land." Together with third- and fourth-generation American Jews, all have found in South Florida a Jewish haven, "a state of mind and a state of being."

Henry A. Green

References and Further Reading
Allman, T. D. 1987. *Miami: City of the Future.* New York: Atlantic Monthly Press.
Bettinger-Lopez, Caroline. 2000. *Cuban-Jewish Journeys: Searching for Identity, Home and History in Miami.* Knoxville: University of Tennessee Press.
Diner, Hasia. 2004. *The Jews of the United States.* Berkeley: University of California Press.
Green, Henry A. 1995. *Gesher Vakesher, Bridges and Bonds: The Life of Leon Kronish.* Atlanta, GA: Scholars Press.
Greenbaum, Andrea, ed. 2005. *Jews of South Florida.* Waltham, MA: Brandeis University Press.

Liebman, Malvina, and Seymour Liebman. 1980. *Jewish Frontiersmen: Historical Highlights of Early South Florida Jewish Communities*. Miami Beach: Jewish Historical Society of South Florida.

Mehling, Harold. 1960. *The Most of Everything: The Story of Miami Beach*. New York: Harcourt Brace.

Millon, Adrienne. 1989. "The Changing Size and Spatial Distribution of the Jewish Population of South Florida." MA thesis, University of Miami.

Moore, Deborah Dash. 1994. *To the Golden Cities: Pursuing the American Jewish Dream in Miami and L.A.* New York: Free Press.

Redford, Polly. 1970. *Billion-Dollar Sandbar: A Biography of Miami Beach*. New York: Dutton.

Sheskin, Ira. 2005. "Ten Percent of American Jews." In *Jews of South Florida*, edited by Andrea Greenbaum, pp. 4–18. Waltham, MA: Brandeis University Press.

Los Angeles

Early in the twenty-first century, Los Angeles Jewry, with a population of nearly 520,000, constitutes 10 percent of the U.S. Jewish population. Jews make up about 5 percent of the population of Los Angeles County. Though Jewish names appear in the census of 1850, and Jews were active in the life of the booming City of Angels in the late nineteenth and early twentieth centuries, it was in the post–World War II era that Los Angeles became the second most populous center of Jewish life in America. By the beginning of the twenty-first century, Los Angeles Jewry had become a vibrant, well-rooted community, serving as a bellwether for emerging trends in Jewish life.

When California became a state in 1850, a census of Los Angeles County included eight recognizably Jewish names (Vorspan and Gartner 1970). Religious services seem to have been held intermittently in Los Angeles starting in 1851, and a Hebrew Benevolent Society was established in 1854. The Hebrew Benevolent Society, which extended aid to Jews and non-Jews, was the first charitable group of any kind to be established in the rough-and-tumble city, and it eventually metamorphosed into the Jewish Family Service of Los Angeles. As in other areas of Jewish settlement, one of the first acts of the society was the acquisition of burial grounds.

By 1860, 100 Jews are estimated to have settled in Los Angeles, constituting fewer than 1 percent of the more than 11,000 residents of the developing county (Vorspan and Gartner 1970). Yet, a synagogue (Congregation B'nai Brith, today's Wilshire Boulevard Temple) was formally established in 1862 with the arrival of Rabbi Abraham Wolf Edelman (of Poland by way of San Francisco), who served as rabbi, *hazzan*, *shochet*, *mohel*, teacher, and ambassador to the larger community. The congregation's first building was dedicated in 1873.

Among the early Jewish residents of Los Angeles were such successful business families as the Newmarks and the Hellmans, whose mercantile interests ranged from wholesale groceries to apparel to banking. Jews were integral to the economic, civic, and social life of the community; indeed, one of the city's first eight Jews, Morris L. Goodman, was a member of the first City Council in 1850. Although most Jews were lax in their religious observance, Congregation B'nai Brith, led by Rabbi Edelman, maintained a traditional ritual—albeit with mixed seating—from its inception to 1884, when it moved toward religious Reform, joining the Union of Hebrew American Congregations (now the Union for Reform Judaism) in 1903.

By 1900, 2,500 Jews lived in Los Angeles within the larger population of 170,000 (Vorspan and Gartner 1970). One-third of these Jews lived downtown, the area of first Jewish settlement, representing one-third of that area's inhabitants (Sandberg 1986). In the ensuing decades, as Los Angeles experienced a population boom, Jews settled in a variety of neighborhoods, including Exposition Park, Central Avenue, Temple Street, West Adams, the Wilshire District, and Hollywood. With rising migration in the 1920s, Boyle Heights—east of downtown—became the largest visibly Jewish neighborhood on the West Coast, though it was also home to large numbers of Latinos, Molokan Russians, Japanese, and African Americans. Secular Yiddishists, political progressives, traditionally observant Jews, and Zionists—American-born and recent immigrants—were to be found in the culturally diverse streets of Boyle Heights.

The growth of the Jewish population of Los Angeles in the 1920s and 1930s outpaced the city's population surge. Although the great majority of Jewish newcomers to the city were Eastern European immigrants—often relocating to Los Angeles after stops in New York or Chicago—Sephardic Jews from Turkey, Greece, and Rhodes also joined the westward migration, many of them settling in South Los Angeles. Each immigrant group established schools, synagogues, and social welfare organizations that primarily served its subcultural population.

During the boom period of the 1920s, Jewish entrepreneurs stood at the forefront of the developing film industry, founding Columbia Pictures, Metro-Goldwyn-Mayer, Paramount Pictures, Warner Brothers, and Universal Studios. Jews were also extensively involved in the clothing industry, as workers as well as manufacturers. Increasing numbers of Jews were engaged in clerical, managerial, and sales occupations. As elsewhere in the country during this period, social prejudice against Jews penetrated all levels of society. Jews were excluded, for example, from the Chamber of Commerce and the California Club, as well as from other communal and civic groups that they had helped to establish.

Jewish social organizations, as well as more than thirty congregations, served the needs of a growing community. By 1940, nearly 2.3 million people lived in Los Angeles County, among them nearly 130,000 Jews (Sandberg 1986); by 1951, 315,000 Jews were among the county's more than 4 million inhabitants (Vorspan and Gartner 1970). In the immediate post–World War II years, 1945–1948, 66,000 Jews are estimated to have settled in Los Angeles (Vorspan and Gartner 1970). Among the army veterans who settled in Los Angeles were many Jews who had been introduced to the area through periods of training at West Coast army bases. A disproportionately high percentage of the Jewish postwar newcomers were from the Midwest.

The San Fernando Valley, sparsely populated before the war, was home to more than 1 million inhabitants by the late 1950s. Jews made up 10 percent of valley residents, though in some areas they constituted 20–30 percent of the local population (Moore 1994). Today, some 250,000 Jews, about 50 percent of the Jewish population of Los Angeles, make the greater valleys area their home (Jewish Federation of Greater Los Angeles [JFGLA] 1998).

In the late 1940s and 1950s, the New York–based Jewish Theological Seminary (Conservative), Hebrew Union College (Reform), and Yeshiva University (Orthodox) all established branch institutions in what was, by 1955, the second-largest Jewish community in the country. Though Yeshiva University eventually closed its Los Angeles Teachers' Institute, the Orthodox-sponsored Touro College launched a Los Angeles branch in 2005. Jewish summer camps were established in the greater Los Angeles area, including the innovative Brandeis Camp Institute (later known as Brandeis-Bardin Institute in memory of its visionary founding director, Shlomo Bardin), operating re-

treat experiences in Jewish living for collegians and adults. An expanded Bureau of Jewish Education (1945) organized and advanced Jewish educational opportunities for children and youth. The Jewish Community Council, an umbrella of local Jewish service delivery organizations (later to merge with the Federation of Jewish Welfare Organizations and to become known as the Jewish Federation-Council), built the Jewish Community Building at 590 North Vermont in 1951. Following the Jewish population, in 1976 it moved west to Wilshire Boulevard on the Beverly Hills border.

In 1953, Rosalind Wiener (later Wyman) became the first Jew elected to the Los Angeles City Council in more than fifty years, only the second woman to be elected to the council and, at age twenty-two, the youngest member ever elected. In the ensuing decades, Jews forged alliances with many of the groups active in Los Angeles political life. Jews played an active role in the region's civil and human rights movements and figured prominently in a coalition of ethnic groups that worked successfully to elect Tom Bradley mayor in 1973. Notable elected officials early in the twenty-first century with deep roots in the Los Angeles Jewish community include congressmen Howard Berman and Henry Waxman and county supervisor Zev Yaroslavsky.

In Los Angeles, large synagogues in developing neighborhoods came to provide many of the social and informal program services performed in some localities by Jewish community centers. At the beginning of the twenty-first century, Jewish community centers in Hollywood–Los Feliz, the West Side, the East Valley, the North Valley, and the West Valley struggled to define themselves, attract a constituency, and develop financial stability.

As in other communities across the United States, Jewish day schools developed on a significant scale in the fifty years after World War II. From one small, struggling day school in 1940, by the beginning of the twenty-first century Los Angeles was home to thirty-six full-day Jewish schools serving nearly 10,000 students in grades K-12. By the end of the twentieth century, more than 12,000 students were enrolled in part-time religious education programs sponsored by fifty-four congregations, while the Los Angeles Hebrew High School (Conservative) and Union Hebrew High School (Reform) provided part-time Hebrew-based instruction to hundreds of high school youth. A growing number of early childhood centers (sixty by the turn of the century) educated 7,000 children. Paralleling national trends, Hillel facilities and programs were expanded at area colleges and universities in the 1990s, and local universities included robust programs in Jewish studies.

By the closing decades of the twentieth century, the Jewish population of Los Angeles was estimated to have reached 519,000 persons. The population had been augmented by migration, including an influx of approximately 25,000 Jews from the former Soviet Union and 17,000 from Iran (JFGLA 1998). Additional immigrant groups included Israelis and Jews from South Africa. With an estimated 1.7 total Jewish fertility rate, Los Angeles's Jewish population is aging; while in 1979 11 percent of Los Angeles Jews were over 65, in 1997 the percentage had risen to 20.4, and it is projected to be 31 percent by the year 2020 (JFGLA 1998).

Yet, there is considerable vitality in Jewish life and culture at the beginning of the twenty-first century. Among the newer institutional expressions of Jewish activity in Los Angeles were the Simon Wiesenthal Center's Museum of Tolerance, the Skirball Cultural Center, which focuses on the American Jewish experience, a number of *Kolelim*—clusters of Talmudic scholars pursuing intensive (traditional) Jewish study and, in many cases, conducting community "outreach" programs—dozens of Chabad-sponsored congregations and schools, and rabbinical ordination programs at the Los Angeles branch of Hebrew Union College–Jewish Institute of Religion, the Ziegler School at the University of Judaism (now independent of the Jewish Theological Seminary, though maintaining academic affiliation with the parent institution), and the Academy for Jewish Religion, California, a nondenominational institution of higher Jewish learning. Notwithstanding the proliferation of Jewish educational and religious opportunities, 1997 data reflected a synagogue affiliation rate of 34 percent, significantly below the national average (JFGLA 1998). Still, there is an ever-expanding marketplace of synagogue options, and Los Angeles is home to such "first of their kind" congregations as the Synagogue for the Performing Arts, Temple Beth Solomon of the Deaf, and Beth Chayim Chadashim (a congregation serving gays and lesbians).

The Jews of Los Angeles are well represented in the fields of medicine, law, arts and entertainment, education, business, real estate, construction, and sales. There are thriving Jewish educational and cultural centers in Los Angeles, and more Jews are more intensively connected with Jewish life than ever before in the city's history. Yet, amid the riches of culture and considerable economic success, there remains the challenge of poverty—the Jewish community's 1997 population survey identified 13 percent of Jewish households (10 percent of the Jewish population) as living below government-defined poverty indices (JFGLA 2000)—an aging population, and weakening identification with Jewish life among many, particularly as the Jewish population becomes more widely dispersed.

Gil Graff and Stephen J. Sass

References and Further Reading

JFGLA. 1998. *LAJPS '97.* Los Angeles: The Jewish Federation.

JFGLA. 2000. *Needs of the Community.* Los Angeles: The Jewish Federation.

Moore, Deborah Dash. 1994. *To the Golden Cities: Pursuing the American Jewish Dream in Miami and L.A.* New York: Free Press.

Phillips, Bruce A. 1986. "L.A. Jewry: A Demographic Portrait." In *American Jewish Year Book 86,* pp. 126–194. Philadelphia: Jewish Publication Society of America.

Sandberg, Neil C. 1986. *Jewish Life in Los Angeles: A Window to Tomorrow.* Lanham, MD: University Press of America.

Sass, Stephen J. 1982. *Jewish Los Angeles: A Guide.* Los Angeles: Jewish Federation Council of Greater Los Angeles.

Vorspan, Max, and Lloyd P. Gartner. 1970. *History of the Jews of Los Angeles.* San Marino, CA: Huntington Library.

Chicago

Until about World War II, Chicago was the third-largest Jewish city in the world. German Jews were among the earliest settlers in the city and were followed by even greater numbers of East European Jews. Through the years, Chicago Jews were very active in Jewish movements, including the founding of the first organized Zionist group in America and the establishment of the Anti-Defamation League. Arriving as poor immigrants, in time they progressed in industry and the professions and became the founders of numerous major corporations. Many became prominent in government, the arts and sciences, and culture, both in the city and nation. Eight received the Nobel Prize.

The first Jews to settle in Chicago came in 1841, shortly after it had been incorporated (1833) as a muddy little lakefront town with 350 inhabitants. These early Jewish settlers came mainly from the German states, especially Bavaria, with smaller numbers from adjacent areas such as Austria and Bohemia. One of these early settlers was Henry Horner, whose grandson and namesake became the first Jewish governor of Illinois almost a century later. Like him, the early Jewish immigrants came mainly because of discrimination and harsh treatment in their homelands and the lure of freedom and opportunity in America. Many started out as peddlers with packs on their backs and later opened small grocery, dry-goods, tailoring, and clothing stores in the downtown area, where they lived behind or above their stores.

The Jews started developing community institutions shortly after their arrival in Chicago. In 1845 the first organized Jewish religious service in the city was held for Yom Kippur, the Day of Atonement, above a Jewish-owned dry-goods store with a bare *minyan* (the required quorum of ten men) present. In the same year, they organized the Jewish Burial Society, and in 1846 they purchased an acre of land for forty-six dollars for use as a Jewish cemetery. In 1847, with a Jewish population of fewer than a hundred, some twenty men organized the first synagogue, Kehilath Anshe Ma'ariv (Congregation of the People of the West, or KAM). One of its founders, Abraham Kohn, had pushed for its formation so the community would have a rabbi and a *shochet* (ritual slaughterer), which would allow his mother to follow her strict kosher dietary laws.

In 1851, as the congregation grew, it built its own wood-frame building, the first synagogue building in Illinois, at a cost of $12,000. Although initially Orthodox, KAM was not sufficiently orthodox for the increasing number of Jews arriving from the Posen area of (Polish) Prussia. In 1852 they broke away from KAM, organized and built their own Orthodox synagogue, Kehilath B'nai Sholom (Congregation Sons of Peace), and used the Polish *siddur* (prayer book). A few years later, another dissatisfied group arose within KAM, who found KAM too orthodox. Thus in 1861, twenty-six men formed the Sinai Reform Congregation and, like the other two congregations, built a synagogue in the downtown area. Its first spiritual leader was Dr. Bernard Felsenthal, who was not a rabbi but was very active in the national Jewish arena. Two of these synagogues still exist. The Jewish community also founded

other organizations. The 1862 city directory listed eleven Jewish organizations, including a B'nai B'rith lodge, a literary association, cemeteries, the Hebrew Benevolent Society, and a number of women's groups—all under the umbrella of the first central Jewish relief organization of Chicago, the United Hebrew Relief Association.

By 1860 there were an estimated 1,500 Jews, mainly from Central Europe, out of a total Chicago population of about 100,000. The Jews rapidly adapted to America. They got along well with their non-Jewish neighbors, who were primarily European immigrants, many also from Germany. By 1861, twenty years after the first permanent Jewish settlers arrived, four Jews had already served in public office, three as aldermen and one as city clerk.

By the time of the Civil War, Jews had made considerable progress in business and in professions such as law and medicine. Over the years, many of their modest early businesses grew into well-known national companies, including Florsheim; Spiegel; Aldens; Kuppenheimer (clothing); Hart, Schaffner and Marx; A. G. Becker (finance); Albert Pick (hotels); Brunswick (recreation equipment); and Inland Steel.

During the Civil War, the Jewish community rapidly organized and financed a complete company of a hundred volunteer soldiers, which fought in the Battle of Gettysburg and other important battles. Dankmar Adler, who was the son of the rabbi of KAM and who later became a renowned architect and partner of Louis Sullivan, was wounded in the war.

The Great Chicago Fire of 1871 hit the Jewish community especially hard. Downtown Chicago, where so many of the Jews lived and had businesses, was devastated. Five of the city's seven synagogues were destroyed, as were four B'nai B'rith lodges and other Jewish institutions, including Chicago's first Jewish hospital, Jewish Hospital, which had opened in 1868. After the fire, a small number of Jews moved north of the Chicago River, forming the nucleus of the city's North Side Jewish community.

The vast majority, who were still mainly German Jews, gradually moved southward, eventually concentrating in the fashionable Chicago lakefront communities of Kenwood, Hyde Park, and South Shore (the Golden Ghetto), as well as in a few nearby communities. On the South Side, they established Jewish institutions to take care of their needs, including Michael Reese Hospital, opened in 1881, the Drexel Home for the Aged, the

Chicago Home for Jewish Orphans, the social Lakeside Club, and the social and civic Standard Club. At its peak just after World War II, an estimated 35,000 Jews lived on the South Side, served by about twenty synagogues, mainly Reform and Conservative, but later including a few Orthodox synagogues as some East European Jews began to move into the area.

Living in the South Side area and known for his antisemitic views is Louis Farrakhan, leader of the Nation of Islam, which is headquartered in Chicago. Through the years, Jewish street peddlers in Chicago have been harassed, *yeshiva* boys have been beaten, Jewish institutional buildings have been defaced and windows broken, and there have been restrictions against Jews in housing, education, and employment. In 1978 American Nazis attempted to march in Skokie, which housed many Holocaust survivors. Today, Jews live in all the major North Shore suburbs, some of which were restricted—closed to—Jews until after World War II. Antisemitic acts are now quite rare.

As the economic status of Jews improved, especially that of the German Jewish businessmen, they became heavy contributors to museums, hospitals, universities, and other philanthropic causes. Julius Rosenwald, chairman of the board of Sears Roebuck and Company, founded the Museum of Science and Industry in 1933, and Max Adler, also with Sears, established the Adler Planetarium in 1930. Jews also contributed heavily to the University of Chicago, which had no Jewish quotas. In the late 1950s, as the racial composition of the area changed rapidly, the South Side Jewish community began to decline in size. Today only a few thousand Jews live on the South Side, mainly in Hyde Park around the University of Chicago, where they are served by two remaining synagogues.

East European Jews started arriving in Chicago after the Great Chicago fire of 1871. By 1880 they constituted only a small part of Chicago's 10,000 Jews. However, after the brutal pogroms in the Russian empire in 1881 and the repressive May Laws of 1882, Russian Polish Jews started coming to Chicago in especially large numbers, along with Jews from other areas of Eastern Europe. By 1900, when the city's Jewish population had reached almost 80,000, about 52,000 were from Eastern Europe, drawn by the numerous economic opportunities offered by the rapidly growing city. By 1930, after Jewish immigration had

peaked, Chicago's Jewish population was about 272,000, about 80 percent of whom were from Eastern Europe. The remainder were largely from Central Europe, with about 2 percent Sephardic Jews from the Middle East and the Mediterranean area. At that time, the Jews constituted about 9 percent of the city's population, and Chicago was the third-largest Jewish city in the world, surpassed only by New York and Warsaw, Poland.

The Eastern European Jews were largely poor *shtetl* (village or small town) Jews, who differed markedly from their German Jewish brethren in religious beliefs, traditions, dress, demeanor, language, and economic status. In autocratic Eastern Europe, they had had little opportunity for secular education, although the men were generally learned in Hebraic studies. The German Jews feared that the presence of hordes of immigrant Eastern European Jews might result in intensified antisemitism. The Eastern European Jews, in turn, perceived that most of the German Jews had strayed from traditional Judaism and were often trying to emulate their Christian neighbors.

On arrival, the Eastern European Jews moved into the Maxwell Street area, just southwest of downtown, an area that had been abandoned by other immigrant groups. Here, from 1880 to almost 1920, was Chicago's largest Jewish community. In the Maxwell Street area, the Eastern European Jews re-created a shtetl atmosphere, including a bazaar-like outdoor market renowned for its variety of new and used merchandise and for bargaining. The market attracted not only the local populace but also customers from the entire metropolitan area, making it at one time the third-largest retail area in the city. Anything could be bought or sold there. The aroma of food and the shouts of the buyers and sellers filled the air. The Maxwell Street area was lined with kosher meat markets, *matzo* bakeries, tobacco stores, groceries, fruit stores, clothing stores, tailor and seamstress shops, peddlers, horse stables, bathhouses, restaurants and snack stands, secondhand stores, a number of Yiddish theaters, and hundreds of pushcarts. Religious institutions included about forty synagogues (all but one Orthodox), numerous Hebrew schools, sacramental wine dealers, Orthodox Yiddish newspaper offices, midwives, *shadchans* (marriage arrangers), *mohels* (for circumcisions), and *shochets*.

Led mainly by Rabbi Emil Hirsch of Congregation KAM and by Julius Rosenwald, the German Jews, who were quite prosperous by this time, tried to improve the conditions of their poorer Eastern European brethren crowded into the Maxwell Street ghetto. They helped build an educational institution (the Jewish Training School), a health facility (the Chicago Maternity Center), a social service and recreational facility (the Chicago Hebrew Institute), and other institutions that would speed their Americanization. The Eastern European Jews made extensive use of these facilities, although some felt they were treated in a paternalistic manner.

The dichotomy between the two groups persisted for many years. Each group had its own neighborhoods, synagogues, social clubs, hospitals, newspapers, fraternal organizations, and children's camps. They also voted differently: German Jews were mainly Republicans; although initially some East European Jews were Republican, later they were largely Democrats. The bitter 1909–1910 garment strike pitted the German Jewish factory owners, including Hart, Schaffner and Marx, against the largely East European Jewish workforce. Until recent decades, intermarriage occurred when a German Jew married an East European Jew.

A long list of prominent people once lived in the Maxwell Street neighborhood. These include Benny Goodman, Supreme Court justice Arthur Goldberg, Admiral Hyman Rickover, radio and television Columbia Broadcasting System founder William Paley, novelist Meyer Levin, Oscar-winning actor Paul Muni, social activist Saul Alinsky, movie mogul Barney Balaban, a number of political figures such as Colonel Jacob Arvey and federal judge Abraham Lincoln Marovitz, and local business entrepreneurs such as Morrie Mages (retail sporting goods), John Keeshin (trucking), and Harris Chernin (retail shoes). Being a tough neighborhood, Maxwell Street produced two world champion boxers, Jackie Fields and Barney Ross, as well as Al Capone's accomplice Jake "Greasy Thumb" Guzik.

Starting about 1910, the East European Jews could afford to leave the densely populated Maxwell Street neighborhood. They moved to better areas on the north and northwest sides—Humboldt Park, Logan Square, Albany Park, and Rogers Park. Small numbers moved into the German Jewish areas on the South Side, but the overwhelming number moved three miles west into the Lawndale area. By 1940, 125,000 Jews, about 40 percent of the metropolitan area's total Jewish population, lived in Lawndale, forming by far the largest Jewish community

Chicago ever had. At its peak, the Greater Lawndale area had sixty synagogues (fifty-eight of which were Orthodox), the Hebrew Theological College, the Jewish People's Institute (JPI), which was a major community center, numerous Hebrew schools, a number of Yiddish theaters, and many Zionist, religious, adult education, and political organizations, as well as Jewish labor unions and dozens of *vereins* or *landsmanshaftn* (organizations of immigrants from the same town in the Old Country). The main commercial street was Roosevelt Road, which for more than a mile contained almost exclusively Jewish-owned bookstores, theaters, restaurants, funeral parlors, banks, meeting halls, cabarets, and a large variety of food, clothing, and furniture stores, interspersed with a number of gambling hangouts.

Yiddishkeit (traditional Judaic customs and traditions) permeated the neighborhood, especially on the Sabbath and Jewish holidays. On those days the synagogues and the boulevards were crowded with Jews dressed in their finest, sometimes dancing and singing, before returning home for the traditional meals. On the morning of Sukkot, men were seen heading to the synagogues carrying the traditional *lulav* (palm branch) and *etrog* (citrus fruit), and on Rosh Hashanah an estimated 40,000 to 50,000 gathered at the Douglas Park lagoon for *Tashlich*, the symbolic casting of their sins into the water. The community was also alive culturally and intellectually, with outdoor soapbox orators of various persuasions endlessly addressing the crowds on Roosevelt Road. Yiddishkeit also thrived in varying degrees in the other Jewish neighborhoods in the city.

After World War II, Jews began to move out of Lawndale. Buoyed by a dynamic economy and government-backed mortgages with low interest rates and small down payments, many could now afford homes of their own, and there were few single-family houses in Lawndale. By 1960, no Jews remained in Lawndale. Some Jews moved to South Shore on the South Side, but most joined their more affluent brethren on the north and northwest sides in Rogers Park along Lake Michigan, in the more diverse Humboldt Park and Logan Square communities where Jewish writers and some radicals lived, and in Albany Park, which, with some 45,000 Jews, was the city's second-largest Jewish community in the immediate post–World War II period. On a somewhat smaller scale, these communities carried on many of the activities and traditions that had been prevalent in Lawndale. Unlike Lawndale, however, which was almost solidly Orthodox, these communities had Orthodox and Conservative synagogues and Reform temples. By the 1960s, many Jews had moved out of these communities, going farther north into West Ridge (West Rogers Park) or the northern suburbs.

In 2004, West Rogers Park, with a population of about 32,000 Jews, was the largest Jewish community left in Chicago and has numerous Jewish institutions. A majority of the Jews are Orthodox, and the rhythm of Jewish life is still visible throughout the neighborhood; indeed, a small stretch of Devon Avenue bears a resemblance to the earlier Roosevelt Road in Lawndale. Many Jewish schools serve the large number of Orthodox children in the area.

Several thousand Jews also live near or along the north lakefront. Many are young professionals, while others are retirees or empty-nesters who have returned to the city after raising their children in the suburbs. Many are especially active in the cultural and political activities of the city.

Recent decades have witnessed a major movement of Jews to the suburbs. In 1950 only about 5 percent of Jews lived in the suburbs; in 2000, the estimate was almost 70 percent. Recently, however, the number of Jews moving from the suburbs to the city has become slightly higher than the number leaving the city for the suburbs, signaling a new, though possibly temporary, trend. The city's Jewish population has also been augmented by an estimated 25,000 immigrants from the former Soviet Union who began arriving in the 1970s, most of whom have continued to reside in the city. Overall, nearly 50 percent of the metropolitan area's Jewish population was born outside the Chicago metropolitan area.

The southern and western suburbs each include an estimated 20,000 Jews. To the south, the largest concentrations of Jews are in Flossmoor, Homewood, and Olympia Fields, and in Hammond and Munster, Indiana. To the west, the largest concentrations of Jews are found in Oak Park, River Forest, and Naperville, the latter a rapidly growing community with increasing numbers of Jews. Overall, however, the southern and western suburban Jewish population is not expanding; in some areas it is even declining.

By contrast, about 150,000 Jews dwell in the northern and northwestern suburbs, which continue to grow selectively, based on location, housing costs, transportation, and Jewish facilities. In the early 1900s, some wealthy German Jews from the South Side of Chicago, led by Julius Rosenwald, established homes in Highland Park and Glencoe, two of the few northern lakefront suburbs that were not closed to Jews. After World War II, with the restrictive covenants mostly removed, large numbers of Jews left their racially changing neighborhoods for the close-in suburbs of Skokie and Lincolnwood, and soon their population was at least half Jewish. This movement continued further outward into Wilmette, Morton Grove, Niles, Des Plaines, Glenview, Evanston, Arlington Heights, Schaumburg, and Hoffman Estates, as well as Highland Park and Glencoe. More recently, Jews have moved still farther out, to Northbrook, Deerfield, Vernon Hills, Wheeling, and Buffalo Grove. Buffalo Grove has grown especially rapidly and now has about ten synagogues. The migration has been fostered, in part, by lower home prices and by parents and grandparents from the city and inner suburbs following their children and grandchildren outward.

With every move farther away from Chicago, Jewish density, political influence, and Yiddishkeit have declined. But whenever there are enough Jews in a suburban area, they have established a synagogue, often followed by Jewish educational institutions and sometimes Jewish community centers. In the outward suburban movement, the Orthodox *shuln* of Maxwell Street and Lawndale have often been succeeded by large Conservative synagogues and Reform temples. Overall, at the beginning of the twenty-first century, there are 140 synagogues, 62 of them Orthodox-Traditional; 37 Reform; 33 Conservative; 3 Reconstructionist; and 5 nondenominational. The Reform and Conservative congregations usually have larger memberships than the Orthodox; consequently, estimates indicate that 35 percent of the religiously affiliated are Reform, 35 percent are Conservative, and the remainder are largely Orthodox-Traditional, except for a small number who are Reconstructionist.

Chicago Jewry has a vast network of important Jewish organizations and movements; indeed, a number of national organizations originated in the city. The National Council of Jewish Women, founded in 1893, grew out of the World's Parliament of Religions held at the World's Columbian Exposition, which took place in the city in that year. The first Herzelian Zionist group in the country was organized in 1895 in Chicago with Bernard Horwich as president. In 1938, renowned Rabbi Solomon Goldman of Congregation Anshe Emet became the first non-easterner to become president of the Zionist Organization of America. In 1913, due chiefly to the efforts of lawyer Sigmund Livingston, the Anti-Defamation League of B'nai B'rith was founded in Chicago to fight antisemitism.

In 1923 the German and East European Jewish charitable organizations merged to form what is today the Jewish Federation of Metropolitan Chicago, with Julius Rosenwald as its first president. Thousands of Jews contribute millions of dollars each year to the Federation—$71 million in 2003. The Federation is an umbrella organization that helps fund overseas Jewry, seniors, education, youth groups, religious and cultural activities, medical facilities, Jewish community centers, and myriad other Jewish causes. Chicago also has active branches of national Jewish organizations such as Hadassah, ORT, B'nai B'rith, various Zionist groups, YIVO Institute for Jewish Research, Hebrew Immigrant Aid Society (HIAS), the American Jewish Committee, and the American Jewish Congress. The Chicago Jewish community supports major educational institutions, including Hebrew Theological College and the Spertus Institute of Jewish Studies with its adjoining Spertus Museum. The once powerful, mainly immigrant organizations—the Workmen's Circle (*Arbeiter Ring*), which had 43 branches and 4 children's schools, the more than 600 landsmanshaftn or *vereinen,* and the more than 30 Jewish trade unions—have all virtually disappeared, as the early immigrants have largely been replaced by their more acculturated descendants, and newer immigrants have created or joined other organizations that meet their needs. The children and grandchildren of the immigrants have neither their progenitors' ties to the Old World nor their experiences as factory workers, craftsmen, or peddlers, as most moved into business and the professions. The Eastern European Jews now generally have the same social and economic status as the German Jews. The old dichotomy has virtually disappeared.

As many Jews prospered, a number became philanthropists. Among the current major contributors to Jewish and non-Jewish causes are the Crowns (who made their wealth in industry), the Pritzkers (in hotels), and the Rubloffs (in real estate).

Chicago Jews became national leaders of labor and liberal organizations. Sidney Hillman, his wife Bessie Abramovitz, Sol Brandzel, Jacob Potofsky, Stan Smith, and Samuel Levin were prominent in the garment workers' unions. Lillian Herstein was a dynamic organizer of the

teachers' union, a founder of the American Civil Liberties Union, and the American representative to the International Labor Organization in Switzerland. U.S. congressmen Adolph J. Sabbath, Sidney Yates, and Abner Mikva were also among the noted liberals of twentieth-century Chicago.

As most Chicago Jews now live in the suburbs, Jews' political clout in the city has declined. In 1971, seven of the fifty city aldermen were Jewish; in 2005, only three. There has never been a Jewish mayor of Chicago, although Jews have held other important city offices. Two Jewish governors of Illinois came from the Chicago area, Henry Horner and Sam Shapiro. Two active liberal Democrats, Rahm Emanuel and Jan Schakowsky, currently represent Chicago in the U.S. Congress.

The city boasted a number of Jewish newspapers, mainly in Yiddish, ranging in political orientation from the Orthodox *Daily Jewish Courier* (1892–1944) to the socialist *Jewish Daily Forward* (1920–1953) to the communist *Der Morgan Freiheit* (1922–1988). And Chicago was home, at least for a time, to many prominent Jewish writers, including Ben Hecht, Edna Ferber, Meyer Levin, Saul Bellow, Albert Halper, Louis Zara, Nelson Algren (who was half Jewish), Studs Terkel, Isaac Rosenfeld, Leo Rosten, Sam Ross, and Maxwell Bodenheim. Others in literary fields are columnists Sydney J. Harris and Irv Kupcinet, playwright David Mamet, movie critic Gene Siskel, and advice columnist Ann Landers (Eppie Lederer).

Among the Jewish artists who called Chicago home were Todros Geller, whose work was imbued with Jewish tradition; sculptor Milton Horn, whose works are displayed in Chicago and elsewhere on public, organizational, and synagogue buildings; and Aaron Bohrod, an American realist painter of international renown. Prominent architects include Alfred Alschuler, Dankmar Adler, Bertrand Goldberg, and Stanley Tigerman. Arthur Rubloff and Philip Klutznick are among Chicago's major real estate developers. Klutznick, who served as a national Jewish leader and high government official, was President Jimmy Carter's secretary of commerce.

A number of talented Jewish conductors, although usually not Chicago natives, have led the Chicago Symphony Orchestra for long periods. These include Fritz Reiner, Sir George Solti, and pianist-conductor Daniel Barenboim. Notable in the field of popular music are Benny Goodman, Art Hodes, Mel Tormé, and Mandy Patinkin. Many comedians came from Chicago, including

Shelley Berman, Morey Amsterdam, Allan Sherman, Jackie Leonard, and the perennial thirty-nine-year-old from Waukegan, Jack Benny. Michael Todd, the movie impresario, came from the Wicker Park neighborhood.

Jews have also been successful in law, medicine, and business. They started many incubator businesses, ranging from Charles Lubin's Sara Lee to Gordon and Carol Segal's Crate and Barrel.

Although Chicago Jews today differ in many ways from their immigrant forebears, many continue to maintain much of their culture, liberalism, and values, albeit in modified form. Although not as dependent on Jewish institutions, they have built a new set of these facilities in the suburbs. Of the many population groups that make up Chicago, Jews are among the best educated, most prosperous, most ardent supporters of the arts and literature, and highest per capita contributors in caring for their own. Some of the old problems—poverty, discrimination, and the friction between German and East European Jews—have largely disappeared, replaced by new problems, including intermarriage and some internal religious friction, for example, between the Orthodox and other Jewish religious groups. The community continues to be concerned about the safety and welfare of Israel and growing international antisemitism, although they are sometimes divided by their approach to these problems.

Irving Cutler

References and Further Reading

Berkow, Ira. 1977. *Maxwell Street*. Garden City, NY: Doubleday.

Bregstone, Philip, D. 1933. *Chicago and Its Jews: A Cultural History*. Chicago: Privately published.

Cutler, Irving. 1996. *The Jews of Chicago: From Shtetl to Suburb*. Urbana: University of Illinois Press.

Cutler, Irving. 2000. *Jewish Chicago: A Pictorial History*. Chicago: Arcadia Press.

Gutstein, Morris A. 1953. *A Priceless Heritage*. New York: Block.

Heimovics, Rachel Baron. 1981. *The Chicago Jewish Source Book*. Chicago: Follett.

Horwich, Bernard. 1939. *My First Eighty Years*. Chicago: Argus Books.

Meites, Hyman L., ed. 1924, 1990. *History of the Jews of Chicago*. Chicago: Chicago Jewish Historical Society/Wellington Press.

Rawidowicz, Simon, ed. 1952. *The Chicago Pinkas*. Chicago: College of Jewish Studies.

The Sentinel Presents 100 Years of Chicago Jewish Life. 1948. Chicago: Sentinel.

The Sentinel's History of Chicago Jewry, 1911–1961. 1961. Chicago: Sentinel.

The Sentinel's History of Chicago Jewry, 1911–1986. 1986. Chicago: Sentinel.

Wirth, Louis. 1928. *The Ghetto*. Chicago: University of Chicago Press.

Philadelphia

Philadelphia is a founding American community that spawned many of the institutions and organizations that define American Jewish communal life. It was the first community in America with two congregations, both formed before 1800—Mikveh Israel (1740) and Rodeph Shalom (1795), the first Ashkenazic synagogue established in the Western Hemisphere. Philadelphia is the sixth-largest city in the United States (2006). Its metropolitan Jewish population (2002) was estimated to be the fourth largest in the United States and the ninth largest in the world, amounting to 285,000 in the Consolidated Metropolitan Statistical Area utilized by the U.S. Census—stretching from Camden, New Jersey, to Wilmington, Delaware, and including Philadelphia proper and its four surrounding counties (Montgomery, Bucks, Chester, and Delaware). Precedent-setting innovation of national significance that defined the infrastructure of American Jewry as a whole stands as the defining characteristic of Philadelphia Jewry from the early nineteenth century until at least the 1920s.

National Innovations

Numerous social and religious structures that came to define American Jewry owe their origins and first successful implementations to Philadelphia. Paralleling the city's role as the first capital of the United States, Jewish Philadelphia established lasting systems of religious observance, social support, publishing, and education. Philadelphia's Jews translated classical Jewish texts into lucid English and melded Jewish tradition with American democratic ideals. Although many American Jewish institutions first emerged in Philadelphia, its lasting contributions lie in the establishment of communal structures that subsequently became the standard throughout the United States.

During the nineteenth century, Philadelphia served as the incubator of Jewish communal innovations. This phenomenon was no accident. Philadelphia benefited from social and political acceptance, relative economic stability, and a consistent record of leadership by a cadre of inventive and intelligent communal leaders. First among them was undoubtedly Isaac Leeser (1806–1868), the *hazzan* (professional religious leader) of the city's founding congregation, Mikveh Israel. Leeser's American Jewish innovations include *The Occident,* the first successful American Jewish newspaper, which also served as a magazine and forum for debate; a Jewish publication society (1845), whose successor organization continues today; the first Hebrew high school (the Hebrew Education Society, 1849); and the first Jewish theological seminary, Maimonides College (1867). He also was a leader in the Board of Delegates of American Israelites (1859), the first American Jewish defense organization. Beyond institutional structures, Leeser lent his intellectual control of both Jewish sources and the English language to the publication of numerous translations and commentaries that made classical Jewish texts accessible to an American Jewish community that generally lacked fluency in Hebrew or familiarity with Jewish literature beyond the Bible. Addressing these challenges, Leeser produced translations of the Sephardic and Ashkenazic prayer books, the first English translation of the entire Hebrew Bible by an American Jew (1853), the first volumes of sermons delivered by an American Jewish leader (1837–1867), and the first Hebrew textbook for children published in the United States (1839).

In Philadelphia, Isaac Leeser was not alone as an innovator of American Jewish religious institutions. His local contemporaries and protégés, men and women, were creators in their own right. Indeed, after Leeser's death in 1868, other "firsts" that Philadelphia subsequently contributed to the American Jewish community often emerged from the concepts and actions of leaders whom he had inspired. Thus, the Jewish Theological Seminary was founded in 1886 in New York by a Philadelphia rabbi, Sabato Morais, who was its first president. Gratz College, the first Jewish teachers' college in the United States, was established through a trust provided by Hyman Gratz (1776–1857). Dropsie College (later University), the first postgraduate institution for Jewish learning in the world, was opened in 1907 and named for Moses Dropsie, with Cyrus Adler as its president. In addition, such institutions

as the American Jewish Committee, the Jewish Chautauqua Society, the American Jewish Historical Society, and many elements of the Conservative movement were first formed in whole or in part in Philadelphia.

Women as Innovators and Leaders

Philadelphia's Jewish community is also striking for the early, substantive roles that women played in leadership and learning. The quintessential exemplar of this trend was Rebecca Gratz (1781–1869). She was the most prominent among a number of generally middle- and upper-class Jewish women of central and western European descent who were members of Mikveh Israel and who devoted themselves to volunteer charitable work. Their efforts concentrated on social welfare and education. They were particularly innovative and successful between 1840 and 1900. Nineteenth-century American women from comfortable families often found outlets outside the home limited to charitable volunteering. Gratz and her coworkers were noteworthy for their development of communal structures that became the norm throughout the American Jewish community. In 1819, basing their new organization on the model of nonsectarian women's welfare organizations, these women established the first American Jewish charitable organization outside a synagogue. The Female Hebrew Benevolent Society first sought to aid indigent families but developed other targeted welfare organizations, including the Female Hebrew Sewing Society (1838) and the Jewish Foster Home (1855). During the Civil War, the Female Hebrew Benevolent Society established offshoots to address the needs of soldiers and their families.

Under Rebecca Gratz's leadership, Philadelphia Jewish women inaugurated religious educational systems that were later copied by other American communities. In 1838, inspired by Protestant models, they established the first Hebrew Sunday school in America. Philadelphia's Hebrew Sunday School set a precedent even for its non-Jewish analogues by admitting girls on an equal basis with boys. That innovation laid the groundwork for more advanced Jewish educational institutions. When Gratz College was established in 1895, it became the first Jewish institution of higher education to accept and encourage women on an equal basis with men. Despite these progressive policies, the lives of the female leaders often represented a choice. Rebecca Gratz—and most of the women who led with her—never married. Neither did Isaac Leeser.

The Philadelphia Group

The successors to Leeser and Rebecca Gratz in precedent-setting Jewish leadership have been categorized as the "Philadelphia Group." Exclusively male and primarily traditional or Orthodox in their religious orientation, they tended to be well educated in Jewish and general areas, and intellectual and scholarly by inclination and accomplishment. In this, they differed from Jewish leaders in New York, who came largely from the ranks of business and the law and possessed great wealth. At the core of the Philadelphia Group were:

Judge Mayer Sulzberger (1843–1923), a disciple of Leeser and the senior member of the Philadelphia Group, who was a founder of the Jewish Publication Society (1888) and the American Jewish Committee (AJC) (1906), and who played a key role in the Conservative movement by bringing Solomon Schechter to the Jewish Theological Seminary and providing the foundation for the Seminary's preeminent Jewish library. Sulzberger was also the first president of the AJC.

Cyrus Adler (1863–1940), an Assyriologist who became librarian of the Smithsonian Institution; a founder of the Jewish Publication Society, the American Jewish Historical Society (1892), the AJC, and the United Synagogue of America; an editor of the *American Jewish Year Book* (1899–1905), *The Jewish Encyclopedia* (1901–1906), and the *Jewish Quarterly Review* (1916–1940); president of Dropsie College (1908–1940) and later, simultaneously, the Jewish Theological Seminary (acting, 1915–1924; permanent, 1924–1940).

Moses Aaron Dropsie (1821–1905), a scholar and author of legal history and Roman law; active supporter of Philadelphia's short-lived Maimonides College; an opponent of the Jewish Theological Seminary and of Reform Judaism. Dropsie left his wealth to establish Dropsie College (later University) as an independent, nontheological, academic institution that provided graduate instruction and facilitated research in Jewish and related branches of learning.

Rabbi Sabato Morais (1823–1897), Leeser's successor at Mikveh Israel and the leading traditional rabbi in the United States following Leeser's death. He was the pivotal figure in the founding of the Jewish Theological Seminary.

Dr. Solomon Solis-Cohen, a physician and medical researcher as well as a Jewish scholar, poet, and Hebrew translator. He was a founder of the Jewish Publication Society and the *American Hebrew*, another organ of news and debate.

Louis Edward Levy (1846–1919), a newspaper editor who invented "Levytype," which allowed newspapers to print halftone pictures. Levy committed himself to the needs of Jewish immigrants and became a founder and president of the Association for Relief and Protection of Jewish Immigrants (1884).

Rabbi Bernard L. Levinthal (1865–1952), who was trained and ordained by the leading lights of Lithuania and came to Philadelphia in 1891, soon thereafter becoming the rabbinic leader of its Orthodox Jewish community. A founder of the Union of Orthodox Rabbis of the United States and Canada (1902), he was its first president. He served as president of Yeshiva University's Rabbi Isaac Elchanan Theological Seminary, but was also a founder of the AJC and of the Mizrachi Organization of America, and an honorary vice president of the Federation of American Zionists.

On the edge of the Philadelphia Group were:

Rabbi Joseph Krauskopf (1858–1923), rabbi of the Reform Congregation Keneseth Israel and a leader of Radical Reform and its Pittsburgh Platform (1885), and later president of the Central Conference of American Rabbis (1903–1905). Originally an anti-Zionist, he modified his views in later life.

Rabbi Henry Berkowitz (1857–1924), rabbi of Congregation Rodeph Shalom and founder of the Jewish Chautauqua Society; he was a key proponent in the establishment of Philadelphia's Federation of Jewish Philanthropies (1901).

Abraham S. Rosenbach (1876–1952), a bibliophile and book dealer who served as president of the American Jewish Historical Society, he was a benefactor of Gratz College and the Jewish Division of the New York Public

Library. He was a founder and first president of the American Friends of the Hebrew University.

Horace Stern (1879–1969), justice of the Pennsylvania Supreme Court (1935–1957; chief justice, 1952–1957); he was director of the Philadelphia Federation of Jewish Charities, briefly president of Dropsie College, and vice president of the Jewish Publication Society of America, 1914–1965.

The Philadelphia Group did more than innovate. Its membership is characterized by unusual or productive alliances between scholarly lay leaders who possessed considerable but not generally great wealth and rabbis of national significance, between staunchly Orthodox religious leaders and those who were radically Reform, between non-Zionists and Zionists. They were linked by broad intellectual acumen and by a commitment to transform visionary ideals into practical realities by establishing effective national organizations to which they devoted their personal time, as well as often the bulk of their financial resources.

Philadelphia and the Jewish Movements

Despite often-positive personal associations, Philadelphia's religious leaders were by no means unified theologically. Indeed, the community helped to define and separate American Jewish movements. Like Leeser and Morais, Levinthal often maintained warm ties with the broad stretch of the Philadelphia Jewish communal leadership and its associated organizations such as the AJC and the American Jewish Congress. Yet, he saw his role as establishing the communal institutions that would guide American Orthodoxy. From local *kashrut* agencies and rabbinical courts to the leading institutions of American Orthodoxy, Levinthal played a central role. Though a close associate of Dr. Cyrus Adler, he eschewed a possible merger between the Jewish Theological Seminary and Yeshiva University in 1926 when the two were in parallel positions of leadership in their respective movements and seminaries. Known as the "Dean of Orthodox Rabbis" (Philip Rosen in Friedman 1993), he did not hesitate to espouse positions that were controversial within his own community, including strong advocacy of Religious Zionism.

Philadelphia's early and defining impact on the Conservative movement is well documented in the leadership of Cyrus Adler and Sabato Morais. Yet, Philadelphia's centrality continued throughout the twentieth century, during which the community became the bastion of Conservative Judaism. By 1970 there were 110 Jewish congregations in the Philadelphia area, approximately 50 of which were Conservative, 45 Orthodox, and 15 Reform, leading to the characterization that in Philadelphia "the dominant religious thrust of the community was Conservative" (Korn 1972). By the mid-1990s, there were 94 synagogues: 40 Conservative, 29 Orthodox or Traditional (20 Orthodox, 3 Sephardi, 6 Traditional), 19 Reform, 5 Reconstructionist, and 1 Progressive. By 2007, there were 87 synagogues: 31 Conservative (26 affiliated with the United Synagogue of Conservative Judaism and 5 that define themselves as Conservative), 29 Orthodox or Traditional (20 Orthodox, 3 Sephardi, 6 Traditional), 8 Reconstructionist, 1 Jewish Renewal, 16 Reform (11 affiliated with the Union for Reform Judaism and 5 that define themselves as Reform), 1 Humanistic, and 1 unaffiliated. Thus, while Reform and Reconstructionist congregations held their own or expanded and Orthodoxy stemmed its earlier losses, Conservative Judaism in Philadelphia saw a significant continuing decline in congregations, a phenomenon that is consistent with national trends, but is particularly dramatic in Philadelphia due to its historic centrality for the Conservative movement.

Despite the dominance of Conservative Judaism and the national leaders of Orthodoxy, Philadelphia played a central role in the advancement of the Reform movement nationally through two defining congregations, Rodeph Shalom and Keneseth Israel, and through a series of rabbis who facilitated and refined the ideals of the Reform movement. Beyond Krauskopf and Berkowitz, David Einhorn—who fled Baltimore for Keneseth Israel near the outbreak of the Civil War because of his abolitionist views—set the tone for Reform liturgy throughout the first three-quarters of the twentieth century. In the twentieth century, rabbis such as Bertram Korn and David Wice personified the rabbi as scholar and advocate on the national Reform scene.

Philadelphia's ongoing centrality to the varieties of Jewish religious experience is perhaps best demonstrated by the Reconstructionist movement, which consciously placed its seminary and the seat of its congregational movement in Philadelphia. Avoiding the vastness of the New York Jewish community, the seminary's founder,

Rabbi Ira Eisenstein, felt that to succeed, the new rabbinical school would require a vibrant Jewish community, access to universities, and economical housing. "Only Philadelphia satisfied all three requirements" (Dan Rottenberg in Friedman 2003).

Despite the challenges affecting American Jewry in the twenty-first century, Philadelphia has continued to attract leading rabbis in all four movements who both mold their congregations and participate in the continuing redefinition of their respective communities nationally. Like their predecessors, they are active in the dialogue of their movements and of Judaism generally. Their work is supplemented by major academic scholarship in Jewish studies taking place at the University of Pennsylvania, Temple University, Gratz College, the Reconstructionist Rabbinical College, and other academic institutions within the Greater Philadelphia area.

Funding the Future

The effective alliance between scholar-activists and visionary philanthropists that made Philadelphia's national contributions to American Jewish life so successful has seen modification over the last century. In 1901, six years after Boston established the first Jewish federation, Jacob Gimbel, the department-store heir, became the first president of the new Federation of Jewish Charities (FJC), a coalescence of earlier Jewish charitable societies such as the United Hebrew Charities (1869). From its inception, the FJC was led by scions of the German Jewish elite, who tended to be non- or anti-Zionists. In 1938 the Allied Jewish Appeal was formed to provide funds for the budding Jewish settlement in the Land of Israel. By 1956 the Zionist controversies had dissipated sufficiently to permit the merger of the Federation of Jewish Charities and the Allied Jewish Appeal to form the Federation of Jewish Agencies (FJA). In 1990 the FJA adopted the name Jewish Federation of Greater Philadelphia (JFGP). Despite these amalgamations, the JFGP witnessed a continuing decline in its annual campaign for unrestricted contributions. Many leading Philadelphia Jewish philanthropists continued to provide support to the JFGP, particularly for emergency funds for Israel. In addition, under the leadership of philanthropic activists Joseph and Connie Smukler in alliance with Natan (Anatoly) Sharansky, one of the leading Prisoners of Conscience, Philadelphia took a preeminent na-

tional role in the battle for Soviet emigration. Nevertheless, significant numbers of Federation supporters, together with other major Jewish funders without Federation involvement, contributed the bulk of their philanthropic resources to non-Jewish causes or to specific Jewish projects and agencies of their choice.

To address these trends, the JFGP established a Strategic Philanthropy Committee in 2003. Its report acknowledged that "[the] Federation (like many others) has lost its edge." It established new priorities for support: creating "an *inspired* Jewish Community . . . [for] our under-affiliated population and by making high quality education available to children"; "building a *caring* Jewish Community by expressing important Jewish values and reducing Jewish poverty, providing safety net services and expanding social action and volunteering"; and developing "a *connected* Jewish Community that links us to each other, Israel and Jews around the world." In a departure for an organization previously known as the Federation of Jewish Agencies, the Federation rejected a system based on allocations to constituent agencies. "Accordingly, Federation funding for those agencies and grantees whose work falls outside the scope of Federation's stated priorities will, after a reasonable period of transition, be reallocated toward the fulfillment of those priorities and away from historical funding patterns; where agency and grantee work cannot be realigned within the priorities, funding will be greatly reduced or terminated." The report suggested that once such priorities are met, funders will increase their giving generally (*Strategic Philanthropy Plan* 2003).

As of 2006, many constituent agencies had reordered their activities to meet the new priorities of the JFGP, and its bold change in approach had allowed the Federation to begin to redirect its limited resources. However, Philadelphia's Jewish communal agencies generally witnessed substantial reductions in financial support from the JFGP, despite the fact that many of those agencies have long been in the forefront of their fields nationally. In addition, hoped-for increases in major gifts had not materialized for unrestricted allocable funds, though significant restricted and directed funds have been secured.

Whether Philadelphia will return to its role as America's precedent-setting Jewish community remains unknown. The dramatic challenges affecting American Jewish life—that is, broad societal acceptance and material success on the one hand and the appeal of assimilation, aided by ignorance of heritage and culture on the other—require creative and effective responses. The JFGP's strategic plan represents one such effort. If it or another facilitating approach succeeds, Philadelphia Jewry could well return to its historic primacy in American Jewish leadership and innovation and may thereby again advance the future of American Jewry itself.

Jonathan Rosenbaum

References and Further Reading

Ashton, Diane. *The Philadelphia Group: A Guide to Archival and Bibliographic Collections,* http://www.temple.edu/feinsteinctr/d.Philadelphia/g1.html#phili (accessed June 27, 2006).

Friedman, Murray, ed. 1983. *Jewish Life in Philadelphia, 1830–1940.* Philadelphia: Institute for the Study of Human Issues.

Friedman, Murray, ed. 1993. *When Philadelphia Was the Capital of Jewish America.* Philadelphia: Balch Institute Press.

Friedman, Murray, ed. 2003. *Philadelphia Jewish Life, 1940–2000.* Philadelphia: Urban Archives at Temple University and the Philadelphia Jewish Archives Center/Temple University Press.

Harrison, Andrew. 2001. *Passover Revisited: Philadelphia's Efforts to Aid Soviet Jews, 1963-1998.* Madison, NJ: Fairleigh Dickinson University Press.

Korn, Bertram W. 1972. "Philadelphia." In *Encyclopedia Judaica,* cols. 268–276. Jerusalem: Keter.

A Strategic Philanthropy Plan for the Revitalization of Greater Philadelphia Jewish Community. 2003. Philadelphia: Jewish Federation of Greater Philadelphia.

Sussman, Lance J. 1995. *Isaac Leeser and the Making of American Judaism.* Detroit, MI: Wayne State University Press.

Tabak, Robert P. 1990. "The Transformation of Jewish Identity: The Philadelphia Experience, 1919–1945." PhD dissertation, Temple University.

Wertheimer, Jack. 2005. "Judaism and the Future of Religion in America: The Situation of Conservative Judaism Today." *Judaism* 54 (Summer–Fall): 131–136.

Jews in the South

Since earliest colonial times, Jews have settled across the South, although their numbers were rarely significant. Jews readily acculturated, yet they remained outsiders. The Jewish experience in the South was ambivalent. Jews were white people in a biracial society, but they were neither Christian nor Anglo-Saxon.

Whether the region's Jews created a distinctly Southern Jewish ethnic identity has been much debated. Eli Evans, in his portraits of Southern Jews, depicts a culturally unique people rooted in a region and to a history (Evans 2005). Mark Bauman argues that the narrative of Southern Jews more closely resembles that of American Jews than that of Christian Southerners (Bauman 1996). Stephen Whitfield refers to Southern Jews as having a "braided identity," hybrids whose various ethnic strands remained distinct rather than blended (Whitfield 1988). Behind these questions lies the problematic identity of the South—whether the region is one place or many and whether it differs culturally from mainstream America. Southern Jewry includes both the Russian-born storekeeper in an Appalachian coal town, and the Old South, Sephardic aristocrat in Charleston. Jews in agrarian market towns in the Mississippi Delta or the Carolina Piedmont had different experiences from those in metropolitan centers such as Memphis, Atlanta, or Baltimore, which supported vibrant Jewish communal and institutional life.

Many attributes that commonly define Southern Jews—isolation, neighborliness, and heightened group and religious awareness—are typical of small-town Jews regardless of region. And Southern Jews, like other American Jews, arrived in multinational waves of migration. Their high rates of geographic mobility also challenge the claim that Southern Jews are a uniquely rooted people. In most communities, Jewish newcomers outnumber natives. Jews moved readily across regional borders in search of economic opportunity, and family and commercial networks linked them to Northern Jews. Like Jews generally, Southern Jews' sense of communal responsibility extended beyond their locales to embrace global Jewry.

Prior to forming communities, small numbers of Jews settled the southern coast in patterns typical of colonial Jewry. The colonies on Roanoke Island in 1585 and at Jamestown as early as 1621 each included a Jew. Trade and family kept Southern port Jews connected to Jews in Newport, Rhode Island, the Caribbean, and London. Jews began settling in Charleston in 1695. In 1733, one year after a debtor's colony was established in Georgia, the Bevis Marks congregation of London sent forty-two impoverished, mostly Sephardic, Jews to Savannah. A community formed in Richmond in the late 1700s. In the 1820s, the planter Moses Levy, who owned vast Florida lands, aspired to create a utopian colony there for distressed Jews.

Jews found the South in the colonial and early national periods relatively tolerant by contemporary standards. By 1800 three of America's five synagogues—Savannah (1735), Charleston (1749), and Richmond (1789)—were located in the South. In 1820 the Charleston Jewish community of seven hundred was the largest in America. In 1786 Virginia passed a Statute for Religious Freedom at a time when virtually all states had constitutional religious tests against Jews holding public office. Still, Maryland did not enact a Jew Bill until 1826, and North Carolina eliminated the disqualification only in 1868. When Francis Salvador was elected to the South Carolina Provincial Congress of 1775, he became the first American Jew elected to public office. David Emmanuel served as governor of Georgia in 1801. Philip Phillips was elected to Congress from Alabama (1853), and Henry Hyams was lieutenant governor of Louisiana (1859). The first Jewish mayor of an American city was Mordecai DeLeon of Columbia, South Carolina, elected to the first of his three terms in 1833.

From the port cities of first settlement, Jews followed the nation's expansion westward. Entrepreneurs Jacob Cohen and Isaiah Isaacs of Richmond financed Daniel Boone to survey their Kentucky land claims. The 5 Jews in Louisville of 1830 grew to 2,000 in 1860. Alsatian and Bavarian Jewish immigrants settled along the Mississippi. As the port of New Orleans expanded with the cotton trade, its Jewish population increased from 35 in 1827 to 2,000 in 1860. With the German second-wave migration, Baltimore's Jewish community grew to 8,000 in 1856. Peddlers and merchants fanned southward.

In response to abolitionism, the South defended slavery, defining itself as a region distinct in its interests and identity. Jews were neither conspicuous nor significant as slaveholders or traders. About one-quarter of Southern Jews owned slaves, a figure comparable to the general Southern population. Their practices were typical of Southerners of their class, occupation, and place of residence, which was largely urban. Very few Jews were planters. The 1820 census reveals that, in four states, the average Jewish household held four slaves, a roughly normative figure (Webb 2001). As Civil War approached, 30,600 Jews were estimated to be living in the thirteen states that would be claimed by the Confederacy, fewer than 0.5 percent of the white population. Several thousand demonstrated their loyalty by serving in Confederate armies. Two U.S. senators of Jewish origin, David Yulee (né Levy) of Florida and Judah P. Benjamin of Louisiana, were ardent secessionists. Intermarried and assimilated into Christian society, they remained Southern patriots even as antisemites excoriated them. Benjamin, a confidant of Jefferson Davis, served the Confederacy as attorney general, secretary of war, and secretary of state. Rabbis Simon Tuska of Memphis and Maximilian Michelbacher of Richmond sermonized on "Southern rights," and Rabbi James Gutheim fled occupied New Orleans rather than swear allegiance to the Union.

After the ruin of Civil War and the end of Reconstruction, proponents of a New South called for industrial progress, racial harmony, and political reform. Welcomed for their capital and commerce, Jews created networks that helped bring the region into the national economy. Jews often began as peddlers and were highly mobile in their search for opportunity. Following a national pattern that dated from antebellum days, Jewish settlement followed channels of economic distribution. Such cities as Cincinnati, Baltimore, St. Louis, and New Orleans, linked to New York and European markets, served as credit and distribution centers for a dry-goods network that extended along rivers, roads, and railroads into the small-town South. The store was a way station for country peddlers. The storekeeper purchased agrarian produce, particularly cotton, which could be brokered in urban markets. The ties between Jewish manufacturer, wholesaler, and retailer were secured by ethnic and family bonds. A Jew in an urban center financed and supplied a son, nephew, or landsman to peddle or open a store in a new territory. An 1878 census revealed Jewish population in 290 towns in the South, and nearly a fifth of America's 250,000 Jews lived there. A newspaper, *The Jewish South* (1877–c. 1881), published by Rabbi E. B. M. Browne to advocate the "interests of Southern Judaism," reported from 177 communities in 13 states.

As was customary among Jews, the first act of communal organization was to purchase a cemetery. Burial or benevolence societies were founded on European communal models. They organized worship, cared for the poor, sheltered strangers, and ensured ritual burial. In 1784 Charleston's Jews formed the Hebra Gemilut Hasadim (Society for Deeds of Loving Kindness), and in 1801 they organized the Hebrew Orphan Society. Both these societies were the first of their kind in America. Ladies' benevolence societies formed in Savannah in 1853 and in Mobile in 1861. With increasing members and prosperity, benevolence societies typically evolved into congregations. Memphis had a cemetery in 1847, a benevolence society in 1850, and a congregation in 1853. The Gemilath Chesed of Atlanta, founded in 1860, became the Hebrew Benevolent Congregation, now known as The Temple, in 1867. The formation of congregations followed the national model as successive waves of immigrants—Sephardic, Bavarian, Prussian, and Russian—organized worship according to their traditional rites. All began as orthodox, but with acculturation, religious practice liberalized, and congregational lines were redrawn by religious ideology.

In 1824 Charleston hosted the first formal effort to establish Reform Judaism in America. Led by playwright Isaac Harby, twenty-four younger Jews split from K. K. Beth Elohim to organize the Reformed Society of Israelites. They aspired to bring Protestant decorum to Jewish worship. The Charlestonians were aware of European Jewish reform efforts, but more decisive were local factors, including generational conflicts, missionary activity, and a Unitarian challenge. An acculturated, American-born youth aspired to forms of worship that reflected their own enlightened, republican values. They were also responding to the Second Great Awakening, a Christian evangelical movement that appealed especially to women. The Reformers included women's voices in Jewish worship. Nine years later, they rejoined Beth Elohim, which dedicated a new temple in 1841, and liberalized their services. Worship there included organ music and liturgical hymns by local poetess Penina Moise.

Jews who settled on the Southern frontier lived apart from both rabbinic and communal authority. Orthodox Jews, such as Rabbi Bernard Illowy of New Orleans, complained of religious laxity when they settled or traveled in the South.

The South was an arena for contention between Isaac Mayer Wise of Cincinnati, who advocated an American Reform Judaism, and Isaac Leeser, mentor of traditional Judaism, who had first settled in Richmond. Wise sympathized with the South, where he found half the subscribers to his journal the *Israelite*. In 1840, Bavarian-born Abraham Rice—the first American rabbi with a verifiable, traditional ordination—arrived at the Baltimore Hebrew Congregation. The presence of a scrupulously Orthodox rabbi provoked reformists in Baltimore to organize Har Sinai Congregation. Its rabbi, German-born David Einhorn, promulgated a Radical Reform that modernized ritual and excised references to a

personal messiah and restoration of temple sacrifices and Zion. Einhorn, whose newspaper *Sinai* expressed abolitionist views, fled to Philadelphia after a proslavery mob destroyed his press in 1861.

When Wise convened a Union of American Hebrew Congregations (UAHC) in 1873, nearly half the delegates were Southerners. By 1900, 73 percent of the South's Jewish communities had a Reform temple, and by 1907, 41 percent of the UAHC congregations were Southern (Weissbach 1997). The success of Reform in the South is due to several factors. In a society that was pervasively Protestant, acculturated Southern Jews wished to minimize their religious difference and adapted religious practices that emphasized decorum and social accommodation. Orthodox life was also difficult to sustain where kosher food was not readily available, and the Sabbath occurred on market day or the mill workers' payday. The Reform movement also had a geographic advantage. From its centrally located base in Cincinnati, the UAHC dispatched rabbinic circuit riders, including students from Hebrew Union College, into the Southern hinterlands.

The end of Reconstruction was marked by white racial backlash. The Jews' place in the Southern social and racial hierarchy was questioned. With the advent of Jim Crow, which coincided with the migration of East European Jews, racial antisemitism intensified in the South. In Atlanta, elite clubs, which included Jews among their founders, began excluding them. For poor whites displaced from farm to factory, Jews were symbols of urbanity, commerce, and finance. Jewish country stores, which held crop liens, were burned in Louisiana and Mississippi when markets fell in the 1890s. Populist demagogue Tom Watson exploited antisemitic sentiments against Leo Frank, the Jewish factory manager who was lynched in 1915 for allegedly murdering a working girl. Shortly thereafter, the Ku Klux Klan revived. The Southern proclivity for racist violence occasionally ensnared Jews, even in such places as Atlanta, where Jews were prosperous and well established.

The third-wave immigration of 2.5 million Jews from East and Central Europe occurred as the South was urbanizing and industrializing. Often starting as peddlers, Jews settled in growing mill and market towns across the South. The Baltimore Bargain House supplied and financed young immigrants, pointing them to new territories. Birmingham's Jewish population increased from 20 in 1878 to 1,400 in 1905. In 1880 one Russian Jew resided in Atlanta; in 1910 there were 1,283. Sephardic Jews from Rhodes established enclaves in Atlanta and Montgomery. From 1900 to 1917, the Galveston Plan, sponsored by B'nai B'rith and the Baron de Hirsch Fund, directed 10,000 immigrants to Texas.

"Jew stores" proffered groceries and dry goods at low prices to farmers and industrial workers, both black and white. In Alexandria, Louisiana, twenty-two of thirty-one East European Jews owned stores (Weissbach 1997). Jews were upwardly mobile, and peddlers became storekeepers, some achieving wealth as merchants and industrialists. Jewish department stores, such as Rich's in Atlanta, anchored downtowns. In the late 1890s, Moses and Caesar Cone of Greensboro began building textile mills in the Carolinas.

Communities were fluid as Jews pursued economic opportunity or sought metropolitan areas with larger Jewish populations. The second generation was especially mobile as college-educated youth aspired to careers beyond their parents' storekeeping. Southern state universities, although not free of discrimination, were more welcoming to Jews than Northern schools were. At the University of North Carolina in the 1930s, the percentage of Jews in the student body was twenty times greater than the percentage of Jews in the state (Rogoff 2001). UNC president Frank Graham in 1933 forced the medical school dean to resign after he admitted that he kept a Jewish quota. In absolute terms, Jewish numbers at Southern universities remained too small to be perceived as a threat. When Jewish scholars fled Nazi Europe, Southern institutions, including African American colleges, welcomed them to enhance their academic stature. World War II drew more Jews southward to military bases and to growing camp and industrial towns.

Southern Jews maintained links to national and global Jewry through local affiliates of B'nai B'rith (1843) and the National Council of Jewish Women (1893). From 1905 to 1913, federations of Jewish charities formed in Atlanta, Baltimore, Dallas, Little Rock, Memphis, and New Orleans. By the 1930s, nineteen more had organized. Although the South is often regarded as anti-Zionist because of its German and Reform legacy, two of the nation's most prominent Zionists—Louis Brandeis of Louisville and Henrietta Szold of Baltimore—had Southern roots. The anti-Zionist American Council for Judaism enlisted prominent Southern rabbis, but Southern Jewry more typically supported the Zionist cause. After 1900 Zionist societies arose in six Southern states. By 1933 the South claimed twenty-four Hadassah chapters.

In the Protestant, fundamentalist South, Jews were viewed as a biblical people, and the synagogue was respected as the Jewish church. For Southerners, church and Sunday school attendance were marks of respectability, regardless of faith. Southern folklore describes Christians who sought Jewish peddlers or storekeepers to discuss the Bible with them or to bless them or their children in Hebrew. Southern Christians often cited the Jewish origins of their savior. In many communities, Christians contributed to the building of synagogues just as Jews donated to the construction of churches. Southern Jews had higher rates of religious affiliation than national norms. Politically, they tended to be more moderate than Northern Jews but more liberal than white Southern Christians (Reed 1982). Disproportionate numbers of Southern Jews have been elected to political office. B. F. Jonas was elected to the U.S. Senate from Louisiana in 1879, as was Richard Stone from Florida in 1974. David Sholtz was elected governor of Florida in 1933, and Marvin Mandel won the first of two terms as governor of Maryland in 1969. Sol Blatt served as speaker of the South Carolina House of Representatives from 1937–1973. Large cities and small towns alike have had Jewish mayors, including E. J. Evans, who served six terms (1951–1963) in Durham.

Despite their civic integration, Jews continued to confront prejudice and isolation. Social segregation persisted at sundown. Country clubs and civic societies were often closed. The hospitality that Southerners extended to their Jewish neighbors did not preclude generic antisemitism. Senator Theodore Bilbo of Mississippi expressed friendship for his Southern Jewish friends while vilifying New York Jews. A significant strain of Protestant fundamentalism damned Jews as unsaved or as Christ-killers. The Southern Baptist Convention passed resolutions condemning antisemitism and professing love for Jews, but in 1980 its president declared that God did not hear the prayers of a Jew. The ardent Zionism of Southern fundamentalist Christians owed to a millennialism that saw the ingathering of Jews in Israel as a prelude to their conversion to Christianity.

The civil rights movement brought the varied loyalties of Southern Jews into conflict. Jewish peddlers and storekeepers often catered to the black trade and, within the limits of a segregated society, adopted liberal racial policies in service, hiring, and extending credit. They also were mindful of their white clientele, which was often agrarian or working class. While Northern Jewish activists flocked southward and national Jewish defense agencies supported civil rights, Southern Jews, given their precarious economic position, were conflicted and more circumspect. White extremists planted dynamite at synagogues in a half-dozen cities. A few prominent Jews were avowedly segregationist; more commonly, Southern Jews expressed sympathy for black aspirations, but in "quiet voices" (Bauman and Kalin 1997). Some Southern Jews, especially rabbis, were courageously outspoken. In Little Rock, among other communities, Jewish women worked to keep open newly integrated public schools. Relative to other white Southerners, Jewish support for integration was significant (Webb 2001).

The Sun Belt, a term applied to the South and the Southwest beginning in the 1970s, reflected the transformation of the South from a diseased, ill-educated, racist backwater into an economically ascendant region with an appealing climate. With the changing economy, rural Jewish communities withered while metropolitan, academic, high-tech, and retirement centers flourished. Atlanta Jewry increased from 14,500 in 1960 to 76,000 in 1996. According to the National Jewish Population Survey (1990), about one-fourth of American Jews now live in the South. The region has seen considerable Jewish institution building—including day schools, high schools, and community centers—and the United Jewish Communities, the national organization of local Jewish federations, now counts fifty-six Southern affiliates.

Southern Jews acknowledge their difference. Writers Ed Cohen, Judith Goldman, Roy Hoffman, Steve Stern, and Stella Suberman penned novels and memoirs that evoked a rich Southern Jewish folklife. They portrayed Jews who were woven into their hometown fabric yet remain different. Dramatist Alfred Uhry, most notably in *Driving Miss Daisy*, depicted Jews who eagerly assimilated to Southern mores yet resisted a total accommodation as they confronted antisemitism and, in Miss Daisy's case, dissented from racial codes. Eli Evans's memoir (2005) portrayed a culturally distinct people. Local and regional Jewish societies and museums host exhibitions or publish community histories that emphasize a unique acculturation. A Southern Jewish Historical Society sponsors conventions and an academic journal; a Museum of the Southern Jewish Experience in Mississippi preserves remnants of lost communities. The museum spawned an Institute for Southern Jewish

Life. Jewish Studies programs flourish on Southern campuses, beginning with Duke in 1943.

With high rates of mobility and low rates of persistence, the question remains whether Sun Belt immigrants are Southern by culture or only by geography. The large Jewish population of southern Florida, for example, is primarily of Northern origin. Miami now holds the nation's third-largest Jewish community, while Boca Raton–West Palm Beach ranks eighth. Moreover, with racial integration, the rise of mass media, and a national population redistribution, the regional distinctiveness of the South has been attenuating. A core of distinctly Southern Jews born and bred in the South—some with Confederate ancestors—persists, but the greater population consists of a mobile people drawn to the Sun Belt by climate, lifestyle, and opportunity.

Leonard Rogoff

References and Further Reading
Bauman, Mark. 1996. *The Southerner as American: Jewish Style.* Cincinnati, OH: American Jewish Archives.
Bauman, Mark, and Berkley Kalin, eds. 1997. *The Quiet Voices: Southern Rabbis and Black Civil Rights, 1880s to 1990s.* Tuscaloosa: University of Alabama Press.
Dinnerstein, Leonard, and Mary Dale Palsson, eds. 1973. *Jews in the South.* Baton Rouge: Louisiana State University Press.
Evans, Eli. 2005. *The Provincials: A Personal History of Jews in the South.* Chapel Hill: University of North Carolina Press.
Reed, John Shelton. 1982. *One South: An Ethnic Approach to Regional Culture.* Baton Rouge: Louisiana State University Press.
Rogoff, Leonard. 2001. *Homelands: Southern Jewish Identity in Durham and Chapel Hill, North Carolina.* Tuscaloosa: University of Alabama Press.
Webb, Clive. 2001. *Fight against Fear: Southern Jews and Black Civil Rights.* Athens: University of Georgia Press.
Weissbach, Lee Shai. 1997. "East European Immigrants and the Image of Jews in the Small-Town South." *American Jewish History* 85, 3 (September): 231–262.
Whitfield, Stephen. 1988. "The Braided Identity of Southern Jewry." *American Jewish History* 71, 3 (March): 363–387.

Jews in the West

On the Pacific shore from Canada to Mexico, Jewish communities were integral parts of the cities and towns of the

American West. From San Diego to Seattle, Jews established businesses based on international, national, and interregional trade and the area's diverse natural resources. The Jewish experience in the West was characterized by continual migration, the presence of multiethnic neighbors, and relatively little antisemitism. Because Jews often arrived during the settlement period, they were founders of the secular, as well as the Jewish, communities and institutions. This led to their strong identification as Westerners. Their lives and their communities developed differently from those of their eastern brethren.

Especially in the nineteenth century, the Pacific West functioned as an interdependent region with San Francisco, the city with the largest Jewish population, as its hub. Transformed from a sleepy port town into a cosmopolitan city almost overnight, San Francisco became the commercial, institutional, and social center of the region for Jews and non-Jews alike. The Golden Gate welcomed Jews from all over the world who sought to play a role in the new western economy, an economy based on gold, agriculture, and, most important, commerce. Most merchants and goods traveled from Europe and the eastern United States by ship to San Francisco and from there spread throughout the region. Families became regional, often with one brother in San Francisco, another in a mining town of the mother lode, and a cousin or nephew in the new town of Portland. Goods, marketing advice, credit, and social introductions circulated freely among family members throughout the region. Some organizations were also regional: San Francisco's Hebrew Orphan Asylum and some Jewish periodicals served, and were supported by, the entire region.

Introduction to the West

Without the California Gold Rush fueling economic development, the nineteenth-century West would have attracted few Jews. Jewish men and women from England, Germany, France, Poland, and Russia came to California in the 1850s, 1860s, and 1870s seeking to participate in the new western economy. Most came through a process of chain migration—a brother, cousin, or friend came first and family members followed later. Some were new immigrants, while others were acculturated to American life by the time they reached the West. Many had moved one, two, or three times before settling in the West. Levi Strauss, who was born in Bavaria, first lived in New York with his merchant brothers, then peddled notions in Kentucky before his brother-in-law suggested in 1853 that he join him in San Francisco. With years of experience behind him, Strauss, like many Jewish migrants, was familiar with American business and social practices by the time he reached the West and therefore rose quickly in the Jewish and secular communities. It was to meet prospectors' needs for durable work clothes that Strauss first developed Levi's.

Who came west? Historian Ellen Eisenberg concluded that the West attracted many Jews who had worked with non-Jews in Europe or the United States and therefore did not feel compelled to live in Jewish enclaves. The pull of the West was also felt by many American-born Jews, including Sephardim whose families had lived in the United States for generations. Because they were Americans, not foreigners, they were more likely to assume leadership roles, defending new immigrants, speaking against Christian-oriented textbooks, and protesting laws that required all businesses to close on Sundays. The latter were damaging to Jewish businesses that chose to close on the Jewish Sabbath.

The California Gold Rush came at the right time to draw Jews who were already seeking to leave Europe. Jewish newspapers in Europe printed accounts of the Gold Rush—most significantly, articles about Jews who remained observant on the Pacific shores. Germany's *Allgemeine Zeitung des Judentums (General Journal of Judaism)* reported in 1850 that many Jews had immigrated to California; London's *Jewish Chronicle* noted in 1851 that young men in San Francisco had kept a strictly kosher Passover; and Paris's *Archives Israelites* in 1855 informed its readers that Jews could be found in most California communities. All these articles stimulated immigration to the Far West. As Jewish immigrants to the United States were familiar with ocean travel, most journeyed to California by sea. Boarding ships in New York, some sailed around South America's Cape Horn to reach the Pacific; others took steamers to Nicaragua or Panama and then trekked across the isthmus to the Pacific coast, where they boarded ships to San Francisco. A few journeyed overland, where they joined wagon trains crossing the plains and the mountains to gold country.

Most early migrants were young, single men who became merchants or clerks, occupations with which they were familiar in Europe. Few migrants were professionals except the American-born Sephardim, many of whom were lawyers. Although Jewish men outnumbered Jewish women in the West for many years, Jewish women, married and single, began to arrive in the 1850s, especially in San Francisco. Restrictive laws and failed revolutions in Central Europe had made it difficult for Jews to make a living and start families in towns that had quotas on new Jewish households. Therefore, young women as well as men left Europe. By the 1860s and 1870s, many communities were family oriented; men over thirty, established in their occupations, often married younger women. However, the ratio between men and women varied according to the size of the population and the economic stability of the community.

Jews in the West generally enjoyed a positive relationship with their multiethnic neighbors, which reinforced their identity as Westerners. As founders and as civic and business leaders, many Jews became prominent citizens not only of their Jewish communities but also of their cities. Divisions in the Far West were more often between property owners and laborers than between European American ethnic groups.

Although the western communities were interdependent, each was distinct, its differences deriving from the decade in which it was founded, its size, economy, resources, location, and ethnic composition.

San Francisco

San Francisco sprang to life as a result of the Gold Rush. With a population of fewer than 1,000 in 1848, it grew to 20,000 by 1851. By 1860, 5,000 Jews lived there—about 8 percent of the city's population. In 1849, San Francisco's Jews formed the First Hebrew Benevolent Society; soon afterward, Jewish mutual aid societies, newspapers, fraternal organizations, social clubs, and congregations were established. After failing to find common ground, two congregations, Sherith Israel and Emanu-El, were founded in 1851. Sherith Israel, made up of Jews from England, Poland, and Posen and American-born Sephardim, followed the Polish *minhag* (prayer ritual), while Emanu-El, whose members were Bavarian, French, and American-born Sephardim, followed the German minhag. Both were what today would be called Orthodox congregations, with separate sections for men and women. Although there were more men than women, the women's gallery was oc-

cupied, and by 1851 weddings were held in the synagogues. The congregations provided for their members' needs by authorizing *shochets* (ritual slaughterers) to supply kosher meat and bakers to make *matzoh* for Passover. Although not every Jew was observant, by 1851 there were several kosher butchers and a number of kosher boardinghouses for young, unmarried men.

In 1854 Emanu-El hired its first rabbi, Julius Eckman, a Posen-born, German-trained rabbi. He arrived just in time to dedicate two synagogue buildings as Emanu-El and Sherith Israel moved into their first permanent structures. Emanu-El seated 800; Sherith Israel, 400. Both were architecturally similar to the churches of the city. By 1859 Sherith Israel had also hired a rabbi, London-trained Henry A. Henry, a perfect fit for his cosmopolitan congregation. He conducted services in English, was a Freemason, and became a leader in the wider Jewish community. Eckman, by contrast, did not fit with Emanu-El, whose members wanted to change traditions, for example, to allow men and women to sit together. By 1864 Emanu-El would be considered Reform; much later in the century, Sherith Israel also became Reform.

After leaving Emanu-El, Eckman in 1857 published and edited one of the first Jewish newspapers in the West— at times there were as many as four Jewish newspapers in the city. Eckman's paper, the *Gleaner,* informed Jews (and non-Jews) from Oregon to Nevada about Jewish issues and local, national, and international events. It was published in English, although words such as *kosher* were in Hebrew type. In addition to his popular Sabbath school, in 1861 Eckman established a free day school. Thus, at this early date in the city's history, Jewish boys and girls enrolled there could study German, French, and music as well as the subjects taught in public school. Exemplifying the mobility that characterized the West, Eckman later served as the rabbi for both Beth Israel and Ahavai Shalom in Portland. By 1870 there were four prominent congregations and a number of small prayer groups in San Francisco.

As founding fathers, San Francisco Jews worked with non-Jews to create the civic community. Abraham Labatt, a Sephardic Jew from Charleston, became both the first president of Congregation Emanu-El and an alderman. Solomon Heydenfeldt, also from Charleston, served on the California Supreme Court and chaired the Mortara proceeding in 1859, when 3,000 San Francisco Jews and Protestants protested the kidnapping in Italy of Edgardo

Mortara, a Jewish child who was taken from his family by agents of the pope because a Catholic nursemaid had secretly baptized him when he was a small child. A thousand more protested in San Francisco than in New York. Jews also joined with non-Jews for other causes. In 1851 and 1856, Jewish and non-Jewish businessmen formed Vigilance Committees, which took the law into their own hands to try to stabilize the often-violent city. Non-Jews also attended Jews' social activities, including weddings and other life-course events.

World Jewry recognized the West Coast, especially California, as a place with a significant Jewish community involved with national and international issues. When leaders of Jerusalem's Jewish community sent messengers to the United States seeking support for the poor of Jerusalem, they singled out the "magnificent State of California" for special attention. While the messengers were in San Francisco, local Jewish leaders founded Ohabai Zion (Lovers of Zion), whose sole purpose was to support Jerusalem's poor. The messengers also traveled inland, raising funds in the small mining communities and river towns.

In the interior, Jews settled in the towns that dotted the hills and waterways of gold country. In the 1850s, Jewish communities were established in Stockton, Sacramento, Jackson, Sonora, Mokelumne Hill, Nevada City, Grass Valley, and Placerville. High Holidays and Passover were celebrated in private homes, Masonic and Odd Fellows halls, and, in some communities, newly built synagogues. The larger communities hired rabbis. However, the mining economy was unstable, and many businesses failed. Fires, bankruptcies, and personal hardships often caused Jews to move on. Some returned to bustling San Francisco, while others moved up or down the coast. Small Jewish communities developed in Oakland, San Jose, Los Angeles, and San Diego. And less than a decade after the Gold Rush, Jews set out for the growing communities of Oregon.

Portland

Merchants and dreamers who did not realize their expectations in San Francisco or the tumultuous mining towns looked to Oregon to begin again. The Oregon economy was more stable because it was based on timber and agriculture, not gold. Also, because Oregon's communities were filled with brick buildings, not the wooden tents of California's mining towns, they were not as likely to be destroyed by fire. In mining country, stores could be destroyed in an evening, their suddenly destitute owners often forced to move on. In the 1850s, Caroline and Philip Selling operated a small store in the mining town of Sonora. When a fire swept through town one night, they were left with nothing. Miners took up a collection so that they could buy necessities. By 1862 the Sellings had resettled in Portland. Their son, Ben, who grew wealthy by purchasing goods manufactured in the Northwest and controlling the supply chain, became an important philanthropist, donating generously to the city's First Hebrew Benevolent Association, which assisted new immigrants, and working with the Industrial Removal Office in New York to reunite immigrant families in the West.

Portland's economy was small-scale compared to San Francisco's. Like all Jewish communities in the Pacific West, Portland's relied on San Francisco for merchandise and social activities, and it was there that it hired the educators, rabbis, or experts it needed. It was also to San Francisco that young Jewish men and women went to find Jewish spouses. By the 1870s, Jews composed 5 percent of Portland's population.

Jewish observance in Portland was institutionalized in 1858 with the establishment of Congregation Beth Israel. Among the congregation's founders were several former members of San Francisco's Temple Emanu-El; its first spiritual leader was Samuel Laski (an educated layman), followed by Herman Bien (he pretended rabbinical ordination), both formerly of San Francisco, followed soon by Julius Eckman, who had been San Francisco's first rabbi. The city's second congregation was organized less than ten years later, when some members left the original, predominantly German, congregation. Although both congregations followed the German style of prayer, their members were from different parts of Central Europe—Beth Israel's from traditionally Germanic territories, Ahavai Shalom's predominantly from the province of Posen. The newly formed congregation was named Ahavai Shalom (Lovers of Peace)—a typical name when members of one congregation left to form another where they felt more comfortable. By the late nineteenth century, Portland's Jews demonstrated their prominence with the construction of noteworthy synagogues. In 1887 Beth Israel built a large wooden synagogue that was architecturally similar to Emanu-El (1866), which dominated San Francisco's skyline.

As in cities across the West, German Jews and the "others" in Portland formed separate social circles, with the Germans establishing exclusive, elite clubs. The separation was not complete, however, and often did not extend to fraternal organizations. As the historian William Toll noted, the two groups mingled at B'nai B'rith meetings, where young men built business relationships and formed community bonds. Many of Portland's new East European immigrants had previously lived in the East—were not "greenhorns"—and because they worked in the trade sector, they therefore had common interests with the more established Jewish merchants. As in other western cities, Portland's Jews also belonged to non-Jewish organizations, joining their fellow merchants in Masonic and other lodges.

In Portland, as in cities across the West, Jews were founders and early settlers and played an important role in maintaining economic and political stability. As small merchants, they supplied nearby farms with the goods and services they required. Jewish women also played a significant role in late nineteenth-century Portland. As they Americanized, they, like non-Jewish women, engaged in community work. The Hebrew Ladies Benevolent Society worked solely with the Jewish community, while the National Council of Jewish Women undertook projects such as Neighborhood House, where both Jewish and other immigrants could encounter the settled Jewish community.

Seattle

The Jewish community of Seattle organized much later than that of San Francisco or Portland. The first congregation was established in 1889. Although Jews had lived in Washington Territory since at least 1853, when Congress separated it from Oregon, their numbers remained small. In the 1880s, when Seattle's population was 3,500, only about 100 were Jews. By contrast, San Francisco's Jews numbered 16,000 out of a total population of 233,959. In the nineteenth century, Victoria, British Columbia, was the center of Puget Sound Jewish life. With regular steamships to San Francisco, Victoria became a home for merchants seeking to supply gold miners, fishermen, and the Alaska fur trade. The Victoria Jewish community grew as an extension of San Francisco Jewry. As early as 1863, it numbered about 100, and a synagogue was built with funding

coming in part from San Francisco Jews. As Seattle grew, a strong relationship developed with other western Jewish communities. Seattle's Jews traveled to Victoria for their weddings and burials and brought men back to Seattle to lead services. Others went to Portland and San Francisco for life-course ceremonies and to buy merchandise for personal use and resale. Some, like Abraham Schwabacher, stayed in San Francisco, purchasing goods for Schwabacher brothers' Washington stores, and businesses often advertised "San Francisco prices."

Because of their access to San Francisco, Portland, and Victoria, Seattle's first Jews, many of whom were nonobservant, delayed establishing a congregation. Passover and other holidays could be celebrated at home or provided a reason to visit a larger Jewish community.

The 1880s brought considerable change: the transcontinental railroad reached Seattle, bringing reduced transportation costs, an end to relative isolation, and a larger Jewish population. In the 1890s, gold was discovered in the Yukon and Alaska, and Seattle became a supply town. Because Canada required that prospectors have $1,000 in provisions before they were allowed to enter Canadian territory, new stores sprang up in Seattle. During these years, the community grew more observant, as East European and Sephardic Jews arrived. Soon there were kosher bakeries and meat markets. By 1909 Seattle was home to three Orthodox congregations and one Reform; the Jewish community numbered close to 4,500.

During World War I, some Jewish immigrants came directly to Seattle via Asia, as German submarines threatened Atlantic travel. Others arrived from Canada or the eastern United States. Seattle grew to be the second-largest Sephardic community in the United States. Following a pattern of chain migration, most came directly to Seattle, where Sephardim became known for selling fish, produce, and baked goods in the city's markets. Remaining apart, they formed their own congregations, organizations, and self-help associations.

By the early twentieth century, San Francisco, Portland, and Seattle all had well-established Jewish communities. Attracted by the climate and economy, Jews of all backgrounds continued to make their way west. There were divisions between the founders and more recent arrivals. Because the influx of immigrants was relatively small, however, the newcomers did not overwhelm the Jewish or gentile communities.

As founders of multiethnic western cities with relatively little antisemitism, Jews were involved in governance. They held civic and leadership positions throughout the region. Bernard Goldsmith was elected mayor of Portland in 1869, and Bailey Gatzert, Seattle's sixth mayor, in 1875. In 1894 Adolph Sutro was elected mayor of San Francisco on the People's Party ticket. Julius Meier, heir of Portland's Meier & Frank department store, was governor of Oregon from 1931 to 1935. Westerners also elected Jews to national office. In 1899 San Franciscans sent Julius Kahn to Congress, where he served for more than twenty years. On his death in 1924, his wife Florence Prag Kahn won a special election for his seat, becoming the sixth woman in the House of Representatives and its first Jewish woman, serving until 1937.

Nationally, 1924 was a watershed year; the National Origins Immigration Act virtually cut off Jewish immigration to the United States. But in the West, communities continued to expand because the region's climate and economic growth drew migrants from other parts of the country. In 1925 the Jewish population of San Francisco was 25,000; by 1937 it was more than 40,000.

Second- and third-generation American Jews, many born in the West, extended the functions of Jewish institutions. Some synagogues became more than places of worship, adding theaters, schools, and recreational centers. In San Francisco, with a large and highly stratified Jewish population, the pioneer generation and its offspring often encountered new immigrants only in settlement work, where many assumed paternalistic roles. In smaller cities such as Portland, by contrast, the sons and daughters of founders and newer immigrants worked together in fraternal and voluntary associations. As the Progressive Era took shape, women increasingly moved from involvement with self-help organizations and charities to organizations with broader purposes, such as the National Council of Jewish Women, and temple sisterhoods. In subsequent decades, early settlement houses became community centers, with professionals hired to supervise activities. The West continued to function as a region during World War II, with professionals training in one city and moving to supervisory positions in another. Because of family, social, and business relations, Jews in the West continued to work together in organizations. In the 1920s and 1930s, the Jewish welfare agencies in Portland, San Francisco, Los Angeles, and Oakland kept track of transients who traveled between cities seeking aid.

Within the West, Jews differed on how they viewed the emerging Zionist movement. San Francisco's classical Reform leadership clung to an anti-Zionist position. As a deeply rooted community, many did not want to appear to have dual loyalties. Although some supported Zionism, San Francisco became known as an anti-Zionist city. With larger percentages of recent Sephardic and East European immigrants, Portland and Seattle were stronger supporters of Zionism.

Beginning in the years leading up to World War II, the West and western Jewish communities were forever changed. The military buildup brought hundreds of thousands of workers and large, new industries, reshaping the Jewish communities in many western states over the next fifty years.

Ava F. Kahn

References and Further Reading

Cline, Scott. 1987. "The Jews of Portland, Oregon: A Statistical Dimension, 1860–1880." *Oregon Historical Quarterly* 88, 1: 5–25.

Cone, Molly, Howard Droker, and Jacqueline Williams. 2003. *Family of Strangers: Building a Jewish Community in Washington State.* Seattle: University of Washington Press.

Eisenberg, Ellen. 2000. "Transplanted to the Rose City: The Creation of East European Jewish Community in Portland, Oregon." *Journal of American Ethnic History* 19, 3: 82–97.

Kahn, Ava F., ed. 2002a. *Jewish Life in the American West: Perspectives on Migration, Settlement, and Community.* Los Angeles: Autry Museum of Western Heritage and Heyday Books.

Kahn, Ava F., ed. 2002b. *Jewish Voices of the California Gold Rush: A Documentary History, 1849–1880.* Detroit, MI: Wayne State University Press.

Kahn, Ava, and Marc Dollinger, eds. 2003. *California Jews.* Hanover, NH: University Press of New England.

Kahn, Ava F., and Ellen Eisenberg. "Western Reality: Jewish Diversity during the 'German' Period." Forthcoming.

Levinson, Robert E. 1994. *The Jews in the California Gold Rush.* Berkeley, CA: Commission for the Preservation of Pioneer Jewish Cemeteries and Landmarks of the Magnes Museum.

Levy, Harriet Lane. 1996. *920 O'Farrell Street: A Jewish Girlhood in Old San Francisco.* Berkeley, CA: Heyday Books.

Lowenstein, Steven. 1987. *The Jews of Oregon, 1850–1950.* Portland, OR: Jewish Historical Society of Oregon.

Rischin, Moses, ed. 1979. *The Jews of the West, the Metropolitan Years.* Waltham, MA: American Jewish Historical Society for the Western Jewish History Center of the Magnes Museum, Berkeley, CA.

Rischin, Moses, and John Livingston, eds. 1991. *Jews of the American West*. Detroit, MI: Wayne State University Press.

Rochlin, Harriet, and Fred Rochlin. 2000a. *Pioneer Jews: A New Life in the Far West*. Boston: Houghton Mifflin.

Rochlin, Harriet, and Fred Rochlin. 2000b. *Visions of Reform: Congregation Emanu-El and the Jews of San Francisco, 1849–1999*. Berkeley, CA: Magnes Museum.

Rosenbaum, Fred. 1976. *Free to Choose: The Making of a Jewish Community in the American West*. Berkeley, CA: Magnes Museum.

Toll, William. 1982. *The Making of an Ethnic Middle Class: Portland Jewry over Four Generations*. Albany: State University of New York Press.

New Mexico

During a time of American expansion, Jews traveled from Missouri to New Mexico down the Santa Fe Trail, which connected the eastern United States, the West, and Mexico. Although crypto-Jews may have settled in this region of New Spain in the fifteenth and sixteenth centuries, and although during the Mexican period, individual Jews traded in the territory, the Jewish community was founded in the 1840s and 1850s by Ashkenazi Jews primarily from Germany. Some Jews peddled, but because of the long distances and the need to transport large amounts of goods, most settled down. They became clerks and merchants, building commercial relationships with the U.S. Army, Hispanics, Indians, and new immigrants alike. Santa Fe commerce was tied to the trail and lasted until 1879, when it was supplanted by the railroad, which bypassed the city, and Jewish communities expanded in the railroad towns throughout the state. The Jewish population in New Mexico was never large: 108 in 1878, 800 in 1905, and just over 1,000 by 1927, when a few Eastern European Jews had settled and the native-born population was several generations old (Marcus 1990). It remained small until World War II and the establishment of military research facilities, including the Los Alamos laboratories, which brought Jewish scientists and professionals to the state.

Unlike many places where Jews lived, New Mexico was primarily Catholic because of its Spanish heritage; Jews forged working and social relationships with the Protestant minority, the Hispanic Catholic majority, and Indian peoples. In this remote and sparsely settled region, there was little antisemitism, and Jews were often viewed as part of the larger Anglo population.

Most Jews followed family chains to New Mexico, with brothers and cousins leading the way. Many of the families were related by marriage. These families became local royalty; the names Ilfeld, Jaffa, and Spiegelberg are still remembered today. The Spiegelberg family's history is illustrative of Jewish life in the early years of the state. Solomon Jacob Spiegelberg, eldest of five brothers, arrived in Santa Fe from Bavaria in 1844. Soon his four brothers joined him. The family brought goods from the East and supplied locals, Indians, and most lucratively, the U.S. Army. The family first sold retail groceries and dry goods; soon they grew to become large-scale wholesalers. In 1872 they established the Second National Bank of New Mexico, and their business expanded into mining and real estate. They were related by marriage to many of the Jewish mercantile families in the state.

Like Jews everywhere, New Mexicans gathered for High Holiday services, and the first *bar mitzvah* took place in Santa Fe in 1876. Santa Fe's first Yom Kippur service was at the home of Levi and Betty Spiegelberg in 1860. Some men returned to Germany or the East to marry, while others married local women. Solomon Bibo married an Acoma Pueblo woman and became governor of the pueblo. As children were born, the community became more observant, and in 1882 Flora Spiegelberg established a Sabbath school in Santa Fe. Two Reform temples were built in the late nineteenth century, Temple Montefiore in Las Vegas and Temple Albert in Albuquerque, where in 1921 a second congregation, B'nai Israel, an Orthodox (later Conservative) synagogue, was established. The birth of B'nai Israel is evidence of a small Eastern European population; when founded, it had seventeen members.

With the arrival of the railroad in 1879, Santa Fe's economic dominance declined along with its Jewish population. By the beginning of the twentieth century, some of the pioneer founders and their families had left Santa Fe. Indeed, some of the Spiegelbergs moved to eastern cities for business opportunities and to live in closer proximity to Jewish institutions. The cities of Las Cruces, Las Vegas, and Albuquerque grew, with Albuquerque sustaining the largest Jewish population, 240 by 1927 and 2,000 by 1960 (Marcus 1990).

Jews helped build the civic communities as well. The youngest Spiegelberg brother, Willi, was elected mayor of

Santa Fe in 1880, and five years later Henry N. Jaffa became the first mayor of Albuquerque. When New Mexico achieved statehood in 1912, Jews were community, civic, and political leaders, although they were never more than 0.6 percent of the total population (Marcus 1990).

Most Jews continued to be involved in commerce; however, some also were involved in ranching and agriculture. One such woman was Yetta Goldsmith Kohn, a widow with four children, who arrived in New Mexico in 1902 and became a successful rancher, store owner, and businesswoman. Kohn homesteaded along the railroad tracks west of Tucumcari. By 1927 Tucumcari was home to forty-one Jews (Marcus 1990). In Las Cruces, Louis E. Freudental, a founder's son, turned to commercial agriculture, growing vegetables and nut trees in addition to raising poultry.

Ava F. Kahn

References and Further Reading
Jaehn, Tomas, ed. 2003. *Jewish Pioneers of New Mexico.* Santa Fe: Museum of New Mexico Press.
Marcus, Jacob Rader. 1990. *To Count a People: American Jewish Population Data, 1585–1984.* Lanham, MD: University Press of America.
Tobias, Henry J. 1990. *A History of the Jews in New Mexico.* Albuquerque: University of New Mexico Press.

Jews in Small Towns in America

Historians of American Jewry have focused on the adaptation of immigrants and their offspring in big cities, largely ignoring the experience of Jews in small towns. Although from the early phases of their settlement in America Jews tended to concentrate in large cities, a significant proportion—between 20 and 30 percent, depending on the period and region—lived in small towns. Jewish experience there differed from that of their coreligionists in big cities. It also differed considerably from town to town, depending on the size, socioeconomic, and civic–political characteristics of the locality, and on the number, religious orientation, and organization of resident Jews.

During the industrial period of American history, from the 1880s through World War II, the experience of Jews in small towns—defined by urban historians as containing fewer than 75,000 residents—differed from that of their big-city fellow ethnics in four main aspects. Whereas in large cities between 40 and 60 percent of Jewish immigrants worked in light manufacturing, and the American-born second generation moved en masse into middle-class, white-collar occupations, in small towns 60 to 80 percent of the employed Jewish population—immigrants and second generation alike—worked in small, family-run or coethnic businesses. Second, the opportunities for occupational advancement were much more limited in the small towns than in the large cities. Third, because of their low numbers, Jews in small towns were unable to build extensive, institutionally diverse communities like those enjoyed by their big-city coreligionists. Fourth, small-town Jews who participated in local mainstream civil–political affairs did so as individual citizens, not as representatives of their ethnic group's interests, as Jews in big cities with large Jewish populations did at least occasionally (Morawska 1996, bibliography).

Although different from the lives of their big-city fellow ethnics, the experience of Jews in small towns also varied considerably from town to town. It reflected, in part, the divergent characteristics of the surrounding environment, including the size of the town, the nature of the local economy, the social structure, the ethnic/religious composition of the population, ethnic residential segregation, the exclusive or inclusive civic–political climate, hierarchical or competitive ethnic relations and politics, public recognition of Jews who were among the town's pioneer settlers, the social distance of dominant groups from outsiders and Jews, antisemitic incidents, and the local relevance of race. Characteristics of the local Jewish group also accounted for the variety of experience, including the size of the Jewish group, its share of the town's population, its position in the socioeconomic structure, the Jews' sense of a shared past with local high-status groups, their participation in local civic–political organizations and affairs, or in the informal social activities of the dominant groups. The Jewish experience also depended on Jews' residential concentration, their residential stability, the availability of absorbing intragroup networks and activities, the Jews' religious and/or ethnic commitment, their self-separatism, the proportion of American-born Jews, and the degree of separation between German and East European Jews.

These factors differently shaped the Jews' economic position and involvement in civil–political activities; the religious orientation, organization, and inclusiveness of local Jewish communities; and the prevalent types of collective Jewish identity. Some of these diverse patterns can be seen through a comparison of the experiences of Jews in Greensboro, North Carolina; Charleston, South Carolina; Muncie, Indiana; and Johnstown, Pennsylvania. (Unfortunately, sporadic data for the first three towns preclude a comparison of the occupational pursuits and public roles of Jewish women.)

Greensboro, North Carolina, with a population of 55,000 in 1930, including about 500 Jews—1 percent of the total—had, since the turn of the twentieth century, grown into a thriving center of textile manufacturing and wholesale trade. Local Jewish merchants, both German (with larger capital) and East European (on a smaller scale), had been instrumental in this development. By 1920, representatives of both groups (although the majority were German) belonged to the town's economic elite, and the industry owned by one Jewish family employed more than one-tenth of Greensboro's working population. The rest of the Jewish families occupied solidly middle-class positions. Since the local government closely cooperated with the economic elite, Jews had access to political positions.

The longtime presence of Quakers and their influence on Greensboro public affairs sustained a tradition of tolerance, and almost no antisemitism existed. (The same tradition also made white attitudes toward, and treatment of, local blacks much more enlightened than the Southern norm.) The town's pride—the local colleges, especially the University of North Carolina branch and Guilford College—also contributed to the liberal civic climate.

Greensboro's Jews were residentially dispersed, but from the turn of the twentieth century until World War II, one Reform congregation gathered in most of them, both Germans and East Europeans. Uncommon at the time, this religious symbiosis between the two groups, which were about equal in size, can be explained by the facts that most of the East Europeans were old-time residents and in 1930 two-thirds were already second generation, and by the two groups' close economic ties and shared participation in the town's civic–political and social life. Aside from the temple, there were few Jewish organizations in town that could have reinforced the ethnic identity of members; those that existed were practical rather than social–cultural or ideological (e.g., Zionist) in character. Instead, the local rabbi and his wife organized social and cultural events to bring the gentile and Jewish communities together. As old-time established residents and pillars of the town's economic

well-being, Greensboro's Jews also belonged to local country clubs and other high-status associations. Due to these combined circumstances, except on special religious occasions, the Jews' ethnic identity was not particularly relevant as a cultural or social boundary in daily life.

Attenuated both by conditions in the local society and in the Jewish group, the "thin" ethnic identity of Greensboro's Jews, in turn, weakened their need to associate with fellow ethnics or to sustain group institutions and increased their readiness to participate in mainstream local organizations, further eroding a sense of commonality and separateness.

The old Southern city of Charleston, South Carolina, had a population of 62,000 in 1930, of which 2,300, or about 3 percent, were Jews. Unlike in Greensboro, the Jews' high social position and integration into Charleston society did not derive from their economic might. Largely unaffected by the rapid industrialization of the late nineteenth century, Charleston's economy had been rather stagnant. The town had neither a superwealthy class (the white population was distributed across the upper-to-lower-middle strata) nor the tough competition for socioeconomic success characteristic of contemporary urban centers in the Northeast. As a result, "parvenu" Jews were not perceived as a status threat. In a distinctly Southern, premodern status system, the elevated position of local Jews had its origins in the long and illustrious pedigree of the town's Jewish residents, who dated back to colonial times. Sephardic Jews who arrived in Charleston in the late 1660s were among the city's recognized founders, and they had also been patriot–heroes of the American Revolution and devoted soldiers of the Confederacy, to which both old-time Sephardi and more recent Ashkenazi German Charlestonians pledged allegiance. Jews' integration into the local society had been further facilitated by the significance of race as the main social divider (blacks constituted about one-half of Charleston's population.)

Most East Europeans had arrived later and without merits comparable to those of their predecessors. Because of the long-term honorific status of their established coreligionists, however, and, more important, the absence of resistance or social distancing from them, East European Jews were accepted as good American and Charlestonian citizens. The unproblematic integration of East Europeans was facilitated by the absence of sharp economic divisions or residential concentration by class or origin in the already-established Jewish group. Perhaps more important was the religious orientation of Charleston's Jewry: a bizarre mix, peculiar to the place, called Orthodox Reform, wherein both components of Judaism were practiced, albeit with the laxity characteristic of Southern culture.

Beth Elohim, the oldest congregation, was Reform in name, but (lax) Orthodox in practice. Established around 1750, one century later it considered itself Reform, but the members' religious behavior indicates that it was "old wine in a new bottle." When German Jews—the majority from Polish lands—arrived in Charleston in the nineteenth century and erected a synagogue, they retained the Sephardi rite of their predecessors because of the Sephardim's local status and their own sense of decorum. The Brith Shalom, or "Polish synagogue," as it was called, did not have daily services, and its members did not observe the Sabbath, but men wore hats during services, and their wives kept kosher homes. By the interwar period, however, the elements of Orthodox practice diminished further, and Reform elements became more numerous.

Similarly, Beth Israel, the Orthodox synagogue established by East Europeans at the beginning of the twentieth century to make observance stricter than that practiced at Brith Shalom, had by the 1920s become pluralistic and tolerant of deviation. The permissiveness in religious observance of the two synagogues also reflected the high proportion (nearly 70 percent) of American-born in the local Jewish population. That a considerable number of congregants, Germans and East Europeans alike, held multiple memberships in these synagogues or circulated between them further contributed to the blurring of religious and social boundaries within the Jewish group.

Contacts between Charleston's Jews and members of the local society were frequent and cordial. Jews actively participated in civic affairs and gentile social clubs and, much more unusually, invited and received gentiles at Jewish celebrations (e.g., the annual Purim Ball was anxiously anticipated and eagerly attended by Charleston business and professional classes). "Rarely [have Jews] attained so high a degree of integration in the general life of a town," noted a contemporary observer (Sherman 1951).

Reflecting their position in the local mainstream society, the extent and intensity of Charleston Jews' ethnic identity attenuated over the period considered here. As in Greensboro, most did not consider their ethnic member-ship relevant to their everyday lives as Charlestonians. Nevertheless, unlike Greensboro Jews, Charleston Jews—like all residents of this traditional town—considered themselves religious (however lax their observance). Historians of Jewish American life in large urban centers during the pre–World War II era have pointed to the progressive severing of the traditionally indivisible ethnic and religious components of Judaism—the ethnic sphere gaining social and cultural autonomy and, gradually, primacy over the religious dimension. (Synagogues turned into Synagogue-Centers, which then became Social Centers with synagogue attachments.) The reverse, however, seems to have occurred in prewar Charleston—an attenuation of the ethnic, and maintenance of the religious, elements of Jewishness. Shaped by circumstances in the local society and within the Jewish group, the de-ethnicized religious identity of Charleston Jews contributed to their increased participation in the local civic–political process and informal social activities, which, in turn, sustained their de-ethnicized collective identification.

Greensboro and Charleston in the Carolinas represent small towns where Jews' successful integration into local communities during the 1880–1940 period attenuated their group ethnic identity. In Muncie, Indiana, and Johnstown, Pennsylvania, by contrast, the economic and political marginality of the local Jews, along with their (albeit dissimilar) in-group characteristics, resulted in the persistence of "alert," though differently textured, collective identities.

Muncie, Indiana—the famous Middletown described by sociologists Robert and Helen Lynd (1929, 1937) as representing the typical America of the period (a claim criticized in a number of subsequent studies)—had a population of 47,000 in 1930, of which Jews constituted no more than 200, or about 0.5 percent. The first Jews arrived in Muncie from Alsatia in the middle of the nineteenth century, although they did not remain very long. German settlers in the 1870s were followed in the 1890s by East Europeans resettling from larger East Coast and Midwestern cities. From the beginning of the twentieth century, they constituted the majority of the town's small Jewish population.

Muncie's economy, primarily focused on the production of durable goods, diversified by the interwar period to include foundry products, wire, glass, automobile and machine parts, and metal household furniture. Just before the

Great Depression, about one-half of the town's gainfully employed worked in manufacturing and 15 percent in trade. Muncie's Jews concentrated in small family- and ethnic-run retail businesses in the lower strata of the local trade sector.

The town's political system, described by the Lynds (1937) as an "antiquated machine" alternating between Republican (dominant) and Democratic bureaucrats, carried on its "Byzantine politics" with little involvement of an apathetic citizenry. Reflecting the composition and prevalent orientation of the residents—more than 85 percent of whom were second- or third-generation Protestant Americans of rural midwestern origins—a mixture of evangelical Protestantism and American nativism permeated the town's civic culture and public institutions throughout the period considered here. This exclusionary ideology and political practice were exacerbated by the "loud" activities of Muncie's Ku Klux Klan (KKK). Although short-lived (1923–1925), public displays of the Klan's aggressive xenophobia had enduring consequences for the town's civic climate and for the sense of insecurity of the local groups—Catholics, blacks, and Jews—that were the objects of its chauvinism. Historical sources indicate that the KKK's hostility was directed mainly against local blacks and Catholics rather than the few, largely invisible, nonthreatening Jews. Indeed, old-time Jewish residents perceived local Klansmen as domesticated predators who patronized Jewish stores and said "hallo" on the street. However mild and subdued, the town's antisemitism was, the Lynds observed, like "tinder ready for kindling if and as Middletown wants a bonfire to burn a scapegoat" (1937). And local Jews remained acutely aware of this ever-present possibility long after the Klan was silenced in Muncie.

Unlike in Charleston and Greensboro, in Muncie neither a pedigree as pioneer settlers, a strong economic position, nor an inclusive civic–political process facilitated Jews' participation in town politics. And Jews themselves, anxious not to alienate the customers of their small businesses by taking public stands on local issues, "tried to keep a low profile" (Rottenberg 1997) and refrained from involvement in political affairs. Until the postwar era, the Jewish presence in municipal politics was confined to one person, the uncommonly outgoing "activist" Charles Indorf, owner of the Muncie Loan Company and King's Clothing Shop.

Jewish merchants' membership in the Muncie Chamber of Commerce was nominal, and they were not welcome in the prestigious Delaware Country Club or in service clubs such as Rotary, Lions, or Kiwanis. Except for business-related contacts with customers, Jews remained outside mainstream social life. Too small to form a ghetto, they were, nevertheless, residentially concentrated in the downtown (business) section, and their attempts to move into the prestigious North Side were met with resistance from realtors and residents. The tacit rule of "the five o'clock shadow," practiced by native-born American Munsonians, routinely separated the residents along ethnoreligious lines after work hours. The Jewish small merchants, preoccupied with making a living, worked long hours in their stores, and this, along with their in-group social engagement, further contributed to the separation.

Founded in the 1870s as the Beth El Reform Congregation and renamed Emanu-El in the 1920s when the temple was built, the Jewish religious community in Muncie was officially affiliated with the Hebrew Union College (Reform), even though the majority of its East European immigrant members came from Orthodox homes. The reasons for this uncommon alliance, however, were different from those in Greensboro. Fewer Jews lived in Muncie, and their concentration in small businesses did not provide the funds necessary to support a second (Orthodox) congregation. In addition, Muncie East Europeans were lax in their religious observance, practicing a private religion, as local residents put it; many felt Jewish, but not very religious. This abandonment of Orthodox precepts may have resulted from their prior sojourns in larger American cities, where traditional practices were often undermined. This tendency was certainly furthered in Muncie, however, by the scarcity of religious services, which were provided only by part-time rabbinical students from the Hebrew Union College in nearby Cincinnati. Muncie Jews' anxious avoidance of exposing their otherness may also have contributed to this "privatization" or minimization of their religious affiliation. If not the religious center, the temple was, however, the hub of local Jews' social life, in part because of their externally imposed isolation from Muncie's mainstream society and also because, given the climate of the town, they preferred to stay among their own.

Thus, local circumstances combined with Jews' small numbers and marginal position in Muncie to sustain their ever-anxious group ethnic identity (Lynd and Lynd 1937,

Gordon 1964, Rottenberg 1997). Impossible to shed in a small town where "everybody knew each other," this uneasy identity was, for its bearers, perhaps a joy in private life, but a persistent burden in public.

Johnstown, Pennsylvania, in 1930 had a population of 67,000, including about 1,250 Jews, fewer than 2 percent. Self-contained amid the hills of western Pennsylvania, Johnstown was dominated by one industry and one powerful employer—the Cambria Steel Company, later Bethlehem Steel—with about three-quarters of its male population in manufacturing and mining. Nonunionized, ethnically fragmented, and tightly controlled by the established Anglo-Protestant elite, until World War II Johnstown remained fundamentally an autocratic town. Mercantile activities were essentially limited to feeding and clothing employees of the Bethlehem Company and its subsidiaries, and the prosperity of local merchants varied directly with the fortunes of local steel and coal enterprises and their employees. Although less aggressive than in Muncie, the Christian-nativist orientation of Johnstown's native-born American population and its industrial elite sustained a civic–political climate resistant to the integration of the predominantly working-class South and East European immigrants and their children—still referred to as "foreigners" in the 1930s—who constituted one-third of the town's population.

The first Jews from Germany settled in Johnstown in the 1860s, followed in the 1880s by East European Jews, who by the beginning of the twentieth century made up about 90 percent of the local Jewish community. German as well as East European Jewish households earned their livelihoods from business. The enterprises of the German Jewish merchants, who were established earlier and had extensive trade connections with fellow ethnics in Philadelphia, were generally larger and more prosperous than those of the East Europeans, who concentrated in small retail businesses. Unlike their Muncie counterparts, whose downtown stores catered to a native-born American clientele, in a replica of the traditional pattern of Old Country economic interdependence the majority of East European Jewish businesses in Johnstown served Slavic and Hungarian peasant immigrants and their offspring—about 20 percent of the town's population and 60 percent of its industrial workforce—in their "foreign" sections of town. Johnstown's heavy-industrial economic structure combined with the confinement of Jewish businesses to an East

European (multi-)ethnic economic niche to marginalize the Jews even more than in Muncie.

The civic–political and social situations of the Johnstown Jews and the Muncie Jews were, however, similar. The exclusionary, autocratic political system dominated by a white Anglo-Protestant industrial elite precluded the participation of Johnstown's Jewish residents in local politics and mainstream social life. From the 1880s until World War II, they held only a few low-level municipal political offices. Except for a couple of more affluent Germans, they were excluded from the more influential country clubs. Their attempts, during the interwar period, to move into Westmont, the most prestigious neighborhood in town, were resisted by native-born American residents (although Jews eventually managed to carve out a part of it for themselves). And, except for practical encounters, they had almost no social relations outside their own group.

A clear undercurrent of antisemitism—couched in traditional Christian symbolism rather than in the secular images of the Jew as economic predator, overbearing social arriviste, or Bolshevik common in large American cities in the interwar period—combined with the economic marginality and political and social exclusion of Johnstown's Jews, sustained their separate ethnic identity. As in Muncie, its integral element was the perception of group vulnerability. But there was an important difference.

Throughout the interwar period, Johnstown hosted three Jewish congregations, each with an array of affiliated associations: Rodef Sholom, the largest and initially Orthodox, had by the 1930s become "Consorthodox," with a small, strictly Orthodox offshoot, Ahavath Achim, and the "German" Reform Temple Beth Zion. A much larger Jewish community than in Muncie was, of course, the precondition for Johnstown Jews to support three congregations. Another reason, however, was that Johnstown's synagogues—especially Rodef Sholom, with which more than 80 percent of the East European Jewish majority were affiliated—were the centers of the inseparable religious-and-social life of the community. Religious observance of East European Jews in Johnstown, both public and private, was far more extensive than that of their fellow ethnics in Muncie, and so was the importance they assigned to the religious dimension of their group membership.

At least three factors account for the enduring religious observance and strong religious identification of Johnstown Jews (Morawska 1996). Most came from traditional, semirural *shtetls;* most had moved directly to Johnstown within three or four years of their first stopover in America. In the context of Johnstown's geographic isolation, general cultural parochialism, and sharp ethnic segmentation, the East European Jews' economic, civic–political, and social marginality combined with their unusually high rate of residential persistence—in contrast to the mobility of the Muncie Jews—contributed to the maintenance of their religious traditionalism. It was further enhanced by the sharp social and religious divisions (absent in Muncie) between German and East European groups that were sustained through the interwar period. Although Johnstown Jews perceived their situation as vulnerable and preferred to remain inconspicuous, they were less tormented by their Jewishness or accepted it more as a natural condition—a result of the inseparability of its ethnic and religious dimensions—than did their fellow ethnics in Muncie. This comparison suggests that, in an unfriendly or even hostile environment, a collective identity solidly anchored in communal ethnoreligious practices makes Jewish lives less stressful than group membership based solely on ethnic (social and cultural) bonds.

In the post–World War II era, the diversity of Jewish experience in American small towns did not disappear (Gordon 1964; Lavender 1977; Rose 1977; Schoenfeld 1970; Shosteck 1953), but it has progressively diminished. Three common tendencies became increasingly visible over time. After a period of growth and diversification from 1945 through the 1950s—the result of the arrival of new Jewish residents—small-town Jewish communities began to dwindle in size and vitality. By the 1990s, an estimated 2.5 percent of American Jews lived in towns with populations of fewer than 100,000 (calculated from data in Goldstein 1992; Goldstein and Goldstein 1996). Those Jews who remained became increasingly integrated—economically, civically, and socially, including intermarriage—into local mainstream societies. And the decline of Jewish communal life and the integration of resident Jews increasingly individualized or rendered optional (Waters 1990) Jewish religious and/or ethnic identities and practices.

A confluence of external and in-group circumstances led to these developments. Rapid advances in transportation and communication technologies compressed geographic distances, facilitating contacts and residential mobility. These changes were accompanied by the increasing receptivity of mainstream Americans and their institutions to different ethnic groups and traditions. At the same time, second- and third-generation American Jews, more educated and with higher achievement aspirations and broader cultural ambitions than their parents, saw few acceptable opportunities in small towns and moved to large cities. At the other end of the age structure, a growing number of retirees—the core of old-time Jewish communities—have been leaving for Florida and, more recently, for California.

As testified in numerous memorial books published by dwindling small-town congregations across America, in which old-time residents tell their stories of "how it was," the era of diverse and vibrant Jewish life in small towns is quickly coming to a close. Time will show whether new circumstances will revive such communities.

Ewa Morawska

References and Further Reading

American Jewish Year Books. 1919/1920, 1927/1928, 1929/1930, 1938/1939, 1941/1942. "Statistics of Jews" and "Local Organizations": Charleston, South Carolina; Johnstown, Pennsylvania.

Goldstein, Sydney. 1992. "Profile of American Jewry." *American Jewish Year Book* 92: 77–176.

Goldstein, Sidney, and Alice Goldstein. 1996. *Jews on the Move: Implications for Jewish Identity.* Albany: State University of New York Press.

Gordon, Whitney. 1964. *A Community in Stress.* New York: Living Books.

Kipp, Samuel. 1977. "Old Notables and Newcomers: The Economic and Political Elite in Greensboro, 1880–1920." *Journal of Southern History* 43: 372–394.

Lavender, Abraham, ed. 1977. *A Coat of Many Colors: Jewish Subcommunities in the United States.* Westport, CT: Greenwood Press.

Lynd, Robert, and Helen Lynd. 1929. *Middletown. A Study in American Culture.* New York: Harcourt Brace & World.

Lynd, Robert, and Helen Lynd. 1937. *Middletown in Transition.* New York: Harcourt Brace & World.

Morawska, Ewa. 1996. *Insecure Prosperity: Smalltown Jews in Industrial America, 1880–1940.* Princeton, NJ: Princeton University Press.

Robison, Sophia, ed. 1943. "Jewish Population Studies." *Jewish Social Studies* III, Special Issue.

Rose, Peter. 1977. *Strangers in Their Midst: Small-Town Jews and Their Neighbors.* Merrick, NY: Richwood.

Rottenberg, Dan. 1997. *Middletown Jews.* Bloomington: Indiana University Press.

Schoenfeld, Eugene. 1970. "Small-town Jews' Integration into Their Communities." *Rural Sociology* 35: 174–190.

Sherman, Bezalel. 1951. "Charleston, S.C. 1750–1950." *Jewish Frontier* 18: 14–16.

Shosteck, Robert. 1953. *Small-town Jewry Tell Their Story.* New York: B'nai B'rith Vocational Service.

Waters, Mary. 1990. *Ethnic Options: Choosing Identities in America.* Berkeley: University of California Press.

Zweigenhaft, Richard. 1978. "The Jews of Greensboro: In or Out of the Upper Class." *Contemporary Jewry* 4: 60–76.

Jewish Agricultural Colonies

Between 1880 and 1910, East European Jewish immigrants established approximately seventy planned farming communities, or colonies, throughout the United States. Based on strategies developed in Russia to address the "Jewish problem," these colonies aimed to "normalize" the Jewish occupational profile through agrarian labor and to serve as models of communal or cooperative life. Established German American Jews supported the colonization movement as a way of diverting immigrants from eastern cities and promoting their Americanization. Although few colonies survived for more than a few years, they played an important role in opening new areas of the country to Jewish settlement, and former colonists provided leadership in these emerging Jewish communities.

When the hopes of Jewish intellectuals for Western-style emancipation in Russia were shattered by pogroms in 1881–1882, many turned to new strategies, including revolutionary movements, emigration, and agrarianism. The *Am Olam* (Eternal People), founded in Odessa in 1881, combined elements of these ideologies by arguing that the "Jewish problem" could be solved through the establishment of socialist, agrarian colonies in the United States. Members believed that antisemitism was based in part on the "abnormal" occupational structure of Jews in Europe, where Jews had generally been prohibited from owning and cultivating the land. They argued that farming represented a pure and productive form of labor that would "normalize" Jewish life. Like the founders of the parallel movement to establish agricultural settlements in Palestine, Am Olam members believed that their colonies would demonstrate to the world both the value of communal living and Jews' capacity for productive labor.

Am Olam members founded the initial wave of colonies in 1881–1882. Intact chapters established a few colonies, such as New Odessa in Oregon; heterogeneous groups, which also included some whose connections to the organization are unclear, founded others. Established

American Jews, eager to divert immigrants from eastern cities, provided financial support. Approximately twenty-four colonies, with populations ranging from a few dozen individuals to sixty families or more, had been established by 1884. The most significant and best documented of these were located in Louisiana, the Dakotas, Oregon, Kansas, and New Jersey, and additional colonies were founded in Colorado and Arkansas.

Several of these colonies were initially established with communal ownership. For example, all holdings of the New Odessa Colony in Oregon and the Bethlehem Judea Colony in South Dakota were owned collectively; members lived together in a single household, and all shared the community's work equally. Such organization, however, proved temporary in nearly all of the colonies: within two years, settlers at Bethlehem Judea had divided the land into individual parcels. This transition from communal ownership to private property was a response to disagreements in some colonies but was built into the design of others. Indeed, the constitution of the Sicily Island Colony in Louisiana stipulated that land would be held collectively for two years and then divided into family holdings. Some colonies—particularly those on land obtained under the Homestead Act (1862), which had no provision for collective ownership—were based on private property from their inception.

Although it has been widely assumed that the colonists had no prior agricultural experience, fragmentary evidence of the settlers' occupational backgrounds suggests that a sizable portion—about one-fifth—of colonists had experience in farming (Eisenberg 1995). Despite the widespread prohibitions on Jewish farming and land owning in Europe, these areas were open to Jews in some parts of the southern Pale, where Jewish agricultural colonies existed during the nineteenth century. In addition, there were a number of colonists who had been merchants trading in agricultural products. Others were students, scholars, and professionals. Reflecting the Jewish occupational profile in the South Pale, relatively few were industrial workers or artisans.

Colony life centered on agricultural labor. Several colonies required that all members engage in farming, and at least one banned commercial activity. Colony life also focused heavily on intellectual and cultural development. In New Odessa, for example, the strict regimen included time set aside daily for "intellectual activity," including sessions on mathematics, English, philosophy, current events, and equal rights for women. Many of the colonies had regular lecture programs and concerts as well as social activities such as dances. Some organized choirs. Notably missing in many of these colonies was organized religious life. Many of the intellectuals attracted to the colonies had rejected traditional Judaism while still in Russia. Although accounts from several colonies indicate some degree of religious observance, such as the celebration of a Passover *seder,* in others religious law was not only ignored but flouted by such practices as raising pigs. Contemporary observer Rabbi Judah Wechsler of Minnesota wrote of the New Odessa colonists, "they do not observe the Sabbath. They desecrate the Holidays and they told me directly that they are completely disinterested definitely in Judaism" (Eisenberg 1995). Although many colonies were entirely Jewish, in some cases non-Jews also lived within the settlements, and in the case of New Odessa, a non-Jew with experience in communal living was recruited to lead the colony.

The overwhelming majority of the colonies were extremely short-lived, lasting five years or fewer. A number fell victim to harsh conditions typical of their regions: malaria in the Arkansas colony; flooding at Sicily Island; and grasshoppers, blizzards, and hailstorms in the Dakota colonies. Others were torn by internal disputes, as at New Odessa, where the community was split by a controversy over the recruited leader. In some cases, as at Cremieux, South Dakota, and Beersheba, Kansas, disputes between colonists and sponsors were critical. For example, financial sponsors in Cincinnati attempted to control Beersheba Colony through a supervisor and objected when the colonists made financial decisions without consulting them. Misunderstandings over whether aid provided by sponsors was intended as a gift or a loan plagued a number of settlements.

Exceptional among the colonies in terms of longevity were those in central New Jersey, near Vineland, which survived well into the twentieth century. Alliance Colony, founded in 1882 by a group that included several Am Olam leaders, had a brief period of communal living followed by division of holdings among the families. The proximity of this colony to New York and Philadelphia made it attractive to newcomers who, while not subscribing to the ideologies of the colony movement, were eager to leave urban areas and establish themselves in an all-Jewish settlement. In addition, proximity to the wealthy and prominent German American sponsors enabled them to exercise considerable control. Through their loan policies, sponsors shaped the colony as one based on individual landholdings and introduced industrial enterprises, such as garment factories, to attract additional immigrants to the area. Although their support was essential to the survival of Alliance and neighboring colonies, sponsor goals were at odds with those of the early settlers. While settlers had established agrarian colonies based on cooperative (if not communal) principles, sponsors saw the colonies as an outlet for "removal" policies aimed at relocating immigrants from urban ghettos to rural areas and as an arena for "Americanizing" the immigrants through cultural programming and loan policies aimed at teaching the colonists financial responsibility. In Carmel Colony, several miles from Alliance, where the initial sponsor was more in accord with settler goals, communal tendencies continued longer, with land purchased collectively as late as 1889.

Sponsor policies led to the founding of additional colonies in southern New Jersey in the early 1890s, including the industrially based settlements of Norma and Brotmanville, which grew around factories established earlier at either end of Alliance, and Woodbine in southern Cape May County. Sponsors believed factories would draw Jewish industrial workers to the settlements, aiding the goal of removal, while creating a local market for the agricultural goods grown and providing employment for farm families during the winter. These developments contributed to the survival and growth of the South Jersey colonies, which reached their peak population in the mid-1910s, while altering them significantly. Newcomers drawn by factories did not share the distinctive regional and ideological background of the early colonists. As the settlements grew, the cooperative elements and the sense of mission that had characterized them earlier dissipated, as they evolved from colonies to communities whose distinctiveness lay primarily in their rural location rather than in their ideological orientation.

Although the most active period of colony formation occurred in the 1880s and 1890s, Clarion Colony, Utah, was founded in 1911. It mimicked the earlier Am Olam settlements in its ambition to model a new mode of Jewish life and in its plan to move from communal organization to individual holdings. While the community grew quickly to 156 people, it was devastated by floods and sold to creditors after a few years.

Woodbine, New Jersey, Jewish agricultural community. (American Jewish Historical Society)

Despite the short-lived nature of most colonies, they were critical in establishing migration streams that brought independent Jewish farmers and other Jewish immigrants into rural areas and small towns in states ranging from New Jersey to Kansas. For example, in North Dakota, new Jewish settlers replaced the colonists beginning in the late 1880s and continuing into the 1910s. These newcomers settled not as colonists but as individual farm families concentrated in the district where the colonies had been; they were followed by Jewish immigrants who settled in the towns of the same region. At Painted Woods, where the Jewish farm population had dwindled to 3 families by 1900, there were approximately 40 more families by 1906 and a total of 250 by 1912. Ultimately, approximately 800 Jewish farm families filed homestead claims in North Dakota, only about half of whom had been members of organized colonies (Eisenberg 2002).

As early settlers, colony veterans frequently became leaders of Jewish communities that emerged in these rural areas, the small market towns that served them, and the larger cities of second settlement. This pattern is clearly visible in Portland, Oregon, which attracted a number of colony veterans whose organizational experience, language skills, and relative acculturation propelled them into leadership positions in institutions ranging from synagogues and schools to B'nai B'rith lodges.

Ellen Eisenberg

References and Further Reading
Eisenberg, Ellen. 1995. *Jewish Agricultural Colonies in New Jersey, 1882–1920.* Syracuse, NY: Syracuse University Press.
Eisenberg, Ellen. 2002. "From Cooperative Farming to Urban Leadership." In *Jewish Life in the American West,*

edited by Ava F. Kahn, pp. 113–131. Los Angeles: Autry Museum of Western Heritage.

Goldberg, Robert. 1986. *Back to the Soil: The Jewish Farmers of Clarion, Utah, and Their World.* Salt Lake City: University of Utah Press.

Herscher, Uri. 1981. *Jewish Agricultural Utopias in America, 1880–1910.* Detroit, MI: Wayne State University Press.

Jews in Suburbia

In the decades leading up to World War II, Jews experienced suburbanization as individuals, with isolated families relocating out of the urban core to the metropolitan periphery. Then, for about four decades after World War II, a period of communal suburbanization saw the whole of the Jewish communal infrastructure leave older urban neighborhoods for newer suburban ones. Since the 1980s, the Jewish community has entered a matured period in which suburbia is taken for granted.

Individual Suburbanization

Prior to World War II, suburbia had not yet become a cultural ideal for middle-class Americans. Suburbs were generally seen as wealthy residential cloisters dominated by Protestants (Chicago's North Shore or Philadelphia's Main Line), as working-class towns dominated by ethnic immigrants (Chicago's Cicero), or sleepy, rural hamlets on the edge of the big city (Skokie, outside Chicago). For American Jews, moving to suburbia meant abandoning the dense Jewish infrastructure of the urban immigrant neighborhoods. Such places as Boston's Blue Hill Avenue, Chicago's Maxwell Street, and Toronto's Kensington held the heart and soul of the urban Jewish community. Here were the first homes of the hundreds of thousands of European immigrants. Here were the dense agglomerations of synagogues, Hebrew schools, Jewish businesses, and most other communal institutions. Leaving this core for a newer and larger home in a mostly non-Jewish suburb held little appeal for most Jews. Instead, Jews who relocated usually moved to adjacent urban neighborhoods, returning to the older neighborhood for their communal needs.

Those Jews who moved to the suburban periphery did so on an individual basis, with little expectation that the whole of the Jewish infrastructure—the synagogues, the Hebrew schools, the kosher butcher shops—would relocate with them. There were, of course, exceptions to this trend, and before World War II one could find small Jewish communities sprouting in the suburbs of New York (Nassau County) and Boston, where as early as 1911 enough Jews had moved to Brookline to form their own *minyan*. By the late 1930s, more than 18,000 Jews called Nassau County home, but this was still a small minority compared to the 100,000 living in Queens (Vincent 2005).

Communal Suburbanization

After World War II, vast areas of farmland on the peripheries of every major metropolitan region were transformed into new suburban neighborhoods. William Levitt, a Jewish real estate developer, was responsible for creating the modern subdivision through his innovative building methods. Using an assembly-line method of house construction, Levitt and his imitators were able to build houses rapidly and cheaply, thus opening the metropolitan frontier to millions of Americans—thousands of Jews included—who in previous decades would not have been able to afford a suburban home.

Unlike the earlier period of individual suburbanization, the years after World War II saw the entire infrastructure of the Jewish community relocate to the metropolitan periphery. In every major city, suburbanizing Jews brought their synagogues along with them, and in time Jewish schools moved with their students, and kosher butcher shops and bakeries and other Jewish institutions followed their clientele. The movement to suburbia also sparked the formation of new institutions, as many Jews wanted a fresh start in their new environment. In Nassau County, Long Island, for example, more than eighty new synagogues were founded in the eight years after World War II.

This wholesale relocation of Jewish communities to the suburban frontier was not without its problems. Suburbanizing synagogues faced questions about how to serve those members who were staying behind. Moreover, the suburban neighborhoods into which Jews moved did not always welcome the newcomers; anti-Jewish sentiments still dominated many small communities on the metropolitan fringe. Legal entanglements over the construction of synagogue buildings were frequent in the 1950s, with prominent lawsuits between synagogues and towns in Beachwood, Ohio, and Indianapolis, Indiana, for example.

Sadly, though they often faced discrimination, Jews were not entirely exempt from their own prejudices. In many cities, Jewish suburbanization coincided with the movement of African Americans into Jewish urban neighborhoods. In places such as Boston's Roxbury and Chicago's West Side, white flight equaled Jewish flight as whole neighborhoods emptied of Jews seemingly overnight. Then, when they arrived in suburbia, many Jewish families wanted no part of integration. William Levitt's salesmen were infamous for refusing to sell homes to African Americans. To Levitt, religion and business were separate. "As a Jew I have no room in my mind or heart for racial prejudice," Levitt explained, but "I have come to know that if we sell one house to a Negro family, then ninety to ninety-five percent of our white customers will not buy into the community" (Halberstam 1993). Ironically, many of the 1960s social activists who championed racial equality were Jews who had grown up in Levitt-style neighborhoods in the previous decade.

Jewish movement into postwar suburbia was a socioeconomic process as well as a geographical movement, with Jews consciously making their institutions and religious practices more compatible with a "modern," upwardly mobile way of thinking. Perhaps the best example of how religion was reshaped to fit the new suburban environment was the 1950 ruling by the Conservative Rabbinical Assembly's Committee on Jewish Law and Standards to permit riding in automobiles on the Sabbath. Recognizing that its member families were violating traditional prohibitions against Sabbath driving, the Committee allowed families to drive on the Sabbath—as long as they drove to synagogue and not to other activities such as shopping. Of course, this declaration did not cause a sudden outbreak of Sabbath driving; driving on Saturdays—to services and everywhere else—had already become a normal pattern for many suburban Jewish families.

The modernization of Jewish religious behavior extended to the roles of children and women in suburbia as well. Suburban families affiliated with synagogues "for the children's sake," with the congregational Hebrew school seen as essential to providing a basic Jewish education—at least through the *bar mitzvah* age. With the growth of synagogue "centers" that were as much social institutions as religious ones, women became more involved in communal life than they had ever been. Synagogue sisterhoods and national organizations such as Hadassah provided an outlet for women's participation. This period also saw the increase in women's involvement within the sanctuary, with most Reform and Conservative synagogues allowing full and equal participation by women in prayer services by the 1980s.

Wrapped up as it was with social mobility and the shedding of religious traditionalism, the era of Jewish communal suburbanization was ripe for social satire. Philip Roth, in works such as *Goodbye, Columbus* (1960), mocked the conspicuous consumption of suburban Jews, who demonstrated ample ability to "keep up with the Cohens," whether in the kinds of cars they drove, the country clubs they belonged to, or the lavishness of their children's bar mitzvah parties.

Social scientists and other observers of the Jewish community saw these suburban transformations as a crucial stage in the development of American Judaism. Studies such as Albert Gordon's *Jews in Suburbia* (1959) and Marshall Sklare's *Jewish Identity on the Suburban Frontier* (1968/1979) focused on the movement from Judaism to Jewishness, with traditionalist observance giving way to cultural identity. These works argued that suburban Jews saw themselves as different from their non-Jewish neighbors but expressed their cultural distinctiveness within the framework of a shared, modern, middle-class lifestyle. Thus, eating only kosher food was rejected because it was "too different," whereas Chanukah was deemed an appropriate Jewish equivalent to Christmas.

Though Sklare and others were generally accurate in depicting the impact of suburbanization on Jewish communities, they underestimated the continued influence of religion. They did not foresee the explosion in Orthodox Jewish suburbanization, mostly because the presence of traditionalist Jews in a consumerist environment did not fit with a model of religious declension and cultural assimilation. The reality is, however, that the blossoming of American Orthodoxy has coincided with—and has even been abetted by—the movement to suburbia. Affluence among suburban Orthodox Jews facilitated the expansion of Jewish day schools, a trend that reflected in equal parts the religious desire for an intensive Jewish education and a middle-class suburban demand for quality general education. Upward mobility also eased the burdens of maintaining a religiously observant home. With affluence, a family could afford a larger kitchen with two sinks, ovens, and even dishwashers, which separate meat and dairy according to laws of *kashruth*. Extra disposable income could also go toward other aspects of "kosher consumerism," such as adorning one's home with artistic Judaica, eating out in upscale kosher restaurants, and enjoying award-winning kosher wines.

Matured Suburbanization

Today, Jewish suburbia has matured to the point that it is entirely taken for granted. It is no longer necessary to identify Jewish communities as "suburban," because almost every major American Jewish community is centered in suburbia. Other than New York City, no other major community in the United States has a majority of Jews living in urban neighborhoods. The Jewish communal infrastructure is fully suburban as well, with most Jewish community centers, day schools, federation offices, and kosher butchers, bakeries, and grocery stores based in suburban neighborhoods.

With suburbia so "normal," there is now a trend in many communities back to the urban neighborhood. Yet this renaissance of urban Jewry merely emphasizes the extent to which Jewish geography has been flipped on its head—suburbia is now the stable core, and urban neighborhoods are the pioneering periphery.

Though one might think that, after several decades of settlement on the metropolitan periphery, the Jewish community would be comfortable in its suburbanization, tensions remain. Battles over the display of a *menorah* on public property have become an annual ritual in many communities, with Orthodox Jewish groups such as Chabad seeking to erect a menorah and liberal Jews fighting to keep such overt religious symbols from entering the public space. Many places have witnessed legal battles over the construction of an *eruv*, the enclosure within which one is permitted to carry objects on the Sabbath. Orthodox Jews, who adhere to strict Sabbath observance, will only carry things in public in neighborhoods that have an eruv. In most cases, an eruv is unobtrusive, constructed out of existing utility wires and fences. Yet even a proposal to construct an eruv raises eyebrows, particularly among less traditional suburban Jews who fear the ghettoization of their neighborhoods. Though many communities have constructed eruvim without controversy, places such as

Tenafly and Lakewood in New Jersey have witnessed lawsuits and political fighting. The irony is that, in most cases, the development of a strong Orthodox Jewish neighborhood raises property values because homes within the eruv and closest to the synagogue become more desirable.

Finally, an examination of suburban Jewry should note that one of suburbia's central icons has Jewish roots as well. Specifically, the shopping mall, a hallmark of suburban consumerism, resulted from the design efforts of Victor Gruen, an Austrian Jew who fled Nazi Europe in 1938. Gruen created a consumerist sensation in 1956 by designing Southdale, the nation's first enclosed shopping mall, in suburban Minneapolis. Gruen recognized the consumerist trends of suburban society and tailored his mall to an automobile culture. The result: a two-story, indoor shopping arcade anchored by large department stores and filled with smaller retail tenants in the middle, all surrounded by acres of free parking. This model of suburban materialism was later imitated and then perfected by other Jewish real estate developers, including Alfred Taubman, the Simon brothers (Minneapolis's Mall of America), and the Ghermezian family (West Edmonton Mall).

Etan Diamond

References and Further Reading
Diamond, Etan. 2000. *And I Will Dwell in Their Midst: Orthodox Jews in Suburbia*. Chapel Hill: University of North Carolina Press.
Gladwell, Malcolm. 2004. "The Terrazzo Jungle." *New Yorker* (March 15).
Gordon, Albert I. 1959. *Jews in Suburbia*. Boston: Beacon Press.
Halberstam, David. 1993. *The Fifties*. New York: Villard Books.
Mittleman, Alan. 2002. "From Jewish Street to Public Square." *First Things* 125 (August/September): 29–37.
Rand, Robert. 2001. *My Suburban Shtetl: A Novel about Life in a Twentieth-Century Jewish–American Village*. Syracuse, NY: Syracuse University Press.
Sklare, Marshall. 1979. *Jewish Identity on the Suburban Frontier: A Study of Group Survival in the Open Society*. 2nd ed. Chicago: University of Chicago Press.
Vincent, Stuart. 2005. "From the Shtetl to the Suburbs: The Story of Long Island's Jews across Two Centuries." http://www.newsday.com/community/guide/lihistory/ny-eJewish–shtetl,0,4199529.story?coll=ny-lihistory-navigation (accessed August 24, 2005).

Antisemitism in America

Antisemitism in American Literature before 1960

Literary characterizations of Jews both reflect the perceptions of them in the culture and help form these perceptions. In the United States, literature and Christian theology have worked hand in hand to create a negative image of the Jew that served as the basis for actions against Jews, and for the lack of action when the European Jews were desperate for help during the Holocaust.

Even though American Jews have experienced a much greater level of toleration and freedom than their European coreligionists, even in the United States Jews have often found themselves regarded as aliens in a Christian land. As Michael Dobkowski observed, Jews, Judaism, and Jewishness "were interpreted in literature and by social commentators as being anathema to America's Christian heritage" (1979).

The portrayal of the Jew in American literature combined the negative economic motif with that of the deicidal Jew-Devil and contrasted "anachronistic" Judaism with "triumphant" Christianity. Even when Jews were occasionally treated positively, they were seen not as real people but as stereotypes.

Some literary figures—among them the abolitionist poet Julia Ward Howe and the novelist Edward Bellamy—credited the Jews for their contributions to Christianity and to the secular world. But the work of most major American writers of the nineteenth century contains anti-Jewish material based on traditional Christian stereotypes.

The earliest group of significant American poets were the nineteenth-century Fireside Poets. All wrote from a Christian point of view when they discussed Jews, and all but John Greenleaf Whittier employed hostile stereotypes.

A friend of the philosemitic Unitarian abolitionist Lydia Maria Child, Whittier believed that there was truth in all religions. In "The Two Rabbins" (1865), he observed, "when at last they rose to embrace / Each saw God's pardon in his brother's face!"

For William Cullen Bryant, however, the Jews had "an unquenchable lust for lucre" and a "lust for money"; they were like snakes "in search of prey." Even when he on occasion praised Jews, calling them "noble" and "spiritual," with great contributions to the world in religion, law, poetry, and music, he still saw only a bundle of stereotyped traits. As he himself indicated, his "admiration" was indeed "reluctant" (Gould 1991).

Henry Wadsworth Longfellow's Hiawatha comments on "How the Jews, the tribe accursed / Mocked him, scourged him, crucified him." In "The Jewish Cemetery at Newport" (1852), the Jewish names in the cemetery seem un-American, "strange" and "foreign." He concedes that the Jews arrived on these shores because of a "burst of Christian hate," yet, like St. Paul, he pictures these Jews as the "Ishmaels and Hagars of mankind," refers to "the deep mark of Cain," and observes that "dead nations never rise again."

In "Bibliolatres" (1849), James Russell Lowell regards the Jewish Bible as useless and rigid, broken and dead, unconnected with the living God. He addresses the Jews as "blind [and] unconverted," Judaism as merely a "dry and sapless rod," the Torah as an "idol-volume" used "to coop the living God."

As American ambassador to Britain, Lowell wrote and spoke of "Jewish blood." In his address to an English audience on October 6, 1884, entitled "Democracy," he explained,

> The Jews [were] perhaps the ablest, certainly the most tenacious, race that had ever lived . . . a race in which ability seems as natural and hereditary as the curve of their noses, and whose blood, furtively mingling in the bluest bloods of Europe, has quickened them with its own indomitable impulsion. We drove them into a corner, but they had their revenge. . . . They made their corner the counter and bankinghouse of the world, and thence they rule it with the ignobler scepter of finance. (Lowell 1904)

His identification of Jews with money was evident to many. A guest at a Lowell dinner party observed that

> the Jews [were] almost a monomania with him. He detected a Jew in every hiding place and under every disguise. . . . It appeared that this insidious race had penetrated and permeated the human family more universally than any other influence except original sin. [Lowell proclaimed:] 'And when the Jews have got absolute control of finance, the army and navy, the press, diplomacy, society, titles, the government, and the earth's surface, what do you suppose they will do with them—and with us?' (*Atlantic Monthly* 1897)

An advocate of religious toleration, Oliver Wendell Holmes observed, "[T]here are many mansions in the Father's earthly house as well as in the heavenly one." Holmes noted that, as a young man, "I shared more or less the prevailing prejudices against the persecuted race," which he traced to Christian teaching and Puritan exclusiveness. In a remarkable poem, rewritten in 1874 as "At the Pantomime" but originally entitled "A Hebrew Tale," Holmes demonstrates how he overcame his early antisemitism. He recounts the story of attending a play and being hemmed in by Jews, whose very appearance he found distasteful:

"The beak that crowned the bistered [swarthy] face/ Betrayed the mould of Abraham's race. . . ." He thought of their deicide, their perfidy, their usury, their murder of Christian children: "Up came their murderous deeds of old / The grisly story Chaucer told / And many an ugly tale beside / Of children caught and crucified. . . ." But when Holmes looks more closely into the faces of the Jews surrounding him, he thinks that Jesus must have looked like them. He realizes that his scorn is supercilious and misplaced. And so he concludes: "From thee the son of Mary came / With thee the Father deigned to dwell—Peace be upon thee, Israel" (Holmes 1895).

Of the American Renaissance writers, Henry Thoreau did not deal with Jews at all. Like him, Emily Dickinson probably never met any Jews, yet she fleetingly mentioned them in images of greed and wealth.

Despite rejecting many aspects of Christianity, Ralph Waldo Emerson's early sermons reflected his belief that the Jews were responsible for murdering Jesus, the founder of a set of religious beliefs far superior to those of Judaism. In January 1827, he observed, "We [Christians] are standing on a higher stage . . . instructed in a better philosophy, whose greater principles explain to us the design. . . . We leave the ritual, the offering, & altar of Moses. We cast off the superstitions that were the swaddling clothes of Christianity." In the spring of 1832, he wrote that "the Jewish Law answered its temporary purpose & was set aside. Christianity is completing its purpose as an aid to educate man" (Gilman 1960–1969). Elsewhere, he saw the "Jewish idea" as a stumbling block to authentic human liberation. The Jewish God was cruel; the Jewish Law was stifling. What was bad about Christianity was its Jewish substance.

Although in 1867 he called attention to the responsibility of Christianity for the Jews' suffering, Emerson bemoaned his brother's becoming "the vulgarest man of business who has no correspondence for any but the Jews. . . ." And he asked him whether he did "not die of the Jews to whom you pay usance?" (Rusk 1939). In his journal entry for July 3, 1839, Emerson wrote, "In the Allston gallery the Polish Jews are an offense to me; they degrade & animalize" (Gilman 1960–1969). In his essay "Fate," he commented, "The suffrance which is the badge of the Jew, has made him, in these days, the ruler of rulers of the earth" (Emerson 1888).

Walt Whitman was an admirer of ancient Judaism and the Hebrew Bible, but looking at the scene on Broadway,

New York, in August 1856, he wrote about "dirty looking German Jews ... with a sharp nasal twang and flat squalling enunciation to which the worst Yankee brogue is sweet music" (Whitman 1936).

Redburn, Herman Melville's only novel with Jewish characters, describes a Jewish pawnbroker as "[a] curly-headed little man with a dark oily face, and a hooked nose, like the pictures of Judas Iscariot." In *The Confidence Man,* Melville concludes a list of criminals, "a horse-thief, an assassin, a treaty-breaker, and a judicial murderer," with "a Jew with hospitable speeches cozening some fainting stranger into ambuscade, there to burk him, and account it a deed grateful to Manitou [Mammon], his God." An entry in his journal refers to the Jews in Palestine: "In the emptiness of the lifeless antiquity of Jerusalem the emigrant Jews are like flies who have taken up their abode in a skull" (Melville 1955).

Melville's long poem *Clarel* denigrates several Jewish characters aside from Jewish women, whom he (following tradition) seemed to regard positively: Nathan was a convert from Christianity; Margoth was a self-hating apostate Jew; the Lyonese, a "toy of Mammon," an assimilated Jew anxious to discard his Jewish identity; Abdon was an Indian Orthodox Jew whose life was essentially over, simply waiting to die in Palestine. There was not among them a born Jew who experienced his Judaism as a living faith with a future.

Perhaps the most egregious examples of antisemitism in nineteenth-century literature occur in the work of Nathaniel Hawthorne. (His son, Julian, was a popular antisemitic novelist at the end of the century.) In *The Marble Faun,* Hawthorne refers to the Jews as "the ugliest, most evil-minded" people, "resembling ... maggots when they over-populate a decaying cheese." Hawthorne's essay in his *English Notebooks* provides the clearest expression of his hatred for the Jews. The first Jewish Lord Mayor of London, Sir David Solomons, invited Hawthorne to a formal dinner in 1856. Hawthorne described the Lord Mayor's elder brother Philip as

> the very Jew of Jews; the distilled essence of all the Jews that have been born since Jacob's time; he was Judas Iscariot; he was the Wandering Jew; he was the worst, and at the same time, the truest type of his race, and contained within himself, I have no doubt, every old prophet and every old clothesman, that ever the tribes produced; and he must have

been circumcised as much as ten times over. I never beheld anything so ugly and disagreeable, and preposterous, and laughable, as the outline of his profile; it was so hideously Jewish, and so cruel, and so keen. (Stewart 1941)

Of the four "Western" writers of the late nineteenth century, Joaquin Miller in his poem "To Russia" asked, "Who gave thee / Your Christian creed? Yea, yea / Who gave your very God to you? Your Jew! Your Jew! Your hated Jew!"

Bret Harte, himself one-quarter Jewish, wrote a satirical poem, "That Ebrew Jew," attacking the Grand Union Hotel in Saratoga Springs, New York, for refusing to rent rooms to Jews and for distinguishing between Jews and Hebrews: "For the Jew is a man who will make money through ... / And an Ebrew's a man that we Gentiles can 'do.'"

Ambrose Bierce observed that he "hated Hebrews but adored Shebrews."

Providing an insight into the origins of his anti-Jewish feelings, Mark Twain wrote, "I was raised to a prejudice against Jews. Christians always are, you know. ..." (Smith 1962). In November 1853, the sixteen-year-old Twain wrote from Philadelphia that the Jewish presence had "desecrated" two historic homes there. And in a newspaper article of April 10, 1857, he asserted, "the blasted Jews got to adulterating the fuel." In 1879 he observed that "the Jews are the only race who work wholly with their brains and never with their hands" (Foner 1958). He ignored the realities of impoverished Jews and exploited Jewish labor in American cities.

Twain wrote his famous essay "Concerning the Jews" in Vienna in 1898. Vienna's mayor was Karl Lueger, a powerful and popular Christian antisemite who would be much admired by Adolf Hitler. Although Twain praised the Jews for their charity, close family life, hard work, and "genius," he repeated the slander that the Jews had an "unpatriotic disinclination to stand by the flag as a soldier." His solution was for regiments of Jews—and Jews only—to enlist in the army, to disprove the charge that "you feed on a country but don't like to fight for it" (Neider 1963). In reaction to angry letters from American Jews who read the essay, Twain later retracted this statement in a postscript and noted that, despite having to endure American antisemitism, Jews fought widely and bravely in America's wars.

In the same essay, Twain ignored historical realities to recount how the Jews had cheated, exploited, and dominated poor and ignorant Christians in the American South, czarist Russia, and medieval England, Spain, and Austria: "There was no way to successfully compete with [the Jew] in any vocation, the law had to step in and save the Christian from the poorhouse. . . . [The Jew] has made it the end and aim of his life to get [money]" (Neider 1963).

Twain opposed Theodor Herzl's plan for a homeland for the Jews in Palestine. He argued that "if that concentration of the cunningest brains in the world was going to be made in a free country . . . , I think it would be politic to stop it. It will not be well to let that race find out its strength." For Twain, there was evidently no place in this world for the Jews, within Palestine or outside it. At the close of his essay, he observed, "By his make and ways [the Jew] is substantially a foreigner wherever he may be, and even the angels dislike a foreigner" (Neider 1963).

Of the American Realists, Harold Frederic devoted more of his work to Jews than any other Realist. He wrote of the Jews who "have imposed the rule of their ideas and their gods upon us for fifteen hundred years." He complained that it was the Jewish spirit that had ruined Catholicism. He differed from the racists in seeing that some Jews were good, but they had to be "of the right sort" (Harap 1974).

William Dean Howells repeatedly associated Jews with money. Although he claimed to be ridiculing this belief, the irony was lost on some. He had a character say that the Jews "have got in. . . . And when they get in, they send down the price of property. Of course, there ain't any sense in it. . . . You tell folks that the Savior himself was one, and the twelve apostles, and all the prophets . . . and it don't make a bit of difference. . . . Prices begin to shade when the first one gets in." And "Oh, yes, they've all got the money" (Howells 1884). Some Jews complained about these gratuitous passages. Cyrus L. Sulzberger, editor of the *American Hebrew,* wrote Howells in 1885, "The introduction of the lines in question cannot even be excused on the ground that it serves a literary purpose, for no such end is accomplished. The sentiment is violently dragged in for no other ascertainable reason than to pander to a prejudice. . . ." (Liptzin 1966). Although Howells argued that he was simply reflecting what most Americans believed, he did cut the offending passages from later editions of his work.

Associated with Howells were the aristocratic writers. Whereas William James was a profoundly humanistic thinker, his brother Henry was a confirmed antisemite. With an air of disdain, Henry James seemed to regard the Jews, especially immigrants, as hardly human. To him the Jewish "denizens of the New York Ghetto" seemed like "small, strange animals . . . snakes or worms . . . who, when cut into pieces, wriggle away and live in the snippet as completely as in the whole." At other times, James seemed to fear the Jews. They were "hard," lived in New York "for race, and not, as it were, for reason"; and he worried about "the extent of the Hebrew conquest of New York," about "what the genius of Israel may, or may not, really be 'up to'" (Harap 1974).

The grandson and great-grandson of presidents, Henry Adams also responded with fear and hatred to the large influx of Orthodox Jewish immigrants entering the country from Eastern Europe. His writing reflected the conflict he saw between his traditional Christian and American values and what he regarded as the Jewish values that were contorting modern society. He feared that "[w]e are in the hands of the Jews. They can do what they please with our values" (Samuels 1958). In the economic crisis of 1892, he wrote, "I detest them and everything connected with them, and I live only and solely with the hope of seeing their demise, with all their accursed Judaism. I want to see all the lenders at interest taken out and executed. . . ." (Samuels 1958). From Vienna in 1900, he complained that economic disaster had come upon him and his friends like "the devil on a broomstick in the shape of a mob of howling Jews who upset my world" (Ford 1930). Adams believed that the Jews conspired to control the world.

Adams's letters from Europe and the United States called architecture that he did not like (the Gothic arch) "the legitimate child of the Jews," exploitative and grasping; of Jewish art collectors, he wrote, "anything these Jews touch is in some strange way vulgarized"; from Warsaw he wrote disgustedly that the city was "mostly Jew. [The Jew] makes me creep" (Ford 1930); and in *The Education of Henry Adams,* he described the Orthodox religious Jew "in all his weird horror." In his view, even the Virgin Mary, though born a Jew, "disliked Jews, and rarely neglected a chance to maltreat them" (*Mont Saint Michel and Chartres*). He regarded the Spanish Inquisition as "a noble aim" (Samuels 1958).

The most significant religious author at the turn of the century was Lew Wallace, whose *Ben-Hur: A Tale of the Christ* was the most popular novel of the period. Wallace associated the Jews with deicide, for which they had to suffer, and he made Judaism appear as merely the groundwork for Christianity, a pure elaboration of Christian triumphalism in a modern novel. To Wallace, the Jewish people were responsible for the Crucifixion. They "stared at each other aghast. . . . They beat their breasts and shrieked with fear. His blood was upon them!" Wallace maintained that only the Jews "could have cried, Better a law without love than a love without law. . . . Revenge is a Jew's of right; it is the law." Ben-Hur and his family "saw the light" and, after having wrongly adhered to Judaism, were saved as Christians.

Several twentieth-century writers were either positive or neutral toward the Jews—O. Henry, Sinclair Lewis, Edmund Wilson, John Dos Passos, James T. Farrell, James Jones, and Lincoln Steffens. Sherwood Anderson, William Faulkner, Thomas Wolfe, and F. Scott Fitzgerald expressed ambivalence about Jewishness. Their early work was antisemitic, yet their later writing treated Jews realistically.

In the 1920s, Fitzgerald was disgusted with Jews, whom he associated with new money, power, and the corruption of culture. In "Echoes of the Jazz Age," Fitzgerald compared Jews with mental defectives, animals, and marine invertebrates.

In *The Great Gatsby,* Fitzgerald portrays Meyer Wolfsheim, a "small, flat-nosed Jew," as diabolical, with no redeeming traits. He is "one man [who] could start to play with the faith of fifty million people." The Wolfsheims are described as "villainous" and "rude," and they make Gatsby's kitchen "a pigsty." Fitzgerald portrayed no other Jewish characters in the novel. As Milton Hindus noted, "the novel reads very much like an antisemitic document." When Edith Wharton wrote to Fitzgerald to congratulate him on his book, she noted that in Wolfsheim, Fitzgerald had created "your *perfect* Jew . . ." (*Commentary* 1947).

Fitzgerald, however, apparently changed his attitude toward Jews, most likely because his antipathy to Nazism and his experience in Hollywood taught him that a variety of real, complicated Jews lived in the world, not just stereotypes. In his uncompleted novel, *The Last Tycoon,* Fitzgerald drew several different kinds of Jewish characters, both good and evil.

Katherine Anne Porter's novel *Ship of Fools* contains one despicable Jewish character, Julius Lowenthal, without any counterbalancing positive Jewish figure. Aside from two Catholic priests, Lowenthal is the only character identified by his religion. His aggressive Jewishness and stereotypical Jewish looks match his intolerance of Christians. Passing by a shipboard celebration of the Mass, Lowenthal

> restrained his impulse to spit until he had passed beyond the line of vision of the worshipers; then, his mouth watering with disgust, he moved to the rail and spat like a landlubber into the wind, which blew it back in his face. At his curse being thus returned to his very teeth, his whole body was suffused with superstitious terror, it scurried like mice in his blood, it shook his nerves from head to foot. 'God forbid,' he said aloud, with true piety.

Phyllis Robinson, Willa Cather's biographer, pointed out that Cather had a "deep-seated" prejudice against Jews. "She romanticized other nationalities and cultures, . . . but where Jews were concerned, she seemed to have a blind spot." Cather's description of the Jewish millionaire, Stein, was that "he was a vulture of the vulture race." She may have had a few "good Jews" in her fiction, but overall she exemplified "a typical Midwestern bias against Jews" (Robinson 1983).

Hemingway's biographer, Jeffrey Meyers, points out that he was "fashionably" antisemitic, which occasioned his hostility toward Robert Cohen in *The Sun Also Rises.* A letter from Hutchins Hapgood, a Christian defender of Jews, challenged Hemingway's portrait of Cohen. Hapgood, who knew the man who had served as the model for Cohen, wrote, "It has never seemed to me to be fair to put into an unfavorable picture of a human being the factor of race as a causal relationship." Hemingway's attitude toward Bernard Berenson changed, but then, Berenson had converted to Christianity. Whereas in 1928 Hemingway had called Berenson "an empty asshole and kike patron of the arts," by 1949 he regarded Berenson as "one of the living people that I respect the most" (Meyers 1999).

For e. e. cummings, Jews were the most utterly repulsive of creatures. "There are some specimens of humanity," he wrote of a Jew he called the Fighting Sheeny, "in whose presence one instantly and instinctively feels a profound revulsion." In *XAIPE* (1950), Cummings associated the Jews with money, manipulation, and corruption: "a kike is the most dangerous/ machine as yet invented/ by even yankee ingenu/ ity (out of a jew a few/ dead dollars and some twisted laws)/ it comes both prigged and canted" (Firmage 1991).

Theodore Dreiser's Jewish characters were "wrecks and cripples," a molester and murderer of little girls, and a Shylock. In his play *The Hand of the Potter*, Dreiser recapitulates the medieval ritual-murder defamation in describing the murder of an eleven-year-old Catholic girl by a Jewish man.

In 1922, Dreiser wrote his friend and kindred spirit, H. L. Mencken, that New York was "a Kyke's dream of a Ghetto." Dreiser's letters from the mid-1930s described the Jews as stubbornly holding onto their religion and "race," and sharply "money-minded." He opposed tolerance for Jews because it would allow them to "possess America by sheer numbers, their cohesion, their race tastes and, as in the case of the Negro in South Africa, really [to] overrun the land. [Once he] invades [a country,] he is still a Jew. He's been in America all of two hundred years, and he has not faded into a pure American by any means . . ." (Elias 1959, letter of October 10, 1933).

Hutchins Hapgood accused Dreiser of ignorance, barbarity, and indecency, noting that Dreiser's letter could have been written by a member of the Ku Klux Klan or a representative of Adolf Hitler. In his reply, Dreiser conceded that Jews are "a brilliant and gifted people." But their "crucifixion in Germany" is due to their "mistaken [attempt] to establish themselves as Jews, with their religion, race characteristics, race solidarity and all, in the bosom . . . of almost every country the world over. . . . Being as gifted as they are, they so rapidly rise to power and affluence wherever they go" (Elias 1959, letter of December 28, 1933). He offered two solutions to the "Jewish problem": drive them out of the United States or force every Jew to marry a Christian.

H. L. Mencken wrote, in his "Treatise on the Gods," "The Jews could be put down very plausibly as the most unpleasant race ever heard of. . . . they lack many of the qualities that mark the civilized man: courage, dignity, incorruptibility, ease, confidence. They have vanity without pride, voluptuousness without taste, and learning without wisdom. . . ."

References to Jews frequent his diaries: "[T]here is a shrewd Jew in him at bottom," "it appeared to me, in the rather dim light, that many of them were Jews," "did not enjoy being bracketed with two Jews." In August 1942, he mused about how foreign he felt in America and how good his life in Germany could have been. A year later, he ruminated about America's role in the war as typical American folly; he hoped that catastrophe would overtake Americans. And yet he termed the United States "this great Christian country" (Fecher 1989). In a letter of May 29, 1919, he wrote prophetically, "There is a good ground for hoping that, as a Jew, [Freud] will fall a victim to some obscure race war in Vienna" (Bode 1977).

One of the most politicized antisemites of the twentieth century was Ezra Pound. Although he later repudiated his Protestant background and often wrote against the churches, his major accusations against the Jews may have initially derived from his Christian upbringing and Sunday school education. He stated that he had "read the Bible daily in childhood," and that as an adult he longed for the Catholic Middle Ages, when the Jew was clearly regarded as an alien in the *corpus Christi*.

Some of Pound's ideas mirrored those of the leading antisemite Father Charles Coughlin, who celebrated Hitler's invasion of Russia and railed against "the British–Jewish–Roosevelt war on Germany and Italy." Pound condemned Jews in almost all of the more than 120 wartime broadcasts he made on Rome Radio. He blamed the Jews for starting the war and corrupting the world. England, France, Russia, and the United States were all "under yidd control. Lousy with kikes." He noted, in Nazi metaphors, "You let in the Jew and the Jew rotted your empire, . . . And the big Jew has rotted EVERY nation he has wormed into. . . . It were better you were infected with typhus." Americans "are now ruled by Jews, and by the dirtiest dirt from the bottom of the Jew's ash can." The Talmud "is the code of vengeance, of secret means unto vengeance. AIMED specifically at the destruction of all non-kike order. . . . OUT of it came the Bolsheviki. Out of it came the determination to ruin Europe, to break down Christianity. . . . Destroy everything that is conducive to civilization." On April 27, 1943, he told his audience that "the sixty Kikes who started this war" got their inspiration from the Talmud (Doob 1978).

In *The Pisan Cantos*, Pound argued again that the war was caused by the Jews, who sacrificed gentile lives for profit: "the yidd is a stimulant, and the goyim are cattle/ . . . and go to saleable slaughter/ with the maximum of docility." He called the Duke of Wellington "a jew's pimp" and blamed the American Civil War on the Jews (Pound 1971). Pound insisted that a few hundred American Jews and FDR should be hung for their crimes and insisted that "all the kike congressmen" should be "bumped off" without delay (Doob 1978). George Orwell recalled a wartime broadcast "in which [Pound] approved the massacre of East European Jews and 'warned' the American Jews that their turn was coming presently" (*Partisan Review* 1949).

Robert Michael

References and Further Reading

Bode, Carl, ed. 1977. *The New Mencken Letters.* New York: Dial.

Dobkowski, Michael. 1979. *The Tarnished Dream.* Westport, CT: Greenwood.

Doob, Leonard, ed. 1978. *"Ezra Pound Speaking:" Radio Speeches of World War II.* Westport, CT: Greenwood.

Elias, Robert, ed. 1959. *Letters of Theodore Dreiser: A Selection.* Philadelphia: University of Pennsylvania Press.

Emerson, Ralph Waldo. 1888. *The Conduct of Life.* Boston: Houghton Mifflin.

Fecher, Charles, ed. 1989. *The Diary of H. L. Mencken.* New York: Knopf.

Firmage, George, ed. 1991. *Complete Poems, 1904–1962.* New York: Norton.

Foner, Philip. 1958. *Mark Twain.* New York: International.

Ford, Worthington C., ed. 1930. *The Letters of Henry Adams.* Boston: Houghton Mifflin.

Gilman, William H., Alfred R. Ferguson, George P. Clark, and Merrell R. Davis, eds. 1960–1969. *The Journals and Miscellaneous Notebooks of Ralph Waldo Emerson.* Cambridge, MA: Harvard University Press.

Gould, Allan. 1991. *What Did They Think of the Jews?* Northvale, NJ: J. Aronson.

Harap, Louis. 1974. *The Image of the Jew in American Literature.* Philadelphia: Jewish Publication Society of America.

Holmes, Oliver Wendell. 1895. *The Complete Poetical Works of Oliver Wendell Holmes.* Boston: Houghton Mifflin.

Howells, William Dean. 1884. "The Rise of Silas Lapham." *Century Magazine* (November).

Liptzin, Sol. 1966. *The Jew in American Literature.* New York: Bloch.

Lowell, James Russell. 1904. *The Complete Writings of James Russell Lowell.* Cambridge, MA: Riverside Press.

Melville, Herman. 1955. *Journal of a Visit to Europe and the Levant.* Princeton, NJ: Princeton University Press.

Meyers, Jeffrey. 1999. *Hemingway: A Biography.* New York: Da Capo.

Michael, Robert. 2005. *A Concise History of American Antisemitism.* New York: Rowman & Littlefield.

Neider, Charles, ed. 1963. *The Complete Essays of Mark Twain.* Garden City, NJ: Doubleday.

Pound, Ezra. 1971. *The Cantos of Ezra Pound.* New York: New Directions.

Robinson, Phyllis. 1983. *Willa: The Life of Willa Cather.* New York: Holt, Rinehart & Winston.

Rusk, Ralph. 1939. *The Letters of Ralph Waldo Emerson.* New York: Columbia University Press.

Samuels, Ernst. 1958. *Henry Adams: The Middle Years.* Cambridge, MA: Harvard University Press.

Smith, Janet, ed. 1962. *Mark Twain on the Damned Human Race.* New York: Hill and Wang.

Stewart, Randall, ed. 1941. *The English Notebooks.* New York: Modern Language Association of America.

Whitman, Walt. 1936. *New York Dissected.* New York: R. R. Wilson.

Leo Max Frank (1884–1915)

Victim of One of the Most Infamous Antisemitic Crimes in the History of the United States

For his first twenty-nine years, Leo Frank led an ordinary though generally successful life. By his mid-twenties, he had received a college degree, married, and was the manager of a factory employing more than a hundred workers in a large southern city. Not long after his twenty-ninth birthday, a murder took place in that factory, a crime for which he was convicted and sentenced to death. For nearly two years, he and his lawyers struggled to keep the execution from taking place. He narrowly avoided judicial execution through a commutation of his death sentence to life in prison, only to be kidnapped from prison and lynched, a fate he alone among American Jews has suffered.

Leo Frank was born in Cuero, Texas, on April 17, 1884; his father, Rudolph Frank, was born in Germany, and his mother, Rachel Jacobs Frank, was born in New York of German Jewish parents. When Leo was about three months old, his family moved to Brooklyn, where he attended public schools and the Pratt Institute before entering Cornell University in the fall of 1902. He received his bachelor's degree in mechanical engineering in June 1906 and was employed in two positions before accepting an offer to manage a pencil factory in Atlanta. Frank spent nine months in Europe learning the business, then moved to Atlanta in August 1908 to become the superintendent of the National Pencil Factory. In October 1910 he married Lucille Selig, from a prominent German Jewish family in Atlanta; Frank later described his "married life" as "exceptionally happy . . . the happiest days of my life."

Leo Frank, wrongly accused of murder in 1913 and lynched by an antisemitic mob in 1915. (Library of Congress)

Those happy days ended on April 26, 1913 (Confederate Memorial Day), when a thirteen-year-old worker, Mary Phagan, was murdered around noon in the factory he superintended. Her body was not found until early the next morning, and Frank did not learn about the murder until several hours later, when the police telephoned him at the home of his in-laws, with whom he and his wife lived. The police sent a car and drove Frank to the funeral home to which Phagan's body had been taken. Though he could not remember her name, Frank was able to identify her as an employee of the pencil factory, as he recalled that she had picked up her pay the previous day around noon. Thus began a nightmare for Frank and his family that would end only some twenty-eight months later with his death at the hands of a lynch mob, the identity of whose members remained secret until only a few years ago, after the death of all those involved. As for Atlanta Jewry, the Leo Frank case would linger in its collective memory for several generations.

At first the police were perplexed by the crime, and, for want of any other suspect, they took the Negro watchman, Newt Lee, who had discovered the body, into custody. On April 30 Frank hired the Pinkerton National Detective Agency on behalf of his employer to aid the police in the apprehension of the murderer, a decision that he would later regret. Rumors and speculations continually appeared in all three Atlanta daily newspapers suggesting one person or another as a possible suspect. Of more enduring consequence as clues were the two notes found near the body of the Phagan girl, which appeared to have been written by her between the time she was attacked and the time she died.

Among those under suspicion were the Negro factory sweeper (or janitor), James Conley, and Frank, both of whom had been taken into custody and not released. On May 24, 1913, Frank was indicted; no action was taken at this time against Conley, although he eventually served a year on the chain gang for being an accessory after the fact in the murder. The indictment of Frank was for murder only, though it was widely believed that Mary Phagan had been raped.

During May the prosecution worked to perfect the testimony of Jim Conley and to develop his relationship to the mysterious notes. At first Conley, who claimed that he could not read or write, was generally overlooked by investigators. When it was discovered that he was literate (ironically, it was Frank who informed the Pinkerton detectives of this) and that his handwriting matched that on the notes, the prosecution began an intense interrogation of Conley. Ultimately, Conley would make four sworn statements (five, if his testimony as a witness is included) as to his involvement in the murder of Phagan. In these statements, he claimed that Frank had dictated the murder notes and that Frank had paid him for his help in shielding Frank from the murder charge.

Frank's trial for the murder of Mary Phagan took place in Fulton County Superior Court from July 28 to August 26, 1913, before Judge Leonard Strickland Roan. Judge Roan was not well at the time of the trial; he died in March 1915, though not before he wrote the governor, John Slaton, a letter expressing his reservations about Frank's guilt. The trial record has been lost, though a fairly accurate transcript of the proceedings has been pieced together from newspaper accounts, which often quoted the trial testimony, as well as from appellate documents. More than a million words were spoken during the trial by the dozens of witnesses.

Although Frank's lawyers—Luther Z. Rosser and Reuben R. Arnold—were considered among the most able in Georgia, their overconfidence, combined with the "native cunning" of the prosecutor Hugh M. Dorsey and his associate Frank Hooper, secured Frank's conviction for murder. The prosecution was aided greatly by the "ugly-tempered crowds" both in the courtroom and in the streets, whose applause and cheers certainly influenced the twelve male jurors and the outcome of the trial.

At first Frank's lawyers seemed to be defending him effectively. On the third day of the trial (July 30, 1913), city detective John Black, a prosecution witness who had worked with Pinkerton detective Harry Scott, turned out to be quite valuable to the defense. Under careful and insistent questioning, Rosser was able to cast doubt on almost all of Black's testimony against Frank. So thorough was Rosser's cross-examination that, near the end of testimony, Black declared, "I don't like to admit that I'm crossed up, Colonel Rosser, but you have got me in that kind of fix and I don't know where I'm at." Unfortunately for the defense, Detective Scott, who followed Black on the witness stand, proved to be a much more difficult witness for Rosser to deal with and was the first witness to aid the prosecution's case against Frank.

The prosecution's case took a decisive turn against Frank with the testimony of the sweeper, Jim Conley. Conley testified that, several times in the past, Frank had paid him to "watch out" for him, while he "chatted" with female visitors in his office. Conley also intimated that Frank was, by the mores of the day, a sexual deviant; so graphic was Conley's testimony that Judge Roan had to clear the courtroom of women and children spectators during this part of Conley's testimony. According to Conley, on the morning of April 26, Frank again asked him to watch out for him and, when he was with a woman, Conley was to lock the front door of the factory. After Mary Phagan had been with Frank for a while, Conley was summoned to the second floor; and there, Conley testified, he saw the dead body of Phagan on the floor and a very nervous Frank, who explained to Conley that Phagan had refused his advances and that she had struck her head on a machine. Conley then described how he and Frank wrapped the body in a sack, how the body was too heavy for Conley to carry alone, how the two of them removed the body to the base-

ment by way of the elevator, and how Conley had dragged the body to another part of the basement, where it was found the following morning by Newt Lee. The two then returned to Frank's office, where Frank offered Conley money to write (with Frank dictating) the two notes that were found near Phagan's body. For the next two days (August 5 and 6), Conley was cross-examined by defense counsel Rosser, but to no avail. Even with the earlier contradictory statements by Conley, Rosser was not able (as he had done earlier with Black) to break Conley's story.

The rest of the trial was a confusing mixture of testimony: arguments about the time of Phagan's death, based on the contradictory medical opinions about how well digested were the contents of her stomach; and character witnesses for Frank, who included relatives, members of the Jewish community of Atlanta, college chums, and female employees of the pencil factory, who testified to his good character and to the propriety of his relations with them. To counter this, the prosecution called several former female workers, who, though short on specific examples of his immoral behavior, testified to their bad opinion of Frank. Other testimony involved Frank's emotional state after the murder of Phagan but before the body was discovered by Newt Lee. Prosecution witnesses described a nervous, distraught Frank, while defense witnesses pictured Frank as being his usual self.

On August 18, in something of a surprise move, Frank took the stand. Under the rules then in effect in Georgia criminal courts, Frank's testimony was not under oath, and he could not be cross-examined. He spoke for four hours. After giving a brief sketch of his life, Frank calmly but firmly explained his story: how Mary Phagan came to his office shortly after the noon hour on April 26 to collect her pay; how she returned after only a few minutes to inquire as to whether the "metal" had been delivered, as her job was to attach the metal tips to the pencils, and no "metal" meant no work. After she left, he worked on the monthly financial statement, went home for lunch, and returned to the factory to finish the financial report. Around 6:30 p.m., he left the factory for the day after checking with the watchman, Newt Lee.

Frank said that he never saw Conley on the day that Phagan was murdered and called Conley's testimony against him lies. He also accused the detectives who worked on the case, Black and Scott, of distorting his conversations with them with the intent to incriminate him.

Frank concluded his statement with the declaration, "Some newspaper men have called me 'the silent man in the Tower.' Gentlemen, this is the time and here is the place! I have told you the truth."

After a couple of anticlimactic days of testimony, the final arguments began. First was prosecutor Hooper, followed by defense attorneys Arnold and Rosser. The last to speak was the lead prosecutor, Hugh Dorsey. His summation was spread over three days, beginning on August 23 and ending at noon on August 25. With the bells of the nearby Church of the Immaculate Conception sounding the noon hour, Dorsey repeated "guilty" between each successive toll of the bell until it ceased. So rife with antisemitic sentiments were the closing statements of the prosecution that, under present judicial rules, a mistrial would have very likely been declared on that basis alone. Near the beginning of his closing statement, prosecutor Dorsey declaimed, "They [the Jews] rise to heights sublime, but they also sink to the lowest depths of degradation."

Then Judge Roan charged the jury, and deliberations began at 1:35 p.m. The jury returned to the courtroom shortly before 5 p.m. Neither Frank nor his attorneys were present; Judge Roan had asked them not to be there, as he claimed that the court could not guarantee their safety if the jury returned anything but a guilty verdict. The jury found Frank guilty of the murder of Mary Phagan. By this time, thousands had thronged the streets outside the courtroom, and when Dorsey appeared, the cheering crowd hoisted him on its shoulders and carried him to his nearby office. The next day, in a secret session, Judge Roan sentenced Frank to hang.

Appeals of Frank's death sentence began almost immediately, first to the Georgia courts and then to the federal courts, culminating on April 19, 1915, in a seven-to-two decision against Frank in the United States Supreme Court in *Frank v. Mangum.* Writing for the minority of himself and Justice Charles Evans Hughes, Justice Oliver Wendell Holmes Jr. stated, "Mob rule does not become due process of law by securing the assent of a terrorized jury. We are not speaking of mere disorder, or irregularities in procedure, but of accounts where the processes of justice are actually subverted." Holmes explained, "Supposing the alleged facts to be true, it is our duty to declare lynch law as little valid when practiced by a regularly drawn jury as when administered by one elected by a mob intent on death." Notably, less than a decade later,

the minority opinion of Justices Holmes and Hughes became the majority opinion in the case *Moore v. Dempsey,* which marked the beginning of the federal courts' scrutiny of state criminal court procedures with reference to the constitutional rights of the accused.

During the almost two years in which his lawyers struggled to save their client, the Frank case became a *cause célèbre* in the national press and among American Jews. Unfortunately for Frank, the stridency of national opinion was more than matched by the defensiveness and hostility of public opinion in Georgia, where it was widely felt that the rich northern Jews were trying to protect one of their own and were prepared to "buy" Frank's freedom if necessary.

With no further appeals to the courts possible, Frank's attorneys filed a petition for clemency with the Georgia Prison Commission, which was denied on May 31, 1915, by a vote of two to one. This left only one hope for Frank: a commutation from Governor John M. Slaton. After thoroughly studying the written record of the case and visiting the National Pencil Factory to examine the scene of the crime firsthand, Governor Slaton, in an act that would ruin a very promising political career, commuted Frank's sentence to life in prison on June 20, 1915, his last full day in office. Frank had been transferred from the Fulton County jail in Atlanta to the state penitentiary in Milledgeville the night before. When news of the commutation became known, riots broke out in Atlanta, prompting a march on the governor's residence, which was broken up by the state militia. So reviled was Slaton, who was hung in effigy in at least two places in Georgia, that he and his wife took an extended vacation from Georgia, returning only months later.

Starting in December 1914, former congressman and populist leader Tom Watson, in his weekly newspaper *The Jeffersonian,* wrote scurrilous, antisemitic editorials against Frank and the Jewish community for its support of Frank. After Governor Slaton's commutation, Watson essentially called for the citizens of Georgia to carry out the death sentence of Frank. This almost happened on July 18, 1915, when William Creen, a fellow prisoner, slashed Frank's throat. Only the timely intercession of two other prisoners, both physicians, prevented Frank from bleeding to death.

The end for Frank came the next month. On the night of August 16, 1915, twenty-six men in eight automobiles traveled from Cobb County to the penitentiary in

Milledgeville. After cutting the telephone wires to the prison, they overpowered the guards and kidnapped Frank. Ample evidence exists of collusion between the lynchers and the staff at the state prison, but exactly which prison staff were involved remains a matter of conjecture. The kidnappers drove Frank to Frey's gin, on the outskirts of Marietta, Cobb County, Georgia, girlhood home of Mary Phagan, where they lynched him the next morning (August 17) just after dawn. Before Frank's body could be removed, many thousands had visited the scene of the lynching, and his corpse came perilously close to being mutilated when a member of the crowd stomped on his face. Only the intervention of Newton Morris, who has been identified as one of those who planned the lynching, prevented further mutilation and allowed Frank's body to be spirited away to an Atlanta undertaker, where the remains were viewed by thousands more after an unruly crowd demanded to see the corpse. The following day, Frank's body, accompanied by his wife, was shipped to New York, and on August 20, 1915, Frank was buried in Mount Carmel Cemetery in Brooklyn, New York.

The most immediate results of the lynching of Frank were the founding of the Anti-Defamation League (ADL), the first organization established in the United States specifically to combat antisemitism, by the Jewish fraternal organization B'nai B'rith, and the revival of the Ku Klux Klan, celebrated in the recently released movie *Birth of a Nation*. Hugh Dorsey capitalized politically on his prosecution of Frank; he was elected governor of Georgia twice, in 1916 and 1918, but in 1920 lost a bid to become United States senator to Tom Watson, who had supported him in his races for governor.

For the Jewish community of Atlanta, as well as for the South, the Frank lynching cast a pall that lasted for more than a generation. Some Jews left Atlanta, one of them the father of the future Librarian of Congress Daniel Boorstin. The younger Boorstin later wrote that his father thought that being Jewish in Georgia at that time would hinder his career as a young lawyer, so the family moved to Tulsa, Oklahoma. Most Jews stayed, though there was an unwritten social rule that the Frank case was not to be discussed, even among themselves, lest the demons of antisemitism be unleashed again. Occasional stories appeared in the local press, though it would be a half-century before a full-length book—Harry Golden's *A Little Girl is Dead* (1965)—appeared. This was followed a few years later by the scholarly study *The Leo Frank Case* (1968) by Leonard Dinnerstein.

The case again made the news in the spring of 1982. Alonzo Mann, who had worked at the National Pencil Factory in 1913 as an office boy and was then in failing health, came forward to claim that, on the day of the murder, he had seen Jim Conley carrying the limp body of Mary Phagan through a trap door to the basement of the factory. Not only did this directly contradict the testimony of Conley but, if true, would certainly point to Conley as the murderer of Mary Phagan. Mann further claimed that when Conley saw him, he threatened his life, and at the urging of his mother, the then fourteen-year-old Mann did not go to the police. Mann testified at Frank's trial that he had been at the factory on the day of the murder of Mary Phagan but had left at 11:30 a.m.; unfortunately, Frank's attorneys did not know that this young boy had knowledge that could exculpate their client.

Using Mann's testimony, which was given on videotape, and a lie detector, which confirmed the veracity of Mann's statement, the ADL, the American Jewish Committee, and the Atlanta Jewish Federation applied for a posthumous pardon for Frank in 1983, but the Georgia Board of Pardons and Paroles denied this request. A second pardon request was granted on March 11, 1986, not to absolve Frank of the crime, but because the state failed to protect Frank while he was in its custody, thereby foreclosing all further efforts of Frank and his attorneys to prove his innocence.

Those involved in the lynching were never brought to justice, and until recently their identities remained a closely guarded secret among their relatives, friends, and descendants in Cobb County. A coroner's jury empaneled shortly after the lynching concluded that Frank had been murdered by "persons unknown." The identity of twelve of the lynchers was made public on the Internet in 2000 by Stephen Goldfarb. A longer, though not complete, list appeared three years later in the most comprehensive, but not definitive, history of the case *And the Dead Shall Rise* (2003) by Steve Oney. As had long been rumored, those involved in the lynching were among the leading citizens of Cobb County, including judges, prosecutors, state legislators, law enforcement officers, and businessmen, as well as a former governor of Georgia.

Antisemitism of a particularly vicious kind runs through the entire Frank case. Unlike the more traditional antisemitism that is associated with Christian beliefs, this form was shaped by the New South industrialization, which uprooted families like the Phagans and sent them to the city to work in the factories. Between the time of the murder of Phagan and the lynching of Frank, there was a particularly tumultuous strike at the Fulton Bag Company in Atlanta, which pitted working-class whites, most from rural areas, against Jewish owners.

Very early in the investigation of the Phagan murder, Frank was singled out by Detectives Scott and Black, as well as the prosecutor Dorsey, over the more logical choice of Jim Conley. Conley was known to have lied to investigators and to have a criminal record that included public drunkenness and disorderly conduct as well as more serious crimes, such as armed robbery. What is certain is that the successful prosecution of Frank was a good "career move" for many of those involved. Even before Tom Watson whipped up the fires of antisemitism, both Hooper and Dorsey had fanned those flames with their closing arguments. Perhaps no better explanation for what befell Frank can be found than the statement made by Luther O. Bricker, who had been the minister of the church that Mary Phagan had attended as a child in Cobb County. More than a quarter-century after the lynching, he wrote that, at the time of the lynching, he felt, as did many others, that the execution of a Negro "would be poor atonement for the life of this innocent little girl"; however, Leo Frank, "a Jew, and a Yankee Jew at that . . . would be a victim worthy to pay for the crime."

Stephen J. Goldfarb

References and Further Reading

Dinnerstein, Leonard. 1968. *The Leo Frank Case.* New York: Columbia University Press.

Dinnerstein, Leonard. 1996. "The Fate of Leo Frank." *American Heritage* 47 (October): 98–109.

Frey, Robert Seitz, and Nancy Thompson-Frey. 1988. *The Silent and the Damned: The Murder of Mary Phagan and the Lynching of Leo Frank.* Lanham, MD: Madison Books.

Golden, Harry. 1956. *A Little Girl Is Dead.* New York: World.

Goldfarb, Stephen J. 1996. "Framed: A Newly Discovered Document Casts a Disturbing Light on Exactly How Frank's Prosecutor Won His Case." *American Heritage* 47 (October): 108–113.

Goldfarb, Stephen J. 2000. "The Slaton Memorandum: A Governor Looks Back at His Decision to Commute the Death Sentence of Leo Frank." *American Jewish History* 88: 325–339.

Lawson, John Davison, ed. 1914–1936. *American State Trials: A Collection of the Important and Interesting Criminal Trials Which Have Taken Place in the United States from the Beginning of Our Government to the Present Day.* 17 vols. F. H. Thomas Law Book Co. "Leo M. Frank." 10: 182–414.

MacLean, Nancy. 1991. "The Leo Frank Case Reconsidered: Gender and Sexual Politics in the Making of Reactionary Populism." *Journal of American History* 78: 917–948.

Melnick, Jeffrey. 2000. *Black-Jewish Relations on Trial: Leo Frank and Jim Conley in the New South.* Jackson: University Press of Mississippi.

Oney, Steve. 2003. *And the Dead Shall Rise: The Murder of Mary Phagan and the Lynching of Leo Frank.* New York: Pantheon Books.

Phagan, Mary. 1987. *The Murder of Little Mary Phagan.* Far Hills, NJ: New Horizon Press.

Henry Ford and the Jews

The root causes of Henry Ford's virulent, sustained—and disturbingly irrepressible—bias against "the Jew" (he preferred the singular form) are difficult to establish. There was no single "tipping point" that marked his transformation into the most influential antisemite in modern American history but, rather, ideological signposts along the road to the flowering of his full-blown, public animus—publication and dissemination of the pernicious forgery *The Protocols of the Elders of Zion* and Ford's concomitant veneration by Adolf Hitler. Ten years before he ascended to power as chancellor, the wall behind Hitler's desk in the Munich headquarters of the National Socialist German Workers' (Nazi) Party was adorned with a massive photographic portrait of "Heinrich" Ford.

Henry Ford (1863–1947) was born on a prosperous farm near Dearbornville in southeastern Michigan. He was the second of eight children and the grandson of John Ford, a Protestant English tenant farmer who had come to America from Ireland during the great potato famine of 1847. Henry's father, William, worked eighty acres of wheat and hay, tended sheep, cows, and pigs, and was a part-time carpenter. Henry's mother, Mary Litogot, was an upstanding Christian of either Dutch or Flemish parentage. Before he entered the country school at age seven, Mary read to her son at the fireside every evening from *The Illustrated Family Christian Almanac for the United States,* wherein he learned that Jesus, the ultimate symbol of goodness, was vilified and persecuted by the Jews; and from the popular *McGuffey Reader* about the adventures of "righteous, honest boys" who grew up to be devout, hard workers with fear of God in their hearts. Mary died when Henry was thirteen.

He labored his way through adolescence, escaping the drudgery of farm life to odd jobs in the factories and warehouses of Detroit, where he became known among his mates as an inveterate tinkerer who preferred to spend the lunch hour taking apart engines and putting them together again. By the age of twenty, from scrounged parts he built a car-locomotive with a kerosene-heated boiler. Friends described him as dogmatic and stubbornly focused. His supervisor at the Detroit Edison Company, electrical engineer Arthur Dow, said, "[Henry] would get his mind running on something and think of it to the exclusion of everything else. When Ford gets set, he is 'set,' and that is all there is to it."

In 1888 he married Clara Jane Bryant, daughter of a farmer. The couple moved to Detroit, where their only child, Edsel, was born. On the rainy morning of June 4, 1896, Ford drove his four-horsepower gasoline quadricycle around the block and changed automotive history forever. He founded a small shop, the Detroit Automobile Company, followed soon thereafter by the Henry Ford Company, "Builders of High Grade Automobiles and Tourist Cars." His friend and partner at the time, the draftsman Oliver Barthel, characterized the young "Mr. Ford" in later years as "tough and mean . . . in order to get along with him, you had to have a little mean streak in your system."

Episcopalian by upbringing, Ford had yet to meet a Jew, but he was exposed to the medieval stereotype. In the ubiquitous *McGuffey Reader,* he had read—and memorized—Shylock's famous "If you prick us, do we not bleed?" soliloquy from *The Merchant of Venice.* Spontaneously during social occasions, Ford would defiantly recite the speech by "the hook-nosed Jew with his bag of gold, carrying the curse of usury," word for word. In 1901, when the death of President McKinley traumatized the nation, Ford turned for solace to Orlando J. Smith's inspirational pamphlet, *A Short View of Great Questions,* a tract he carried in his vest pocket for years, testifying that it "changed [his] outlook on life." The author "did not have patience with . . . the mythology of the Jews [which] discredits the immortality of the soul." Smith drew freely upon Arthur Schopenhauer's *Die Welt als Wille und Vorstellung (The World as Will and Idea,* 1859), sharing

with Schopenhauer the conviction that "the Jewish race . . . resist[ing] the consoling belief of metempsychosis," obstructed the integration of purer, ideal values of classical antiquity into the modern world. To the impressionable Ford's delectation, Smith also drew deeply from an earlier exponent of German race-thinking, Gotthold Lessing, invoking him as "the Luther of German literature, German drama, German art." In Lessing's seminal work *Die Erziehung des Menschengeschlechts (The Upbringing of Mankind,* 1780), he stated that it was imperative for the truly religious man to choose between two starkly different paths—that of "the sensual Jew, or the spiritual Christian."

As Ford emerged as a leading automobile manufacturer, his earliest and most enduring prejudice was reinforced, and he came to believe that a dominant, increasingly regulatory banking network instigated by Jews threatened his fortune. Defying the economic panic of 1907, the four-year-old Ford Motor Company prepared to launch the Model-T the following spring, promising nothing less than "the car for the great multitudes." It was the car that would make Ford fabulously wealthy. In November 1907, the distinguished German Jewish banker, Paul M. Warburg, a partner in Jacob Schiff's firm, Kuhn, Loeb & Company in New York, published a seminal article in *The New York Times Annual Financial Review* calling for a revamping of the nation's banking system. It would be another six years before President Woodrow Wilson authorized Warburg's "Plan for a Modified Central Bank" as the Federal Reserve System. Over these years, as Ford made many millions of dollars, his resentment of what he later called the "*Jewish Idea* of a central bank for America" simmered. The "private" (i.e., in Ford's opinion, secret) nature of the Federal Reserve made it all the more insidious.

At the brink of the Great War, Henry Ford had already presided over the manufacture of more than a million motor cars. Bored with the stress of factory life, Ford delegated the hands-on management to Ernest Gustav Liebold, his personal secretary, chief financial officer, self-styled "watchdog," corporate spokesman, and—it soon became evident—conscientious antisemite. On April 10, 1915, eight months after the guns of August thundered, Henry Ford gave an interview to the *New York Times* magazine, his first documented public dictum on the "war problem." "Moneylenders and munitions makers cause wars," he declared. "The warmongers urging military preparedness in America are the Wall Street bankers." This initial diatribe was followed by a series of bombastic outbursts extending through that anxious summer and fall, revealing Ford's dangerous inclination to blur the boundaries between international banking and profiteering. Two months later, in reponse to the sinking of the unarmed Cunard passenger ship *Lusitania,* torpedoed in Irish waters by a German U-boat, Ford made an ominous entry in one of the "jot-book" diaries he kept close at hand: "People who *profitt* [*sic*] from war must *go.* . . . War is created by people who have no country or home except Hadies [*sic*] Hell and live in every country."

On November 17, 1915, Ford made his most emphatic statement on the preoccupying "Jewish question." A meeting was convened in the Highland Park factory with the ostensible purpose of providing an opportunity for Ford to hear a fund-raising appeal by Hungarian pacifist and women's rights advocate Rosika Schwimmer, in the midst of a lecture tour aimed at galvanizing American grassroots support for an end to the conflict in Europe. Schwimmer had barely begun her talk when Ford burst out, "I know who caused the war—the German-Jewish bankers!" He slapped his breast pocket. "I have the evidence here. Facts! The German-Jewish bankers caused the war. I can't give out the facts now, because I haven't got them all, but I'll have them soon." Ford's tone shifted, Schwimmer recalled, and his voice became "flat as a pancake as he came forth with this cheap and vulgar statement. . . . A strange shadow crept across his face as he uttered the disconnected phrase."

Ernest Liebold was not in the meeting, but more than three decades later he matter-of-factly elucidated Ford's assertion: "The international Jewish interests play behind the scenes and carry on different activities, [men] such as Mr. Ford referred to as warmongers . . . [those] who were interested in carrying on the war for profit. Mr. Ford's definition of Wall Street was the Jewish interests who operated on that type of proposition. . . . That's even happening today [1950]," he continued. "You can read *The Protocols of the Elders of Zion* and find out exactly what's going on. I think I have it around [my office] because I never wanted it to get out of my hands."

By the spring of 1916, Henry Ford was a household name. Despite insisting he would "never do anything [as] outlandish" as stand as a candidate for president, the Republican Party of Michigan put him on the presidential preference list, and Ford was placed in nomination at the Republican National Convention, where he received thirty-

two votes on the first ballot but did not survive a second ballot. Two years later, switching parties to run as Michigan's Democratic candidate for the U.S. Senate, Ford lost by a hair's breadth. Although unsuccessful, both forays demonstrated to Ford that even in defeat he could come out ahead as an outspoken pundit when he took his case directly to "the common man." Therefore, Ford decided that his best platform would be a personal soapbox, a weekly forum for his ideas directed to "plain Americans." Thus on Armistice Day 1918 were sown the seeds for the *Dearborn Independent* newspaper, subtitled "The Ford International Weekly," with its motto, "Chronicler of the Neglected Truth."

The journal was intended to be "a private apparatus for molding public opinion" and would be guided by an intimate group of editors in addition to "The Boss," since he did not intend to write any of the articles himself. He preferred to depend upon a few men handpicked to set his rambling thoughts into cogent type. Aside from Liebold, this team consisted of Edwin G. Pipp, hired away from the editorship of the Detroit *News,* and William J. Cameron, the *News* chief editorial writer. An unordained preacher and a member of the British Israelite sect who believed that the "Modern Hebrews . . . the tribe of treacherous Judah" stole their "chosen people" status from the rightful Aryan claimants, Cameron later co-founded the Anglo-Saxon Federation of America.

By the spring of 1919, the fledgling newspaper had begun to veer away from its soft news, local gossip, and features-driven mission. Boris Brasol, former member of the antisemitic "Black Hundred" organization that instigated the blood-libel ritual murder trial of Mendel Beilis in Kiev in 1913, and now a disaffected czarist emigré and vice chairman of the Russian Officers' Union in America, submitted an essay to the *Independent,* "The Bolshevik [Communist] Menace in Russia." Brasol warned that "this country, too, will have to decide whether it would be prepared to see American homes looted [and] the American flag trodden down. . . . Why should humanity submit its will to a tyranny, which is worse than Oriental autocracies which ruled over mankind at the dawn of its history?" As the Red Scare caught fire in the Midwest, Ford's "Own Page," directly facing the editorial page, began to assume a similarly feverish, paranoid, and reductive pitch, lashing out against the "Dark Forces—whether political, military or capitalistic. . . . What *about* those aliens who have given

Henry Ford's newspaper, The Dearborn Independent, *which widely circulated* The Protocols of the Elders of Zion. *(American Jewish Historical Society)*

us so much trouble, those Bolsheviki messing up our industries and disturbing our civil life."

Brasol had been working for more than a year, in collaboration with physician and avowed nativist Dr. Harris Ayres Houghton, on the first translation on American soil from the original Russian into English of the fourth edition of *The Protocols of the Elders of Zion* (*Protocols*). This twenty-four-part "spurious document" purported to be the proceedings of a Jewish conclave led by the Grand Rabbi during the time of the First Zionist Congress in Basel, Switzerland, in 1897. The purpose of this secret convention of the "innermost circle" of worldwide Jewish leadership was to structure a subversive "blueprint" for world economic and political domination—a "Super-Government" reducing all non-Jews to slavery—and then to set a schedule for subsequent gatherings every one hundred years by an unbroken succession of "autocrats of the House of David. . . . The mark of the serpent's evil will be

stamped on every man's brow," the *Protocols* warned, "and none will be able to make the sign of the cross."

In the issue of May 22, 1920, *The Dearborn Independent* published the first of ninety-one consecutive weekly articles devoted to examining "The International Jew: The World's Problem." Liebold claimed credit for the overall rubric of the series, but he credited the inspiration of "Mr. Ford [who] intimated to me that he was going to show up this group. . . . He said, 'We are going to print their names. We are going to show who they are.'" The inaugural article was called "The Jew in Character and Business," and everyone who came to the factory to meet with Henry Ford for the next several years was required first to spend fifteen minutes reading an offprint in the waiting room.

In mid-June 1920, a typescript of the English translation of the *Protocols* arrived at Liebold's office. On June 26, the *Protocols* began to appear in Ford's newspaper, starting with the "Seventh Protocol," a manifesto about the compulsion of "the secret Jewish Sanhedrin," a "newspaper militia," to unleash the "Great Power" of the press, "already entirely in our hands . . . [to keep] the governments of the *goyim* in Europe in check. . . . Let them amuse themselves until the hour strikes." Liebold insisted, "If the *Protocols* had not been authentic, we never would have published them. . . . We took the *Protocols* at their face value." For the ensuing three months, the document was serialized in the *Independent.* Two years later—by which time he had resigned the editorship in disgust—E. G. Pipp asserted that "Henry Ford had the files of the correspondence . . . [showing] just how [Liebold] worked to give the man with Brasol's Russian record a standing in the newspaper." It is impossible now to determine the extent to which Brasol, Liebold, and Ford had already been in contact, or who first approached whom about the *Protocols,* because the corporate files were destroyed in the 1960s (Jacobs and Weitzman 2003).

By the fall of 1920, "the International Jew" had escalated to become "the world's *Foremost* problem," featured in the first of four paperbound anthologies published over the next eighteen months, in which were gathered all of the pertinent *Dearborn Independent* articles. Much of each printing of 200,000–500,000 copies was mailed *gratis* by Ford's Dearborn Publishing Company to "influential citizens, especially clergymen, bankers and stockbrokers." Never copyrighted, within five years the booklets were translated into sixteen languages. As the historian Norman

Cohn pointed out in his definitive 1967 study, *Warrant for Genocide*, "*The International Jew* probably did more than any other work to make the *Protocols* famous." Twenty-one printings of *Der internationale Jude: ein Weltproblem* (*The International Jew: A World Problem*) appeared in Germany during 1921 and 1922. The publisher was Hammer Verlag of Leipzig, under the direction of Theodor Fritsch (1852–1933), known for decades as the tireless *Altmeister* (Grand Master) of antisemites. Fritsch's preface lauded Henry Ford for the "great service" he had provided to America and the world by attacking the Jews. "The younger generation looked with envy to the symbols of success and prosperity like Henry Ford," recalled the Reich Leader of the Nazi Students' Federation and eventual Hitler Youth leader, Baldur von Schirach. "And if Henry Ford believed that the Jews were to blame, why, naturally we believed him" (Cohn 1967).

Arriving for their appointment with Hitler, visitors could peruse copies of *Der internationale Jude* arrayed on a coffee table in the anteroom of his Munich office. Hitler's documented approval of Ford's behavior can be found as early as the fall of 1923 when, in a dialogue (*zweigensprach*) with his mentor Dietrich Eckart, his attention veered toward America, "where [the Jews] have had the country by the throat for quite awhile . . . as Ford well knew." In his blueprint for the future, *Mein Kampf*, Hitler paid tribute in volume II to "only a single great man, Ford, [who], to [the Jews'] fury, still maintains full independence [from] the controlling masters of the producers in a nation of one hundred and twenty millions." Hitler eagerly devoured the German edition of Ford's memoirs when it was given to him as a birthday gift in 1925. Twenty years later, during the American occupation of Munich, a small collection of the Fuehrer's books and papers was salvaged from his workroom in Nazi Party headquarters. Only one of the literary artifacts showed evidence of thumbing and marginalia—the well-worn copy of *My Life and Work* (*Mein Leben und Werk*) by Heinrich Ford.

On the home front, the factionalized Jewish community in America was faced with a complex dilemma: how to counter the dissemination of Ford's antisemitic views without exacerbating the problem. Rabbi Henry Pereira Mendes, Sephardic spiritual leader of Congregation Shearith Israel in New York City, poignantly summed up the quandary in a letter on October 1, 1920, to Louis Marshall, president of the American Jewish Committee: "To

answer [Ford] feeds the vehemence of the attacks," Mendes wrote. "Not to answer seems unmanly, and gives the enemies a chance to say our silence acknowledges our guilt." The *Independent* also cast aspersions upon the leaders of the Zionist movement, especially calling into question the scruples of Rabbi Judah Magnes. Founder of the American Zionist Federation, Magnes believed that cosmopolitans and *Yiddishists* must work together under his New York *Kehillah*. The *Independent* castigated this banner for communal Jewish life as "the Judaized Tammany Hall," a "whispering gallery" on the corrupt East Coast that kept Jewish organizations "interlaced and dovetailed."

The response of the Jewish press ranged from that of the *Forward*, which continued to accept Ford's advertising dollars for the Model-T, to the left-wing *Der Veg*, which pushed for a consumer boycott of Ford products. Not only were "downtown" *yidden* pitted against "uptown" German elitists over the Ford matter, there was also disagreement within the ranks of "Our Crowd." Philanthropist Jacob Schiff of Kuhn, Loeb took a restrained stance, cautioning Louis Marshall and Cyrus Adler, his colleagues on the American Jewish Committee (AJC), to "take no notice" of the articles in the *Independent*. Adler, in turn, urged Marshall, a fellow attorney, to "denounce [the newspaper] for the fraud that it is." In desperation, the Central Conference of American Rabbis (CCAR), the National Council of Jewish Women, and B'nai B'rith turned to the Anti-Defamation League in Chicago, beseeching that organization—founded in 1913—to speak out against Ford. The League published a pamphlet by Sigmund Livingston, *The Poison Pen*, "Being an exposure of the hoax which is being foisted upon the American public by Henry Ford." Toward the end of 1920, in response to another petition for united action issued by the Zionist Organization of America, the Union of American Hebrew Congregations, the Union of Orthodox Jewish Congregations, the CCAR, and half a dozen other groups, the AJC published *The Protocols, Bolshevism, and the Jews: An Address to their Fellow-Citizens by American Jewish Organizations*, funded by the Sears Roebuck magnate Julius Rosenwald. It was followed by *The Jew and American Ideals* by John Spargo, a Fabian social reformer who had joined the settlement house movement and taken up residence on the Lower East Side. In the new year, Spargo raised funds from "more than one hundred citizens of Gentile extraction and Christian faith" for a lengthy petition-advertisement against Ford,

The Perils of Racial Prejudice, signed and published in newspapers across the country under the banner headline, "President Wilson Heads Protest against Anti-Semitism."

Ford's wife Clara and son Edsel, frustrated by their fruitless attempts to convince him to cease the relentless attacks, resigned in protest from the board of the Dearborn Publishing Company. Not even this dramatic action by his own family slowed Ford's momentum. He asserted again that his "educational campaign" would result in an "investigation . . . of the *facts* of the Jewish question, then everyone can operate for the general good." As historian Leo P. Ribuffo has shown, the years 1922–1925 marked a "second wave" of damaging essays in the *Independent,* for example, praising admissions quotas for Jews at Harvard; naming the "wire-pullers" in the federal government with the temerity to oppose Calvin Coolidge; and criticizing Julius Rosenwald for encouraging Negro migration to Chicago, thereby bringing about "a tide of white dispossession" (Ribuffo 1980).

However, in Ford's eyes the most abhorrent transgression of all was the "Jewish Exploitation of Farmers' Organizations—Monopoly Traps Operat[ing] under the Guise of 'Marketing Associations.'" When Aaron Sapiro (1885–1959), a labor attorney trained for the rabbinate, set out to organize agricultural cooperatives in rural southern California, Ford became incensed, ordering up a series of "exposés" accusing "Oriental financiers" of infiltrating the most cherished outpost of Jeffersonian democracy—the farm. In the spring of 1925, Sapiro—hailed in the press as a latter-day David with the courage to step up against the "Tin Lizzie–plated Goliath of Detroit"—retaliated by filing a $1 million libel suit against Henry Ford and the Dearborn Publishing Company for defamation of character, "to vindicate myself and my race."

Depositions took a year, and Ford's attorney moved for further continuances so that the matter did not come to trial until March 15, 1927. First Cameron, then Liebold, then other staff members took the stand, trying to take the fall for "Mr. Ford," but Sapiro's lawyers pressed forward and made a motion to call "The Boss" himself to testify. As the noose tightened, Ford, in seclusion, summoned a young aide, Fred Black, to his mansion. Ford expressed concern that the negative publicity generated by the trial—complete transcripts were running daily in the Hearst newspapers—would hinder company plans to release a brand-new car in time for Christmas. "I want to stop this *Dearborn Independent!*" Ford ordered Black, and continued without pause: "Of course, you know about us bringing out this new car?" The Model-A was intended to be the successor to the eighteen-year reign of the Model-T and a challenge to the up-and-coming General Motors. The future of the Ford Motor Company was on a collision course with the antisemitic path of its founder, who seemed to have arrived at the expedient realization that in the end the company must survive. There was no way Henry Ford could successfully bring a new generation of motor cars to market with the stigma of Jew-hatred and its (real or imagined) economic implications hanging over his head.

In mid-June 1927, much to his surprise, Louis Marshall received word via two emissaries of Henry Ford that he was now ready to do "whatever [Marshall] thought was right." Marshall stipulated that, if Ford wanted a clean slate, he must make "a complete retraction . . . see to it that such attacks are not made in the future . . . and make amends for the wrongs." Ford responded that Marshall should write the statement for him. "I don't care how bad it is," he said, "you just settle up." Ford did not read the final draft and authorized close aide Harry Bennett to forge his signature. The apology was released to the press on July 8, a day on which Louis Marshall told Cyrus Adler he felt "a great *Nachas Ruach* (spiritual satisfaction)" passing through him.

In the eight-paragraph text, Ford expressed mortification that the *Independent* articles, *International Jew* pamphlets, and *Protocols* had been brought out over the past seven years "delegated to men whom I placed in charge." He professed never to have seen the antisemitic materials prior to publication and expressed "shock" at their content. He asked forgiveness for "the mental anguish . . . [and] harm that I have unintentionally committed," and promised that "the pamphlets which have been distributed throughout the country and in foreign lands will be withdrawn from circulation." He said that he was "fully aware of the virtues of the Jewish people as a whole."

Ford's settlement was quickly negotiated, and Aaron Sapiro received the Richard Gottheil Medal from B'nai B'rith for the most distinguished service to the cause of Judaism in 1927. However, Henry Ford continued with his chronic "antilocution." Gordon Allport, in the classic work *The Nature of Prejudice,* defines this syndrome as the compulsion to talk openly about one's personal biases. Indeed, soon after the *Dearborn Independent* shut

Henry Ford accepts the Grand Cross of the German Eagle from the Nazi government, July 30, 1938. (Corbis)

down, Ford reflected with like-minded friends at the Dearborn Country Club that "by taking a club to [the Jews] I thought I might be able to change some of their obnoxious habits. . . ." (Allport 1979).

Ford took no steps to withdraw *The International Jew* from circulation. He did not hesitate to attribute trade union agitation to "certain bankers." Into the Depression years, Ford made notes in his jot-books such as "The Jew is out to enslave you." On his seventy-fifth birthday, July 30, 1938, Ford was honored to be the first American recipient of the Grand Service Cross of the Supreme Order of the German Eagle (*Verdienstkreuz Deutscher Adler*), created by Hitler in 1937 as "the highest honor given by Germany to distinguished foreigners." Three months later, Ford's friend Charles Lindbergh received the same medal from the founder of the Gestapo, Hermann Wilhelm Goering, in

gratitude for the world-famous pilot's assistance with the development of the Luftwaffe's newest airplanes. Into the late 1930s, Fritz Kuhn of the German-American Bund and the "Radio Priest" Father Charles Coughlin and his National Union for Social Justice/Christian Front picked up Ford's banner. In the early 1940s, Ford provided funding for white supremacist and "America First" activist Gerald L. K. Smith to broadcast weekly radio speeches over WJR, the largest radio station in Detroit. Thirteen years after his "apology," Ford "show[ed] no regret" and told Smith that he "hope[d] to publish *The International Jew* again some time."

Neil Baldwin

Unless otherwise noted in the text, citations in this essay are derived from *Henry Ford and the Jews: The Mass-Production of Hate* by Neil Baldwin (New York: Public Affairs, 2001).

References and Further Reading

Allport, Gordon. 1979. *The Nature of Prejudice.* Reading, MA: Addison-Wesley.

Bronner, Stephen Eric. 2000. *A Rumor about the Jews: Reflections on Antisemitism and the Protocols of the Elders of Zion.* New York: St. Martin's Press.

Bryan, Ford. 1993. *Henry's Lieutenants.* Detroit, MI: Wayne State University Press.

Cohen, Naomi W. 1972. *Not Free to Desist: A History of the American Jewish Committee, 1906–1966.* Philadelphia: Jewish Publication Society.

Cohn, Norman. 1967. *Warrant for Genocide.* New York: Harper & Row.

The Dearborn Independent. 1920–1922. *The International Jew: The World's Foremost Problem.* Vols. 1–4. Detroit, MI: The Dearborn Independent. Reprinted 1999 by GSG Associates, San Pedro, CA.

Jacobs, Steven Leonard, and Mark Weitzman. 2003. *Dismantling the Big Lie: The Protocols of the Elders of Zion.* Los Angeles: Simon Wiesenthal Center.

Mendes-Flohr, Paul, and Jehuda Reinharz, eds. 1995. *The Jew in the Modern World: A Documentary History.* New York: Oxford University Press.

Nevins, Allan, and Frank Ernest Hill. 1954–1962. *Ford: The Times, the Man, the Company.* New York: Charles Scribner's Sons.

Pipp, Edwin Gustav. 1922. "The Real Henry Ford." Detroit, MI: *Pipp's Weekly.*

Ribuffo, Leo P. 1980. "Henry Ford and *The International Jew.*" *American Jewish History* (June): 413–453.

Wistrich, Robert. 1991. *Antisemitism: The Longest Hatred.* New York: St. Martin's Press.

Zeskind, Leonard. 1986. *The "Christian Identity" Movement: Analyzing Its Theological Rationalization for Racist and Anti-Semitic Violence.* Atlanta: Center for Democratic Renewal.

Antisemitic Violence in Boston and New York during World War II

During World War II, marauding bands composed largely of Irish-American youth terrorized Jewish communities in Boston and New York, repeatedly assaulting Jews in the streets and parks, desecrating synagogues and Jewish cemeteries, and damaging Jewish stores. Yiddish journalist and Zionist leader Dr. Samuel Margoshes referred to the violence in Boston as a "series of small pogroms" (Norwood 2003). The attacks peaked in 1943 and 1944, as marauders left Irish-American districts contiguous to Jewish neighborhoods to go "Jew hunting." They challenged individuals they encountered by demanding to know whether they were Jewish. If the answer was affirmative, they beat, stabbed, or even mutilated the victim. They sometimes tore the clothes off Jewish girls. In late 1943, state senator Maurice Goldman, who represented the Dorchester-Mattapan-Roxbury district, where most of Boston's Jews resided, informed Massachusetts governor Leverett Saltonstall that his constituents lived in "mortal fear" of antisemitic assault (Norwood 2003). Jewish spokespersons in both cities, joined by concerned non-Jews, declared that the violence was part of an organized antisemitic campaign inspired by the Coughlinite Christian Front. The savage wartime beatings of Jews in Boston and New York constituted the most sustained wave of overt antisemitic violence in American history.

Both Boston and New York were Coughlinite strongholds. Michigan-based priest Charles Coughlin was one of the nation's most influential antisemites, who spoke every week to millions of Americans across the nation over the radio. In 1938 he reprinted the *Protocols of the Elders of Zion,* a long-discredited forgery purporting to demonstrate a Jewish conspiracy to take over the world, in his newspaper *Social Justice,* sold in front of churches and at street corners throughout both cities. Coughlin organized the Christian Front in 1938 to propagate his antisemitic views. It recruited many members from the Boston and New York police forces. The Christian Front urged shoppers not to patronize Jewish-owned stores. Both the Christian Front and an offshoot called the Christian Mobilizers, whose rhetoric was explicitly violent, regularly staged street-corner meetings denouncing Jews.

From the late 1930s through World War II, the Christian Front advanced an antisemitic isolationism. Prior to U.S. entry into the war, Boston Christian Front leader Francis Moran charged that Jews schemed to draw the country into the European conflict in order to advance their economic interests. Labeling Jewish interventionists "bloodsuckers," Moran deliberately invoked the medieval charge that Jews murdered Christian children to obtain blood to mix with Passover matzoh. Although the federal government banned *Social Justice* as seditious in 1942, and Coughlin's archbishop, under U.S. Justice Department pressure, ordered him to withdraw from political activity, the Christian Front continued its antisemitic, isolationist campaign behind newly created front groups. It circulated massive quantities of antisemitic literature, including some that falsely accused Jews of avoiding military service. The

Charles Coughlin, Michigan-based Roman Catholic priest and leader of the virulently antisemitic Christian Front. (Library of Congress)

antisemitic priest Edward Lodge Curran, the "Father Coughlin of the East," visited Irish-American South Boston during the war to denounce America's ally Britain at heavily attended, city-financed celebrations of Evacuation Day (which commemorated British withdrawal from Boston during the American Revolution). John Roy Carlson, one of America's leading authorities on hate movements, described wartime Boston as "seething with anti-Semitism and defeatism" (Norwood 2003).

In October 1943, antisemitic violence in Boston and New York was suddenly brought to national attention when Arnold Beichman wrote several articles about it in the New York daily *PM.* The mainstream press in the two cities had failed to report the antisemitic assaults and vandalism. Boston Irish-American anti-fascist Frances Sweeney, who for several years had investigated and documented the beatings and vandalism, had contacted Beichman and provided data on the Boston antisemitic outbreaks. Beichman also

drew on affidavits that the American Jewish (AJ) Congress and the Anti-Defamation League (ADL) had collected from victims. Scores of Jews testified that the police repeatedly ignored their complaints of antisemitic assault and harassment and sometimes joined in it. Shortly after Beichman's articles appeared, the AJ Congress announced that beatings of Jews and synagogue desecrations had reached epidemic proportions in New York. New York's ADL assembled a detailed record of them.

Beichman's initial report in *PM,* headlined "Christian Front Hoodlums Terrorize Boston Jews," provided specifics on numerous cases of antisemitic assault, intimidation, and vandalism, and accused Governor Saltonstall, Boston mayor Maurice Tobin, the police, and the press of ignoring a massive outbreak of violent antisemitism. Members of the state legislature from the Dorchester-Mattapan-Roxbury district, joined by some local rabbis, backed Beichman's charges. Frances Sweeney, along with several journalists writing in leading mass circulation magazines, sharply criticized the Catholic Church hierarchy for remaining indifferent to the beatings of Jews and for its unwillingness to use its influence to discourage them.

In both Boston and New York, Jews at the neighborhood level reacted by organizing volunteer patrols to combat the antisemitic marauders. Their objectives included protecting elderly Jews, who were unable to attend synagogue services because they feared leaving their homes, and Jewish children, many of whom the marauders had injured. In Boston, Jewish Girl Scout troops had called off meetings because members were frightened of street attacks. The New York Yiddish newspaper *Tog* (*The Day*) compared the patrols to the ghetto defense groups that Jews in czarist Russia had organized to combat pogromists. The formation of neighborhood defense units was probably also inspired by the Warsaw ghetto fighters' heroic resistance against the Nazi army earlier in 1943.

In January 1944, the Jewish-owned New York *Post,* among the few newspapers that refused to accept advertising from hotels and resorts that excluded Jews, urged its readers to provide it with detailed reports of antisemitic beatings, synagogue desecration, and antisemitic graffiti on stores and apartment buildings and in subways. The *Post* used the evidence it gathered from readers to pressure police to take action against the antisemitic outbreaks.

Violence against Jews in Boston and New York declined after World War II, although it remained alarming into the early 1950s, especially in Boston. The annihilation of six million Jews in the Holocaust heightened some Americans' awareness of the danger of antisemitism. Liberal groups joined with Jewish organizations in sponsoring educational efforts to promote tolerance in schools and among policemen and the public. In Boston, a new cardinal, Richard Cushing, whose brother-in-law was Jewish, also made an effort to foster intergroup understanding, in sharp contrast to his predecessor, William O'Connell, who died in 1944. O'Connell had remained silent during the wartime antisemitic outbreaks. Postwar migration of Jews out of urban neighborhoods contiguous to Irish Catholic districts also reduced the possibility of marauding antisemitic youth encountering Jews.

Stephen H. Norwood

Reference and Further Reading

Norwood, Stephen H. 2003. "Marauding Youth and the Christian Front: Antisemitic Violence in Boston and New York During World War II." *American Jewish History* 91 (June): 233–267.

Antisemitism and Right-Wing Extremist Groups after 1960

American antisemitism has continued to exist as a social problem since 1960, but its magnitude has been much less than during the previous four decades, the 1920s through the 1950s. Although numerous very small extreme-right organizations featuring anti-Jewish ideology have been extant since 1960, only three have had more than ten thousand members—the Liberty Lobby, the Nation of Islam, and the United Klans of America. In addition, a few small groups have garnered publicity far out of proportion to their size: the American Nazi Party, The Order, the Church of the Creator, and the National Alliance. The leader of this last group, Dr. William Pierce, wrote a novel, *The Turner Diaries,* which may have influenced others to commit terrorist acts, including Timothy McVeigh and Robert Matthews, founder of The Order. A spin-off from Aryan Nations, The Order believes in Christian Identity, a strange theology positing that the true Israelites are Nordic Caucasians ("Aryans") and that Jews are descendants of Cain, who was conceived in a sexual liaison between Eve and the

Serpent. There is also the John Birch Society, which had antisemites in its ranks but never included anti-Jewish beliefs in its ideology.

Religious antisemitism existed for hundreds of years before political antisemitism first appeared in the latter part of the nineteenth century. Typical of the earlier form of antisemitism was the assertion by Pope Gregory the Great (590–604) that Jews actually knew Jesus was the Messiah but rejected him because their hearts were corrupt (Johnson 1987). Political antisemitism, which posits a Jewish conspiracy to take over the world, did not hit full stride, however, until the early twentieth century, when the infamous fabricated document *The Protocols of the Learned Elders of Zion* appeared. Concocted in Russia around 1903, principally by Sergus Nilus, a czarist attorney, the *Protocols* provided excuses for actions Jew-haters would have taken anyway but also helped to push fence-sitters over to the antisemitic side.

Supposedly a master plan for Jewish world conquest, the *Protocols* were in part plagiarized from an 1864 work, *Dialogue in Hell between Machiavelli and Montesquieu* by Maurice Joly, that had nothing to do with Jews but was a satire on the despotism of Napoleon III. Almost half of it was incorporated into the *Protocols,* as Nilus and his collaborators attributed words Joly had put into Machiavelli's mouth to leading (but anonymous) Jews.

In the United States, it was Henry Ford who widely disseminated the *Protocols* during the 1920s in his *Dearborn Independent,* although he later disavowed the document as spurious. That in 1921 the *London Times* exposed the *Protocols* as fraudulent had little or no effect on its use by antisemitic groups in the United States or elsewhere. Today, most Americans have never heard of this mendacious document.

The first important twentieth-century group harboring a strong antipathy toward Jews was the second Ku Klux Klan, formed in 1915 principally by W. J. Simmons. Although he called himself "Colonel," the title had nothing to do with the military but was his rank in the fraternal group Woodmen of the World. The reborn Klan was not only the largest twentieth-century extremist group (about 2 million members by the mid-1920s, when the U.S. population was less than 110 million) but also the most violent. It may accurately be described as "terrorist," with Jews, recent immigrants, blacks, Catholics, and violators of prohibition as its primary targets. Clergy and law enforcement personnel were prominent members.

During the Depression of the 1930s, other antisemitic extremist groups gained notoriety and influence: the Black Legion, the Silver Shirts, the German-American Bund, the Christian Nationalist Crusade, and Defenders of the Christian Faith, whose leader, Gerald B. Winrod, a Kansan, was known as the "Jayhawk Nazi." The Christian Front, headed by the antisemitic radio priest Charles Coughlin, was also influential. Members of these and similar smaller groups believed in the existence of an all-encompassing, worldwide, Jewish conspiracy as delineated in the *Protocols*, and a significant number were sympathetic toward the sociopolitical systems and leaders of fascist Italy and Nazi Germany.

These organizations began to lose influence and, in effect, went into a tailspin after Japan bombed Pearl Harbor on December 7, 1941. In 1944, a number of well-known antisemitic rightists were tried for sedition (*U.S. v. McWilliams*), an action decried by a majority of, but far from all, civil libertarians. (Although this trial was aimed at extreme rightists, it helped to justify later prosecutions of extreme leftists—who had earlier strenuously supported the trial!) The prosecution of the rightists resulted in a mistrial, and the effort to prosecute was later abandoned.

During World War II and its aftermath, the Jew-hating right was dealt a blow from which it never recovered. By the 1960s, very few right-wing extremist groups that were ideologically antisemitic had memberships exceeding 10,000; the great majority had fewer than 1,000. Among the exceptions were the Liberty Lobby, the Nation of Islam, and the United Klans of America.

The most influential post-1960 anti-Jewish organization was a group originally called Liberty and Property, formed by California businessman Willis Carto. This was essentially a paper organization for Carto's publication *Right,* which summarized information from numerous far right sources. In August 1957 *Right* announced the formation of what would become probably the best financed antisemitic extremist group of the last half of the twentieth century, Liberty Lobby. One of the first endorsers of the new group was the well-known novelist and active John Birch Society member, Janet Taylor Caldwell.

Right became defunct in 1960 and was superseded by *Liberty Letter,* which attained a circulation of about 200,000. In 1975, however, *Liberty Letter* was discontinued and replaced by *National Spotlight,* later renamed simply *Spotlight,* which continued until July 2001. With a paid circulation close to 90,000, it was quite possibly read by three times that number. As with most extremist groups, membership figures for Liberty Lobby are difficult to determine, since all these groups, as well as those who detest them, exaggerate. Around 1990, Liberty Lobby claimed 25,000 members—but this writer and two others were counted as members for subscribing and sending stamps when requesting information. One was even listed on Liberty Lobby's Board of Policy for a few years.

Willis Carto's clandestine anti-Jewish activities first received wide exposure in a 1966 column by Drew Pearson, the most widely read American columnist at that time. Jeremy Horne, a Liberty Lobby employee, discovered letters from Carto to various right extremists, including two black nationalists. One letter mentioned shipping blacks "back to Africa," while another revealed pro-Nazi views: "Hitler's defeat was the defeat of Europe and America. . . . The blame . . . must be laid at the door of the International Jews. . . . If Satan himself . . . had tried to create a . . . force for destruction of all nations, he could have done no better than to invent the Jews." Disturbed, the "mainstream conservative" Horne informed the FBI (although no lawbreaking was involved) and Drew Pearson, who published excerpts from the letters. Liberty Lobby took Pearson to court twice, even appealing to the U.S. Supreme Court, and lost. Carto also asserted that Horne was a spy whom Pearson had planted in his organization. Horne told this writer that he had never had previous contact with Pearson and had acquired the job with Liberty Lobby by replying to a newspaper ad seeking an individual who wanted to work for a "conservative" organization.

The factor most responsible for cementing Willis Carto's sympathy for Nazism and belief in a worldwide Jewish conspiracy was probably his brief connection with the enigmatic Francis Parker Yockey. This unstable intellectual, a 1941 honors graduate of Notre Dame and a minor assistant to Nuremberg prosecutors, authored a sort of "neo–*Mein Kampf* for neo-Nazis" entitled *Imperium*. The 619-page effort was supposedly written in six months. It was published in 1948 using the pseudonym Ulick Varange and dedicated "To the hero of the Second World War." The "hero" was, of course, Adolf Hitler. *Imperium* is a most difficult book to read, and few in the world of the anti-Jewish right have actually perused much of it.

In the late 1940s, Yockey's requests to renew his passport were denied, and from 1949 to 1960 he traveled in both the United States and Europe using fabricated documents. During this time, he did not have an occupation, and a number of far rightists have maintained that sympathizers gave him money. Yockey related grandiose tales of his organization, the European Liberation Front (ELF), which was supposedly doing much to counter "the nefarious machinations of the International Jews." There is no evidence that the ELF was much more than a paper organization—and thus a scheme to support the mentally disturbed Yockey, who may well have believed his own outlandish tales.

In 1960 Yockey flew to San Francisco but left a suitcase in Fort Worth. Airline employees opened it to determine the owner and found seven birth certificates, German press credentials, and three passports (U.S., Canadian, and U.K.) displaying Yockey's photo. He was arrested on a passport violation and placed in the San Francisco jail, where Willis Carto visited him. After a week and a half, Yockey committed suicide with a cyanide capsule. With the exception of his attorney, the last to see him was Carto, who thereafter made Yockey a cause célèbre. In the July 1960 issue of *Right*, Carto asserted that Yockey was a "great creative genius" who had been "persecuted" to the point that he took his own life. Despite this, Carto averred, his "great" work, *Imperium*, would "live a thousand years." This prediction proved inaccurate; only forty years later, few had read it, and fewer, if any, have understood much of it.

The most surprising characteristic of Carto's hero, Yockey, is that he was probably a paid Soviet agent. This writer's 1970 interview with a self-described fascist who knew Yockey rather well included the following exchange:

George: Why was the FBI after him so much? They had him under surveillance for about eleven years. Did he really have . . . Nazi connections in Europe or not?

X: He had Soviet connections.

George: Oh, he did?

X: Yes. The current bunch who exploit him don't want to hear about that angle.

George: What was he doing with the Soviets?

X: I think he was a coordinator of some sort. I think the Russians, particularly in Germany, were encouraging some of those radical rightist groups and parties for their own purposes.

This statement about Yockey's Soviet connections is supported by other evidence that also suggests that he

was quite anti-American and considered the West a greater threat to European culture than the Soviet Union. With the collapse of the Soviet bloc, East German intelligence documents revealed that its version of the KGB, the Stasi, had agents posing as neo-Nazis and even formed neo-Nazi groups in West Germany. Yockey may have been just the sort of fellow the Soviets wanted. He, conversely, probably believed that he was using them (George and Wilcox 1996).

Other Willis Carto actions included the 1966 takeover of the *American Mercury* (cofounded by H. L. Mencken) and the creation of the National Youth Alliance (NYA) in 1969. The NYA, which was actually a takeover and makeover of Youth for Wallace (supporters of the 1968 American Independent Party candidate for president, George Wallace of Alabama), attracted a number of stalwarts of the anti-Jewish right as sponsors, including these:

Dr. William Pierce, formerly of the American Nazi Party, whose fictional account of a white racial nationalist seizure of the United States, *The Turner Diaries,* so impressed Oklahoma City bomber Timothy McVeigh. Pierce, a physics professor, died in 2002.

Louis Byers, who left the John Birch Society mainly because of its stated opposition to antisemitism.

Admiral John Crommelin, longtime Jew-hater, who in the 1960s ran for both the U.S. Senate and the office of vice president under the auspices of the neo-Nazi group the National States Rights Party.

The NYA did not last very long, principally because of the far right's "prima donna factor"—namely, that having numerous unstable, idiosyncratic, megalomaniacal personalities in an organization is not conducive to group cohesion.

The part of the "Carto Complex" that attracted the most attention was the Institute for Historical Review (IHR), founded in 1978. It became the most widely known "Holocaust revisionist" or "Holocaust denial" organization. The group asserted that probably no more than 200,000 Jews died at the hands of the Nazis during World War II and that most died fighting Hitler's minions or perished from disease in concentration camps. They insist that there was no plan to exterminate Jews, gypsies, or others, but only to deport them "to the East." The Institute's main publication, the *Journal of Historical Review,* has provided a forum for British pseudohistorian David Irving, who lost a libel suit he filed against Penguin Books and American historian Deborah Lipstadt. (Irving objected to Lipstadt's branding him a Holocaust denier.) Also featured have been antisemites Michael Hoffman and David McCalden (who claimed to have founded the IHR under the name Lewis Brandon), and posthumous articles by Yockey. It was McCalden who in 1981 goaded the IHR into offering a $50,000 prize for proof that gas chambers existed in Nazi concentration campus. An Auschwitz survivor, Mel Mermelstein, laid claim to the reward, which the IHR rejected. Mermelstein sued in Los Angeles County Superior Court and was awarded the $50,000, the judge taking "judicial notice" that people were gassed at Auschwitz. The IHR appealed, then decided the judicial battle would be expensive, and settled with Mermelstein for $90,000.

Fratricidal battles within the IHR resulted in the ouster of Carto, and the group severed all ties with Liberty Lobby in 1993. Carto also lost control of the umbrella corporation, Legion for the Survival of Freedom, which sued him and won in 2000. Due to Carto's financial shenanigans, he eventually owed more than $2 million. By mid-2001 the final issue of *Spotlight* was published, and the Liberty Lobby was defunct. Little has been heard from Willis Carto since.

Another antisemitic and even anti-Caucasian group is the Nation of Islam (NOI), which from the early 1960s to the present has probably had more than 10,000 but fewer than 20,000 members. The NOI has been inaccurately labeled extreme left by some commentators, usually people on the right. From its inception, however, the organization has been ethnically exclusive ("racist"), quite religious (a variation of Islam), separatist, capitalist, and intensely racial nationalist—hardly leftist traits. Founded in the early 1930s by W. D. Fard, who called himself W. Farad Muhammad, the NOI was quickly taken over by Elijah Muhammad (né Poole) after Fard simply disappeared in 1934. Elijah headed the group until his death in the mid-1970s. Not long after Elijah's demise, his son, Warith Deen Muhammad, disbanded the NOI and instructed his followers to join mainstream Islamic groups. Into the void stepped Louis Farrakhan (né Wolcott) who appropriated the name Nation of Islam and revived the antiwhite, anti-Jewish rhetoric that had been abandoned by Warith Muhammad.

Farrakhan always had charisma, although not nearly as much as Malcolm X (né Little) who was murdered in February 1965 by two NOI members and a third assassin in front of hundreds of witnesses in Harlem's Audubon Ballroom. Malcolm had been the major catalyst for the growth of the NOI during the early 1960s, and Farrakhan had always been jealous of him and his reputation, going so far as to justify his murder—"and, if we dealt with him like a nation deals with a traitor, what the hell business is it of yours?" (*Brother Minister* 1993). And as is typical of antisemitic agitators, Farrakhan has blamed Jews for virtually every bad action taken against blacks. Indeed, he has gone so far as to insist that Jews were predominantly responsible for the slave trade. This absurd charge was answered quite adequately by Harold Brackman in his concise work, *Farrakhan's Reign of Historical Error: The Truth Behind "The Secret Relationship between Blacks and Jews."*

In the early 1960s, there were also about a dozen Klan groups, whose total membership, according to the Anti-Defamation League, exceeded 50,000—only a shadow of the single Ku Klux Klan of the 1920s. Largest among them was Robert Shelton's United Klans of America, with more than 40,000 members. By the mid-1970s, membership in all the groups combined had declined to about 5,000. One of the main KKK claims was that Jews instigated and controlled the black civil rights movement of the sixties.

Klan groups received what they regarded as a "treasonous" blow when the House Un-American Activities Committee (HUAC) investigated them in 1965 and 1966. The various Klans had consistently and strongly supported all actions of HUAC, and they considered it a "stab in the back" to be called before it to answer hostile questions. Observers of the extremist scene found this situation ironic, even darkly humorous, and some believed the Klansmen got what they deserved. Consistent civil libertarians, however, took the position that any illegal actions committed by them should be the business of law enforcement rather than a controversial committee of the U.S. House of Representatives.

The magnitude of the infighting and backstabbing within and among Klans from the mid-1960s into the 1990s was difficult to exaggerate. The phenomenon was exacerbated by the growing presence of informants for law enforcement and for organizations that monitored Klan groups. The infiltration was such that, from the late 1960s through the mid-1970s, nearly all officers of the Indiana Klan were paid informants for law enforcement. Bill Wilkinson, chief of the Invisible Empire, Knight of the Ku

Klux Klan, was a paid FBI informant for a number of years. Not only did Wilkinson incite dissension and rivalry among KKK groups, but he also gave Klan records and membership lists to the FBI (George and Wilcox 1996).

By the end of the twentieth century, membership in all Klans amounted to no more than 5,000 in a U.S. population approaching 290 million—an enormous decline from an estimated 2 million Klansmen in the 1920s. Moreover, instead of an overrepresentation of law enforcement officers and Christian clergy as was the case in the earlier period, the recent Klans contained hardly any police and sheriffs and a considerably smaller percentage of preachers than the Klan of the 1920s.

The John Birch Society (JBS) is another right extremist group of more than 10,000 that found notoriety during the 1960s and 1970s. Although accused of being antisemitic, and it did have some antisemitic members, the JBS was never ideologically antisemitic; it made pronouncements against such beliefs and claimed about 500 Jewish members. Indeed, the exposure of a Bircher as a Jew-hater, followed by expulsion from the Society, was a fairly common occurrence during the 1960s and 1970s. Robert H. W. Welch Jr., Birch founder and leader until his death in 1985, even warned his flock that antisemitism was bad and could do considerable damage both to the group's internal functioning and to its public image. The most striking expulsion occurred during a hot July in 1966 at the Birch-sponsored New England Rally for God, Family, and Country in Boston. Dr. Revilo P. Oliver, professor of Classics at the University of Illinois (Urbana), gave a talk to the faithful that can accurately be described as anti-Jewish. This writer and a friend attended and were quite surprised that Oliver said such things publicly. Shortly thereafter, leading Society members insisted that he had to go. It seems a bit strange that these Birchers were evidently unaware (or weren't bothered) that Dr. Oliver, in a 1959 talk before the Illinois Daughters of the American Revolution, had referred to Cuba as "an island largely populated by mongrels" (George and Wilcox 1996).

Throughout the 1960s, a number of antisemites informed this writer that they considered the John Birch Society a fertile recruiting ground (although one called it "kid stuff") but that most Birchers were uninformed and quite naive about the "International Jewish Conspiracy." And while Robert Welch did believe in the Illuminati Conspiracy, according to these antisemites, he "just couldn't see

that it was simply a tool of the International Jews." This illustrates the differences between the outlook of typical antisemites and that of Welch and the great majority of his followers, who did not accept the idea of a long-lasting, overarching Jewish conspiracy. Still, Welch held other conspiratorial beliefs—for example, that President Eisenhower, his brother Milton, Secretary of State John Foster Dulles, his brother, CIA director Allen Dulles, General George Marshall, and many others were all Communist agents and part of a greater conspiracy that uses Communism. Birchers referred to these conspirators as the "Insiders." To Welch, the Insiders were a continuation of the Illuminati "conspiracy" founded in 1776 by Adam Weishaupt in Bavaria. Although the group was abolished in 1785, belief in an Illuminati conspiracy has occupied the imaginations of conspiracy-minded extremists for well over two hundred years.

Numerous very small anti-Jewish organizations have appeared and disappeared during the past half-century. Largely because of their outrageous pronouncements, a few achieved the notoriety so cherished by the leaders and their followers. The best known was the American Nazi Party (ANP). Organized in 1959 by former U.S. Navy commander George Lincoln Rockwell, the American Nazi Party (later renamed the National Socialist White Peoples Party) attracted more attention than other neo-Nazi groups. Although the National Renaissance Party had been formed ten years earlier, its leader, James Madole, had neither the intelligence nor the public relations ability of the clever but rather unbalanced Rockwell. While the ANP's swastikas, Sam Browne belts, and little "fascist" hats upset many people, at no time did this group have even two hundred actual members, and some of them were informants. Rockwell was assassinated in 1967 by John Patler, a disgruntled party member who felt that the "American Fuehrer" was not paying enough attention to him. Patler was sentenced to twenty-two years in prison for his crime.

Another small neo-Nazi group that garnered much more than its rightful share of publicity was the National Alliance. Formed in 1974 by Dr. William Pierce, the National Alliance probably never had as many as five hundred members. Pierce got his neo-Nazi start with Rockwell's American Nazi Party but was expelled from the organization in 1970 by Rockwell's successor, Matt Koehl. In the late 1970s, Pierce used a religious front group, the Cosmotheist Community Church, to gain tax-exempt status.

In 1983 a federal court of appeals revoked this status. The following year, Pierce achieved greater notoriety when it became publicly known that he was the author of the highly controversial novel *The Turner Diaries*. This book, which Pierce wrote under the name Andrew McDonald, details a violent racial-nationalist takeover of the United States by antisemitic whites. His description of the overthrow includes the killing of blacks, "race traitors," and, of course, Jews. Among those highly impressed with the novel, which Pierce intended to be prophetic, was Timothy McVeigh, who in 1995 murdered 168 people in Oklahoma City with a bomb. He was executed in 2002.

Another who drew inspiration from Pierce's hate book was Robert Matthews, who belonged to the small neo-Nazi group Aryan Nations led by the Reverend Richard Butler and headquartered in Hayden Lake, Idaho. In 1983 Matthews formed a spin-off grouplet he dubbed The Silent Brotherhood, better known as The Order. Purposely keeping his creation highly secretive and limited to a small number (fewer than thirty), Matthews led his minions into actions shunned by the overwhelming majority of American political extremists, even those with intense anti-Jewish proclivities. These actions included counterfeiting, robbery, and murder. Thus, unlike its parent organization Aryan Nations, The Order became a terrorist group. Emulating the most extreme American Marxist–Leninist fringe by robbing armored cars and banks, these racial-nationalists also committed at least two murders: Denver radio talk show host Alan Berg was gunned down in his driveway, and Order compatriot Walter West was killed deep in the woods because Matthews came to believe that he was an informant for law enforcement. (The odds are that West was not an informant. Groups such as the Silent Brotherhood know they have infiltrators, but they are seldom able to determine who they are.) All Order members were eventually arrested and sentenced to prison, with the exception of Matthews, who was killed in a December 1984 gun battle with FBI agents.

The World Church of the Creator is another very small organization. Founded in 1973 by Ben Klassen, who committed suicide in 1993, the World Church of the Creator was taken over in 1996 by Matt Hale, who continued the group's hostility toward Jews, blacks, Asians, Latinos, and even Christians. The credo of the organization has been "To Serve The One Living God Who Has Placed A Trust In Us." After losing the right to use the name World Church of the Creator, Hale settled for the name Creativity. It has been described as a "racial religion whose goal is the survival, expansion, and advancement of the white race."

During 1999 some exceedingly bad publicity descended on Hale and his Creativity movement when a member named Benjamin Smith shot eleven people (Jews, Asians, and blacks), two of whom died. Hale immediately claimed only casual contact with Smith, but this assertion rang hollow, since he had given Smith the "Creator of the Year" award not many months prior to the shootings. Hale also discovered that plotting to have a federal judge killed would result in time behind bars. Hale's plot was exposed because an FBI informant had successfully infiltrated Creativity and won his confidence. At its zenith, Creativity probably did not have one thousand members.

Thus, the great majority of post-1960 anti-Jewish groups have been not only quite small but also populated by loud, cruel, generally maladjusted, self-destructive people who have been more of a danger to themselves than to Americans in general or Jews in particular. The only group with any real influence in the twenty-first century is the Nation of Islam. Most black political figures have been reluctant to criticize Louis Farrakhan strongly, and most blacks know nothing of his hatred for Malcolm X, much less his 1993 justification of Malcolm's murder.

John George

References and Further Reading

Aho, James. 1990. *The Politics of Righteousness: Idaho Christian Patriotism*. Seattle: University of Washington Press.

Anti-Defamation League. 1983. *Extremism on the Right*. New York: Anti-Defamation League.

Anti-Defamation League. 1984. *Hate Groups in America*. New York: Anti-Defamation League.

Brackman, Harold. 1992. *Farrakhan's Reign of Historical Error: The Truth Behind "The Secret Relationship Between Blacks and Jews."* Los Angeles: Wiesenthal Center.

Brother Minister (Film). 1993. Videotape of excerpts owned by John George.

Dobratz, Betty, and Stephanie Shanks-Meile. 1997. *White Power, White Pride! The White Separatist Movement in the United States*. New York: Twayne Publishers.

George, John, and Laird Wilcox. 1996. *American Extremists: Militias, Supremacists, Klansmen, Communists, and Others*. Amherst, NY: Prometheus Books.

Johnson, Paul. 1987. *A History of the Jews*. New York: Harper & Row.

Marsden, Victor, trans. n.d. *The Protocols of the Learned Elders of Zion*. Distributed by Christian Nationalist Crusade.

Mintz, Frank P. 1985. *Liberty Lobby and the American Right: Race Conspiracy and Culture*. Westport, CT: Greenwood Press.

Perry, Bruce. 1991. *Malcolm: The Life of a Man Who Changed Black America*. Barrytown, NY: Station Hill.

Shermer, Michael, and Alex Grobman. 2000. *Denying History: Who Says the Holocaust Never Happened and Why Do They Say It?* Berkeley: University of California Press.

Varange, Ulick [Francis Parker Yockey]. 2000 [1948]. *Imperium*. Newport Beach, CA: Noontide Press.

African American Antisemitism in the 1990s

In recent decades, the college campus has become a major venue for antisemitic rants. In the 1990s, before Israel and Zionism became the central focus of the attacks, campuses echoed with charges that Jews dominated the Atlantic slave trade. In truth, as David Brion Davis, Sterling Professor of History at Yale University and a leading historian of slavery, and other scholars have shown, Jews had only a "very marginal place" in the history of the slave trade. The absurd claims that rocked the campuses were drawn from a tract anonymously authored by the Historical Research Department of the Nation of Islam (NOI), *The Secret Relationship between Blacks and Jews* (*SR*). Notably, Davis would characterize the volume as "the extreme example of anti-Semitic accusations masquerading as a documented history of Jewish involvement in the slave trade" (1994). Several scholars have exposed the methods used in *The Secret Relationship* as consistently fraudulent. The tract commonly cited and misquoted scholars in support of the very positions they had refuted. It identified notorious antisemites as "respected historical authorities" and presented as fact long-discredited myths that had been used to justify pogroms. It drew inferences that flouted all rules of logic and routinely made wild extrapolations, often from preposterous "evidence." Indeed, one commentator wrote of the "sense of authorial derangement" one gets from reading the last ninety-nine pages, "a historical manhunt for a Jewish Simon Legree" (Conlon 1995). Despite the *SR*'s gross violation of the historical record, however, the media gave wide circulation to its allegations, promul-gated on college campuses, while failing to dismiss them as spurious.

Even before *The Secret Relationship* exploded on college campuses, a number of universities, mainly on the east and west coasts, were roiled by conflicts over the issue of black antisemitism. In February 1991, *Nommo,* the magazine of UCLA's Black Student Organization (BSO), published an article that embraced the *Protocols of the Elders of Zion,* with its revelations of the Jews' secret plans for world domination, as historical "truth." "The fact remains," the student wrote, "that the *Protocols* have never been refuted," adding that hatred of Jews had been "good for Hitler . . . good for Stalin and . . . [was] good for *Nommo.*" Unlike the confusion or ambivalence that later greeted *The Secret Relationship,* the response of a number of faculty was immediate and unequivocal. Historians Gary Nash, Robert Dallek, Regina Morantz-Sanchez, et al., wrote an open letter denouncing the article as libelous. Although, later, professors of Judaic studies would be largely absent from the affray, Steve Zipperstein even wrote a long, well-argued article on the history of the *Protocols* in the school paper. Emboldened in part by faculty support, Jewish students condemned the *Nommo* piece as malicious and uninformed. Thrown on the defensive, the BSO refused to meet with the Jewish student organization, accusing the Jewish students of "disrespect." Upon the arrival of *The Secret Relationship,* however, black students resumed the offensive with a vengeance. Accusing Jewish students of ignorance of their dominant role in slavery, they challenged Hillel, the campus Jewish organization, to a debate.

Elsewhere, for the two years before *The Secret Relationship* began to circulate, BSOs invited numerous bigoted speakers to campus. Provided platforms in elite colleges, they leveled their antisemitic charges to packed houses that resounded with cries of "Teach!" At Columbia, the rapper "Professor Griff" taught that Jews "have a history of killing black men," and explained that Jews were responsible for "the majority of the wickedness that goes on across the globe" (*Spectator* 1991). Khalid Muhammad enlightened students about the iniquities of "Columbia Jewniversity," the "*Jew York Times,*" and "*Jew York City,*" although he also peddled his videotape, "The White Woman Is a Bitch and a Two-Legged Dog" (*Spectator* 1991; *Independent* 1993). Leonard Jeffries, keynoter of Race Relations Week, electrified the house with his charges of Jews' responsibility for the slave trade even before he had *The Secret Relationship* in hand. A few days after he spoke, sixty mezuzahs were torn from the doors of Jewish students' rooms. Jewish students wrote a stream of letters to the school paper protesting the antisemitic bile, but, for the most part, they wrote alone. In a time of identity politics, other students chose not to speak out on what they considered a Jewish issue. Only because Jeffries had called Henry Louis Gates Jr., head of African-American studies at Harvard, a "faggot" did the Lesbian Bisexual Gay Coalition join the Jews' protest. Jeffries had told the Harvard *Crimson* that "whites had introduced homosexuality to blacks," remarking that Europeans often "offered their wives to me in exchange for a blow job" (*Spectator* 1991). Nor did faculty, who spoke at rallies against rape and sexism and at forums lionizing Malcolm X, openly question the choice of speakers or condemn their outrageous charges. Later, when Abraham Foxman, executive director of the Anti-Defamation League (ADL), came to the campus, he spoke pointedly of the "new tolerance for intolerance" (*Spectator* 1991). Black campus activists, increasingly members or fellow travelers of the NOI, had brought overt antisemitism back to the university, and many professors and students hesitated to speak out lest they be accused of racism.

Released late in 1991, *The Secret Relationship* landed on college campuses a year later, and for the next four years the reverberations were felt everywhere, even at schools heretofore isolated or obscure. For many blacks, *The SR* became the little red [really, blue] book of the 1990s. They frequently consulted it, cited it, and soon were writing articles, quoting chapter and verse. NOI spokesmen and sympathizers now made their charges while insisting, "It's right here in the book!" Students were impressed. The editor of the Kean College newspaper boasted, "Unlike the musicians who sang of protest to the youth of the sixties, the modern cultural icons have titles such as Dr. and scholar. They support their views with quotable sources and teach the youth heterodoxy" (*Independent* 1993–1994). The scholars to whom he was referring were Khalid Muhammad and Louis Farrakhan, whom students addressed as Dr., although neither had finished college, and Leonard Jeffries, whom they lauded, incorrectly, as a distinguished historian. Waving *The Secret Relationship*, students now challenged all comers to a debate on the iniquity of Jews. When Richard Cohen, the *Washington Post* columnist, wrote of the Howard University audience who wildly cheered Muhammad and Malik Shabazz, the student

leader who had invited him, as "brimming with ignorance, led by Pied Pipers of racism . . . down the sucker's road to nowhere," Shabazz demanded a debate. With *The Secret Relationship* as his guide, he promised to "destroy Richard Cohen . . . using primarily Jewish scholars" and the "Jewish Talmud" as his sources (*Washington Post*, March 1, 1994; *Hilltop* 1994).

Others, drawing heavily from *The Secret Relationship*, penned articles in which the major role in the genocide of both Native Americans and African Americans was ascribed to Jews. Writing in the magazine of the Black United Students at Kent State, a student explained that, after the Jews had completed the "slaughter" of the Indians, which they had accomplished with "no remorse, no scruples," they moved on to effect "the greatest human tragedy history knows," the African slave trade. "According to their own scholars," he wrote, "Caucasian Jews were right there at the top, financing, trafficking, slaughtering, trapping and hauling millions of defenseless Africans like a herd of sheep." "The immense wealth of the Jews," he instructed, "was acquired only by the brutal subjugation of Black Africans. . . ." Indeed, in the American South, he informed his readers, "Caucasian Jews outnumbered their Caucasian Christian brethren in the number of slaves owned by almost two to one." He concluded with the warning that "Caucasian Jewry . . . should not expect anyone to respect or protect their humanity or even shed a tear when something catastrophic happens to them" (Shropshire 1995).

This student had learned the prattle of *The Secret Relationship* well. But until students could take over the task, Khalid and other NOI supporters crisscrossed the country, hawking the tract and preaching its message, Khalid sometimes stopping at three different colleges on a single day. On the anniversary of *Kristallnacht* in 1992, he returned to Columbia, where, to "continued applause," he charged Jews with culpability for "the Black Holocaust." When a Jewish student in the audience protested the false claims, he was silenced by NOI goons and accused by black students of "disrespecting" their religious leader. When Jewish students expressed horror at the timing of the event, blacks rejoined that every night was a *Kristallnacht* for them. When Jack Greenberg, dean of the college, wrote a letter to the school newspaper "condemning" BSO's invitation to the bigot to speak, Columbia's student council censured the dean. A sponsor of the resolution explained that, by his action, the dean was impeding the free "flow of ideas" (*Spectator* 1992).

At many schools, students and not a few faculty welcomed the falsifiers of history as a positive good, their antisemitic rant recast only as a controversial view. Students claimed that college was "exactly the place where these ideas ['of the gentleman from the NOI'] need to be expressed." One student insisted that "[a]nytime your views are challenged, it's a positive thing" but could not indicate which of his beliefs Farrakhan or Muhammad had caused him to question. Some African-American students complained that they were not "given credit for being . . . critical and analytical thinker[s] who could determine what to take from the speech." But although they wrote countless op-ed pieces, few ever indicated any historical allegation with which they found fault. When pressed, one countered only that critical thinking had led her to reject Muhammad's call to "kill all the white babies" in South Africa (*Independent* 1993–1994). Notably, students knew so little of the history of the Jews that when Khalid Muhammad told a Howard audience that Jews were never "stripped of their names, culture, religion, land, and family, like black people were," no one dissented (*Hilltop* 1994). It seemed credible to them.

Some students, such as the editors of Howard University's paper, endorsed the right of the hatemongers to speak, since "it is through public discourse [and 'debate'] . . . that truth will emerge" (*Hilltop* 1994). The "debate," however, was always kept within very narrow bounds. Howard canceled a lecture by Yale professor David Brion Davis, former president of the Organization of American Historians, who had written on slavery for twenty-five years, because he was a Jew. The columnist Nat Hentoff, a supporter of unrestricted free speech, advised that these talks, "full of egregious distortions of history," required "immediate rebuttal," that they must "be discussed and analyzed when students met in classes the next day. All kinds of classes" (Hentoff 1994). But when he surveyed students, he found this was never done. At Kean College, where Muhammad appeared at the end of November 1993, Rabbi Avi Weiss was brought in at the beginning of the next semester to challenge his views. But although Weiss came prepared with much evidence and careful argument, he was not a scholar, and many black students dismissed his case as merely the biased opinions of a Jew. Some were outraged that he had

been allowed to speak in February, the month that belonged to them.

Yet even if Weiss were a historian—and had come in a different month—it is unlikely that he would have led many students to modify their views. Many had come to accept that the idea of the scholar's disinterested pursuit of proximate truth was a Euro-American ideology that obscured the scholar's racist point of view. There were only different biases and agendas. Many administrators and some professors had spoken repeatedly of diverse perspectives, usually privileging the minority worldview. An editorial in the Kean College paper heralded "Dr. Khalid" as a hero, a savior bringing "unorthodox viewpoints" to a campus that had only given lip service to "multiculturalism" (*Independent* 1994). Indeed, for some, Khalid had become the public face of this new curriculum and *The Secret Relationship,* one of its texts. Faculty and administrators had expected and even encouraged blacks to rewrite their own history, but few had anticipated that it would embody an antisemitic worldview.

The Secret Relationship both reflected and augmented historical black antisemitism. The many who persist in referring to its alleged antisemitism appear not to have perused it or listened to its hawkers. Indeed, its impact was so powerful because it drew so heavily on classical as well as traditional black, anti-Jewish myths. In March 1995, the *Donahue Show* featured Tony Martin, professor of Africana Studies, who assigned *The Secret Relationship* to his students at Wellesley College. (Indeed, in 1994 Martin wrote *The Jewish Onslaught,* issued by his own publishing company, which detailed what he called the "escalating Jewish onslaught against Black people." According to Martin, *Onslaught* "spent several months in 1994 at the top of the Black book industry's bestseller list," and "was named 'Best Book of the Year 1994' at the annual Black Literary Awards held in Hampton, Virginia" [*Blacks & Jews at Wellesley News,* March 1995].) The trailer for the *Donahue Show,* played again and again, pictured only an African American woman declaiming that, when she heard about Jews and the slave trade, she knew it was true because wherever there is money, there are Jews. When Khalid Muhammad explained to his rapt audience that "Swindler's List," directed by "Steven Stealberg," was just another attempt "to divert attention from Jews' complicity in the African slave trade," it resonated with the belief in the greedy and duplicitous Jew. Indeed,

The Secret Relationship itself presented the acquisition of wealth "not just [as] the ambition of the Jews, but the [very] purpose of Judaism": "Europe's experience with Mosaic Law was that it very closely resembled business law, and that money, not worship, was the main objective" (*In These Times* 1994; Conlon 1995).

Those who preached the message of *The Secret Relationship* linked it closely to traditional antisemitism. Across the flyer advertising Khalid Muhammad's appearance at Kean College was a nativity scene, and immediately below it, the title of his sermon, "The Secret Relationship between Blacks and Jews." The reference was unmistakable: those who killed Christ killed the blacks. Indeed, Muhammad reminded his listeners that Jesus was black, so the Jews had been murdering blacks for a very long time. When he came to Howard to preside over what Richard Cohen tagged a "Nuremberg Rally," classical antisemitism was further blackened. When law student Malik Shabazz in his introduction conducted a deafening call-and-response, he asked not only who killed Nat Turner, who killed Martin Luther King, but who had killed Jesus. In each case, the answer was the same. Indeed, Shabazz made the message explicit: those responsible for the death of Jesus had killed blacks' more recent saviors as well. Other proponents of this new black bible warned blacks that Jews only posed as their friends; in the end, they will sell you out; they will betray you; they will, in effect, crucify you. This is what *The Secret Relationship*, with its message of Jewish perfidy, had wrought. Shabazz would tell a reporter, "If we [blacks] were violent, they [the Jews] would have been dead a long time ago" (*Hilltop* 1994; *Emerge*, February 1994).

Even Farrakhan's motives in commissioning *The Secret Relationship* appear explicitly anti-Jewish. In 1984, Farrakhan became furious when Jesse Jackson's antisemitic slur became public, and Jews' demand that he apologize for "the Hymie remark" threatened to derail his presidential campaign. It was the Jews, Farrakhan railed, who should apologize to blacks, for their role "in the slave trade that caused 100 million black lives to be lost." Seven years later, with the publication of *The Secret Relationship*, he would have his revenge. Farrakhan was also outraged, he explained at the time, that Jews "put it all on the Arabs," writing of the Arab slave trade (*Emerge* July/August 1994). (The Arab slave trade had, in fact, lasted far longer, was likely more lethal, and transported more blacks across the Sahara and the Red Sea than were shipped across the At-

lantic.) As a Muslim, Farrakhan was close to the Arabs—the next year, the Libyan dictator Colonel Muammar Gadhafi would offer him a $5 million, interest-free "loan"—and the NOI had not even commented when Saudi Arabia finally outlawed slavery in 1962. Strongly anti-Israel, he was distressed that it was the Arabs, not the Jews, who were maligned for their role in slavery.

The Secret Relationship is also a product of Farrakhan's move away from the preoccupation with white devils and white supremacy favored by his mentor Elijah Muhammad to an obsession with Jew-devils and Jewish domination of the world. At Kean College, a black in the audience rejected Rabbi Weiss's portrayal of Jews' extremely marginal role in the slave trade as merely the teachings of the "devil." Indeed, those who disseminate the teachings of *The Secret Relationship* routinely refer to Jews as sons of Satan. In a 1995 article written in the Columbia University paper by an NOI supporter, Satan is a synonym for Jew: "You [Jews] hate me because I understand that Satan can never want or yearn to support a march that will uplift blacks"; "Farrakhan and Chavis are only two of our spiritual leaders who are choosing not to stand with Satan," unlike King, who stood with the Jews (*Spectator* 1995). Indeed, some of Farrakhan's followers believe that Jews are literally the descendants of the devil, offspring of an illicit copulation of Satan and Eve. Thus, contrary to all evidence, they stress that it was the Jews who were responsible for the slave trade. Only those doing the work of the devil could have perpetrated "the Black Holocaust," the world's most heinous deed.

Alternatively, those who proclaim the gospel of *The Secret Relationship* refer to the "imposter Jews," "so-called Jews," or, for the media-savvy, "European Jews." Here they embrace the view that, if Jews are not the progeny of Satan, they are descended from Khazars, a tribe of amoral warriors who, in the eighth century CE, enslaved and killed the Jews, then converted en masse to Judaism themselves. Who but they could have been capable of the world's most pernicious deed, the African slave trade? Thus on the anniversary of *Kristallnacht*, Khalid Muhammad explained that when Farrakhan spoke of Judaism as a "gutter religion" [dirty religion], he was "only referring to the Judaism practiced by whites," that is, by the imposter Jews; he would never impugn the religion of the "black Hebrews," the true Jews, who flourished while the white Jews became Khazar barbarians, "roaming around Europe in caves" (*Spectator*

1992; *In These Times* 1994–1995). Thus Farrakhan and his acolytes can accuse Jews of much of the evil in the world while insisting they are not antisemitic, since today's (white) Jews, and the Jewish slave-traders, were never "Semites" at all.

If Jews once dominated the slave trade, the Jews, according to Farrakhan, now controlled the world. On Savior's Day 1995, one of the holiest days of the NOI year, he preached that Jews were now "at the root of the control of the banking system of the Federal Reserve." The faithful learned that Jews are also at the root of world conflict, which they provoke so they might profit even more. But, he warned his fellow victims, the ADL will destroy "anybody who would expose" these modern nefarious Jews (*In These Times* 1995). What could one expect from those who had financed the slave trade and then tried to cover it up?

Although the national media gave the NOI's allegations wide coverage, the discussion was framed largely around questions of free speech, around whether the campus speakers were antisemitic, and if their harangues inflamed ethnic hatred. For the most part, however, the media did not address the absurdity of the claims. Because the charges were so egregious and dangerous—and remained unanswered—two historians, Eunice G. Pollack and Stephen H. Norwood, asked the American Historical Association (AHA) to take a stand. In January 1995, in an action virtually unprecedented in its 111-year history, the AHA issued a policy resolution (applauded in and by the press and even in the U.S. Senate) that "condemns as false any statement alleging that Jews played a disproportionate role in the Atlantic slave trade." A statement published along with the resolution, written by David Brion Davis and Seymour Drescher, professor at the University of Pittsburgh, noted experts on the history of slavery and the slave trade, along with Eunice G. Pollack, concluded that these "claims so misrepresent the historical record . . . that we believe them only to be part of a long anti-Semitic tradition that presents Jews as negative central actors in human history."

On October 16, 1995, Farrakhan held what he promoted as a Million Man March on the Mall in Washington, D.C. On the day before the rally, large numbers of antisemitic tracts were made available to those in attendance. In his keynote address, Farrakhan treated the crowd to his strange facts and stranger reasoning, as he taught that the first slaves landed in Jamestown in 1555, which was a "1"

placed in front of the height of the Washington Monument. (Jamestown was not founded until 1607, and the first blacks arrived in 1619.) The *Washington Post* reported that 87 percent of those in attendance had "a favorable impression" of Farrakhan (October 17, 1995). Apparently, they were able to overlook, or were indifferent to, the obsessive antisemitism that was central to his stature and renown.

After 1999, prostate cancer somewhat curtailed Farrakhan's ability to disseminate his message, as did the death of his disciple Khalid Muhammad in February 2001. Still, when Farrakhan appeared before his followers on subsequent Savior's Days, his antisemitic invective remained undiminished: "Listen, Jewish people don't have no hands that are free of the blood of us," he railed (February 27, 2005) (www.adl.org).

Eunice G. Pollack

References and Further Reading

Alexander, Edward. 1994. "Multiculturalists and Anti-Semitism." *Society* (September/October).

Alexander, Jeffrey C., and Chaim Seidler-Feller. 1992. "False Distinctions and Double Standards." *Tikkun* 7 (January/February): 12-13.

Brackman, Harold. 1994. *Ministry of Lies: The Truth Behind the Nation of Islam's "The Secret Relationship between Blacks and Jews."* New York: Four Walls Eight Windows.

Cohen, Richard. 1994. "What Happened at Howard?" *Washington Post* (July 19).

Columbia University *Spectator*. August 1991–November 1995.

Conlon, Edward. 1995. "The Uses of Malice." *American Spectator* (April).

Davis, David Brion. 1994. "The Slave Trade and the Jews." *New York Review of Books* (December 22).

Hentoff, Nat. 1994. "Black Bigotry and Free Speech." *The Progressive* (May).

Hentoff, Nat. 1995. "Sunlight the Best Disinfectant." *Spectator* (November 1).

Howard University *Hilltop*. March–April 1994.

In These Times. January 1994–October 1995.

Kean College *Independent*. December 1993–February 1994.

Muravchik, Joshua. 1995. "Facing Up to Black Anti-Semitism." *Commentary* (December).

Novick, Peter. 1988. *That Noble Dream: The "Objectivity Question" and the American Historical Profession.* Cambridge: Cambridge University Press.

Pollack, Eunice G. 1996. "Slavery and Jews: Letter to Editor." *Atlantic Monthly* (February).

Pollack, Eunice G., and Stephen H. Norwood. 1995. Letter to Editor. *Journal of American History* 82 (December).

Puddington, Arch. 1994. "Black Anti-Semitism and How It Grew." *Commentary* (April).

Shropshire, Terrence. 1995 (orig. 1994). "The Paradox of European Jewry." *Uhuru Na Mazungumzo* (Spring).

Tyrell, R. Emmett, Jr. 1993. "Public Radio's Anti-Semites." *American Spectator* (June).

University of California at Los Angeles *Daily Bruin*. February 1991–November 1993.

Whitfield, Stephen. 1994. "An Anatomy of Black Anti-Semitism." *Judaism* 43 (Fall).

The Crown Heights Riot

The Crown Heights riot of August 19–22, 1991, in the Crown Heights neighborhood of Brooklyn in New York City was the most serious antisemitic incident in American history. The riot has been the topic of movies, television shows, and plays. For nearly three days, the city police seemed powerless to prevent attacks on Jews and their property by black rioters. One Jew was murdered, another committed suicide, six stores were looted, and property damage was in the millions of dollars. Although the loss of life and property was minuscule when compared to other American riots, its impact on Jews was traumatic. The riot also affected the politics of New York City by bringing into question the widely held assumption that blacks and Jews were natural political allies. The riot took place on the watch of David N. Dinkins, a Democrat and the city's first black mayor. Dinkins lost his bid for reelection to Republican Rudy Giuliani in November 1993, and Dinkins's response to the riot was one of the most important issues during the bitter campaign.

Crown Heights was an upscale neighborhood of spacious homes and apartments in which upwardly mobile Jews had settled after World War I. By the late 1940s, there were some two hundred thousand Jews living in Crown Heights, including prominent physicians, lawyers, and politicians, and the area contained dozens of synagogues and other Jewish institutions. During the 1950s and 1960s, however, there was an influx of poorer blacks into Crown Heights, and most Jews left the area. Many of the blacks who settled in Crown Heights came from the West Indies, and by the 1970s the neighborhood had become the center of West Indian culture in America.

There was also a smaller migration of Jews into Crown Heights during the 1950s and 1960s. These were members of the Lubavitch Hasidic sect, which had its headquarters on Eastern Parkway. They settled in Crown Heights to be close to their spiritual leader, to other Lubavitchers, and to Lubavitch institutions. Crown Heights, in fact, was the only primarily black area in the city that attracted a sizable number of Jews. These three migrations help explain the sociological dynamics that led to the riot. The neighborhood had a large number of alienated West Indian youth torn between the values they absorbed in the street and the values they learned in their conservative families. The Lubavitch Hasidim, who constituted about 15 percent of the population of Crown Heights, wanted little cultural or social interaction with the other residents living in the area. This insularity, which was necessary if the Lubavitchers were to maintain their religious traditions unsullied by outside influences, was resented by their black neighbors. They believed it reflected contempt for anyone who was not part of the Lubavitch community.

The poverty of Crown Heights' residents, Jews and blacks alike, worsened the situation. Per capita income in Crown Heights was lower than in most Brooklyn neighborhoods. Many younger Lubavitchers were involved in religious study and not gainfully employed, and many blacks found it difficult to find employment because of poor educational backgrounds and unfamiliarity with the job market. A struggle within Crown Heights for antipoverty dollars and other emoluments of the welfare state exacerbated the tensions within the neighborhood, as did attacks on Jews by blacks, including several that resulted in murder. In addition, there was a fierce competition for housing caused by the flow of West Indians and Lubavitchers into Crown Heights and by the large size of Lubavitch families, which required larger living quarters. This tension also reflected a general worsening relationship between blacks and Jews in New York City during the 1970s and 1980s manifested in quarrels over affirmative action, mandatory school busing, and the placing of public housing projects in the Jewish neighborhood of Forest Hills in the borough of Queens, and the antisemitic and anti-Israel rhetoric of a small group of black nationalists.

The Crown Heights riot began a little after 8 p.m. on Monday, August 19, when a car struck Angelina Cato and her cousin Gavin Cato, members of a Guyanese family, who were playing outside their apartment house near the northwest corner of President Street and Utica Avenue. Gavin Cato was killed, and Angelina Cato was injured. The car was driven by Josef Lifsh and was part of a three-car procession bringing Rabbi Menachem Mendel Schneerson, the head of the Lubavitch Hasidic sect, back from one of his frequent visits to the Lubavitch cemetery in the borough of Queens. The first automobile in the procession was a police car, the second contained Schneerson, and Lifsh's car brought up the rear. The first two cars in the procession, which was traveling west along President Street, crossed Utica Avenue. By the time Lifsh's car reached the intersection, the light had changed to either yellow or, most likely, to red. Lifsh was eager to remain close behind Schneerson's car, and he hurried to cross the street. His automobile was struck by a car traveling north along Utica Avenue; he lost control, and the automobile plowed into the Cato children.

Ambulances and police cars arrived at the scene a few minutes after the accident. The Cato children were taken to a local hospital, and Lifsh and the other occupants of his automobile were escorted from the area. By then a crowd had gathered and was being stirred up by agitators. They accused Lifsh of having intentionally run into the Cato children, charged that a Jewish ambulance service had refused to aid the Cato children, and demanded revenge. By coincidence, a concert attended by hundreds of young blacks had just ended, and they learned what had happened. The conditions became combustible, and soon gangs of young blacks were rampaging through the neighborhood, throwing rocks at Jewish-owned homes and attacking Jews. This rioting continued until the morning of August 22.

One of these gangs encountered Yankel Rosenbaum a little after 11 p.m. on August 19. Rosenbaum, an aspiring Australian academician, was living in Brooklyn while doing research in New York libraries for his doctoral dissertation in European Jewish history. Although not a Lubavitch Hasid, Rosenbaum was easily identified by his beard and his clothing as an Orthodox Jew. About a dozen young blacks surrounded him and began beating him. According to witnesses, the attack was preceded by shouts of "Let's get the Jew." One of Rosenbaum's attackers was Lemrick Nelson, who stabbed Rosenbaum several times with a knife. The police soon arrived, arrested Nelson, and saw to it that Rosenbaum was transported to a hospital.

Mayor Dinkins had been immediately informed of the riot and Rosenbaum's stabbing. The mayor proceeded to Brooklyn, where he visited Rosenbaum in the hospital shortly after midnight. Doctors assured Dinkins that Rosenbaum was well on the way to recovery. Less than two hours later, the Australian was dead, a victim, seemingly, of gross incompetence. The staff in the emergency room had treated Rosenbaum for the wounds on the front of his body, but, inexplicably, they never turned his body over to treat the wounds on his back. Governmental investigations of Rosenbaum's death severely criticized the quality of medical care he received.

The second fatality arising from the rioting was also puzzling. On August 26, sixty-eight-year-old Brokha Estrin, who lived on President Street across from the scene of the accident, jumped out of a window in her apartment to her death. Estrin's family could not explain her action. She was, however, a Holocaust survivor, and some observers speculated that the continuous incitement of the crowd across the street from her home brought to the surface painful memories of World War II that she had tried to suppress. There were also questions regarding another fatality that was perhaps related to the riot. On September 5, 1991, sixty-seven-year-old Anthony Graziosi, a hardware salesman, was murdered by a group of young blacks. Graziosi had a beard and was wearing a dark suit, and his family and Jews in Crown Heights believed that he had been mistaken for a Jew. But Graziosi was parked in his car, and it was close to midnight at the time of the attack. It is thus problematic whether his assailants identified him as a Jew. The police did not think Graziosi's murder was a bias crime, and no one was prosecuted for it.

Lemrick Nelson did stand trial in state court for Rosenbaum's murder. Nelson had admitted his guilt to the police a few hours after being arrested. A bloody knife was found in his pants pocket, and his pants were stained with blood of the same type as that of Rosenbaum. A guilty verdict seemed inevitable. The Brooklyn District Office was astonished when a predominantly black jury came in with a "not guilty" decision in late October 1992. (Nelson would later be found guilty of violating Rosenbaum's civil rights and sentenced to twenty years in prison.) Although the verdict seemed outrageous and an example of jury nullification, it was not unreasonable in view of the serious mistakes made by the police and the prosecution. In the wake of the Nelson verdict, Governor Mario Cuomo of New York ordered an investigation into the circumstances surrounding the Crown Heights riot and the subsequent trial. The investigation produced a two-volume report in July 1993 that emphasized the failings of the police and the prosecution. By this time, the mayoralty election campaign was well on its way.

Giuliani, who had made his reputation as a federal prosecutor, claimed that Dinkins and Lee Brown, his black police commissioner, had been selective in enforcing the law during the riot and had left the Jews of Crown Heights to their own resources. Giuliani's charges resonated within the city's white population. There was a widespread feeling among the city's Jews, and particularly among the twenty thousand Jews of Crown Heights, that Dinkins was at best incompetent and at worst an antisemite, and this had seemingly been confirmed by the state's report.

The soft-spoken Dinkins was certainly not a bigot, but he had been unable to reassure the city's whites that he would move with equal vigor against blacks as well as whites who broke the law. On this issue, the mayor had to be as innocent as Caesar's wife, and Dinkins's justification of his actions during August 1991 failed to convince. Dinkins's margin of victory over Giuliani in 1989 had been a little over 2 percent, or 46,000 votes out of approximately 1.75 million votes cast. He lost by the same margin in 1993. There were too many issues in the campaign to say that the Crown Heights riot was "the" factor responsible for Dinkins's defeat. But the riot was certainly important in strengthening doubts about the mayor's managerial abilities.

Apart from politics, the riot did not have any lasting effects. Relations between the Lubavitcher Hasidim and their neighbors have not fundamentally changed since August 1991. Although the Lubavitchers use the word *pogrom* to describe the riot, they did not leave Crown Heights, in contrast to the Jewish family in the musical *Fiddler on the Roof*, who were forced to leave the mythical Anatevka after a pogrom. In fact, the Lubavitch population of Crown Heights has grown, and the price of housing in the neighborhood has escalated. Lubavitch families are now living north of Eastern Parkway, for years the northernmost boundary of their community. Much to their surprise, many Lubavitch families with modest incomes have become wealthy because of the increased value of their houses. The riot did not change the religious outlook of the Lubavitchers or the image they have of their community. They felt beleaguered prior to 1991, and the riot merely confirmed this. The riot reinforced their distrust of the Jewish establishment, which, they believed, had not spoken up forcefully enough during the riot and its aftermath. The riot also did not weaken the Lubavitch commitment to spread Torah throughout the world. If there was a watershed event in the recent history of the Lubavitch community of Crown Heights, it was not the riot but the death of Schneerson in June 1994.

Edward S. Shapiro

References and Further Reading

Goldschmidt, Henry. 2000. "Peoples Apart: Race, Religion, and Other Jewish Differences in Crown Heights." PhD dissertation, University of California at Santa Cruz.

Kasinitz, Philip. 1992. *Caribbean New York: Black Immigrants and the Politics of Race*. Ithaca, NY: Cornell University Press.

Lardner, James, and Thomas Repetto. 2000. *NYPD: A City and Its Police*. New York: Henry Holt.

Mintz, Jerome R. 1994. *Hasidic People: A Place in the New World*. Cambridge, MA: Harvard University Press.

Rieder, Jonathan. 1995. "Reflections on Crown Heights: Interpretative Dilemmas and Black–Jewish Relations." In *Antisemitism in America Today: Outspoken Experts Explode the Myths*, edited by Jerome A. Chanes, pp. 348–394. New York: Birch Lane Press.

Shapiro, Edward S. 2002. "Interpretations of the Crown Heights Riot." *American Jewish History* 90 (June): 97–122.

Shapiro, Edward S. 2006. *Crown Heights: Blacks, Jews, and the 1991 Brooklyn Riot*. Waltham, MA: Brandeis University Press.

Zionism in America

American Zionism to the Founding of the State of Israel

Zionism, or the movement to reestablish a Jewish homeland in the area that was ancient Palestine, grew out of a confluence of nineteenth-century European nationalism and the ages-old messianic belief that Jews would eventually be restored—by God—to their ancestral home. Zionism had great appeal in Eastern Europe, home to millions of Jews who still, at the beginning of the twentieth century, lived under the economic, social, and political burdens of official antisemitism. But it had little appeal to Jews in Western Europe, who had been emancipated beginning in the Napoleonic era, or to Jews who had emigrated to the United States, which had never had any official policies aimed against the Jews. Even recent immigrants from Eastern Europe, although scarred by their experiences there, wanted to make their home in America, not Palestine. For Zionism to take hold in the United States, it would need a cause and a leader who would be able to "Americanize" the movement and give it a meaning that would appeal to those Jews who had no interest in relocating to Palestine.

Modern Zionism actually begins in the 1880s with a group known as *Hibbat Zion* (Love of Zion), a response to the bloody pogroms that shook the Russian empire at the time. The *Hovevei Zion* (Lovers of Zion), however, were not Zionists. They wanted to establish colonies in Pales-

tine, so that some Jews could go there and escape persecution. They did not consider themselves a movement, nor did they seek to bring all Jews to *Eretz Yisrael* (the land of Israel), nor did they have a consistent philosophy. But they did succeed in launching the first *aliyah,* and between 1882 and 1903 some 25,000 men and women went to live and work in the Holy Land. The initial group landed in Jaffa in 1882 and established the first modern Jewish settlement in Palestine, Rishon L'Tzyon.

Although they received support from some wealthy western Jews, such as the Baron de Rothschild, who helped establish viniculture in Palestine, the movement's greatest accomplishment, aside from the settlements it founded, was to make known to Jewish groups around the world that an opportunity existed. In the United States messengers (*shluchim*) who came asking for money found interested audiences—although not much cash—among recent immigrants from Eastern Europe. But they, and millions like them, had already made their aliyah—to the United States, where they lived free from the persecution they had known in the Old World and where opportunity awaited those with talent and the willingness to work hard.

True Zionism begins with Theodore Herzl, the publication of *The Jewish State* in 1896, and the convening of the First Zionist Congress in Basle, Switzerland, the following year. Herzl reflected the belief among many Jews that the Emancipation had failed to solve the Jewish problem.

He himself had been a reporter at the trial and degradation of Captain Alfred Dreyfus, the most notorious case of antisemitism in Western Europe in the late nineteenth century and in supposedly the most "enlightened" country in Europe. There the delegates adopted what came to be known as the Basle Program, calling for the creation of a Jewish homeland in Palestine, the colonization of that country by Jews, and the eventual establishment of an independent Jewish state. The Zionist Congresses have met ever since, interrupted occasionally by war, and, until the creation of the State of Israel in 1948, served as the main forum for debating Jewish problems and for guiding the growth of the *yishuv,* the Jewish settlements in Palestine. After that first Congress, Herzl wrote in his diary, "At Basle I founded the Jewish State. If I were to say this today, I would be met by universal laughter. In five years, perhaps, and certainly in fifty, every one will see it."

In the United States, a few small chapters of Hibbat Zion had managed to establish themselves in large centers of immigrant Jewish population such as New York and Philadelphia. Following the publication of *The Jewish State*

Theodor Herzl, founder of modern Zionism. Herzl organized the First Zionist Congress, held in Basle, Switzerland, in 1897. (Library of Congress)

and news of the Zionist Congress, small groups of men friendly to the idea created Zionist chapters, primarily to debate Jewish issues and to raise small sums of money to send to the yishuv. A few Americans even attended the early Zionist Congresses, but the movement did not catch fire among the nearly three million Jews who lived in the United States, a great majority of them immigrants or the children of immigrants.

First of all, leadership of the American Jewish community at that time resided with the German American Jews, who had begun to come over to the United States in the 1840s. By the turn of the new century, they dominated all the communal institutions, which they had founded, and assumed to speak for the entire community through the American Jewish Committee, which they had established to safeguard Jewish interests in 1906. Known as *yahudim* (as opposed to the *yidden,* the downtown Jews who had come from Eastern Europe), they opposed Zionism because they believed it conflicted with their allegiance to the United States. Zionism, as they saw it, called for all Jews to be loyal to this Jewish state-in-the-making, and this meant they could not be loyal to the United States. This idea of divided loyalty carried a great deal of weight not only with the yahudim but also with the yidden. They had chosen to come to the United States, they wanted to become *Amerikaners,* and they took seriously the warning that they were jeopardizing not only their own future in the *goldine medine,* the "golden country," but the fortunes of all American Jews already there as well as those who might come in the future.

How strongly this argument played and how little Zionism managed to attract American Jews can be seen in the fact that the Federation of American Zionists (FAZ), a loose coalition of various Zionist and Hibbat Zion groups, had a combined membership of only twelve thousand on the eve of World War I, out of three million Jews in the United States.

While the American Jewish Committee (and its offshoot, the Joint Distribution Committee) raised funds to help Jewish communities in eastern and central Europe devastated by the war, it had little interest in aiding the Palestine colonies. The FAZ, therefore, called a meeting at the Hotel Marseilles in New York at the end of August 1914 to raise money for the yishuv. It invited the noted Boston attorney, Louis D. Brandeis, to chair the meeting. The organizers assumed that he would make a speech

Louis D. Brandeis, who became chairman of the Federation of American Zionists in 1914. (Library of Congress)

asking for money (he did), that he would give a generous contribution himself (he did), and that he would then retire. But Brandeis, who had joined the movement only a year earlier and had not been active, took over the chairmanship of the FAZ and, over the next four years, energized the movement.

First, he brought to the task skills he had learned both as a successful attorney and as a Progressive reformer. His motto—"Men! Money! Discipline!"—called upon the Zionists to stop debating abstract questions of theory and to do real work: bring in new members, raise money for the yishuv, and work together to influence public opinion regarding the movement. By the end of the war in November 1918, the FAZ counted 186,000 members and had chapters in every major Jewish community in the country. Affiliated with the FAZ was Hadassah, the women's Zionist organization founded by Henrietta Szold, which ran health programs in Palestine. In addition, American branches of the Socialist Zionist movement (*Poalei Zion*) as well as the religious Zionists (*Mizrachi*) worked with the FAZ.

Brandeis's greatest contribution, however, was to create a philosophy that negated the fears of dual loyalty raised by the yahudim and in fact made it patriotic and

American to be a Zionist. Brandeis saw Palestine as a great opportunity, one in which an egalitarian society modeled along Jeffersonian ideas of democracy could be established. He paid practically no attention to the neomessianic aspects of Zionism but concentrated on the practical aspects. American Jews need not go on aliyah; their job would be to help those persecuted Jews of Europe build a new and free life in Palestine. Dual loyalties, he argued, were only a problem if they conflicted; but in America everyone had dual loyalties—to home, to community, to lodge, and to country. In his merger of Zionist and American ideals, he created what has become known as the Brandeisian synthesis: "To be good Americans, we must be better Jews, and to be better Jews, we must become Zionists."

Brandeis, by removing the feared stigma of dual loyalties and placing Zionist idealism squarely in the tradition of Jeffersonian democracy, made Zionism respectable in the United States. The ultimate proof that one could be a Zionist and a good American came in January 1916, when President Wilson named Brandeis to the U.S. Supreme Court.

Brandeis dominated American Zionism until 1921 and, even after his appointment to the Court, worked through trusted lieutenants such as Stephen Wise, Julian Mack, and Felix Frankfurter to guide the movement. Over the objections of the State Department, they secured Wilson's approval of the Balfour Declaration, in which Great Britain promised the establishment of a Jewish homeland in Palestine after the war. At the Paris Peace Conference, they helped secure the trusteeship of Palestine for Great Britain. What had once been a weak and ignored fringe group had become the most powerful voice within the American Jewish community.

But the ideas that made Zionism acceptable to Americanizing Jews, the emphasis on the practical and the dismissal of the religious, antagonized not only European Zionists but many of the recent Eastern European immigrants as well. In emphasizing the practical, the material, and the financial work to be done, Brandeis totally ignored the religious, spiritual, and messianic aspects of Zionism, a mistake that Herzl almost made but did not. To religious Jews, and not just the Orthodox, a Jewish state had to be a Jewish entity as well as a political one. It is not clear that the secular-minded Brandeis ever understood this. Brandeis and Chaim Weizmann, the leader of

Chaim Weizmann, an accomplished scientist who worked tirelessly to advance the Zionist movement. (Library of Congress)

European Zionism, clashed at the two Zionist meetings in London in 1919 and 1920; then, in 1921, Weizmann-led forces voted against the Brandeis group at the Pittsburgh meeting of the Zionist Organization of America (ZOA), the successor to the FAZ. Brandeis and his lieutenants immediately resigned. Weizmann's support came from Eastern European Jews, for whom he was the embodiment of *Yiddishkeit*. He stood for all those aspects of Zionism Brandeis had ignored.

The 1920s, which should have been a golden time for American Zionists, proved a disaster. Under the leadership of Louis Lipsky, Weizmann's handpicked spokesman, the ZOA lost membership every year. Hadassah, which remained loyal to Brandeis and his ideas, withdrew from the ZOA and successfully expanded its medical program in the yishuv. Despite the prosperity of the era, monetary contributions declined along with membership. About the only positive note was the reconciliation of the American Jewish Committee to the Zionist idea—a reconciliation based on Brandeis's ideas and in which he played a behind-the-scenes role—and the creation of the Jewish Agency in 1927. The agency became the official body, under the man-date, to represent Jewish interests in Palestine, a role it would play until 1948. But despite the air of triumph following the establishment of the Agency, Zionism continued to founder in the United States.

The World Zionist Organization kept creating unrealistic budgets and expecting the ZOA to pay 75 percent of it. It treated the leaders of the ZOA, even Lipsky, as low-level employees who could not do the one thing they were supposed to do—raise money. The ZOA could not even bring in enough funds to cover its own expenses, and, beginning in 1922, it operated with a growing annual deficit. Then came the Depression in 1929. Donations disappeared, and membership, with the exception of Hadassah, shrank back to the prewar levels. By 1931 rank-and-file Zionists were demanding Lipsky's resignation and the return of the Brandeis group.

Brandeis himself, now seventy-five, informed emissaries from the ZOA that he personally could not head the organization but would give his support and advice to leaders who believed in and carried out the ideas he had articulated during the war years. So, during the 1930s, the ZOA would be headed by Brandeis's lieutenants, including Wise and Mack, but the decade proved to be one of the darkest in Zionist and Jewish history.

The Depression, which continued until 1941, adversely affected any fund-raising that the new ZOA leadership attempted. The simple fact was that most American Jews, who were either small retailers or laborers, did not have any money in the 1930s, and what little they had went to provide food and shelter for their families. While membership increased slightly, the amount brought in by dues did not cover the basic overhead of the ZOA.

Whereas in 1919 American Zionism had been a strong voice in international affairs, it was impotent in the 1930s to stop two great tragedies. One was the British perfidy of reneging on the Balfour promise and the mandate and, in order to appease the Arabs, closing the gates of Palestine to further Jewish immigration. This came at the same time as Hitler's rise to power in Germany and the persecution of German Jews. Then war broke out in 1939, causing hundreds of thousands of Jews to try to flee the Nazis but to no avail, and most of them perished in the death camps established by the Third Reich to eliminate Jews from Europe.

The war and returning prosperity galvanized American Zionism. Members flooded back into ZOA ranks, and somehow or other money was transferred to assist the yishuv during the war. Most important, a new and more militant leadership arose to take over the reins of the movement. Where Weizmann, Brandeis, Stephen Wise, and the older leaders had placed their faith in Great Britain and as a result felt cruelly betrayed, people such as David Ben-Gurion, the leader of the yishuv, and Abba Hillel Silver, the new head of the ZOA, had no faith in the English at all. (Brandeis died in 1941; Wise and Weizmann would live to see Israel established.)

The turning point came at the Biltmore Conference in May 1942. Whereas previously Zionism had adhered to the Basle Program with its indefinite idea of a future homeland, and then after 1919 had relied on the British mandate, Zionists now demanded that an independent Jewish state be created immediately after the war. Despite a show of unity in which Wise and Weizmann played prominent roles, it was clear that their time was over. While each would continue to make important contributions to the cause, Zionism would now be headed by two militant communities, one in Palestine and the other in America. The Holocaust destroyed European Zionism as well as the communities that had nourished it.

During the war, American Jews could do little about the Holocaust, although Wise, Silver, and others tried in vain to influence the Roosevelt administration. Silver himself recognized that little would be done, and he urged American Zionists to focus on what would happen after the war. He wanted them to be strong and well organized so that, when the peace conference came, Zionists could demand the creation of a Jewish state.

But while Zionists seemed to be more unified, they found themselves besieged by opponents both within the movement and from outside. The Revisionist Zionists, a group founded by Vladimir Jabotinsky, demanded that work on Palestine should be tied to demands for the salvation of European Jewry, and their leaders denounced the ZOA for its alleged failure to act. While the ZOA, led by Wise and then Silver, recognized that they had to work within the confines of American politics during wartime, the Revisionists felt no such constraints. Unlike the bulk of American Zionists, whose prime concern as Americans was winning the war, the Revisionists had as their prime concern European Jewry. The Revisionists put on a number of showy demonstrations, but in the end their loud demands had no effect on the administration. For Roosevelt

and for Churchill, the best way—the only way—to save European Jewry was to defeat the Third Reich.

The renewed vigor of Zionism also triggered a new wave of Jewish anti-Zionism. Classical Reform Judaism had always opposed the idea of a return to Zion, but in the light of European Jewry's plight in the 1930s, the Reform movement had adopted a pro-Zionist stance. This led ninety Reform rabbis to form the American Council for Judaism in 1942, but within a short time most of them had resigned. They explained they had formed the Council for religious reasons but found it "hijacked" by lay leaders who vehemently opposed Jewish nationalism. They claimed that they did not believe Jewish nationalism was compatible with the universalistic interpretation of Jewry put forth by classic Reform. They discovered that the laypeople had no interest in religious ideas but only in countering the idea of a Jewish state so they would not be accused of disloyalty to the United States. The rabbis resigned because the laypeople ran the Council in such a way that it had become a war of one set of Jews against another. The rabbis saw this more as an argument within the family, in which they themselves were calling Reform Jews back to their roots. They refused to be part of a vitriolic campaign against other Jews. The American Jewish Committee, which supposedly had made peace with Zionism in the 1920s, now had a rigid anti-Zionist, Joseph Proskauer, as its head. At the American Jewish Conference in 1943, both the Council and the Committee were routed. As one of the Zionist leaders put it, American Jews, thanks to Hitler, were becoming "Zionized."

After the war, the ZOA, led by Rabbi Silver, provided the greatest ally the yishuv had in its fight for independence. Along with Ben-Gurion, Silver testified at numerous hearings held by both the United Nations and the U.S. Congress; Zionists worked tirelessly to recruit Christian support for establishing a Jewish homeland in Palestine; and Zionists took the lead in raising millions of dollars to help the nascent Israeli army purchase arms, some of it done clandestinely and occasionally illegally, although sympathetic American officials, including J. Edgar Hoover, often looked the other way. When Israel declared its independence in 1948, American Zionists helped persuade President Harry S Truman, over the objections of the State Department, to recognize the new state.

The establishment of Israel in May 1948 marked both the triumph of American Zionism and the beginning of its decline. Whereas prior to 1948 the Jewish Agency had spoken for the yishuv—and in many instances that meant Silver or another American alongside Ben-Gurion—now the independent nation would speak for itself. Israel needed people, not just the refugees from Europe, and looked to American Jews to make aliyah. Aside from a few idealists who had fought in the Israeli army during its war for independence, American Jews had no interest in leaving the United States. They would give generously of their time and money and would visit Israel, but they would remain in America.

The Brandeisian synthesis, which made the success of Zionism in America possible, also carried within itself the seeds of its downfall. By concentrating on organization, fund-raising, and political lobbying, American Zionism proved a powerful ally to the Jewish settlers of Palestine. But by ignoring the religious aspect of Zionism, the neomessianic call for return, American Zionists neither understood nor shared the fervor that motivated aliyah and the sacrifices made by the yishuv. Brandeis never intended American Zionism to become merely philanthropic, but the success of the movement in Zionizing American Jewry made political and monetary support for Israel the least common denominator that tied all American Jews together.

Another important element in American Zionism was Labor Zionism, closely allied with the *Histadrut* (trade union organization) and Poalei Zion in Palestine. Like them, Labor Zionism wanted a Jewish state founded on socialist as well as democratic principles. Although Labor Zionism attracted a significant number of first-generation Eastern European Zionists, it had no lasting impact on the movement after that generation died out.

American Zionism left a rich legacy in making Israel the tie that binds together much of the contemporary American Jewish community. Organizationally, however, with the exception of Hadassah, Zionist groups have withered away. Hadassah has made medical work its *raison d'être*, a mission that it easily carried over from the yishuv to the state. The other Zionist groups had little to offer American Jews that they could not get from the United Jewish Appeal and other general fund-raising groups.

Melvin I. Urofsky

References and Further Reading
Cohen, Naomi. 2003. *Americanization of Zionism, 1897–1948*. Hanover, NH: University Press of New England.

Feinstein, Marnin. 1965. *American Zionism, 1884–1904*. New York: Herzl Press.
Gal, Allon. 1991. *David Ben-Gurion and the American Alignment for a Jewish State*, trans. David S. Segall. Bloomington: Indiana University Press.
Halpern, Ben. 1987. *A Clash of Heroes—Brandeis, Weizmann, and American Zionism*. New York: Oxford University Press.
Shapiro, David H. 1994. *From Philanthropy to Activism: The Political Transformation of American Zionism in the Holocaust Years, 1933–1945*. New York: Pergamon Press.
Urofsky, Melvin I. 1975. *American Zionism from Herzl to the Holocaust*. Garden City, NY: Anchor Doubleday.

Revisionist Zionism in America

Revisionist Zionism was founded by Russian Zionist leader Vladimir Ze'ev Jabotinsky in 1925 as a faction within the world Zionist movement dedicated to revising the political approach of the Zionist leadership, which he regarded as excessively cautious. The following year, a small U.S. branch was established in New York. Revisionist themes such as the need for Jews to undergo military training and mass immigration to Palestine resonated in East European regions rife with antisemitism but attracted few followers in America in the Roaring Twenties, as Jewish immigrants focused on climbing the socioeconomic ladder. The American Zionist movement as a whole dwindled during this period, and the tiny Revisionist group struggled to take root.

After the 1929 Arab massacres of Jews in Palestine, however, U.S. Revisionists could point to the violence and the weak British response as vindication of their warnings that the English were backtracking on their pledge to help establish a Jewish national home. The rise of Hitler to power in Germany in 1933 seemed to confirm the Revisionists' expectation that severe antisemitism in the Diaspora was inevitable and that mass Jewish emigration to Palestine was the only answer. By the early 1930s, the U.S. Revisionists had perhaps a thousand members, a monthly magazine, an American wing of Jabotinsky's Betar youth movement, a summer camp, and their first national conference. Revisionism was still tiny compared to the rest of the American Zionist movement, but it was finally on the map.

Still, the U.S. Revisionists faced many obstacles in trying to win support during the 1930s. While sympathy for

Vladimir Ze'ev Jabotinsky, founder of Revisionist Zionism.
(American Jewish Archives)

labor unions was strong among American Jews, the Revisionists opposed strikes on principle and criticized the hegemony of the socialist *Histadrut* trade union in Palestine. The arrest of Revisionists in Palestine in connection with the 1933 assassination of Labor Zionist leader Haim Arlosoroff further tarnished the image of the Jabotinsky movement, although the suspects were eventually cleared. Some opponents went so far as to allege a resemblance between the Revisionists' brand of Jewish nationalism and the rising ultranationalist movements in Europe. The secession of the Revisionists from the World Zionist Organization in 1935 intensified accusations that the Jabotinskyites were fomenting divisions at a time when the Jewish world needed more unity. Ongoing conflicts between Revisionists and Labor Zionists in Palestine did not serve the Jabotinsky movement well among American Jews, who perceived the Laborites as admirable pioneers rebuilding the Land of Israel in the face of adversity.

The fortunes of American Zionism typically rose and fell in relation to events in Palestine and Europe, and Revisionist Zionism in America was similarly affected. With the renewal of mass Palestinian Arab violence in the late 1930s and the increasing persecution of Jews in Germany and Austria, the U.S. Revisionists—now known as the New Zionist Organization of America (NZOA)—gained more adherents and more attention for their arguments. In addition, the support of a prominent Reform rabbi, Louis I. Newman of New York City's Temple Rodeph Shalom, who served as NZOA president from 1937–1939, gave the movement a measure of respectability it previously lacked.

Beginning in 1937, the Revisionist movement in Europe initiated a program known as *aliyah bet,* or unauthorized immigration to Palestine in defiance of British restrictions. The U.S. Revisionists raised funds to help sponsor this effort and made it one of the features of their public information campaigns. Although this, too, became a point of conflict with Labor Zionists—who accused the Revisionists of endangering Zionist relations with the British and bringing in individuals physically unsuited to life in Palestine—the American Revisionists found in aliyah bet an issue that resonated in the U.S. Jewish community. The Revisionists appeared to be at the forefront of action to rescue Jews from the rising dangers of European antisemitism.

With the eruption of World War II, Jabotinsky shifted his focus from London to Washington, convinced that England's need for U.S. assistance would give the Americans a potentially decisive voice in determining the future of Palestine. In the spring of 1940, the Revisionist leader traveled to the United States to seek support for Zionist goals from the administration, Congress, and the public, beginning with the establishment of a Jewish army that would fight alongside the Allies against Nazi Germany. He believed that a military Jewish contribution to the war effort would facilitate attaining Jewish statehood after the war and that a Jewish armed force could be the nucleus of the future Jewish state's army.

Jabotinsky's stature and the public controversies he engendered pumped new life into the NZOA. The campaign for a Jewish army in the spring and summer of 1940 brought publicity and new members to the movement. At the same time, the army campaign stirred opposition among some mainstream Jewish leaders, who feared it would provoke antisemites to accuse American Jews of trying to drag the U.S. into overseas conflicts.

Significantly, Jabotinsky dispatched to America a number of talented young Revisionist leaders from Europe and Palestine, among them Hillel Kook, Benzion Netanyahu, and Eliahu Ben-Horin. Other key Jabotinsky followers, including Yitshaq Ben-Ami, Alexander Rafaeli, and Joseph Schechtmann, also arrived shortly before or after the war broke out. They provided dynamic new leadership for the U.S. Revisionists. During their first months in the United States, these activists focused on the Jewish army issue and attracted the support of numerous intellectuals and political figures, including some officials of the Roosevelt administration. Their efforts also helped revive the previously dormant American wing of the Revisionist movement.

Jabotinsky's sudden death in August 1940 threw the movement into disarray. A faction led by Kook, Ben-Ami, and Rafaeli left the NZOA and created an independent political action committee focusing on the Jewish army issue. Netanyahu worked with the Kook group for some months but left in 1941 in a dispute over tactics. Kook believed that public criticism of the British might backfire, while Netanyahu was convinced that openly challenging London was the most effective way to influence British policy.

In early 1942, Netanyahu became executive director of the U.S. Revisionist Zionists. Under his leadership, the Revisionists undertook high-profile public information campaigns aimed at pressuring the British to open Palestine to Jewish immigration. Formerly the editor of the Revisionist newspaper *Ha-Yarden,* in Palestine, Netanyahu believed that "words are the most effective means of political warfare," and he put that approach into action by publishing a militant Zionist magazine, *Zionews,* by organizing public rallies, and by authoring large newspaper advertisements sharply critical of British policy toward Palestine.

Kook's Committee for a Jewish Army of Stateless and Palestinian Jews employed similar tactics but enjoyed greater success because the idea of a Jewish army both fired the imagination of some American Jews and impressed many non-Jews as a potential asset to the war effort. Kook's newspaper ads featured long lists of endorsements from prominent American political figures, intellectuals, and Hollywood celebrities. Mainstream Jewish organizations later took up the army proposal and lobbied British government officials behind the scenes. Kook's public pressure and the establishment's private efforts combined to eventually convince London to establish the Jewish Brigade, which saw action on the European battlefield during the final months of the war. Many Brigade veterans subsequently took part in smuggling Holocaust survivors to

Palestine and served in the Israeli Army during the 1948 War of Independence.

Kook called himself Peter H. Bergson in the United States in order to shield his family, which included some of the most prominent rabbis in Palestine, from public controversy. The political action committees he established were popularly known as the Bergson group. The Bergsonites had no official connection to the U.S. Revisionist movement, the NZOA, although leaders of the two factions maintained friendly relations and, in the public eye, the Bergson group was often referred to, by sympathizers as well as critics, as Revisionists or Jabotinskyites.

When confirmed information about the Nazi genocide reached the United States in 1942–1943, Kook refocused his attention on a campaign for U.S. intervention to rescue Jewish refugees and created a new group, the Emergency Committee to Save the Jewish People of Europe. To alert the American public to the Nazi genocide, Bergson's committee sponsored a dramatic pageant called *We Will Never Die,* authored by his close ally, the Academy Award-winning screenwriter Ben Hecht. During the spring and summer of 1943, the pageant was performed at Madison Square Garden in New York City and then in Philadelphia, Washington, D.C., Chicago, and Boston, and at the Hollywood Bowl in Los Angeles. More than 100,000 Americans attended the performances. The Bergson group placed more than 200 full-page advertisements in newspapers around the country, with eye-grabbing headlines such as "How Well Are You Sleeping? Is There Something You Could Have Done to Save Millions of Innocent People from Torture and Death?" and "Time Races Death: What Are We Waiting For?" The committee also organized protest rallies, including a march of 400 rabbis to Capitol Hill and the White House to plead for rescue.

Both the Bergson group and the NZOA also actively lobbied Congress. While the established Jewish leaders had built few relationships on Capitol Hill beyond congressional supporters of the administration, the Jabotinskyites found considerable success in wooing Republicans and disaffected Democrats who, for political or personal reasons, found common cause with militant Zionism.

The Bergson group was uniquely successful in recruiting cultural and political figures to support its campaigns. The group's letterhead and newspaper ads overflowed with the names of liberal as well as conservative intellectuals, Democratic as well as Republican politicians, and an array of colorful Hollywood celebrities. Their participation attracted public attention and lent credibility to Bergson's cause.

In the autumn of 1943, Bergson persuaded prominent U.S. senators and representatives from both parties to introduce a resolution calling for the creation of a government agency to rescue Jewish refugees. The well-publicized congressional hearings on the resolution, combined with behind-the-scenes lobbying for rescue by Treasury Secretary Henry Morgenthau Jr. and his aides, convinced President Roosevelt to establish the agency the resolution had demanded—the War Refugee Board. The board played a major role in the rescue of more than 200,000 Jews from Hitler.

Bergson's activities aroused opposition from many mainstream Jewish leaders. Some feared that the Bergson group's vociferous protests would provoke antisemitism. Others were concerned that Bergson's criticism of Allied policy would embarrass President Roosevelt, whom they strongly supported. There were also concerns among Jewish leaders that the Bergson group was usurping them by appearing to the public as the only organization actively seeking to rescue refugees. Several Jewish leaders privately urged the administration to draft or deport Bergson in order to curtail his political activity, but Bergson's allies in Congress helped shield him.

While Bergson focused on rescue, the NZOA concentrated on Palestine. Netanyahu cultivated relations with leading Republicans, which facilitated efforts to include a strongly pro-Zionist plank in the GOP's 1944 platform. This helped enshrine support for Zionism as a principle of both major political parties and facilitated the ability of future Jewish lobbyists to influence American foreign policy.

In 1943–1944, Bergson established two additional organizations: the American League for a Free Palestine, to rally American public support for Jewish statehood, and the Hebrew Committee of National Liberation, to serve as a government-in-exile for the future Jewish state. Zionist leaders denounced the creation of the Hebrew Committee as an attempt to usurp the authority of the world Zionist movement and the Palestine Jewish leadership. The NZOA also criticized the Hebrew Committee initiative.

Using newspaper advertisements, lobbying Congress, soliciting the support of celebrities, and staging dramatic theatrical productions, the League and the Hebrew Committee helped build up public and political pressure on the British to withdraw from Palestine. A particularly effective tactic was the League's staging, in 1946–1947, of Ben Hecht's explosive play, *A Flag Is Born*. After ten weeks on Broadway, *Flag* was performed in major cities around the country, providing tens of thousands of Americans with a gripping introduction to the plight of Holocaust survivors and the harsh policies of the British regime in Palestine. Funds raised by the play were used by Bergson to purchase a ship, renamed the *S.S. Ben Hecht,* to bring Jewish refugees from Europe to Palestine.

Both the Bergson group and the NZOA labored to rally American public support for Jewish national independence in Palestine, with an emphasis on explaining and defending the armed Jewish revolt against the British authorities. This was a struggle particularly close to the hearts of the Jabotinskyites in America, some of whom had been previously affiliated with the *Irgun Zvai Leumi*, the underground Jewish militia spearheading the battle. A handful of activists from both the Bergson group and the NZOA took part in clandestine efforts to smuggle weapons from the United States to the Irgun.

In their torrent of newspaper ads, rallies, publications, and speeches, the militant Zionists frequently drew analogies between the Jewish fight against the British in Palestine and America's own struggle for independence from British rule. Bergson adopted the slogan "It's 1776 in Palestine" as the theme of his campaign. This approach helped many Americans make sense of an otherwise bewildering fight between Jews, Arabs, and Englishmen thousands of miles away. A groundswell of humanitarian sympathy for the Jews in the wake of the Holocaust also played a major role in winning over the American public.

The aggressive public campaigns by the NZOA and the Bergson group undoubtedly contributed to the psychological pressure on Britain to leave Palestine. Anxious to maintain U.S. support, especially in order to secure economic aid for postwar reconstruction, London monitored the militant Zionist agitation and grew increasingly worried that American public and congressional opinion were being turned against them.

The postwar period saw a gradual rapprochement between the mainstream Jewish leadership and the Revisionists. Grassroots Jewish anger over the Nazi massacres and the British closure of Palestine fueled the rise of the activist-minded Rabbi Abba Hillel Silver to the leadership of the American Zionist movement. Privately sympathetic to the

Irgun's fight against the British, Silver generally refrained from his predecessors' attacks on Bergson and actively sought close relations with Netanyahu and the NZOA. In 1946 the Revisionist movement rejoined the World Zionist Organization, and the U.S. Revisionists became an official part of Silver's American Zionist Emergency Council, the coalition of all major American Zionist groups.

Any hopes the Jabotinskyites may have entertained about becoming a numerically significant movement in America were dashed, however, as Silver mounted a nationwide campaign of rallies and aggressive political lobbying. Hundreds of thousands of American Jews, energized by the Palestine struggle and the plight of Holocaust survivors in Displaced Persons camps in Europe, sought an activist response. But most found it in the mainstream, respectable, yet increasingly militant campaigns led by Silver, not in the ranks of the tiny Revisionist group, whose platform now hardly differed from that of the establishment. Silver even hired three of the Revisionists' foremost intellectuals, Eliahu Ben-Horin, Benjamin Akzin, and Joseph Schechtmann, to assume leading roles in his lobbying and public information efforts. At their peak, the Revisionists never numbered more than 5,000 in the United States, as compared to the estimated 250,000 members of the Silver-led Zionist Organization of America in 1948.

The late 1940s marked the zenith of Revisionist Zionism in America. After the creation of Israel, the Bergson group disbanded, key activists such as Kook and Netanyahu moved to the new Jewish state, and the U.S. Revisionist movement lapsed into a long period of sharply reduced activity, its main goal having been accomplished. The Revisionist youth movement Betar, however, continued its efforts to promote immigration to Israel and to train young Zionists according to the teachings of Jabotinsky. The United Zionists-Revisionists of America, as it was known (later it became Herut USA and then Likud USA), enjoyed a brief revival after the election of former Irgun commander Menachem Begin as prime minister of Israel in 1977. Unable to sustain that momentum for long, the U.S. wing of the Jabotinsky movement soon returned to its status as a minor force among the numerous American Zionist factions, several of which adopted nationalist agendas that effectively usurped the Revisionists' traditional role as standard-bearer of maximalist Zionism.

Rafael Medoff

References and Further Reading

Medoff, Rafael. 2002. *Militant Zionism in America: The Rise and Impact of the Jabotinsky Movement in the United States, 1926–1948*. Tuscaloosa: University of Alabama Press.

Wyman, David S., and Rafael Medoff. 2002. *A Race against Death: Peter Bergson, America, and the Holocaust*. New York: The New Press.

Golda Meir (1898–1978)

Zionist Leader and Prime Minister of Israel

Golda Meir was prime minister of Israel from 1969 to 1974. Born in the Ukraine and raised in America, she was a lifelong Zionist and a member of the upper echelon of Israeli politics for fifty years. She is best remembered for her foreign policy and for her handling of the Yom Kippur War of 1973.

Goldie Mabovitch was born in Kiev, Russia, in 1898 and later moved to Pinsk. She claimed that her earliest memory was of a pogrom that did not materialize. "I remember how scared I was and how angry that all my father could do to protect me was to nail a few planks together while we waited for the hooligans to come," she said. "And, above all, I remember being aware that this was happening to me because I was Jewish" (Meir 1975).

Her household was traditional and celebrated all the Jewish holidays, but talk of religion or God was rare in her home. By contrast, Zionism was a frequent topic of discussion, and Mabovitch's older sister, Sheyna, at fourteen was already a dedicated member of the socialist-Zionist movement in Europe. Sheyna allegedly wore black for two years following the death of Theodore Herzl until the family arrived in Milwaukee in 1906. Goldie Mabovitch's father, Moshe, did odd jobs, while her mother, Blume, ran a grocery store in which Sheyna refused to work due to her socialist principles. Her father also participated regularly in Labor Day celebrations. In short, Goldie Mabovitch had been born into a politically idealistic family.

After an adolescent dispute with her family, Mabovitch ran away to Denver in February 1913 to join her sister Sheyna, who was staying temporarily at the Jewish Hospital for Consumptives. Despite the physical frailty of its patients, the hospital was a hotbed of anarchism, socialism, and socialist-Zionism. Meir later remembered, "They talked about the anarchist philosophy of Emma Goldman and

Golda Meir, Zionist leader and prime minister of Israel from 1969 to 1974. (Library of Congress)

Peter Kropotkin, about President Wilson and the European situation, about pacifism, the role of women in society, the future of the Jewish people . . . but when they talked about people like Aaron David Gordon, for instance, who had gone to Palestine in 1905 and helped found Degania (the kibbutz established three years later on the deserted tip of the Sea of Galilee), I was absolutely fascinated and found myself dreaming about joining with pioneers in Palestine" (Meir 1975).

It was through American leftist and Jewish nationalist politics that Meir learned about the Zionist ideal, an ideal deeply influenced by the religion of labor espoused by A. D. Gordon. As she later recalled, "No modern hippie, in my opinion, has ever revolted as effectively against the Establishment of the day as those pioneers did at the beginning of the century. Many of them came from homes of merchants and scholars; many even from prosperous assimilated families. . . . But they were radicals at heart and deeply believed that only self-labor could truly liberate the Jews from the ghetto and its mentality and make it possible for them to reclaim the land and earn a moral right to it, in

addition to the historic right. . . . [W]hat they all had in common was a fervor to experiment, to build a . . . society in Palestine . . . that would be better than what had been known in most parts of the world" (Meir 1975).

Due to another spat, this time with her sister, Goldie Mabovitch returned to Milwaukee in 1914, where she soon became involved in the nascent *Poalei-Zion* (Labor Zionist) movement. After high school, she attended Wisconsin State Normal School in Milwaukee to train as a teacher, but she spent most of her time organizing for Poalei-Zion and rose quickly in its Milwaukee ranks.

Moshe (now Morris) Mabovitch also became increasingly involved in Labor Zionism and B'nai B'rith. Meir remembered, "Most of the people who slept on our famous couch during those years were socialists (Labor Zionists) from the East. . . . Of the many people whom I first met or first heard speak in public then, some were to become major influences not only on my life, but . . . on the Zionist movement, particularly on Labor Zionism. And some of them were . . . among the founding fathers of the Jewish state" (Meir 1975).

Goldie Mabovitch was quickly recruited by Poalei-Zion's larger Chicago organization, and she moved there with her new husband, Morris Meyerson. Goldie Meyerson tried to join the Jewish Legion to fight with the British in World War I but discovered that it did not accept women (Meir 1975). In 1921 the Meyersons emigrated to Palestine and joined Kibbutz Merhavia, where they worked for three years. They then moved to Tel Aviv, where she became secretary of the *Moetzet Hapoalot*, the Working Women's Council of Palestine's primary labor organization, the *Histadrut*. From this position, in 1930 Meyerson became one of the founders of *Mapai*, the Labor Party of the Land of Israel.

In 1932 Mapai leaders asked her to become secretary of Pioneer Women, a U.S.-based, worldwide Labor Zionist women's organization founded in 1925 to provide welfare services for women, children, and recent immigrants in Palestine. The organization was a mix of American Zionism, *Yiddishkeit,* and feminism, which suited Meyerson's background well. Her main task was to raise money by speaking at Pioneer Women engagements across America. Meyerson became known as a very effective fund-raiser and speaker (in both English and Yiddish), and she toured America periodically throughout her entire career.

In 1940 Meyerson was appointed head of the political department of the Histadrut and, in 1946, to the same position in the Jewish Agency, the de facto government of the Jewish people in Palestine. In 1949 she became minister of labor of the new Israeli state. In June 1956, just before the Sinai Campaign, she became Israel's foreign minister and, at the request of David Ben Gurion, changed her name to Golda Meir. In 1966 she became secretary general of the Mapai party. According to an acquaintance, she was known as an ideologue, "a person of monolithic mind who took her cue from what the Labor Party said. She . . . helped to formulate what the party said, but once it was said, she followed it blindly" (Martin 1988).

On March 17, 1969, at age seventy, Meir became Israel's fourth prime minister. She enjoyed very high approval ratings until the outbreak of the Yom Kippur War (1973), when some Israelis faulted her for allegedly acquiescing to demands of the American government not to launch a preemptive strike against Egyptian and Syrian military buildups. No record of such a request is known to exist, and Meir always took sole responsibility for the decision not to preempt. However, it is reasonable to believe that in light of Israel's preemption during both the Sinai Campaign (1956) and the Six Day War (1967), the American government warned of the difficulty of providing political support and munitions were Israel to act preemptively once more. On June 4, 1974, shortly after reaching cease-fire agreements with both Egypt and Syria, Meir retired from government work and gave up the seat in the Knesset she had held for twenty-five years. She died on December 8, 1978.

Michael Alexander

References and Further Reading
Martin, Ralph G. 1988. *Golda: Golda Meir, the Romantic Years.* New York: Scribner.
Meir, Golda. 1975. *My Life.* New York: Putnam.
Syrkin, Marie. 1969. *Golda Meir: Israel's Leader.* New York: Putnam.

Marie Syrkin (1899–1989)

Zionist Intellectual-Activist, Social Critic, Educator, Poet

Marie Syrkin's strong advocacy of the Labor Zionist movement had a far-reaching impact on Jewish American intel-

Marie Syrkin, Labor Zionist, educator, and poet. (American Jewish Archives)

lectual life and communal priorities. Unlike other American Zionists such as Horace Kallen and Louis Brandeis, whose ideology was often confused and contradictory, Syrkin had arrived at her Zionism almost organically, as the daughter of Bassya Osnos Syrkin (1878–1915), a feminist revolutionary activist and Zionist, and Nachman Syrkin (1867–1924), the founder and theoretician of Labor Zionism, whose ideas inspired the kibbutz movement. By the time he came to the United States in 1908, Nachman Syrkin had an international reputation as a scholar-intellectual and a Zionist theorist. Horace Kallen later adopted his socialist ideas, though in a less doctrinaire form.

Born in Berne, Switzerland, Marie Syrkin came to the United States after having lived in Germany, France, and Russia during the years when her father was active on behalf of socialist Zionism there. Her friend and biographer, Carole S. Kessner, remembered her remarking that "Papa was always getting exiled—so we traveled a lot" (Kessner

1994). In childhood, Syrkin encountered village children in Vilna who warned her to paint a cross on her house if the killing began. Later she recalled that, when she repeated this advice to her father, he had offered a different remedy: "The answer I was taught and grew up believing lay in a socialist society and a socialist Jewish state" (Syrkin 1980). But after fleeing the czarist authorities, Nachman Syrkin took his family not to Palestine but to America, where he had been invited to edit *Das Volk* (*The People*), the Zionist journal of the Socialist-Territorial movement.

Working closely with public intellectuals such as Hayim Greenberg, Horace Kallen, and Maurice Samuel, Syrkin initially used her father's intellectual legacy, and later her own widely respected rhetorical gifts, to shore up support for the Jewish state-in-the-making. She remained a staunch defender of Israel even years after Labor Zionism's influence had greatly diminished in this country subsequent to the ascent of Menahem Begin and the Likud Party in the late 1970s. Situated in the social context of the period between the world wars and during World War II, her life and writings provide important perspectives on Jewish American ideology during a time of material and existential crisis. Syrkin was devoted to both collective destiny and group identity. For Syrkin—since the Jewish people in *Galut* (Exile) were inevitably linked to political institutions and policies that betray them—the most logical hope for the Jews' continuity was through a state of their own.

Syrkin was nine years old when she reached the United States, and her family settled in the Bronx. While attending Cornell University, she met and married a biochemist named Aaron Bodansky. She had two sons (the older died in 1924, after the couple separated) and lived in New York City, where she taught high school English in the public schools for twenty-five years. Syrkin's first book, *Your School, Your Children* (1944), was a highly praised critique of the city's high school system based on her own teaching experience. Shorter works of social criticism on subjects such as her advocacy of a meritocratic system appeared in venues such as the *New York Times Magazine*. In 1930, she married the Objectivist poet Charles Reznikoff and remained married to him until his death in 1976.

In spite of being excluded from most (predominantly male-authored) official histories of Zionism, Syrkin warrants consideration as one of the most influential Jewish American women writer–activists of the twentieth century,

a figure whose public reputation surpassed that of her husband, the poet Reznikoff. Her early years in czarist Russia, her interviews with survivors in the displaced persons camps of postwar Europe, and her frequent sojourns to Israel as a public figure in the Zionist movement culminated in numerous essays on the modern Jewish condition, particularly in the years following the Holocaust. Besides contributing to the *Menorah Journal*, she wrote for *Commentary*, *Midstream*, and *The New Republic* during a career that lasted more than fifty years. Respected by American intellectuals for her withering critique of Hannah Arendt's response to Zionism and the Holocaust (*Jewish Frontier*, 1963), she had already achieved a reputation for her intelligent coverage of the Moscow Trials (*Jewish Frontier*, 1937). Her anthology of often-acerbic essays, *The State of the Jews*, testifies to her lifelong concern with the enigma of the twentieth-century Jewish experience, offering candid reflections on such topics as the Holocaust, Israel and its relations with the Palestinian Arabs, and especially Jewish culture in America. After her first trip to Palestine in 1933, she joined the staff of the *Jewish Frontier*, Eventually she would write Zionist speeches for Chaim Weizmann and Golda Meir. Among her books is a famous oral biography of Meir (*A Land of Our Own, An Oral Autobiography by Golda Meir*, 1973). Syrkin and Meir became such intimates that she was a guest in Meir's home while she researched her biography of her father (*Syrkin* 1961).

Syrkin's inherited variant of Eastern European Zionism, unlike the American brand espoused by Kallen and Brandeis, was not sanguine about the consequences of the Jews' emancipation from European ghettos and their transformation by the culture of individualism. The disillusionment that shaped Syrkin's perspective on Christian Europe eventually diminished her confidence in the Jews' position in America as well. Marked by a complete loss of trust in the host society, this ideology led to a fundamental lack of confidence in the possibilities of Jewish participation in Western culture. This sense of loss culminated in a series of irrefutable principles: "that the Jewish people is viewed as alien everywhere in the diaspora; that the Jewish bourgeoisie invented the deception of assimilation to promote its power of exploitation; that a profound moral contradiction exists between the bourgeois lie of assimilation and the revolutionary truth of socialism; that the Jewish socialist is duty bound to aid the Jewish people and to accept Zionism as the instrument for the emancipation of the Jewish people and the spiritual redemption of the individual Jew" (Syrkin 1961).

In October 1934, Syrkin, together with Hayim Fineman, chaired a committee to discuss plans for a new publication that would bring the message of Labor Zionism and the reality of Jewish settlement in Palestine directly to the Jewish American public on a greater scale than ever before. In December the *Jewish Frontier*'s premier issue appeared. Besides presenting translations of the Hebrew nationalist poetry of Haim Nachman Bialik and Nathan Alterman and Hebrew articles by Palestinian leaders such as David Ben-Gurion and Berl Katznelson that were otherwise unavailable to English readers, the journal attracted such writers as Maurice Samuel, Mordecai Kaplan, Will Herberg, Hannah Arendt, and Ludwig Lewisohn. The founders readily acknowledged the contemporary tension between Jewish socialists and those who had wholeheartedly embraced the American Dream. Moreover, they foresaw the unifying role that Zionism would eventually play in Jewish American culture after the Holocaust.

Syrkin and the other writers of the *Jewish Frontier* often took editorial stands on the politics of Palestine. Over the course of nearly a decade, the *Frontier* waged an impassioned, often bitterly ideological campaign in its pages against what it considered the hate-mongering right-wing Revisionist Zionist press, implicitly linking Labor Zionism with American liberalism, and Revisionism with American xenophobia and nativism. Syrkin's own essay, "The Essence of Revisionism: An Analysis of a Fascist Tendency in Jewry" (1940), was representative of this editorial trend toward the left.

From the beginning, similar confrontations with Jewish and non-Jewish adversaries of Jewish culture and Zionism marked Syrkin's public life, gradually leading her to conclude that only the latter could promise a safe haven for the former. Syrkin's defensive responses to American anti-semitism underscore the success with which hostile forces drove home the Jews' irreconcilable otherness in these years. Following World War II, Syrkin went to Germany as a representative of B'nai B'rith Hillel Foundations to find suitable applicants for Hillel scholarships to American universities among survivors of the Holocaust. She traveled to displaced person camps and interviewed numerous survivors. Her book, *Blessed Is the Match: The Story of Jewish Resistance* (1957), grew out of these experiences and is believed to be the first work in English about Jewish resistance under the Nazis. Syrkin joined the faculty of Brandeis University in 1950, teaching humanities and literature, a post she held until retiring in 1966 as professor emerita. As Brandeis's first female professor, she developed the first courses on the literature of the Holocaust ever taught on a college campus. In the 1960s, she served on the World Zionist Executive and as honorary president of the Labor Zionist movement in the United States. A lifelong friend of Israel's Prime Minister Golda Meir, Syrkin wrote her biography, *Golda Meir: Israel's Leader* (1969).

By the time of her death, on February 2, 1989, Syrkin had earned a reputation as a gifted thinker and educator who consistently engaged and experienced the political world as a Jew. Facing the historical forces of political anti-semitism, her response was to produce prose and poetry intended to counter fascism and defenselessness. The Holocaust—and the decaying remnant of a rootless Diaspora—confirmed her belief that Jewish survival in the modern world, including the United States, required the aggressive politics of Zionism. Whereas Syrkin's most influential and widely read essays appear in *The State of the Jews, Gleanings: A Diary in Verse* (1979) is the poetic record of Syrkin's activities. Its title is apt, for the work represents the great themes of her life: her great loves, losses, resentments, and political battles, and above all, her devotion to realizing the dreams of Zionism. Her mission-oriented poetry and polemics alike are angrily invigorated by a coherent and unified vision of a meaningful Jewish destiny.

Ranen Omer-Sherman

References and Further Reading

Kessner, Carole S. 1979. "Behind the Polemics: A Woman." *Reconstructionist* 45 (July).

Kessner, Carole S. 1994a. "Marie Syrkin: An Exemplary Life." In *The "Other" New York Jewish Intellectuals.* Edited by Carole S. Kessner. New York: New York University Press.

Kessner, Carole S. 1994b. "Matrilineal Dissent: Emma Lazarus, Marie Syrkin and Cynthia Ozick." In *Women of the Word: Jewish Women and Jewish Writing,* edited by Judith R. Baskin, pp. 197–215. Detroit, MI: Wayne State University Press.

Omer-Sherman, Ranen. 2002. *Diaspora and Zionism in Jewish American Literature.* Hanover, NH: Brandeis University Press/University Press of New England.

Syrkin, Marie. 1961. *Nachman Syrkin, Socialist Zionist: A Biographical Memoir.* New York: Herzl Press.

Syrkin, Marie. 1980. *The State of the Jews.* Washington, DC: New Republic Books.

The Holocaust and America

America's Response to Nazism and the Holocaust

The response of the United States to the Holocaust fell far short of measuring up to the nation's underlying human and democratic values. In the pre-extermination years (1933–1940), many hundreds of thousands of European Jews could have reached safe haven if the United States and other countries had been willing to open their doors. The United States could have set the example by a temporary widening of its immigration quotas. Instead, even the small quotas that were legally available were not allowed to be filled, except from mid-1938 to mid-1940. Then, in the extermination years (1941–1945), immigration was made even more difficult. Not until January 1944, fourteen months after it had incontrovertible evidence that genocide was occurring, did the U.S. government begin to take even limited steps toward rescue.

The three main factors that lay behind America's failed response were the Great Depression, nativism, and antisemitism. In 1933, at the worst point in the Depression, unemployment in the United States reached 25 percent. Even by 1938, it was still above 15 percent. The decade of the 1930s was one of insecurity, fear, and anxiety. Many Americans worried that foreigners would enter the country and take their jobs. During World War II, when war production eliminated unemployment, there was still widespread apprehension that the Depression would return with the end of hostilities.

Nativist attitudes, which were particularly widespread in the 1920s, remained prevalent in the 1930s and 1940s. A great many Americans disliked foreigners of any kind and wanted to end or significantly reduce the small flow of immigration that still existed. The issue was partly one of job competition, but many Americans also harbored fears of the cultural impact of foreigners on the United States.

Antisemitism, already on the rise in the 1920s, increased dramatically in the 1930s and reached its peak in American history in the late 1930s and the World War II years. The view that Jews constituted an "undesirable race" was widely accepted. Another strong force in those years was a political antisemitism that argued that there was a world Jewish conspiracy that secretly wielded vast international economic and political power. Jews supposedly manipulated the capitalist system through their stranglehold on international finance and simultaneously controlled the Soviet Union as well as the international Communist movement. Their alleged objective was to increase their power to the point where they could rule the world. While the theory as a whole was too extreme for very wide acceptance, parts of this mythology spread through American society: for instance, that the Jews were Communists and that they were at the same time capitalist manipulators intentionally imposing the Depression on the country.

217

Antisemitic mass movements and demagogues spread fear and hatred throughout the United States. By 1940, more than a hundred antisemitic organizations had appeared, led by the Silver Shirts, the German-American Bund (American Nazis), and the Defenders of the Christian Faith. By far the most influential among the antisemitic demagogues was the Catholic priest Charles Coughlin, whose weekly radio broadcasts reached several million Americans. Opinion polls from 1940 through 1945 indicated that about 33 percent of the American public was antisemitic. (This figure does not include individuals who harbored antisemitic sentiments but were reluctant to reveal them to those taking the polls.) Of those polled, 12 percent were prepared to support an antisemitic campaign, and an additional 20 percent expressed sympathy for such a movement. During the war years, the rhetoric of hate turned into violence in several northeastern cities, where a number of incidents occurred in which teenage gangs assaulted Jewish schoolchildren.

Troubling though the antisemitism of the 1930s and 1940s was to American Jews, those who were hurt most by it were the Jews of Europe. Antisemitism in the 1920s had helped to bring about the Immigration Act of 1924, which all but closed America's doors. But the antisemitism of the 1930s and 1940s was crucial in keeping them closed. However, despite the strength of the antisemites, their victory in the struggle concerning American refugee policy was not a foregone conclusion. The opinion polls of 1940 to 1945 also showed that, if a campaign had been launched against Jews, almost one-third of Americans would have actively opposed it. Clearly, a reservoir of sympathy for endangered Jews existed in American society. But almost no leadership emerged to try to convert this concern into political pressure. President Franklin D. Roosevelt and most of the rest of the political leadership made no effort to mobilize it. Very few Christian church leaders called for action to help the European Jews. Almost none of the mass media offered such leadership; in fact, most of the media failed even to bring the Holocaust to the public's attention. Jewish leaders called on non-Jewish America for help, but few listened and even fewer acted.

Still, criticism of U.S. refugee policy from individual newspaper columnists such as Dorothy Thompson and a small but vocal number of congressmen worried the administration, especially in the wake of the extreme persecution of Jews and anti-Nazis following on the heels of Germany's annexation of Austria in March 1938. Fearing that such criticism would now become "exceedingly strong and prolonged," State Department officials decided that the best way to elude the pressure for refugee action would be "to get out in front and attempt to guide it," by inviting thirty-two countries to send representatives to a conference in Evian, France, in July 1938 (Wyman 1968). To assure both Americans and foreigners that no country would be called upon for major sacrifices, the administration's invitation and other pronouncements regarding the conference stressed that "no country would be expected or asked to receive a greater number of immigrants than is permitted by its existing legislation" (Wyman 1968). To make matters worse, the U.S. acquiesced in the British position that there should be no discussion of Jewish refugee immigration to Mandatory Palestine, which England intended to restrict in order to appease Palestinian Arab rioters. As a result, the Evian Conference failed almost completely in its main task, that of finding places to which refugees could go.

In the autumn of that year, Hitler's persecution of German Jewry took a new and violent turn with a series of government-sponsored pogroms on the night of November 9 and 10, known as *Kristallnacht*, a reference to the vast amount of glass from the shattered windows of Jewish homes and businesses. Some one hundred Jews were murdered, tens of thousands were incarcerated in concentration camps, thousands of Jewish-owned businesses were demolished, and most of Germany's synagogues burned while firemen acted only to protect nearby non-Jewish property. In a sharp statement of denunciation, President Roosevelt said, "I myself could scarcely believe that such things could occur in a twentieth-century civilization" (Wyman 1968). He temporarily recalled the American ambassador from Germany and announced that the government would allow the 12,000–15,000 German refugees already in the United States on visitor's visas to remain by means of extensions of their permits. As for the possibility of relaxing the immigration laws, however, Roosevelt said that was "not in contemplation" (Wyman 1968).

Nevertheless, some members of Congress did contemplate bringing more refugees to the United States. The Wagner-Rogers Bill, introduced in early 1939, proposed to admit 20,000 refugee children from Germany outside the quota system. Although a number of prominent Americans backed the bill, their support could not overcome vigorous lobbying by nativists and isolationists and the tide of public opinion, which still ran strongly against the idea of increasing immigration despite the German pogroms. The president's cousin, Laura Delano Houghteling, who was the wife of the U.S. commissioner of immigration, articulated the acerbic sentiment of many opponents of the bill when she remarked that "20,000 charming children would all too soon grow into 20,000 ugly adults" (Breitman and Kraut 1987). While the Wagner-Rogers Bill was being squelched in Congress, the refugee issue again came into the limelight as the German cruise ship *St. Louis,* carrying more than nine hundred Jewish refugees, was denied permission to land its passengers at Havana. The ship hovered for days off the coast of Florida, its passengers hoping to be granted haven in the United States. Instead, the refugees were sent back to Europe.

During the spring of 1940, as the German war machine moved rapidly across Western Europe, a near-hysteria swept America concerning the threat of Nazi spies and saboteurs infiltrating the United States. It was fueled by rumors that Germany's shockingly swift defeat of France had been significantly abetted by such internal subversion. The American media burst with stories of "Trojan Horses," "enemies within our gates," and "Hitler's slave spies in America" (Wyman 1968).

The threat of subversion was a legitimate concern. Care had to be taken to keep Nazi agents and collaborators out. But instead of adding reasonable screening precautions to the immigration procedures, the State Department greatly exaggerated the problem and used it as a device to cut in half the use of the already small quotas. In view of anti-immigration, anti-alien, and antisemitic attitudes then current in the State Department, it is evident that the subversion issue was far from the only factor behind the new policy. Since his appointment as an assistant secretary of state in early 1940, Breckinridge Long had been in charge of refugee policy. Long was virulently anti-alien as well as antisemitic. He kept President Roosevelt posted on his policies, and the president approved, or at least accepted, the steps that Long took. In an internal State Department memorandum in June 1940, Long outlined the methods used to implement the drastic reduction of immigration:

We can delay and effectively stop for a temporary period of indefinite length the number of immigrants into the United States. We could do this by simply advising our consuls to put every obstacle in the way and to require additional evidence and to resort to various administrative advices which would postpone and postpone and postpone the granting of the visas. (Wyman 1968)

The policy change was kept secret, but within weeks refugee aid organizations in the United States realized what had happened. They protested to President Roosevelt to no avail.

The 50 percent cut in immigration in mid-1940 was not the last of Long's changes. In the months that followed, he and the State Department concluded that there was increasing danger of foreign agents entering the United States disguised as refugees. In July 1941, Long further tightened visa procedures. Use of the quotas dropped to 25 percent (for a total of about 15,000 immigrants per year). This time, the State Department made the new procedures public. There were many protests. A small group of distinguished Americans met with President Roosevelt and requested changes. But the new policy remained in place.

American Jewish leaders were deeply troubled by the plight of their brethren in Nazi-occupied Europe and by America's restrictive immigration policy but refrained from urging liberalization of the quota system. The anti-immigrant mood and the prevalence of antisemitism intimidated many of them. They feared that a public effort to bring more refugees to the United States would stimulate even more antisemitism and possibly provoke nativist congressmen to push for more severe restrictions.

There was a second group of American Jews who were potentially in a position to influence U.S. refugee policy. These were Jews who served in senior government positions or were part of Roosevelt's inner circle of advisors, such as speechwriter Samuel Rosenman, Supreme Court justice Felix Frankfurter, and Secretary of the Treasury Henry Morgenthau Jr. But the Jews closest to the president tended to be highly assimilated, self-conscious about their Jewish identity, and therefore unwilling to be seen as engaging in "special pleading" on behalf of specifically Jewish concerns, such as the plight of refugees from Hitler (Wyman 1984).

The nature and extent of the Jewish refugee problem worsened drastically in the summer of 1941. As the new, tighter American visa policy was taking effect, the earlier German policy of forced emigration of the Jews was changing to one of physical extermination. With the German invasion of the Soviet Union in June 1941, special mobile killing units (*Einsatzgruppen*) operating directly behind the front lines began systematically to destroy the hundreds of thousands of Jews in the newly conquered areas. For the most part, the method was mass gunfire, carried out at the sides of ditches. By the end of 1942, the Einsatzgruppen had killed more than 1.3 million Jews in eastern Poland, the Baltic states, and the western Soviet Union. The decision to extend the genocide policy to all the European Jews was probably reached during the summer of 1941, certainly by October 1941. To kill the Jews outside the Eastern European regions where the Einsatzgruppen operated, six killing centers with large gas chambers were brought into operation by spring 1942. In the next three years, about three million Jews from across Europe were deported, mostly via freight train, to the killing centers to be put to death in the gas chambers.

For many months, only scattered information about the mass killings arrived in the West. By mid-August 1942, however, strong evidence of systematic annihilation had reached the State Department. But only in late November 1942 did the State Department decide that it had obtained adequate confirmation. It then authorized Rabbi Stephen Wise, president of the American Jewish (AJ) Congress, to make the dreadful truth public. The extermination news, now amply documented and confirmed by the U.S. government, received only minor attention in the American mass media. This pattern continued throughout the war, making it difficult for those who advocated government rescue action to build public support for it.

On December 17, 1942, Great Britain, the United States, the Soviet Union, and eight other nations issued the Allied War Crimes Declaration. The declaration condemned Germany's policy of extermination of the Jews and pledged that the perpetrators would be brought to justice. But despite their condemnation, neither the British Foreign Office nor the American State Department was willing to attempt to rescue Jews. The British recognized that any significant flow of Jews out of Axis Europe would place great pressure on them to reverse their policy of tightly restricting Jewish immigration to Palestine. They had established the policy in the White Paper of 1939 in response to Arab pressures and were unwilling to modify it in the years that followed. The State Department feared a large-scale exodus of Jews from Nazi Europe because it would put pressure on the United States to open its doors, at least to some extent. For both governments, the real policy, albeit unannounced, was the avoidance of rescue.

Despite limited coverage by the news media, information about the mass killing of the Jews circulated in the United States and Great Britain from November 1942 on. In Britain, Christian church leaders and many members of Parliament joined Jews in calling for rescue action. Some pressures for governmental rescue steps also arose in the United States. For several months, an effort to bring about American government action was carried on by the Joint Emergency Committee on European Jewish Affairs (JEC), a coalition of prominent mainstream Jewish organizations, including the AJCommittee, the AJCongress, B'nai B'rith, the Jewish Labor Committee, Agudath Israel of America, and the American Emergency Committee for Zionist Affairs. The JEC developed an eleven-point list of specific rescue proposals and sought to publicize them through a series of forty mass meetings held in twenty states during the spring of 1943. The committee also sought help from sympathetic members of Congress and tried but failed to persuade the State Department to give serious attention to its rescue program.

In early December 1942, a campaign for U.S. government rescue action was also initiated by a handful of maverick Jewish activists from Palestine. Known as the Bergson group after their leader, Peter Bergson, most of these young men had been connected to the Irgun Zvai Leumi, a Jewish underground militia based in Palestine. They originally came to the United States during 1939–1940 to promote the idea of establishing a Jewish army to fight alongside the Allies against the Nazis; they soon built their Committee for a Jewish Army into an effective political action organization through the use of newspaper advertisements, public rallies, and celebrity endorsements. Once aware of the systematic annihilation of the Jews in Europe, they worked to publicize the terrible news and to build popular and political support for U.S. government rescue action, centering their efforts on the call for creation of a special rescue agency. The Bergson group pressed its cause with full-page newspaper advertisements, intensive lobbying in Washington, and a striking pageant called *We Will Never Die*, which played to large audiences at Madison Square Garden, the Hollywood Bowl, and elsewhere. The Bergson activists sought to join their efforts with those of the Joint Emergency Committee but were turned down.

"Boycott Nazi Germany" demonstration in New York, 1937. (Library of Congress)

Confronted with increasing calls for action in both Great Britain and the United States, the British Foreign Office and the State Department devised a stratagem for undermining the pressures for rescue. Representatives of the two governments met for twelve days in Bermuda in April 1943. The ostensible purpose of the conference was to look into ways to rescue the Jews who could still be saved. The findings of the Bermuda Conference were kept secret, but the diplomats announced that several recommendations for action had been sent on to the two governments.

In reality, the Bermuda Conference recommended almost nothing in the way of rescue proposals. Nevertheless, its real objective was accomplished: it undermined the pressures for action by giving the appearance of planning steps to rescue Jews. Neither the American nor the British government wanted any significant number of Jews to get out of Hitler's Europe, because they saw no places to put

tens of thousands of Jews if they did come out. They knew no other nations were willing to let the Jews in, which meant that, if the Jews came out, especially if the Allies took the initiative to get them out, the responsibility to take them would fall upon Britain and the United States. But Great Britain was not willing to take Jews into the country, and the British were adamant that the doors of Palestine would be kept almost completely closed to Jewish immigration. The State Department was equally unwilling to consider any substantial influx of Jewish refugees into the United States (not more than 6,000 per year).

For both Britain and the United States, the policy was not rescue but avoidance of rescue. For example, consider the March 1943 meeting at the White House between British Foreign Minister Anthony Eden, President Roosevelt, Secretary of State Cordell Hull, and a few others. Hull raised the issue of perhaps helping the 60,000 Jews in

Bulgaria. Eden replied "that the whole problem of the Jews in Europe is very difficult and that we should move very cautiously about offering to take all Jews out of a country like Bulgaria. If we do that, then the Jews of the world will be wanting us to make similar offers in Poland and Germany" (Wyman 1984). No one there questioned Eden's position. In a similar vein, a State Department official, some months later, put the problem this way:

> There was always the danger that the German Government might agree to turn over to the United States and to Great Britain a large number of Jewish refugees. . . . In the event of our admission of inability to take care of these people, the onus for their continued persecution would have been largely transferred from the German Government to the Allied nations (Wyman 1984).

The failure of the Bermuda Conference to produce meaningful rescue action stimulated opposition to the administration's policy toward refugees. Members of Congress such as Senator William Langer (R-ND) and Representative Emanuel Celler (D-NY) increased their criticism of U.S. policy, the Bergson group sponsored large newspaper advertisements denouncing Bermuda as a "cruel mockery," and mainstream Jewish leaders were unusually forthright in their criticism (Wyman and Medoff 2002). The failure of the conference also provoked a widening split within the JEC. Pessimists such as Wise and Joseph Proskauer, president of the politically cautious AJCommittee, now believed there was nothing more they could get out of the administration and opposed calls for more action. Activists, including some from Wise's own AJCongress, began pressing for bolder protests. The minutes of JEC meetings from the summer and fall of 1943 chronicle an increasingly vigorous struggle between the two camps. By November, Wise engineered a 5-to-4 vote by the JEC to dissolve itself and turn over its functions to the Rescue Commission of the American Jewish Conference, an agency over which he exercised tighter control.

Despite the impact of the Bermuda Conference, the struggle for American government action persisted. By summer 1943, the main effort had shifted to the Bergson group. In July 1943, it sponsored a special Emergency Conference in New York City where, working with many important American leaders, it developed rescue proposals and discussed ways to persuade the American government to take the lead in carrying them out. Bergson and his colleagues formed a new organization, the Emergency Committee to Save the Jewish People of Europe, to supersede their Committee for a Jewish Army. The Emergency Committee used full-page advertisements, mass meetings, editorial support by newspapers, and lobbying in Washington. In October 1943, it organized a march in Washington by four hundred Orthodox rabbis, which gained additional publicity for the rescue issue and galvanized Bergson's congressional supporters.

Months of lobbying on Capitol Hill resulted, in November, in the introduction in Congress of a rescue resolution calling on President Roosevelt to establish a government rescue agency independent of the State Department. By the end of 1943, substantial support for the legislation was building in Congress. Meanwhile, in an unrelated set of developments, Treasury Department officials had discovered that the State Department not only had failed to pursue rescue opportunities but had even obstructed rescue efforts that American Jewish organizations had attempted on their own. Treasury officials also learned that Breckinridge Long and the State Department had secretly cut immigration to less than 10 percent of the quotas and had taken steps in early 1943 to stop the transmission of information from Europe about the Nazi genocide. The Treasury officials revealed these and other findings to Secretary of the Treasury Henry Morgenthau Jr. in a thoroughly documented report entitled "Acquiescence of This Government in the Murder of the Jews."

Morgenthau brought the information to President Roosevelt in January 1944. Roosevelt, recognizing that an explosive scandal was imminent and realizing that the State Department's record would be debated within days when the rescue resolution reached the Senate floor, decided to avoid the impending crisis by accepting Morgenthau's recommendation that he establish a government rescue agency by executive order. The new agency was named the War Refugee Board (WRB).

The WRB received little support from President Roosevelt and his administration. It became largely a Treasury Department operation in collaboration with private Jewish organizations. In planning its rescue programs, the board worked closely with American Jewish groups, and most of its overseas projects were implemented by Jewish organizations in Europe. In addition, government funding for the WRB was very small; consequently, 91 percent of the board's work was paid for by American Jewish organizations.

Some of the board's efforts produced only meager results. Its months-long campaign to persuade President Roosevelt to offer temporary shelter to large numbers of refugees ultimately yielded just one such shelter, for 982 refugees, in upstate New York in 1944. The board's repeated requests to the War Department to order the bombing of either the rail lines leading to Auschwitz or the gas chambers and crematoria themselves were consistently rejected. War Department officials claimed they had undertaken a study of the bombing proposal and found it was militarily unfeasible because it would divert resources essential to the war effort. In fact, no such study had been conducted, and the refusal to bomb Auschwitz was rooted in the War Department's secret decision, back in January 1944, not to use military resources "for the purpose of rescuing victims of enemy oppression." In the months during which these bombing requests were being rejected, more than 2,800 U.S. heavy bombers struck industrial targets within forty-five miles of Auschwitz. Among them were 127 Flying Fortresses that, on August 20, 1944, bombed the Auschwitz industrial complex, *not five miles from the gas chambers*. On September 13, Liberator bombers hit the same industrial complex. On December 18 and also on December 26, American bombers again pounded the Auschwitz industries. The railways or the gas chambers themselves could readily have been bombed had the Allied leadership wanted to do so.

Yet the WRB also had to its credit numerous significant lifesaving achievements. In its sixteen months of action, the board played a crucial role in saving the lives of about 200,000 Jews. About 15,000 were evacuated from Axis territory (as were more than 20,000 non-Jews). At least 10,000, and probably thousands more, were protected within Axis Europe by WRB-financed underground activities, including the safeguarding of holders of Latin American passports. WRB diplomatic pressures, backed by psychological warfare such as radio broadcasts and dropping leaflets warning of Allied retribution for war crimes, were instrumental in bringing about the removal of 48,000 Jews from imminent danger in the Transnistria region of Romania to safe areas in that country. Similar pressures helped end the German deportations from Hungary to Auschwitz, saving 120,000 Jews in Budapest. Nonetheless, as the WRB's director concluded years later,

"What we did was little enough. . . . Late and little, I would say" (Wyman 1984).

America's response to the Holocaust was the result of action and inaction on the part of many people, but in the forefront was Franklin D. Roosevelt. He could have aroused substantial public backing for a significant rescue effort by speaking out on the issue. Even a few forceful statements by the president would have brought the extermination news out of obscurity and into the headlines. But he said little about the problem and gave no priority to rescue. After one brief meeting with Jewish leaders in December 1942 about the recently confirmed news of extermination, he refused Jewish requests to discuss the crisis and even left the White House to avoid the rabbis who marched in Washington in October 1943. He gave the State Department free reign with regard to immigration. He established the WRB only when he was forced to do so by the pressure on Capitol Hill and by the danger that a major scandal would erupt over the State Department's persistent obstruction of rescue.

Roosevelt's response to the Holocaust was deeply affected by political expediency. Because there was considerable opposition to immigration, much of it rooted in antisemitism, a prorefugee stance could have lost him votes. In addition, the overwhelming majority of Jewish voters were strongly attached to the Democratic Party and were virtually certain to support FDR as they had in previous elections. Thus, an active rescue policy appeared to offer Roosevelt little political advantage. Still, the United States has a long and noble tradition of concern for the oppressed, and Roosevelt in particular portrayed himself as the champion of people in need. In the end, however, the era's most prominent symbol of humanitarianism turned away from one of history's most compelling moral challenges.

David S. Wyman and Rafael Medoff

References and Further Reading

Breitman, Richard, and Alan M. Kraut. 1987. *American Refugee Policy and European Jewry, 1933–1945.* Bloomington: Indiana University Press.

Leff, Laurel. 2005. *Buried by the Times: The Holocaust and America's Most Important Newspaper.* New York: Cambridge University Press.

Medoff, Rafael. 1987. *The Deafening Silence: American Jewish Leaders and the Holocaust.* New York: Steimatzky-Shapolsky.

Penkower, Monty Noam. 1983. *The Jews Were Expendable: Free World Diplomacy and the Holocaust.* Urbana: University of Illinois Press.

Penkower, Monty Noam. 1994. *The Holocaust and Israel Reborn: From Catastrophe to Sovereignty*. Urbana: University of Illinois Press.

Wyman, David S. 1968. *Paper Walls: America and the Refugee Crisis, 1938–1941*. Amherst: University of Massachusetts Press.

Wyman, David S. 1984. *The Abandonment of the Jews: America and the Holocaust, 1941–1945*. New York: Pantheon.

Wyman, David S., and Rafael Medoff. 2002. *A Race against Death: Peter Bergson, America, and the Holocaust*. New York: The New Press.

Zucker, Bat-Ami. 2001. *In Search of Refuge: Jews and U.S. Consuls in Nazi Germany, 1933–1941*. London: Vallentine Mitchell.

Holocaust Survivors and Their Children in America

The fourth wave of Jewish immigration to America, namely, that of the *she'erit hapletah*, the surviving remnant of the destruction of European Jewry, is part of the collective memory of American history, for America is a land of immigrants (Wieseltier 1993). From liberation until the early 1950s, approximately 150,000 Jewish Holocaust survivors were given refuge in the United States. This figure does not include German Jews who escaped the Third Reich in the 1930s or those who miraculously fled German-occupied countries and arrived in the United States before 1945. In subsequent decades, the Holocaust survivor population was augmented by thousands of others who fled to the United States from Poland, Hungary, Romania, Czechoslovakia, and other countries, and more recently from former republics of the Soviet Union. Although initially silenced, at the beginning of the twenty-first century the Holocaust survivors are encouraged and applauded for being vocal and visible. As a result, the contributions of Holocaust survivors and their heirs to America and American Jewish life have been immeasurable.

At the end of World War II, the U.S. government was not eager to be flooded with Europe's refugees. In December 1945 Josef (Yosel) Rosensaft, former inmate of Auschwitz and Bergen-Belsen and leader of the survivors in the Belsen displaced persons (DP) camp and in the British Zone of Germany, was the first survivor invited to address the United Jewish Appeal (UJA) in Atlantic City, New Jersey. His impassioned speech galvanized the American Jewish community to allocate funds and manpower to aid the remnants of European Jewry.

While each wave of Jewish immigrants was discriminated against to some extent by the previous wave, Holocaust survivors were shunned and told to forget about the past. The presence of Holocaust survivors in the late 1940s made some American Jews uneasy because they were a reminder of what could happen in America if the current already high level of antisemitism were to intensify. American Jews were reminded of the complacency or silence of many in their community when millions of Jews were being killed. Survivors felt so ostracized that, in Cincinnati and Pittsburgh, they felt compelled to form their own synagogue and community center.

In the 1940s, 1950s, and 1960s, artistic expressions of the persecution of Jews in German-occupied Europe were not embraced by the Jewish community or by American audiences. *Long Is the Road*, a feature film made in the DP camps in 1948, was considered too graphic for American audiences. Most of the film shows life after the liberation. It was shortened and used by the UJA as a fund-raising tool to raise money for Israel for a very brief period. *The Juggler*, with Kirk Douglas (1953), also did not have much of an audience. This film focuses on the aftermath of the Holocaust and portrays the survivor with all his emotional wounds, including post-traumatic stress disorder, the symptoms of which were not understood at the time. *The Diary of Anne Frank* was published in 1957, but its Jewish component was minimized. John Hersey's *The Wall* (1950) and Leon Uris's *Mila 18* (1961) had wider audiences because of their heroic narratives.

In 1961 the Eichmann trial had a major impact in Israel, but this was not the case in the United States, where Jewish leaders were concerned that all the gruesome details would exacerbate antisemitism. To preempt this backlash, Jewish defense agencies worked to present the Eichmann trial in a univeralistic language of hatred and totalitarianism.

In 1973, when the Warsaw Ghetto Resistance Organization (WAGRO) attempted to organize a community-wide Holocaust commemoration, major synagogues that were approached in New York City refused it space. The organized community retained the earlier frame of mind of not emphasizing the destruction. Religious institutions were also concerned that if one dwelt on the *Hurban* (Destruction), God's existence would be questioned and other theological issues raised that would detract from faith and practice. The handful of organizers eventually held the event in Carnegie Hall with well-known actors and dignitaries. In 1975, however, New York's prestigious Temple Emanu-El volunteered its sanctuary for the annual commemoration because of the success of the previous star-studded events.

For the most part, survivors healed themselves by joining *landsmanshaftn* or establishing groups that derived from their experiences during the Nazi years—for example, various partisans groups and the survivors of the Lodz ghetto. The World Federation of Bergen-Belsen Associations (WFBBA) was the first of this genre; it was established by Josef Rosensaft, Norbert Wollheim, and Sam Bloch after the survivors of that concentration and DP camp had resettled in Israel, the United States, Canada, and elsewhere. Rosensaft's foresight helped instill a sense of hope and created a new extended family for most survivors, who had lost everything.

The American Jewish community remained in denial about the destruction of European Jewry until the late 1970s. When Elie Wiesel's novel *Night* was published (in France in 1958) in the United States in 1960, only his close friends took note. The WFBBA honored him with its Remembrance Award in 1965. But when he spoke at one of the first Holocaust commemorations, at a synagogue in Riverdale, New York, in the late 1960s, only a handful of people—mainly survivors—came. In 1972 Elie Wiesel taught his first Holocaust course at City College in New York. It was not until President Jimmy Carter appointed Elie Wiesel chair of the President's Commission on the Holocaust in 1978 and, later, chair of the United States Holocaust Memorial Council that his voice began to have moral power. The survivor community was at last becoming visible in America. The council also included other prominent survivors, seated next to members of the House of Representatives—including Tom Lantos (D-CA), a survivor from Hungary—policymakers, academics, business executives—such as Miles Lerman, Sigmund Strochlitz, and Benjamin Meed, who chairs the American Gathering of Jewish Holocaust Survivors (AGJHS)—and Abraham Foxman, head of the Anti-Defamation League (ADL).

With the televising of Gerald Green's docudrama *Holocaust* in 1978, the survivors' pain, suffering, and losses were validated. This validation gave survivors permission to start talking about their ordeals. In 1979 Yaffa Eliach, a historian and child survivor, started the first oral history project at a Center for Holocaust Studies, Documentation and Research in Brooklyn, currently housed at the Museum of Jewish Heritage in New York. Her students at Brooklyn College interviewed local survivors, liberators, and rescuers. In 1981 Judith and Milton Kestenberg started an International Study of Organized Persecution of Children under the auspices of Child Development Research. Holocaust child survivors were interviewed worldwide. In 1994, the Eliach interviews and the Kestenberg interviews (currently housed at Florida Atlantic University) became models for the Steven Spielberg Survivors of the Shoah Foundation's interviews (housed at the University of Southern California).

To give Holocaust survivors a greater voice, some 5,000 survivors and their children gathered in Jerusalem in 1981. The World Gathering of Holocaust Survivors was conceived of in Auschwitz by Ernest Michel, the head of the New York United Jewish Appeal-Federation, and his fellow Auschwitz survivor, Pise, who had emigrated to a kibbutz in Israel. This gathering captured the world's attention, with coverage by television crews, filmmakers, and newspaper reporters. Participants and observers reported that the event restored the dignity survivors had lost during the years of persecution and genocide. The World Gathering was the catalyst for the establishment of the American Gathering of Jewish Holocaust Survivors (AGJHS), led by Benjamin Meed, Sam Bloch, Norbert Wollheim, and Roman Kent. In 1983, the AGJHS organized a gathering of more than 10,000 survivors and their children in Washington, D.C. Many described this gathering as giving the survivors a feeling of belonging to the United States. To be personally thanked for their contributions to American society by President Ronald Reagan was a healing experience of the highest order.

In the mid-1980s, Dr. Judith Kestenberg, Milton Kestenberg, and Eva Fogelman started meetings for child survivors of the Holocaust in New York; these meetings developed into the National Association of Jewish Child Holocaust Survivors, Inc. (NAHOS). Meetings also mushroomed in Los Angeles, Chicago, Baltimore–Washington, and Miami. National conferences are now held annually.

Myriam Abramowicz, director of the film *As If It Was Yesterday* (on the rescue of children in Belgium), sought to unite all those who were hidden as children during the German occupation. With seed money from the Kestenbergs's

Child Development Research, hidden-child survivors were found worldwide. In 1991 a historic gathering took place in New York City under the auspices of the newly formed Hidden Child Foundation of the ADL.

With growing international and national recognition of the survivors' resilience and achievements, the organized Jewish community started embracing survivors as spokespersons for communal causes and charities. Survivors helped raise funds for institutions in Israel, working with the American Friends of Yad Vashem and the American Friends of Beth Hatefutsoth, the Museum of the Diaspora in Tel Aviv.

The academic rabbinical colleges have benefited from the wisdom of a few surviving scholars. Alfred Gottschalk made a mark as chancellor of Hebrew Union College (HUC); Abraham Joshua Heschel of HUC and later the Jewish Theological Seminary (JTS), author of such classics as *The Sabbath,* was also a prominent civil rights activist. Heschel accompanied the Reverend Martin Luther King Jr. on the march from Selma to Montgomery (1965). Columbia University Professor David Weiss Halivni founded the Academy for Traditional Judaism and recorded his war experiences in *The Book and the Sword.*

Holocaust survivors are represented in all areas of American life. Louis Begley, a prominent New York attorney, also succeeded as a novelist and became president of PEN. Jerzy Kosinski was a social psychologist who became a world-class novelist. Gerda Weissmann Klein, who married her liberator, an American Jewish soldier, won an Academy Award for a film based on her life story. Among the survivor artists are Joshua Neustein, Ephraim Peleg, Ruth Rintel, Samuel Bak, and Irene Lieblich, who illustrated Isaac Bashevis Singer's *A Tale of Three Wishes* and *The Power of Light: Eight Stories for Hanukkah.* Andrew Grove, a child survivor from Hungary, was head of the Fortune 500 company Intel. Dr. Henry Krystal, an Auschwitz survivor, became a prominent psychoanalyst. In academia, Randolph Braham, a distinguished professor at the Graduate Center of the City University of New York, has written definitive works on Hungarian Jewry. Nobel laureate Elie Wiesel pioneered Holocaust studies at the City College of New York in 1972.

The major contribution of the survivor generation in the United States was in Jewish education. Survivors built and supported Jewish schools in order to reestablish the link to the European Jewish community that was de-stroyed. Without the driving force of the remnants of European Jewry, *yeshivot* and other Jewish day schools would not have flourished in the twenty-first century.

Continuity, for Holocaust survivors, also meant ensuring biological continuity. Indeed, in the mid- to late 1970s, young adults in America whose parents had survived Nazi persecution realized a collective identity of their own. Despite their heterogeneity, they share the bond of a shattered family heritage. Those born after liberation have diverse religious backgrounds, political attitudes, and socioeconomic and educational levels. Although the circumstances of their parents' survival varied, they all suffered immeasurable loss of community, family, and identity. Whether survivors talked about their dehumanization and grief or remained silent, their losses were nonetheless reflected in the socialization of their children.

The emergence of a second-generation consciousness and the development of an identifiable group had its origin in the larger "roots" movement in the United States in the mid-1970s, in the increasingly manifest antisemitism in Europe in the early and mid-1980s, and in the restored dignity of Holocaust survivors in Israel.

It was during the social, religious, and political activism of the late 1960s and early 1970s that a number of Jewish graduate students began exploring what it meant to be children of Holocaust survivors. They shared the dynamics of the relationships with their parents, a worldview as children of survivors, and different perceptions from those of their Jewish American peers. These early discussions appeared in the *Bergen-Belsen Youth Magazine* (1965), edited by Menachem Rosensaft, and in *Response* (1975), a forum for alternative Jewish views, edited by William Novak. These discussions inspired psychiatric social worker Bella Savran and psychologist Eva Fogelman to develop awareness groups for children of Holocaust survivors. Independently, WAGRO persuaded its children to meet and form the Second Generation Organization in New York City. Psychoanalysts in New York formed the Group for the Psychoanalytic Study of the Effects of Second Generation, and after much resistance, the American Psychoanalytic Association agreed to have a study group for this population. These heretofore small and invisible group efforts achieved national visibility in Helen Epstein's watershed *New York Times Magazine* article, "Heirs to the Holocaust" (June 19, 1977). In the spring of 1979, Epstein's *Children of the Holocaust: Conversations with Sons and*

Daughters of Survivors continued to galvanize these young adults to talk to each other.

Several grassroots efforts facilitated the meetings of children of survivors, which reduced their sense of isolation and increased their ability to reach political, educational, psychological, commemorative, and creative goals. In 1979 the first major event was the First Conference on Children of Holocaust Survivors, held under the auspices of Zachor, a unit of the National Jewish Resource Center, CLAL. More than 600 children of survivors attended, and the conference resulted in the formation of groups and organizations throughout the United States. More than 1,000 children of survivors joined their parents in Jerusalem in 1981 at the World Gathering of Holocaust Survivors and took a pledge at the Western Wall to commemorate, educate, work toward preventing future genocides, and ensure Jewish continuity. Following this gathering, the children of the survivors established their own umbrella organization, the International Network of Children of Jewish Holocaust Survivors, under the leadership of Menachem Rosensaft, a New York attorney born in the Bergen-Belsen DP camp.

Among many Second Generation members, there is a sense of moral authority that comes from confronting the injustice of the Holocaust and the silence or complicity of the peoples of the world. Through the International Network, children of survivors as a group became a moral voice in the American Jewish community and in the international political arena. Menachem Rosensaft wanted to make sure that the Second Generation would not be introverted but would also recognize human and social issues affecting the community as a whole. Thus, the International Network was the first group to organize a rally in New York City (1982) on behalf of Ethiopian Jewry. Rosensaft also led the opposition to President Reagan's decision to visit the German military cemetery at Bitburg in 1985. The International Network consistently and vocally opposed the president's laying of a wreath at the graves of members of the Waffen-SS in Bitburg. On May 5, 1985, Rosensaft led a demonstration of Second Generation members at Bergen-Belsen against what he called Reagan's "obscene package deal" of Bitburg and the mass graves of Bergen-Belsen. The International Network was also instrumental in ensuring the deportation of Nazi war criminal Karl Linnas to the Soviet Union in 1987. Beginning in 2000, Rosensaft has spearheaded the Holocaust Survivors Memoirs Project, an initiative of Elie Wiesel, which collects and publishes the memoirs of Holocaust survivors jointly with Yad Vashem in Jerusalem.

Other children of survivors lend their voices on behalf of a range of causes. The social and literary critic Leon Wieseltier of *The New Republic* has spoken on behalf of the memory of the Holocaust dead. When the issue of the Carmelite convent and crosses at Auschwitz was raised in 1988, Wieseltier wrote, "It appears that Auschwitz has lost none of its power to derange. Nobody dies there anymore; but decency still does" (*New York Times,* September 3, 1989).

Social science research directly or indirectly related to the destruction of European Jewry reflects the commitment of Second Generation scholars to remember the past and its consequences. More than 150 children of survivors have written doctoral dissertations on the psychological results of growing up with Holocaust survivor parents. Others have written about the Holocaust and its aftermath in fiction, plays, screenplays, poetry, and nonfiction. Actors, singers, directors, filmmakers, media stars, and visual artists have drawn on their Holocaust family backgrounds to sensitize audiences to what happened to the Jewish people and others who were persecuted during the German occupation. They include Aviva Kempner, producer and cowriter of *Partisans of Vilna;* Annette Insdorf, author of *Indelible Shadows: Film and the Holocaust;* television news correspondent Wolf Blitzer; author and performance artist Lisa Lipkin; actor and writer Mark Ethan; singer and songwriter Billy Joel; singer and actress Rosalie Gerut; filmmaker Menachem Daum; director Steve Brandt; and author, psychologist, and filmmaker Eva Fogelman.

Other Second Generation adults find meaning by educating the next generation about inhumanity. As a result of the efforts of Rositta Kenigsberg of Miami's Documentation and Education Center, Holocaust education is mandatory in Florida. In the United States, Holocaust centers, whose main mission is education, are flourishing because of Second Generation adults.

Because Holocaust survivors now receive the public recognition they deserve, the Second Generation has been empowered to identify with their parents not only as victims but as human beings who had lives before the destruction of European Jewry. This identification is now channeled into socially constructive programs that perpetuate Jewish continuity and make a difference in the world for all.

Eva Fogelman

References and Further Reading

Burstin, Barbara Stern. 1989. *After the Holocaust: The Migration of Polish Jews and Christians to Pittsburgh.* Pittsburgh, PA: University of Pittsburgh Press.

Epstein, Helen. 1979. *Children of the Holocaust: Conversations with Sons and Daughters of Survivors.* New York: G. P. Putnam's Sons.

Fogelman, Eva. 1984. *Breaking the Silence: The Generation after the Holocaust.* Produced by Edward A. Mason and Eva Fogelman. Waltham, MA: National Jewish Film Center, Brandeis University.

Helmreich, William. 1992. *Against All Odds.* New York: Simon & Schuster.

Hoffman, Eva. 2004. *After Such Knowledge: Memory, History, and the Legacy of the Holocaust.* New York: Public Affairs.

Insdorf, Annette. 2003. *Indelible Shadows: Film and the Holocaust.* 3rd ed. New York: Cambridge University Press.

Novick, Peter. 1999. *The Holocaust in American Life.* Boston: Houghton Mifflin.

Peck, Abraham J., and Uri D. Herscher. 1989. *Queen City Refuge: An Oral History of Cincinnati's Jewish Refugees from Nazi Germany.* Springfield, NJ: Behrman House.

Pilcer, Sonia. 2001. *The Holocaust Kid.* New York: Persea Books.

Wieseltier, Leon. 1993. "After Memory." *The New Republic* (May 3).

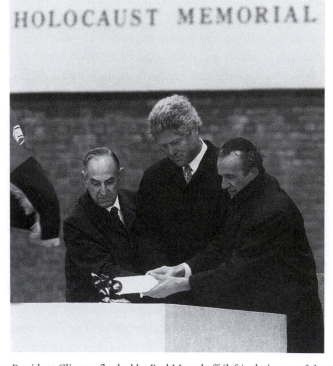

President Clinton, flanked by Bud Meyerhoff (left), chairman of the U.S. Holocaust Memorial Council, and Elie Wiesel (right), founding chairman of the U.S. Holocaust Memorial Council, light an eternal flame during the dedication ceremony for the U.S. Holocaust Memorial Museum in Washington D.C., April 22, 1993. (AP/Wide World Photos)

The Making of the United States Holocaust Memorial Museum

April 22, 1993, witnessed the highly publicized opening of the United States Holocaust Memorial Museum adjacent to the nation's ceremonial center, the Washington Mall. The opening of the museum brought to fruition a fifteen-year struggle begun during the administration of President Jimmy Carter.

The idea for a federally sanctioned Holocaust memorial in the United States came about because of political realities and popular interest. Politically, the Carter administration was deeply concerned about increasingly frayed relations with the American Jewish community, and understood commitment to some kind of Holocaust memorial as a part of a larger attempt to heal the rift as well as an appropriate act of remembrance for aging Holocaust survivors and American liberators.

Culturally, by the late 1970s, the Holocaust had become a benchmark of evil. Holocaust survivors—notably Elie Wiesel, who would receive the Nobel Peace Prize and

would become chairman of both the President's Commission on the Holocaust and the United States Holocaust Memorial Council—had become popular witnesses, offering testimony about their experiences that held "lessons" for a society fascinated and frightened by the specter of genocide. Increasing attention to the Holocaust in American popular culture converged with the Carter administration's concerns. On May 1, 1978, President Carter announced the formation of the President's Commission on the Holocaust, tasked with recommending an appropriate national Holocaust memorial.

From the beginning, almost everything was a "razor's edge" issue. There was bitter contestation over representation on the commission: How many Jews? What about representatives of Eastern European nations that had both been victims of Nazi terror *and* killed Jews? Should the working definition of the Holocaust focus on the sacred number "six million" Jews, or the more universalist "eleven million" (Jews and "other" victims)?

After a commission trip to Holocaust sites in Eastern Europe and to Israel, on September 27, 1979, Elie Wiesel presented the group's report to President Carter in the Rose Garden of the White House. The report made four major recommendations: the creation of a "living memorial," including a museum, educational outreach, and a committee on conscience to warn about ongoing acts of genocide; the creation of an annual civic ritual of Holocaust remembrance, "Days of Remembrance of Victims of the Holocaust"; the ratification of the Genocide Treaty; and, largely because of their experiences in Eastern Europe, the commission asked that the State Department urge foreign governments to care for the oft-neglected ruins of Jewish cemeteries.

On May 2, 1980, the United States Holocaust Memorial Council—the commission's successor body—began its work. Throughout the history of this project, there have been two major challenges: issues of location of Holocaust memory in the United States and issues of representation of Holocaust memory. The first issue regarding location was whether or not the Holocaust was in any way an American memory and whether or not it was appropriate for there to be a federally sponsored and supported memorial. Some argued that the Holocaust should certainly be remembered at sites throughout Europe and in Israel but that it was a memory "out of place" in the United States. Further, they argued, there was a troublesome fascination among many who were interested only in how Jews were murdered. Rather than a memorial to the Holocaust, they argued, what about an institution that celebrated the rich history of Judaism in the United States, an institution that focused on life rather than death?

Supporters of a Holocaust memorial responded that thousands of survivors came to the United States, that several thousand American soldiers encountered and liberated the western camps and brought these memories home with them, that many perpetrators had also fled to the United States, and that the nation had a complex relationship—complicit bystander as well as liberator—to reflect upon. A Holocaust memorial, they argued, could be not only a site of mourning but also a site from which the transformative power of Holocaust education would spread and a site that would remind visitors what can happen when democracies fail.

Once it was decided that there would be a federal Holocaust memorial, the Council faced the challenge of deciding where, in what city, and what *kind* of memorial. Some survivors thought New York City was the most ap-

propriate location, given its large Jewish population. Others argued for Washington, D.C, the nation's capital. Once it was selected, a number of different sites in the city were considered, among them the Auditor's Complex adjacent to the Washington Mall, next to the Bureau of Printing and Engraving, which would become the site of the museum.

For many survivors, locating the institution at the ceremonial core, alongside the narratives of war and politics expressed on the mall, meant that the Holocaust would take its place as a central American narrative, and federal sponsorship and support offered them solace, in the face of Holocaust denial, that the United States government would remember the reality of the Holocaust. For survivors, of utmost importance were both this guarantee of remembrance and the sentiment that the museum was a symbolic burial site for Holocaust victims.

Yet another issue of location was the physical shape of the institution. In 1984, the Council received permission to tear down old annex buildings on the site and then struggled with several architectural designs that did not evoke enthusiasm. Finally, in 1986, the distinguished New York City architect James Ingo Freed was hired to design the museum. Moved by his own trip to Auschwitz, Freed believed that the building itself had to be, in his words, "expressive of the event." There was pressure from some members of the Commission of Fine Arts for Freed to "soften" his building; nevertheless, the highly praised design located and housed Holocaust memory in an eloquent, brooding design that brings visitors to the nation's center and then displaces them from that center as they ride elevators to the fourth floor to begin their descent through three floors of an intense Holocaust exhibition.

Throughout the planning of the permanent exhibition, those tasked with its creation struggled with the challenge of Holocaust representation. With what photographs does one begin? If they are too horrifying, will it dissuade visitors from continuing? If they do not adequately express the horror of the Holocaust, will they be untrue to the event? Does the display of genitalia victimize the dead yet again? If Nazi music, flags, and speeches are seen and heard, will they perhaps move some visitors to a dangerous identification with the perpetrators and not the victims? How should the exhibition represent perpetrators? Do Nazi ghetto photographs allow visitors to view the dying and dead in the ghetto only through the eye of the perpetrator? Should the exhibition fully and frankly talk about

Christian complicity in the Holocaust, or would this upset too many visitors, who bring with them an understanding that religion is, by definition, a force for good, not evil? What kinds of material artifacts should be used? Does the inclusion of a Polish railcar of the type used to transport Jews to Treblinka, part of a women's barrack from Auschwitz, prisoner's uniforms, a huge pile of shoes from Majdanek, a canister of Zyklon-B gas, a mass of eyeglasses, for example, help American visitors touch the reality of the Holocaust, or are these volatile artifacts that should never have been allowed to defile American shores? Should the exhibition display women's hair brought to the museum from Auschwitz, or was this too personal, too sensitive? (Eventually, the museum's director, Shaike Weinberg, honored the commemorative sensibilities of several female survivors who deeply objected to plans for this display, and the hair is not included in the permanent exhibition.)

Another issue of representation revealed an enduring tension in the museum project: the relationship between Jews and "other" victims. Was the Hall of Remembrance, the hexagonal memorial space, a place for ritual remembrance of all Holocaust victims, or just Jews? Should the permanent exhibition inform visitors about the Armenian genocide as a precursor to the Holocaust, or would this dilute the museum's commitment to being specifically a Holocaust museum and lead inexorably to a transformation of the museum into one of comparative genocide? How should the exhibition represent various groups of victims: homosexuals, the mentally retarded, non-Jewish Poles, and Gypsies, for example?

Since this was a United States Holocaust Memorial Museum and not a private Jewish museum, commitment to the pluralistic imperative was not in doubt. Nevertheless, the tensions not only over who received attention in the exhibition but who owned the "right" to the means of production, who got to tell the story, were revealing.

The museum is, in Shaike Weinberg's words, a "storytelling" museum, and the intense narrative, shaped by film and video, text, photographs, and artifacts, is designed to bring about civic transformation: ideally, visitors will experience this intense story and emerge "born again," sensitized to the evils of antisemitism, racism, and other ills of the time. The museum is a model of an activist memorial environment, and subsequent institutions, notably the Oklahoma City National Memorial, are modeled after it.

Since opening in 1993, the museum has offered a rich variety of public programs and educational outreach programs and resources. The Center for Advanced Holocaust Studies offers fellowships and seminars. Several exhibitions, including "Remember the Children: Daniel's Story," "Varian Fry, Assignment: Rescue 1940–1941," and "The Nazi Olympics Berlin 1936," have toured the nation. Public programs have focused not only on a variety of Holocaust-related subjects but on issues of contemporary genocide as well. Programs have included, for example, such topics as "Homophobia and Sexual Politics in Nazi Germany," "The Churches and the Holocaust," "Second-Generation Holocaust Literature," "The Nazi Persecution of Deaf People," "Crisis in Sudan," "The Modernity of Genocide: Race, War and Revolution in the Twentieth Century," and "Freedom on Fire: Human Rights Wars and America's Response." There continue to be presentations by authors and a chamber music series focusing, the museum's website informs, not only on pieces that "convey themes related to Holocaust history," but also featuring "works by composers who suffered under the Nazi regime, or whose works were banned during the Nazi era."

The museum continues active collections programs of artifacts, documents, photographs, oral histories, and film footage. Also, the President's Commission's original vision of a Committee on Conscience, envisioned as a body to warn policymakers and the public about ongoing or possible acts of genocide, was realized only in 1995.

Policymakers were not keen on an independent institution injecting itself into foreign policy, nor were some—who were convinced that the Holocaust was a "unique" event—eager to blur the boundaries between the Holocaust and contemporary genocides. In 1995, however, the committee was created. In 2001, Rabbi Irving Greenberg, chairman of the United States Holocaust Memorial Council, declared that the committee was "intended to be the expression of a memory that is committed to improving the world. Its function is to reassert the witness of those who were killed and of those who went before us that life is meaningful and that the world will yet be redeemed" (Greenberg 2001). Whether—and how—the museum can influence foreign policy, whether it can transform what has been enduring policy indifference to genocide, remains an open question.

The United States Holocaust Memorial Museum, like similar institutions around the world—Holocaust museums and education centers, the Gulag Museum in Russia, the District Six Museum in South Africa, for example—has become part of an ever-expanding civic landscape of conscience, an institution that is much more than just a museum, a forum as well as a shrine. It freezes a shattering moment in recent history as a warning. Its existence is an enduring and compelling protest against the anonymity of mass death in the twentieth century.

Edward T. Linenthal

References and Further Reading

Berenbaum, Michael. 1993. *The World Must Know: The History of the Holocaust As Told in the United States Holocaust Memorial Museum.* Boston: Little, Brown.

Greenberg, Irving. 2001. "Remembrance and Conscience: A Sacred Bond." http://www.ushmm.org/conscience/analysis/details.hp?content+2001-12-05&menupage=History+%26+Concept (accessed February 7, 2007).

Linenthal, Edward T. 2001. *Preserving Memory: The Struggle to Create America's Holocaust Museum.* 2nd ed. New York: Columbia University Press.

Novick, Peter. 1999. *The Holocaust in American Life.* Boston: Houghton Mifflin.

Stier, Oren Baruch. 2003. *Committed to Memory: Cultural Mediations of the Holocaust.* Amherst: University of Massachusetts Press.

Weinberg, Jeshajahu, and Rina Elieli. 1995. *The Holocaust Museum in Washington.* New York: Rizzoli.

Young, James. 1993. *The Texture of Memory: Holocaust Memorials and Meaning.* New Haven, CT: Yale University Press.

Meyer Levin was responsible for bringing Anne Frank's diary to the attention of the English-speaking public. (Corbis)

Meyer Levin (1905–1981)

Reporter, Novelist, Filmmaker

Meyer Levin spent a lifetime trying to understand what it meant to be a Jew in secular America, to live in the shadow of the Holocaust, and at the time of the establishment of Israel, the first Jewish nation in over two and a half millennia. He viewed his life as embedded in this pivotal historical moment, and Levin not only wrote about the events that were reshaping world Jewry but experienced some of them firsthand. Most known for bringing Anne Frank's diary to the attention of the English-speaking public, Levin also wrote numerous novels, plays, and film scripts. In his

memoir *In Search* (1950), he explicitly stated the themes on which his work focused, the themes that shaped his life. He sought to examine and "follow . . . out the sometimes conflicting elements of the Jewish question within myself," as well as to explore "my relationship to America" and "to the world."

Levin was born to East European immigrant parents in Chicago on October 8, 1905. His father managed to lift the family out of poverty only for brief moments. Levin later wrote of his youth and that of his friends, all first-generation American Jews, in his thinly fictionalized novel set in Chicago, *The Old Bunch* (1937). In some one thousand pages, he traced how the Bunch made their way from penury and embarrassment over their parents' foreign ways to tentative positions in middle-class America—only to see their hard-won places lost in the Depression. Having abandoned their cultural heritage and youthful ideals for a place at the American table, they were now also left spiritually afloat. It had been too great a sacrifice. Though he, too, had been briefly tempted, in the end Levin had refused to follow their course.

Entering the University of Chicago at fifteen, Levin became a reporter for the Chicago *Daily News* while still a student and remained there for a year after graduation. After experimenting with puppetry (including script, set design, and performance) as a new means of expression, in 1925 he moved to Paris to study painting. There he met Marek Swarcz, a Hasidic Jew turned sculptor and the soon-to-be-outcast member of the Jewish Artists' Circle of Montparnasse. Swarcz sought the fulfillment of traditional messianic promises in a strain of Catholic mysticism then gaining influence among a small coterie of Parisian artists and intellectuals. Levin was drawn to the Hasidic tales his mentor related to him, a side of Judaism and Jewish life he had never known, but dismissed his Christological interpretations. With the publication of *The Golden Mountain* (1932), Levin brought these tales to the attention of the larger world, Jew and gentile alike.

Having experienced 1920s Paris and found some of the spiritual meaning for which he was searching, he returned to Chicago and his job at the *News.* But just as his first novel, *Reporter* (1929), was about to appear, he sailed for Palestine to seek out another part of the puzzle. A second, less distinguished work of fiction, the love story *Frankie and Johnnie* (1930), was published while he was living on a collective farm there. Out of this experience came *Yehuda* (1931), the first fictional account of life in the *yishuv* by an American Jew. It signaled Levin's lifelong concern for the Zionist enterprise, which culminated in 1959 in his partial resettlement in Israel.

The move was partial because he could never fully leave America or disengage from the larger Western struggle for social, political, and economic justice. Returning to Chicago, Levin not only continued to address Jewish issues of assimilation, cultural survival, Zionism, and increasing antisemitism, but also became involved in the general social activism of his time. As a writer and reporter for *The Nation, Esquire,* and *Saturday Evening Post,* he joined a number of protests, culminating in his active role in the bloody Republic Steel strike in Chicago in 1937. He expressed his outrage at the murder of several strikers by the authorities in what some consider his finest novel, *Citizens* (1940).

In 1934, Levin married Mabel Scamp Foy, who shared his socialist ideas as well as his love of puppetry as a medium of protest. They went to Spain during that country's civil war, although she returned to the United States in the late stage of her pregnancy. Now on his own, he found journalistic camaraderie on the battlefield with Martha Gellhorn and her husband, Ernest Hemingway. But as a Jew, Levin (more clearly than many of his colleagues) recognized the broader implications of the struggle against fascism being waged in Spain.

When the United States entered the war against the Axis powers in 1941, Levin joined the Office of War Information as a filmmaker. Later he worked as a war correspondent, first for the Overseas News Agency, then for the Jewish Telegraphic Agency. In this latter capacity, he participated in the liberation of a number of concentration camps, including Dachau and Buchenwald, often riding in the lead jeep ahead of the troops. Overwhelmed by what he found, he went from camp to camp accompanied by a survivor photographer, filing countless dispatches based on interviews with survivors and compiling lists of their names in an effort to reunite families and friends as he crisscrossed the area, moving from one location to another.

Levin never recovered. His exposure to the horrors of the Holocaust shaped, distorted, and clouded his life until his death nearly four decades later. Unwilling merely to record events, he was fully engaged in the struggle to ensure that such a catastrophe would never again befall his people. It was in the wake of these efforts that *In Search* (1950) emerged, detailing his smuggling of survivors through the British blockade and into Palestine. He drew on this experience in his semidocumentary film, *The Illegals* (1948), and his Zionist novel, *My Father's House* (1947), which chronicled a survivor's life in the camps and subsequent journey to recovery in Palestine. Levin produced Israel's first feature film, based on this novel, for which he wrote the screenplay.

Levin's most life-altering experience occurred when he was introduced to the diary written by a young Jewish victim from Holland, Anne Frank. Her stirring voice communicated the tragedy of the Holocaust more powerfully and poignantly than the works of those who had not experienced it directly. Levin succeeded in bringing the diary to the English-speaking world, but his subsequent struggle to stage her story failed, despite the promise of Anne's father,

Otto, that he could dramatize it. *Obsession* (1973) is Levin's account of his efforts. Mostly accurate in its basic outline of how he had been prevented from presenting the play, Levin's book revived the controversy that had surrounded the production two decades earlier and opened him once again to accusations of mental instability and Red baiting. It was, in fact, the misuse of the diary that had driven Levin to distraction and depression during these years, forever upsetting his four children—the son from his first marriage, the stepdaughter from his second (to Tereska Torres, Marek Swarcz's daughter, whom he had first met when he was an art student in Paris and she a small child), and the two sons he and Torres had together. Much to Levin's distress, Lillian Hellman, a Stalinist, in keeping with Soviet antisemitic policies, engineered the cutting of nearly all the Jewish content from the diary by feeding her handpicked playwrights a long series of changes throughout the dramatization process. Theatrical profit-seekers among her circle of friends further Americanized the characters and story line by overly emphasizing domestic tensions. The Holocaust now played so insignificant a role that critics commented that the Pulitzer Prize–winning play hardly differed from any dramatization of adolescent-parent conflict. Levin successfully sued Otto Frank, the playwrights, and the play's producer for plagiarizing portions of his original playscript, but he never received the acknowledgment he deserved. Nor was Anne Frank recognized for the subtlety and complexity of her thoughts as a consciously Jewish victim questioning God's justice and the world's inhumanity.

Levin obsessively sought allies in his fight to produce his dramatization of the diary, although, as part of a settlement reached during the endless series of appeals by the deep-pocketed defense, in frustration he had signed away his rights. Nonetheless, he continued to be a highly productive writer. He wrote his most popular work, *Compulsion* (1956), a fictionalized account of the Leopold and Loeb Chicago murder case of 1924, which was adapted for the stage and then made into a film. With the exception of his final book, only *Compulsion* was not centered on the themes he had set out in *In Search*. Everything else was about Zionism and Israel, the Holocaust, or Jewish history and culture both religious and secular. Even when well written, the more than a dozen works that followed—among them *Eva* (1959), *The Fanatic* (1964), *The Stronghold* (1965), *The Story of Israel* (1967), *Gore and Igor* (1968), *The Haggadah, Retold* (1968), *The Settlers* (1972), *The Spell of Time* (1974), and *The Harvest* (1978)—were received at best tepidly by critics. Levin became convinced that the same literary crowd that had undermined his efforts with the diary was now blacklisting him. Increasingly, he spent his time at his home in Israel, though each year he made extended trips to New York and Paris.

Still, Levin returned to Chicago for his final authorial effort, on a completely non-Jewish subject, a novelistic account of a figure based on Frank Lloyd Wright entitled *The Architect*. Published a few weeks after his death on July 9, 1981, by the time he wrote the book, Levin had come full circle. Although a curious choice of subject, it was perhaps his final attempt to reach out to the wider world and call for its reconstruction. It was, he seemed to say, not enough for the Jews alone to rebuild their community. All the world had this need, and the Jews' self-restoration could serve as encouragement toward this larger end. As he had earlier written in *In Search*, "[t]he example of Jewish history in the past few years can give courage to all of humanity."

Ralph Melnick

References and Further Reading

Melnick, Ralph. 1997. *The Stolen Legacy of Anne Frank: Meyer Levin, Lillian Hellman, and the Staging of the Diary*. New Haven, CT: Yale University Press.
Rubin, Steven Joel. 1982. *Meyer Levin*. Boston: Twayne.

Jewish Organizations

The Workmen's Circle

In its heyday, the Workmen's Circle, founded in New York in 1892, was a major fraternal order. It was established by East European Jewish immigrants and initially attempted to woo potential members not only by offering mutual aid benefits but also by sponsoring educational activities.

Though the organization proclaimed early on that German would be the language in which meetings were conducted and in which publications would appear, Yiddish rapidly became the language in which the Workmen's Circle conducted most of its activities. Many of the early members were sympathetic to socialism. The Workmen's Circle was not, however, formally affiliated with a political party, and in its early years it attracted anarchists and other critics of the existing order as well as socialists.

In 1900 the Workmen's Circle—with a total of 300 members in three branches—reorganized as a nationwide order and entered a period of rapid growth. By 1910 membership stood close to 39,000; five years later, at almost 50,000.

Particularly visible among those who became members in the post-1905 era were a number of onetime adherents of the Jewish Workers' Bund. The Bund, established in the Russian Empire in 1897, had a Marxist, anti-Zionist, and anti-clerical orientation and played a significant role in the Russian Revolution of 1905. The crushing of that revolution led some Bundists to flee Russia for the United States; many eventually became activists in the Workmen's Circle.

The earliest leaders of the Workmen's Circle tended to be cosmopolitan and generally thought of Yiddish as at best a tool through which to reach rank-and-file members. The Bundists, however, had a somewhat stronger Jewish consciousness and supported the development of secular Yiddish culture. While the Workmen's Circle had non-Bundist members (and some Labor Zionist and other anti-Bundist members), by the 1920s a number of the major national offices within the Workmen's Circle were filled by former members of the Bund.

Members of the Workmen's Circle were intimately involved in the development of the trade union movement, including the International Ladies Garment Workers Union (organized in 1900) and the Amalgamated Clothing Workers of America (created in 1914). The Workmen's Circle, which supported strikes and organizing efforts by these and other unions, became known as "the Red Cross of the labor movement"—and was proud of this nickname. The Declaration of Principles adopted by the order in 1922 underscored that "every member of the Workmen's Circle should belong to the union of his trade" (Hurwitz 1936).

During a crucial period in its history, the Workmen's Circle was highly supportive not only of the unions but also of the Socialist Party. Membership in the Jewish Socialist Federation—the Socialist Party's Yiddish-language section from 1912 to 1921—overlapped with that of the Workmen's Circle. This helps to explain why the Workmen's Circle played a pivotal role in the election campaigns of Meyer London, the Workmen's Circle's attorney, who repeatedly ran for Congress on the Socialist ticket. In 1915, when the Socialist Party took an uncompromising stand against World War I, the Workmen's Circle followed suit.

One did not have to be a Socialist to be a member of the Workmen's Circle, but support of bourgeois parties put one beyond the pale. In 1901 a member was expelled from the order for supporting the Republican Party.

Determined to express solidarity with all like-minded people, the Workmen's Circle never restricted its membership to Jews. Norman Thomas, the non-Jewish, long-term leader of the Socialist Party, for example, was a member at one point. During the Nazi era, the Solidaritaet Branch of the Workmen's Circle—Branch 424E—included non-Jewish social democratic refugees and exiles from the German-speaking lands.

In an attempt to combat tuberculosis, a scourge among working-class immigrants at the beginning of the twentieth century, the Workmen's Circle opened a sanatorium, which operated from 1910 to 1955. The Workmen's Circle also created a medical department and offered numerous other services to members.

In 1918, the Workmen's Circle opened the first of what eventually became a network of Jewish secular schools for children. The schools, which were supplementary rather than day schools, initially stressed study of the Yiddish language, Jewish history, "the life of the workers," and "the struggle for freedom in world history" (Trunk 1976). In 1939 there were 125 elementary schools, 5 high schools, and 17 additional entities offering high school classes in the Workmen's Circle school network, with an enrollment of approximately 8,000. The Workmen's Circle established summer camps, a mandolin orchestra, choruses, and a dramatic society; it also sponsored lectures and supported concert tours.

Though the Workmen's Circle had been formed in part because its founders perceived that existing *landsmanshaftn* (mutual aid organizations made up of immigrants from the same town, city, or region) did not meet the needs of politically aware workers, many branches of the Workmen's Circle were organized along the same lines as the landsmanshaftn. Many branches consisted of individuals from the same part of Eastern Europe.

Membership in the Workmen's Circle peaked at approximately 85,000 in 1920–1926. Changes in American immigration law, however, cut off the supply of immigrants from Eastern Europe, impeding the continued growth of the order. The organization was also hurt by sharp differences of opinion within its ranks over the policies of the Communist Party.

The Workmen's Circle was initially sympathetic to the Soviet regime, as reflected in its organ, *Der fraynd (The Friend)*. Though the Workmen's Circle was critical of the Soviet government's repression of non-Bolshevik socialists, in December 1922 the order expressed "greetings and brotherly wishes to the Russian soviet regime on its fifth anniversary" (Hertz 1950). Support for the American Communist Party and for the pro-Bolshevik Workers' Party of the United States (founded in December 1921) was far more controversial. A large majority of the leading figures in the Workmen's Circle's New York schools and in Camp Kinderland (established by Workmen's Circle school activists in 1923) was sympathetic to the Communist Party (or to the Workers' Party). Many other Workmen's Circle activists were bitterly opposed. Throughout much of the 1920s, the Workmen's Circle's national leadership attempted to avoid a definitive rift between the order's right- and left-wing members. In 1929, however, thousands of the pro-Communist members left the Workmen's Circle. Shortly thereafter, these men and women helped to create a rival group—the International Workers' Order.

By then, the Workmen's Circle's membership had declined to just over 70,000. The Great Depression also made it difficult to attract new members or to retain existing members. By 1939 the average age of Workmen's Circle members was over forty.

The Workmen's Circle was exceptionally active in antifascist and anti-Nazi activities in the years leading up to and during World War II. In 1934, representatives of the Workmen's Circle participated in the founding meeting of the Jewish Labor Committee (which went on to aid numerous anti-Nazi and antifascist refugees) and continued to play a significant role in that group in the following years. In 1937 the Workmen's Circle also provided direct material support to the anti-Nazi underground and became involved with the Joint Anti-Nazi Boycott Council. It purchased a considerable quantity of war bonds during

World War II and was recognized for this by having bombers stenciled "Spirit of the Workmen's Circle."

The antiwar position taken by the Socialist Party in the period preceding Japan's attack on Pearl Harbor ultimately led the order to distance itself from the party. The Workmen's Circle declined to endorse Norman Thomas, the party's candidate for president in 1940. A year later, the order formally refused to permit a Socialist Party representative to greet the Workmen's Circle's convention.

When they entered the armed forces during World War II, many young Jews who had been educated in Workmen's Circle schools or who had attended Workmen's Circle summer camps left the inner-city immigrant neighborhoods of their youth and never returned. Those who did return were estranged, in a number of instances, not only from the Socialist Party but also from socialist ideals. While the Workmen's Circle continued to make room in its ranks for social democrats and democratic socialists and formally echoed its earlier commitments to socialism in the latter half of the 1940s, the positions it adopted in the post–World War II decades were generally liberal, not radical—closer to those of the Democratic Party than the Socialist Party.

Bundist (anti-Zionist) sentiment also became weaker within the order, particularly after the founding of the State of Israel. The Workmen's Circle has been consistently supportive of Israel—it has repeatedly encouraged members to purchase Israel bonds and has arranged tours of Israel for its members. At the same time, it has remained officially non-Zionist in its orientation, because it did not—and does not—agree with what it perceived as the derogation of Yiddish by the Zionist mainstream, and because it did not—and does not—endorse the Zionist goal of immigration by all Jews to the Jewish state.

The leadership of the Workmen's Circle attempted to adapt to new circumstances—to the geographic dispersion of the Jewish population and its linguistic acculturation. While the order continued to disseminate *Der fraynd,* in 1933 it also began to issue an English-language organ, the *Call.* In the years after World War II, branches and supplementary schools were created in suburban areas. However, a variety of factors, especially the diminution in the size of the American Jewish working class, made the Workmen's Circle less attractive to post–World War II youth than it had been to previous generations of American Jews. The average age of the order's members was 55 in 1969, and total membership did not exceed 60,000 in the 1970s.

In recent years, the Workmen's Circle has completed its transition from an immigrant-based group to a group of primarily American-born Jews. Though the school system of the Workmen's Circle is no more than a shadow of the system that existed decades ago, a handful of supplementary schools maintain their affiliation with the order. The Workmen's Circle currently operates one summer camp for children (Camp Kinder Ring), a summer resort for adults, and several homes for the elderly. It agitates on behalf of liberal or left-of-center political positions and fosters ties with like-minded organizations, including the Forward Association, the Jewish Labor Committee, the Congress for Jewish Culture, and the Folksbiene Yiddish Theater. Recently, the Workmen's Circle has stripped itself of some of its traditional functions, such as selling insurance policies, putting somewhat greater emphasis on cultural and political programming and less on mutual aid benefits. Though originally the Workmen's Circle did not have explicitly Jewish goals, it now underscores its Jewish identity and highlights that it is "dedicated to Jewish community." It is a major bastion of those committed to sustaining and developing secular Yiddish culture.

Membership in the organization has declined steadily and is now fewer than 20,000. Nevertheless, the Workmen's Circle currently has branches in a number of major American Jewish communities and has modest pockets of strength in New York, Boston, and elsewhere.

Jack Jacobs

References and Further Reading
Epstein, Melech. 1969. *Jewish Labor in the U.S.A.: An Industrial, Political, and Cultural History of the Jewish Labor Movement.* 2 vols. n.p.: Ktav.
Hertz, J. S. 1950. *50 yor arbeter-ring in yidishn lebn* [50 years of the Workmen's Circle in Jewish Life]. New York: Der natsionaler ekzekutiv-komitet fun arbeter-ring.
Howe, Irving. 1976. *World of Our Fathers.* New York: Harcourt Brace Jovanovich.
Hurwitz, Maximilian. 1936. *The Workmen's Circle: Its History, Ideals, Organization and Institutions.* New York: The Workmen's Circle.
Liebman, Arthur. 1979. *Jews and the Left.* New York: John Wiley and Sons.
Shapiro, Judah J. 1970. *The Friendly Society: A History of the Workmen's Circle.* New York: Media Judaica.
Trunk, Isaiah. 1976. "The Cultural Dimension of the American Jewish Labor Movement." *YIVO Annual* 16: 342–393.
Zaks, A. Sh. 1925. *Di geshikhte fun arbeter ring 1892–1925* [The History of the Workmen's Circle 1892–1925]. 2

vols. New York: Der natsionaler ekzekutiv komite[t] fun arbeyter ring.

The Jewish War Veterans of the United States of America

The Jewish War Veterans of the United States of America (JWV), established under that name in 1929, grew out of earlier Jewish veterans' organizations, the first of which, the Hebrew Union Veterans Association (HUVA), was formed in 1896 by Jews who had served in the Union army during the Civil War. The JWV, like its predecessors, focused not merely on veterans' concerns but on distinctively Jewish issues. The HUVA protested against antisemitism before the founding of the major Jewish defense organizations—the American Jewish Committee (AJC), the Anti-Defamation League, and the American Jewish (AJ) Congress. Almost immediately after Hitler assumed power in Germany, the JWV called for aggressive mass demonstrations against Nazism and a boycott of German goods. Its combative approach led to confrontations in which its members exchanged blows in the streets with domestic fascists. The JWV formally backed the establishment of a Jewish state in Palestine in 1942 and strongly supported Israel after it became a nation in 1948. After World War II, the JWV criticized West Germany's leniency toward Nazi war criminals. During the 1960s, it opposed the mainstream Jewish organizations' quarantine policy of avoiding public clashes with the American Nazi Party, which was intended to deny it publicity. The JWV was the only veterans' organization to openly align itself with the African American civil rights movement. Of the major Jewish organizations, it offered the steadiest support for the Vietnam War, shifting to a critical stance only in 1971.

The JWV's earliest predecessor, the HUVA, was established at a meeting of Jewish Union army veterans in New York in 1896 at a time of rising antisemitism. In the Christian and Islamic worlds, Jews were frequently depicted as cowardly, were denied officers' commissions in some national armies, and were sometimes even prohibited from bearing arms. Extensive American press coverage, which began in 1894, of the arrest and trials in France of Captain Alfred Dreyfus, who was falsely accused of selling military secrets to Germany, focused attention on antisemites' long-

Logo for the Jewish War Veterans of the United States. (Jewish War Veterans of the United States)

standing efforts to impugn Jews' patriotism. The HUVA was determined to publicize and honor the significant participation of Jews in all of America's wars.

In 1904–1905 the HUVA erected a monument in Brooklyn to Jewish soldiers who died fighting for the Union during the Civil War; this monument became the nation's preeminent Jewish military memorial. At the unveiling, legendary General Nelson Miles, of Indian Wars fame, commanding general of the U.S. Army during the Spanish-American War, praised Jewish soldiers' bravery and Jews' unparalleled contribution to world civilization.

The outbreak of the Spanish-American War in 1898 sparked intense patriotic display among American Jews, a significant proportion of whom had recently immigrated from Eastern Europe. Many Jews considered the conflict a war of revenge against Spain for its expulsion of Europe's largest Jewish population several centuries before and for the Inquisition's torture of conversos and Jews. The press described a "wonderful war excitement" in such cities as New York and Chicago among Russian Jews, who clamored to go to Cuba "rifles in hand" (*New York Times,* May 1, 1898). In New York, prominent philanthropist Nathan Straus chaired a meeting called to organize two Jewish regiments to fight the Spaniards. When the battleship *Maine* exploded in Havana harbor, 15 Jews died; and more than

4,000 served in the armed forces during the Spanish-American War, many of them participating in combat in Cuba and the Philippines. Several of Theodore Roosevelt's Rough Riders were Jews.

Jewish Spanish-American War veterans established their own organization immediately after the war, which soon took the name Hebrew Veterans of the War with Spain (HVWS). The HVWS and the HUVA joined to express public outrage over the Kishinev pogrom in Bessarabia in 1903 and urged President Theodore Roosevelt, an honorary HVWS member, to issue a strong official protest to Russia's czarist government. HVWS head Maurice Simmons, also briefly national commander of the United Spanish War Veterans (USWV), damaged his chances of being reelected to the latter office by pressing for the desegregation of USWV posts. In the period immediately preceding U.S. intervention in World War I, Simmons protested the refusal of several New York National Guard units to accept Jews.

After World War I, in which Jews served in numbers higher than their proportion in the American population, recently demobilized Jewish veterans joined with those of the Civil War and the Spanish-American War in a new Hebrew Veterans of the Wars of the Republic (HVWR). This organization included Jewish veterans of the Boxer Rebellion, the Philippines campaigns, and General Pershing's 1916 incursion into Mexico, as well as Americans who had joined the Jewish Legion of the British army, which had fought the Turks in Palestine during World War I. In such cities as New York and Boston, large numbers of Jewish veterans participated in mass protest parades and assemblies against the postwar pogroms in Poland, Galicia, Rumania, and the Ukraine. The HVWR was also concerned with ensuring that Jewish soldiers killed in action in World War I who had been buried in France had a Star of David marking their graves rather than a cross. The HVWR renamed itself Jewish Veterans of the Wars of the Republic (JVWR) in 1924 and began issuing a newsletter, *The Jewish Veteran*, in 1925, which is still published today as a magazine. *The Jewish Veteran* has devoted much attention to publicizing Jews' significant combat role in America's wars and to condemning antisemitism in Europe and the Middle East.

The JVWR, renamed the Jewish War Veterans of the United States of America in 1929, focused on mobilizing American opposition to the Nazis almost immediately after they assumed power in Germany in January 1933. The JWV was the first Jewish organization to call for a boycott of German goods, in March 1933. It participated in picketing stores and assembled information on where to find products that could be substituted for those from Germany. In April 1933, the JWV strongly criticized both the AJC and the AJCongress, which initially opposed the boycott, alleging they were overly cautious, even timid. The JWV claimed that the AJC's strategy for combating Nazism involved "cringing, begging, and praying," while the AJCongress's leadership had become too "old [and] . . . conservative" to speak effectively for Jews (Delman 1933). In March 1933, the JWV led the first mass street demonstration against Nazism, in New York. After the march, JWV leaders appeared at the British consulate, calling for that government to waive immigration quotas to Palestine so that Jews could escape from Germany. The JWV spoke out against the decision of many American universities to send delegates to Nazi Germany in 1936 to help celebrate the University of Heidelberg's 550th anniversary, and against American participation in the Olympic Games in Berlin that year. It also protested the 1939 New York World's Fair's invitation to Nazi Germany to set up a pavilion.

After World War II, in which the rate of American Jews' armed forces participation again surpassed that of the nation's population as a whole, the JWV engaged in efforts to combat racial and ethnic discrimination. It lobbied for a postwar fair employment commission, supported armed forces desegregation, and, alone among national veterans' groups, joined in the civil rights March on Washington in 1963.

During the 1950s and 1960s, the JWV strongly opposed U.S. government support for paroling Nazi war criminals, including Waffen SS general Sepp Dietrich, commander of Hitler's bodyguard. Known as the "Butcher of Malmédy," Dietrich was responsible for the execution of several hundred American prisoners of war during the Battle of the Bulge. In 1964–1965, the JWV protested West Germany's plan to impose a statute of limitations that would prevent prosecution of Nazi war criminals still at large. It drew attention to Egypt's harboring of Nazi war criminals, who, as scientists and technicians, worked to develop advanced weaponry for use in the Arab nations' war against Israel. In 1985 the JWV denounced President Reagan's laying of a wreath in a German military cemetery at Bitburg where Waffen SS soldiers were buried. In the same year, it sharply criticized members of an American World War II infantry division who staged a reunion with German Waffen SS veterans.

Stephen H. Norwood

References and Further Reading

Delman, J. David. 1933. "Haman, 'Yemach Shemoh'!" *The Jewish Veteran* (April).

Mosesson, Gloria R. 1971. *The Jewish War Veterans Story.* Washington, DC: The Jewish War Veterans.

Norwood, Stephen H. 2004. "Legitimating Nazism: Harvard University and the Hitler Regime, 1933–1937." *American Jewish History* 92 (June): 189–223.

Raymond, Harry. 1954. "300 Years of Fighting for Freedom." Jewish War Veterans, 59th National Convention. Archives, National Museum of American Jewish Military History, Washington, DC.

Simonelli, Frederick J. 1999. *American Fuehrer: George Lincoln Rockwell and the American Nazi Party.* Urbana: University of Illinois Press.

Spivak, Michelle, and Robert M. Zweiman, eds. 1996. *The Jewish War Veterans of the U.S.A.: One Hundred Years of Service.* Paducah, KY: Turner Publishing.

The American Jewish Committee

The American Jewish Committee (AJC) is the oldest Jewish defense organization in the United States, established in 1906 "to prevent the infraction of the civil and religious rights of Jews, in any part of the world." Growing directly out of concerns about conditions in czarist Russia, especially the 1903 Kishinev pogrom, the AJC was one response to the search for a central representative organization of American Jews.

The Committee initially consisted of a small group drawn from the established German Jewish community, who had migrated in large numbers to the United States beginning in the 1830s. As German Jews became well established, they wanted to be able to respond to matters of concern on behalf of American Jews. Its founders included Jacob Schiff, Mayer Sulzberger, Louis Marshall, Oscar Straus, and Cyrus Adler, men prominent within the German stratum of the Jewish community, and who, out of a sense of *noblesse oblige,* combined philanthropic activities and *hofjude* ("court Jew") diplomacy on behalf of their fellow Jews. Oligarchic in design, the Committee—literally, a "committee"—limited its membership to 60 American cit-

izens (expanded by 1931 to 350), with offices in New York, and remained a small group for many years. The AJC was self-selected and had a sense of the "elitism" of the German Jewish community.

Two ideas have characterized the work of the AJC throughout its history. First, the notion of stewardship, the idea that a Diaspora-based group of Jewish stewards—a "committee"—could enhance the collective welfare of the Jewish people; second, in recent decades, the notion that no "defense" agency is effective unless it promotes as well the internal vitality of the Jewish people. In this second objective, the AJC carved out a path that was different from its fellow defense groups.

The AJC's agenda shifted in response to changing developments, from a focus early in the twentieth century almost exclusively on the condition of Russia's Jews to antisemitism and immigration policy in the United States, to the destruction of European Jewry, to (1950s and 1960s) civil rights and the concerns of pluralism and ethnic identity, and finally to Israel and international affairs.

Public affairs informed the agenda of the AJC from its beginnings. The plight of Russian Jewry before World War I prompted the AJC's strong defense of a liberal American immigration policy. In 1911 the Committee conducted a successful campaign for the abrogation of the Russo-American treaty of 1832. Not only did the AJC object to the Russian discrimination against the entry of American Jews into Russia, which it considered a violation of the treaty, but it hoped that by its abrogation Russia would inevitably be compelled to free its own Jews. At the outbreak of World War I, the AJC sparked the organization of the American Jewish Relief Committee, which set up a central relief fund for Jewish war victims.

Opposed to the idea of a democratic and nationalist American Jewish movement presenting the Jewish demands to the Paris Peace Conference in 1919, under public pressure the Committee nonetheless joined the first American Jewish Congress (AJCongress) there. However, the minority rights secured for Jewry in the new successor states of Europe were largely the result of the work of Julian Mack, Louis Marshall (who served as AJC president from 1906–1929), and Cyrus Adler, who operated as individual intercessors in Paris. The Committee welcomed the 1917 Balfour Declaration, but—consistent with its anti-Zionist stance, which prevailed almost until the creation of the State of Israel in 1948—underscored the provision that the Declaration would in no way prejudice the liberties of Jews who were citizens of other countries.

During the 1920s, the Committee centered its attention on domestic matters in the United States. It fought the popular "Jew-Communist" charge circulated in the infamous *Protocols of the Learned Elders of Zion* and further propagated in Henry Ford's *Dearborn Independent*. Marshall, as president of the Committee, formulated the terms for Ford's retraction of his antisemitic campaign in 1927. The approach of the AJC, both strategically and tactically, differed sharply from that of the AJCongress, which was more confrontational and which relied—especially after 1945—on litigation as a primary vehicle for social action. The AJC's approach reflected Louis Marshall's idea that discreet lobbying best served the interests of American Jews. This nonconfrontational strategy reflected the fear that the AJC would be perceived as a "Jewish lobby" with interests at odds with those of other Americans.

The rise of Nazism led to intensified activities on two fronts. In an effort to ameliorate the situation of German Jewry, the AJC applied pressure upon the Roosevelt administration, the Vatican, the League of Nations, and even individual German officials. The objective of halting the Nazis through aroused public opinion failed, and the AJC turned increasingly to plans of rescue and emigration for German Jews. The outbreak of the war halted independent operations, leaving the fate of Jewry contingent upon the Allied war effort. Upon learning of the mass murders, the Committee, along with other American organizations, staged protests and appealed for concrete assistance from the Bermuda Conference on Refugees (1943). The Committee also cooperated in the efforts of the War Refugee Board. Simultaneously, the AJC fought the alarming rise in organized antisemitism in America, emphasizing education and "prejudice-reduction" programs. In developing new techniques both to measure and to influence general and Jewish opinion, the Committee discarded the traditionally apologetic Jewish reaction to antisemitism and demonstrated that antisemitism is used to undermine the foundations of democratic society. The AJC also investigated the operations of virulent hate groups and disclosed their connections to the Nazi regime. The AJC pioneered an approach to combating antisemitism in the communities, promoting the idea that every Jewish community needed to have a "volunteer fire brigade" to counter antisemitism.

While the AJC joined the Zionists in protesting Britain's curtailment of immigration into Palestine as a result of the White Paper, the AJC denounced the concept of "Diaspora nationalism" inherent in the programs of the AJ Congress and the World Jewish Congress. Any Jewish nationalist position, especially Zionism, was abhorrent to the avowedly anti-Zionist, German Jewish leadership of the Committee. The AJC hoped that the future of Jewry would be secured by universal recognition of human rights to be protected by the United Nations (UN), and it lobbied for an international commitment to that principle in 1945 at the San Francisco Conference at which the UN charter was prepared. By 1946 the Committee realized that the problem of the displaced persons could be solved only by the creation of a Jewish state, and, modifying its traditional anti-Zionist stance, it cooperated with Zionist groups in advocating the partition of Palestine into Jewish and Arab states.

After 1948 the Committee worked consistently to ensure American sympathy and diplomatic aid to the State of Israel, and by agreement with Israeli statesmen, it officially kept Israel's interests distinct from those of Diaspora Jewry. This dynamic was exemplified in the 1950 "entente" between Israeli prime minister David Ben-Gurion and AJC president Jacob Blaustein following reports that Ben-Gurion had called for large-scale immigration to Israel by American Jewish youth. Ben-Gurion acknowledged that American Jews "have only one political attachment, to America," and in effect admitted that the "ingathering of exiles" as a central Zionist principle did not apply to American Jewry.

The AJC also assumed a role in several extended projects relating to the Holocaust: prosecution of Nazi war criminals, material restitution by Germany to the Jewish community, and rehabilitation of Jewish cultural life within Europe. In the postwar period the Committee concentrated on combating the persecution of Jews within the Soviet orbit and documented Kremlin-inspired antisemitism. The eruption of antisemitism in the Muslim countries and South America involved the Committee in tasks of relief and emigration with respect to the former and tasks of self-defense in the latter.

After World War II, the AJC expanded markedly in size and function. A chapter plan adopted in 1944 slowly changed the oligarchic cast and elitist control of the organization. The AJC's approaches to litigation as a vehicle for achieving its goals changed as well. The Committee had long believed that litigation was confrontational and would damage the interfaith relationships that Jews had formed. Louis Marshall's view was that individuals, not groups, were constitutionally protected from prejudicial action. (The ADL, by contrast, maintained that Jews had every right to oppose group defamation.)

A turning point came in 1943 when John Slawson became AJC executive. He believed that, consistent with the AJC tradition of viewing rights for Jews as part of the larger struggle for rights for all minorities, the AJC needed to be transformed into a vibrant civil rights agency. From 1947 on, the AJC participated, through litigation, educational campaigns, and community projects, in the black struggle for equal rights. Work to break down the barriers in education, housing, employment, and public accommodations led to pioneering efforts against anti-Jewish discrimination in clubs, fraternities, and the "executive suite."

The AJC's focus on human relations resulted in new approaches to intergroup cooperation and intercultural education. It labored successfully for the revision of prejudiced teachings about Jews in Christian textbooks and for the historic papal declaration on the Jews—*Nostra Aetate*—approved by the Second Vatican Council in 1965. The Committee consistently emphasized the need for research in the behavioral sciences to guide its action program. It sponsored the "Studies in Prejudice" series. The watershed volume *The Authoritarian Personality* (1950) emphasized the psychological, rather than the socioeconomic, forces at work in group prejudice. The annual *Survey of American Jewish Public Opinion,* conducted by the Market Facts agency, provides valuable data for social scientists and policymakers.

The Six Day War (1967) convinced the AJC that it should not be on the sidelines during a fateful period of Jewish history. Thus began the "mainstreaming" of the AJC.

In terms of institutional dynamics, during the 1960s and 1970s, under the stewardship of executive directors John Slawson and especially Bertram Gold, the AJC resembled not a single agency but a collection of related fiefdoms, each directed by a leader in his respective field. Collectively they contributed to the shaping of the contemporary community-relations agenda: Marc Tanenbaum in interreligious relationships; Yehuda Rosenman in Jewish communal affairs; and Hyman Bookbinder, the highly visible director of the AJC's Washington office, in

contouring the agency's public-affairs agenda. Milton Himmelfarb shaped the AJC's research agenda and edited the *American Jewish Year Book.*

Since the early 1980s, the AJC has redefined its mission and function. Following a period of institutional and financial instability, in 1990, with David Harris as the new executive director, the AJC turned aggressively toward the international arena, positioning itself, in effect, as an international diplomatic corps for the Jewish people. By joining the Conference of Presidents of Major American Jewish Organizations (the designated voice of the organized American Jewish community on Israel and other international matters) in 1991, the AJC signaled that international affairs now had primacy on its agenda. The AJC's leadership had long avoided formal affiliation with the Presidents' Conference, in early years because the conference adhered to a Zionist and Israel-based agenda to which the AJC did not subscribe; more recently, because the Committee's agenda was focused on domestic issues.

In recent years, with the decline of antisemitism in the United States and full acceptance of Jews into American society, the AJC's agenda has expanded beyond matters of defense to include questions of Jewish continuity.

Jerome A. Chanes

References and Further Reading

Chanes, Jerome A. 1991. "The Voices of the American Jewish Community." In *Survey of Jewish Affairs 1991.* London: Institute for Jewish Affairs.

Cohen, Naomi W. 1972. *Not Free to Desist: The American Jewish Committee, 1906–1966.* Philadelphia: Jewish Publication Society of America.

Schachner, N. 1948. *The Price of Liberty: A History of the American Jewish Committee.* New York: AJC.

Svonkin, Stuart. 1997. *Jews against Prejudice: American Jews and the Fight for Civil Liberties.* New York: Columbia University Press.

Zelin, Richard David. 1992. "Ethnic and Religious Group Politics in the United States: The Case of the American Jewish Committee, 1982–1987." PhD dissertation, University of Wisconsin.

The Anti-Defamation League

The Anti-Defamation League (ADL) was founded in 1913 in response to rampant antisemitism and discrimination against Jews in the United States. Although antisemitism was pervasive in mid-nineteenth-century America, as waves of Jewish immigrants arrived in the late nineteenth and early twentieth century, private prejudice and social ostracism escalated into public ridicule, stereotyping, discrimination, and contempt. Sigmund Livingston, a lawyer, believed that such bigotry, if left unchallenged, would lead to more virulent and violent forms of Jew-hatred. Believing that equality must apply to all Americans, ADL's founders—the Independent Order of B'nai B'rith—outlined a mission in its charter: "to stop the defamation of the Jewish people . . . to secure justice and fair treatment to all citizens alike . . . to put an end forever to unjust and unfair discrimination against and ridicule of any sect or body of citizens."

In 1881, at age nine, Livingston emigrated from Germany with his parents, settling in Bloomington, Illinois. After receiving a law degree from Illinois Wesleyan University, he practiced law from 1894 to 1926. Offended by the portrayal of Jews in the arts and the press, in 1908 he suggested to B'nai B'rith, the Jewish fraternal organization, that a group be formed for the purpose of "eliminating the caricaturing and ridiculing of the Jew in literature, art, drama, and the press."

The ADL began in 1913 in Livingston's law office in Chicago with a $200 budget. The same year a Jew, Leo Frank, was unjustly convicted in an Atlanta court of the murder of a young girl in the pencil factory he managed. Though, in 1915, Governor John Slaton commuted Frank's death sentence to life imprisonment after conducting a thorough investigation into the evidence, which convinced him of Frank's innocence, a mob broke into the jail, dragged Frank from his cell, and lynched him. The Frank case dramatically underscored the threat of antisemitism in America and the need for an organization to combat it, providing an impetus for the ADL's growth. In the 1980s, an eyewitness to aspects of the crime came forward, revealing the murderer to be factory janitor Jim Conley, and the ADL succeeded in obtaining a posthumous pardon for Frank.

Early on, the ADL took several steps to combat the negative images of Jews in print and the stereotyping of Jews on stage and in film. The League was still in its infancy when Adolph S. Ochs, publisher of the *New York Times,* joined the ADL in writing a memo to newspaper editors nationwide discouraging the use of "objectionable and vulgar" references to Jews.

With the coming of World War I, antisemites targeted Jews as cowards, "slackers," and "war-profiteers," responsible for many of the country's ills. A U.S. Army manual read, "Foreign born, especially Jews, are more apt to malinger than the native born" (Dinnerstein 1994). The ADL protested to President Woodrow Wilson, who ordered the entire edition destroyed. The ADL also provided Americans with the facts about Jews' military and civilian contributions to the war effort.

During the 1920s, the ADL began using the weapon of exposure to battle the bigotry of the Ku Klux Klan. The Klan boycotted Jewish merchants, vandalized their stores, and burned crosses outside synagogues and other Jewish institutions. In 1923, the KKK Imperial Wizard condemned Jews as an "absolutely unblendable element" (*Time,* November 5, 1923).

The League protested Henry Ford's circulation of the antisemitic forgery, *The Protocols of the Learned Elders of Zion,* which he reprinted in his newspaper, *The Dearborn Independent.* The ADL countered with *The Protocols—A Spurious Document* and *The Poison Pen,* pamphlets by Sigmund Livingston targeting *The Dearborn Independent.* The League called on Woodrow Wilson and William Howard Taft to denounce Ford's antisemitism. After years of calumny, Ford publicly apologized to the Jewish people. In a letter to the ADL's Livingston, he expressed hope that "hatred of the Jews, commonly known as anti-Semitism, and hatred against any other racial or religious groups, shall cease for all time" (Baldwin 2002). Despite his apology, Ford continued to promote antisemitism during the pre–World War II period, maintaining close ties with Nazi Germany and claiming that "international financiers"—a euphemism for Jews—wanted war.

Antisemitism was also expressed in classified ads that openly discriminated against Jews in employment and housing. Colleges, universities, and medical, professional, and graduate schools imposed quotas limiting the admission of Jews. The ADL educated the public about discrimination and the quotas and sought legal remedies not just for Jews but for all minorities.

A major strain of antisemitism emanated from the Christian community through propagation of the charge that Jews killed Jesus. This was reinforced by Cecil B. DeMille's 1928 film, *The King of Kings.* The portrayal of Jews as responsible for the death of Jesus led to an immediate outcry from Jewish organizations, some Catholics, and others. The ADL met with representatives of the producers, who eventually agreed to some revisions. In addition to making the suggested changes to titles and scenes, DeMille inserted a foreword in which he exculpated the Jews for the death of Jesus.

During the Great Depression, an array of anti-Jewish forces emerged in Europe, and Hitler's rise to power provided the impetus and often the money for a variety of American fascist groups. The German-American Bund, led by Fritz Kuhn, paraded in swastikas, waved Nazi flags, and ardently peddled its antisemitic message. In February 1939, it held a mass rally in New York's Madison Square Garden. The Catholic priest Charles E. Coughlin, leader of the pro-fascist Christian Front, reached a mass audience through his antisemitic radio broadcasts and his publication *Social Justice*, which was filled with anti-Jewish screeds, including *The Protocols of the Elders of Zion*. Throughout the decade, the ADL, laboring under a small budget, tried to awaken Americans to the danger represented by the groups whose antisemitism masked a virulent hatred of democracy.

The ADL joined a coalition to produce a monograph that analyzed Coughlin's propaganda. The monograph thoroughly refuted Coughlin's antisemitic charges and showed that one of his articles was lifted verbatim from an earlier speech by Nazi propagandist Joseph Goebbels. This evidence of Coughlin's sympathy for Nazism helped discredit him in the eyes of many Americans.

During the 1930s, the ADL began a fact-finding operation to monitor and investigate the rapidly multiplying fascist groups in the United States, amassing a vast storehouse of credible information on extremist individuals and organizations. It exposed the links of several of them to Nazi Germany.

In the post–World War II period, the ADL sought the enactment of civil rights laws. The League fought against discrimination in housing, employment, and education, waging a successful "crack the quota" campaign against anti-Jewish discrimination in college and university admissions. The ADL filed its first amicus curiae brief with the U.S. Supreme Court in 1947 in *Shelley v. Kramer*, in which the Court held that restrictive covenants in housing were unenforceable. The ADL also began its effort to reform the harsh immigration quotas that had prevented the rescue of many European Jews during the Holocaust.

Exploring new frontiers in social and judicial reform, the League filed its first church/state-related amicus brief in 1948 in *McCollum v. Board of Education*, in which the ADL questioned the constitutionality of released time for religious instruction held in public school classrooms. Since then, the ADL has been amicus in practically every major church/state case, consistently arguing for the separation of church and state. At the same time, the League has championed every American's right to the free exercise of religion.

On May 14, 1948, as a result of the decision of the United Nations to partition Palestine, the State of Israel was born, bringing hope to a people shattered by the Holocaust. Holocaust survivors began rebuilding their lives in the fledgling Jewish state. Yet the Jewish homeland became the target of a new movement—anti-Zionism. Arab anti-Jewish sentiment intensified as a result of the existence of the new state; others who had previously scorned Jews for being stateless now excoriated Jews for having a state.

Citing Israel as their enemy, leaders of Arab states stepped up their antisemitic activity. Egypt's leader, Gamal Abdel Nasser, distributed *The Protocols of the Elders of Zion* to foreign journalists; Syria's longtime minister of defense, Mustafa Tlas, wrote *The Matzoh of Zion*, which claimed that Jews were engaged in ritual murder, a charge embraced by Saudi Arabia's King Faisal. Many also became Holocaust deniers, insisting that the Jews fabricated the Holocaust to take land from Arabs. To counter these charges, the ADL embarked on an educational campaign aimed at government officials, media, and the American people.

At home, the ADL continued its drive to stamp out prejudice and bigotry. When the League learned that the Georgia Ku Klux Klan was planning a revival of its anti-black terror, it joined forces with a sympathetic southern journalist who infiltrated the Klan. For two years, the journalist, using a fictitious name, supplied information to the League, which made it available to law enforcement authorities and the press. This exposure assisted the ADL in securing the passage in southern states of its model statute to unmask the Klan.

In the early 1950s, antisemitism intensified, as Jews were accused of being Communist subversives. President Dwight D. Eisenhower used the ADL's fortieth anniversary dinner in 1953 to make his first public condemnation of McCarthyism, although he refrained from mentioning

Senator McCarthy by name. Subsequently, the ADL embarked on a campaign against McCarthyism.

During this decade, President Eisenhower signed the first civil rights bill to be passed by Congress since Reconstruction. The ADL joined the struggle for civil rights and filed an amicus brief in the landmark case of *Brown v. Board of Education,* which ended the legality of "separate but equal" schools. The ADL also embarked on a campaign to expose widespread discrimination by resorts and hotels. The League employed the dual-letter test—sending identical letters, one with a Jewish name and one with a non-Jewish name—as well as other methods to prove that many resorts were closed to Jews. In the 1960s the ADL worked hard for the passage of the landmark Civil Rights Act of 1964 and the Voting Rights Act of 1965 as well as for open housing legislation.

Feeding on fears of Communism, a powerful Radical Right movement emerged that used divisive tactics and hurled baseless accusations. Widely read ADL reports and publications revealed the dangerous ideas spread by groups such as the John Birch Society and the Liberty Lobby. When anti-Catholicism emerged as a factor in the 1960 presidential campaign of John F. Kennedy, the ADL countered that bias as well. In 1964 the publication of *Danger on the Right* by ADL general counsel Arnold Forster and ADL national director Benjamin Epstein exposed the Radical Right extremist movement as a threat to American democracy.

In 1964 the ADL commissioned a team of researchers at the University of California to investigate all aspects of antisemitism and prejudice in American life. The study ultimately yielded nine books and numerous other publications and critiques. Documenting prejudice in children, and analyzing political extremism, the impact of the 1961 Eichmann trial on the American public, and other topics, the research underscored the link between religious teachings and antisemitism. Subsequent to the first report, later published as a book, *Christian Beliefs and Anti-Semitism,* the Vatican Council adopted *Nostra Aetate* (1965), a papal encyclical that repudiated collective Jewish responsibility for the death of Jesus and denounced "hatred, persecutions, displays of anti-Semitism, directed against Jews at any time by anyone."

Countering a flood of anti-Zionist Arab propaganda in the aftermath of the Arab-Israeli Six Day War of 1967, the ADL informed the public that the United States and Is-

rael, the sole bastion of democracy in the Middle East, shared common values. Following the Yom Kippur War of 1973, the League intensified its Middle East education program. The ADL condemned the United Nations' notorious resolution equating Zionism with racism (1975) and battled the Arab boycott of U.S. firms doing business with Israel, playing a key role in the passage of the 1977 Anti-Boycott Bill prohibiting American participation in the Arab blacklist.

By the end of the 1970s, the ADL had become an international agency. In addition to regional offices from coast to coast, the League opened offices in Israel and Europe. In the United States, the ADL initiated its *Annual Audit of Anti-Semitic Incidents* in 1979, documenting personal attacks, vandalism, and harassment.

The plight of the millions of Soviet Jews took priority in the 1970s and 1980s. Conducting a media campaign, the ADL created and disseminated materials decrying Soviet violations of human rights and urging the USSR to allow Jews to emigrate to Israel. The League worked with congressional leaders and administration officials on behalf of Soviet Jewish Prisoners of Conscience and tens of thousands of "refuseniks," Jews who had been denied permission to emigrate. In October 1986, at the summit meeting in Reykjavik, Iceland, the American government presented the ADL's publication, *A Uniquely Jewish List: The Refuseniks of Russia,* to Soviet leaders in an appeal for their right to move to Israel.

Countering not just antisemitic acts but all hate crimes, the ADL developed the penalty-enhancement approach for bias-related crimes, which levies an additional penalty for crimes motivated by bias. Continuing its mission to unmask and condemn bigotry, the League exposed the antisemitism of former KKK leader David Duke and Nation of Islam leader Louis Farrakhan.

A growing religious Right movement prompted the ADL to release reports warning that the traditional wall of separation between church and state was becoming "transparent." The ADL filed amicus briefs in cases dealing with Christmas observances in public schools, publicly sponsored sectarian displays, and federal aid to parochial schools.

In December 1987, the Palestinian uprising in the West Bank and Gaza, the "*intifada,*" erupted, prompting a rise in anti-Israel sentiment, especially on college campuses across the United States. The ADL publicized antisemitic incidents on campuses and provided guidelines for students, faculty, and administrators in confronting extremist speakers spreading anti-Israel and anti-Jewish propaganda. When Holocaust deniers flooded campus newspapers with advertisements claiming that the Nazis had not exterminated six million Jews, the ADL exposed the deniers and counseled student editors on the line between upholding free speech and spreading messages of hate.

As the Internet expanded, the ADL recognized that bigots and hate groups utilized it for their ends. Hundreds of hate sites exploded on the Web, many camouflaged to recruit new members, some specifically targeting children. The ADL created an Internet Monitoring Unit to track, document, and expose the bigots while also working with Internet providers to keep hate off their sites. In 1996 the ADL launched its own website—www.adl.org—and in 1998 developed HateFilter® as a tool for parents.

In the 1990s, ADL activities resulted in the enactment by forty-six states and the District of Columbia of hate crimes legislation based on the model statute of penalty enhancement, which the U.S. Supreme Court upheld in 1993. The organization also played a central role in the first White House Conference on Hate Crimes, held at George Washington University in November 1997.

As terrorism escalated in the 1990s, the ADL provided expert testimony to Congress and urged states to enact anti-paramilitary training laws. Six months before the 1995 Oklahoma City bombing, an ADL report, *Armed and Dangerous: Militias Take Aim at the Federal Government,* alerted the nation to the growing menace of antigovernment extremist groups.

Religious intrusion into public life increased significantly in the late 1990s with attempts to pass a so-called Religious Freedom Amendment, which the ADL argued violated the First Amendment. The proposed amendment would have allowed teachers to organize and supervise religious activities during school hours, would have permitted tax dollars to flow to parochial schools, and would have promoted the display of religious objects, such as crosses, in courtrooms.

The ADL introduced "Confronting Anti-Semitism: A Family Awareness Project," an interactive workshop on how to respond to antisemitism. The ADL also launched its Annual Youth Leadership Mission to Washington, D.C., bringing youths to the U.S. Holocaust Memorial Museum to teach them about the depths to which hatred can sink

and the responsibility each person bears for others. The ADL's "Bearing Witness," a joint project with the Archdiocese of Washington, D.C. and the U.S. Holocaust Memorial Museum, teaches Catholic educators about the Holocaust and how to convey its lessons to their students.

Responding to the 1996 epidemic of arson against black churches in the South, the ADL launched a campaign to provide funds to help rebuild the churches. In 1999, troubled by Kosovo's "ethnic cleansing," the ADL formed the Fund for the Refugees of Kosovo, eventually donating more than $800,000 for direct assistance to victims.

The twenty-first century began with an increase in terrorism and the resurgence of antisemitism. The UN World Conference against Racism, held in Durban, South Africa, August 31–September 7, 2001, was hijacked into a forum to attack Jews, Jewish nationalism, and Israel's right to exist. Zionism was declared racism, delegitimizing the national self-determination of the Jewish people, and Israel was branded an apartheid state. Equally troubling was the failure of countries (except the United States) and long-term nongovernmental organizations to protest the display of antisemitism.

The ADL recognizes that Americans today must be concerned with antisemitism as a global phenomenon. In response to the September 11, 2001, terrorist attacks on the World Trade Center and the Pentagon, the ADL shared its information on terrorist and extremist groups with law enforcement agencies, government, and media, and promoted counterterrorism legislation, along with the protection of minorities. While Americans understood that the attacks were aimed at their democratic way of life, many in the rest of the world blamed Jews. A big lie spread that Jews and Israel were behind the attacks and that Jews had been forewarned about them. This big lie originated on Al-Manar, the television station of the terrorist group Hezbollah, based in Lebanon; it was spread throughout the world on the Internet and satellite TV. While the big lie gained credence across the Arab and Muslim worlds, it was embraced by antisemites and Israel bashers everywhere. After Amira Baraka, New Jersey's poet laureate, recited a poem he wrote incorporating the big lie, the state eliminated the position. A constant drumbeat of anti-Israel and anti-Jewish incitement emanated from the Arab/Muslim world—equating Zionism with Nazism, the blood libel, the deicide charge, Holocaust denial, classic stereotypes, quoting the infamous *Protocols of the Learned Elders of*

The Anti-Defamation League (ADL) civil rights counsel Michael Sheetz holds up the ADL's annual "Audit of Anti-Semitic Incidents" at a news conference in Boston on March 24, 1999. (AFP/Getty Images)

Zion—which contributed to an explosion of antisemitism in Europe.

Jews and Jewish institutions were attacked in France, Belgium, and England. France suffered the majority of attacks and the most violent, including an assault by Muslim youths on a Jewish teenager at an ice-skating rink, an attack on a rabbi and his young son after Sabbath services, the stabbing of a Jewish youth by a man shouting "*Allah Aqbar!*" ("God is Great" in Arabic), the desecration of Jewish cemeteries, and arson attacks on synagogues. Norway's largest labor union called for a boycott of Israeli products. Portugal's Nobel laureate in literature, after visiting Jenin, the site of a so-called "massacre" that never happened, called it Auschwitz. An Israeli-owned hotel in Mombasa, Kenya, was attacked by a suicide car bomber on November 28, 2002; on the same day, two surface-to-air missiles narrowly missed an El Al jetliner as it lifted off from Moi International Airport in Kenya. Two synagogues were bombed in Istanbul on November 15, 2003.

The ADL's Conference on Global Anti-Semitism in New York, October 31–November 1, 2002, brought together Jewish community representatives, government officials, and diplomats from European and other countries. Nobel laureate Elie Wiesel gave the keynote address, and Germany's foreign minister, Joschka Fischer, said his nation would fight against rising antisemitism.

Surveys revealed that antisemitism in the United States had increased for the first time in ten years. The ADL's *2002 Survey of Anti-Semitism in America* found that 17 percent, or 35 million adults, harbor antisemitic views and that anti-Israel sentiments fuel—and rationalize—antisemitism. ADL surveys conducted in Europe in 2002 and 2004 showed that large numbers still accept a wide range of traditional antisemitic stereotypes. Unlike Americans, Europeans are often indifferent to antisemitism, deny that it exists in their countries, or blame it on the politics of the Middle East.

The ADL recognizes that antisemitism has a unique resilience. By exposing antisemitism and educating people about it, the ADL hopes to keep this hatred unacceptable and at bay.

Abraham H. Foxman

References and Further Reading

Baldwin, Neil. 2002. *Henry Ford and the Jews: The Mass Production of Hate.* New York: Public Affairs.

Church, Forrest, ed. 2004. *The Separation of Church and State: Writings on Fundamental Freedoms by America's Founders.* Boston: Beacon.

Dinnerstein, Leonard. 1994. *Antisemitism in America.* New York: Oxford.

Dworkin, Susan. 2000. *Miss America, 1945: Bess Myerson and the Year That Changed Our Lives.* New York: Newmarket Press.

Foxman, Abraham H. 2003. *Never Again? The Threat of the New Anti-Semitism.* San Francisco: HarperSanFrancisco.

Lawrence, Frederick M. 1999. *Punishing Hate: Bias Crimes under American Law.* Cambridge, MA: Harvard University Press.

Lipstadt, Deborah. 1993. *Denying the Holocaust: The Growing Assault on Truth and Memory.* New York: Free Press.

Rosenbaum, Ron, ed. 2004. *Those Who Forget the Past: The Question of Anti-Semitism.* New York: Random House.

Stern-LaRosa, Caryl, and Ellen Hofheimer Bettmann. 2000. *The Anti-Defamation League's Hate Hurts: How Children Learn and Unlearn Prejudice.* New York: Scholastic.

Svonkin, Stuart. 1997. *Jews Against Prejudice: American Jews and the Fight for Civil Liberties.* New York: Columbia University Press.

Wolf, Michael. 1998. *Religion in the Workplace: A Comprehensive Guide to Legal Rights and Responsibilities.* Chicago: ABA Publishing.

The American Jewish Congress

The American Jewish Congress is one of a number of "defense" organizations that serve the American Jewish polity and that perform a range of community-relations functions. The genesis, early development, and growth of the American Jewish Congress ("AJCongress" or "the Congress") are classic examples of American pluralism and associationalism.

The American Jewish Congress was established by a group that was dissatisfied with the American Jewish Committee (AJC or "the Committee"). This group, largely of Eastern European origin, felt that the "aristocratic" German Jewish leadership of the Committee was a self-appointed, self-perpetuating body with no mandate from American Jewry and that AJC was paternalistic in its dealings with Eastern Europeans. The debate played out the larger one between East European and German Jews and between Zionists and anti-Zionists, and was primarily over the establishment of a congress that would represent American Jewish interests at the peace conference following World War I. The result was an ad hoc "congress" that would act as an umbrella for Jewish groups and represent Jewish interests.

Institutionally, the present AJCongress was an outgrowth of the first American Jewish Congress, which assembled in Philadelphia in December 1918. A written agreement entered into by a number of organizations stipulated that the Congress was to dissolve as soon as it fulfilled its task of formulating a postwar program for the Jewish people, named a delegation to the peace conference in Versailles, and received the delegation's report. This agreement was implemented at the second and last session of the Congress in Philadelphia in 1920. However, some delegates from religious, Zionist, and fraternal organizations and from *landsmanshaftn* reassembled the next day under the chairmanship of Stephen S. Wise and laid the foundation for the present AJCongress, which was fully organized in 1928. Although the initial constituency of the American Jewish Congress was mainly Zionist, additional positions were voiced following the 1928 reorganization. In sum, while the American Jewish Committee and other organizations wanted the Congress to go out of business—and it did formally dissolve itself in 1920—the pressure for a permanent representative organization resulted in the formation of the present Congress, which came into being in 1922, originally as a council of agencies. AJCongress evolved into a membership organization in the 1930s.

The initial twin goals of AJCongress, which together molded the agency's subsequent ideology, were to provide humanitarian relief for European Jews in the aftermath of

Rabbi Stephen S. Wise, Zionist and leader of the American Jewish Congress. (American Jewish Historical Society)

World War I and to restore a political Jewish presence in Palestine. The AJCongress is the only community-relations agency that has been pro-Zionist throughout its history and that on a number of issues (for example, a boycott of German goods in the 1930s) was arguably more representative of the views of grassroots American Jewry than the other "defense" and community relations agencies. The early AJCongress leaders, Louis Brandeis and Stephen S. Wise, believed that only a democratic structure would allow maximum participation in Jewish affairs by Jews and not just by German Jews. Moreover, they fervently rejected the views that Jews should not organize along ethnic lines, that Jews should restrict their lobbying efforts to "behind the scenes," and that Jews should not engage in vigorous advocacy. Wise, a key American Zionist leader as well as a founder of the National Association for the Advancement of Colored People (NAACP) and the American Civil Liberties Union (ACLU), was a driving force in the AJCongress from its provisional organization until his death in 1949. The AJCongress's view of pluralism was different from that of the American Jewish Committee or the Anti-Defama-

tion League (ADL): AJCongress articulated the view that group, and not individual, interests needed to be advanced through appropriate organizational channels and not merely through a few well-connected individuals. Wise especially offered a vision of American Jewry as both religious and ethnic and maintained that, as a people possessing a distinct cultural history, American Jews should openly advocate their interests.

The AJCongress set goals related to American and world Jewish affairs, including Palestine. In the 1930s, the AJCongress emerged as a leading force in the anti-Nazi movement and in efforts to aid the victims of fascism. It sought to arouse American public opinion and to combat manifestations of antisemitism in America. With the Jewish Labor Committee, AJCongress organized the Joint Boycott Council directed against German goods and services.

In the mid-1930s, AJCongress led in the formation of the World Jewish Congress (WJC) and shortly thereafter changed itself from a body representing organized groups into one based on individual membership. National Jewish organizations found that group affiliation alongside individual membership was untenable and therefore withdrew to form the American Section of the World Jewish Congress, which was designed to give a voice to the WJC in the United States. The AJCongress is also an affiliate of the WJC.

The AJCongress pioneered in the use of law and social action as tools in combating prejudice and discrimination. This strategy—opposed by other Jewish communal groups, especially the AJC and the ADL, who believed in quiet diplomacy and social relations—led to the creation in the 1930s of a number of "commissions" within the agency to examine the utility of litigative action to secure constitutional protection of equal rights. While the image of AJCongress was one of a creative and aggressive advocate for Jewish interests, there was, in fact, little substantive difference between AJCongress and the ADL and AJC until after World War II.

In 1945 the AJCongress embarked on a program based on proposals submitted by Alexander H. Pekelis that broadened the focus of the agency. Proceeding from the premise that the well-being of Jews depended on a liberal political and social climate, the AJCongress became increasingly involved in the promotion of social legislation and in activities designed to strengthen American democracy, eliminate racial and religious bigotry, and advance civil liberties. AJCongress in 1945 created its Commission on Law and Social Action (CLSA, a merger of two commissions, on discrimination and law and legislation) to implement this goal. The CLSA was created for the purpose of formulating and implementing direct action strategies that would promote legislative and judicial measures to redress constitutional grievances of American Jews.

The program of advocacy implemented by the CLSA had been fermenting within the AJCongress for some years. Underpinning CLSA advocacy was the view that AJCongress should not limit its work to attacking governmental infringements on the rights of Jews, but should fight discriminatory practices by large private institutions such as universities and corporations, and in doing so should enter into coalition with like-minded groups such as the NAACP and the ACLU. Moreover, the direct action method—law and litigation—would concentrate on fighting legal discrimination and not prejudicial attitudes. This approach was a major departure from that of the ADL and the AJC, both of which were committed to educational programs and goodwill campaigns to educate Americans about Jewish interests, and to "quiet diplomacy" to redress grievances. Indeed, the creation of the CLSA created shock waves that reverberated throughout these American Jewish organizations.

Contributing to the widening gap between AJCongress's commitment to legal reform and the ADL's and AJC's preference for the "social relations" model was the towering figure of Leo Pfeffer, for many years the director of CLSA. Pfeffer's uncontested emergence as the Jewish community's chief strategist on church–state matters was accompanied by his exercise of almost complete authority over the Jewish community's litigation agenda.

CLSA activity over the years led AJCongress to view itself as the "lawyer" for the American Jewish community. Indeed, the AJCongress took a pioneering stand and a leading role in Jewish–community involvement in landmark Supreme Court cases on First Amendment (especially church–state separation) and civil rights issues. Major advocates, such as Alexander Pekelis, David Petegorsky, Will Maslow (executive director, 1960–1972), and above all Leo Pfeffer, put their stamp on AJCongress's agenda and, beyond the agency, on American Jewish communal activities in these arenas. Notably, the first woman to serve as professional head of a major national Jewish organization, Naomi Levine, was executive director of AJCongress from 1972–1978.

In Zionist affairs, the Congress has adopted a pro-Israel position and indeed is the only American Jewish group (aside from Zionist organizations) to be pro-Zionist from its beginnings. It organized annual "dialogues" in Israel between U.S. and Israeli intellectuals and sponsored regular tours of its members to Israel. Changes with respect to Israel emerged under the professional leadership of Henry Siegman in the 1980s and 1990s, and AJCongress veered sharply to the "left" on Israel-related issues, departing in some cases radically from consensus positions of the Jewish community on the Jewish settlements and the peace process.

The recent history of the AJCongress can be divided into three periods. In the first, with Henry Siegman as executive director (1978–1994), the Congress, adopting a sharply "leftist" stance, aggressively took issue with the policies of the State of Israel. An AJCongress mission to Saudi Arabia in 1992—a singular event for American Jewish communal agencies—was one example of the Congress's ideological independence in these years. Siegman's approach was nonetheless entirely consistent with the long tradition of the AJCongress as the "idiosyncratic" agency.

In the second period, from 1994 to 2002, Phil Baum, *contra* Siegman, made an effort, for the first time in AJCongress's history, to position the Congress as a mainstream Jewish organization, in effect reinventing the Congress as a "mirror" of the American Jewish Committee. During the years of Baum's tenure, AJCongress expressed increased support for Israeli policies and generally developed positions and programs on a range of issues that were more consistent with consensus positions of other defense agencies. During these years, however, there was a measure of internal conflict in AJCongress, with the geographically important Southwest region pulling out of the agency (1996) to form an independent activist group. The Southwest region wanted to play a significantly more activist role in economic justice matters than the Congress's national office was interested in doing.

In the third period, since 2002, Neil Goldstein has been the AJCongress executive, and the agency has enjoyed a new financial lease on life, in large measure as the result of the sale of the Stephen S. Wise Congress House in 2004. The agenda of the AJCongress has shifted to reflect chang-

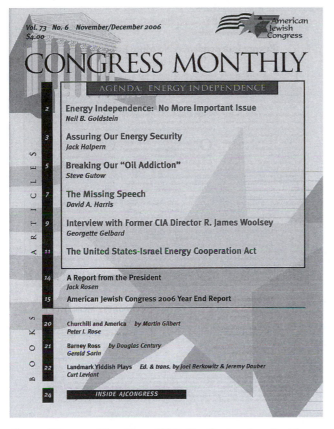

Cover of Congress Monthly, *published by the American Jewish Congress. (American Jewish Congress)*

ing realities of the twenty-first century. Israel again absorbs more agency resources, and American domestic changes have resulted in the Congress often adopting a reactive and defensive, rather than aggressive, posture on issues of concern. AJCongress is currently reexamining a number of its stances, including its strong "separationist" position in church–state affairs.

The AJCongress has approximately 40,000 members. In 2005 the Congress operated out of fifteen chapters, with offices in Jerusalem and Paris, and a presence in Moscow and Brussels. Its budget in 2005 was $6.5 million, raised from membership dues, independent campaigns, allocations from Jewish federations ($300,000 annually), and other sources. The small budget—relative to the ADL and the AJC—is deceptive. During the 1990s many predicted the demise of AJCongress, particularly after merger talks with the AJC broke down—analysts suggest that the Congress leadership was unhappy about the prospect that their "movement-based" agency would be submerged into the AJC, and thereby lose its highly distinctive history and identity. However, while it is clearly in the "second tier" of

defense agencies, AJCongress in the first decade of the twenty-first century is hardly moribund. The core of its operation, CLSA, is active, and AJCongress has added a Jewish Life office. AJCongress holds national conventions annually. The publications *Congress Monthly* and the scholarly *Judaism,* which for many years was one of the premier intellectual journals in American Jewish life, are produced under AJCongress auspices.

Jerome A. Chanes

References and Further Reading

American Jewish Congress. 1936. *American Jewish Congress, What It Is and What It Does.*

American Jewish Congress. 1943–1944. *Confidential Congress Reports.*

American Jewish Congress. 1949–1951. *Reports to the National Convention.*

American Jewish Congress. 1959–1961. *Fortnightly Newsletter.*

Chanes, Jerome A. 1991. "The Voices of the American Jewish Community." In *Survey of Jewish Affairs 1991.* London: Institute for Jewish Affairs.

Fommer, Morris. 1978. *The American Jewish Congress: A History.* PhD dissertation, Ohio State University.

Ivers, Gregg. 1995. *To Build a Wall: American Jews and the Separation of Church and State.* Charlottesville: University Press of Virginia.

Svonkin, Stuart. 1997. *Jews Against Prejudice: American Jews and the Fight for Civil Liberties.* New York: Columbia University Press.

The Jewish Labor Committee

Founded in the mid-1930s, the Jewish Labor Committee (JLC) began as an umbrella group of Jewish (and Jewish-led) trade unions and fraternal organizations with the aim of organizing aid for victims of Nazism and fascism in Europe and enlisting the American Federation of Labor (AFL) in the struggle against Hitler. In the post–World War II years, the organization's primary focus shifted to antidiscrimination and civil rights work in the U.S. labor movement, but the Committee's increasingly professional staff also became engaged in educational, lobbying, publicity, and advisory work on a wide variety of issues from the defense of Soviet Jewry to Holocaust education. In the face of profound shifts in the class makeup of the American Jewish population and in the ethnic composition of U.S. trade unions, the JLC continues to act as a Jewish presence in the

Delegate Assembly for Civil Rights. Roy Reuther (left) of United Automobile Workers, AFL-CIO; Clarence Mitchell (center), director of NAACP Washington bureau; and Charles Zimmerman (right) of the Jewish Labor Committee. (Library of Congress)

councils of American labor and a labor voice in the organized Jewish community.

The founding meeting of the JLC, held at the Central Plaza on New York's Lower East Side on February 25, 1934—just a year after Hitler's rise to power in Germany—brought together more than a thousand delegates. They represented the International Ladies' Garment Workers' Union (ILGWU), the Amalgamated Clothing Workers of America, a number of smaller unions, the United Hebrew Trades, the Workmen's Circle, the Jewish Daily Forward Association, and the Left Labor Zionists. Baruch Charney Vladeck, general manager of the *Forward* and the prime mover behind the gathering, was elected president; David Dubinsky of the ILGWU was chosen as treasurer; Joseph Baskin of the Workmen's Circle, secretary; and Benjamin

Gebiner, also of the Workmen's Circle, executive secretary. There was considerable overlap in membership between the constituent groups, but potentially they represented a base of several hundred thousand Jewish workers, workers' family members, and middle-class sympathizers. In the face of developing anti-Nazi efforts by Rabbi Stephen Wise and his American Jewish (AJ) Congress, by Communist-led groups, by the Jewish War Veterans of the United States, and by non-Jewish liberals, Vladeck and Dubinsky wanted to create their own powerful political force that could respond effectively to the looming catastrophe in Europe.

Holding that only a broad-based workers' movement could overthrow Hitlerism, the JLC emphasized its labor orientation and nonsectarian philosophy. Its immediate aims were to support Jewish civil and human rights everywhere, to support progressive and democratic antifascist groups, to aid refugees, and to educate the American labor movement (and the general public) about the Nazi threat.

By 1934, B. C. Vladeck (1886–1938), a Russian-born socialist known for the elegance of his Yiddish oratory, was experienced in New York City politics. He had served as a Socialist Party member of the New York Board of Aldermen and was soon to be elected to the City Council on the American Labor Party ticket. Like many of the early generation of Jewish American labor and socialist leaders, he had served his political apprenticeship in the famous General Jewish Workers' Union of Lithuania, Poland, and Russia, the Jewish Labor Bund. In many respects, the founders of the JLC were translating and adapting lessons learned in the ranks of the Bund for use in the very different social milieu of America. The Bund's central tenets—support for democratic socialism, bitter opposition to Communism, anti-Zionism, secularism, and the nurturing of Yiddish-based Jewish culture—were central tenets of JLC ideology through its first decade. In later years, these core beliefs developed unevenly: some faded, some hardened, and some were reshaped in response to changing times.

David Dubinsky had cultivated the friendship of AFL president William Green and sat as the only Jewish member of the AFL's Executive Council. Vladeck and Dubinsky arranged for Vladeck and Walter Citrine, secretary of the Trades Union Congress of Great Britain and a staunch anti-Nazi, to address the September 1934 AFL convention in San Francisco. In response to their pleas, the AFL leadership created a Labor Chest to aid the victims of fascism. Participation was entirely voluntary, but the project gave the AFL imprimatur to an endeavor that Jewish trade unionists embraced with passion, recruiting allies where they could. The Labor Chest funded a number of JLC-inspired educational and aid projects. The JLC handled much of the editorial work for the Labor Chest News Service, organized mass meetings, and produced Labor Chest pamphlets in several languages, aimed at non-Jewish immigrant workers.

In an era when American Jewish organizations were deeply divided on matters of ideology and tactics, the JLC was relatively open to collaboration with other national and local Jewish groups engaged in anti-Nazi work. One of its early concerns was to build support for a boycott of Nazi goods both in the labor movement and among the general public. Putting aside its disagreement over Zionism, the JLC joined with the AJCongress to form the Joint Boycott Council, which operated from 1938 to 1941. When the United States Olympics Committee ignored widespread protests against U.S. participation in the Berlin Olympics of 1936, the JLC, with the Workmen's Circle and the ILGWU, staged a World Labor Athletic Carnival, also known as the Counter-Olympics, in New York City in August 1936. The event drew top college athletes as well as teams organized by unions, and it proved so successful as a publicity venture that a second "carnival" was held in the summer of 1937.

The premature death of B. C. Vladeck, struck down by a heart attack in October 1938, was a heavy blow to the Committee. But its work continued, now under the presidency of Adolph Held of the Amalgamated Clothing Workers and executive secretary Isaiah Minkoff.

Another urgent concern was the fate of refugees. Neither the U.S. government nor the AFL was open to proposals for relaxing immigration controls, so the JLC had to press for special ad hoc measures. In 1939–1940, after the Nazi invasion of Poland and the fall of France, immediate action was needed to save European socialist and labor leaders, who would be prime targets of the Gestapo. The JLC compiled a list that included Jewish and non-Jewish labor leaders and socialists, as well as Yiddish writers and other activists deemed to be in immediate danger. Securing more than 800 emergency visitors' visas from the U.S. Department of State, the JLC was able to bring some 1,500 individuals to safety. Through a network of courageous underground couriers, money was smuggled into Nazi-occupied territory to sustain the scattered remnants of East European Jewry in hiding.

The JLC also supported exiled representatives of European unions and socialist parties who took refuge in New York, where they met under JLC auspices to plan for the political future of their respective countries. During these years, the Committee became a conduit for U.S. government financial support of some of these groups as well; these contacts and practices laid the groundwork for a more shadowy role for the JLC in abetting the labor component of Cold War diplomacy, under the direction of such figures as George Meany, Jay Lovestone, and Irving Brown in the late 1940s and 1950s.

The prewar atmosphere of cordial cooperation between the JLC and other national Jewish organizations suffered a temporary setback in August 1943, when an American Jewish Conference was called to meet in Pittsburgh. The conference was organized by Zionists, and the JLC was apprehensive that the issue of a Jewish homeland in Palestine would overshadow the urgent need for coordination on the rescue of Holocaust victims. Soon, both the American Jewish Committee (AJC) and the JLC withdrew from the conference, citing the domination of a Zionist agenda and, in the case of the JLC, the admission of representatives of Communist groups.

As the war drew to a close, the immediate needs of Holocaust survivors became the JLC's prime concern. By 1944 it was spending close to $1 million a year, mostly on European relief. But the rescue and relief work of the JLC was not measured in dollars alone. Intangibles were just as important: knowledge of conditions in Europe; links to the underground; the ability to find jobs, homes, and care for emigrés; the mobilizing of union locals to solicit large quantities of free clothing, toys, and other goods from employers; and the thousands of hours of labor donated to anti-Nazi efforts by JLC supporters.

In the spring of 1945, the JLC presented an exhibition entitled "Heroes and Martyrs of the Ghettos" at the Vanderbilt Gallery in New York. It opened on April 19, the second anniversary of the destruction of the Warsaw ghetto, and was the first exhibit dealing with the Holocaust and Jewish Resistance to be seen in New York—perhaps the first in America. Beginning in 1945, JLC officers and trade union leaders, among them Nathan Chanin, David Dubinsky, Charles Zimmerman, Jacob Pat, and Paul Goldman, visited European communities and displaced persons (DP) camps and sent back searing accounts of the condition of Jewish survivors and the destruction of Jewish life. By 1947 there were still an estimated 850,000 people living in DP camps, and it was obvious that few Jewish survivors would return to their former homes. Bella Meiksin and Nathan Gierowitz were assigned as full-time JLC representatives working in the camps of the U.S. Zone of Germany. JLC offices in Brussels and Stockholm served thousands of refugees waiting to be permanently resettled. Across Europe soup kitchens, cooperative workshops, Yiddish schools and libraries, day nurseries, and clinics were supported by JLC funds.

In New York the JLC helped prepare lists of those who perished and those who survived and established elaborately cross-referenced card files on people seeking loved ones. Making ample use of the columns of the *Forward* and of the Forward Association's Yiddish-language radio station WEVD, the JLC tried to reunite families and publicized the needs of victims of Nazism and anti-Jewish persecution around the world. The JLC also organized a so-called Child Adoption Program. Its aim was not adoption in the usual sense but rather to provide a mechanism by which Americans could contribute to the care of destitute children (mostly Jewish and non-Jewish Italians) living in Europe or Mandatory Palestine. At a cost of $300 per year, a union shop or local, fraternal society, Workmen's Circle branch, women's club, or any other group or individual could "adopt" a child. The money was used to supply clothes, school supplies, toys and gifts, and special food parcels. Donors received a photo of their "adoptee(s)," a biography, progress reports, and sometimes letters from the children.

By the late 1940s, the JLC began to feel a need to redirect its efforts toward a domestic agenda and to carve out a distinct role for itself, both within the postwar labor movement and in the newly configured world of U.S. Jewish organizations. It determined to make itself the center for antidiscrimination work in the labor movement, and the link between organized labor and community relations activity in the Jewish community.

In the immediate postwar years, the JLC created its own Anti-Discrimination Division, under the leadership of Charles Zimmerman of the ILGWU and national field director Emanuel Muravchik, who joined the staff in 1947. Muravchik, who later served for many years as JLC executive director, was the first top official of the JLC who was American-born and whose first language was English. JLC civil rights work was led by Muravchik, who worked closely with field staff such as Julius Bernstein in Boston, Max Mont and William Becker in Los Angeles, Lillian Herstein and Aaron Aronin in Chicago, Alex Wollod in Philadelphia, and others. Setting up field offices in most major cities, the JLC developed local labor coalitions; ran seminars and summer schools for trade unionists; published pamphlets, newsletters, and reports; conducted research; and testified before legislative and judicial bodies on behalf of Fair Employment Practices laws, equal opportunity in education, and proposals for integrated housing. Its *Labor Reports* news service distributed antidiscrimination material to the labor press throughout the United States and Canada. JLC staff monitored right-wing hate groups, especially those targeting union members, and compiled voluminous annual clipping files on anti-semitism and racism within the labor movement.

On the international scene, the JLC found its position on the creation of a Jewish homeland in Palestine evolving rapidly. In the shadow of the Holocaust, and in consideration of increasing Zionist sentiment among Jewish labor leaders, the JLC became actively involved in lobbying at the United Nations for the establishment of the State of Israel. For many years, the Committee sent direct aid to Holocaust survivors in Israel and funded labor cooperatives, Yiddish libraries and schools, and a number of other projects in the new nation. Pro-Israel educational efforts have become more and more prominent on the JLC's agenda, and in recent years it has regularly sponsored specialized tours of Israel for American trade unionists.

In the early 1950s, JLC president Adolph Held served on the Claims Commission, which negotiated reparations agreements on behalf of Holocaust survivors with the German and Austrian governments. In this effort, Held made effective use of the long-standing ties between the JLC and the German and Austrian Socialist parties. The Committee was also prominent in early efforts to make the American public (and political leaders) aware of discrimination against Jews in the Soviet Union and Eastern Europe.

In 1955 Charles Zimmerman was tapped to become the first head of the Civil Rights Department of the newly merged AFL-CIO, and he, in turn, brought in Donald Slaiman of the JLC's Detroit office as assistant director. Both Zimmerman and Slaiman eventually returned to serve as JLC national presidents. Over the years, the JLC gave direct aid to rural black schools and sharecropper organizing projects in the South, developed the Labor Advisory Committee on Puerto Rican Affairs and the National Trade Union Council on Human Rights, picketed discriminatory employers, mobilized Jewish community support for the farm workers' grape boycott, and built close working relationships with civil rights leaders A. Philip Randolph, Roy Wilkins of the NAACP, and James Farmer of CORE. Under the direction of longtime JLC ally Bayard Rustin, JLC staff worked behind the scenes to coordinate the 1963 March on Washington for Jobs and Freedom.

By the early 1960s, with Fair Employment Practices Committee (FEPC) legislation on the books in many states, *Brown v. Board of Education* in place, and a strong federal Civil Rights Act in the offing, it appeared that the JLC could take considerable satisfaction in the progress of its agenda. But there were ominous signs of strain within the fragile alliance the JLC had tried to forge between labor, the civil rights movement, and the organized Jewish community. In 1959 A. Philip Randolph lashed out bitterly at the AFL leadership for its sluggishness in dealing with Jim Crow practices in affiliated unions. A rancorous exchange between Charles Zimmerman and NAACP labor secretary Herbert Hill on alleged discrimination in the garment unions led to Zimmerman's resignation from the NAACP's Legal Defense Fund in 1962.

The stubborn refusal of the AFL-CIO Council to endorse the March on Washington, in contrast to the enthusiastic participation of many individual unions such as the United Auto Workers and the Hospital Workers, Local 1199, revealed deep political fissures within the ranks of labor, which the Vietnam War exacerbated. Although it took no official position on the war and worked hard behind the scenes to shift the "old guard" of labor on civil rights issues, the JLC was perceived by a new generation of militants as being on the wrong side of many New Left debates. The emergence of such new-style civil rights organizations as the Student Nonviolent Coordinating Committee and strong nationalist tendencies in African American communities brought intergenerational and political confrontation, both within the civil rights movement and between the movement and many of its Jewish supporters. Worsening relations between African Americans and Jews came to an explosive head in the 1968 Ocean Hill–Brownsville dispute over community control versus union rights in the New York City school system.

For the JLC, the 1970s ushered in another period of revising organizational goals and reevaluating long-standing relationships. A series of new JLC initiatives developed in the 1980s and 1990s were designed to expand the JLC's traditional field of action and reconnect younger generations of American Jews with a fast-receding past of immigrant struggle and labor solidarity. Liberal-minded rabbis and Jewish college students have been recruited to fight sweatshops, oppose anti-labor legislation, and support striking workers. Hundreds of non-Jewish teachers have studied the history of the Holocaust and Jewish resistance through JLC-sponsored summer seminars in Poland and Israel. And the JLC's popular nationwide program of Labor Seders offers opportunities for labor activists of every ethnicity to meet with Jewish communal leaders in a setting that balances ancient tradition and shared ideals of social justice.

Gail Malmgreen

References and Further Reading

Berlin, George L. 1971. "The Jewish Labor Committee and American Immigration Policy in the 1930s." In *Studies in Jewish Bibliography, History and Literature in Honor of I. Edward Kiev,* edited by Charles Berlin, 45–73. New York: Ktav.

Brooks, Thomas R. 1973. "Forty Years of Fighting Bias." *American Federationist* (December): 19–21.

Carew, Anthony. 1996. "Conflict within the ICFTU: Anti-Communism and Anti-Colonialism in the 1950s." *International Review of Social History* 41: 147–181.

Draper, Alan. 1994. *Conflict of Interests: Organized Labor and the Civil Rights Movement in the South, 1954–1968.* Ithaca, NY: Cornell ILR Press.

Gottlieb, Moshe R. 1982. *American Anti-Nazi Resistance, 1933–1941: An Historical Analysis.* New York: Ktav.

Herling, John. 1939–1940. "Baruch Charney Vladeck." *American Jewish Year Book:* 79–93.

Jacobs, Jack. 1996. "A Friend in Need: The Jewish Labor Committee and Refugees from the German-Speaking Lands, 1933–1945." *YIVO Annual* 23: 391–417.

Kelman, Sidney. 1990. "Limits of Consensus: Unions and the Holocaust." *American Jewish History* 79 (Spring): 336–357.

Kranzler, David. 1984. "The Role of Relief and Rescue during the Holocaust by the Jewish Labor Committee." In *American Jewry during the Holocaust,* edited by Seymour Maxwell Finger, Appendix 4–2: 1–20. New York: Holmes and Meier.

Lebowitz, Arieh, and Gail Malmgreen, eds. 1993. *Archives of the Holocaust, Volume 14: Robert F. Wagner Labor Archives, New York University–Records of the Jewish Labor Committee.* New York: Garland.

Malmgreen, Gail. 2000. "Comrades and Kinsmen: The Jewish Labor Committee and Anti-Nazi Activity, 1934–41." In *Jews, Labor and the Left, 1918–48,* edited by Christine Collette and Stephen Bird, 4–20. Aldershot, UK: Ashgate.

Shapiro, Edward S. 1985. "The World Labor Athletic Carnival of 1936: An American Anti-Nazi Protest." *American Jewish History* 59 (March): 255–273.

The Simon Wiesenthal Center

A not-for-profit educational and research institution dedicated to the exploration of the Holocaust and other genocides, the Simon Wiesenthal Center was the first institution established in North America to link Holocaust remembrance to the defense of human rights. It was founded by Rabbi Marvin Hier in 1977, a third of a century after the full extent of the Nazi annihilation of 6 million Jews and millions of others became known. Headquartered in Los Angeles, with regional offices in New York, Chicago, Florida, Toronto, Paris, and Jerusalem, the Center is supported by more than 500,000 member families.

The Center was named for Nazi-hunter Simon Wiesenthal, who, having survived four concentration camps, emerged from Mauthausen in 1945 committed to tracking down the tens of thousands of mass murderers who escaped judgment at Nuremberg. Rather than return to his prewar profession of architect, he built the Jewish Documentation Center, first in Linz, Austria, and then in Vienna, to collect information that would help in this effort. In the early 1960s, Wiesenthal earned international renown for his contribution to Israel's capture and trial of Adolf Eichmann, the bureaucratic architect of "The Final Solution." The Center was committed to educating the public about the Holocaust and to helping track down Nazi war criminals still at large.

According to best estimates, 10,000 war criminals from Germany and its numerous puppet states escaped postwar justice to the United States, 3,000 to Canada, and thousands more to Latin America, Australia, New Zealand, and Arab states. Lesser functionaries, including death camp guards, achieved entry under false papers as displaced persons. Fascist underground networks such as ODESSA assisted elite personnel, including high-ranking officers and rocket scientists, to escape from Europe. The Pentagon's Operation Paperclip even recruited some Nazi war criminals, giving them free entry, citizenship, and lucrative jobs. Hence, Simon Wiesenthal's sardonic verdict that fugitive Nazis were "the real winners of the Cold War."

In 1978 the Wiesenthal Center initiated its first international campaign to persuade the Federal Republic of Germany not to end prosecutions. Had West Germany invoked its statute of limitations, there could have been no justice for fugitive war criminals. The petition drive to abolish the German statute of limitations on war crime prosecutions deluged President Jimmy Carter with 200,000 letters and postcards and Chancellor Helmut Schmidt with 1 million signed appeals. In March 1979, the Center's first mission to Germany brought Chancellor Schmidt and other German parliamentarians the message "Justice has no time limit!" The lobbying campaign influenced the Bundestag's 255 to 222 vote in July 1979 to abolish the statute of limitations. In 1981, a German court sentenced Hermine Braunsteiner Ryan to life imprisonment, the first person extradited from the United States to face war crimes charges. She was known as "the Mare" for trampling Majdanek prisoners to death with her jackboots.

The campaign to end West Germany's statute of limitations on war crimes crystallized the Center's role as a link between grassroots and governmental efforts in the United States to bring the unpunished to justice. The Center's first director, Holocaust scholar and Nazi-hunter Ephraim Zuroff, launched a Survivor Registry to elicit the recollections of victims of the Shoah. Ultimately, it evolved into *Testimony to the Truth,* an ongoing video history project to preserve survivor testimonies for future generations. The Registry also provided testimony about the identity of war criminals for the Office of Special Investigations (OSI). Since its inception in 1979, the OSI has stripped more than 60 Nazi collaborators of their U.S. citizenship and is still investigating almost 300 others.

Rabbi Hier's oft-repeated observation—that hatred was not buried at Auschwitz—reflected the Center's realization that a new breed of neo-Nazis, Klansmen, and skinheads was revitalizing the antisemitic right in the 1980s. The Center closely monitored such groups as Tom Metzger's White Aryan Resistance (WAR), organized in 1978, and the Order, responsible for the murder in Denver of Jewish radio talk show host Alan Berg. It also worked with Morris Dees and the Southern Poverty Law Center, which used the innovative tactic of civil litigation on behalf of hate victims to bankrupt the United Klans of America in 1987 and WAR in 1990.

Following Louis Farrakhan's rise to prominence during Jesse Jackson's 1984 presidential campaign, when the Nation of Islam (NOI) leader called Hitler "a great man" and Judaism "a gutter religion," the Center commissioned the first national poll gauging Farrakhan's impact on African-Americans. As Farrakhan's influence mounted, culminating in the 1995 "Million Man March," Center consultant Dr. Harold Brackman exposed the NOI's outrageous antisemitic allegations that the AIDS virus was invented by Jewish doctors to infect black children and that Jewish merchants had dominated the Atlantic slave trade.

As dangerous as extremist threats against people and property was the violence against history and memory propagated by Holocaust deniers. The Institute for Historical Review (IHR), organized in 1978 and bankrolled by Willis Carto, a notorious antisemite and racist, the next year held its first "Revisionist Conference," where crackpots posing as scholars argued that the Nazi gas chambers were a Jewish–Zionist myth designed to victimize Germans and Palestinians. The Center combated the tactics of Holocaust deniers such as Bradley Smith, which included placing Holocaust-denying ads in college newspapers and disrupting Simon Wiesenthal's speaking engagements. Polls from the 1980s showed that as many as 30 percent of Americans and perhaps an even higher percentage of young adults were not sure that the Holocaust had occurred. The Center developed Holocaust curricula for colleges and secondary schools at a time when Holocaust education was virtually unknown on the West Coast. It also supported Holocaust survivor Mel Mermelstein, who in 1981 successfully sued the IHR to honor its promise of $50,000 to anyone who could prove that Jews had been gassed at Auschwitz.

The Center developed media projects to educate the public about the Holocaust. It produced the film *Genocide,* narrated by Elizabeth Taylor and Orson Welles, that told the story of the Holocaust largely in the words of the victims. It won the 1981 Academy Award for best documentary feature. A second award followed in 1998 for *The Long Way Home,* a chronicle of the experience of Holocaust survivors between 1945 and 1948.

The Center held its first International Conference on Antisemitism in Paris in 1983. In the wake of an attack on the historic Rue Copernic Synagogue, the Center's delegation discussed the connection between the French government's pro-Arab tilt in the Middle East and the rising tide of antisemitic incidents in France with Larent Rapin, director of the French Foreign Ministry's Middle East Desk, and Justice Minister Robert Badinter. The Center was accorded official observer status at the war crimes trial of Lyons SS chief Klaus Barbie (1987).

The Center also combated bigotry in rap and other forms of music popular among youth. In the late 1980s, Guns N' Roses and Public Enemy—one group militantly "white," the other militantly "black"—brought songs promoting race hate into the musical mainstream. The Center placed open letters in *Daily Variety* and the *Hollywood Reporter* decrying the trend. Public Enemy's album *Welcome to the Terrordome,* for example, was crudely antisemitic: "Crucifixion ain't no fiction, so-called chosen, frozen . . . they got me like a Jesus" (Harrington 1989).

As the Cold War wound down, a new threat—state-sponsored terrorism by Middle Eastern countries—took center stage in late 1985 and early 1986. The Palestinian terrorist group led by Mohammed Abbas seized the liner *Achille Lauro* and murdered wheelchair-bound Jewish American Leon Klinghoffer. Abu Nidal masterminded murderous attacks on the El Al counters at the Vienna and Rome airports. A Berlin discotheque bombing resulted in the deaths of two American servicemen and the injury of many more. At an Arab League meeting attended by UN Secretary General Javier Pérez de Cuéllar, PLO representative Farouk Kaddoumi suggested that Klinghoffer's wife may have pushed him "into the sea to have his insurance," while the Italian government gave Mohammed Abbas safe passage (*New York Times*, December 5, 1985).

The Center's contribution to the fight against terrorism included convening the International Conference on Terrorism in Los Angeles in 1986 with experts from the United States, Europe, and Israel. Subsequently, the Center was among the first to publicize the threat of weapons of mass destruction from states like Iraq that used poison gas against both Iran and its own Kurdish minority. It was the moving force behind the historic 1989 Conference on Jewish Solidarity with Israel, where 1,300 Jewish leaders from 42 countries came to Jerusalem to show support for the beleaguered Jewish state.

The new state-sponsored terrorism of the 1980s invariably combined antisemitism and anti-Americanism. As early as 1986, the Center spotlighted the increasing Jew hatred in the Arab world by exposing Syrian defense minister Mustafa Tlas's book, *The Matzah of Zion*, which revived the old blood libel. In 1988 the Center revealed the stunning popularity of *The Protocols of the Elders of Zion*, the antisemitic document forged by czarist agents, in Cairo, the capital of Israel's ostensible "peace partner" Egypt. That same year, the Center translated into English the charter of the then-little-known Muslim fundamentalist group Hamas, whose antisemitic mindset inspired future suicide bombers.

The new global antisemitism extended beyond the Middle East and Europe. As early as 1987, the Center became concerned about the phenomenon of "Jew hatred with almost no Jews" in Japan. After a fact-finding mission to Tokyo in 1988, Center associate director Rabbi Abraham Cooper reported, "Virtually every one of the two dozen bookstands I visited featured popularly priced books which blamed international Jewry for every conceivable problem, from the overvaluation of the yen to a purported cover-up of the Chernobyl nuclear disaster" (Cooper 1988).

In 1993 the Center acted to counter the rising tide of antisemitism in Central Europe. Yaron Svoray, an Israeli citizen and child of Holocaust survivors, volunteered on behalf of the Center to pose as right-wing Australian journalist "Ron Furey" in order to penetrate the leadership of German hate groups. In addition to such venerated icons as Hitler's bodyguard and the children of Himmler and Goering, Svoray/Furey won the confidence of contemporary celebrities such as Frank Rennicke, the "Elvis" of the German radical right, and of shadowy, sinister figures such as Nationalistic Front leader Meinolf Schoenborn and FAP leader Friedhelm Busse. His investigation revealed a neo-Nazi movement larger and more organized than previously believed, benefiting from the tacit support of some local police and with worldwide links. These disturbing findings—recounted in the book *Hitler's Shadow* and dramatized in the television film *The Infiltrator*—were aired in hearings before the U.S. House Subcommittee on International Security, International Organizations and Human Rights.

In the wake of the Gulf War, Kenneth R. Timmerman's Wiesenthal Center–commissioned study, *The Poison Gas Connection*, confirmed what the Center had suspected for years: that Western, mostly German, firms were exporting chemical weapons precursors to Libya and Iraq. I. G. Farben—a manufacturer of Zyklon B during the Holocaust—also supplied Saddam Hussein. "You Germans have assembled so much information about the gassing of Jews—that interests us. We would like to know how this knowledge can be put to use in the destruction of Israel," an Iraqi general told Karl Heinz Lohs, director of the Institute for Poisonous Chemicals, Leipzig (London *Guardian*, October 26, 1990).

The Center urged world governments to stop transferring to dictatorships technology relevant to building weapons of mass destruction, especially to those in the volatile Middle East. It also helped pressure Illinois-based Baxter International, the world's largest hospital supply firm, to cancel a deal to build a "pharmaceutical" plant in Syria that the Assad regime could have converted into a weapon against Israel.

During the 1990s, the Center became involved in several initiatives involving Africa. In the wake of the 1994 Rwandan genocide, which claimed the lives of 500,000 people and resulted in 2.5 million refugees, the Rwandan ambassador to Israel requested the aid of the Center's Israel director Zuroff in documenting the atrocities and prosecuting perpetrators. Zuroff helped make Rwanda's case for expedited trials before the chief prosecutor of the International Criminal Tribunals for Former Yugoslavia and Rwanda. The UN Tribunal's difficulties in arraigning suspects, including priests and nuns accused of participation in genocide, echoed Simon Wiesenthal's struggles in bringing Nazi war criminals to justice. In 1999 the Center's Museum of Tolerance (MOT) in Los Angeles also hosted an international conference on slavery and the slave trade today in Mauritania and Sudan.

The information superhighway permits hatemongers to reach a vast audience. Over 1,000 websites promote their racist and antisemitic agendas. Currently, the Center devotes 80 percent of its research manpower to monitoring online hate groups. The effort began in 1994, when the Center asked supporters to alert it to propaganda postings on electronic bulletin boards so that an "early warning system" could be established.

The carnage at the Murrah Federal Building in Oklahoma City in April 1995 dramatized the threat. Timothy McVeigh was a cyberspace junkie code-named "Mad Bomber." The apocalyptic novel—*The Turner Diaries* by William Pierce of the neo-Nazi National Alliance—that was McVeigh's inspiration and blueprint for the bomb plot was readily available for Internet download, as was that perennial favorite, *The Protocols of the Elders of Zion*. The Cyberspace Minutemen, Stormfront, the Aryan Resistance Center, and White Resurgence were just a handful of the more than 250 American, Canadian, and European hate groups that the Center discovered were recruiting in cyberspace. Resistance, Inc., the corporate front for racist rock groups, was creating a multimedia empire including independent music and video production, desktop publishing, shortwave radio, satellite hookups, citizen access television, and fax networks, as well as computer billboards on the Internet. The Net was awash in lethal recipes, including how-to manuals for making ammonium nitrate bombs, chlorine bombs, car bombs, pipe bombs, hand grenades, C–4 plastic explosives, and even sarin nerve gas. Extremists also used the Internet to identify enemies on their "hit lists" by name and address.

The Center issued a manual, *The New Lexicon of Hate*, to better inform law enforcement and community leaders about the changing language and tactics of America's extremist movements. When fourteen neo-Nazi skinheads were convicted of plotting to bomb synagogues and black churches in Los Angeles in 1992, a federal court ordered them to undergo tolerance education at the Center's MOT as part of their sentence. After the 1995 murder by skinhead soldiers of an African American couple in Fort Bragg, North Carolina, the Pentagon requested the aid of the Center's National Task Force against Hate. The Center sent Tom Leyden, a former neo-Nazi recruiter who had undergone a change of heart, to help the military promote tolerance in the ranks. These efforts did not go unnoticed by the haters. In 1998 the FBI foiled a national plot by members of the neo-Nazi "New Order" to bomb the Center's Los Angeles headquarters as well as offices of the Anti-Defamation League and Southern Poverty Law Center.

The Center's MOT opened in 1993 and has hosted more than 2 million visitors. It utilizes hands-on computer stations, interactive displays, graphics, films, and videos to explore the history of the Holocaust and intolerance in America. The MOT not only exposes visitors to historical issues but challenges them to confront the problems of contemporary bigotry and racism. The Center is linking the MOT by fiber-optic network to the 50,000 videotaped survivor testimonies compiled by Steven Spielberg's Shoah Foundation. The result will be an exhaustive, eyewitness "instant history" of the Holocaust available to every computer user who seeks to know what happened and why it must never be allowed to happen again.

In the twenty-first century, a heightened focus is the growing linkage of anti-Americanism with antisemitism and hatred of Israel, which the Center highlighted even before the terrorist attacks of September 11, 2001.

Harold Brackman

References and Further Reading

Cooper, Rabbi Abraham. 1988. "What Sparked the Wave of Anti-Semitism in Japan?" *Toronto Star* (August 16): A17.

Harrington, Richard. 1989. "Public Enemy's Rap Record Stirs Jewish Protests." *Washington Post* (December 29): D1.

Prosise, Theodore O. 2003. "Prejudiced, Historical Witness, and Responsible: Collective Memory and Liminality in the Beit Hashoah Museum of Tolerance." *Communication Quarterly* 51, 3 (Summer): 355–371.

Simon Wiesenthal Center. Archives. Los Angeles. www.wiesenthal.com

Jews and the Press

The Early Yiddish Press in the United States

The Yiddish press was arguably the most important institution in immigrant Jewish life. Although characterized by repeated failures during the 1870s and 1880s, the American Yiddish press came into its own during the 1890s, as the quantity, diversity, and popularity of Yiddish newspapers and journals increased dramatically. The development of a ramified Yiddish press occurred alongside the emergence of a mass Yiddish readership at the end of the nineteenth century. By 1900, the majority of immigrant Jews, especially in New York City, the capital of the American Yiddish press, either read Yiddish newspapers or regularly listened to them being read by friends, relatives, or coworkers. "All you have to do is go down to the Jewish quarter," a correspondent for the Russian journal *Voskhod* (*Dawn*) reported in 1894, "and you will hear sellers hawking Jewish newspapers; you will see the newspapers being bought up; wherever you go [Jewish immigrants] are reading and they discuss what is read" (Michels 2005).

Ten years later, a correspondent for *Der fraynd* (*The Friend*), Russia's first Yiddish daily, similarly observed, "It has become a necessity to have a newspaper at home. . . . Newspapers have become the main intellectual food of the Jewish immigrant in America" (Michels 2005). Correspondents for Russian publications expressed amazement at the huge readership of Yiddish newspapers (the combined circulation of Yiddish dailies reached 66,000 in 1900 and 120,000 two years later) because a commercial Yiddish newspaper market did not yet exist in the Russian empire, where most European Jews lived. Although several Yiddish newspapers had appeared in Russia since the 1860s, the Russian government largely suppressed Yiddish publications until the establishment of *Der fraynd* in 1902. Not until the outbreak of the 1905 revolution did a popular Yiddish press come into existence in the Russian empire. (A number of short-lived Yiddish publications had also appeared in Austria-Hungary and Rumania in the second half of the nineteenth century.) The Yiddish press was, to a great extent, an American invention.

Yiddish newspapers did not simply report daily events, but rather fulfilled several functions at once. They provided education to those who could not read English or attend school. Articles on subjects such as biology, hygiene, civics, and history filled the pages of the American Yiddish press. The press also provided the main venue for Yiddish fiction, poetry, and criticism. Yiddish writers, from the best to the worst, published most of their work in the newspapers. Finally, Yiddish newspapers functioned as "agents of acculturation," introducing and interpreting American society, politics, and culture for their readers. Commentators agreed that the Yiddish press played the major social, cultural, and political role in immigrant Jewish life. "In the

Yiddish press," the sociologist Robert Park wrote in his classic study, "the foreign-language newspaper may be said to have achieved form. . . . No other foreign language press has succeeded in reflecting so much of the intimate life of the people which it represents, or reacted so powerfully upon the opinion, thought, and aspiration of the public for which it exists" (Park 1922). According to Irving Howe, the Yiddish press functioned as both "kindergarten and university" (Howe 1976).

The rise of the Yiddish press entailed at least two basic changes in Jewish cultural practices and social organization. It consolidated both a popular Yiddish readership and a Yiddish-writing (though often Russian- or English-speaking) intelligentsia. These twin phenomena were distinctly American inasmuch as they were not transplanted from Eastern Europe, but they defy "Americanization" in any conventional sense. Most writers for Yiddish newspapers in the late nineteenth century did not, prior to immigration, write in Yiddish; a significant number did not even know the language well enough to be able to do so. Not until settling in the United States did most writers become "yiddishized." By the same token, few immigrants (regardless of their literacy skills) were accustomed to reading Yiddish newspapers; indeed, they had never seen one before coming to the United States. Reading a newspaper, for nearly all immigrants arriving before the early 1900s, was a habit developed in the United States, and with considerable effort.

Newspapers encouraged new, often secular, identities; transformed the Yiddish vernacular into the primary language of intellectual discourse and literary creativity (thereby overturning the traditional language hierarchy of Ashkenazic Jews that placed Hebrew above Yiddish); and established new types of leaders: editors and writers, including secular and politically radical intellectuals. Similar developments were already under way in the Russian empire by the late nineteenth century. But in American cities they were greatly accelerated and extended due to freedoms of speech and assembly, the absence of entrenched communal structures, an exceptionally large and concentrated Jewish population in New York, and the city's prevailing secular atmosphere.

In terms of circulation, the American Yiddish press would reach its peak in the 1920s, the decade in which Congress implemented highly restrictive quotas on immigration. Yet the foundation of the Yiddish press was set in place by the end of the nineteenth century.

The history of the Yiddish press in the United States began on March 1, 1870, when a businessman and communal activist in New York City, Y. K. Bukhner, published the first issue of *Di yidishe tsaytung* (*The Jewish Newspaper*), a lithographed weekly "paper of politics, religion, history, science and art." Although the newspaper appeared irregularly and its meager contents belied its lofty subtitle, *Di yidishe tsaytung* paved the way for future efforts. Five months after its debut, a Hebrew writer, Tsvi Hirsh Bernshteyn, decided to start a second Yiddish newspaper, *Di post* (*The Post*). In April 1871, an aspiring politician, Yankev Cohen, founded the *Hebrew News*, an English-German-Hebrew-Yiddish newspaper. By the end of the decade, no less than seven Yiddish newspapers had appeared in New York and one in Chicago.

Several factors contributed to the birth of the Yiddish press in the 1870s. First, the Yiddish-speaking population in New York grew significantly during that decade, reaching perhaps as many as 15,000 on the Lower East Side by 1880. Enterprising individuals perceived a potential readership within New York's rapidly increasing Yiddish-speaking population and therefore a potentially lucrative market. Events overseas, especially wars, further stimulated interest in Yiddish newspapers. *Di post*, for example, was started in the wake of the Franco-Prussian War, and the *New Yorker Izraelit* (*New York Israelite*) was founded in 1877 after the outbreak of the Russo-Turkish War. Local politics provided a third stimulus. The Tammany Hall Democratic Party, for example, understood that Yiddish language newspapers could be an effective means to reach Jewish voters and funded newspapers, such as the *Hebrew News*, whose editor ran for municipal office in 1871.

Nonetheless, the story of the Yiddish press in the 1870s was primarily one of failure. Most of the early Yiddish newspapers appeared irregularly and were short-lived. Only twelve issues of *Di yidishe tsaytung*, for example, appeared between March 1870 and October 1873. Very few immigrant Jews were accustomed to reading newspapers in Yiddish or any language. Most immigrants saw little need for a paper: they got along without one in the old country, why bother in the new? Immigrant Jews typically viewed reading Yiddish newspapers as a luxury. Furthermore, most immigrants found reading Yiddish newspapers exceedingly difficult. Few individuals could simply pick one up and read it. Most had to learn how to read. It is true that a relatively high rate of literacy characterized immigrant

Jewry, particularly in comparison with non-Jewish immigrants from Eastern Europe. Russia's 1897 census reported that 64–66 percent of male Jews and 32–37 percent of female Jews over the age of ten could read in some language. But most immigrants, male and female, possessed only rudimentary reading and writing skills.

The principal educational institution in Jewish society was the *kheyder,* which taught little more than the Hebrew alphabet, prayers, and the Bible to boys under the age of thirteen. Girls sometimes attended kheyder with their brothers for the first two years, and, in scattered instances, they attended special *khedorim* for girls, but generally girls received instruction at home in reading and writing Yiddish. The privileged minority of Jewish boys and girls who attended a government school in Russia were taught to read and write in Russian, not Yiddish. Consequently, immigrant Jews found it difficult to read Yiddish newspapers in the 1870s, and indeed immigrants would continue to find reading a challenge well into the twentieth century. In short, a readership did not exist; this had to be created.

Apart from their limited education, the peculiar language of Yiddish newspapers confronted readers with a major problem. In the 1870s, most journalists wrote in a highly Germanized Yiddish that came to be known as *daytshmerish,* characterized by a semi-German syntax, a preponderance of German vocabulary, and German-influenced orthography. (A single sentence in an 1873 article in *Di yidishe tsaytung,* for example, contained no less than eighteen German words adapted to the Yiddish alphabet's Hebrew characters.) Even words native to Yiddish were usually spelled in such a way as to make them sound more like German: *shprakhe* rather than *sphrakh* (language) or *haben* rather than *hoben* (to have). Readers thus had to learn a kind of newspaper language that was very different from the Yiddish they spoke. Referring to *Di yidishe gazetn* (*The Jewish Gazette*), one of the leading Yiddish newspapers in the 1870s and 1880s, a commentator wrote, "It would be much easier and less time-consuming for you to make sense of Egyptian hieroglyphics than to understand this journal of 'literature'" (Michels 2005).

Yiddish newspapers employed daytshmerish for at least four reasons. First, a number of early editors and writers came from a region of Poland near the Prussian border where the German influence was strongly felt. They spoke a blend of German and Yiddish called *Kalvalier daytsh* and transferred it to the pages of American Yiddish

newspapers. A second factor had to do with negative perceptions of Yiddish. Many pioneer Yiddish journalists were, ironically, frustrated Hebraists who had taken up Yiddish because the Hebrew-reading public was too small. Many of them regarded Yiddish as a corrupted version of German and incorporated as much German as possible with the goal of "purifying" and "elevating" the Jewish vernacular. Third, owing to the fact that Yiddish journalism was such a recent invention, the Yiddish language did not yet possess a vocabulary to describe events, ideas, and institutions specific to the United States. Nor did Yiddish newspapermen (few women wrote for the Yiddish press during the early years) possess generally agreed-upon rules of spelling and grammar. In the absence of a standardized, literary Yiddish (this would not come into existence until the twentieth century), early Yiddish journalists relied on German American newspapers for vocabulary and as a source of articles. A host of factors thus gave rise to daytshmerish during the Yiddish press's formative period.

Of the early Yiddish newspaper publishers, Kasriel Tsvi Sarasohn (1834–1905) was far and away the most successful. A rabbi and conservative *maskil* (proponent of the *Haskalah* or Jewish Enlightenment) from Lithuania, Sarasohn immigrated to the United States in 1869 and tried his hand at newspaper publishing in 1872. His first Yiddish newspaper, *Di nyu-yorker yidishe tsaytung* (*The New York Jewish Newspaper*), went out of business after only four or five months, but in 1874 Sarasohn made a second, successful attempt with the weekly *Di yidishe gazetn* (*The Jewish Gazette*). This time, he raised enough money from investors (a wealthy relative chief among them) to keep the new paper alive. *Di yidishe gazetn* was, in fact, the only Yiddish newspaper to survive the 1870s. In 1881, following the outbreak of pogroms in the Russian empire and the subsequent jump in Jewish immigration, Sarasohn tried to turn *Di yidishe gazetn* into a daily.

The Yiddish readership, however, was not yet large or mature enough to support a Yiddish daily, forcing *Di yidishe gazetn* to return to a weekly schedule after a matter of months. Not until early 1885 did Sarasohn, with his son and business partner Yehezkl, succeed in publishing what is considered the first viable Yiddish daily, *Dos yidishes tageblat* (*The Jewish Daily*). The *Tageblat* actually appeared only four or five times per week until 1894, when it began coming out every day except *shabes*. Nonetheless, during its first nine years, the *Tageblat* published more frequently than any other Yiddish newspaper. (*Di yidishe gazetn* continued as a weekly all along.)

In addition to launching the first successful Yiddish daily, the Sarasohns changed the way Yiddish newspapers were distributed. Prior to 1885 Yiddish newspapers were sold mostly in grocery stories and kosher butcher shops. The Sarasohns, however, hired newsboys to sell their papers in the streets in the custom of English-language newspapers. Although initially Jewish newsboys, seeing Yiddish as a marker of foreignness, felt too embarrassed to hawk Yiddish newspapers in public (thereby compelling the Sarasohns to hire non-Jews), Yiddish newspaper vendors soon became fixtures in immigrant Jewish neighborhoods.

Kasriel and Yehezkl Sarasohn dominated the American Yiddish newspaper market during the 1880s and 1890s. By the turn of the century, the *Tageblat*'s circulation climbed to almost 40,000, surpassing all competitors. Furthermore, the Sarasohns purchased competing Yiddish newspapers in Boston, Chicago, New York, and Philadelphia. (They also published several unsuccessful Hebrew-language publications.) Sarasohn can be considered, in the words of one historian, the first Yiddish press "magnate" (Marmor 1944).

Yet the Sarasohns faced growing competition during the late 1880s and 1890s. A precipitous rise in Jewish immigration (caused by the 1881–1883 pogroms in Russia, tightened legal restrictions on Russian Jews, and, above all, the generally deteriorating economic fortunes of Eastern European Jews) greatly increased the number of potential Yiddish newspaper readers. A parallel increase in the number of businesses catering to Yiddish speakers supplied newspapers with needed advertising revenue. Technological innovations (such as the Linotype machine) enabled publishers to print more copies and reduce prices from six cents in the 1870s to a penny in the 1890s. And, above all, people increasingly wanted to read Yiddish newspapers. Immigrants recognized that the Yiddish press could help them both adapt to their new country and stay informed about *der alter heym* (the old country). Local events (such as strikes and elections) and events abroad (such as wars and pogroms) played an especially important role in stimulating demand. A slow move from daytshmerish toward colloquial Yiddish, starting in the late 1880s, made Yiddish newspapers somewhat more accessible to average immigrants.

Of the Sarasohns' competitors, the Jewish labor movement's socialist leaders were the fiercest and ultimately most successful. Socialists rejected the very premise behind the *Tageblat* and the Sarasohns' other publications. The Sarasohns defined the *Tageblat* as a *kol yisroel* (all Jews) newspaper that represented the interests of the Jewish people as a whole rather than a particular segment of it. The *Tageblat*, Yehezkl Sarasohn explained in 1894, "is not a newspaper of a class against a class, it is a newspaper for all Jews [kol yisroel]" (Michels 2005). With the rise of the Jewish labor movement in 1885–1886, the *Tageblat* often denounced socialists for dividing the Jewish people. The newspaper showed sympathy for the plight of "honest" workers, but the Sarasohns wanted to contain class conflict as much as possible and sometimes even sided with employers during labor conflicts. (During a bakers' strike in 1899–1900, an angry mob rallied outside the *Tageblat*'s offices and smashed its windows in protest against the newspaper's antilabor position.) As part of the Sarasohns' attempt to cast the *Tageblat* as a proponent of Jewish unity standing above destructive partisan divisions, they defended Jewish religious Orthodoxy against its socialist critics and the general drift away from strict observance. Yet, at the same time, the *Tageblat* encouraged readers to adapt to their new country. The Sarasohns thus attempted an uneasy balance between tradition and change, Jewish unity and justice for Jewish workers.

Jewish socialists, by contrast, objected outright to the idea of kol yisroel. In a society divided by irreconcilably hostile classes, they argued, Jewish unity was a chimera that served the interests of bosses. Socialists viewed the press as a means to provide secular education ("enlightenment"), to agitate for a particular ideology (such as Marxian social democracy or anarchism), and to mobilize public opinion behind the labor movement. While the Sarasohns appealed to tradition for legitimacy (but deviated from it when considered necessary), socialists advocated radical change to solve current problems.

Socialists entered the Yiddish newspaper market in the middle of the massive, nationwide strike wave known as the Great Upheaval. They began inauspiciously in June 1886 when Abraham Cahan (who eventually became the dominant figure of the Yiddish press) and his friend Charles Raevsky founded *Di naye tsayt* (*The New Era*), an inconsequential weekly that survived just a few weeks. The socialist Yiddish press really began with *Di nyu-*

yorker yidishe folkstsaytung (*The New York Jewish People's Newspaper*, named after the German-language daily *New Yorker Volkszeitung*, but with the appropriate modification), which appeared shortly after *Di naye tsayt*. The newspaper's editors, Abba Braslavsky and Moyshe Mints, were both leading members of the Yidisher Arbeter Fareyn (the Jewish Workers' Association), which was the first Yiddish-speaking socialist organization in the United States, founded in 1885. The *Folkstsaytung*'s editors promised to "show the Jewish worker its correct place in the family of workers of the entire world, his duty to his suffering brothers, to open his eyes to his economic situation, to enlighten and show him what kind of world he lives in, why he suffers, and how he can overcome it" (Michels 2005).

In addition to bringing radical political ideas to the Yiddish reading public, Braslavsky and Mints introduced a new level of professionalism in Yiddish journalism. They kept the *Folkstsaytung* free of the outdated news items and sensationalistic stories that were typical of the *Tageblat* and other Yiddish newspapers. Furthermore, Braslavsky and Mints used a more colloquial form of Yiddish than was considered appropriate at the time. The *Folkstsaytung*'s circulation reached about 4,500 and was read in cities as far away as Burlington, Vermont, and Milwaukee, Wisconsin. Although considered moderately successful during its own time, the *Folkstsaytung* survived only three and a half years because of growing ideological divisions between anarchists and social democrats in the Jewish labor movement. Its final issue appeared in December 1889. By that time, no less than five radical Yiddish newspapers had come and gone due to lack of money, inexperience, or political infighting.

Despite its shaky beginning, the Yiddish socialist press grew into a powerful force during the 1890s. The founding of *Di arbeter tsaytung* (*The Workers Newspaper*) in March 1890 marked the turning point. A group of prominent socialist intellectuals and activists—Abraham Cahan, Morris Hillquit (then still known by his family name Hilkovits), Louis Miller, and Bernard Vaynshteyn among them—launched *Di arbeter tsaytung* after rejecting a proposal by anarchists to start a joint, bipartisan newspaper. The new weekly, unlike the defunct *Folkstsaytung*, defined itself as a strict Marxian newspaper allied with the Socialist Labor Party (SLP) (the major socialist party in the United States at the time, dominated by German immigrants).

Di arbeter tsaytung also differed from the *Folkstsaytung* in that it was owned collectively by a "publishing association" (like the German-language *Volkszeitung*) rather than by private individuals. Only members of the SLP, the United Hebrew Trades, or an affiliated union could join the Arbeter Tsaytung Publishing Association (ATPA). Members were responsible for raising money (most of which came from German American trade unionists), selecting *Di arbeter tsaytung*'s editor, and overseeing the newspaper's affairs. The ATPA imported Philip Krants from England to serve as the first editor. A veteran of the Russian revolutionary movement, Krants had coedited London's *Arbeter fraynd* (*The Workers' Friend*) between 1885 and 1889 and was widely respected among New York's Jewish socialists.

As its name implied, *Di arbeter tsaytung* viewed itself not as a Jewish newspaper but as a workers' newspaper in the Yiddish language. As such, it put forward no specifically Jewish goals, but rather pledged "to help the workers in their political and economic struggles against the capitalists at every step; to awaken in them a spirit of freedom, independence, and class-consciousness" (Michels 2005). A typical issue of *Di arbeter tsaytung* included news about labor and socialist movements in the United States and Europe; an essay on contemporary events, socialist thought, or an aspect of revolutionary history; and fiction and poetry by Yiddish authors on both sides of the Atlantic (such as Morris Rosenfeld, Sh. Y. Abramovitsh, Y. L. Perets, and Dovid Pinsky). European literature regularly appeared in translation. From a literary standpoint, *Di arbeter tsaytung* was the best Yiddish newspaper in the United States.

It was also important as the newspaper in which Abraham Cahan honed his talents as a Yiddish journalist. Cahan replaced Krants in the summer of 1891 and remained editor of *Di arbeter tsaytung* until it ceased publication in 1897. Cahan lent the newspaper a folksy, popular flair. He possessed a superior command of Yiddish and a knack for presenting socialist ideas in an accessible style. Thus Cahan used to explain to readers that a union card was like a *mezuze* that could protect workers from harm. Rather than resort to daytshmerish, Cahan mined the Yiddish lexicon for appropriate terms or coined new ones (such as *pasirung*, or event) that had an authentic Yiddish flavor. He insisted that his colleagues write in simple, understandable language or what he called *yidishe yidish*. If they did not know Yiddish well enough (as held true for many socialist intellectuals), then Cahan tutored his writers in plain *mame-loshn,* the immigrants' mother tongue. Cahan's most distinctive contribution to *Di arbeter tsaytung,* starting in 1890, was the *Sedre* or commentary on the weekly Torah portion, in which Cahan (under the guise of The Proletarian Preacher) commented on current events in the style of an Old World *magid* (preacher). In later decades, as editor of the *Forverts* (*Forward*), Cahan achieved enormous success by combining his folksy socialism with American yellow journalism.

Di arbeter tsaytung, established during the second major strike wave since the Great Upheaval of 1886, won immediate approval from the immigrant Jewish public. The premier issue sold out and, a month later, the newspaper expanded from four to eight pages. Estimates of its circulation range between 6,000 and 8,000 copies, an impressive figure for that time. The actual number of readers was certainly larger since single copies typically passed from hand to hand and were read collectively in small groups. Moreover, *Di arbeter tsaytung* paved the way for *Dos abend blat* (*The Evening Sheet*), the world's first socialist Yiddish daily, in the fall of 1894. Started during yet another huge strike wave, *Dos abend blat* struck a chord with the public. Philip Krants, the paper's editor, boasted in February 1895 that the daily had 36,000 "worker-readers."

In truth, not all of *Dos abend blat's* readers were workers or even socialists. The Yiddish readership did not divide neatly into rigid ideological or political camps. Some readers might read both *Dos abend blat* and the *Tageblat,* regardless of whether they agreed fully with the contents of either. People read a given newspaper for any number of reasons: for its literary offerings, practical information, entertaining feuds between writers, whatever. Nonetheless, it was remarkable that tens of thousands of people (most without prior exposure to radical ideas or without experience reading newspapers in Eastern Europe) showed a willingness to read an avowedly Marxian newspaper every day, regardless of whether or not they agreed with its editorial line or the entirety of its content. *Dos abend blat* still trailed behind the *Tageblat,* but its considerable popularity can be understood as a barometer of rapid cultural change occurring among immigrant Jews and, indeed, as a contributor to it.

A factional struggle within the ATPA led to the demise of *Di arbeter tsaytung* in 1897 and *Dos abend blat* in 1902. They would be replaced by the *Forverts,* founded in April

1897, which would grow into the most successful Yiddish daily of all time under Cahan's editorship. Anarchists met with less success in the Yiddish newspaper market. The anarchist group, Pioneers of Liberty, founded *Di fraye arbeter shtime* (*Free Voice of Labor*) in July 1890 but struggled to keep it afloat during much of the decade. Lacking a strong base of support in the trade union movement, anarchists faced chronic problems in raising sufficient funds. The paper was forced to cease publication in 1892 and again in 1893. Not until 1899 would anarchists manage to publish *Di fraye arbeter shtime* (refashioned by its editor Shoel Yanovsky into a paper of high literary merit) on a regular weekly basis, which they did until 1977.

Beyond the left-wing Yiddish press, the quantity and diversity of Yiddish publications increased across the country during the 1890s. In addition to the *Tageblat, Dos abend blat,* and *Forverts,* five other dailies representing different ideological perspectives appeared between 1894 and 1899: *Der teglekher herold* (*The Daily Herald,* 1894), *Der teglekher telegraf* (*The Daily Telegraph,* 1895), *Di teglekhe prese* (*The Daily Press,* 1898), *Di teglekhe folkstsaytung* (*The Daily People's Newspaper,* 1899), and the *Nyuyorker yidishe abendpost* (*The New York Jewish Evening Post,* 1899). In 1892, the Sarasohns bought out Chicago's *Der yidisher kurier* (*The Jewish Courier*), founded in 1887, and turned it into the city's first Yiddish daily. (While New York newspapers dominated the national market, Baltimore, Boston, Chicago, Newark, Philadelphia, Pittsburgh, and San Francisco were home to Yiddish newspapers of their own.)

A variety of specialized newspapers and journals (albeit mostly short-lived) also appeared during the late 1880s and 1890s. There was a newspaper for women (*Di vayberishe tsaytung* [*The Women's Newspaper*]), satirical journals (*Der yidisher puck* [*The Jewish Puck*], *Der litvakl* [*The Little Lithuanian Jew*], *Di groyse baytsh* [*The Big Whip*]), a theater newspaper (*Di fraye yidishe folksbine* [*The Free Jewish People's Theater*]), Zionist newspapers (*Di tsayt* [*The Times*], *Der tsionist* [*The Zionist*]), a science journal (*Natur un lebn* [*Nature and Life*]), a publication for matchmakers (*Der shadkhen* [*The Matchmaker*]), and others. A number of left-wing educational/political/literary journals also came out during the decade, such as the Pioneers of Liberty's *Di fraye gezelshaft* (*The Free Society*), Alexander Harkavy's *Der nayer gayst* (*The New Spirit*), and, most important, the monthly *Di tsukunft* (*The Future*).

Founded by the SLP's Yiddish-speaking branches in 1892 for the purpose of educating ("enlightening") Jewish workers, *Di tsukunft* aimed to popularize secular knowledge for readers who knew no other language than Yiddish and who had no formal secular education. The journal (edited first by Krants and then by Cahan) published articles on political economy, philosophy, biology, zoology, anthropology, astronomy, pedagogy, physics, psychology, religion, and literature. Nowhere else could immigrants learn about a wide array of scientific subjects written in a relatively good Yiddish. By 1897, *Di tsukunft*'s circulation reached about 3,500 with an actual readership of about 10,000, according to one contemporary estimate.

Di tsukunft and similar, less successful journals reflected a maturation of the Yiddish reading public. These journals helped to cultivate a relatively small, but growing stratum of readers who wanted to expand their intellectual horizons beyond the newspaper page. This "advanced" segment of the Yiddish readership assumed organizational form in the numerous self-education societies that sprung up in immigrant Jewish centers during the 1890s. Members of self-education societies (mostly young men and women active in the Jewish labor movement) formed reading groups, organized lectures, built informal libraries, and raised money for journals (such as *Di tsukunft*) and for the publication of Yiddish pamphlets. Some groups even trained their members to become public speakers. Many such societies eventually merged into the Arbeter Ring, established as a national fraternal order in 1900, which combined mutual aid with self-education. The Jewish labor movement's first, stable mass-membership organization, the Arbeter Ring gained almost 40,000 members in 1910 and more than twice that in the 1920s.

As the Yiddish readership matured, so too did Yiddish journalism as a profession. In the 1870s, the number of people who made a living from the Yiddish press could be counted on one hand. Typically, a single editor wrote or translated most of his newspaper's copy and often served as the typesetter as well. (This also held true for the early English-language press in the United States.) The few people who could be labeled Yiddish journalists usually had to supplement their income with other occupations, such as teaching in Jewish religious schools (itself a low-paying occupation). By the mid-1880s, however, there were signs that Yiddish writers had started to think of themselves as a distinct group or profession. In October 1885, a meeting was called to create the Nyu-yorker zhargoner prese klub (New York Yiddish Press Club) for the purpose of "mutual assistance, both material and moral, between Yiddish writers" (Khaykin 1946). However, no such organization came into existence. The number of professional Yiddish journalists (people who supported themselves by writing full-time for Yiddish newspapers) was still quite small in the late 1880s. The total number of professional or semiprofessional Yiddish journalists, as of 1889, probably totaled no more than ten.

But, with the expansion of the Yiddish press in the 1890s, the number of professional writers grew steadily. The Yiddish press drew writers from other languages, such as Hebrew and Russian, which failed to sustain viable newspapers in the late nineteenth century. A few writers, such as the Stanford University–educated William Edlin, even chose Yiddish over English. A growing number of journalists and creative writers immigrated to the United States—either by invitation from a specific newspaper or on their own initiative—to take advantage of the burgeoning audience and financial possibilities afforded by the Yiddish press. The list included Philip Krants, Dovid Pinsky, and Morris Vintshevsky, all of whom played a pioneering role in the development of Yiddish letters on both sides of the Atlantic. (A poet in both Hebrew and Yiddish, Vintshevsky was known as the grandfather of Jewish socialism.) For the first time, writers and editors could earn a decent living from Yiddish journalism in the 1890s. On the high end, the *Tageblat*'s editor, Johann Paley, earned $30 per week and its staff writers, about $10 per week. The highest-paid writer in the Yiddish press was Getsl Zelikovitsh, who made $18 per week. A number of fiction writers, such as Shomer and Moyshe Zeyfert, earned as much as $8 to $12 per week writing for the *Tageblat*. Socialist Yiddish newspapers paid substantially less than the Sarasohns because of lower profits. Krants's official salary from the ATPA was $12 per week in 1890 and Cahan's was $10. Rarely, however, was either person paid regularly or in full, at least not in the early years of the publishing association. (Socialist writers could earn extra money giving lectures to Jewish socialist or labor organizations.)

Professional self-consciousness among Yiddish writers also took the form of strikes. Starting in the 1890s, Yiddish writers occasionally went on strike against their employers, leading to attempts at unionization. In 1915,

Yiddish writers formed the Y. L. Perets Fareyn, the first successful union of Yiddish writers.

Thus, in the late nineteenth century, a full-fledged commercial Yiddish press had come into existence in the United States, years before one developed in Europe.

Tony Michels

References and Further Reading

Howe, Irving. 1976. *World of Our Fathers.* New York: Harcourt Brace Jovanovich.

Khaykin, Y. 1946. *Yidishe bleter in Amerike.* New York: Author.

Marmor, Kalman. 1944. *Der onhoyb fun der yidisher literature in Amerike (1870–1890).* New York: IKUF.

Michels, Tony. 2005. *A Fire in Their Hearts: Yiddish Socialists in New York.* Cambridge, MA: Harvard University Press.

Park, Robert E. 1922. *The Immigrant Press and Its Control.* New York: Harper and Brothers.

Rischin, Moses. 1970. *The Promised City: New York's Jews, 1870–1914.* New York: Harper & Row.

Shtarkman, Moyshe. 1945. "Vikhtikste momentn in der geshikhte fun der yidisher prese in Amerike." In *75 yor yidishe prese in Amerike.* New York: Y. L. Perets Shrayber Fareyn.

Abraham Cahan (1860–1951)

Editor of the *Jewish Daily Forward* and Novelist

A radical labor organizer, brilliant orator, novelist, translator, and journalist, Abraham Cahan is best known as the indefatigable editor of the Yiddish-language, socialist newspaper, *The Jewish Daily Forward* (*Forvarts*). Over the course of nearly half a century, from 1903, when he assumed the helm at the *Forward,* to his death in 1951, Cahan turned a drab, virtually unreadable Yiddish daily into a landmark of American journalism. Instead of emphasizing theoretical pieces in his socialist paper, Cahan presented the class struggle in the form of stories and news from the marketplace, home, and factory. With his keen eye for the intrinsically interesting in the many complex and intersecting worlds of urban life, and with his commitment to social justice and to the "whole truth in life and literature," Cahan constructed a *Forward* that remained attractive to nonsocialist as well as socialist Jews and

reached a circulation of more than a quarter million. The paper was the world's greatest immigrant, Jewish, and socialist daily, and it helped make Cahan possibly the single most influential figure in the cultural life of millions of Jewish immigrants and their families during his lifetime.

Born July 7, 1860 in the *shtetl* of Podberezya, Byelorussia, Cahan was the only child of Shachne and Sarah Goldarbeiter Cahan. When he was five, his family moved to nearby Vilna, the capital of rabbinic learning and the seat of a growing modernization movement. Here the elder Cahan, a relatively poor shopkeeper and Hebrew teacher, and the son of an itinerant rabbi, was torn between his desire to prepare his own son for a career through secular education or through religious school (*heder*).

Cahan went to religious school and studied the tractates of the Talmud, but he also voraciously read secular works in the Vilna Public Library. Through intense self-study, he learned Russian and gained admission to the Vilna State Teachers Training College in 1878. The school was a center for student radicalism, and by 1880 Cahan had had significant contact with revolutionary students and was converted to socialism. He was taken with radical literature, which he described as "a forbidden object."

> Its publishers are those people . . . who live together like brothers and are ready to go to the gallows for freedom and justice. . . . I took the pamphlet in hand as one touches a holy thing I will never forget it. . . . All of this became part of my new religion, and had a great effect on my feelings. After my conversion to Socialism, I withdrew from all foolishness. I was definitely a better, more serious and philosophical man.

In 1881, Cahan, now a certified schoolmaster in Velizhi, Lithuania, and a member of an underground revolutionary cell, had to flee the police, whose suspicions had been aroused by the young teacher's radical associations. He thought of emigrating to Switzerland and even to Palestine, but Cahan finally joined an Am Olam group, which in the wake of nearly 200 pogroms in Ukraine was going to the United States to experiment with Jewish agricultural communalism.

Cahan arrived in Philadelphia on June 6, 1882, but settled in New York the very next day. He worked for a while in a cigar factory and then for an even shorter time

Abraham Cahan, editor of the Yiddish-language socialist newspaper The Jewish Daily Forward. *(Library of Congress)*

in a tin shop. He found the labor exhausting and monotonous. His joy came from teaching English to groups of his East Side neighbors at night. To learn the language better himself, the twenty-two-year-old Cahan worked with English newspapers and a rudimentary grammar, and sat among twelve- and thirteen-year-olds (mostly non-Jews) in an elementary school on Chrystie Street.

Aspiring to a career as a writer and anxious to escape the oppression of the shops, Cahan sent his first article, a critique of czarism, to the *New York World*. Though unsolicited, the piece was published on the front page. Cahan continued to teach English classes to immigrants for ten more years, all the while encouraging acculturation, but his main contribution came in labor activism and journalism, particularly the pioneering of popular Yiddish journalism. As early as the summer of 1882, Cahan had discovered a growing immigrant audience responsive to Yiddish. Unlike many of his colleagues among the radical Jewish intelligentsia, who were addressing Yiddish-speaking immigrants in Russian, Cahan began to deliver popular political harangues in the so-called folk vernacular. Relatively quickly, others saw the practicality of this, and Yiddish became the primary medium of communication among Jewish radicals. Lecturing in Yiddish and English in 1884 and 1885, Cahan helped organize a Jewish tailors union and a Jewish cloakmakers union. This was the beginning of Cahan's lifelong association with the militant labor movement.

For some time the consensus continued to be that Yiddish was strictly an expedient in the conducting of Socialist labor activity and not a value in itself. Many radicals, however, came to love the "despised jargon," and Cahan would champion Yiddish to journalistic and literary heights, even as he tried to transcend the Yiddish-speaking community with articles and stories in the English press and with several English-language novels. Among the most important of these is *Yekl: A Tale of the New York Ghetto* (1896), a classic exploration of the urban experience, which focuses on the conflicts and tensions inherent in the American immigrant struggle for new identity. And *The Rise of David Levinsky* (1917), considered by critics to be Cahan's greatest work, is a first-person retrospective assessment of a poor immigrant who became a successful garment manufacturer—rich, but filled with both pride and regret.

Abraham Cahan's early politics resembled an eclectic stew of European ideas strongly flavored with the ethical and moral ingredients of his Jewish religious background. After his association with Am Olam, which he ultimately rejected as "utopian," Cahan described himself as an anarchist *and* a socialist. For a while he preached the violent "propaganda of the deed" and advised the poor to "march with iron bars and axes on Fifth Avenue and . . . seize the palaces of the rich." But after the Haymarket affair in 1886–1887, when seven radical agitators were sentenced to death and four were executed for the murder of seven policemen killed in the course of a violent melee at an anarchist meeting, Cahan became convinced that the anarchists were "adventurers," and he committed himself more firmly and exclusively to socialism.

To make the appeal to socialism effective, Cahan and other journalists, organizers, and activists believed recruits would have to see social strain and discontent and the need for collective economic and political action in terms of their own cultural heritage. Cahan constantly wove biblical references and Talmudic aphorisms into his calls to labor unionism and socialism. In 1886, in the first issue of *Neie Tseit* (*New Times*), which he coedited, Cahan used the theme of Shevuot (the festival of weeks, associated with the receiving of the Law) to illustrate socialist principles, and he remained interested throughout most of his career in using Jewish tradition and folk-religious forms in this way. He understood and applauded the fact that the rigid mores of Jewish Orthodoxy had already undergone a loosening in Eastern Europe and that in the United States, the *trefene medina* (unkosher land), there was further erosion. But Cahan knew how thoroughly Jewish values and traditions were embedded in the Jewish imagination, even in that of a professed atheist like himself. Ethnic attachments, in the

richest sense of that term, operated even on those who thought they had discarded them as "backward," and they were certainly meaningful to the average Jewish worker who read Cahan's journalism.

In 1890, Abe Cahan began a weekly column in the *Arbeiter Tseitung* (*Workers Newspaper*) known as the *Sedre*, the portion of the Pentateuch read each week in Sabbath services. He always began with a formal element in the liturgy, but soon took off into a discussion of socialist matters. Cahan's pieces proved so popular that even the anarchists tried to imitate them in the *Freie Arbeiter Shtimme* (*Free Voice of Labor*). *The Jewish Daily Forward*, which Cahan edited at its founding in 1897 and to which he returned permanently in 1903, became under his leadership the educator of the Jewish immigrant masses, a critical component of the Jewish labor movement and Jewish socialism, and a defender and patron of Yiddish literature and modern culture. Among the authors sustained by the *Forward* were Sholem Asch and Isaac Bashevis Singer.

One of the *Forward*'s best-read innovations was the *Bintel Brief* (bundle of letters), started in 1906. Letters from readers about poverty and sickness, love and divorce, unemployment, intermarriage, socialism, generational conflicts, and declining religious observance were printed daily. The responses, written by Cahan in the early years and increasingly by his staff as well, tried to suggest that the immigrants should not make excessive demands on themselves, that they should even enjoy life a little. Cahan did not advise immigrants to give up their religious or ideological preconceptions entirely, but he did encourage the newcomers to make the needs of everyday life in America primary.

As part of the Americanization process, Cahan also tried to acquaint *Forward* readers with English. Opening himself to the charge of corrupting the Yiddish language, Cahan encouraged his writers to follow the general custom of incorporating English words into their Yiddish articles. And in 1923 he went so far as to introduce a multipage English language insert. At its height in 1920, the *Forward* published twelve metropolitan editions from Boston to Los Angeles, and its circulation was close to 300,000. A large part of the profits went to social causes.

A moderate socialist, Cahan's anticapitalist views were tempered by American conditions and by the increasing tyrannies of militant Bolshevism. At the outset of the Russian revolution in 1917, Cahan had proclaimed, "Russia is free." But the *Forward* became increasingly anti-Communist as the excesses of Soviet authoritarianism became apparent. In addition, Cahan continued to be interested in the particular oppression of Jews. As early as 1891, when Cahan was a delegate of the United Hebrew Trades at the Brussels congress of the Second International, he explained that the federation of unions he represented had "nothing to do with religion or nationality" and that the word *Hebrew* was adopted "only because of the language spoken by all its members." At the same time, however, he introduced a resolution condemning antisemitism.

In April 1903, when the news of the Kishinev pogrom reached Cahan in Connecticut, he was bird-watching, a hobby he had developed as a break from writing. Field glasses and bird manual in hand, he immediately rushed for a New York train. "I felt an urge to be among Jews," he explained in his autobiography. Partially in response to Kishinev, Cahan wrote his little-known novel *The White Terror and the Red*, which was published in 1905. The story, set in the early 1880s, explores the conflicts of young Jewish revolutionaries and deals with their unfortunate attitudes toward the Jewish people and the pogroms that victimized them.

In 1925, after attending the Socialist Congress at Marseilles, Cahan visited Palestine for the first time and wept at the Western Wall. Jewish "crises" continued to agitate him. After the 1929 anti-Jewish riots in Palestine, which a handful of radicals applauded as the beginning of "revolution," Cahan made certain his paper did a thorough and sensitive job covering the impact of the events on the Jewish community there. Although he did not consider himself a Zionist, he paid tribute to the courage and idealism of Zionist pioneers. Throughout the 1930s and 1940s Cahan continued to be productive and creative. Only after suffering a stroke in 1946 at the age of eighty-six did he stop appearing at the *Forward* office on a daily basis.

In a series of letters written between 1883 and 1884, Abraham Cahan had complained of a lack of "orientation" and a "firm foundation." He was tormented over his "divided mood." Despite his marriage to Anna Bronstein in 1886, an educated and cultured woman from Kiev who brought sensibilities to the relationship that helped sustain Cahan for sixty years of a turbulent career, he never completely transcended the divided mood. He was, after all, a refugee from Russia observing revolutionary sacrifice from afar and an assertive promoter of Americanization wedded to Yiddish journalism.

Cahan as a Socialist could integrate his Old World and New World selves. But Cahan the exile—hailed along with Stephen Crane and Hamlin Garland as the harbinger of a new literature, and whose *Forward* was described as "America's most interesting daily"—never fully came to terms with his becoming something of the "successful American." The ambivalence he continued to experience showed clearly in his semiautobiographical novel, *The Rise of David Levinsky*. David is also a "success," but reflects: "I cannot escape from my old self. David, the poor lad swinging over a Talmud volume at the Preacher's Synagogue, seems to have more in common with my inner identity than David Levinsky, the well-known cloak manufacturer." By the time Cahan died of heart failure at the age of ninety-one, however, this complex, often troubled man was recognized as a great journalist, a legendary teacher to a people in the process of acculturation, and a persistent defender of the cause of labor and socialism.

Gerald Sorin

References and Further Reading
Chametzky, Jules. 1977. *From the Ghetto: The Fiction of Abraham Cahan*. Amherst: University of Massachusetts Press.
Hapgood, Hutchins. 1967. *The Spirit of the Ghetto*. Cambridge, MA: Belknap/Harvard University Press.
Howe, Irving. 1976. *World of Our Fathers*. New York: Harcourt Brace Jovanovich.
Marovitz, Sanford E., and Lewis Fried. 1970. "Abraham Cahan (1860–1951): An Annotated Bibliography." *American Literary Realism* (Summer): 197–243.
Rischin, Moses. 1962. *The Promised City*. Cambridge, MA: Harvard University Press.
Rischin, Moses. 1985. *Grandma Never Lived in America: The New Journalism of Abraham Cahan*. Bloomington: Indiana University Press.
Sanders, Ronald. 1969. *The Downtown Jews*. New York: Harper & Row.
Sorin, Gerald. 1992. *A Time for Building: The Third Migration, 1880–1920*. Baltimore: Johns Hopkins University Press.
Stein, Leon, Abraham Conan, and Lynn Davison, trans. 1969. *The Education of Abraham Cahan*. Philadelphia: Jewish Publication Society.

The American Jewish Press

Rabbi Stephen S. Wise referred to U.S. Jewish newspapers as "weaklies," and Brandeis professor Jonathan Sarna noted that the history of American Jewish journalism showed, "at least until recently, a story of marked decay" (Sarna 2004). Despite these justifiably critical comments, the American Jewish press has had a rich and complex history. In the more than 160 years of American Jewish journalism, an estimated 2,500 newspapers and magazines have appeared, with at least one publication in most states. Although these American Jewish publications have appeared in German, Yiddish, Hebrew, Russian, and Ladino (Judeo-Spanish), the English publications constitute the oldest segment of American Jewish journalism. In 1880, although about two-thirds of the 250,000 American Jews had German ancestry, the English-language Jewish publications "outnumbered those in German and survived longer" (Goren 1987). According to Arthur Goren, the influx of Yiddish-speaking East European Jews at the end of the nineteenth century contributed to the further expansion of the Anglo-Jewish press, as the "established Jews" sought to secure their status as English speakers. In the decades after immigration restriction (1924), as the number of Jews able to read Yiddish declined precipitously, the English-language Jewish press once again became the most widely read.

The difficulties of defining an American Jewish publication are akin to those of defining a Jew. The earliest publication with a Jewish name is *Cohen's Gazette and Lottery Register*. Yet this Baltimore journal, which began publication in 1814, was Jewish in name only: "[I]t was, in essence, a gambling sheet" (Sarna 2004). A New York journal, *The Jew*, was published in 1823 to counter Christian missionary efforts, but contained little substantive news. It lasted only two years. From 1817 through most of the 1830s, Mordecai Manuel Noah, a leading American Jewish editor, playwright, lawyer, and politician, wrote about many issues of Jewish concern, but these articles appeared in the New York–based *National Advocate*, New York *Evening Star*, and other non-Jewish publications.

The first identifiably Jewish publication was the *Occident and American Jewish Advocate*. Founded in April 1843 by Isaac Leeser, the *hazzan* of Congregation Mikveh Israel in Philadelphia, this journal soon emerged as the place where American Jews found "answers to questions regarding Jewish behavior and identity in this new world" (Libo 1987). The journal published news from Jewish communities throughout the country and reprinted articles from European Jewish periodicals. The *Occident* also published book reviews, editorials, fiction, poetry, political and reli-

gious philosophy, documents, and historical essays. Stating its aim as the "diffusion of knowledge on Jewish literature and religion," it was "one of the finest journals that the American Jewish community has ever produced" (Sarna 2004). Nevertheless, Sarna suggests that the *Occident* foreshadowed a persistent problem in American Jewish journalism: "a tension between the Jewish journalist as a reporter of news and . . . a shaper of community." In the years preceding the Civil War, Leeser would not publish diverse Jewish views about slavery, fearing this might have bad effects on the welfare of the entire Jewish community. The refusal to publish vigorous debate about a controversial issue is not unique to this era. A century and a half later, some community activists and Jewish journalists denounced American Jewish newspapers and magazines for not printing articles critical of the policies and actions of Israeli right-wing governments.

Although New York did not emerge as the preeminent American city for Jews until the late nineteenth century, America's largest metropolis became the home of the first important Jewish periodical in 1849. Edited by a businessman, Robert Lyon, *The Asmonean* published articles on a wide variety of Jewish and secular topics, but lasted less than a decade.

In 1854, the growth of Reform Judaism spawned the *Israelite*, later renamed the *American Israelite*, now the oldest continuously published Jewish newspaper in the United States. Founded by Rabbi Isaac Mayer Wise of Cincinnati, this was the first American Jewish publication propounding the ideology of a Jewish religious denomination. Rabbi Wise wrote articles critical of anti-Jewish discriminatory practices and hailed the legal and religious freedom accorded Jews in this country (Libo 1987). The *American Hebrew*, founded in 1879, published Israel Zangwill, Emma Lazarus, and Henrietta Szold, among other literary and intellectual figures, and emerged as a significant journal fostering both Jewish and American values.

By the end of the nineteenth century, almost every American city with a sizable Jewish population had a weekly English publication covering Jewish news in the United States and abroad. Although the rapid growth of American Jewish publications was impressive, it never matched—even to this day—the circulation and influence of the Yiddish-language American press, which in the 1920s sold an estimated 600,000 daily copies in New York City alone (Libo 1987). Occasionally, the English-language

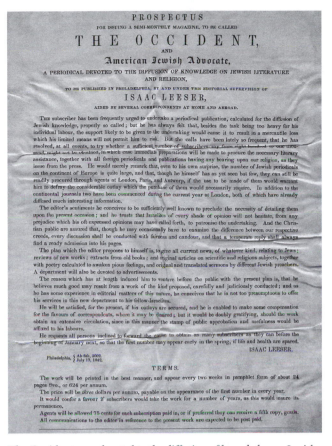

The Occident *was devoted to the diffusion of knowledge on Jewish literature and religion. (American Jewish Historical Society)*

Jewish press voiced the hostility of some American-born Jews to their East European coreligionists and their language. The *Jewish Times* characterized *Di Yiddishe Zeitung* as "just as ridiculous as its language," and the *American Israelite* objected to *Di Post* because Judaism "is degraded by being clothed in such a language" (Silverman 1963).

The professionalization of Jewish journalism began in the twentieth century with the creation of two organizations. In 1917, Viennese Jewish journalist Jacob Landau founded the Jewish Telegraphic Agency (JTA, originally the Jewish Correspondence Association) to provide news that was not covered by the major wire services—for example, the impact of World War I on Jewish communities throughout the world. The JTA covered the anti-Jewish riots in Palestine in the 1920s and the rise of Nazism in the 1930s. It also launched an Overseas News Agency to get news from Nazi-held areas, where Jewish correspondents were forbidden (Libo 1987). Many distinguished American Jewish journalists worked at the JTA, including Daniel Schorr, Theodore White, David Schoenbrun, Elie Abel, and

Meyer Levin. Formerly disseminating much of its news by the print *JTA Daily Bulletin,* the agency now features a website covering news about Jews in the United States, Israel, and throughout the world. The second organization, the American Jewish Press Association (AJPA), founded in April 1944, is composed of Jewish Federation–affiliated and independent newspapers, magazines, and, recently, electronic media.

Reflecting the religious, political, cultural, intellectual, and social interests of the community, the American Jewish press now boasts a remarkably eclectic range of newspapers, newsletters, magazines, journals, and websites. Each denomination has at least one publication— *Tradition* (Orthodox), *Conservative Judaism, Reform Judaism, The Reconstructionist,* and *Humanistic Judaism.* Political, religious, and cultural Zionism are propagated and discussed in many periodicals and newsletters, including *Hadassah Magazine* (1921), one of the largest circulating American Jewish journals, and *Midstream* (1955), a political and cultural magazine issued by the Theodor Herzl Institute. Almost every Zionist organization publishes a journal or newsletter, ranging from the left-wing *Israel Horizons,* issued by the American branch of the Israeli political party Meretz, to the right-wing *Outpost,* published by Americans for a Safe Israel.

The *American Jewish Year Book* includes an extensive list of publications, but even this authoritative source omits some specialized periodicals. If, for every Jew, there are two opinions, nowadays there are—at least—two periodicals. American Jewish stamp collectors, for example, could subscribe to two publications: the *Judaica Philatelic Journal* and *Judaica Post.* Jews who observe religious dietary laws have savored the contents of several journals over the years, including *Kosher Outlook, Kosher Home, Kashrus Magazine, Kosher Spirit,* and *Kosher Gourmet Magazine.*

More than thirty-five years before Daniel Glickman was appointed the first Jewish secretary of agriculture, Jewish grangers subscribed to the *Jewish Farmer,* published by the Jewish Agricultural Society for almost fifty years. The *Paper Pomegranate,* the quarterly journal of the national Pomegranate Guild of Judaic Needlework, features articles on needlework techniques, Jewish holiday projects, and other material related to the fiber arts. Since 1996, the National Yiddish Book Center, based in Amherst, Massachusetts, has published the beautifully designed *Pakn Treger*

(*Book Peddler*). Unique among U.S. publications, it is aimed at a general Jewish audience interested in the multilingual facets of Jewish literature and culture.

While readers with an appetite for intellectual issues were never offered a wide fare, a few major journals have greatly stimulated religious, literary, cultural, and philosophical discussions on the nature of American Judaism. Once described as "one of the most exciting episodes in the history of the American-Jewish intellectual community," the *Menorah Journal* featured the writings of prominent intellectuals and literary figures, including Cecil Roth, Salo Baron, Harry Austryn Wolfson, Lionel Trilling, Louis Untermeyer, and Rabbi David de Sola Pool (Alter 1965). Founded by Harvard College students, this widely quoted journal with a small circulation was published from 1915 to 1962. A managing editor, Elliot Cohen, later became the editor of the premier U.S. Jewish intellectual journal *Commentary*, published by the American Jewish Committee. After the writer Norman Podhoretz assumed the editorship in 1960, *Commentary* gradually emerged as a voice for neoconservatism, publishing essays that greatly influenced Jewish communal life and even American government policies. Jeane Kirkpatrick's November 1979 essay reportedly so impressed President Ronald Reagan that he appointed her U.S. ambassador to the United Nations.

As a lonely journalistic voice challenging the veracity of the most powerful government on earth, *I. F. Stone's Weekly* may have been unique, but it has counterparts among some Jewish journals that attempted to do battle with major Jewish leaders and organizations. Trude Weiss-Rosmarin, founder of the New York–based School for Jewish Women, published the *Jewish Spectator*, which for more than a half century offered iconoclastic views on many issues of Jewish interest. Begun in 1936, the *Jewish Spectator* was originally billed as a "typical family magazine, with a special appeal to the woman" (Moore 1994). Yet Weiss-Rosmarin, an early Jewish feminist, published a variety of pathbreaking articles, from attacks on American complicity with Nazi Germany to debates on the nature of Zionism. Although it was a secular and cultural publication, almost a thousand rabbis subscribed in the 1950s. Weiss-Rosmarin died in 1989, and the publication folded in 2002.

Starting in 1970, a small collective of dissident rabbis, communal leaders, and activists contributed to Rabbi Eugene Borowitz's *Sh'ma, A Newsletter of Jewish Renewal*. Articles addressed a wide range of topics, from Jewish feminism to Jewish attitudes toward affirmative action. One issue was devoted to Jewish intramarriage, for example, Sephardi–Ashkenazi and secular–religious. Contributors ranged from Rabbi Meir Kahane, who claimed that Judaism and liberal democracy were incompatible, to attorney Henry Schwarzschild, who resigned from all Jewish organizations to protest the Israeli incursion into Lebanon. In the 1980s the newsletter had 6,000 subscribers.

Author and journalist Leonard Fein offered his perspective on American Jewish and Israeli issues in *Moment*, a glossy magazine with a much larger circulation than the newsletter. Named in honor of *Der Moment*, one of the leading pre–World War I Yiddish dailies in Warsaw, the magazine is noted for its interviews with major Jewish personalities, including Nobel laureate Isaac Bashevis Singer, Israeli diplomat Abba Eban, and the preeminent American Jewish historian Jacob Rader Marcus.

Started in 1986 by Michael Lerner as the "liberal alternative to *Commentary* and the voices of Jewish conservatism," the San Francisco area–based *Tikkun* magazine has published essays critical of both American and Israeli foreign policy and the rightward drift of many American Jews.

Anglo-Jewish newspapers, weeklies, or biweeklies, mostly funded by the local Jewish federations, have frequently been attacked for offering mainly wire reports from the JTA, instead of original local coverage. These publications have also been criticized for avoiding controversial issues affecting their communities. Announcements of births, bar and bat mitzvahs, engagements, marriages, and deaths, originally confined to synagogue bulletins, have become the mainstay of these newspapers. Former Boston *Jewish Advocate* editor Joseph Weisberg mocked the community leader who rushes "to get into print news and pictures dealing with family *simchas*—and even his election to the lodge—but then refuses to subscribe to the paper because there is too much social news" (Altschiller 1980).

Recently, however, there has been a noticeable change in some publications. Founded in 1990, the English-language *Forward*, which currently has about 28,000 subscribers, has enlivened American Jewish journalism with its brash and investigative style. (The Yiddish-language *Forverts*, started in 1897 under the legendary author Abraham Cahan, is still published, but it is read by only a few thousand elderly native speakers.) Ironically, this venerable socialist newspaper was reconstituted in English by Seth Lipsky, a neoconservative *Wall Street Journal* editor who sought to "analyze local politics, the Middle East, the economy, immigration and a range of other 'secular' topics from a sophisticated and uniquely Jewish perspective" (Beckerman 2004). But his politics turned out to be too conservative for the publishers, and in May 2000 the Forward Association forced Lipsky to resign. He was replaced by J. J. Goldberg, a liberal and left-wing Zionist.

The *Forward* is not unique in printing dissenting articles about the Jewish community. In 1973, the now defunct *Present Tense* magazine published pieces critical of the rightward drift of American and Israeli Jews. Edited by Murray Polner, a writer and former teacher, *Present Tense* published several controversial articles, including a condemnation of some Jewish nursing home operators, who were convicted of crimes against their patients.

At about the same time, an emerging Jewish student movement also criticized established Jewish leaders. Although inspired by the 1960s radical movements, these Jewish activists, unlike some of their comrades on the Left, refused to shed their ethnic and religious background. They published newspapers that protested U.S. foreign policy, but also criticized Jewish organizations' meager allocations for Jewish education and mocked Jewish *machers*' (big shots) deference to the American WASP establishment by presenting "Uncle Jake" awards. Often produced on a shoestring budget, these newspapers— numbering around forty—included *genesis 2* (Boston), *Chutzpah* (Chicago), *Exodus* (San Francisco Soviet Jewry activists), *Jewish Liberation Journal* (New York), and *Jewish Radical* (Berkeley). The student journalists also started their own wire service, the Jewish Student Press Service (JSPS). While most of these papers lasted only through the 1970s, *genesis 2* was published until 1989. *Response: A Contemporary Jewish Review,* however, has appeared almost continuously since 1967. The only other current Jewish student publication is the bimonthly *New Voices*, first appearing in 1991 and published by the JSPS.

In 1976, Jewish feminists founded the still published *Lilith* magazine, to protest and help redefine the often subordinate role of Jewish women in religious and communal life. Although many of these ideological publications accurately reflected the social, political, and cultural ferment of their times, they were read mainly by committed activists and seldom by the broader Jewish community.

In recent years some mainstream papers have addressed controversial issues. Probably the most controversial and consequential recent article was "Stolen Innocence" in *Jewish Week* (June 23, 2000). Written by editor and publisher Gary Rosenblatt, this 4,000-word article is about a prominent New Jersey rabbi accused of sexually abusing and harassing teenagers in his charge over a period of two decades. Rosenblatt documented how some Jewish clergy and organizations attempted to cover up the crimes. His investigative article sparked a bitter debate in the Jewish community about airing "dirty laundry" in public. The *New York Times* and other media picked up the story, and some claim this coverage led to the prosecution and imprisonment of the perpetrator. This case demonstrates the quandary facing the American Jewish press and journalists. Rosenblatt summarized it nicely: "The First Commandment of the journalist is to probe, uncover, explore. The first commandment in the Jewish organizational world is pretty much the opposite: to present the united front: 'We are one.' That crystallizes the dilemma" (Barringer 2000).

For many years, debate has simmered about Jewish Federations' funding of their community newspapers. Critics have charged that this support not only compromises their editorial independence, but also creates unfair competition for independent papers, which constitute a small minority of the Jewish press.

Since more than a hundred ethnic groups in the United States publish newspapers, magazines, and journals, it is difficult to compare the American Jewish press to such a wide range of publications. There are, however, some similarities. The debate about diaspora–homeland relations—e.g., whether the American Jewish press should criticize Israel—finds echoes elsewhere. Chinese-American newspapers have long battled over whether they have the right to openly support Taiwan or the People's Republic of China, and the Armenian diaspora press has argued over the idea of a "greater" Armenia. The concerns of the Jewish and Armenian presses are probably the most similar of all American ethnic groups because of the parallels in their national histories—genocide and their ambiguous and occasionally conflicted relations with their homelands.

Nevertheless, the American Jewish press may be unique in some ways. Jews constitute both an ethnic and religious group, and this is reflected in the huge number of religious, ecumenical, fraternal, social, cultural, political, academic, Zionist, anti-Zionist, and non-Zionist publications. In his classic study of the immigrant press, the sociologist Robert Park, who was not Jewish, commented, "The Jew brings with him a civilization" (Park 1922). The number of Jewish journals and magazines that have published anthologies of their articles may also be unique. To paraphrase the classic Jewish joke: Jewish publications are like other ethnic publications. Only more so.

Research Note: Singerman's extensive bibliography of Jewish serials includes invaluable material for further research. The *Index to Jewish Periodicals* provides access to Jewish publications that had never before been listed in standard library indexes.

Donald Altschiller

References and Further Reading

Alter, Robert. 1965. "Epitaph for a Jewish Magazine: Notes on the *Menorah Journal.*" *Commentary* (May): 51–55.

Altschiller, Donald. 1980. "Problems and Prospects of Jewish Journalism." In *The Sociology of American Jews: A Critical Anthology,* 2nd rev. ed, edited by Jack Nusan Porter, 160–167. Lanham, MD: University Press of America.

Barringer, Felicity. 2000. "Paper Seen as Villain in Abuse Accusations against Rabbi." *New York Times* (June 23).

Beckerman, Gal. 2004 "Forward Thinking: So What If the Goyim Are Looking? A Jewish Newspaper Lets It All Hang Out." *Columbia Journalism Review* 42, 5 (January–February): 33–36.

Ford, Luke. 2004. *Yesterday's News Tomorrow: Inside American Jewish Journalism.* New York: iUniverse.

Goren, Arthur A. 1987. "The Jewish Press." In *The Ethnic Press in the United States: A Historical Analysis and Handbook,* edited by Sally M. Miller, 203–228. Wesport, CT: Greenwood Press.

Libo, Kenneth. 1987. "History of Jewish Journalism in America." In *People in Print: Jewish Journalism in America,* 31–49. Philadelphia: National Museum of American Jewish History.

Moore, Deborah Dash. 1994. "Trude Weiss-Rosmarin and the *Jewish Spectator.*" In *The "Other" New York Jewish Intellectuals,* edited by Carole S. Kessner, 101–121. New York: New York University Press.

Park, Robert E. 1970 [1922]. *The Immigrant Press and Its Control.* Westport, CT: Greenwood Press.

Sarna, Jonathan. 2004. "A History of Jewish Journalism in the United States" In *Yesterday's Tomorrow: Inside American Jewish Journalism,* edited by Luke Ford, 321–332. New York: iUniverse.

Silverman, David Wolf. 1963. "The Jewish Press: A Quadrilingual Phenomenon." In *The Religious Press in America,* edited by Martin E. Marty, 125–172. New York: Holt, Rinehart, and Winston.

Singerman, Robert. 1986. *Jewish Serials of the World: A Research Bibliography of Secondary Sources.* Westport, CT: Greenwood Press/*Supplement,* 2001.

American Jews in Political and Social Movements

American Jews in Politics in the Twentieth Century

Jews constitute barely 2 percent of the U.S. population. But because of their education, organization, and affluence, they are able to wield considerable political influence. While there is no single political doctrine to which all Jews subscribe, generally speaking, Jews have used their political influence to promote a liberal social agenda, to combat discrimination, and to further such communal interests as American support for the State of Israel. For the most part, Jews support the Democratic Party in national politics, and the Jewish community constitutes an important force within the Democratic political coalition.

How Jews Acquired Political Influence in America

The political influence of America's Jewish community dates from the 1930s and Franklin D. Roosevelt's New Deal. Before the Roosevelt presidency, American Jews were politically weak and the victims of considerable discrimination. During the New Deal era, however, the government's needs and the capacity of the Jewish community to serve them provided the starting point for the Jews' climb toward political influence and social acceptance. When Roosevelt came to power in 1933, he was opposed by much of the nation's established Protestant elite. As a result, the administration turned to Jewish intellectuals and professionals to develop and administer its ambitious agenda of domestic programs.

One of Roosevelt's key Jewish advisors was Harvard law professor and later Supreme Court Justice Felix Frankfurter, who played a key role in formulating New Deal programs and in recruiting large numbers of Jewish professionals, known as Frankfurter's happy hot dogs, to staff New Deal agencies. Among Frankfurter's protégés was Benjamin Cohen, who wrote many important pieces of New Deal legislation. These included the 1933 Securities Act, the Federal Communications Act, the Wagner Act, and the Minimum Wage Act, all of which remain cornerstones of American public policy. Other Jews who were prominent in the Roosevelt administration include Supreme Court Justice Louis Brandeis, who advised the administration on ways of securing the Court's approval for its legislative enactments; Treasury Secretary Henry Morgenthau; and Securities and Exchange Commission Chairman Jerome Frank. The term *New Deal* itself was coined by one of Roosevelt's Jewish aides, Samuel Rosenman. Such was the importance of Jews in FDR's camp that his opponents sometimes denounced the New Deal as the *Jew Deal* and claimed—falsely—that Roosevelt, himself, must be of Jewish descent. Service with New Deal agencies gave Jewish professionals a considerable measure of political influence and also provided them with expertise and contacts that were invaluable in the private sector. Corporations and firms that had engaged in discriminatory hiring practices before the New Deal began to open their doors, albeit slowly, to Jewish attorneys and other professionals, thus beginning the fuller integration of Jews into American society.

The relationship between Jews and the Roosevelt administration also led the Jewish community to give FDR and his political party their allegiance, and, to this day, most Jews remain firmly in the Democratic political camp. Before Roosevelt, much of the American Jewish community and such communal leaders as Louis Marshall and Felix Warburg had identified with the Republican Party. This identification dated from the Civil War as well as from the linkage between the Democrats and Populism, a movement associated with nativism and antisemitism. Since Roosevelt, Jews have been pillars of the Democratic coalition. In recent years, Democratic presidential, senatorial, and congressional candidates have typically received 80 percent of the Jewish vote as well as a great deal of Jewish money and energy. This is especially remarkable given the growing affluence of the Jewish community, which should lead it to join other wealthy American groups in the Republican Party. One Republican president, Ronald Reagan, made a concerted effort to attract Jewish support, and a small but influential group of Jewish intellectuals, the so-called Neoconservatives, has become prominent in Republican ranks. For most Jews, however, identification with the Democratic Party not only has a strong historic basis in the New Deal, but has also been reinforced by subsequent events. Since the Roosevelt presidency, Jews have assumed an increasing number of leadership positions and an ever-growing stake in the success of the Democrats.

The New Deal represented a political beginning for American Jews. Yet Jews did not fully enter the American political mainstream until the 1960s when they assumed a prominent role in the so-called New Politics, or public interest movement. Between the 1930s and the 1960s, Jews had served mainly as advisers, staffers, operatives, "idea men," and powers behind the throne. Indeed, Roosevelt had told many of his Jewish staffers to maintain a low profile to avoid provoking an antisemitic backlash against his administration. Tragically, Jews had not been sufficiently influential to induce the American government to open the nation's doors to refugees from Nazi Germany before or even during World War II. During the 1960s, however, Jews assumed visible positions of leadership in the civil rights and anti-Vietnam War movements. In the 1970s, Jews led or were influential in virtually all of the political reform, feminist, consumer rights, gay rights, environmental, and other public interest groups, as well as in the related foundations and think tanks that arose during this period. Jews continue to play important roles in a diverse group of liberal political and public interest organizations such as Common Cause, People for the American Way, the Children's Defense Fund, the Women's Legal Defense Fund, and hundreds of others.

The importance of liberal activist groups within the Democratic coalition waxed as the strength of other Democratic entities waned. Economic change undermined the power of organized labor, for decades an important force in the party. By the 1970s, moreover, old-fashioned political party "machines" had all but disappeared in the United States. Candidates for office now relied on ad hoc regiments of volunteers rather than the old-time phalanxes of party workers to staff their campaigns. Increasingly, the public interest movement became the spearhead of the Democratic Party's political army, providing the activists and workers needed for campaign efforts. As the most active of liberal activists and a key element in the leadership cadré of the public interest movement, Jews became increasingly important in Democratic Party politics.

The political weight of these activist groups was further enhanced by the various political reforms that they, themselves, helped to bring about during the 1970s. Changes in the presidential nominating process, starting with the so-called McGovern-Fraser reforms of 1972, gave issue-oriented activists an important voice in the presidential selection process. Citizen-suit provisions included in hundreds of federal regulatory statutes enacted since the 1970s allowed activist groups to use the courts to press their agendas in such areas as environmental protection, consumer affairs, and civil rights.

Perhaps most important, a series of changes in campaign finance rules made activist groups important conduits for campaign funds, particularly for Democratic Party candidates who are not as able as their Republican rivals to depend on the largesse of America's business corporations. The most recent reform of campaign finance laws, the 2002 Bipartisan Campaign Reform Act (BCRA), outlawed the so-called soft money contributions to political parties that had been a major vehicle for funneling corporate money into political campaigns. But while soft money contributions were prohibited by BCRA, the law allows nonprofit groups to form what are known as "527 committees," named for the section of the tax code that grants them tax-exempt status, and to use such committees to raise money for political drives. This proved quite advantageous to liberal activist groups, which quickly formed 527 committees that soon directed tens of millions of dollars into Democratic political efforts. Wealthy Jewish liberals have long been among the most important contributors to the Democratic Party's efforts, and Jewish political activists quickly assumed leadership roles in many of the new fund-raising groups, including America Coming Together, MoveOn.Org, and The Media Fund, which together raised and spent more than $50 million in support of Democratic candidates in 2004.

As Jews became more and more important in the Democratic Party, they increasingly sought and won both elections and appointments to high national offices under Democratic auspices. Before the New Deal, only six Jews had ever served in the U.S. Senate, and only one, Theodore Roosevelt's Commerce Secretary Oscar Straus, had ever been a member of a presidential cabinet. Today Jews commonly hold high national office, almost always as Democrats. In 2004, for example, ten Jews served in the U.S. Senate. Nine of the ten were Democrats. One of these Democratic senators, Joseph Lieberman of Connecticut, was the party's vice presidential candidate in 2000. During the same year, twenty-seven Jews held seats in the U.S. House of Representatives. Only two were Republicans. Also in 2004, two Jews sat on the Supreme Court, both appointed by a Democratic president. In a similar vein, no Jews served as cabinet secretaries in the Republican administrations of George W. Bush, George H. W. Bush, or Ronald Reagan. Indeed, since America's founding, only four Jews have ever been members of Republican cabinets. In addition to Oscar Straus, these were Eisenhower's Commerce Secretary Lewis Strauss, Nixon's Secretary of State Henry Kissinger, and Edward Levi, attorney general under Gerald Ford.

By contrast, Democrat Jimmy Carter, alone, appointed four Jewish cabinet secretaries and Bill Clinton appointed five. The Carter appointees were Treasury Secretary W. Michael Blumenthal, Defense Secretary Harold Brown, Transportation Secretary Neil Goldschmidt, and Commerce Secretary Philip Klutznick. Clinton named Labor Secretary Robert Reich, Treasury secretaries Robert Rubin and Lawrence Summers, Agriculture Secretary Dan Glickman, and Commerce Secretary Mickey Kantor. This pattern of presidential appointments reflects the importance of Jews in the Democratic coalition more than the several presidents' personal feelings about them. Thus Carter, who was not especially friendly to the State of Israel and did not have good relations with the American Jewish community, appointed many Jews to his cabinet, while Ronald Reagan, a staunch supporter of Israel and friend of the American Jewish community, appointed none.

Thus, since the New Deal launched the Jewish community on the path of political influence, Jews have risen to positions of considerable political prominence. That they have done so under Democratic Party auspices helps to explain the continuing loyalty of the Jewish community to the Democrats. To abandon the Democratic Party would be to abandon the institution that continues to provide American Jews with access to political power and position.

Jewish Policy Priorities

While there are many areas of disagreement within the Jewish community, Jews have generally made use of their positions of influence to promote policies to end racial and ethnic discrimination, strengthen the separation of church and state, expand domestic social programs, and maintain American support for the State of Israel. During the 1930s and 1940s, when Jews first won access to policy-making institutions, the chief goal of Jewish political leaders was to bring an end to the discriminatory practices to which Jews had long been subjected. To this end, in 1944, several major Jewish organizations, including the American Jewish Committee, the American Jewish Congress, and the Anti-Defamation League, joined together to form the National Jewish Community Relations Advisory Council (CRC) to combat discrimination against Jews in employment, education, and housing. The CRC succeeded in persuading a number of state legislatures to enact laws prohibiting housing and employment discrimination and in 1965 convinced President Lyndon B. Johnson to issue an executive order prohibiting firms holding federal contracts from discriminating on the basis of religion or race. Johnson later expanded the scope of his order to include banks holding federal funds and insurance companies serving as Medicare carriers.

Jews were also in the forefront of the effort to reinforce America's constitutional separation of church and state. As a religious minority, Jews felt threatened by government-sponsored prayer in the public schools and the display of religious symbols in public places. Accordingly, Jewish organizations backed a campaign of litigation aimed at ending both practices. Often Jewish groups worked from behind the scenes for fear of provoking anti-semitism. For example, the heavily Jewish American Civil Liberties Union (ACLU) found non-Jewish plaintiffs and attorneys for its eventually successful effort in the case of *Zorach v. Clausen* to have the courts strike down a New York state law providing for released time from school for religious instruction.

Jewish organizations made an especially concerted effort to ban ethnic discrimination in the realm of education. After World War I, major American colleges and universities had imposed strict quotas on the admission of Jews to their undergraduate and professional programs. As a result, the proportion of Jewish students at such prestigious institutions as the Harvard Medical School and Columbia's College of Physicians and Surgeons fell from more than one-third of the class to barely 5 percent of each school's student body. Similarly, major institutions refused to hire Jewish faculty and administrators. Jewish organizations used their growing influence to launch two federal investigations of discriminatory practices by universities. These investigations, coupled with a series of lawsuits, forced colleges and universities to dismantle their quota systems in the early 1960s.

In their battles against discrimination, Jews made common cause with African Americans. Throughout the 1960s, Jewish organizations and individuals played an important role in the civil rights movement. For example, Stanley Levison, a Jewish attorney, was one of Dr. Martin Luther King's chief advisers and Kivie Kaplan, a retired Jewish businessman, was one of his chief financial backers. The NAACP Legal Defense Fund, which won many important victories in the courts, was led by Jews, and Jews also constituted a majority of the white participants in civil rights sit-ins and protest marches. Jews were especially visible among the Southern whites who publicly supported the cause of civil rights and, as a result, were sometimes attacked by racist thugs. To this day, most Southern Jews re-

main Democrats even though many other Southern whites shifted their political allegiance to the GOP when Republicans opposed the Democratic Party's liberal stance on matters of race. From the Jewish perspective, support for the civil rights movement was both a matter of moral principle and communal interest. The principle was clear. Racial discrimination was morally reprehensible. The interest was also clear. The elimination of discrimination against African-Americans would also do away with discrimination against other minorities, including Jews.

Jews' political alliances also help to explain another major focus of their political efforts, the expansion of domestic social programs. During the 1930s, many Jews were poor and supported the New Deal agenda of social programs as a matter of necessity. As Jews have become increasingly affluent, they have nevertheless continued to back government-sponsored housing, employment, pension, and health care programs. Part of the reason that one of the nation's most affluent communities supports programs designed to help the poor is that the Democratic political coalition, in which the Jews play such a prominent role, includes large numbers of minority and poor Americans. For the Jews, maintaining the organizational coherence and power of the Democratic Party is an important end, and domestic social programs are an important means to that end.

Finally, Jews have used their influence in American politics to sustain American support for the security of the State of Israel. In the post–World War II period, the Jewish community was able to induce President Harry S Truman to sanction the creation of a Jewish state despite the opposition of the State Department and America's most important ally, Great Britain. Over the ensuing decades, the efforts of such Jewish groups as the American Israel Public Affairs Committee (AIPAC) have helped to maintain a steady flow of American military and economic aid for Israel, even as reluctance to offend Arab oil producers impelled other Western nations to distance themselves from the Jewish state.

Change and Continuity

For most American Jews, political participation and Democratic politics have been synonymous since the New Deal. In recent years, however, some cracks have developed in this bedrock of Jewish political involvement. One source of stress has been a fraying of the once close relationship between Jews and another loyal Democratic constituency, African Americans. Jews have been offended by antisemitic remarks attributed to a number of prominent African American politicians, including Jesse Jackson and Al Sharpton. Blacks, for their part, have expressed resentment at what they regard as Jewish efforts to intrude in the affairs of the African American community. In 2002, for example, Jewish organizations worked against black Democratic congresswoman Cynthia McKinney of Georgia, whom they viewed as antisemitic, by supporting another African American woman, Denise Majette. After McKinney's defeat, a number of other black politicians complained that she had been unfairly singled out by a "special interest group."

Jewish allegiance to the Democratic Party has also been shaken by the increasingly anti-Israel stances of some liberal Democrats. On a number of college campuses, including Harvard and Columbia, liberal students and faculty have mounted petition drives urging these schools to divest their stock holdings in companies doing business with Israel. In a 2002 speech, Harvard president Lawrence Summers lamented the fact that "profoundly anti-Israel views are increasingly finding support in progressive intellectual communities" (Singer and Grossman 2003). At the same time, moreover, that some liberal Democrats have turned against Israel, some of the most conservative groups in the Republican coalition have emerged as unswerving supporters of the Jewish state and its policies. Evangelical Protestants, long viewed with suspicion by most American Jews, strongly back Israel against its Arab enemies and have helped to ensure that Republican administrations continue America's pro-Israel policies.

Despite these strains, however, the American Jewish community remains firmly, if not always happily, within the Democratic camp. Membership in the Democratic coalition continues to allow Jews to exercise considerable political influence and has provided them with access to important political and social institutions. Three-quarters of a century ago, Franklin D. Roosevelt gave America's Jews a political home they are not yet ready to leave.

Benjamin Ginsberg

References and Further Reading
Chesler, Phyllis. 2003. *The New Anti-Semitism.* New York: Jossey-Bass.

Dershowitz, Alan. 1998. *The Vanishing American Jew.* New York: Touchstone.
Freedman, Samuel. 2001. *Jew v. Jew: The Struggle for the Soul of American Jewry.* New York: Simon & Schuster.
Friedman, Murray. 1995. *What Went Wrong? The Creation and Collapse of the Black-Jewish Alliance.* New York: Free Press.
Gerber, David A., ed. 1986. *Anti-Semitism in American History.* Urbana: University of Illinois Press.
Ginsberg, Benjamin. 1993. *The Fatal Embrace: Jews and the State.* Chicago: University of Chicago Press.
Goldberg, J. J. 1997. *Jewish Power: Inside the Jewish Establishment.* Reading, MA: Addison-Wesley.
Maisel, L. Sandy, and Ira N. Forman, eds. 2001. *Jews in American Politics.* Lanham, MD: Rowman & Littlefield.
Sachar, Howard M. 1992. *A History of the Jews in America.* New York: Alfred A. Knopf.
Sarna, Jonathan, and David Dalin. 1997. *Religion and State in the American Jewish Experience.* Notre Dame, IN: University of Notre Dame Press.
Singer, David, and Lawrence Grossman, eds. 2003. *American Jewish Year Book.* New York: American Jewish Committee.

American Jewish Involvement in Public Affairs

American Jews, individually or as a polity, have engaged in public affairs—in issues of concern to the larger society—in an effort to enhance Jewish security. The question, however, is what makes any given issue a priority to American Jewish groups?

Organized public affairs activity by American Jews dates back to the 1858 Mortara episode when, at the Vatican's behest, police in Bologna seized a Jewish child, removing him from his family, because a Catholic servant girl claimed that, unbeknownst to his parents, she had personally baptized him when he was an infant; Pius IX subsequently refused to return him to his family. In response, the Board of Delegates of American Israelites was formed (1859), modeled on the Board of Deputies of British Jews, which had been established (1840) as a response to the Damascus blood libel accusation. The agency was short-lived, however, and in 1873 it was incorporated into the newly formed Union of American Hebrew Congregations (now the Union for Reform Judaism), the Reform congregational body.

The twentieth-century history of American Jewish involvement in public affairs can be divided into five periods.

From the early twentieth century to the mid-1950s, the primary focus of the American Jewish community was on combating antisemitism, both in the United States and, after the rise of Nazism, in Europe. Combating the corollary of antisemitism—anti-Jewish discrimination, which was pervasive—was also a priority on the Jewish communal agenda. Although discrimination was severe both in employment and higher education, the Jewish "defense" agencies disagreed on how to attack it. The American Jewish Committee (AJC) favored its leader Louis Marshall's view that discreet lobbying would best serve the interests of American Jews. This nonconfrontational strategy reflected the fear that AJC would be perceived as a Jewish lobby, having interests at odds with those of other Americans. The American Jewish Congress (AJCongress), on the other hand, preferred more aggressive tactics, involving the use of social action and the courts. Nonetheless, there was unanimity among Jewish groups that antisemitism was salient.

From the early 1950s to the mid-1960s, the struggle for civil rights became the priority issue on the Jewish communal agenda. Although the civil rights initiative developed into a movement spearheaded by a coalition of blacks and Jews, along with a third important actor, the trade union movement, the struggle for civil rights for blacks did not at first blush appear to be a struggle for Jewish interests. Why, therefore, was it a priority issue for Jewish groups? Indeed, early on Jewish groups did not express unanimous support for making common cause with blacks, and the wisdom of coalition building stirred debate. It was Rabbi Stephen S. Wise, an AJCongress and NAACP leader, who made the case for involvement based not on the principles of liberalism (to which the Jewish community was in large measure committed), but on Jewish self-interest. The Wise rationale—that combating and ending prejudice in any sector of society strengthened the fiber of society and thereby benefited Jews—became the basis for American Jewish involvement in spearheading the movement.

Local Jewish community relations councils and chapters of the NAACP embraced coalition building. Both communities relied on the relatively new strategy, pioneered by the AJCongress, of using the law and social action. The approach was not aimed at converting individual bigots, but at using the U.S. Congress and the federal courts to radically change the central institutions of society, especially in education, employment, and housing, as well as the electoral process.

While civil rights was the priority issue during the 1950s, the separation of church and state and immigration reform were of significant concern as well. From 1948 through the early 1960s the landmark cases decided by the U.S. Supreme Court—often spearheaded by Jewish groups, especially the AJCongress—gradually broadened church–state protections. Repeal of the National Origins Quota System (1965) was also an important issue for Jewish groups in these years.

Two events in the mid-1960s radically changed American Jewish priorities: the emergence of the Soviet Jewry movement in the United States in 1963 and the Six Day War in 1967. American Jews became preoccupied with Israel and Soviet Jewry, and moved away from the broad range of domestic advocacy issues—from social and economic justice—as priorities on the Jewish agenda. Almost overnight, the Jewish advocacy agenda became more particularistic, more "Jewish." Also noteworthy in terms of changing priorities for American Jews was the rise of a black nationalist movement—with its significant expression of antisemitism—in which erstwhile allies were viewed as enemies.

At the beginning of the 1980s, the Jewish community started moving back to the broader agenda. The first Reagan administration led many in the Jewish community to fear a potential crisis with respect to constitutional protections and that the administration's restrictive policies would undermine economic justice. Additionally, with the organizing of the Moral Majority in 1979 and the rise of an aggressive religious Right, the Jewish community began to fear a "Christianization" of America. The Jewish community therefore again reordered its priorities and began returning to a larger agenda. A new round of church–state cases and federal legislation threatening the separation of church and state captured the attention of Jewish groups.

One issue early in the Reagan administration suggested that the Jewish community was one to be reckoned with, both on the Hill and in the administration. It was the struggle over the $8.5-billion sale of airborne warning and control system surveillance aircraft (AWACS) to Saudi Arabia, which, it was feared, could use them in a war against Israel. This was a highly significant instance of pro-Israel advocacy, because the organized Jewish community realized that it could mobilize a national advocacy effort. While the Jewish groups failed to stop the sale, their ability to act in a coordinated manner to develop a grass-roots and national advocacy effort left a deep impression on the Hill, and was a watershed event in Jewish public affairs advocacy.

Beginning in 1990—and fueled in some measure by the findings of the 1990 National Jewish Population Survey, which highlighted high rates of intermarriage and low rates of cultural literacy—American Jewry once again reevaluated its communal agenda. Levels of both behavioral and attitudinal antisemitism were on the decline, despite dramatic individual manifestations of antisemitism during the decade. In any case, antisemitism posed no threat to the ability of Jews to participate fully in American society. With the collapse of the Soviet Union in the early 1990s, the Soviet Jewry issue no longer constituted an agenda for political and international advocacy, but for social services.

The Israel agenda, long the most critical for Jewish advocacy groups, underwent changes. Whatever the pitfalls of the peace process, the issues that commanded the most attention during the 1990s were related more to the relationship between Israel and American Jews than to the physical security of Israel, which no longer had the salience for many American Jews that it had in the previous decade, and in the 2000s the issue of disengagement became significant. At the same time, concerns about Jewish identity suggested to many that the true threat to Jewish security was the endogenous issue of Jewish continuity rather than the exogenous issue of physical security. The concern of many American Jews has turned increasingly inward, to American Jewry's own values and indeed to its own continuity.

In the 2000s, with the administration of George W. Bush, a new set of challenges to constitutional protections—especially church–state separation—and to social and economic justice once again nudged many in the increasingly polarized Jewish community back to the national affairs agenda.

Over the decades, a central organizing principle for issues on the Jewish public affairs agenda emerged. Issues selected as priorities are those for which there is a consensus in the community that they affect Jewish security. Over the years, and intensifying in the 2000s, there has been debate within the Jewish community over the parameters of the "Jewish security" rubric. The public affairs agenda can be viewed as a series of concentric circles. At the center are issues immediately and directly related to Jewish security: antisemitism, Israel, and the security of Jewish communities abroad. These issues lie at the core of Jewish public affairs advocacy.

One concentric circle out, in the penumbra of Jewish concerns, are First Amendment and other Bill of Rights and political freedom protections—especially the separation of church and state, which is a central guarantor of Jewish security in the United States. The construct for this category is what government cannot do to an individual and what one individual cannot do to another.

The next level of concentric circles includes issues that are important to the health of the society and therefore to enhancing American Jewish society. The questions are not of restraint but of positive beneficence: what government can and should do for the individual. Social and economic justice, the environment, and other such issues fall into this category. As the agenda expands—as it has over the past fifty years—the question of priorities continues to be salient for American Jews.

Jerome A. Chanes

References and Further Reading

American Jewish Year Book. Annual. New York: American Jewish Committee.

Chanes, Jerome A. 1998. "Jewish Involvement in the American Jewish Public-Affairs Agenda." In *A Portrait of the American Jewish Community,* edited by Jerome A. Chanes, David A. Schnall, and Norman Linzer. Westport, CT: Praeger.

Maisel, L. Sandy, and Ira N. Forman, eds. 2001. *Jews in American Politics.* Lanham, MD: Rowman & Littlefield.

National Jewish Community Relations Advisory Council. Annual. *Joint Program Plan.* New York: NJCRAC/JCPA.

Svonkin, Stuart. 1997. *Jews Against Prejudice: American Jews and the Fight for Civil Liberties.* New York: Columbia University Press.

American Jews in the Socialist and Communist Movements

Jews have been overrepresented in most radical movements in America, including Socialism and Communism, since at least the 1890s. The vast majority of Jewish Americans have *not* been radicals, but a significant minority in the modern period actively helped shape the American Left. Jews, although only 3 percent of the population of the United States, provided about 15 percent of the membership of the Socialist Party (SP) through the 1920s and about 40 percent of the Communist Party (CPUSA) rank and file in the 1930s.

The leadership of the SP was also disproportionately Jewish. Morris Hillquit and Victor Berger, each of whom served as national party chair after World War I, were Jews. The two men exercised great influence over party operations, mainly because the party's recurrent presidential candidate, Eugene V. Debs, avoided organizational issues. In addition, the only Socialists ever elected to Congress were Jews: Berger from Milwaukee and Meyer London from New York.

The SP's most successful institutions were also often Jewish. There was, first and foremost, *The Jewish Daily Forward,* which had a circulation of nearly 300,000, making it the largest socialist paper in America. *The Forward* was, in addition, a major financial contributor to SP causes and election campaigns. Also closely tied to the Socialist Party was the *Arbeiter Ring,* or Workmen's Circle, a mutual aid organization of Jewish laborers that grew to more than 80,000 members by 1924. The United Hebrew Trades, a confederation of largely Jewish labor unions, was also saturated in socialism. This was especially true for the needle-workers' unions, like the International Ladies' Garment Workers' (ILGWU) and the Amalgamated Clothing Workers, whose leaders, including David Dubinsky and Sidney Hillman, were affiliated with the SP.

The CPUSA was also often led by Jews, including Benjamin Gitlow and Jay Lovestone (born Jacob Liebstein), both of whom served as the party's general secretaries in the late 1920s. And throughout the 1930s and 1940s, more than 33 percent of the Central Committee of the CPUSA were of Jewish background. Moreover, the *Freiheit,* the party's Yiddish-language paper, was not only the first Communist daily published in the United States; it had, for some time, an even larger circulation than the English-language *Daily Worker.* The Jewish People's Fraternal Order was the largest ethnic bloc in the CPUSA's umbrella organization, the International Workers' Order. And several unions with huge Jewish memberships were strongly influenced by communism, including the American Federation of Teachers and the Fur and Leather Workers' Union, whose president, Ben Gold, was a Jew and an avowed Communist.

Jewish radical movements in America were in large part products of two or three generations of East European Jewish immigration. The great mass of gainfully employed Jews in Eastern Europe had been small businessmen and independent craftsmen for generations. The development of working-class consciousness among them began in earnest only in the late nineteenth century when large numbers of petit bourgeois Jews suffered precipitous economic displacement and were forced to work for wages. The making of the Jewish working class continued, and intensified, with immigration to the larger American cities, where most Jewish newcomers confronted an even more highly industrialized environment than they had begun to experience in Eastern Europe. Subjected to intense economic pressures, living in poverty, and uprooted from a traditional way of life, the immigrants were also exposed, especially in New York and several other large cities, to a growing left-wing culture. Here the implications of Jewish proletarianization were articulated and reinforced by the activities of a remarkable group of radical intellectuals and organizers—Jewish young men and women, mostly former students—who provided leadership and a persuasive and attractive socialist critique of capitalism.

Socialism, then, was a vigorous and vital theme in Jewish immigrant life almost from the beginning, and thousands of Jewish workers made their first entry into American political life in association with the movement. In 1886 the Jewish Workingmen's Association formally affiliated with the Socialist Labor Party (SLP), which was led by a Sephardic Jew, Daniel DeLeon. In the same year the Association joined a coalition of liberals and socialists to support the New York mayoral candidacy of Henry George. In 1887, two "Jewish" foreign-language federations were formed in the Socialist Labor Party: section 8 for Yiddish speakers, and section 17 for the Russians. Fourteen more Jewish sections were added in the 1890s, and as early as 1889 the party press celebrated the rapid development of socialist influence among Jewish workers.

Later, in 1901, Morris Hillquit, Eugene V. Debs, labor lawyer Meyer London, and Milwaukee's Victor Berger, "evolutionary socialists" who demurred at the "intransigent revolutionary determinism" of DeLeon, became "founding fathers" of the Socialist Party of America. One of the factors that sparked the withdrawal from the SLP and the creation of the new party was DeLeon's emphasis on dual unionism. The brilliant but unbending class warrior demanded that several unions in the coalition of United Hebrew Trades detach themselves from the American Federation of Labor to join the Knights of Labor, an organization DeLeon hoped to control and use as a revolutionary base. Dissidents from the Socialist Labor Party who moved into the Socialist Party maintained that socialism was dependent on the support of *existing* trade unions. They also believed, in contrast to the followers of DeLeon, that working to ameliorate the conditions of the working class through reforms of capitalism was not counterrevolutionary.

Jews came to support the candidates of the new party in increasing and disproportionate numbers. In 1908, Jews, who made up about 39 percent of SP membership in Manhattan and the Bronx, organized enormous campaign meetings on the East Side for Eugene V. Debs, the Socialist candidate for president. This is not as impressive as what Jewish votes would do later for the SP, but it was possible for an American journalist to believe in 1909 that "most Jews of the East Side, though not all acknowledged socialists, are strongly inclined toward socialism."

At the same time that the SP was attracting increasing numbers of Jews, the socialist-led Workmen's Circle (WC) was doing the same. A nationwide fraternal order, the WC, organized in 1892, had only 872 members in 1901. But in 1905, after the society received a charter from New York State, and could offer safer and more attractive medical and insurance benefits, its membership grew to nearly 7,000. The worker members, most of whom were not socialists, accepted the long-range socialist goals of the radical leaders, as well as the fact that the WC helped finance the socialist movement. In turn the leadership gave first priority to meeting the immediate needs of workers. By 1908, the WC boasted 10,000 members, the vast majority of whom were sympathetic to the socialist movement.

Even more important to the socialist movement was the *Jewish Daily Forward,* which Abraham Cahan edited at its founding in 1897 and to which he returned permanently in 1903. In Cahan's hands the *Forward* became, along with the United Hebrew Trades (UHT) and the Workmen's Circle, a critical component of the Jewish labor movement and of Jewish socialism. Cahan quickly changed the somewhat formal language of the paper to the Yiddish of the streets and shops. If "you want the public to read this paper and assimilate Socialism," he told his staff, "you've

got to write of things of everyday life, in terms of what they see and feel."

The editor tersely summed up the essentials of the new socialism, to be elucidated in the daily paper as "justice, humanity, fraternity—in brief, honest common sense and horse sense." Karl Marx's postulates were tapered to fit. In principle, labor was still the source of all value, and rent was still seen as robbery. But in practice, the *Forward* insisted that, so long as capitalism endured, it was better to deal with "honest landlords" and "honest bosses."

Despite their cosmopolitanism and class-war vocabulary, the "liberated" radical leaders and Jewish labor militants did not secede from the ethnic community. Union organizers, intellectuals, journalists, and political activists, in their efforts to mobilize the Jewish proletariat, tried to synthesize the essential values of Jewish culture with the modern goals and values of the socialist movement. They consistently wove biblical references, Talmudic aphorisms, and prophetic injunctions into their socialist appeals. They wrote and spoke particularly about the concept of *tsedaka* (righteousness and social justice), and implicitly drew on the obligation of *tikkun olam,* the commandment to repair or improve the world. In all they emphasized communal responsibility and secular messianism. And they helped Jewish workers in their struggle to create new identities out of traditional materials in a modern context. This struggle was not always conscious or simple. But it was made a good deal easier between 1905 and 1910 when large numbers of Bundist socialists reached New York after the collapse of the 1905 revolution in Russia.

The Bundists, like the radicals who preceded them to American shores, also celebrated the breakup of religious hegemony, but they strongly resisted further assimilation. They desired to remain Jews—atheists and socialists—but Jews. They brought with them to America sophisticated ideological defenses for this position, and they articulated them with spirit and dedication. They were effective. By 1906 there were 3,000 members in Bund branches in America, more even than the enrollment in the Jewish branches of the SP.

The newspapers, union activists, socialists, and even more so the Bundists furnished the language and the terms of a powerful discourse. They helped immigrant workers, on their way to becoming Americans, keep their balance between the revitalized values of an ancient past and a nearer past falling to pieces. They were effective because in addition to confronting the objective conditions of American life and avoiding abstraction, the Bundists tapped into and refurbished something that was still alive in Jewish workers—Jewish ethical practice derived from Judaic precepts.

Visions of proletarian solidarity would dim over time, to be overshadowed by the remarkable upward mobility of Jewish immigrants and their children. In the meantime the socialists furnished the Jewish labor movement with important vehicles of worker education and mobilization—the United Hebrew Trades, the Workmen's Circle, and the *Jewish Daily Forward*. With these institutions, the East European immigrants built the first consciously Jewish power base in America. With that base, the socialist movement set out through strikes and union-building to solve some of the more practical problems of the workers.

The years from 1909 to 1914 saw increased activity among working-class people throughout America, but the militancy of Jewish workers was particularly intense. In several major cities tens of thousands of Jewish workers struck for higher wages, better conditions, and union recognition. The United Hebrew Trades experienced a phenomenal growth. In 1910 there were fewer than ninety constituent unions with approximately 100,000 members; by 1914 there were more than a hundred unions in the federation with 250,000 members. The American labor movement was growing, but the Jewish trade unions grew faster. The Jewish garment unions alone increased membership by 68 percent between 1910 and 1913, a rate of growth greater than that of any other labor union in the country.

In the same period Jewish socialists broadened their influence in several Jewish communities, especially New York. In addition to actively building and strengthening unions, many Jewish socialists worked for the Socialist Party, recruiting membership and garnering votes for socialist candidates. Socialists rarely received more than 3 percent of the votes in New York, but, between 1910 and 1914, Jewish assembly districts in the city delivered 10 to 15 percent of their votes to SP office seekers, and after 1914 the figure climbed past 35 percent. Socialism never captured the entire community, but with its explicit appeal to moralism and justice, it was an important force on the Lower East Side. Indeed, the rise of the SP vote in the United States from 16,000 in 1903 to more than 118,000 in 1912 was partly the consequence of increasing Jewish support.

Socialist candidates were especially attractive to Jews when they represented a combination of ideological and ethnic interests. In this regard a comparison of the congressional campaigns of Morris Hillquit and Meyer London is instructive. Socialist Morris Hillquit, who was defeated in the 1908 congressional race, though Jewish, had not openly identified with specific Jewish interests. This, at a time when East Side residents were upset by the police commissioner's report implying that Jews generated 50 percent of the crime in New York City; when the "special interest" issue of immigration restriction was being hotly debated in the U.S. Congress; and when the relatively restrictionist position of the SP on that issue was not attractive to East Side Jews who still had relatives desperate to escape from pogrom-ridden Russia. Like the English conservative Edmund Burke who, over a century earlier, had run as a representative not of his constituents but of the "realm," the radical Morris Hillquit was roundly defeated.

Meyer London, who replaced Hillquit as the SP's candidate, openly identified himself as a Jew and a Socialist and allied himself with the vital interests of the Lower East Side. Though London lost a bid for a congressional seat in 1910, he outran the rest of the SP ticket two to one. By 1914 London had developed enough support in the district to win. It was rare, even from the Lower East Side, for Socialists to be sent to Congress, yet London was reelected twice, in 1916 and 1920.

Combining socialist ideology and class interest with ethnic interest played a vital role in these victories. London told a crowd of 15,000 after his first election: "We shall not rest until every power of capitalism has been destroyed and the workers emancipated from wage slavery." But in the same speech, London, proud to work for specifically Jewish interests, also said, "I hope that my presence will represent an entirely different type of Jew from the kind that Congress is accustomed to see."

Socialist pacifism after America's entrance into World War I dampened enthusiasm for Socialist candidates generally, and the national party garnered fewer than 80,000 votes in 1917. But the Socialists in Jewish New York were still strong, electing in that year ten state assemblymen, eleven aldermen, and a municipal judge. Once again, however, the strength of the SP in the Jewish community should not be overstated. Socialists certainly received disproportionate support from the Jewish electorate, but still most Jews were not Socialists. Moreover, in 1914 of eleven Jews elected to the New York State Senate, two were Republicans and nine were Democrats. In the same year seven Jews sat in the Assembly; only two were Socialists, the rest Republicans.

One of the more remarkable dimensions of American political culture from 1917 to about 1924 was Jewish attraction to the Soviet revolution. The Communist regime in Moscow seemed eager to recruit Jewish talent, and the hope of progress and modernity inherent in Communist ideology found resonance in Jewish political life in America. It was estimated that in the 1920s, Jews in the United States gave 4–5 percent of their votes to Communist candidates, at the same time that they were giving approximately 12–15 percent to Socialists, both figures substantially higher than the national average.

About 15 percent of the members of the CPUSA in the 1920s were Jewish (Finns were at that time about 50 percent of the CPUSA). And in 1924 a small but determined Communist group, with the help of numerous sympathizers, had gained control of three locals of the heavily Jewish ILGWU. They were also strong in Waistmakers Local 25, which had a predominantly Jewish membership and a long history of radicalism. And during the 1930s the radical student movement, with its Communists and Socialists of varying stripes, was strongest on campuses with large numbers of Jewish students—City College of New York, Columbia University, New York University—and a significant percentage of the leaders were Jewish.

Abetted by the "united front" policy of making alliances with other left-leaning and liberal groups (which in New York were also disproportionately Jewish) and a strategy of infiltrating Jewish organizations, the Communist Party increased its Jewish membership to an estimated 40 percent during the Depression. Also, 5,000 of 13,000 members of the Young Communist League were Jewish. Jews were clearly overrepresented in the Communist movement, but only a very small percentage of Jews were Communists. This, however, did not stop antisemites from speaking of "Judeo-bolshevism," which became a buzzword of the Right in the interwar period.

By the mid-1920s, much of the enthusiasm among Jews for Communism was already dissipating. Lenin had earlier ordered an end to antisemitic movements in Russia and the Ukraine that had left 75,000 Jews dead between 1918 and 1920. But this did not exempt the Jewish bour-

geoisie from being considered "class enemies" of the revolution, and the general antibourgeois, antireligious policies of the Soviets under Stalin continued to create desperate conditions for Russian Jewry, including the wanton destruction of Jewish cultural and religious institutions and the imprisonment of thousands of Jewish leaders.

By 1928 Jewish leaders of liberal or socialist persuasion in America, like Lillian Wald, Horace Kallen, and David Dubinsky, realized there were antisemites among the Stalinist heirs of Lenin's mantle. Socialists like Baruch Vladek, managing editor of the Forward, and Morris Hillquit, head of the National Committee of the Socialist Party, became so disaffected that they refused even to support extending diplomatic recognition to the Soviet Union.

The ravages against Jews in the Soviet Union, coupled with the drive of Communists in the United States to co-opt Jewish unions and cultural institutions, continued to diminish Communism's mystique. Many Jewish union members supported the Communist factions in their organizations, because elements of the established leadership were corrupt and the Communists promised "democratization." But Communist behavior diluted goodwill. In a general strike in the cloak trade in 1926, for example, the workers had elicited a favorable offer from management. The Communist Party, however, forced a continuation of the strike, which ended in a disaster. After twenty-six weeks of unemployment for the workers and an expenditure of $3.5 million by the unions, the ILGWU was compelled to settle for virtually the original terms. The ILGWU was temporarily broken, but so was the Communist faction.

The Jewish unions distanced themselves from the more radical left-wingers. So did the vast majority of ordinary Jews. Communist support of Arab riots in Palestine in 1929, the purge trials of the 1930s in Moscow, and the Non-Aggression Pact between Nazi Germany and the Soviet Union in 1939 also cut into Jewish support of the Communists. CPUSA membership dropped by more than a third in 1939, and most of those who departed were Jews, virtually all of whom had been attracted to the party in the thirties because they believed it to be the only effective enemy of fascism. Of an estimated 800,000 Jewish votes cast in New York State in the 1930s, only 50,000 went to Communist candidates. This was very meager considering that the Jewish population had been intensely targeted by the party.

With the Communist group out of the way, the needle trades unions, after 1928, could get on with improving conditions for workers rather than fighting for the remote realization of a classless society. The unions also paid more attention in the 1930s to progressive issues that were also particularly Jewish. For example, the Jewish Labor Committee was formed in 1933 to counteract antisemitism in the United States and the Nazi threat in Europe. There was a small irony in this new "Jewish orientation" in the fact that Jewish membership in the garment industry unions in the 1930s had dropped below 50 percent. But the leaders were Jewish and still considered themselves part of the progressive non-Communist left.

Many Jewish writers also had leftist leanings in this era. Yiddish-speaking secularists such as Chaim Zhitlovsky, a champion of Jewish cultural nationalism, Nachman Syrkin, the foremost spokesman for labor Zionism, Shmuel Niger, the literary critic, and Hayim Greenberg, essayist and editor, constituted a small cadre of Yiddish intellectuals who manifested a strong interest in Jewish national resurgence. But most expected that resurgence to come associated with, or through a synthesis with, socialism. Sidney Hook, Horace Kallen, Harry Wolfson, Lewis Mumford, and others associated with Elliot Cohen's *Menorah Journal* were also inclined to support a "humanistic social order." And a third group of Jewish writers on the left, the New York Intellectuals, included Philip Rahv, Lionel and Diana Trilling, Meyer Schapiro, Harold Rosenberg, and Irving Howe. They expressed themselves mainly through the *Partisan Review* and later *Dissent* magazine, and were held together by their utter revulsion against the Soviet experiment under Stalin, with which some of them had initially flirted; but they clearly maintained their socialist sensibilities, especially in the face of the strident antisemitism of the Right in the 1930s. If this last group of cosmopolitan intellectuals were on their way to losing varying degrees of their Jewish identity, there was still something familiarly Jewish in their penchant for a kind of Talmudic argumentation, in their assumption of the inherent worth of intellectual pursuits, and in their left-leaning proclivities.

A good number of Jewish writers of fiction were also on the left in the 1930s, several radicalized by the Depression and its attack on the American Dream. Henry Roth joined the Communist Party in 1933. Mike Gold, who had joined some ten years earlier, became even more enthusiastic in the 1930s, especially about enlisting writers and artists for the revolutionary struggle. And Daniel Fuchs, Samuel Ornitz, and Edward Dahlberg, under the influence of the socialist realism school, were harshly judgmental of the low level of class consciousness, and the high level of materialism and exploitation they perceived in American and Jewish society.

The preceding account hints at the temporary character of Jewish radicalism. Indeed, by the middle of the twentieth century, with the decline of antisemitism, the intensification of Jewish economic and social mobility, increasing acculturation, and even assimilation, and given the excesses of the Communists in the United States and abroad, Jewish political values changed. Starting as early as 1912 there was a gradual shift of Jewish votes at the presidential level from Republican and Socialist to the Democratic Party. The shift was reinforced by the liberal, progressive role played by Louis Brandeis as President Woodrow Wilson's advisor, especially after Brandeis became head of the American Zionist Movement in 1914. Wilson was also advised by Rabbi Stephen S. Wise and Henry Morgenthau, Sr., the real estate tycoon, who served the president in a variety of positions including ambassador to Turkey. Later Wilson's crusade for the League of Nations appealed to the universalism and internationalism in modern Jewish political culture, and his initial support for the Balfour Declaration, promising a Jewish homeland in Palestine, further strengthened Jewish links to the Democratic Party.

In 1924 Jews voted 51 percent for John Davis, the Democratic candidate, and 22 percent for Robert La Follette, the Progressive candidate, who received 16 percent nationwide; and in 1928 they gave 72 percent to Democrat Al Smith. Smith had recognized what he called "Jewish brains," he spoke a little Yiddish, he was one of the few Democratic leaders with courage to advocate an anti-KKK plank in the campaign of 1924, and he had helped engineer the appointment of Benjamin Cardozo, a Jew, as chief justice of the New York State Court of Appeals. Above all he was an intelligent legislator and a reformer. What else could a Jew ask? Not surprisingly, during the election of 1924, Smith, who had won the affection of the Jewish voters, was reelected governor of New York State and ran ahead of presidential candidates Calvin Coolidge and John Davis in several Jewish election districts.

The Jewish community was proud of the growing number of high government officials who were Jewish, such as Eugene Meyer, a member of the Federal Farm and Loan Board, on whom Coolidge depended for advice, and the Jewish advisors around Al Smith such as Belle Moskowitz. But the parochial aspect of ethnicity—the narrow group interest or group pride dimension—was more often blunted by the strong universalist strain in Jewish political culture. The Jewish community had an uncommonly broad interpretation of its group interest, and Jews repeatedly crossed ethnic lines and even party lines to support candidates they felt best upheld the liberal values they cherished. Fiorello La Guardia in 1920 and Franklin Delano Roosevelt in 1928 both defeated more conservative Jewish opponents with the help of a very sizable Jewish vote.

Consistent loyalty to the Democratic Party manifested itself most powerfully in the 1930s during the Depression and New Deal (sometimes called by its enemies the Jew Deal). The Socialist Party lost virtually its entire Jewish mass base in 1936 when socialist union leaders like David Dubinsky and Sidney Hillman took the lead in forming the American Labor Party (ALP) in New York and gave their backing to Franklin Delano Roosevelt. Continued support for Roosevelt's programs led many onetime Jewish Socialists and even Communists to become liberal Democrats. And Jews, whether former socialists or not, gave Roosevelt an extraordinary proportion of their votes, always hovering around 90 percent; they were the only ethnic group in the United States to increase its support for him over the four elections through 1944.

Jews proved to be a unique force in American politics, exhibiting the capacity to vote and act beyond both their class interest and the narrow interests of their group. A survey of Jews in Chicago in the 1950s indicated that 67 percent of the respondents answered the question, "What is a good Jew?" with statements like someone who "supports all humanitarian causes" or someone who is "liberal on political and economic issues." The consistency of Jewish liberalism was simply unmatched by other groups. One highly reputable study on religion and politics in Detroit, also in the 1950s, showed black Protestants to be liberal on questions of the welfare state and civil rights, but less so in regard to international affairs and civil liberties. White Protestants were relatively hostile to racial integration and to government intervention in the economy. Catholics also opposed civil rights and were moderate, but not liberal, on questions of freedom of speech, foreign aid, and government regulation of the economy. Only the Jews could be classified as liberal in all categories, especially when civil rights for blacks were at stake.

In the early 1960s, a substantial percentage of the New Left was Jewish. And Jewish presence, and indeed leadership, in the movements for civil rights and women's equality, as well as against the Vietnam War, was manifestly obvious. Later, emerging tensions between blacks and Jews, partly generated by different economic and social mobility rates and by the politics of ethnic identity, increasingly challenged what had actually been a relatively uneasy and unequal alliance from the start. And the New Left's increasing hostility toward Israel discouraged a revival of radicalism in the Jewish American community. Nonetheless, the political vision of Jews, even into the fourth generation, remained focused on social justice, urban welfare, civil rights, civil liberties, and internationalism. These values reflected a distinctive American faith that was equated with the left wing of the Democratic Party. But it was a faith held so tenaciously by Jews, a substantial majority of whom were still connected to the traditions of communal responsibility, mutual aid, *tsedakah*, and *tikkun olam*, that liberalism could be seen as the political ideology of Jewish American ethnicity.

Gerald Sorin

References and Further Reading

Dubofsky, Melvyn. 1968. *When Workers Organize*. Amherst: University of Massachusetts Press.

Fox, Richard W. 1974. "The Paradox of Progressive Socialism: The Case of Morris Hillquit, 1901–1914." *American Quarterly* 26,1: 127–140.

Frankel, Jonathan. 1981. *Prophecy and Politics: Socialism, Nationalism and the Russian Jew, 1862–1917.* Cambridge: Cambridge University Press.

Glazer, Nathan. 1961. *The Social Basis of American Communism*. New York: Harcourt Brace.

Howe, Irving. 1976. *World of Our Fathers: The Journey of the East European Jews to America and the Life They Found and Made*. New York: Harcourt Brace Jovanovich.

Johnpoll, Bernard, and Harvey Klehr, eds. 1986. *Biographical Dictionary of the American Left*. Westport, CT: Greenwood Press.

Klehr, Harvey. 1984. *The Heyday of American Communism: The Depression Decade*. New York: Basic Books.

Mendelsohn, Ezra. 1970. *Class Struggle in the Pale*. Cambridge, UK: Cambridge University Press.

Moore, Deborah Dash. 1981. *At Home in America: Second Generation Jews in New York*. New York: Columbia University Press.

Quint, Howard. 1953. *The Forging of American Socialism*. Indianapolis, IN: Bobbs-Merrill.

Sanders, Ronald. 1987. *The Downtown Jews.* New York: Dover Publications.

Shannon, David. 1955. *The Socialist Party of America.* Chicago: University of Chicago Press.

Sorin, Gerald. 1985. *The Prophetic Minority: American Jewish Immigrant Radicals, 1880–1920.* Bloomington: Indiana University Press.

Sorin, Gerald. 1992. *A Time for Building: The Third Migration.* Baltimore, MD: Johns Hopkins University Press.

Sorin, Gerald. 1997. *Tradition Transformed: The Jewish Experience in America.* Baltimore, MD: Johns Hopkins University Press.

Sorin, Gerald. 2002. *Irving Howe: A Life of Passionate Dissent.* New York: New York University Press.

Weinstein, James. 1960. "The Socialist Party: Its Roots and Strengths, 1912–1919." *Studies on the Left* 1 (Winter): 5–27.

Ethel and Julius Rosenberg ride to separate jails on March 29, 1951, after being convicted of espionage. (AP/Wide World Photos)

The Rosenberg Case

An espionage case that became a cause, and then engendered a bitter controversy that endured for decades, the trial, conviction, and execution of Julius and Ethel Rosenberg as Soviet spies constituted one of the most dramatic legal proceedings of the early Cold War era. The trial of a Communist Jewish couple for allegedly "stealing the secret of the atomic bomb" for the benefit of the Soviet Union—what FBI Director J. Edgar Hoover labeled the "crime of the century"—aroused considerable anxiety in the American Jewish community, fearful that the images of Jew and Communist and traitor would merge in the public mind. Although that dire consequence did not ensue, the prominence accorded the Rosenbergs' Jewishness in the campaign to save their lives ensured that their religious affiliation would play a major part in the ongoing debate about their case.

The Rosenberg Case began in the summer of 1950 when Julius and Ethel Rosenberg were arrested and charged with conspiracy to commit espionage on behalf of the Soviet Union. The couple (Julius was thirty-two years old, Ethel was three years older) had married in 1939, had two young sons, and were living in modest circumstances in a housing project on Manhattan's Lower East Side. The Rosenbergs had Communist Party ties dating back to Julius's days as an engineering student at City College during the Depression, when he had been active in the Young Communist League. Julius joined the Communist Party in 1939 and served as a civilian employee of the Army Signal Corps during World War II, until he was discharged in 1945 for having concealed his Party membership. In the winter of 1943–1944, Julius began organizing an espionage network to collect military-related scientific intelligence on behalf of the Soviet Union.

The arrest of the Rosenbergs in the summer of 1950 followed that of David Greenglass, Ethel's younger brother and a recent partner of Julius's in an unsuccessful electronics business venture. Greenglass had served in the army as a machinist at the highly classified Los Alamos weapons laboratory that had been charged with the development of an atomic bomb—the Manhattan Project—during World War II, and had recently been identified by Soviet courier Harry Gold as one of his espionage contacts. Greenglass admitted his guilt and told investigators that he had been recruited as a spy by his sister Ethel and brother-in-law Julius in November 1943. He confessed that, at their direction, he had passed along top secret information about atomic bomb design that he had learned while working at Los Alamos, using his wife Ruth as a conduit, and that Julius had continued to engage in espionage in the postwar years. Atomic Energy Agency officials who later reviewed his testimony were impressed by the range and accuracy of the information he had been able to obtain, despite his lack of technical knowledge and relatively low-level position. Greenglass secured immunity for his wife and a promise of leniency for himself, but the Rosenbergs refused to cooperate.

In January 1951 the Rosenbergs were indicted for conspiracy to commit espionage, along with Morton Sobell, who was alleged to be a member of the spy ring operated by Julius but who was not implicated in the atomic espionage directed at Los Alamos. The indictment listed ten overt acts in furtherance of the conspiracy, including the receipt by Julius Rosenberg from Ruth Greenglass of a paper containing written information after a trip by Ruth to New Mexico, and the additional receipt by Julius from David Greenglass of a paper containing sketches of experiments conducted at the Los Alamos Project.

The Rosenbergs' trial opened on March 6, 1951, in federal court in lower Manhattan. The trial judge was Irving Kaufman. The prosecution was led by Irving Saypol, the U.S. Attorney for the Southern District of New York, assisted by future Joseph McCarthy aide Roy Cohn, among others. The Rosenbergs were represented by Emanuel Bloch and his father, Alexander. The younger Bloch was an experienced trial attorney with a solid track record as an advocate for left-wing causes, but the defense team proved to be badly overmatched in the face of the relentlessly aggressive Saypol and the generally unsympathetic trial judge.

As was often noted, all of the trial's principals, including not only the defendants and the principal witnesses against them, but also the judge and both lead prosecuting and defense attorneys, were Jewish. The one exception was the jury—something that has often looked suspicious, given that New York was the world's largest Jewish city. In response to the claim that only antisemitism in the trial process could account for this disparity, it has been pointed out that a number of potential jurors who may have been Jewish were excused from service, so that the impanelment of a non-Jewish jury reflected nothing more than the normal working of the selection process. One commentator calculated that, of 156 persons sworn for potential jury service, "fifteen names were *obviously* Jewish; . . . of these, ten were excused by the court for personal reasons, four were challenged by the defense, and one was challenged by the government" (Dawidowicz 1952a). However, the argument that has also been advanced that the lack of Jews on the jury is not surprising because the federal court's district did not encompass the entire city, but included only Manhattan and the Bronx, and extended northward into the largely non-Jewish counties of the lower Hudson Valley, is not convincing. Given the large Jewish populations of Manhattan, and especially of the Bronx, and the much smaller overall populations of the constituent counties outside the city, the percentage of Jews in the federal court's district was about the same as in New York City as a whole.

In any event, it is not clear whether the lack of Jews on the jury helped or hurt the defendants. Rosenberg supporters have frequently accused trial judge Kaufman of being unduly harsh precisely because he was Jewish and wanted to avoid any appearance of favoritism or sympathy toward Jewish defendants, whom he regarded as traitors. The one disturbing, but inconclusive, bit of evidence that the non-Jewish jury may have harbored antisemitic attitudes came from a piece of paper with the word "Jude" written on it that was found on the table in the jury room after the trial. But the significance of that scribbled note or what it referred to is unknown (Radosh and Milton 1997).

The jury was quickly impaneled and the trial proceeded with remarkable rapidity, concluding with a verdict of guilty on March 28. The prosecution presented a case that was much more streamlined than its lengthy witness list had promised. The crucial testimony was provided by David and Ruth Greenglass. They testified to David's recruitment by the Rosenbergs, the information David acquired at Los Alamos (including a description of the implosion process that was critical to the design of the atomic bomb), the delivery of that material via both Ruth and Harry Gold, and, in a last-minute addition to their prior version of events, Ethel's direct involvement in the espionage effort by typing up some of that information before it was passed along to the Soviets. David also produced replicas of the sketches of the bomb design that he said he had delivered during the war. The Greenglasses' testimony was corroborated by Soviet courier Harry Gold. A Manhattan Project scientist testified to the classified nature of the information obtained and transmitted by Greenglass, vouching for the "reasonable" accuracy of Greenglass's sketch and the potential usefulness of that information to outside scientific experts, although the prosecution did not call the top Manhattan Project officials (including J. Robert Oppenheimer and General Leslie Groves) who had been identified as potential witnesses.

Elizabeth Bentley, the tabloids' Red Spy Queen, testified to her own Soviet spymaster's relationship to a certain "Julius," who could be identified as Rosenberg, but she also appeared as an expert witness on the loyalty of American Communists to the Soviet Union. This testimony was central to the prosecution's theory of the motive for the Rosenbergs' activities, and Communism all but eclipsed the formal charge of espionage as the dominant theme of the trial. Prosecutor Saypol was relentless in driving this point home. As he told the jury:

> the allegiance of the Rosenbergs and Sobell were not to our country, but that it was to Communism, Communism in this country and Communism throughout the world. . . . The evidence will show their loyalty to and worship of the Soviet Union and by their rank disloyalty to our country these defendants joined with their co-conspirators in a deliberate, carefully planned conspiracy to deliver to the Soviet Union, the information and the weapons.

It was an exceedingly difficult time for a defendant to be on trial as an accused spy for the Soviet Union. The Korean War was raging. United Nations forces had only recently recovered from the intervention by Chinese Communist forces that had threatened to drive UN troops off the peninsula entirely, and had yet to recapture Seoul. Joe McCarthy's charges of widespread Communist infiltration of the government were generating headlines daily. Alger Hiss was in prison, having been convicted on perjury charges the year before in the same federal courthouse in which the Rosenbergs were on trial. The Soviet Union's initial testing of an atomic bomb in the summer of 1949, several years before American intelligence had predicted it, made the plight of defendants accused of facilitating that breakthrough—and the fears of nuclear confrontation that it triggered—all the more desperate.

But even considering these unfavorable circumstances, the Rosenbergs' defense was a debacle. The Rosenbergs offered no plausible alternative to the detailed testimony of David and Ruth Greenglass, and their credibility was shattered by unconvincing denials of Communist Party affiliations or the even more damaging refusal to answer such questions on fifth amendment grounds. The challenge to Greenglass's testimony as falsely motivated by bad blood arising from a business dispute with Julius was unconvincing, given the enormity of the stakes for Greenglass's own sister. By deciding not to cross-examine Harry Gold, the defense passed up an opportunity to probe that important witness's psychological peculiarities. Perhaps most damaging of all, Emanuel Bloch's motion—that palpably astonished both the judge and the prosecutor—to impound Greenglass's sketches may have been a desperate bid to score patriotic points with the jury, but it dramatically underlined the argument that the information at issue was just what the prosecution claimed it to be: highly secret even years after the fact and still vital to the security of the nation.

It was true that the prosecution's case lacked one prominent feature of other espionage cases of the time: the actual, hard evidence of what the defendants were accused of turning over to the Soviets. In the Alger Hiss and Judith Coplon cases, the prosecution presented the actual documents that the defendants had passed; in the Rosenberg case, the bomb design sketches entered into evidence were David Greenglass's reconstructions (while in custody) of what he said he had turned over to the Rosenbergs.

Moreover, the case against the Rosenbergs was built on claims and tactics that have not withstood the test of time. Prosecutor Saypol's contention that the Rosenbergs had been able to "steal through David Greenglass this one weapon [the atomic bomb]" grossly exaggerated the actual trial testimony about the value and extent of the classified information provided by Greenglass. As the government knew, the German émigré and Communist physicist Klaus Fuchs had provided the Soviets with the detailed technical data that constituted the true "atomic secret." Although Greenglass's sketches "may not have been extremely helpful in themselves . . . they confirmed that Fuchs was telling the truth when he claimed the United States had now settled on the plutonium, implosion-type bomb, abandoning the uranium model as a dead end. This information . . . could well have enabled the Russians to avoid the highly expensive and elaborate duplicate efforts undertaken by the United States" (Radosh and Milton 1997).

On cross-examination of Ethel Rosenberg, the prosecution repeatedly used her invocation of the fifth amendment in grand jury testimony to impeach her denials at trial. Although this practice was allowed under the then current rules of evidence (and not challenged by the defendants on appeal), it was held improper by the U.S. Supreme Court in an unrelated case a few years later. However, given the plausibility of the prosecution's case, founded as it was on the apparently sincere testimony of the defendants' own close relatives, whose credibility was buttressed by the fact that their testimony might send the defendants to their death, along with the weaknesses, verging on incompetence, of the defense, it is hard not to conclude that guilty verdicts were fully justified by the evidence and inevitable. On April 5, 1951, Judge Kaufman sentenced the Rosenbergs to death and Sobell (who had not been implicated in atomic espionage) to thirty years in prison.

Given the gravity of the charges, the overwhelming strength of the evidence of guilt, and the wartime atmosphere, the imposition of the maximum penalty on the Rosenbergs occasioned little surprise or protest, although it exceeded the government's own position at the time (supported by FBI Director J. Edgar Hoover) that Julius, but not Ethel, be executed. Ultimately the decision to invoke the death penalty was that of Irving Kaufman alone. The judge's sentencing statement rested on his conclusion that, by stealing "the secret of the atomic bomb," the Rosenbergs had committed a crime "that was worse than murder" and thereby triggered the Korean War. This claim rested on no evidence presented at trial, but—apart from its single-minded focus on the Rosenbergs—has been more or less sustained by recent disclosures. These have confirmed the Soviet Union's crucial role in unleashing North Korea's invasion of the South and Stalin's reversal of an earlier veto of that attack plan after the Soviets' first atomic bomb test. John Haynes concludes, "It is unlikely that [Stalin] would have approved North Korea's invasion of South Korea in 1950 had the American atomic monopoly still existed" (Haynes 1996). Judge Kaufman, while acknowledging Ethel's subsidiary role in the conspiracy, noted that she was older than Julius and labeled her the decisive influence on her younger brother, David Greenglass, without whom the Rosenbergs' atomic espionage activities would not have been possible.

Other suggested motivations remain speculative. Critics have suggested that the judge was bidding to win governmental favor and advance his career, but, as noted, sentencing Ethel to death exceeded what the government desired. It has also been charged that Judge Kaufman was driven by the need to prove that Jews, such as himself, were reliable patriots who could be counted on to repudiate the defendants' treasonous activities, a need that some have attributed to the fact that his wife's maiden name was Rosenberg. A more prosaic explanation for the sentences may be found in the context of a time when the death penalty was inflicted far more often and routinely than would be the case thereafter. In 1951, there were one hundred executions in the United States; in New York State alone in the first months of that year, while the Rosenberg trial and sentencing unfolded, eight people were executed, including one woman. Within a few years the infliction of the death penalty would drop so sharply that the execution of the Rosenbergs could readily appear excessive in retrospect, although it was fully consistent with sentencing practices at the time. Whatever the reasoning behind the imposition of death sentences on both Julius and Ethel, it was the specter of the electric chair, and the consequent orphaning of their young sons, that provided the emotional energy to transform their legal case into a passionately embraced—and passionately rejected—cause over the two years that ensued before their execution in June 1953.

The Rosenbergs were both Jews and Communists. If their Communist affiliations and beliefs took center stage at their trial, it was their Jewish identity, virtually unmentioned in the courtroom, that dominated the campaign to overturn their convictions or, at the least, avert their executions. Immediately after the Rosenbergs were sentenced, the anti-Communist Yiddish press raised questions about the imposition of the death penalty. On April 6, 1951, the *Forward,* while acknowledging the Rosenbergs' guilt and the severity of their crime, pronounced the sentence as "too horrible," adding that "every Jew felt the same way." The *Day* concurred in criticizing the death sentences and faulted Judge Kaufman's handling of the case. The criticisms of these anti-Communist Jewish papers were then quoted by the Communist Party–allied monthly *Jewish Life,* which also charged in its May issue that "the Jewish community felt that the judgment had the odor of the pogrom." According to *Jewish Life,* "The shock [at the death sentences] was particularly deep on New York's East Side where the Rosenbergs were born and brought up . . . and where they lived up to the time of their arrest." These protests escalated into Communist charges that the Rosenbergs had been targeted as Jews and that the death sentences were motivated by antisemitism.

In the summer of 1951, the *National Guardian* published a series of articles challenging the Rosenbergs' conviction and first broached the possibility of antisemitism in the court proceedings by highlighting the lack of any Jews on a jury despite their large numbers in New York City. A National Committee to Secure Justice in the Rosenberg Case, with a largely Jewish membership, was organized in response to the *National Guardian* articles, and Jews were exhorted: "The Rosenbergs shall not die. . . . Raise your voices, all you Jews, rich and poor!" (Dawidowicz 1952a). The January 1952 issue of *Jewish Life* featured editor Louis Harap's article, "Anti-Semitism and the Rosenbergs," arguing that "a lowering cloud of anti-Semitism hangs over the death sentence of Julius and Ethel Rosenberg":

> The country had had trials of a number of confessed traitors like Axis Sally and others; a number of alleged atomic spies were deemed more important than the Rosenbergs. *Yet no one received the death sentence until two East Side Jews were tried. Why?*

Two months later, the executive secretary of the Communist-dominated Civil Rights Congress warned, "The lynching of these two innocent American Jews . . . will serve as a signal for a wave of Hitler-like genocidal attacks against the Jewish people throughout the United States" (Dawidowicz 1952a). The Rosenbergs' "Death House Letters," initially published in the spring of 1953 to rally support for their last-minute clemency campaign, portrayed them as an average Jewish couple on New York's Lower East Side and were studded with references to their Jewish religious practices, faith, and holiday observances even while imprisoned and awaiting execution.

While the Rosenbergs' supporters and Communist-allied publications were attempting to garner sympathy by claiming that the couple were victims of an antisemitic frame-up, the Communist Party itself (which had been silent during the Rosenbergs' trial) gave little organized support to the Rosenberg defense campaign. That changed in November 1952. That month, deposed Czechoslovak Party Secretary Rudolf Slansky and other Czech Communist leaders were put on trial in Prague on trumped-up charges of orchestrating a capitalist–Zionist conspiracy with U.S. President Harry S Truman and Israeli Prime Minister David Ben-Gurion to overthrow the communist

regime. Eleven of the fourteen defendants (including Slansky) were Jewish; the indictment formally identified them as of "Jewish origin."

The flagrantly antisemitic thrust of the purge provided a grim harbinger of intensifying antisemitism, culminating in the fabricated Doctors' Plot charges against mostly Jewish Kremlin physicians, that would mark the months before Stalin's death in March 1953. With American public opinion, led by President Truman and President-elect Dwight D. Eisenhower, denouncing the Prague trial as (in Eisenhower's words) "a political act designed to unloose a campaign of rabid anti-Semitism through Soviet Russia and the satellite nations of Eastern Europe" (*New York Times*, December 22, 1952), American and European Communist parties seized upon the Rosenberg case to redirect accusations of antisemitism away from the Soviet Union and toward the United States.

It was then that the Communist Party threw its full weight behind the Rosenberg defense. New members flooded into the defense committee. A worldwide campaign was quickly mobilized. The charge of antisemitism found a particularly receptive audience in Europe. The Rosenbergs did indeed prove a handy lightning rod to deflect concerns about the events in Prague. Prominent Communist historian Herbert Aptheker argued that Slansky was guilty, but that the Rosenbergs were the innocent victims of an antisemitic frame-up. Writing in the French Communist newspaper, *L'Humanité*, in November 1952, American Communist novelist Howard Fast claimed that "the Jewish masses of our country" had detected "the stale smell of fascism" in the case. Alleging that the Rosenbergs "have been judged by Jews" and "sent to death by other Jews," Fast charged that it was "exactly the old technique of the Jewish Tribunal employed by Hitler" (Radosh and Milton 1997).

The perception that the Rosenberg defense effort was being orchestrated to serve as an instrument of Soviet and Communist propaganda elicited an increasingly vehement response from Jewish organizations and intellectuals anxious to dispel any Communist taint from the American Jewish community. There was reason for such concern. Not only were all the alleged and admitted Soviet spies involved in the Rosenberg trial Jewish, but the common perception that the American Communist Party contained a disproportionately high number of Jews was well-founded (Glazer 1961). And the one increase in the overall downward trend in antisemitic attitudes since World War II occurred between 1951 and 1953, the years when the Rosenberg case unfolded (Dinnerstein 1994).

The anti-Communist Jewish community mobilized to counteract Rosenberg defense efforts, perceiving that the campaign was facilitating the equation of Jews with Communism. As Lucy Dawidowicz wrote, "because a spy or a Communist is a Jew, the Communists proclaim that all Jews are collectively involved" (Dawidowicz 1952a). In March 1952 the *Anti-Defamation League Bulletin* published an article "Anti-Semitism and the Atom Spy Trial" by Oliver Pilat asserting that antisemitism was encouraged by Communist emphasis on the fact that the Rosenbergs were Jews. In May, the National Community Relations Advisory Council, acting on behalf of the American Jewish (AJ) Committee, the Anti-Defamation League (ADL), the AJCongress, the Jewish War Veterans, the Jewish Labor Committee, and the Union of American Hebrew Congregations, issued a statement that labeled the Rosenberg defense committee a "Communist inspired group" that was wrongly injecting "the false issue of anti-Semitism into the Rosenberg case" (Marker 1972). The AJ Committee deputized staff member Rabbi S. Andhil Fineberg to monitor pro-Rosenberg activities. Rabbi Fineberg wrote *The Rosenberg Case: Fact and Fiction* to affirm the justness of the convictions and executions and to expose "the hurtful impact of one of the most sensational propaganda campaigns ever conducted." He concluded, "the Rosenbergs' case is ended but the evil they did is endless" (Fineberg 1953).

Writing in the *New Leader,* a social democratic publication with a large Jewish readership, Lucy Dawidowicz argued that the Rosenberg defense campaign "serves only one purpose—to intensify the 'hate America' campaign throughout the world" and that commutation of the death sentences would hand the Communists an unwarranted propaganda victory (Dawidowicz 1952b). She faulted even anti-Communist critics of the death sentences for providing a cloak of legitimacy for Communist agitation on the issue (1952a). In his perceptive but pitiless dissection of the Rosenbergs' "Death House Letters," social critic Robert Warshow characterized the couples' repeated references to Jewish tradition and identity as "patently disingenuous." "Since the propaganda built up around the case emphasized the fact that the Rosenbergs were Jewish, they simply adopted the role that was demanded of them" (Warshow 1953).

In the end, the organized campaign to "save the Rosenbergs" did not rally significant support beyond the diminishing ranks of the Communist Party and its remaining sympathizers and auxiliaries. Independent leftist journalist I. F. Stone pointedly explained the failure: "[T]he constant effort of the defense to equate the United States with Nazi Germany; to picture the Rosenbergs as the victims of a racist murder and anti-Semitic plot fit neatly with Soviet propaganda but it hurt the Rosenbergs more than it helped them; it antagonized the American Jewish community; it was poisonous folly" (Stone 1953).

While the Rosenbergs' supporters pressed their claims in the streets, meeting halls, and the press, their lawyers pursued post-trial and appellate remedies in the courts, but without success. The federal court of appeals affirmed their conviction in February 1952, and the U.S. Supreme Court declined to hear the case. Newly inaugurated President Eisenhower denied a petition for clemency. Never a strong possibility for Julius, clemency for Ethel was doomed by the president's belief that the older Ethel was the dominant personality, and that a commutation of her sentence to the term (thirty years) of imprisonment authorized by law as the alternative to death would allow her release in half that time, a sentence he considered unduly lenient. Until the last minute, however, a commutation of the sentences was possible had the Rosenbergs agreed to confess and disclose details of their espionage activities to the government. This they refused to do. "Love for their cause dominated their lives—it was even greater than their love for their children," Judge Kaufman had said in his sentencing statement.

In a final legal twist, just days before the rescheduled June 19, 1953, execution date, Supreme Court Justice William O. Douglas granted a stay to consider a last-minute argument by new counsel, who contended that the Rosenbergs had been wrongly tried and sentenced under a law that had been superseded by the Atomic Energy Act. The more recent statute, it was argued, did not authorize the death penalty unless the jury recommended it; at the Rosenbergs' trial, the death sentence had been imposed by the judge alone. But with the Eisenhower administration now determined to bring the legal proceedings to an immediate close, the U.S. Supreme Court was summoned from its summer recess into special session to review the stay. By a six-to-three vote, the Court overturned the stay at noon on Friday June 19. After a two-year battle in the courts, the execution was cleared to proceed that night.

The Rosenbergs' Jewishness gave their last hours a final twist. While the Supreme Court was deliberating, counsel and Judge Kaufman had agreed that it would be inappropriate to execute the couple as scheduled on the Sabbath (Friday, June 19), at 11 p.m. When the Supreme Court vacated the stay on Friday, the Rosenberg camp assumed that the execution would be delayed for at least a day. Instead, the time for the execution was accelerated to beat the Sabbath deadline. As several thousand supporters gathered in Union Square to await the fatal announcement, Julius, followed by Ethel, went to the electric chair in Sing Sing prison's death house just before sunset. They are the only civilians executed for espionage in the history of the United States. Two days later, the Rosenbergs were buried, in accordance with Jewish ritual, in Wellwood Cemetery on Long Island.

In the aftermath of the executions, the vast bulk of public opinion, including opinion in the Jewish community, considered the case closed and the Rosenbergs guilty as charged. The ferment of the Sixties and the reemergence of the radical Left, however, provided a broader and more receptive audience for critics of the trial. In 1965, Walter and Miriam Schneir's *Invitation to an Inquest* persuaded a wide readership that the charge of atomic espionage had been fabricated by an unscrupulous government. E. L. Doctorow's highly praised novel, *The Book of Daniel*, rendered this theme in fictional terms a few years later. When the Rosenbergs' children, under their adoptive names of Robert and Michael Meeropol, went public with their identities and their protestations of faith in their parents' innocence, an emotional current was added to the growing conviction that the Rosenbergs had been unjustly convicted. The 1975 documentary *The Unquiet Death of Julius and Ethel Rosenberg* argued the case for the Rosenbergs in theaters and on public television. In post-Watergate America, claims of government misconduct and persecution of the innocent on the left resonated with renewed plausibility. However, now it was their status as leftists and not as Jews that was identified as the source of their vulnerability.

The debate on the case was once again transformed by the publication in 1983 of *The Rosenberg File: A Search for Truth* by Ronald Radosh and Joyce Milton. Drawing on a vast array of documentary and oral evidence, including newly available internal FBI documents, Radosh and Milton affirmed the Rosenbergs' guilt and provided a detailed account of the extensive espionage network that Julius had

directed. They argued that Ethel had been prosecuted, convicted, and sentenced to death primarily to pressure Julius into cooperating with the authorities, and questioned the propriety of the death sentence imposed on her. Although questioning the exaggerated claim that the Rosenbergs had stolen "the secret of the atomic bomb," Radosh and Milton showed that the classified material the Rosenbergs had obtained from David Greenglass was of significant value to the Soviet Union's weapons development effort. The weight of informed opinion—liberal and conservative—concluded that the case against the Rosenbergs had now been conclusively established.

Almost from the onset of the case, allusions had frequently been made to conclusively incriminating evidence against the Rosenbergs that could not be presented in court because of national security concerns. Hoover had referred to such evidence in his *Reader's Digest* article on the FBI's investigation of atomic espionage. President Eisenhower's attorney general told him about the existence of the evidence during their discussions about clemency. Beginning in the 1980s, however, a number of accounts, based on highly placed sources, revealed that American intelligence had broken Soviet codes in the 1940s and that these decryptions had provided crucial leads in building the case against the Rosenbergs. In 1995, the U.S. government officially confirmed the existence of that code breaking effort, known as the Venona Project, and released the texts of hundreds of Soviet intelligence messages that had been decoded decades earlier. The leading historian of cryptoanalysis, David Kahn, announced, "the Venona intercepts show one thing beyond doubt, that the Rosenbergs spied for the Soviet Union against the United States" (Radosh and Milton 1997).

The Venona revelations brought any debate about the Rosenbergs' guilt more or less to an end. Even the Schneirs retreated from their prior protestations of innocence and acknowledged that the "Venona messages reveal that during World War II Julius ran a spy ring composed of young fellow Communists" and that they corroborated Julius's involvement in atomic espionage, but insisted it was only "minor" (Schneir and Schneir 1995).

But however dispositive the Venona decrypts were on the issue of guilt, that evidence rekindled doubts about the propriety of the death sentences. Venona, together with other revelations of Soviet atomic espionage activities, demonstrated that Soviet infiltration of Los Alamos was more extensive than had heretofore been publicly acknowledged and involved highly placed scientists who were never prosecuted because evidence that could be used in court was not available. That the Rosenbergs were put to death while other critically important Soviet agents, whose spying activities were arguably even more beneficial to the Soviets, went free raised newly troubling questions about their execution. Venona confirmed that the American investigative agencies had managed to identify the members of the Rosenberg spy ring that the Rosenbergs had refused to implicate. To the extent that the death sentences were intended as leverage to gain the Rosenbergs' cooperation in exchange for clemency, that effort was apparently directed at obtaining admissible evidence for use in further prosecutions, not the identities of the agents themselves.

More than half a century after their deaths, the passions the Rosenberg case once roused have been eclipsed by the end of the Cold War and the demise of the political conflicts that it once encapsulated. From the vantage point of an American Jewish community that is now overwhelmingly affluent and suburban, the human side of their story, that of a young Jewish couple raised in poverty on the Lower East Side and scrambling to maintain a modest livelihood, seems increasingly remote. The fear that the case would trigger a resurgence of antisemitism has proved unfounded. That the case belongs to a world that has irretrievably passed does not, however, mean that it will be forgotten. As Justice Felix Frankfurter wrote, in explaining his decision to issue a lengthy written dissent from the Supreme Court's June 19, 1953, decision although the Rosenbergs had been executed by the time his opinion was completed, "History also has its claims."

Henry D. Fetter

References and Further Reading
Dawidowicz, Lucy S. 1952a. "'Anti-Semitism' and the Rosenberg Case: The Latest Communist Propaganda Trap." *Commentary* 14 (July): 41–45.
Dawidowicz, Lucy S. 1952b. "The Rosenberg Case: 'Hate-America' Weapon." *New Leader* (December 22): 13.
Dinnerstein, Leonard. 1994. *Antisemitism in America.* New York: Oxford University Press.
Fineberg, S. Andhil. 1953. *The Rosenberg Case: Fact and Fiction.* New York: Oceana Publications.
Glazer, Nathan. 1961. *The Social Basis of American Communism.* New York: Harcourt, Brace.
Haynes, John. 1996. *Red Scare or Red Menace? American Communism and Anticommunism in the Cold War Era.* Chicago: Ivan R. Dee.
Marker, Jeffrey M. 1972. "The Jewish Community and the Case of Julius and Ethel Rosenberg." *Maryland Historian* 3 (Fall): 106–112.
Moore, Deborah Dash. 1998. "Reconsidering the Rosenbergs: Symbol and Substance in Second Generation American Jewish Consciousness." *Journal of American Ethnic History* (Fall): 21–37.
Parrish, Michael. 1977. "Cold War Justice: The Supreme Court and the Rosenbergs." *American Historical Review* 82 (October): 805–842.
Radosh, Ronald, and Joyce Milton. 1997. *The Rosenberg File.* 2nd ed. New Haven, CT: Yale University Press.
Roberts, Sam. 2001. *The Brother: The Untold Story of Atomic Spy David Greenglass and How He Sent His Sister, Ethel Rosenberg, to the Electric Chair.* New York: Random House.
Schneir, Walter, and Miriam Schneir. 1965. *Invitation to an Inquest.* New York: Doubleday.
Schneir, Walter, and Miriam Schneir. 1995. "Cryptic Answers." *Nation* (August 14, 21).
Stone, I. F. 1953. "Rosenberg Aftermath: Wild Words Will Not Help Peace." *I. F. Stone's Weekly* (June 27): 2–3.
Warshow, Robert. 1953. "The 'Idealism' of Julius and Ethel Rosenberg." *Commentary* (November): 33–43.

Jewish Anarchism in America

Anarchism as a significant movement among Jews in the United States began in 1886. Before then, there were a few Jewish anarchists, the most well known being Isidore Stein from New Haven, Connecticut. During the first years of its existence (1886–1890), the anarchist movement was probably the largest among Jewish radicals in the United States, and it remained relatively strong between 1900 and World War I. The less radical socialist movement, however, was always more appealing to the masses. The anarchist movement concentrated mainly in the Lower East Side of Manhattan, New York, but also bloomed in the ghettos of cities in Pennsylvania, New Jersey, and New England. It started in the sweatshops, where its adherents took part in the first garment strikes and helped organize some of the first Jewish trade unions, including the New York cloak makers and knee-pants workers. They imparted revolutionary content to popular activities, sponsoring picnics and lectures, organizing clubs, cooperatives, and mutual-aid societies. Anarchism's impact on Jews in the United States was limited to the immigrant generation.

Anarchism among Jews started mainly in Russia, where some Jews adhered to Peter Kropotkin's anarcho-communist doctrine and actively participated in its propaganda by attending meetings, distributing pamphlets, recruiting members, and organizing strikes. Many anarchists joined the vast stream of Jews who left Russia for America following the anti-Jewish riots of 1881 and subsequent years. Few fled specifically because of political persecution. Upon their arrival, these radicals were estranged from the mainstream of American political life. They did not speak English and maintained the Russian radical tradition. They organized themselves as the Russian Progressive Labor Association, not attaching themselves to any specific ideological group. As they learned English and came to understand American political and social issues, they affiliated with the labor movement while staying within the Yiddish-speaking milieu. Soon they formed Jewish political groups, such as the *Rusish-yidisher arbeter fareyn* (Russian-Jewish Workers' Union) on February 7, 1885, and the *Yidisher arbayter fareyn* (Jewish Workers' Union) on April 19, 1885—the first to include immigrants from countries other than Russia and Germany.

The turning point, however, came with the Haymarket Affair (May 4, 1886). That evening a demonstration of labor unions was held at Haymarket Square in Chicago. A bomb exploded, killing one policeman and wounding many. Eight anarchist leaders were arrested, some of whom had not been present. Seven of the accused anarchist leaders were sentenced to death, and one to fifteen years in prison. (On the eve of the execution, the sentences of two of the condemned men were commuted to life in prison.) Although the bomb thrower was never identified, the defendants were charged as accessories to murder: their oral and written statements against the state and the police had allegedly inspired his crime. May 4 caused some radicals to define themselves as anarchists rather than socialists. On October 9, 1886, the day the anarchist leaders were sentenced, the first Jewish anarchist group in the United States, *Pionire der frayhayt* (Pioneers of Liberty), was formed on the Lower East Side of Manhattan. Among its renowned members were Hillel Solotaroff, Moshe Katz, Roman Lewis, Emma Goldman, and the poet David Edelshtat.

Jewish anarchists were drawn almost entirely from the growing ranks of organized Jewish workers, who were concentrated in the needle trades. By 1886, there were fourteen Jewish unions, most of which represented workers in the garment industry. In October 1888, *Fareynikte yidishe ge-*

verkshaftn (United Hebrew Trades) was founded as an umbrella organization to create and strengthen the existing Jewish unions. Another significant Jewish group, founded in 1889 in Philadelphia, was *Riter der frayhayt* (Knights of Liberty). Among its members were the powerful speakers Max Staller, Chaim Weinberg, and Isidore Prenner.

These anarchists leaned toward atheism, believing that religion was an ally of the state and that both were used as instruments to subjugate humanity spiritually, politically, and economically. They therefore rejected traditional Judaism. Their activities included publishing antireligious journals on Yom Kippur (Pioneers of Liberty) and staging Yom Kippur balls, starting in 1889, which featured merry-making and atheistic harangues.

Jewish anarchist groups, like their other American anarchist counterparts, affiliated with the International Working People's Association, an anarchist labor organization. Its American branch was founded in 1883 mainly by Johann Most (b. Germany, 1846–d. United States, 1906), but with the aid of Albert Parsons and other anarchist leaders. Jews in the 1880s began to play a significant role in the movement, which had been dominated by German immigrants and native-born Americans. Johann Most embraced the American Jewish groups, forging close ties between them and the German branch.

Since many Jews immigrated to the United States through England, strong ties developed between the anarchist groups in both countries. London's Yiddish newspaper, *Arbeter fraynd*, also served as a voice for the American Jewish anarchists. Anarchist newspapers published in Boston (*Liberty*) and New York (*The Alarm*) did not address specific issues concerning the Yiddish-speaking group. As a result, in February 1889, the Pioneers of Liberty published *Di Varhayt* (*The Truth*), the first Yiddish periodical in the United States. Among the prominent contributors were Most and Kropotkin. However, after only five months and twenty issues, it ceased to appear, probably due to insufficient funds.

By 1890 disagreements on fundamental issues arose between Jewish anarchists and socialists. The anarchists insisted on a nonparty paper that exposed the readers to all streams of radical ideas to enable them to form their own political opinions, while the socialists argued for a consistent stand on social, political, and economic issues. On December 25, 1889, the first conference of Jewish radicals was convened to discuss the possibility of publishing a newspaper to serve both anarchists and socialists. Arguments over format were put to a vote, resulting in the anarchists' defeat by one vote. The gathering broke up, and the breach between the two camps became irreparable.

On July 4, 1890, the *Fraye arbayter shtime* (*FAS, Free Voice of Labor*) appeared, surviving with few interruptions until December 1977. This Yiddish newspaper played a vital role in the Jewish labor movement. It had high literary standards, featuring the finest Yiddish writers. Its first editor was Roman Lewis (1864–1918), who became one of the leaders of the Jewish anarchist movement in the United States. Later he turned his back on radicalism and became an active member of the Democratic Party. Several months later, on January 9, 1891, the poet David Edelshtat assumed the position, first as co-editor with the Social Democrat Aronovitsh (Dr. Ayzik Hurwitz). When Aronovitsh resigned several weeks later, Edelshtat became the sole editor, turning the paper into an anarchist weekly.

In 1892, during the Homestead strike, Alexander Berkman (b. Vilna, 1870–d. Nice, 1936) attempted to murder Henry Clay Frick, the manager of Carnegie Steel Works in Pittsburgh. This caused friction in the movement; while some were inspired by the act, others repudiated terrorism. Upon his release from prison in 1906, Berkman became, together with Emma Goldman (b. Lithuania, 1869–d. Toronto, 1940), the foremost anarchist in America.

In 1894, the *FAS* suspended publication due to lack of funds and organizational problems, ending the first phase of Jewish anarchism. Nevertheless, a year later the monthly *Di fraye gezelshaft* (*The Free Society*) appeared, printing articles in Yiddish by leading Jewish and gentile anarchists until 1914. The *FAS* was revived in October 1899 under the editorship of the prominent agitator and journalist Saul Yanovsky (b. Pinsk, Russia, 1864–d. United States, 1939) and lasted until 1919. This was a period of rejuvenation for both the paper and for the movement throughout America. The paper's circulation grew steadily, exceeding 20,000 on the eve of World War I, while the movement gained new life, even as the Pioneers of Liberty, Knights of Liberty, and other groups faded away. Jewish anarchists from northeastern cities sent delegates to New York once a year for meetings.

During these two decades, a dozen Yiddish anarchist periodicals were published, although only *FAS* persisted for a long time. Many Jewish groups were formed, like the *Federirte anarkhistishe groupe in Amerike* (Federated Anarchist Groups in America), organized in Philadelphia in December 1910. These groups helped organize unions in all trades that had Jewish workers.

At the same time, during these two decades, Jewish anarchism became less militant. This was in part because anarchists participated in the organization of unions in all trades in which Jews were employed and focused on specific improvements in workers' economic and social conditions. In addition, the assassination of President William McKinley in 1901 shocked anarchists, including Yanovsky, who claimed that violence does not serve anarchism, which calls for harmony and peace. Antireligious agitation was also reduced because it turned away many, who, although no longer religious, were still sentimentally connected to tradition. Those who had previously condemned reformism now adopted a conciliatory attitude. As a result, the movement lost its revolutionary identity. Anarchists even took part in *Arbeter ring* (Workmen's Circle), the socialist-oriented Jewish fraternal order in North America, which emphasized educational and cultural programs, life insurance, and sickness and accident benefits.

When World War I began, the anarchist movement entered a critical period, splitting over whether to support the war or not. Kropotkin backed the Entente, while Yanovsky, in *FAS,* at first opposed the war and signed an International Manifesto denouncing it, together with other prominent anarchists, such as Emma Goldman and Alexander Berkman. Later, however, he shifted his stand to favor an Allied victory, while other anarchists, including Michael Cohn, were pro-German.

This controversy was followed by the repression and deportation of many anarchists, among them leaders of the movement, in the Palmer Raids staged in the winter of 1919–1920. In addition, the immigration of Eastern Europeans declined and then was severely restricted in 1924, reducing potential Yiddish-speaking recruits. The younger generation of Jews, born in the United States, was assimilating and entering the mainstream of American culture. The movement had fallen on hard times from which it never recovered.

The collaboration between the anarchists and socialists between 1923 and 1927 against the communists proved successful when they were able to block the communists from taking over the garment unions. They remained on good terms and shared many concerns. Jewish anarchists organized libraries, reading rooms, and literary clubs.

After World War II, anarchist groups and federations reemerged, but wielded little influence among Jews compared to the earlier movement. This is not surprising because anarchists never stressed the need for organizational continuity.

In the 1960s and 1970s, a new radicalism took root among students and the Left in general in the United States, Europe, and Japan, embracing criticism of elitist power structures and the materialist values of modern industrial societies—both capitalist and communist. This resulted in a renewed interest in anarchism, but only among some students, not workers, who in the late nineteenth and early twentieth centuries had constituted the movement's major source of recruits. The *FAS*'s circulation steadily declined, and it became a biweekly. As the Yiddish readership aged and the number of Jews who read Yiddish sharply declined, the paper's circulation by the 1970s had decreased to less than 2,000. Although switching to English could have increased the paper's circulation, its editors refused to do so for ideological reasons. The closing of the *FAS* in 1977 signaled the end of the Jewish anarchist movement in the United States.

Ori Kritz

References and Further Reading

Avrich, Paul. 1988. *Anarchist Portraits.* Princeton, NJ: Princeton University Press.
Kritz, Ori. 1997. *Poetics of Anarchy.* Frankfurt am Main: Peter Lang.

Commentary and the Origins of Neoconservatism

A New York City–based monthly magazine founded by the American Jewish Committee (AJC) in 1945, *Commentary* has reflected and shaped the changing currents of American intellectual and political discourse, as its perspective moved from liberal to radical to conservative over the years. The magazine made its most notable mark by serving, along with the more policy-oriented *The Public Interest* (edited by onetime *Commentary* associate editor, Irving Kristol), as a flagship publication expressing the disillusionment with the radical turbulence of the 1960s that came to be labeled—initially by its opponents—neocon-

servatism. *Commentary*'s anti-Communist liberalism in the 1950s and radicalism in the early 1960s made it a leading voice of mainstream American Jewish opinion. The magazine's shift to the right thereafter "broke ranks" (in the words of its longtime editor, Norman Podhoretz) with a community that has largely retained its traditional left-of-center allegiances. Ironically, however, *Commentary*'s own political rethinking was animated by specifically Jewish concerns.

Although in the first years of the twenty-first century the public associated neoconservatism almost exclusively with advocacy of the war in Iraq and an assertive program of nation-building in the Middle East, very different issues provided its initial impetus. In a 2003 response to the increasingly prevalent claim that neoconservative views on Iraq are linked to earlier support for the Vietnam War, Nathan Glazer, one of the movement's original spokesmen, pointed out that he opposed the earlier war and wrote that "the 'neoconservatism' of that era had almost nothing to do with the war. It arose out of skepticism over some social policies of the 1960s, from community action to affirmative action, and out of skepticism over the tactics and objectives of the student movement at Berkeley and Columbia" (Glazer 2003). Indeed, in a summation of the tenets of neoconservatism, written in 1979, Irving Kristol, the movement's "godfather," made no mention of foreign policy (Kristol 1983). Examination of *Commentary*'s rightward turn in the aftermath of the 1960s sustains Glazer's contention about the origins of neoconservatism and underlines how marginal foreign policy concerns were to its genesis.

Commentary was established as a successor to the *Contemporary Jewish Record* that the AJC had published since 1938. In the "Statement of Aims" that has appeared in each issue since July 1952, the Committee averred that "in sponsoring *Commentary*," the AJC "aims to meet the need for a journal of significant thought and opinion on Jewish affairs and contemporary issues. . . . The sponsorship of *Commentary* is in line with its general program to enlighten and clarify public opinion on problems of Jewish concern, to fight bigotry and protect human rights, and to promote Jewish cultural interest and creative achievement in America." Less officially, the AJC's sponsorship has been ascribed to a wish to demonstrate that "American Jewish writers and intellectuals had something important to say to the rest of the nation and that the time had finally come for the American Jewish community to contribute to the nation's intellectual life" (Shapiro 1992).

The selection of Elliot E. Cohen as editor proved crucial to the new publication's success. Cohen grew up in Mobile, Alabama, and, after graduating from Yale at the age of eighteen, had edited the *Menorah Journal* in the 1920s. During the 1930s he worked as the public relations director of the Federation of Jewish Philanthropies of Greater New York while maintaining ties to the mostly Jewish, anti-Stalinist radical intellectuals identified with *Partisan Review*. Cohen "had always maintained a great curiosity about Jewish affairs and spoke with pride of his Litvak father, an ordained rabbi, Hebrew scholar, and . . . businessman, at a time when young American Jewish intellectuals generally did not boast of such parochial, genteel origins" (Teller 1968). Although Cohen and the AJC (which described itself as non-Zionist) shared an initial coolness toward the establishment of Israel in 1948, and an enduring hostility toward communism, Cohen enjoyed editorial independence to fulfill his own vision of the journal's role in post-Holocaust American Jewish intellectual life. Cohen hoped "to prove that Jewish identification could be intellectually respectable enough to win over not only educated Jews . . . but specifically the lapsed Marxists of the 1930s" (Sachar 1992).

Cohen assembled a roster of mostly Jewish editors and contributors, which included scholars concerned with Jewish issues (historians Salo Baron and Jacob Marcus) as well as a cadre of formerly Marxist social and literary critics (Clement Greenberg, Robert Warshow, Nathan Glazer, Philip Rahv, Alfred Kazin, Daniel Bell, Irving Howe, Diana Trilling, and Irving Kristol), who were becoming more self-consciously Jewish in their personal identities and increasingly celebrated the virtues of American society. The new magazine "functioned as an invaluable halfway house in which a former 'lost generation' of talented Jews could negotiate their return to Jewish identity and creativity" (Sachar 1992). "The main difference between *Commentary* and *Partisan Review*," Cohen declared, "is that we admit to being a Jewish magazine and they don't" (Shapiro 1992).

Under Cohen's editorship, *Commentary* published the work of writers beginning to make their mark on American letters—Jewish novelists Bernard Malamud, Philip Roth, and Saul Bellow, as well as African-American author James Baldwin—and preeminent Jewish religious philosophers—Franz Rosenzweig, Martin Buber, and Gershom Scholem. It devoted more attention to the Holocaust than was then customary in intellectual or public discourse, and it presented a series of sociological studies exploring "how the Jew has changed yet retained his heritage in communities from West Bronx to San Francisco" (Mitgang 1953). It featured articles on developments in the Soviet bloc, the Hiss and Rosenberg cases, Cold War defense and foreign policy, and civil liberties and McCarthyism, the last of which provoked Irving Kristol's controversial observation that "there is one thing that the American people know about Senator McCarthy; he, like them, is unequivocally anti-Communist. About the spokesmen for American liberalism, they feel no such thing. And with some justification" (March 1952). By the late 1950s the magazine had a circulation of about 20,000 and "kept open communications," as literary critic and *Commentary* contributor Leslie Fiedler later wrote, "between a group of dissident intellectuals and an audience they had seldom reached. Surely no voice was more effective in making the Gentile American aware that the American Jews had become, momentarily, his spokesman at home and abroad. Beginning as a parochial journal of the Jewish community, *Commentary* became more and admired even by those with no stake in Jewish survival or Jewish thought" (Fiedler 1962). Cohen's own verdict was less sanguine, telling a colleague "sadly that *Commentary* is a fine magazine, but it had in no way changed American Jewish habit" (Teller 1968). Cohen struggled with depression for several years before committing suicide in May 1959.

In 1960, thirty-year-old Norman Podhoretz succeeded to the editorship of *Commentary* following Cohen's death, and he served as editor for thirty-five years. Podhoretz grew up in the impoverished, mostly Jewish Brownsville section of Brooklyn and was educated at Columbia University and Jewish Theological Seminary before attending Cambridge. After military service in Germany in the post–Korean War peacetime army, he served an editorial apprenticeship under Cohen at *Commentary* and made his mark as a stylish and combative literary critic, writing for *Partisan Review* and *Commentary*, as well as *The New Yorker* and *Harper's*. "One of the longest journeys in the world," he later wrote, "is the journey from Brooklyn to Manhattan—or at least from certain neighborhoods in Brooklyn to certain parts of Manhattan," and at a notably young age he had "made that journey" (Podhoretz 1967).

Podhoretz assumed the editorship determined to steer the magazine away from what he had come to fault as the "hard anti-Communism" promulgated by Cohen as well as the "disposition . . . to place everything American in a favorable light" (Podhoretz 1967). Podhoretz "immediately pressed the 'new *Commentary*' into articulating and developing the ideas that simultaneously encouraged the emergence of a new radicalism and gave it legitimacy and intellectual respectability" (Podhoretz 1985). Podhoretz launched his new regime by giving extended play to three articles by social critic Paul Goodman, which Podhoretz announced "constitute the first analysis that solidly relates delinquency to the prevailing patterns of respectability, showing how the juvenile criminal and the Organization Man, the rebel and the conformist, are equally symptomatic of the same deep disturbance in American culture" (February 1960). In subsequent issues, the magazine pursued Podhoretz's mandate for change in matters both domestic and foreign, providing a forum for claims that the United States, not the Soviets, was mostly responsible for initiating the Cold War, that the strategy of nuclear deterrence was dangerously misguided, that Kennedy's New Frontier was too conservative to meet the economic and social problems of the 1960s, and that the incipient American military involvement in Vietnam was ill-conceived. Most remarkably, the April 1961 issue featured a "Challenge to the Negro Leadership" that advocated a strategy of armed struggle for civil rights in the South. "Material of special Jewish concern" appeared less frequently (Podhoretz 1967).

As the radicalism of the 1960s gathered strength, Podhoretz and *Commentary* continued to stake out a "left of liberal" position on the issues of the day. Communism was credited "with the ability and will to revolutionize stagnant societies that do not yield readily to conventional liberal treatment." President Lyndon B. Johnson's Great Society was described as "social welfare on the cheap," falling far short of "the program of social action that is desperately needed" for "the restoration of the cities, integration of minorities into the labor force, relief of youth unemployment [and] elimination of the culture of poverty"; *Commentary* assailed American military intervention in the Dominican Republic and Vietnam, and in a final bow to the "spirit" of the Sixties, Podhoretz provided a forum for Norman Mailer's celebratory account of the October 1967 March on the Pentagon. The magazine's provocative content attracted a wider readership, with circulation rising to more than 50,000 by 1966 and peaking at 60,000 at the end of the decade.

There were, however, limits to *Commentary*'s embrace of the new radicalism, and these determined the journal's ultimate political trajectory. Russian revolutionary Leon Trotsky had once belittled American Socialism as the "socialism of dentists," and a New Leftist might have said the same about Podhoretz's revamped *Commentary*. The magazine might review Herbert Marcuse's *One Dimensional Man* favorably, but it was consistently wary of the youthful protestors who claimed to be inspired by Marcuse's portrayal of a repressive contemporary American society. Two early dissents from the escalating militancy of the radical Movement of the Sixties proved especially notable in light of the magazine's later move rightward. In response to the Berkeley Free Speech Movement and the accompanying shutdown of the University of California in the winter of 1964–1965, *Commentary* ran a critical account by Nathan Glazer (then a Berkeley professor) that faulted the direct action tactics of the protesting students as an illegitimate threat to university governance. By contrast, the recently founded *New York Review of Books* had rejected Glazer's piece and published instead an account by two other Berkeley professors who enthusiastically endorsed the protests. As student militancy, community activism, inflammatory rhetoric, and an anti-anti-Communism that morphed into the cult of Fidel Castro, Ho Chi Minh, and Mao Zedong became the defining characteristics of the decade's radical movement, that initial split marked a growing wedge between the two publications. By 1966, *Commentary* was pronouncing the New Left part of the problem of whatever ailed the nation, not the solution. And while the *New York Review* was referred to as "the New York Review of Vietnam" for its relentless, morally impassioned opposition to the war, *Commentary* devoted little space to the conflict. It advocated a negotiated political solution, not unilateral American withdrawal, as a means of ending the war, further distancing it from opinion on the Left.

A second source of *Commentary*'s disenchantment with the radical impulse, and a long-standing concern of the magazine, was tensions in black–Jewish relations. Indeed, *Commentary*'s fourth issue included sociologist Kenneth Clark's unvarnished portrayal of the bitterness felt by blacks in northern cities toward Jews (February 1946), and two years later James Baldwin drew an even starker picture of two groups locked in such "perpetual hostility" that "it seems unlikely that any real and systematic cooperation can be achieved between Negroes and Jews" (February 1948). Even as the magazine turned toward radicalism in the early 1960s, labor journalist Tom Brooks identified the "growing antagonism between the Jewish and Negro labor camps" as a potential "precursor of strained relations between the larger Jewish and Negro defense agencies and ultimately between the two minority communities in general" (September 1961).

In "My Negro Problem—and Ours," Podhoretz positioned himself outside the liberal consensus, describing his "own twisted feelings about Negroes . . . and of how they conflict with the moral convictions I have since developed" (February 1963). Podhoretz acknowledged "the hatred I still feel for Negroes" as a legacy of a childhood of "fearing and envying and hating Negroes," and argued that blacks could not, as a group, emulate the Jewish ability to succeed in American society. He concluded that "Jews . . . were tied to a memory of past glory and a dream of imminent redemption," but that, for American blacks, "his past is a stigma, and his vision of the future is the hope of erasing the stigma by making color irrelevant, by making it disappear as a fact of consciousness." Podhoretz "share[d] this hope," but wrote, "I cannot see how it will ever be realized unless color does in fact disappear: and that means not integration, it means—let the brutal word come out—miscegenation."

Responding to the passage of the landmark 1964 Civil Rights Act, Nathan Glazer anticipated an increase in intergroup tension precisely as a consequence of the dismantling of formal discrimination because "the system of formal equality" that had worked so well for Jewish social advancement "produces so little" for blacks. This was the "crux of Negro anger and the Jewish discomfort. . . . As the Negro masses have become more active and more militant," Glazer explained, "Jewish leaders—of unions, of defense and civil rights organizations—as well as businessmen, housewives, and homeowners, have been confronted for the first time with demands from Negro organizations that, they find, cannot be the basis of a common effort" (December 1964).

Commentary's disquiet with the political direction of the late 1960s Left and the rising tide of black militancy reached critical mass with the confrontation between the Ocean Hill–Brownsville (Brooklyn) School District and the United Federation of Teachers in the fall of 1968. If "a neoconservative is a liberal who has been mugged by reality," it was the New York City teachers' strike that mugged *Commentary.*

What in calmer times might have been a negotiable contractual dispute between the teachers' union and school district officials (newly empowered by a community control pilot program sponsored by the Ford Foundation) over the discharge of nineteen teachers and administrators exploded into a series of strikes that shut down all of the city's schools for months. All but one of the nineteen were Jewish, and, with the heavily Jewish teachers' union aligned against the minority administrators of the largely black and Puerto Rican school district, the conflict generated an upsurge in antisemitic rhetoric and interracial tension. Jewish teachers found themselves accused of the "mental genocide" of black children, and the Anti-Defamation League reported that antisemitism had reached crisis levels "unchecked by public authorities" (Ravitch 1974). In supporting the teachers, *Commentary* found itself virtually alone in a New York intellectual community that ardently embraced the cause of community control, disdained the teachers as instruments of a repressive white power structure, and often minimized or excused inflammatory anti-Jewish rhetoric by black activists.

Education historian and *Commentary* contributor Diane Ravitch noted, "to those who lived through it, the teacher's strike of 1968 will always be remembered as a seismic event" (Rosenberg and Goldstein 1982). It certainly was for *Commentary*—ironically, given the mistrust many neoconservatives eventually came to hold for teachers' unions as opponents of educational reform. "The ultimate legacy of events in the Ocean Hill-Brownsville experimental district was a lingering distrust between two historically sensitive minority groups who had previously been allies: blacks and Jews," observed a chronicler of John Lindsay's mayoralty (Cannato 2001). For *Commentary,* the strike immediately intensified concern about the conflict between blacks and Jews. In March 1969, Milton Himmelfarb, *Commentary*'s longtime observer of Jewish political behavior, limned what would become a recurring motif: the community control experiment funded by the Ford Foundation and initiated by the Lindsay administration heralded an alliance between privileged elites and dispossessed minorities directed against a newly vulnerable Jewish middle class. Norman Podhoretz struck the same note when he later cited the teachers' strike (along with the rise of "anti-Zionism" in the aftermath of the Six Day War) as "one of the two traumatic events which actually led those who are now worried about the position of the Jews in America to feel the way we do." "The strike," Podhoretz wrote in 1971, "brought black anti-Semitism into widespread public view; and . . . exposed in certain elements of what blacks themselves like to call the white power structure an apparent readiness to purchase civil peace in the United States . . . at the direct expense of the Jews."

The moment for "breaking ranks" had arrived. "With the June 1970 issue," Podhoretz wrote, *Commentary* launched "a campaign against the Movement that . . . continued with great intensity for about three years" (Podhoretz 1979). At the same time, *The Public Interest,* edited by sociologist Daniel Bell and onetime *Commentary* editor Irving Kristol, was subjecting liberal social welfare policies to increasingly critical scrutiny. Unlike the traditional free-market, small-government conservatism typified by William F. Buckley, Jr. and the *National Review, The Public Interest* accepted the broad outlines of the post–New Deal order but increasingly questioned whether large-scale governmental intervention in economic and social affairs was solving the problems it was intended to alleviate. In response, socialist leader Michael Harrington (a regular contributor to *Commentary* until February 1970) coined the pejorative term "neoconservative" for what he regarded as backsliding by his erstwhile allies (Isserman 2000). By 1973, the label had found its way into common political discourse. That September, Martin Kilson, a black sociologist, challenged the magazine's opposition to affirmative action policies designed to ensure greater minority (and especially black) representation, often through the imposition of quotas, in universities, labor unions, and the professions. According to Kilson, "on the quota issue—and others too—the American Jewish Committee and *Commentary* ought to come out of the neoconservative closet" (*New York Times Magazine,* September 30, 1973).

A dozen years after "neoconservative" had entered the political lexicon, Podhoretz offered his own definition (Podhoretz 1985). From the vantage point of 1985, Podhoretz concluded that neoconservatism "represented in many essential respects a return to the revisionist or cold-war liberalism of the first post-war decade," but that neo-

conservatives had staked out distinctive ground on two key issues: the economy and foreign policy. First, "Neo-conservatives . . . are not socialists, disguised or otherwise. We believe in capitalism. . . . We have come to recognize that economic freedom is not only good in itself but is also an indispensable protection against totalitarianism. We have also come to recognize that only through economic freedom can wealth be created." Second, "the neo-conservatives do not for the most part share [Cold War liberalism's] faith in containment. Most of us want to see the United States adopt a strategy aimed at encouraging the forces of disintegration already independently at work within the Soviet empire." It is striking how little Podhoretz drew on the concerns that sparked the magazine's original turn toward neoconservatism.

Commentary devoted minimal attention to foreign policy in the early 1970s. When it did, the outlook hardly conformed to neoconservativism's subsequent challenge to Soviet power or advocacy of nation-building overseas. To the contrary, Podhoretz lamented the "wanton American involvement in Vietnam" and the tens of thousands who had been "killed in a war for which even the President of their country now refuses to make any noble or transcendent claim" (July 1970). In May 1971 Podhoretz and Nathan Glazer advocated an immediate withdrawal from Vietnam. As the war wound down, the magazine disclaimed any role for "American power and prestige [in] the maintenance of a desirable world order" (March 1970); and Walter Laqueur, perhaps its most respected commentator on Soviet and Middle Eastern affairs, sympathetically described Henry Kissinger's task as having "to preside over America's decommitment, . . . a long overdue withdrawal from an exposed position, a realistic adjustment to a new world position" (December 1973).

Nor were free-market economics a key theme in *Commentary*'s initial turn to the right. Indeed almost no attention was paid to economics during those years, and there was certainly no celebration of the market as the preferred mechanism for ordering economic life. Instead, the labor movement, with its big-government, high-tax and free-spending agenda, was endorsed as an essential counterweight to the influence of the "new politics" in the Democratic Party.

Commentary's neoconservative turn was, in fact, driven not by foreign policy and economics, but a disenchantment with radical, as well as prevailing liberal, opinion on social and cultural issues. Looking back on the magazine's political odyssey, Podhoretz concluded that "from a political and ideological point of view, the post-1970 *Commentary* in many respects represents a return to the pre-1960 *Commentary* that was created and edited for the most part by Elliot Cohen" (Podhoretz 1985). But the tone of the magazine was quite different. The *Commentary* of the 1950s had been confident, sometimes complacent, about the consensual virtues of American society that had rendered earlier radical critiques irrelevant. In the 1970s, the magazine was an embattled, lonely voice in what was perceived as an uphill struggle to reverse the ascendancy of radical thinking in cultural, social, and political life. The "Rebelling Young Scholar" whom Andrew Hacker admired in November 1960 for embracing the emerging New Left had become Dorothy Rabinowitz's scathing portrait of "The Radicalized Professor" in July 1970.

The initial impetus for *Commentary*'s neoconservative turn was best expressed in the monthly column "Issues" that Podhoretz wrote for three years beginning in June 1970 and that served as the sharp end of *Commentary*'s assault on the radicalism of the 1960s. Podhoretz looked skeptically at Earth Day (identifying "the environment [as] the issue on which the WASP patriciate hopes to regain its primacy" (June 1970); exposed "the new hypocrisies" of the counterculture, writing that its supposed idealism "consists entirely of self-interested action" (December 1970); criticized the media's "disposition to seek out and play up stories that feed the belief that the country is breaking down" (March 1971); lamented the decline of a common culture in the face of the rising tide of ethnic particularism (June 1972); expressed dismay over "bigoted attitudes towards the general American populace that have become so widespread within the intellectual community" (March 1973); and targeted the "new inquisitors" who were stifling the exchange of ideas in the university (April 1973).

That specifically Jewish concerns were inextricably intertwined in this ideological counteroffensive was apparent from Podhoretz's writing and from the contents of the magazine generally. The potential impact on Jews of quota-driven affirmative action policies provoked his longest column. This revived a concern about discrimination against Jews in university admissions that had been expressed in the magazine's first years. The return of quotas, albeit as an instrument of liberal social policy and not of traditional prejudices, provoked renewed concerns

about discrimination against Jews, who were, in proportion to the population, "over-represented" in elite schools and the professions.

The critics of affirmative action quotas, writing in *Commentary* or elsewhere, were by no means exclusively Jewish, but the issue resonated especially sharply in a community that had achieved much of its recent success through more open access to higher education and that had come to believe that such discriminatory practices had been overcome once and for all. The Ford Foundation's Ocean Hill–Brownsville community control initiative cast a persistent shadow, with Jews and blacks seen as pitted against one another by a WASP establishment bidding to preserve its own power. "What emerged from the '68 teachers' strike," Podhoretz's wife, social critic Midge Decter recalled, "was a message sent to the Jews. Up to that point, we had really come to believe that anti-Semitism was more or less finished. . . . [T]he teachers' strike was a reminder that there was a specifically Jewish interest, that anti-Semitism did exist, that it had been suppressed because for a time it had been deemed no longer respectable. The blacks had once more made it respectable" (Rosenberg and Goldstein 1982). A generation earlier, Carey McWilliams had written in *Commentary* (November 1947) that "Jews constitute a marginal class in America," victimized by "social discrimination" in education, business, and professional life. By the late 1960s, that perception of Jewish vulnerability had returned.

In April 1973, Podhoretz stopped writing his column, apparently satisfied that the ideological reorientation of the magazine had been effected. The topics that he had written about, and that *Commentary* had focused on, during those years had been overwhelmingly cultural and social. Not until the Soviet Union's open intervention in support of the Arab states that attacked Israel in the 1973 Yom Kippur War did the magazine turn sustained attention to the Soviet Union and the necessity of combating its power and influence in world affairs. These foreign and defense policy issues would come to redefine neoconservatism.

As *Commentary* tacked right in the early 1970s, circulation held steady at about 60,000, but thereafter began a long decline. It dropped to 45,000 in 1980 and to 35,000 by 1988, even as neoconservatism was achieving a putative intellectual influence within the Reagan administration. In 2004, Podhoretz would be awarded the Presidential Medal of Freedom.

The overwhelming majority of Jewish intellectuals and academics, however—as well as the rank and file of Jewish voters—remained staunchly liberal. Indeed, as Glazer pointed out at the time ("Blacks, Jews & the Intellectuals," April 1969), a large number of the writers and activists who stoked the flames of the black militancy that did so much to crystallize neoconservatism were Jewish. Nor did the Ocean Hill–Brownsville school district lack for Jewish supporters in its cataclysmic confrontation with the teachers' union. But the constellation of concerns that initially shaped the "neoconservative persuasion" had a particular resonance with the Jewish intellectuals associated with *Commentary,* who maintained a religious, or at least an ethnic, identity. Perceptions of increasing antisemitism and hostility to Israel touched a sensitive nerve for those whose own commitment to the Jewish state had acquired a newfound emotional dimension during and after the Six Day War. Quota-driven affirmative action programs threatened the meritocratic policies that had only recently opened elite educational institutions to large-scale Jewish enrollments. The emergence of an apparent coalition of the WASP elite and militant blacks in opposition to middle-class Jewish interests, typified by the racial politics of Mayor Lindsay's New York, rekindled traditional fears of Jewish powerlessness and marginality.

This heightened sensitivity to the precariousness of the Jewish condition, at home and abroad, echoed Elliot Cohen's editorial statement of purpose in *Commentary*'s inaugural issue, where he warned that, while the Jews of Europe were being murdered, "There was a strange passivity the world over in the face of this colossal latter-day massacre. . . . And . . . the kind of thinking and feeling that set loose this nightmare phenomenon still burns high in many countries, and lies latent in all" (November 1945).

In a *Commentary* symposium on "Jewishness and the Younger Intellectuals" (April 1961), *New York Review* founder Jason Epstein had said, "That I am also a Jew seems relatively unimportant. . . . I have the impression that the traditional human groupings are on the way out. . . . Perhaps it would be good to feel oneself engaged in a highly auspicious tradition. But I happen not to and don't feel at one with those who do." Epstein's perspective on Jewish identity was reminiscent of the outlook of Rosa Luxemburg who had once written "Why do you come with your special Jewish sorrows?" It was radically different from that which played such a significant part in turning

the Jewish intellectuals grouped around *Commentary* toward neoconservatism. Although all neoconservatives were not Jewish, as the examples of Daniel Patrick Moynihan, James Q. Wilson, and Jeane Kirkpatrick show, polemics against neoconservatism, from the right or left, have frequently been imbued with an antisemitic tinge. As *New York Times* columnist David Brooks noted, decoding some critiques of the "neocons" requires understanding that "neo" is short for "Jewish." And, contrary to such critics, to the extent there is a Jewish component to neoconservatism, the values thereby expressed have been anything but alien to American traditions.

Henry D. Fetter

References and Further Reading

Cannato, Vincent. 2001. *The Ungovernable City: John Lindsay and the Struggle to Save New York.* New York: Basic Books.

Cohen, Elliot E., ed. 1953. *Commentary on the American Scene: Portraits of Jewish Life in America.* New York: Alfred A. Knopf.

Fiedler, Leslie. 1962. "His World Was New York." *New York Times Book Review* (February 4): 209.

Friedman, Murray, ed. 2005. "*Commentary" in American Life.* Philadelphia: Temple University Press.

Gerson, Mark. 1996. *The Neoconservative Vision.* Lanham, MD: Madison Books.

Glazer, Nathan. 2003. "Neoconservatives, Then and Now," Letter to the Editor. *New York Times* (October 26).

Isserman, Maurice. 2000. *The Other American: The Life of Michael Harrington.* New York: Public Affairs/Perseus.

Kristol, Irving. 1983. *Reflections of a Neoconservative.* New York: Basic Books.

Miller, Merle. 1972. "Why Norman and Jason Aren't Talking." *New York Times Magazine* (March 26).

Mitgang, Herbert. 1953. "A Lox Is a Lox." *New York Times Book Review* (March 8): 24.

Podhoretz, Norman. 1967. *Making It.* New York: Random House.

Podhoretz, Norman. 1979. *Breaking Ranks.* New York: Harper & Row.

Podhoretz, Norman. 1985. "Ideas, Influence and American Politics: The Case of *Commentary.*" *Survey* 29 (Autumn): 20–26.

Ravitch, Diane. 1974. *The Great School Wars.* Baltimore, MD: Johns Hopkins University Press.

Rosenberg, Bernard, and Ernest Goldstein, eds. 1982. *Creators and Disturbers: Reminiscences by Jewish Intellectuals of New York.* New York: Columbia University Press.

Sachar, Howard. 1992. *A History of the Jews in America.* New York: Vintage.

Shapiro, Edward. S. 1992. *A Time for Healing: American Jewry since World War II.* Baltimore, MD: Johns Hopkins University Press.

Teller, Judd L. 1968. *Strangers and Natives*. New York: Delacorte Press.

Jewish Women in the American Feminist Movement

Feminism has a long and a short history. From ancient times, philosophers, poets, and writers have questioned the inferior status assigned to women. Perceptive and prophetic men and women wondered why women were consigned to limited roles in society with little chance to be educated and to play roles in the public arena. But it is only in the late eighteenth, and more important, in the nineteenth century that an organized feminist movement developed in the Western world, particularly in England and the United States. While a few men participated, women, largely from the middle class, led the movement and comprised most of its following. Middle-class status meant that they had adequate educations, leisure time to think about their fate, and sometimes supportive fathers and/or husbands who encouraged them to attend meetings and to consider ways of improving women's status in society. If they were temperamentally and philosophically inclined, they acted on the opportunity.

Through most of the nineteenth century, the American Jewish population was small, so when Jewish women organized activities outside the home, they were usually associated with their synagogue, temple, or benevolent organization. (The same situation applied to Christian women, but, because they were so much more numerous, a small segment of them moved beyond the church-based social activities toward women's and social reform issues.) As long as religious doctrine determined social roles, both Christian and Jewish women were discouraged from speaking in public or questioning their roles as wives and mothers. Moreover, for Jewish women, the desire to maintain a low profile in this new country shaped many of their responses. The fear of antisemitism always played a part for the first two generations of Jewish Americans.

The major exceptions were the Jewish women who embraced Socialism, rejected Orthodox Judaism, and/or came out of the working classes. Secular Jewish women, or those with a liberal Jewish background, participated earlier and more easily in secular reform movements such as fem-

Ernestine Rose, American Jewish advocate for women's rights. (Library of Congress)

inism. Ernestine Rose (1810–1892) is the most prominent example of a nineteenth-century Jewish woman who shared all of these characteristics. Born in Eastern Europe, she came to the United States in the 1840s as a married woman and spoke publicly to women's groups for women's rights. She advocated women's right to vote, to own property after marriage, and to retain custody of children in case of a divorce. Though she never denied her Jewish ethnicity, her philosophy was universalistic, not particularistic. Rose viewed the practice of religion as restrictive and out of step with the modern world.

Rose believed that her Jewish heritage made her sensitive to the plight of other oppressed peoples, and she addressed all of them—women, African Americans, and other minorities. At the third national Woman's Rights

Convention in Syracuse, New York, in 1852, Rose declared, "Yes, I am an example of the universality of our claims; for not American women only, but a daughter of poor, crushed Poland, and the downtrodden and persecuted people called the Jews, 'a child of Israel,' pleads for the equal rights of her sex." From her perspective, being born a Jew classified her as one of the world's oppressed peoples. She eventually moved to England where she died in 1892.

In twentieth-century America, many immigrant Jewish women supported woman's suffrage and the most radical identified as Socialists, attending meetings where the speakers acknowledged their background by addressing them in Yiddish. The major migration of Eastern European Jews from 1880 to 1914 (over 2 million came to the United States) included many women who had become secularized before arriving here, while others became committed suffragists and feminists while working in the garment factories of New York. Indeed, even anarchist Emma Goldman (1869–1940) spoke to her Jewish audiences in Yiddish, using examples from the Jewish prophets to make her case for anarchism. Trade unionist Rose Schneiderman (1882–1972) tied her advocacy of workers' rights to Jewish principles of social justice. Goldman and Schneiderman represent two different outlooks of Jewish women activists in the secular world of the first thirty years of the twentieth century, with Schneiderman's position having many more supporters than Goldman's.

Anarchism embraced the most optimistic view of humankind, arguing that all laws were unnecessary because people would behave humanely without strictures. Emma Goldman became the most famous spokesperson for this view. Born in Russia, she emigrated to the United States in 1882, determined to leave Orthodox Judaism, a tyrannical father, and Russian antisemitism behind. Having a curious mind combined with an intense personality, she drew on her work experience in a factory and Johann Most's anarchist thought to create a comprehensive critique of industrial capitalism, religion, and marriage. The Haymarket Square disaster in Chicago (1886), where workers were killed by the police, and the 1893 Depression convinced her that the entire system was corrupt and needed reforming. Though Goldman later tempered her views, disavowing violence as the way to achieve the humane society, she found her voice as a lecturer, writer, and editor. In her publication *Mother Earth,* she translated Yiddish stories and reported on her extensive lecture tours around America. Starting in

1906, she spent six months a year traveling and speaking about anarchism, Ibsen, birth control, and "Art and Revolution." She also lectured on feminism, presenting the oppression of women as a key feature of capitalist societies.

Goldman found her Jewish audiences most responsive to her message. As she told her readers, the Jewish meeting was always the best and " . . . makes the Trail less difficult" (Goldman 1911). A favorite subject was the horrible treatment of African-Americans. "The persecution, suffering and injustice to which this much-hated race is being constantly subjected can be compared only to the brutal treatment of the Jews in Russia" (Goldman 1907). Known as Red Emma to the police in every city she visited, she remained undeterred until America entered World War I. Goldman was deported in 1919 after being imprisoned and never again lived in her beloved America.

Rose Schneiderman, another Russian immigrant, worked in a cap factory and embraced socialism as the most viable philosophy for working people. In 1910, she became an organizer for the Women's Trade Union League (WTUL). She believed that union membership would lead to the sharing of power with the employers, making industrial capitalism more humane. Schneiderman worked with upper- and middle-class Protestant women who funded the WTUL, as well as with Jewish women unionists such as Pauline Newman (1890?–1986), the first woman organizer for the International Ladies' Garment Workers' Union (ILGWU). Young Jewish women were among the largest group of workers in the new garment factories of New York, and a few joined Jewish men to become leaders in the unions. In Chicago, Bessie Abramowitz (1889–1971) helped to organize the Amalgamated Clothing Workers Union (ACWU), along with her future husband, Sidney Hillman. In 1909 in New York and in 1910 in Chicago, major strikes in the clothing industry—most sparked and staged primarily by women—led to the first successful unions in the industry. Jewish owners and Jewish workers negotiated labor contracts that became models for every industry.

While union women spoke publicly for workers' rights, some of the Jewish women followed Ernestine Rose's path and became advocates for women's right to vote and to hold office. Rosa Sonneschein (1847–1932) applied the message of feminism to Jewish women's roles in the temple. She advocated the full participation of women, including single women, in all aspects of temple worship. Living in Chicago during the 1890s, she edited *The Ameri-*

can Jewess (1895–1899), in which she applied feminist principles to Jewish practices. Sonneschein asked why Christian social worker Jane Addams could speak at Sinai Temple, Chicago's most prominent Reform temple, but no Jewish woman could. Initially a supporter of the newly created National Council of Jewish Women, she became a critic after she observed that it had no central purpose. Sonneschein was an early advocate of Zionism and argued that women were particularly suited to work for a Jewish national home because they have "the time, the inclination and the faculty to pursue great objects" (Sonneschein 1896). She attended the First Zionist Congress in Basel in 1897. Her outspoken views alienated many of the organization women who would have been her supporters, and as a result, her magazine lost funding. In 1899, it ceased publishing and her public life ended.

The middle generations of Jewish American women, those born in America in the first forty years of the twentieth century, devoted their individual and collective energies to adjusting to middle-class life and to coping with the Depression and the World Wars. The organized woman's suffrage movement had splintered after the passage of the Nineteenth Amendment in 1920, and the more radical Woman's Party, which was devoted to passage of an equal rights amendment, found little popular support in the prosperous twenties and the hard thirties. The next time a discernible feminist movement appeared on the horizon was in the late 1960s, and it included many Jewish women who became speakers and writers for feminism. Betty Friedan (1921-2006), Phyllis Chesler (b. 1940), and Shulamith Firestone (b. 1945) are prominent examples.

Friedan, a generation older than Chesler and Firestone, had been a journalist for a left-wing labor union newspaper after college and was very interested in social issues. During the 1950s, she contributed articles to women's magazines as a freelance writer while raising her three children. Surveying her Smith College class ten years after graduation (1959) led her to write the book that became a founding text for the women's liberation movement. *The Feminine Mystique* (1963) describes the "problem with no name"—a problem that seemed to be spreading among dissatisfied, college-educated, middle-class women. On the surface, these women had everything that 1950s America had to offer and yet they were unhappy, trapped, as Friedan put it, in a "comfortable concentration camp." Friedan's study is the first of the modern era to try to explain why.

Friedan joined other professional women—many of them of her generation—who had worked quietly behind the scenes for years to improve women's status in the workplace. In some striking ways, however, all three of these Jewish feminists resemble the first generation of Jewish women activists. Friedan and Chesler, like Rose Schneiderman and the other union women, represent a liberal agenda for women's rights, while Shulamith Firestone, like Emma Goldman, takes a radical position, one far removed from mainstream opinion. It is a testament to the dynamism of Jewish feminism and to its growing popularity that a wide range of views emerges within the larger feminist movement. While the majority of reformers (who themselves are a minority of Jewish women) seek gradual change by democratic means, a small number of feminists reject the methods and goals of the moderates and embrace revolutionary means and aims.

Shulamith Firestone, born to an Orthodox family in Ottawa, Ontario, grew up in St. Louis, Missouri, and attended Yavneh of Telshe Yeshiva near Cleveland. She then went to Washington University in St. Louis and the Art Institute in Chicago. Settling in New York in the late sixties, she became active in the civil rights and antiwar movements. She experienced firsthand the shocking discovery that radical men were traditional when dealing with women. Firestone became a founding member of a number of radical feminist groups in New York City and in 1970 published *The Dialectic of Sex,* her major contribution to feminist discourse. In stark contrast to Friedan's work, which offers tame suggestions for women to find part-time jobs to alleviate their boredom, Firestone argues that women are oppressed in every way in bourgeois society—economically, socially, and sexually. The only way to end male domination is to separate sex from childbearing.

Prophetically, she anticipated the major scientific advances of the last thirty years of the twentieth century, such as in vitro fertilization. In her scenario, the next generation could be produced in the laboratory, and women could design their adult lives as they wished. Most feminists did not embrace Firestone's extreme critique of society or her drastic remedy, but her ideas generated extensive discussion. Marx and Freud had replaced Orthodox Judaism as the primary influence on Firestone. By the mid-1970s, without explanation, she had dropped out of public life. Betty Friedan, by contrast, became world famous after the publication of her book and the founding of the National

Organization for Women (NOW). She is considered the founding mother of the contemporary women's movement and continued to lecture and write on women's topics until her death in 2006. Friedan's goal was a humane society, one in which people of all ages have good health care, affordable housing, and opportunities for professional development.

Phyllis Chesler credits her Jewish upbringing with inspiring her to become a feminist. Raised in an Orthodox family in Brooklyn, she found Orthodoxy too confining for her ambitions. Trained as a psychologist, her first book, *Women and Madness* (1972), became another popular document for the women's movement, selling millions of copies. Chesler called attention to the mental illnesses that plagued women—illnesses, she argued, that arose from the cultural restraints on women's development. Unlike Friedan and Firestone, Chesler's Jewish identity remained intact. She identified as a Jewish feminist, with her commitment to Zionism a major priority. In recent years, she has been concerned with the rise in antisemitism among feminists, particularly in developing countries. At the United Nations Conferences on Women in 1975, 1980, and 1985, she was disturbed by the anti-Zionist resolutions and the verbal attacks on Jewish feminists (*The New Anti-Semitism*, 2003). U.S. congresswoman Bella Abzug (1920-1998) (D-NY) also spoke out on feminist issues, and at the 1975 United Nations conference publicly denounced the antisemitism expressed there.

Jewish institutional life was also affected by the American feminist movement. Jewish women asked to be members of temple boards and to participate in worship services. Though Reform Judaism accepted the idea of women rabbis as early as the 1920s, it was not until Sally Priesand (b. 1946) received ordination in 1972 that the practice gained respectability. Other branches of Judaism—Reconstructionism and Conservative most notably—began to reexamine their practices, with both branches admitting women to their rabbinic seminaries. In 1983, women joined men in the rabbinic training program at the Conservative Jewish Theological Seminary. Orthodox Judaism, though not willing to allow women rabbis, has undergone change as well, primarily because of the initiative of Orthodox women who defined themselves as feminists. These women have created separate prayer *minyanim* and separate study groups to expand their knowledge while abiding by Orthodox law.

Perhaps because Jewish women intellectuals of all denominations appreciated their double minority status in America—as women and as Jews—they were more likely to become leaders and followers of feminism. While some left their Judaism behind, many of them created a new synthesis of their religious commitments and their secular pursuits. The fact that by the 1960s many Jewish American women were well educated and comfortably ensconced in the middle class also enabled them to become active in the women's liberation movement. Granddaughters of immigrants, they were sufficiently removed from the experience of newcomers to feel both part of, and apart from, America. They could criticize the failings of the culture of which they were an integral part and shape a new definition of Jewish women, one that allowed them individuality while preserving communal ties.

June Sochen

References and Further Reading
Antler, Joyce. 1997. *The Journey Home: Jewish Women and the American Century*. New York: Free Press.
Chesler, Phyllis. 1972. *Women and Madness*. Garden City, NY: Doubleday.
Firestone, Shulamith. 1970. *The Dialectic of Sex: The Case for Feminist Revolution*. New York: William Morrow.
Friedan, Betty. 1963. *The Feminine Mystique*. New York: W. W. Norton.
Goldman, Emma. 1906–1912. *Mother Earth*. Vols. 1–7. New York: Greenwood Reprint Corp.
Kessler-Harris, Alice. 1976. "Organizing the Unorganizable: Three Jewish Women and Their Union." *Labor History* 17,1: 5–23.
Lerner, Elinor. 1981. "Jewish Involvement in the New York City Woman Suffrage Movement." *American Jewish History* 70,4: 442–461.
Sochen, June. 1981. *Consecrate Every Day: The Public Lives of Jewish American Women, 1880–1980*. Albany: State University of New York Press.
Sonneschein, Rosa, ed. 1894-1897. *The American Jewess*. Vols. 1-6. New York: American Jewess Publishing.

Emma Goldman (1869–1940)

Jewish Spokeswoman for Freedom

Emma Goldman dedicated her life to the creation of a radically new social order rooted in absolute freedom. She was a passionate advocate of free speech, women's indepen-

Emma Goldman, anarchist and feminist. (Library of Congress)

dence, birth control, and workers' rights. Although her fiery oratory and writings eventually led to imprisonment, deportation, and exile, Goldman never compromised her unwavering commitment to her anarchist ideals and to what she called "everybody's right to beautiful, radiant things" (from "Jewish Women of Valor" poster, a collaborative effort of the Emma Goldman Papers and the Jewish Women's Archive).

She came to America in a wave of migration in 1885, fleeing both the antisemitism of czarist Russia and the constraints on women in the traditional Jewish family of the Old World. Having experienced the stirrings of a budding revolution, she felt at home in a country that took pride in its egalitarian ethos and celebration of individual freedom. The clash between her exalted vision and the harsh realities she confronted in late nineteenth-century industrial America catapulted her into a life of action. She devoted herself to the cause of anarchism—to propagate a concept of freedom that knew no bounds, which extended beyond national borders, and attempted to break away from the restricting categories of race, gender, ethnicity, or religious belief. Yet she, like most who were attracted to an array of universal values, and who believed they could clear the slate of their past, was inevitably influenced by the traditions, including religious affiliation, from which she emerged. A lifelong creative tension between Goldman's self-identification with cosmopolitan-universal ideals and her rejection of the Jewish religious and sectarian community practices of her upbringing deepened her political stance, shaped her life, and underscores the question of whether one can ever escape the defining influences of one's past.

To her "dear friend Rabbi Harry Stern" she inscribed a copy of her autobiography:

> As a heathen my faith in those who speak for religion has not been very strong. You have shown me that one may serve his god and yet be true to man.
>
> If my work will show you that one can serve humanity without a god I shall feel that we have exchanged true compliments—not merely in words (Handwritten inscription in *Living My Life,* Montreal, March 1935).

Goldman believed in "no gods, no masters"—and even joined those among her ranks who dared to posit the challenging idea that Jesus was an anarchist. In her early years in America, she felt closest to militant German and Yiddish anarchists who scorned religion and those who practiced it, who believed that traditional values enslaved the mind and the spirit, and considered the notion of a chosen community an expression of narrowness and insularity. She criticized the practice of *tzedakah,* or charity, among Jews as a form of amelioration rather than a solution to the pervasiveness of poverty.

But she, like most radical Jewish immigrants who rejected the religion of their past, also created and clung to the familiarity of a community of their own in a New World that was often hostile and exploitive to "outsiders." It was not uncommon, for example, for anarchist Jews to gather together on Yom Kippur, the sacred solemn Day of Atonement traditionally marked by fasting, for an afternoon picnic of ham and cheese sandwiches or for a festive evening ball. Goldman was reported to have dressed as a nun dancing "the anarchist slide" into the small hours of the night at one such Yom Kippur Ball. Those acts of sacrilege were whimsical theatrical shows of defiance, in comparison to some of her more intensely antireligious comrades who routinely stood on the steps of the synagogue spitting on the congregants as they left after a day of the reverie of prayer. Yet they all reinforced their connection to their Jewish community by marking rather than ignoring this sacred day and by taking a strong stand against the puritanism of the dominant Christian culture around them.

In Goldman's time there was a flurry of interest in the "Jewish Question" among activists and political theorists. Although her first instinct was to argue against it, in favor of "universal questions," her rigid rejection of Jewish "exceptionalism" softened as her awareness of antisemitism in Russia and of growing Nazi persecution of the Jews in Germany came into full focus. Reluctantly, she took a public stand to defend the special needs of her own people, who were increasingly vulnerable to race-hatred and to violent threats of extermination.

And, although she expanded the definition of "her people" to include the oppressed, wherever and whoever they might be, and pronounced herself an anarchist who did not believe in the state—she was "neither a Zionist nor a Nationalist"—she always "worked for the rights of Jews and against every attempt to hinder their life and development" (1937). In 1938, she defended the right of asylum for Jews "cruelly persecuted in nearly every European country," observing that antisemitism, formerly fostered from the top, had since infested every layer of social life. She entered the debate about the issue of Arabs and Jews in the Middle East. While she believed that "the land should belong to those who till the soil" and lauded the "tens and thousands of [Jews], young and deeply devout idealists [who] reclaimed wastelands and have turned them into fertile fields and blooming gardens," she insisted that "I do not say therefore the Jews are entitled to more rights than Arabs." With some humility as an outsider, she acknowledged that "one cannot decide whether the demand of natives for the monopoly of their country is any more just than the desperate need of millions of people who are slowly being exterminated."

This commitment and determination "to repair the world" might very well have been incubated within the particular traditions of her childhood and the high cultural value Jews placed on the messianic concept and practice of *tikkun olam*.

Goldman emerged from a Jewish culture that valued justice. Her anarchist belief in the potential for creating social harmony unencumbered by government was completely consistent with the pre-Holocaust reality of the Jewish people united by their shared beliefs outside the boundaries of a state. Her experience as a Diaspora Jew who felt part of a community whose cohesiveness came from a common history grounded in religious-cultural traditions, rather than by national identity, confirmed her belief that anarchism was not merely an ideal but a vision of the possible. Her conviction about the benefits of such a world was evident in an article she published in the very first issue of Goldman's magazine, *Mother Earth* (1906–1917), attributing the cosmopolitan open-mindedness of many Jews to the lack of a country of their own—a situation that compelled the formation of voluntary associations.

Even the practice of "questioning authority"—the motto of any good anarchist and certainly Emma's—seemed natural to one whose tradition encouraged lively debate on the myriad of meanings in its most sacred text, always searching for the higher meaning. Weekly readings of the Talmud can also be interpreted as ingrained training for developing arguments, for critical thinking, and for questioning the authority of what came before with yet another new and valued interpretation.

That Goldman ultimately considered herself less an agitator than an educator followed the vein of a tradition that places a high value on learning. Talmudic devotion to scholarship was evident in Goldman's definition of a full life—a belief in rationality also was a prevalent assumption of the Enlightenment. The concept and practice of free expression—a cause to which she devoted herself in America *and* in Bolshevik Russia—were necessary for the advancement of truth, and integral to the anarchist quest for justice, which included the unhindered right to speak one's mind. This was, perhaps, in part because teaching and learning were basics of the Jewish culture from which she emerged. Goldman's role as a public intellectual and political educator, as one who asserted that "the most violent element in society is ignorance," was rooted in her very being (Falk 2003–2009).

To counter centuries of antisemitism, a host of survival strategies were embedded in the Jewish traditions and teachings. Maintaining one's faith in a hostile environment often necessitated performing ritual observances in secrecy. One example was the dreydel game played at Chanukah, signifying the playful and clever reenactment of how Jewish soldiers affirmed their outlawed faith under the watchful eye of authorities. These early, seemingly benign ways to inculcate and normalize clandestine practices in the name of a higher ideal may have functioned as an early contributing factor to Goldman's ease with and attraction to the sub-rosa elements of anarchist politics. That she could espouse both a vision of complete harmony and the inevitability of violence, and that she could praise the heroism of political militants while concealing the depth of her ties to them also can be traced, in part, to her Russian-Jewish background. In her youth, she was steeped in the larger-than-life stories of the Russian women revolutionists who plotted against the czar, and she was imprinted with an early fascination with Judith, the Jewish heroine who cut off the head of Holofernes to avenge the wrongs of her people. This violent undertow that streamed through her life and ideas was not at all foreign to her, and, in fact, was a source of celebration of a culture that prided itself on resilience and survival.

Between the years 1936 and 1938, she chose to devote herself to the Spanish anarchists of the civil war rather than to the growing antisemitism in the world. But when Spain fell, and as the clouds of World War II billowed ominously on the horizon in 1938, Goldman began to take a bolder stand on the link between Nazism, Fascism, and Stalinism—as forms of State domination wreaking havoc in Europe, which, she predicted, were destined to fail. During this period, she spoke primarily about the economic causes of war and portrayed the rampant racial xenophobia in Germany as a smokescreen of prejudice powerful enough to obscure the real causes of desperation and fear. But Goldman did not fully foresee the horrific attempts at ethnic cleansing that would sweep through Germany and Eastern Europe that might have tipped the balance and direction of her efforts against injustice.

In spite of her desire for self-definition and control over how she was perceived, Emma Goldman, who strove to identify first and foremost with all of humanity, who was a woman revered as one of the most eloquent spokespeople for freedom, could not escape antisemitic and sexist descriptions, alternatively as a short, stocky Jewish woman or as "surprisingly attractive." In 1919, when she was cast out of America, deported in a wave of anti-radical hysteria, it was clear that the patriotic fervor accompanying World War I eclipsed any semblance of political

tolerance or multi-ethnic welcome that attracted her to its shores. Yet, in the silence of her absence, and long after her death, she has become a positive symbol of feminism and anarchism, one who danced in the revolution. Emma Goldman's words and actions are a reminder that great American patriots are often "outsiders," like this Russian Jewish anarchist who had the chutzpah and vision to take on the world.

Candace Falk

References and Further Reading
Falk, Candace, with Barry Pateman, Jessica Moran, and Robert Cohen. 2003–2009. *Emma Goldman: A Documentary History of the American Years—1890–1919.* 4 vols. Berkeley: University of California Press.
Falk, Candace. 1999 [1984]. *Love, Anarchy, and Emma Goldman.* Rev. ed. New Brunswick, NJ: Rutgers University Press.
Emma Goldman Papers Project. Available at: http://sunsite.berkeley.edu/Goldman. Accessed March 3, 2007.
Jewish Women's Archive (prepared with the Emma Goldman Papers Project). "Women of Valor: Emma Goldman." Available at: http://www.jwa.org/exhibits/wov/goldman/index.html. Accessed March 3, 2007.

Meyer London (1871–1926)

Socialist Congressman

Meyer London, lawyer, labor leader, and Socialist congressman, worked tirelessly in New York City for striking immigrants and Lower East Side trade unions like the International Ladies' Garment Workers' Union, the International Fur Workers, and the United Hebrew Trades. In Congress, he sponsored numerous bills that later became part of Franklin Delano Roosevelt's New Deal, including minimum wage laws, unemployment insurance, and increased taxes on the wealthy. London fought hard, too, for a liberal immigration policy and for antilynching legislation. Known, and indeed loved, mostly as a progressive politician, London was also widely admired for his general and literary erudition.

Born in 1871 in Russia in the province of Sulvakie, Meyer was the eldest son of Rebecca Berson and Ephraim London. His mother was a devout daughter of a rabbi, but

Meyer London speaking at a labor rally, ca. 1914. (Library of Congress)

his father, although a lifelong student of the Talmud, was an agnostic and a radical in his politics. This rich mix of the traditional religious and the modern secular appears often in the social backgrounds of East European Jews like Meyer London who went on to become socialists. Meyer had himself attended *heder* (religious school), studied Hebrew, biblical interpretation, and Talmud, and then went on to Russian school, where he received a secular education and became proficient in six languages.

Economic instability in Meyer's background was also a factor in shaping his political radicalism. His father occasionally wrote for Hebrew periodicals but had no regular source of income. Without much success, he also tried his hand as a grain merchant in Zenkov, Poltavia, before he left for what he thought would be better opportunity in America in 1888. Here Ephraim London ran an unprofitable anarchist print shop and published a small Yiddish paper. Meyer had been left behind in Russia and was expected to go on with his education. Later he described his challenging years in the Old Country:

I was poor, of course. We were all poor together. I was able to keep up my studies by teaching boys who did not know as much as I did. I belonged to a crowd of young fellows who talked a lot about revolution and had not the least idea what revolution really meant. My father in America heard of my inclination and wrote me that under no condition whatever . . . was I to commit myself on revolutionary matters. I must study, think, observe, and wait until I knew very much more about conditions in the world.

When Meyer London came to New York in 1891 at age twenty to join his father on Suffolk Street in the heart of Manhattan's Lower East Side, he was immediately drawn into radical politics. Immigrant Jews were already giving disproportionate support to the Left, and the elder London, who maintained a close and abiding relationship with his son, was deeply involved with socialist and anarchist groups. But Meyer's developing activism and commitment did not prevent him from continuing his voracious reading or his formal education. He tutored youngsters and worked in a library to put himself through high school. In 1896 he became a U.S. citizen, entered New York University Law School at night, and was nominated by the Socialist Labor Party (SLP) for the New York State Assembly. Running as a neophyte reformer, London, predictably, lost to the candidate of the Tammany machine, which employed bribery, fraud, and pressure tactics to win elections.

By 1897, London, finding himself at odds with the SLP leadership of Daniel DeLeon, went over to the newly organized Social Democratic Party. Ultimately, working with Eugene V. Debs, Victor Berger, and Morris Hillquit, Meyer London became one of the founders of the Socialist Party of America in 1901.

London was a Socialist who acknowledged the legitimacy of ethnic demands as well as class needs, and local interests as well as the interest of the generalized proletariat. He recognized the reality of Jewish oppression within the broader context of economic exploitation. London spent much of his time and energy providing legal services to workers. He accepted only clients and cases that would not conflict with his socialist principles. And he preferred to work pro bono. On one occasion, appreciative striking union members threatened to dismiss him as their counsel if he continued to refuse any recompense.

In 1899 Meyer London married Anna Rosenson. They had one daughter, who remembered a home with little material embellishment, but filled with love and support and many books. London was a modest man who lived his whole adult life on the East Side and who, despite his reading habits, shared the values of his plebian constituency. He served them as adviser, advocate, and sometimes banker. In his law office, amid his own unpaid bills, London handed over the entire $35 balance in his bankbook to strikers in 1912. It was neither the first nor the last time he did this sort of thing. He made little contribution to Socialist theory, but he was loved and respected by the residents of the East Side as the finest example of Socialist man.

London's commitment to the alleviation of particular grievances and his loyalty to the Jewish constituency of the Lower East Side were surely among the reasons that he was eventually successful in his bid for a congressional seat. In 1910 he replaced Morris Hillquit as the congressional candidate of the Socialist Party. Hillquit had lost the election in 1908, and his defeat had been unexpectedly heavy. At the first rally of his campaign, Hillquit had said that if elected he would "not consider [himself] the special representative of the . . . special interests of this district, but the representative of the Socialist Party . . . and . . . the working class of the country."

This was put forward at a time when East Side residents were upset by a police commissioner's report that implied that Jews were responsible for 50 percent of the crime in New York City, when the "special interest" issue of immigration restriction was being hotly debated in Congress, and when the position of the Socialist Party on that issue, favoring some restriction, was not favored by East Side Jews who still had relatives desiring to escape from pogrom-ridden Russia.

Meyer London, unlike Hillquit, openly identified as a Jewish Socialist and allied himself with the interests and vital movements of the East Side. "I deem it a duty of the Jew everywhere," he said, "to remain a Jew as long as in any corner of the world the Jew is being discriminated against." Though failing to be elected in 1910, London garnered 33 percent of the vote and outran his own Socialist Party ticket two to one. By 1914 he won 47 percent of the vote and was victorious. He went on to be elected twice more, in 1916 despite a fusion of the Republicans and Democrats, and in 1920.

London did not substitute ethnic interests for class interests. He combined them. He was not elected *despite* his socialism, but because to the Jewish immigrant masses he was very much *their* Socialist. London told a crowd of 15,000 after his initial election: "I do not expect to work wonders in Congress. I shall, however, say a new word and I shall accomplish the thing that is not in the platform of the Socialist Party. I hope that my presence will represent an entirely different type of Jew from the kind that Congress is accustomed to see." In the same speech, which was met with much enthusiasm, London also said, "We shall not rest until every power of capitalism has been destroyed and the workers emancipated from wage slavery."

London went on in the House of Representatives to introduce bills described as "wild socialist schemes" by his congressional colleagues. "When I made my first speech," London remembered, "one of the most extreme of the Republicans made his way across the House and peered into my face as if to discover what kind of a weird creature from some other world had found its way to this planet." During his three terms, London advocated measures against child labor and against the use of injunctions in labor disputes.

He supported nationalization of the coal industry, improved salaries for government workers, and old-age pensions. He opposed immigration restriction, protectionism, and property qualifications for voting in Puerto Rico. One bill that he introduced, protecting employees of bankrupt firms, became law.

London continued to render service to the Bund, the most important organization of Russian-Jewish Socialists. He favored the March Revolution of 1917 in Russia and criticized the general Allied failure to encourage and support the provisional government there. After the Bolshevik takeover, he spoke on moral and political grounds against the policy of intervention and blockade. In the same years, Meyer London was sharply critical of the "bread and butter" unionism of the American Federation of Labor, and he continued to serve the Socialist needle-trades unions as legal counsel, advisor in matters of union policy, and spokesman in negotiations.

Although all this made London a "moderate" leftist, he was nonetheless the target of virulent anti-Socialist attacks. He also endured critical blasts from his own party, particularly in 1917–1918, for refusing to resist *all* wartime activity. London was clearly antiwar. He had earlier opposed intervention in Mexico and budget increases for the Army and Navy. He strongly resisted U.S. entry into World War I and voted against the conscription and espionage laws, and he vigorously fought efforts to curb civil liberties during the national crisis. He was convinced, however, that the Socialists' St. Louis Declaration, insisting that all workers refuse to heed the calls for help from their respective governments, was too extreme, and once the United States was at war he voted "present"—a way of abstaining, but not impeding the nation's military measures. "I owe a duty," London explained, "to every man who has been called to the service of his country, to provide him with everything he needs [and] to get this fight over as soon as possible." For this the Socialist Left never forgave him, but he was also severely attacked by non-Socialists for his lack of "war patriotism."

London also ran afoul of the Labor Zionists. Although he ultimately supported the Balfour Declaration and looked forward to the establishment of a Jewish homeland in Palestine that the declaration promised, he had evaded a request to *introduce* a resolution supporting the Balfour Declaration, and he had warned against "forcible annexation" of Arab land. No longer the representative of a solidly coherent constituency, London failed to be reelected in 1918. He did run and win again for the last time in 1920. But in 1922 the Republicans and Democrats once more united against him and the Socialist Party, and his district was gerrymandered in such a way that his defeat was assured. He never ran again.

In 1926, while crossing Second Avenue, Meyer London, at age fifty-five, was struck by a taxi and fatally injured. In the ambulance, London, characteristically expressing concern for wage earners, made his wife promise not to sue the troubled cab driver. When he died shortly thereafter, his body lay in state at the building of the *Jewish Daily Forward* on East Broadway. Half a million New Yorkers attended his funeral. "For six hours," the *New York Times* reported, "the East Side put aside its duties, pressing or trivial, to do honor to its dead prophet." Although beloved for his political leadership, London was respected almost as much for his learning. In the pocket of the jacket he was wearing when he was killed was a well-worn anthology of Chekhov's short stories. London was buried in the Writer's Lane section of the Mount Carmel Cemetery, near the grave of Sholom Aleichem and other Jewish cultural heroes.

Gerald Sorin

References and Further Reading

Goldberg, Gordon Jerome. 1971. "Meyer London: A Political Biography." PhD dissertation, Lehigh University.

Gorenstein, Arthur. 1960. "A Portrait of Ethnic Politics." *Publications of the American Jewish Historical Society* 50: 202–238.

Lewbel, Sam R. 1979. "Meyer London and the 67th Congress." MS thesis, Central Connecticut State College.

Meyer London Bibliography. 1957. New York: Tamiment Institute.

Rogoff, Hillel. 1930. *An East Side Epic: The Life and Work of Meyer London.* New York: Vanguard Press.

Sorin, Gerald. 1989. "Tradition and Change: American Jewish Socialists as Agents of Acculturation." *American Jewish History* 79,1: 37–54.

Henry Kissinger (b. 1923)

Diplomat

Henry Alfred Kissinger fled Nazi Germany at age fifteen and eventually became the American secretary of state in

Secretary of State Henry Kissinger conversing with President Gerald Ford on the grounds of the White House in 1974. (Library of Congress)

both the Richard M. Nixon and Gerald Ford administrations. He is credited with implementing a strategy of détente with the USSR, helping to open relations with China and, through shuttle diplomacy, laying the groundwork for the peace agreements between Egypt and Israel after the Yom Kippur War.

Born in Fürth, Germany, Kissinger emigrated to New York in 1938 with his family where he enrolled in George Washington High School. His parents attended K'hal Adath Jeshurun, an Orthodox synagogue, while he participated in the Beth Hillel youth group. He attended City College of New York but in 1943 was drafted into the Army, where he worked for Division Intelligence and Counter-Intelligence. He helped to administer the defeated German town of Krefeld and fulfilled other tasks of the occupying American Army. His letters indicate an intimate knowledge of the death camps and their victims.

Kissinger's childhood under the Nazis and his experience in war-torn Germany sparked his interest in political science. After his service, he enrolled at Harvard with the goal of becoming a political historian. His undergraduate thesis reflected the mood that would come to dominate his political thought: "The generation of Buchenwald and the Siberian labor camps cannot talk with the same optimism as its fathers," he wrote. "Life is suffering, birth involves death. Transitoriness is the fate of existence" (Isaacson 1992).

In his graduate thesis for Harvard's government department, Kissinger adopted the perspective of realpolitik from which he would come to understand world politics. Published as *A World Restored* (1957), the thesis showed how two diplomats, Austrian Prince Klemens von Metternich and British Foreign Secretary Viscount Castlereagh, restored peace to Europe after the defeat of Napoleon and his revolutionary forces at Waterloo. Because of their efforts, Europe knew only limited international conflicts from 1815 to the outbreak of World War I.

To Kissinger, the century-long stability was a result of the complex of international relationships created by Metternich and Castlereagh in which the fates of the major European powers were tied together by pacts of mutual support and deterrence. Kissinger held that this system of realpolitik—the continuous balancing of power among nations based on shared political interests—inhibited aggression because no state would be willing to risk its position by threatening its neighbors, thereby unleashing mutual defense treaties against itself. By making the fate of European states so interdependent, the system of alliances would deter any state from reaching beyond its own borders.

Kissinger's view was conservative in that it sought to maintain the established international order against any revolutionary power that contested it. The moral foundation of his view was simply that disorder brings violence, while order inhibits violence. He argued that political revolution is necessarily violent, since political authority is rarely established by moral or intellectual authority, but rather by the violent demonstration of power. The most significant corollary of this view is that the appeasement of revolutionary forces by established states (e.g., the Western democracies' acquiescence in Hitler's annexation of Austria) is viewed as weakness and therefore breeds further assaults against order. As Kissinger wrote on the first page of his graduate thesis, "Whenever peace—conceived as the avoidance of war—has been the primary objective of a power or a group of powers, the international system has been at the mercy of the most ruthless member of the international community."

Rather than peace, Kissinger held that "stability based on an equilibrium of forces" should be the goal of diplomacy. That equilibrium could only be based on ever-fluctuating real political interests. The success of revolutionary states, such as those of Napoleon and Hitler, was possible only when the defense relationships between neighbors were not based on alliances of realpolitik (e.g., defensible borders, shared waterways), but rather on amorphous connections such as shared ideologies or morals (e.g., democracy, communism). In Kissinger's view, the mores of a state do not determine real mutual interests. Ideologies alone could not trigger the massive military response necessary to protect a troubled ally the way a shared real interest would. Therefore alliances based on real mutual interests, however temporary the confluence of interest might be, were the only alliances that states could be trusted to defend.

Kissinger's study of early nineteenth-century diplomacy was meant as a model for a twentieth-century diplomacy that had failed to prevent two World Wars, both started by revolutionary desires, and that was slow to control the buildup of nuclear arms and the Cold War. In his book,

Nuclear Weapons and Foreign Policy (1957), Kissinger argued against the current U.S. policy of massive nuclear retaliation in the face of Soviet attack and suggested instead that the objectives of realpolitik, including mutual dependencies, could be achieved with nuclear weapons, if those weapons could be reconceived as having smaller tactical applications.

Kissinger became a lecturer in the government department at Harvard in 1957, where he ran the International Seminar and was a recognized expert on nuclear policy. He was promoted to full professor in 1962. Frequent articles in *Foreign Affairs* and *The Reporter* brought Kissinger to the attention of presidential hopeful Nelson Rockefeller, for whom Kissinger acted as a foreign policy consultant before President-elect Nixon in 1968 appointed Kissinger his national security advisor.

In 1972, Kissinger became the first Jewish secretary of state, which Senator Jacob Javits called "a miracle of American history." Gallup polls in 1972 and 1973 ranked Kissinger as one of the "most admired" Americans, while Representative Jonathan Bingham proposed a constitutional amendment to allow foreign-born citizens to run for president. Kissinger's acceptance speech for secretary of state indicated how influential his experience under Hitler had been: "Mr. President, you referred to my background and it is true there is no country in the world where it is conceivable that a man of my origin could be standing here. . . . If my origin can contribute anything to the formulation of policy, it is that at an early age I have seen what can happen to a society that is based on hatred and strength and distrust" (Isaacson 1992).

Kissinger's immediate task was to help Nixon withdraw 550,000 soldiers under combat conditions in Vietnam and still maintain credibility with America's other client states. Kissinger's broader goal was to thaw the Cold War conditions that had created Vietnam in the first place. He was fortunate to be in the service of Richard Nixon, who had a similar worldview. To achieve détente with the Soviet Union, Nixon and Kissinger introduced the balance of power of nineteenth-century Europe to the global arena by initiating an American relationship with China. China did not share America's ideals of freedom and democracy, but both Kissinger and Nixon realized that America and China had a common interest: controlling Soviet expansion. By befriending China, Kissinger and Nixon shifted the global balance from two superpowers to three. In a word, they attempted triangulation. While America established relations with China, the Soviet Union was kept in check, reducing the likelihood of an international incident between the superpowers.

The Nixon administration's active policy concerning Asia meant a certain neglect of policy for the Middle East, so it is remarkable that some of Kissinger's most lasting work was in this area of the world. His first achievement was the introduction of a relationship, based on realpolitik, between Israel and Jordan in the autumn of 1970. In September, the Popular Front for the Liberation of Palestine hijacked four Western planes and brought them to an airfield near Amman, thereby inciting a Palestinian revolt against King Hussein. Fearing Syrian and Iraqi support for the Palestinians, Hussein asked the United States for military protection of Jordan's borders. Instead of promising American protection, Kissinger arranged for Israel to provide air support in the event of Syrian mobilization. In doing so, Kissinger hoped to demonstrate to both Jordan and Israel their mutual political interests. It is plausible (though also debatable) that Kissinger's maneuver helped to reconstitute the relationship between the two countries.

Kissinger's greater achievement was in unhinging Egypt from Soviet client status during the Yom Kippur War, thereby laying the foundation for what would become the peace agreement between Egypt and Israel under American auspices during the Carter administration. Like much of the world, the Middle East had been divided between American and Soviet influence since the 1950s, with the Soviets generally supporting Arab interests while America supported Israel—with significant dissent from those who believed that America was backing the wrong side. Indeed, many State Department officials were in this camp. Though the relationship between America and Israel was surely one of shared ideologies and cultures, it was fundamentally an alliance of realpolitik, in the sense that American military support of Israel continued a general policy to aid any country threatened by the Soviet Union or by a Soviet client. It was American policy that no country should be allowed to succeed in reaching its goals with Soviet support. Kissinger took this general Cold War strategy a step further when he confided to Defense Secretary James R. Schlesinger his specific thinking concerning the Arab–Israel conflict: "Our strategy has to be that when the Soviet Union, the British, and the French press [for Israeli concessions], we stall—so all of them know only we can deliver." Kissinger's objective was to demonstrate that alliances with any state except America were unhelpful to re-

alizing Arab goals, and that America, unlike the Soviet Union, had enough influence in the region to return lands Israel had occupied during the Six Day War of 1967. Kissinger underscored the seriousness of America's position against Soviet gains in the region by favoring a worldwide nuclear alert when the Soviet Union threatened direct intervention on behalf of ailing Egyptian forces at the end of the war. The Soviets did not intervene, and America thereby demonstrated the ineffectiveness of Soviet support compared to American assistance. Shortly thereafter Kissinger was able to comment, "All the Arabs are coming to us." Indeed, through Kissinger's shuttle diplomacy, Egypt effectively became an American client, and America eventually did fulfill its promise to have Israel return seized territory to Egypt. Israel restored the Sinai to Egypt in 1978 as part of the Camp David Agreement negotiated by Israel, Egypt, and the United States. Israel and Egypt have since enjoyed a peaceful border and full diplomatic relations (Isaacson 1992).

Kissinger has been accused by some of having favored Israel too strongly on account of his heritage. Others claim he often requested too much of Israel and hindered it unfairly. He had rocky relationships with prime ministers Golda Meir and Yitzhak Rabin in the aftermath of the Yom Kippur War, when neither felt able to cooperate fully with American peace designs. Despite both hopes and fears that Kissinger treated Israel specially, he always maintained that he advocated only American interests. "I was born Jewish, but the truth is that has no significance for me," he declared. "America has given me everything. A home, a chance to study and achieve a high position. I don't know what other Jews expect of me, but I consider myself an American first" (Isaacson 1992). During the Cold War, his policies benefited both America and Israel, as the Cold War polarized alliances and Israel became an important square for America on the world chessboard.

Michael Alexander

References and Further Reading

Isaacson, Walter. 1992. *Kissinger: A Biography.* New York: Simon & Schuster.

Kissinger, Henry A. 1957. *A World Restored: Metternich, Castlereagh, and the Problems of Peace, 1812–1822.* Boston: Houghton Mifflin.

Kissinger, Henry A. 2003. *Crisis: The Anatomy of Two Major Foreign Policy Crises.* New York: Simon & Schuster.

Schulzinger, Robert D. 1989. *Henry Kissinger: Doctor of Diplomacy.* New York: Columbia University Press.

Jews in Wars and the Military

Jews and the Civil War

Jews clearly did their part in the American Civil War: thousands of Jewish men served in both armies, and countless other Jews aided the war effort at home. Yet they also encountered an outbreak of antisemitism that, though it subsided after the fighting ended in 1865, indicates how close to the surface of American culture this form of prejudice lay.

An estimated 150,000 to 200,000 Jews lived in the United States on the eve of the Civil War (Marcus 1990). There was no official Jewish position on slavery and secession, and the views of individual Jews were influenced more by their region than by ethnicity or religion.

Approximately 15 percent of American Jews lived in the states that became the Confederacy (Marcus 1990). Slaveholding was as common among Jews as among gentiles—about one-fourth of Jewish households owned slaves (Korn 1973)—but Jews were rarely the owners of large plantations and gangs of slaves. Most southern Jews lived in cities and towns, where they were merchants, brokers, artisans, or peddlers. The relatively small number of slaves they owned were domestic servants, laborers in the owner's trade, or workers for hire. Jews also took part in the slave trade, but in negligible numbers: Jews made up only 6 percent of slave dealers and auctioneers in three southern cities (Korn 1973). Jews' involvement in slavery was inci-

dental to their participation in the southern economy, and all evidence points to the conclusion that "slavery would not have differed one whit from historic reality if no single Jew had been resident in the South" (Korn 1973).

Whether they owned slaves or not, Jews lived in a region that did not tolerate dissent on this issue. They thus shared in the South's "pervasive racist sentiment," and southern Jews and their rabbis seldom criticized slavery as an institution (Feingold 1974). When the election of Abraham Lincoln in 1860 appeared to threaten slavery's survival, prominent Jewish elected officials, most notably Senator Judah P. Benjamin of Louisiana, supported secession. According to a rabbi in New Orleans, Benjamin's stand reflected the opinions of his fellow Jews: nearly all Jews in the city were "ardently in favor of secession, and many among them are intense fanatics" (quoted in Allardice 2002). During the Civil War, the majority of southern Jews remained loyal to the Confederacy.

Northern Jews expressed the same wide range of views on slavery as did their gentile neighbors. Antislavery organizations expected Jews to join them because, in the words of one group, Jews had been "the object of so much mean prejudice and unrighteous oppression . . . for ages" (quoted in Feingold 1974); the groups' leaders were distressed that many Jews failed to support the cause. Yet Jews had compelling reasons to keep their distance from the antislavery movement: as onetime victims of European mobs, some Jews were wary of public protests, whereas others were antagonized by antislavery groups' exclusionistic Christian rhetoric. Nonetheless, a number of Jews became prominent in the antislavery effort. Several rabbis denounced slavery to their congregations, other Jews joined John Brown in his antislavery crusade of the 1850s, and Ernestine Rose, daughter of a rabbi, was a leading antislavery lecturer.

An undercurrent of antisemitism circulated through American culture prior to the Civil War, especially in the North. A geography textbook informed students that Jews were "industrious but crafty," a California newspaper described a candidate for office as a "swindling sheeny," and a credit report warned that "prudence in large transactions with all Jews should be used" (quoted in Rockaway and Gutfeld 2001; quoted in Gerber 1982). Jews were caught up among the targets of the nativist frenzy of the early 1850s: in 1850, for example, a mob plundered a synagogue in New York on Yom Kippur. Such incidents inspired the formation of a new group, the Board of Delegates of American Israelites, in 1859. Among its other functions, the Board investigated and protested discrimination against Jews.

Yet the nativist furor subsided, and antisemitism remained more a reflex than a preoccupation of antebellum gentiles. Moreover, antisemitism was considerably milder in the South. One indicator of acceptance of southern Jews is their success in politics—a disproportionate number of Jews, particularly in Louisiana, were elected to political office.

The coming of the Civil War transformed the lives of individual Jews and the scale of antisemitism. Regional loyalties led thousands of Jews to serve in the opposing armies. The precise number of Jewish soldiers is unknown, because neither army collected information on recruits' religion. Estimates suggest that 7,000 to 10,000 Jews served in the two armies (Marcus 1995; Feingold 1974). The Union–Confederate breakdown within these numbers is similarly imprecise, with estimates for Jewish Confederates varying from 1,500 to more than 2,500 (Rosen 2000). There is no firm basis for choosing among these figures; the most that can be said is that Jews achieved a significant mobilization among a relatively small population and that Jews who fought for the Union considerably outnumbered Jewish Confederates.

Because of Jews' small numbers, there were no all-Jewish regiments in either army; there were, however, a few predominantly Jewish companies (a company was approximately a hundred soldiers, with ten companies per regiment). Nonetheless, according to two studies, Jews in both armies preferred to blend in with their friends and neighbors and avoid the image of clannishness (Allardice 2002; Korn 1951).

The typical Jewish Confederate soldier was a volunteer who was born in Germany, Poland, Russia, or Hungary; who owned no slaves; and who had worked as a clerk, peddler, tailor, or small shopkeeper (Rosen 2000). Like most Confederates, he served in the infantry. It is likely that Jewish soldiers in the Union army had similar characteristics, and we can gain an additional detail from military records. Regimental rosters report the ages of recruits in a largely Jewish company of the 149th New York Volunteers, a regiment formed in Syracuse in the summer of 1862. Since most Jewish recruits were recent immigrants, they were likely to be older than native-born soldiers: one-third of enlisted men were over age thirty when they joined the Syracuse company, compared to one-fourth of recruits in the Union army as a whole. Being unusually old for military service did not deter Jews from volunteering.

Like their gentile peers, Jewish soldiers fought for liberty and in defense of their homes and families, out of honor, patriotism, and a sense of duty, but seldom out of any convictions on the slavery issue. Other motives common to most soldiers included loyalty to comrades in arms, the adventure and excitement of war, escape from unappealing jobs, social and peer pressure to enlist, and the desire for praise or fear of censure. One study suggests that there was a "special burden" on Jews to prove their patriotism and courage by joining the army (Rosen 2000).

As the war dragged on, more soldiers on both sides became motivated by hatred for the enemy and a desire to avenge fallen comrades. Among Union fighting men, the opinion on emancipation became more positive, reflected in the changing views of Marcus Spiegel, a Jewish officer from Ohio. Early in 1863, soon after the Emancipation Proclamation took effect, Spiegel was unwilling "to fight for Lincoln's Negro proclamation one day longer"; a year later, he wrote that "I am [in] favor of doing away with the . . . accursed institution. . . . I am [now] a strong abolitionist" (Byrne and Solomon 1985).

Jews participated in every aspect of the war, as foot soldiers and artillerymen, cooks and color-bearers, pickets and teamsters. Few Jewish soldiers served in the cavalry, but Jews' experience in commerce and the professions won them prominent roles in both armies' support services. Abraham Myers attempted the thankless task of supplying clothing and equipment for the Confederacy, and David De Leon served as surgeon general. Phineas Horwitz was surgeon general for the Union army, and numerous other Jewish officers served on both armies' supply and administrative staffs.

A number of Jewish soldiers were recognized for exemplary service. Sergeant Leopold Karpeles received the Congressional Medal of Honor for rallying his comrades at the Battle of the Wilderness, and a superior saluted Confederate colonel Leon Marks's "great gallantry" in repelling a Union attack at Vicksburg (Allardice 2002). Other Jews endured capture and imprisonment, and some proved to be shirkers or deserters. As with all Civil War soldiers, more Jews succumbed to accidents, disease, and exposure than were killed by the enemy.

Both armies commissioned numerous Jewish officers. Like other Confederate officers, the Jews among them were educated and affluent men with important family connections. But in the South, with its smaller number of Jewish soldiers, no Jews rose to become generals, and only a few became colonels. The Union army, on the other hand, appointed eight Jewish generals. One, Frederick Knefler, earned his first star for leadership at the Battle of Chickamauga, and Edward Salomon, who enlisted as a lieutenant, rose to brigadier general after distinguished service at Gettysburg.

The rigors of military service hindered but did not prevent the practice of religion. There are reported instances of Jewish soldiers joining together for Sabbath worship, requesting leave for observing Jewish holidays, conducting camp meetings to discuss mutual problems, visiting wounded Jewish soldiers, and organizing traditional burials for dead comrades.

Jews held responsible government positions on both sides of the conflict. Judah P. Benjamin served the Confederacy as attorney general, secretary of war, and secretary of state; recognizing that the South was running short of fighting men, he became an early proponent of arming slaves to fight for the Confederacy in return for their freedom. Isachar Zacharie, a close friend and confidant of Abraham Lincoln, was sent to Richmond in 1863, apparently in an attempt to negotiate peace.

Jewish civilians served in home relief and humanitarian activities, and they raised money for the war effort. Synagogues engaged in the same kinds of patriotic activities as churches, offering prayers for the success of the cause and for an end to the hostilities, as well as inspirational sermons. Jews contributed to the efforts of the U.S. Sanitary Commission to provide supplies and medical care to soldiers, and they worked with other aid societies that furnished food, fuel, clothing, and money to support soldiers' families. Jewish women nursed the wounded and sewed clothing and other supplies for the troops; the flag of the 149th New York Volunteers bore the inscription of "the Jewish ladies of Syracuse."

In spite of Jews' vital participation, the Civil War set the stage for an eruption of antisemitism in both the North and the South. Jews were especially visible targets for prejudice due to their vulnerability as recent immigrants, the unfamiliar culture and languages of the Central Europeans among them, and their concentration in cities. They became the primary scapegoats for the economic distress, political tensions, and social disruption that plagued societies at war.

In the North, newspaper editors exploited the stereotype of the avaricious Jew to help explain the slow progress of the war. Editors declared that "hooked nose wretches" took pleasure in military defeat, because "it puts money in their purse" (quoted in Dinnerstein 1994). Such suspicions also transformed "shoddy" into an ethnic slur. The term originally referred to inferior material made from scrap wool, but it became associated with Jewish merchants and manufacturers in a remarkable evolution of prejudicial thinking. Nineteenth-century Jews were particularly visible in the needle trades; the Union army contracted for vast quantities of mass-produced goods, including uniforms; the goods, especially the uniforms, were often overpriced and of poor quality; therefore, Jewish avarice must have been at fault. This reasoning was so persuasive that "shoddy" came to include all sorts of alleged Jewish profiteering: in 1864, a serialized poem caricatured the "Shoddy family," whose patriarch boasts of "bleeding the country, but not bleeding for it!" (quoted in Bunker and Appel 1994). Gentiles such as Lincoln's first secretary of war and his cronies also engaged in wholesale profiteering, but "'shoddy' came to represent the quintessential stereotype of the unpatriotic Jew" (Bunker and Appel 1994).

The federal government's wartime treatment of Jews ranged from bumbling to calculated bigotry. In 1862, federal authorities ordered the arrest of Simon Wolf, an attorney affiliated with B'nai B'rith; until the secretary of war obtained Wolf's release, officials insisted that Wolf and his organization were pro-Confederate subversives. A bill passed by Congress in 1861 contained a provision allowing only Christian ministers to serve as chaplains in the military; in one historian's view, this was "the first instance of outright discrimination and legal inequity in a Congressional enactment" in American history (Korn 1951). In 1862, General Ulysses S. Grant issued General Order No. 11 in response to a persistent trade through the lines in cotton and other goods, whose profits could benefit the Confederacy. Although there were few Jewish merchants conducting this commerce, the order applied solely to Jews. It called for the immediate forced removal of *all* Jews from areas in the Mississippi Valley under Grant's jurisdiction, without trial and regardless of actual participation in the alleged wrongdoing. Most subordinates hesitated to carry out the order, but a number of Jews were arrested in northern Mississippi, and a particularly zealous officer forced nearly all the Jewish families of Paducah, Kentucky, to leave the city.

In the South, many of the charges leveled against Jewish civilians were similar to those in the North: politicians and editors accused "Jewish Shylocks" of speculation, profiteering, passing counterfeit money, unfair competition, and "fatten[ing] upon the calamities of the very people who are giving them a home" (quoted in Greenberg 1993; quoted in Rosen 2000). But conditions on the southern home front made antisemitism, which had been relatively benign before the war, worse than in the North. These conditions included a general antipathy toward foreign immigrants, based in part on the belief that the Union forces were made up of foreigners; an agrarian society's suspicion of merchants and storekeepers; a deeper commitment to evangelical Christianity than in the North; and the morale problems attendant on a prolonged war with diminishing chances of victory. Jews were suspect because many of them spoke with an accent, kept to themselves, lived frugally, declined to intermarry, and allegedly engaged in immoral business practices.

In Thomasville, Georgia, citizens met in 1862 to denounce Jewish merchants and peddlers, accusing them of speculation, counterfeiting, and disloyalty to the Confed-

eracy; the meeting concluded with a call to expel local Jews. In Union-occupied areas such as New Orleans under General Benjamin Butler, southern Jews were subjected to worse treatment than other southerners by both the Union army and the northern press. Nor could Judah P. Benjamin's stature as Confederate cabinet member and confidant of Jefferson Davis protect him from ethnic slurs: Congressman Henry S. Foote of Tennessee ceaselessly denounced him as "Judas Iscariot Benjamin," calling him the Confederacy's "Jewish puppeteer," and a Richmond newspaper complained that "the people do not like to be made to choose between Jesus Christ and Judah P. Benjamin" (quoted in Evans 1988; *Richmond Enquirer*, Feb. 9, 1865).

On the other hand, there is little evidence of bigotry against Jewish soldiers in the Confederate army. To be sure, prejudice was not entirely absent: one officer in an Alabama regiment blamed antisemitism for his delayed promotion, and another Jewish officer was harassed by his men. Confederates were notoriously disrespectful to officers, however, and descriptions of the latter officer's treatment contain no explicit slurs. Moreover, the Confederate Congress set no religious barriers to the appointment of chaplains (though there is no record of Jews being appointed), and no Jewish soldiers were court-martialed during the war.

Jews themselves did not remain passive in the face of the rising tide of prejudice, and they were quick to assert their right to equal treatment. Editors of Jewish periodicals, aided by the secular press, reacted immediately to the chaplaincy controversy in the Union military. Jews and Christians alike sent petitions to Congress, and an envoy traveled to Washington to argue against the exclusion of Jewish chaplains. Lawmakers responded by changing the chaplaincy act in 1862: now, chaplains could be appointed from any religious denomination.

Angered by the *group* punishment of Jews, without a trial, for the actions of the mostly non-Jewish *individuals* who inspired Grant's General Order No. 11, Jews wrote letters and editorials demanding fair trials for the persons accused of illegal trading, regardless of their background, and insisting on penalties for the guilty. Protest meetings occurred in major cities, and accusers of Jews were challenged to present their evidence in a public forum. Jewish protests reached the White House, and Lincoln rescinded the order in early 1863.

This action helped to inspire Jewish admiration for Lincoln. A rabbi, visiting the president to convey gratitude for the order's demise, came away "fully convinced ... that [Lincoln] feels no prejudice against any nationality and especially against the Israelites" (quoted in Markens 1909). Citing such traits and Lincoln's Jewish friends, encomiums "claimed for Lincoln personal qualities that made him almost a Jew" (Diner 1992). Contemporary feelings of affinity may have gone too far—for example, Lincoln justified a Sunday observation order by citing "the best sentiment of a Christian people" (*War of the Rebellion* 1899, ser 3, vol. 2)—but his behavior nonetheless demonstrated, as a Jewish acquaintance concluded, that Lincoln was "a man of very broad views" (quoted in Markens 1909).

In the South, Jews in Georgia vigorously protested the antisemitic actions that had occurred in Thomasville. Jewish soldiers in a Georgia regiment wrote a letter in defense of Thomasville's Jews, and a protest meeting in Savannah condemned Thomasville's "slander, persecution and denunciation of a people" (quoted in Diner 1992).

Wartime antisemitism itself had limits. Despite repeated antisemitic harangues by Foote, the Confederate Congress produced no legislation against Jews. The diary of Clara Solomon, who lived in New Orleans during the Civil War, makes no mention of antisemitism against her or her family from schoolmates or others. Marcus Spiegel did not suffer from antisemitism in the Union army; he admired Grant, and he never mentioned General Order No. 11 in his numerous letters.

Jews also had their defenders against the aforementioned invective in the South. The editor of the *Richmond Sentinel* criticized "intolerant and illiberal views and prejudices" against Jews, and an editor in Georgia denied "the charges which we have frequently heard made by our street-corner gossipers and windy patriots" about Jews' wartime conduct (quoted in Korn 1951). In Thomasville, despite the ominous tone of the anti-Jewish rally and its formation of a vigilance committee, the town's Jewish families remained throughout the war without molestation; a study of the incident concludes that "with the exception of this single anti-Semitic outburst, the townspeople lived in harmony" (Greenberg 1993). The vital role that Jewish merchants and tradespeople played in economic life tempered antisemitism and maintained cordial relationships, especially in small towns like Thomasville. One historian

has concluded that, even during the Civil War, "acts of public tolerance offset almost every act of antisemitism" (Diner 1992).

With the war's end in 1865, antisemitism diminished. For Jews, successfully countering the war's challenges to equal rights set a precedent that had far-reaching effects: they learned that public officials could be responsive to efforts to safeguard the rights of minorities and victims of discrimination. Jewish leaders reminded voters of General Order No. 11 when Grant ran for president in 1868, urging them not to "lick the feet that kick them about" (quoted in Diner 1992). Other Jews, however, supported Grant, and after his election they suggested ways in which he could demonstrate positive feelings, which he did by appointing Jews to public office, attending synagogue events, and making other public expressions of goodwill.

Larry M. Logue

References and Further Reading

Allardice, Bruce S. 2002. "'The Cause a Righteous One': Louisiana Jews and the Confederacy." In *Louisianians in the Civil War*, edited by Lawrence Lee Hewitt and Arthur W. Bergeron, Jr., 72–86. Columbia: University of Missouri Press.

Bunker, Gary L., and John Appel. 1994. "'Shoddy,' Anti-Semitism and the Civil War." *American Jewish History* 82: 43–71.

Byrne, Frank L., and Jean Powers Solomon, eds. 1985. *Your True Marcus: The Civil War Letters of a Jewish Colonel.* Kent, OH: Kent State University Press.

Diner, Hasia. 1992. *A Time for Gathering: The Second Migration, 1820–1880.* Baltimore, MD: Johns Hopkins University Press.

Dinnerstein, Leonard. 1994. *Antisemitism in America.* New York: Oxford University Press.

Evans, Eli N. 1988. *Judah P. Benjamin: The Jewish Confederate.* New York: Free Press.

Feingold, Henry L. 1974. *Zion in America: The Jewish Experience from Colonial Times to the Present.* New York: Twayne Publishers.

Gerber, David A. 1982. "Cutting Out Shylock: Elite Anti-Semitism and the Quest for Moral Order in the Mid-Nineteenth-Century American Marketplace." *Journal of American History* 69, 3 (December): 615–637.

Greenberg, Mark I. 1993. "Ambivalent Relations: Acceptance and Anti-Semitism in Confederate Thomasville." *American Jewish Archives* 45: 13–29.

Korn, Bertram Wallace. 1951. *American Jewry and the Civil War.* Cleveland, OH: World Publishing Co.

Korn, Bertram Wallace. 1973. "Jews and Negro Slavery in the Old South, 1789-1875." In *Jews in the South,* edited by Leonard Dinnerstein and Mary Dale Palsson, 89-134. Baton Rouge: Louisiana State University Press.

Marcus, Jacob R. 1990. *To Count a People: American Jewish Population Data, 1585-1984.* Lanham, MD: University Press of America.

Marcus, Jacob R. 1995. *The American Jew, 1585-1900: A History.* New York: Carlson.

Markens, Isaac. 1909. "Lincoln and the Jews." *Publications of the American Jewish Historical Society* 17: 109-165.

Rockaway, Robert, and Arnon Gutfield. 2001. "Demonic Images of the Jew in the Nineteenth Century United States." *American Jewish History* 89: 355-381.

Rosen, Robert N. 2000. *The Jewish Confederates.* Columbia: University of South Carolina Press.

War of the Rebellion: A Compilation of the Official Records of the Union and Confederate Armies. 1880-1901. 128 vols. Washington, DC: U.S. Government Printing Office.

American Jews and World War I

As a result of World War I (1914–1918), American Jews redefined their relationships with each other, with their former homelands, and with American society. America's diverse Jewish communities forged unprecedented levels of unity as they confronted questions over which side to support in the conflict and how to help millions of Jewish refugees suffering abroad. The war also brought the debate about a Jewish homeland in Palestine into the mainstream of American Jewish life. As they wrestled with these issues, the nation's 3 million Jews distanced themselves from their European pasts, tied their aspirations to the United States, and established a more visible presence than in earlier periods.

At the outbreak of hostilities in August 1914, the country's Jewish population was more diverse than it had ever been, and attitudes toward the war were divided. Most Jews of Central European descent, who were well established in the United States, followed the general course of American opinion, moving from neutrality to open support for the Allies. East European immigrants, however, deeply loathed Imperial Russia because of its history of antisemitic brutality. For the first three years of the war they did not desire a German victory so much as the downfall of the czarist regime. With the czar's overthrow in February 1917, most American Jews believed that a democratic society would emerge in Russia. Therefore they supported the new government's decision to continue to fight and the growing American desire to enter the war as an Ally.

Still, when the Wilson administration joined the conflict in April 1917, a large minority of American Jewry remained opposed to U.S. participation. Dissent was strongest in New York, where East European Jews provided much of the support for the country's most significant antiwar organization, the People's Council for Democracy and Peace. Anarchist Emma Goldman was deported for protesting the draft, while Jewish-led unions and the *Daily Forward* heavily backed the Socialist Party's antiwar campaign in the 1917 elections.

A series of landmark events ended this opposition and created a united Jewish position on the war. Most important was the catastrophic outcome of the Treaty of Brest-Litovsk, the peace settlement between Germany and the new Bolshevik government in Russia that had seized power in the October Revolution. Under the agreement, most of the Jewish Pale of Settlement was placed under German military control in early 1918. This harsh treatment contrasted sharply with the Allied diplomatic initiatives, which carefully addressed American Jewish concerns over the welfare and future of Jews in Europe and the Middle East. In November 1917, Britain's Balfour Declaration had expressed support for a future Jewish state in Palestine. Soon after, Woodrow Wilson had proclaimed national self-determination to be a key American war aim. By spring 1918, nearly all on the Jewish left had reversed their positions and endorsed the Allied cause.

While unity on the war issue took years to develop, early in the conflict American Jewry came together to provide relief for Jewish war refugees. Its major constituencies—the Central Europeans, the Orthodox, and labor—created their own organizations and raised $63 million between 1914 and 1924. A single agency, the Joint Distribution Committee, administered the funds; by war's end it sponsored soup kitchens, medical treatment, and schools for 750,000 Jews on the Eastern Front.

Jewish participation in the American war effort was also impressive. Over 200,000 Jews served in the U.S. armed forces, a higher proportion than that of Jews in the American population. In an extraordinary demonstration of Jewish unity, fourteen religious bodies created the Jewish Welfare Board to assist these men and women in uniform. It provided rabbis, social workers, and recreational facilities at training camps nationwide and overseas. In the federal government, financier Bernard Baruch directed the powerful War Industries Board, Congressman Julius Kahn steered the passage of the Selective Service Act, and labor leader Samuel Gompers served on the Council of National Defense. American Jews provided tens of millions of dollars for the country's Liberty Loan, Red Cross, and other mobilization drives, while thousands also worked on draft boards and fund-raising committees.

Even more remarkable was the convergence of American Jewish opinion on establishing a Jewish homeland in Palestine. Before 1914, the Zionist movement in the United States was very limited. But the war's devastating impact on European Jews and the collapse of the empires that governed them made the Zionist objective both a dire necessity and a realistic possibility. This sense of urgency continued in the immediate postwar years, as a wave of pogroms, unleashed by the chaos and civil wars in East Europe, brought death and destruction to hundreds of Jewish communities in Poland, Galicia, Rumania, and the Ukraine. By late 1918, membership in American Zionist organizations had skyrocketed to over 200,000. Even more audaciously, 335,000 Jews across the country had voted to establish the American Jewish (AJ) Congress, which demanded a homeland and legal protection for Jews worldwide at the postwar peace negotiations. Though the Versailles treaty and its guarantees of Jewish rights would soon disintegrate in the interwar years, the efforts of the AJCongress delegation set a dramatic precedent for American Jewish advocacy in international affairs.

Together, these events and actions strengthened the American Jewish community. For the first time since the mass emigration from East Europe, Jews from a wide range of religious, political, and national backgrounds cooperated on a series of critical projects. Their efforts to assist refugees reflected the relative material success and security they enjoyed in the United States; few ever considered returning to their home countries or emigrating to Palestine after the war. Their political activity, whether supporting or opposing the American war effort, or advocating a Jewish homeland, also underscored the relative openness of American society, even during wartime. This political assertiveness and the greater unity American Jews forged during World War I continued to develop even as nativism and antisemitism mounted during the interwar period.

Christopher M. Sterba

References and Further Reading

American Jewish Committee. 1919. *The War Record of American Jews.* New York: American Jewish Committee.

Rappaport, Joseph. 1951. "Jewish Immigrants and World War I: A Study of Yiddish Press Attitudes." PhD dissertation, Columbia University.

Sterba, Christopher M. 2003. *Good Americans: Italian and Jewish Immigrants during the First World War.* New York: Oxford University Press.

Szajkowski, Zosa. 1972. *Jews, Wars, and Communism.* Vol. 1. New York: Ktav Publishing House.

American Jews in the Spanish Civil War (1936–1939)

The Spanish Civil War (1936–1939) gave Jews from around the world the first opportunity for organized armed resistance against fascism and Nazi antisemitism. Most U.S. Jews who volunteered to fight in Spain were not religious: their decision to enlist in the fight against fascism was the result of identification with internationalist, class-based labor and political organizations. Nevertheless, ethnic and cultural identity constituted an important element of their radical politics and fueled their opposition.

At the end of November 1937, while recovering from wounds received in battle, Hyman Katz wrote to his mother in New York in an attempt to mollify her disapproval of his decision to volunteer to fight fascism in Spain:

> Yes, Ma, this is the case where sons must go against their mothers' wishes for the sake of their mothers themselves.
>
> So I took up arms against the persecutors of my people—the Jews—and my class—the Oppressed. I am fighting against those who establish an inquisition like that of their ideological ancestors several centuries ago, in Spain. Are these traits which you admire so much in a Prophet Jeremiah or a Judas Maccabbeus, bad when your son exhibits them? Of course, I am not a Jeremiah or a Judas; but I'm trying with my own meager capabilities, to do what they did with their great capabilities, in the struggle for Liberty, Well-being and Peace (Nelson 1996).

His mother's response to this letter has been lost. The next year, Hyman Katz was killed in action in Spain. Hy Katz's explanation of his motivations, rooted in a Jewish history of exploitation as well as in religious and racial persecution, resonates in the words of other volunteers. In 1939, as part of his testimony before the Dies Committee set up by the U.S. Congress to investigate so-called un-American organizations, Milton Wolff said, in explaining why he enlisted in support of the Spanish Republic: "I am Jewish, and knowing that as a Jew we are the first to suffer when fascism does come, I went to Spain to fight against it." Spain became the battlefield where Jews could confront this raging enemy. "Here, finally," said Gene Wolman, "the oppressed of the Earth are united, here finally we have weapons, here we can fight back. Here, even if we lose, . . . in the weakening of Fascism, we will have won" (Carroll 1994).

During the 1930s, fascist and Nazi expansionism affected the basic context of European politics and diplomacy. Thus, when the Spanish military, backed by Hitler and Mussolini, rebelled against the legally elected republican government, for many around the world the Spanish Civil War came to embody the global struggle against exploitation, oppression, and racism. The clearest example of this connection was the decision by over 35,000 men and women from fifty-two countries to join what became known as the International Brigades to fight in defense of the Spanish Republican government.

According to some recent estimates, Jews comprised from 25 to 30 percent of international volunteers. This high percentage prompted the leadership of the International Brigades to support the publication of the Yiddish language *Botwin* (named for the Polish Jewish Communist martyr, Naftali Botwin) and to consider forming an all-Jewish brigade. The purpose of this unit was to demonstrate the direct participation of Jews alongside other national groups in the fight against fascism. High casualties made this impossible, but a Jewish company was formed within the Polish brigade. Embroidered on the company's flag in Spanish, Polish, and Yiddish was its motto "For your liberty and ours."

While the main contingent of Jewish volunteers came from Poland, the second largest group was from the United States. Of the approximately 3,000 U.S. volunteers who formed the Abraham Lincoln Brigade, some estimates suggest that one-third were Jewish. Many were children of European immigrants, who had arrived in the United States during the early years of the century. They had received an "Americanized" education in school, but still felt family

ties to Europe. Most volunteers came from large cities, where the immigrants had settled.

In October 1938, after two years of fighting, the Spanish government ordered the withdrawal of the surviving members of the International Brigades, hoping that the gesture would press Germany and Italy to remove their troops. But the fascist countries ignored the withdrawal. In March 1939, Francisco Franco's forces captured Madrid and brought the war to an end. For many Jewish volunteers, defeat in the Spanish Civil War meant a continuation of the antifascist struggle on different battlefields. With the onset of World War II scores of former European Jewish brigadiers, among them Connecticut-born nurse Irene Goldin, who after the fall of Spain had remained in France, joined the Resistance against Nazi occupiers and their puppet regimes. Following the U.S. entry into the war, over four hundred Lincoln brigade veterans enlisted in the armed services, while many others served in the merchant marine. As members of the U.S. Army, Jewish Lincoln veterans fought around the world. Several participated in action inside Germany. Some, including veterans Al Tanz, Lou Gordon, Morris Cohen, and Jack Lucid, helped to liberate Nazi concentration camps in 1945.

With the defeat of Hitler and Mussolini, members of the Lincoln Brigade felt vindicated in their struggles against Fascism and Nazism. However, during the Cold War era, both the Veterans of the Abraham Lincoln Brigade (VALB) organization and individual Lincoln vets faced government investigations as well as private harassment by employers. Since about 70 percent of the members of the brigade had been affiliated with the Communist Party (or a related group), all were treated as potential subversives. In the 1960s, the U.S. Supreme Court ruled in favor of the VALB's protest against being listed as a subversive organization. Meanwhile, as individuals and as a group, veterans of the Lincoln Brigade remained political activists, taking public stands in favor of the civil rights movement, against the war in Vietnam, protesting the antisemitic campaigns of the Polish government that followed the Arab-Israeli Six Day War, opposing the Pinochet regime in Chile, providing humanitarian aid for Cuba and countries in Central America, and finally demonstrating against the U.S. invasion of Iraq.

As they aged, Lincoln veterans paid more attention to their personal heritage both as radicals and, in many cases, as Jews. Some, like the composer Lan Adomian, focused primarily on Jewish themes in their work. Another veteran, Albert Prago, presented historical research that questioned whether Communists who were Jews should not also be considered Jews who were Communists. His essay "Jews in the International Brigades" emphasized the role of a Jewish consciousness in inspiring individuals to volunteer in the fight against fascism. Many other surviving veterans acknowledge the importance of Prago's research. "Let us herald the fact," he wrote, "that more Jews, proportionately, fought in Spain . . . than any other minority or any other nationality in Europe!" (Prago 1987).

Fraser M. Ottanelli

References and Further Readings

Abraham Lincoln Brigade Archives. "Jewish Volunteers in the Spanish Civil War." New York: Tamiment Library, New York University.

Carroll, Peter N. 1994. *The Odyssey of the Abraham Lincoln Brigade: Americans in the Spanish Civil War.* Stanford, CA: Stanford University Press.

Diamant, David. 1979. *Combattants juifs dans l'armée républicaine espagnole, 1936–1939.* Paris: Editions Renouveau.

Nelson, Cary, and Jefferson Hendricks. 1996. *Madrid 1937: Letter of the Abraham Lincoln Brigade from the Spanish Civil War.* New York: Routledge.

Prago, Albert. 1987. "Jews in the International Brigades." In *Our Fight: Writings by Veterans of the Abraham Lincoln Brigade,* edited by Alvah Bessie and Albert Prago, 94–103. New York: Monthly Review Press and Veterans of the Abraham Lincoln Brigade.

www.alba-valb.org

American Jewish Soldiers in World War II

Over half a million Jews, more than 10 percent of the American Jewish population, served in all branches of the armed forces of the United States in World War II. Over 10,000 Jews lost their lives in the service, 80 percent of them in battle (Kaufman 1947). Many thousands were wounded. Scarcely a Jewish family did not have a son or brother, father or uncle, in the service. No experience more dramatically reshaped American Jewish identity for men born in the 1920s than U.S. military service. The war transformed this generation. It made them fighters. Military service produced a new American Jew. It took young men who had grown up in working- and middle-class ethnic neighborhoods of large cities, men who recognized themselves as Jewish by virtue of their family and environment, and turned them into self-conscious Jews, aware of their equal rights as American citizens. These new American Jews learned as soldiers to defend their country. In the process, the armed forces also taught them how to defend themselves and their people. Donning an American uniform made Jews both more American and more Jewish.

Few Jewish men set out to transform themselves. Most accepted military service as their duty to their nation. They were eager to defend the United States and to defeat its enemies, especially Nazi Germany. Military service made extraordinary demands on all civilians that often contradicted the values they had cherished in a democratic society. Jews responded in ways that allowed them to retain their Jewishness, internalizing it as a private aspect of their personalities rather than displaying it as a public dimension of their culture. Military life encouraged Jews to revise their understanding of gender roles and hastened Jewish assimilation to American masculine norms. Jews become less visible in the service. They looked just like other American soldiers. Even circumcision did not mark Jews as different since the procedure had become popular among middle-class Americans. In important ways Jews were just like their comrades

Snapshots of American Jewish soldiers during World War II. (American Jewish Historical Society)

in arms, but beneath the common uniforms Jews struggled with a different reality, a Jewish reality.

World War II began on September 1, 1939, when Germany invaded Poland, but the United States did not enter the war until after Japan attacked Pearl Harbor on December 7, 1941. However, in 1940 the United States instituted a peacetime draft that required one year of military service for young men selected by lottery. Most American Jews, like most Americans, entered the armed forces in the months and years after Pearl Harbor. Many spent three years in uniform, others only two, and some spent four or five years in the service. The war in Europe ended on May 8, 1945, with the unconditional surrender of Germany. The war in the Pacific theater ended on August 15, 1945, with the unconditional surrender of Japan. Fighting on two fronts, the United States focused its manpower first on the European and North African theaters of war and then on the Pacific and Asian theaters. Defeating Nazi Germany, which targeted Jews for persecution and extermination, took primacy in the eyes of most American Jews, unlike other Americans who thought it was more important to avenge the bombing of Pearl Harbor.

Jews were not segregated like African Americans. Historians have argued that military service in World War II integrated white ethnics, including Jews, into an American national identity. Because Jews constituted such a small fraction of the American population—less than 5 percent—they represented a similar percentage in the armed forces. This meant that usually there was only a handful of Jews in a unit, and it was not uncommon for a man to find himself the only Jew in his unit. Feelings of isolation became particularly acute in the Pacific theater where units were dispersed. At other times, especially in the European theater, Jews constituted as much as 10 percent of a unit.

The military officially recognized that Jews differed only in their religion. Differences among Jews on political, ethnic, or religious grounds were ignored. The Army allowed soldiers to choose a religious designation to be stamped on their dog tags: P for Protestant, C for Catholic, and H for Hebrew. Informal observation by Jewish chaplains suggests that officers may have been more reluctant to have an H on their dog tags than enlisted men. Jewish fliers based in England often discussed whether they should fly with their dog tags over Germany. Once Jewish soldiers reached the European theater, they worried about the H and whether, if they were captured by German troops, they would be treated as prisoners of war or as Jews and sent to concentration camps. There was no official policy developed by the American military, and most American Jewish soldiers were treated as prisoners of war. Some, however, were persecuted by German troops.

Through its chaplaincy services the armed forces aimed to provide equal recognition to Judaism alongside Protestantism and Catholicism as one of the three fighting faiths of democracy. In the process it created what would come to be called the "Judeo-Christian tradition" after the war. The Judeo-Christian tradition championed belief in God the Father, the Brotherhood of Man, and the individual dignity of men. World War II provided an arena not only for implementing in pragmatic terms the Judeo-Christian tradition as America's faith, but also for translating that religious vision into a commitment of many American military leaders. Worshipping together in uniform gradually came to be accepted by soldiers and sailors as standard operating procedure, the American military norm. The armed forces initiated the performance of ecumenism on the battlefield, in hospitals and camps, and at thousands of memorial services honoring the dead. The military's standard operating procedure for memorial services included three chaplains, one each to represent Protestants, Catholics, and Jews.

In its efforts to integrate Jews and Christians as equal partners in uniform, the armed forces encouraged chaplains to move from cooperative behavior to a common belief in a religious worldview that sustained American democracy. All chaplains were required to report on what they did to minister to men of other faiths as well as their own. Military chapels did not have any distinguishing religious symbols so that anyone could use them. Lifeboats held pocket-sized Protestant, Catholic, and Jewish Testaments, packaged together in a waterproof container. The monthlong chaplaincy training course mixed men of different religions, even aiming to make routine the placement of a Jew, a Catholic, a liturgical Protestant, and an evangelical Protestant as roommates.

The sinking of the *USAT Dorchester* in the North Atlantic in 1943, with the deaths of Protestant chaplains George Fox and Clark Poling, Catholic chaplain John Washington, and Jewish chaplain Alexander Goode, symbolized for many Americans their nation's distinctiveness. The four chaplains came to represent American ideals guiding the country's wartime mission. Similarities outweighed religious differences. Whether one prayed in Hebrew, Latin, or English, the same God heard the prayers. After the war, the postal service issued a stamp commemorating the sacrifice of the four chaplains who gave their life preservers so that other men might live.

The Army established a quota for Jewish chaplains initially at 2 percent based on a 1928 census of Jewish participation in the military. The Jewish Welfare Board (JWB) convinced the Chief of Chaplains that more Jews were serving than reflected in the census. So the Army raised the quota to 3 percent. In 1944 the Committee on Army and Navy Religious Activities (CANRA) requested an increase to 3.7 percent to reflect the percentage of Jews in the United States population. In May 1945 the War Department agreed and raised the quota to accommodate the large numbers of Jews in the armed forces. Judaism ranked fifth in the Army's quota system for chaplains, after Catholic, Methodist, "Baptist, South," and "Baptist, Colored" (Bernstein 1971). In actual numbers, however, most white Protestant denominations exceeded their quotas of chaplains, while Catholic, Jewish, and African American chaplains were underrepresented.

The military delegated the recruitment of chaplains to each religious group. Jews reorganized the CANRA under the auspices of the JWB to oversee the recruitment and supervision of Jewish chaplains, and to provide assistance to them. Under Rabbi Philip Bernstein's guidance, CANRA established a formula of tripartite representation on all of its committees as well as among its officers. CANRA strove for harmony, seeking unanimity for important decisions.

At a time when boundaries between Orthodoxy and Conservatism were fluid, CANRA institutionalized both Jewish denominationalism and cooperation among rabbis. A special responsa committee of three rabbis—Solomon B. Freehof, Leo Jung, and Milton Steinberg, representing Reform, Orthodoxy, and Conservatism—answered religious questions posed by chaplains. The tripartite division of Orthodox, Conservative, and Reform soon became standardized. It allowed the JWB to develop consensus on a wide range of religious matters, including a joint prayer book for military use. The spirit of interdenominational cooperation among Jews, nourished by the exigencies of wartime, was extended into the postwar era, as reflected in the activities of the Synagogue Council of America. CANRA also built on precedents established during World War I, such as the choice of a *magen david* (Star of David) to mark Jewish graves instead of a cross.

Over half of all rabbis in the United States volunteered for military service, an impressive record. However, only 311 of them actually received commissions as chaplains due to the need to be certified first by CANRA and then by the military. CANRA encouraged each of the rabbinical associations to recruit chaplains. Almost half (147) came from the Reform movement, not quite a third (96) from Conservatism, and a fifth (68) from modern Orthodoxy (Slomovitz 1999). Their distribution reflected the guidelines and recruitment process, including standards imposed by CANRA, which were more stringent than the military's. CANRA required both ordination and a college degree. CANRA wanted chaplains who were culturally American as well as Jewish. It also screened prospective candidates for their appearance, speech, religious integrity and flexibility, and psychological approach. CANRA rejected men with accents and those who would be unable to serve diverse types of Jews. They wanted chaplains who were educated in the United States and would not seem foreign to American GIs. Just being a rabbi in uniform would make Jewish chaplains unusual.

The armed forces distributed Jews as it did other soldiers, but stereotypes about Jews and their skills influenced where they served. For example, in the Army Air Corps, Jews were more often classified and trained as navigators and bombardiers than as pilots because Army personnel thought that Jews lacked the leadership skills required of pilots and, conversely, that Jews were good with numbers. Unlike many rural recruits, almost all Jews in military service had graduated from high school and so possessed literacy and typing skills that were valuable for service corps work. Nevertheless, Jews served in all branches of the military and in all theaters of war. Antisemitic canards to the contrary, their distribution largely paralleled military norms. The U.S. Army committed 2.28 million men, or 30 percent, to its combat forces. Approximately 23 percent of Jewish GIs served in the Marines and Army ground forces that saw most of the combat and suffered the highest casualties. Of the 80 percent of Jews who served in the Army, 36 percent served in the vast Army Service Corps, another 23 percent entered the Army Air Forces, and 21 percent served in the ground forces, including 13 percent in the infantry. Sixteen percent served in the Navy (Dublin 1947).

Antisemitism existed within the ranks and among the officer corps. Military service brought millions of Americans together from all parts of the country and all walks of life. Since over 75 percent of American Jews lived in five large cities—with over 40 percent in New York City alone—most Americans had never met a Jew before entering the military. Jews encountered religious stereotypes (e.g., men asked to see their horns) and ethnic stereotypes (e.g., they were considered cowardly). Army lingo included ethnic slurs like "jewboy" and "kike" in male conversation. Antisemitic ditties and songs traveled through the barracks. Jews were also accused of fomenting war to help their fellow Jews in Europe. Top-ranking generals subscribed to notions of a Jewish conspiracy to control the world and to undermine the United States.

Surveys done at the time found that antisemitic feelings peaked during the war years in the United States. Antisemitic sentiments were expressed openly in Congress, in the press, and on city streets. Discrimination against Jews in employment, higher education, housing, and hotels was widely accepted as routine and unremarkable. But in the military, Jews encountered antisemitism as personal, not abstract or institutional. Each Jewish soldier had to decide how to handle the slurs and stereotypes. Many responded by challenging their fellow GIs and fighting for their honor and manhood.

Once overseas, Jewish soldiers, sailors, and marines learned that, despite the common foe, their comrades in arms often retained their antisemitic attitudes. Jews fought to prove their valor to their fellow soldiers and to themselves. Thus they battled on three fronts simultaneously: against enemy troops, stereotypes, and their internalization of negative views of Jews. Many managed to achieve recognition for their bravery under fire. Three Jews received the Medal of Honor: Isadore S. Jachman, staff sergeant, 513th Parachute Infantry Regiment, in Belgium on January 4, 1945; Benjamin Solomon, a dentist/surgeon with the 105th Infantry, in Saipan on July 6, 1944; and Raymond Zussmann, second lieutenant, 756th tank battalion, in France on September 12, 1944. However, bias existed in according Jews recognition for their bravery. Ben Solomon only received his medal on May 1, 2002. Other Jews also sought recognition many years after the war ended when attitudes toward Jewish bravery had changed.

Invidious charges about Jews' unwillingness to fight provoked the urge to document their involvement. After

Isadore Jachman, American Jewish soldier and recipient of the Congressional Medal of Honor during World War II. (National Museum of American Jewish Military History)

the war the JWB collected documentation about Jewish military service. Twenty-four Jews reached the upper echelons of military rank. There were six major generals, thirteen brigadier generals, two admirals, two rear admirals, and one commodore (Dublin 1947). Military service reached all types of American Jews. Uncle Sam recruited fourth-generation, native-born Jews whose grandparents were born in the United States and recent refugees from Nazism who arrived only a few years before they enlisted. Some refugee soldiers worked in counterpropaganda units and in interrogation teams, using their linguistic skills. Their return to their native land wearing an American uniform brought them some sense of justice.

Jewish women volunteered for military service in record numbers. They shared similar motivations with Jewish men who volunteered: a desire to fight Nazism and to contribute to the war effort to defend their country. Some also sought adventure and a chance to escape homes that they considered constricting. Few went overseas, but those who did fulfilled their duties honorably. Some strug-

Raymond Zussman, American Jewish soldier and recipient of the Congressional Medal of Honor during World War II. (National Museum of American Jewish Military History)

gled against anti-Jewish bias or ignorance of Jews among their fellow women in uniform.

No American soldier was prepared for encountering the concentration camps, and no Jewish soldier could anticipate the horror, even though he knew about Nazi antisemitism. The rapid conquest of Germany in the spring of 1945 left little time to dismantle the camps. Allied armies rushing to defeat remnants of the German army did not particularly target them. Few were military objectives. As a result, American soldiers liberated the camps almost by accident. Contemporary accounts reveal shock and horror. The camps stunned these experienced soldiers. Often, infantry and armored units rolled through and spent only a couple of hours. They left the camps' manifold problems for rear echelon troops, who determined what to do with the barely living and recently dead.

The discovery of the death camps changed everything. The sight and smell of a death camp exploded in soldiers' faces. Like burning phosphorus, the fact of the horror stuck to their brains and guts. The experience of liberating the camps, no matter how brief, would endure a lifetime. And the process of liberation would be repeated, often over the course of weeks, as new troops arrived and discovered the horror for themselves. Those who came later often saw more because they entered barracks farther from the entry gates of the camps.

Jewish soldiers responded to the death camps in diverse ways. For some the experience turned them into Zionists, convinced that Jews needed a state of their own because there was no future in Europe. Others were so repulsed by what they saw that they lost their faith in God. Still others sought revenge. They recognized that had they or their parents or grandparents not immigrated to the United States, they might have been suffering and dying in the camps. Meeting survivors strengthened Jewish bonds of solidarity even as it led Jewish soldiers to realize the difference their uniform made. It also forced them to realize the ghastly price paid by Jews. Far more Jews died in World War II than American or British troops.

For the vast majority of American servicemen, the war came to an end on August 15, 1945, when the Japanese surrendered. For 292,000 dead, however, the war had ended before peace arrived. They would never see home, and many remained behind buried in vast military cemeteries on foreign soil. In the American military cemeteries of World War II, endless rows of white crosses stand at attention. Scanning this sea of uniformity, eyes every so often catch an irregularity: an angular, six-pointed white star shatters the symmetry, marking the grave of an American Jewish soldier. His difference and similarity appear in the symbolism used to signify his death. Jewish sacrifice in the United States' armed forces during World War II both erased and memorialized Jewish differences from their comrades.

Beyond their shared commitment with other Americans to defend their nation and to win the war, Jews hoped to prove their loyalties and earn through their heroism a measure of respect. American Jews had much at stake in World War II. The commitment of the United States to the four freedoms—freedom from want and fear, freedom of speech and worship—promised them a future of dignity, as individuals and as a community. It was a future worth fighting for.

Deborah Dash Moore

References and Further Reading

Abzug, Robert. 1987. *Inside the Vicious Heart: Americans and the Liberation of Nazi Concentration Camps.* New York: Oxford University Press.

Bard, Mitchell G. 1994. *Forgotten Victims: The Abandonment of Americans in Hitler's Camps.* Boulder, CO: Westview Press.

Bendersky, Joseph W. 2000. *"The Jewish Threat": Anti-Semitic Politics of the U.S. Army.* New York: Basic Books.

Bernstein, Philip. 1971. *Rabbis at War.* Waltham, MA: American Jewish Historical Society.

Dinnerstein, Leonard. 1994. *Antisemitism in America.* New York: Oxford University Press.

Dublin, Louis I., and Samuel C. Kohs, eds. 1947. *American Jews in World War II: The Story of 550,000 Fighters for Freedom.* 2 Vols. New York: Dial Press.

Kaufman, Isidore. 1947. "The Story the Figures Tell." In *American Jews in World War II.* Vol. 2, 348–356. New York: Dial Press.

Kligsberg, Moses. 1950. "American Jewish Soldiers on Jews and Judaism." *YIVO Annual of Jewish Social Science* 5: 256–265.

Moore, Deborah Dash. 2004. *GI Jews: How World War II Changed a Generation.* Cambridge, MA: Harvard University Press.

Rontch, Isaac E. 1945. *Jewish Youth at War: Letters from American Soldiers.* New York: Marstin Press.

Shapiro, Edward S. 1990. "World War II and American Jewish Identity." *Modern Judaism* 10,1: 65–84.

Slomovitz, Albert Isaac. 1999. *The Fighting Rabbis: Jewish Military Chaplains and American History.* New York: New York University Press.

American Jews and the Law

The Jewish Justices of the Supreme Court

Seven Jews have served on the United States Supreme Court: Louis Dembitz Brandeis (1916–1939), Benjamin Cardozo (1932–1938), Felix Frankfurter (1939–1962), Arthur Goldberg (1962–1965), Abe Fortas (1965–1969), Ruth Bader Ginsburg (1993–), and Stephen G. Breyer (1994–). The Jewish presence on the Supreme Court has far exceeded the Jews' proportion of the population or of the U.S. Congress. Beginning with Louis Brandeis's nomination in 1916, seven of the thirty-eight (18 percent) judges appointed to the Court have been Jews, during a time when the Jewish percentage of the U.S. population peaked at 3.7 percent in the late 1930s and fell to less than 2 percent by the beginning of the current century. By comparison, although Roman Catholics comprised 20–25 percent of the population throughout that period, the number of Jews who served on the high court since 1916 nearly equals the number of Catholics. Twice during these years, two Jewish justices have served simultaneously, Justices Brandeis and Cardozo from 1932 to 1938 and Justices Ginsburg and Breyer since 1994.

The quality of the work the Jewish justices performed on the Court has been no less impressive than their number. Brandeis and Cardozo hold firm places on any "all-star" team of the nine greatest justices, and Frankfurter would be ranked as a "great" judge on more comprehensive lists. Fortas and Goldberg authored significant opinions in their brief tenures on the Court, as have current justices Ginsburg and Breyer, whose careers are still unfolding. All have been highly regarded for their intellect and their contributions to the development of American law.

Louis Dembitz Brandeis (1856–1941)

Brandeis, the first Jew appointed to the United States Supreme Court, was born in Louisville, Kentucky, on November 13, 1856, to a prosperous merchant family who had emigrated from Prague. After graduating from Harvard Law School, where he excelled, he opened a law practice in Boston. After accumulating substantial wealth as a successful corporate lawyer, Brandeis embarked on an innovative career as a "public interest lawyer," waging battles in courtrooms and legislatures on issues ranging from insurance reform to protective labor legislation. Acclaimed the "people's attorney," he became a leading figure in the Progressive movement, defending social legislation from conservative attack in a number of notable cases by preparing what came to be known as Brandeis briefs, which justified the challenged reforms by supplementing formal legal arguments with sociological and economic data. He also coauthored what was probably the most influential law review article ever written, an explication of a

Louis Brandeis, associate justice of the U.S. Supreme Court (1916–1939). (Library of Congress)

novel "right to privacy" that appeared in the *Harvard Law Review* in 1890.

Brandeis was a close adviser to President Woodrow Wilson and helped shape Wilson's New Freedom program, which sought to preserve the competitive environment of small-scale business and agriculture, in contrast to Theodore Roosevelt's New Nationalism, which accepted industrial concentration and looked to the regulation of the trusts to protect the public interest. In January 1916, Wilson nominated Brandeis for a Supreme Court seat, sparking one of the most bitter and protracted confirmation battles of American history. Brandeis's opponents comprised a good part of the American legal and corporate establishment, including seven former presidents of the American Bar Association as well as a committee of Boston Brahmins led by Harvard president A. Lawrence Lowell. They harshly assailed the nominee's ethics, professionalism, and liberal political and social views. The leading historian of the judicial confirmation process concludes that, although "the opposition was directed largely at Brandeis's social and economic record and at his 'sociological ju-

risprudence' . . . there is no question that much of the anti-Brandeis campaign was anti-Semitic in origin" (Abraham 1985). Writing to William Howard Taft, who was orchestrating the opposition to confirmation, George Wickersham (the attorney general in the ex-president's cabinet) railed against the "Hebrew uplifters" who were supporting Brandeis and claimed that "it is a disgusting fact that while many Jews privately criticize the nomination as unfit, none of them will put pen to paper to say so" (Todd 1964). Brandeis himself believed that "the dominant reasons for the opposition . . . are that he is considered a radical and is a Jew" (Mason 1946). Strongly backed by President Wilson, Brandeis was finally confirmed by the Senate in June.

Once on the Court, Brandeis forged a close personal and working relationship with the patrician Oliver Wendell Holmes Jr., who recognized in his younger colleague, despite their divergent backgrounds, a fellow aristocrat of the intellect. Their frequent votes against the Court's conservative, laissez-faire–oriented majority made "Holmes and Brandeis dissenting" a catch phrase of the era. He also maintained cordial relations with former president William Howard Taft, who was appointed Chief Justice in 1921, notwithstanding their differences in judicial philosophy and Taft's active opposition to Brandeis's appointment to the Court. By contrast, President Wilson's prior high court judicial appointee, the far less accomplished James Clark McReynolds, exhibited an unconcealed antisemitism that included a refusal to extend even minimum social amenities to the Court's first Jewish justice.

During his twenty-three years on the Court, Brandeis compiled a record of extraordinary distinction. He broke new ground in expanding protection of the freedom of speech, celebrated the rights of states to engage in social experimentation as the "laboratories of democracy," upheld a right of privacy against government intrusion, and defended the constitutionality of most New Deal efforts to combat the Depression and regulate the economy. Brandeis remained on the Court long enough to see his views on that hotly contested subject prevail by the time he retired from the Court in February 1939.

Benjamin Cardozo (1870–1938)

Cardozo was born in New York City to a distinguished Sephardic family; he was related to the poet Emma

Lazarus. Cardozo received his undergradute and legal education at Columbia University. An otherwise secure childhood was shadowed by his father's resignation from a judgeship on the New York Supreme Court (the state's trial court) to avoid impeachment on corruption charges, a disgrace that weighed on Cardozo's mind throughout his life and that may have inspired him to become a lawyer to redeem the family name. Cardozo quickly established a reputation as a "lawyer's lawyer," handling especially difficult cases that other attorneys referred to him. He was elected to the New York Supreme Court in 1913 and elevated to the state's highest court, the Court of Appeals, the next year. There he served as chief judge from 1926 until his appointment to the U.S. Supreme Court in 1932.

On the New York Court of Appeals, Cardozo proved to be one of the preeminent judges in all of American legal history, writing opinions that transformed legal doctrine on issues ranging from causation in tort law, products liability, the scope of contractual obligation, and fiduciary

Benjamin Cardozo, United States Supreme Court Justice (1932–1938). (Library of Congress)

duty. His extrajudicial speeches and writings, most notably *The Nature of the Judicial Process,* exerted a similar influence on the development of American jurisprudence. In 1932 President Herbert Hoover nominated Cardozo to replace Oliver Wendell Holmes Jr. on the Supreme Court. To date, he is the only Jewish justice to have been appointed by a Republican president. Cardozo's appointment marked "one of the few times in our history that the most qualified candidate to fill a vacancy on the Supreme Court was the one actually picked for the vacancy" (Posner 1990). Cardozo was a pillar of the legal establishment, who was held in the highest regard by both academics and the corporate bar, and his appointment to the Court did not engender the antisemitic reaction that attended that of Brandeis fifteen years earlier. Perhaps Brandeis's earlier suspicion that a Jewish Wall Street lawyer would not have faced the same intensity of opposition was thereby confirmed.

Cardozo served on the Supreme Court during an especially contentious period, as key provisions of the New Deal were held unconstitutional by the court's conservative majority. Cardozo was troubled by the delegation of power to administrative agencies and concurred in the court's invalidation of the National Recovery Act. However, he generally voted to uphold governmental economic and social regulations, believing that courts should defer to congressional and state action in those areas, first in dissent as the majority of the Court struck down such measures, and then as part of the majority that coalesced in 1937 to validate New Deal initiatives on labor relations, Social Security, and interstate commerce. Cardozo also shaped the future development of the then nascent legal issue of the scope of federal constitutional protection for individual rights, contending that the Bill of Rights extended to rights that are "the essence of a scheme of ordered liberty" (*Palko v. Connecticut*). His opinions remain oft-cited models of legal prose, admired for their literary style as well as for their analytical power.

Felix Frankfurter (1882–1965)

Frankfurter was born in Vienna and immigrated to the United States at age twelve. He graduated first in his class from Harvard Law School and embarked on a career as a nationally known—and to many, notorious—teacher, activist, and publicist, comparable only to that of his idol, Louis Brandeis. Beginning his professional career with a

United States Supreme Court Justice Felix Frankfurter (1939–1962). (Bettmann/Corbis)

New York law firm, he left after a few years to serve as an assistant to U.S. Attorney Henry Stimson, moving to a position in the War Department after President William Howard Taft appointed Stimson secretary of war. Frankfurter joined the Harvard Law School faculty in 1913, but returned to Washington during World War I, where he served as counsel to the War Labor Policies Board and on the President's Mediation Commission. Here he established a working relationship with assistant secretary of the navy and future president Franklin D. Roosevelt.

After the war, Frankfurter resumed teaching at Harvard and thrust himself into a wide range of liberal causes. He opposed the deportation of radicals arrested in the Palmer Raids, argued on behalf of reform legislation in the Supreme Court, and wrote a stream of articles on current legal and constitutional issues. Most notably, he emerged as a vigorous defender of the anarchists Nicola Sacco and Bartolomeo Vanzetti in the impassioned, but unsuccessful, campaign to block their executions.

At Harvard Law School, Frankfurter taught innovative classes on utilities regulation and administrative law, attracting a coterie of admiring, talented students. Cement-

ing his ties to Franklin Roosevelt, during the 1930s Frankfurter was a noteworthy "talent spotter" for the New Deal and placed a number of his protégés on the administration's proliferating "alphabet agencies" and the White House staff. Two of the most notable, Benjamin Cohen and Thomas Corcoran, were known as the Happy Hot Dogs in homage to their mentor. Frankfurter himself became a valued counselor to the president, proving his loyalty by working behind the scenes to support the "court packing" plan, despite his private misgivings. When Justice Cardozo died, Roosevelt appointed Frankfurter as his replacement.

With the passing of the Court's existing personnel, President Roosevelt began to shape a New Deal Court—and both those who feared the prospect and those who welcomed it expected Frankfurter to be its intellectual leader. However, as Frankfurter biographer H. N. Hirsch has written, "something went wrong. For the first time in his life, and much to his surprise, Frankfurter was faced with a situation in which he could not triumph, in which he could not overcome opposition to his policies and goals" (Hirsch 1981). To many, Frankfurter "was not as fine a judge as his pre-judicial career promised," falling short of the widely held expectation that he would be another Holmes or Brandeis—a failure that has attracted an amount of psychoanalytic conjecture unique in the annals of judicial biography (Posner 1990).

Formed in an era when courts regularly struck down social and economic reform legislation as unconstitutional extensions of the commerce power or as undue restrictions on the freedom to contract, Frankfurter's philosophy of judicial restraint left him at odds with a developing trend in liberal legal thought that looked to the courts to curb executive and legislative power when governmental action limited individual rights. Frankfurter generally upheld governmental efforts to combat domestic communism, although he did write a strong dissent to the court's opinion sanctioning the execution of the Rosenbergs. He opposed the application of the exclusionary rule in criminal prosecutions, thereby upholding the use at trial of evidence obtained by the police through searches and seizures that violated constitutional safeguards, and deferred to Congress and legislatures on reapportionment questions.

Frankfurter did, however, play a prominent role in what was perhaps the most important case decided during his time on the Court, *Brown v. Board of Education*. Although he did not write the Court's opinion, the decision may count as his most significant accomplishment as a justice. Frankfurter labored persistently behind the scenes to forge what turned out to be the Court's unanimous 1954 decision declaring segregated educational facilities unconstitutional. Indeed, when Chief Justice Fred Vinson, who had been reluctant to depart from the "separate but equal" doctrine, suddenly died at a critical moment in the court's deliberations, the agnostic Frankfurter was moved to say that it was "the first solid piece of evidence I've ever had that there really is a God" (Elman 1987). The often criticized judicial craftsmanship of new Chief Justice Earl Warren's opinion may not have met the exacting standards of Professor Frankfurter, but Justice Frankfurter had largely orchestrated the result.

After suffering a disabling stroke in 1962, Frankfurter resigned from the Court. He died three years later.

Arthur J. Goldberg (1908–1990)

Goldberg was born in Chicago on August 8. Earning a law degree from Northwestern University at twenty-one, Goldberg began his career at a corporate law firm but gravitated to the representation of labor unions in the new field of labor law. After service in the Office of Strategic Services in World War II, he became counsel to the United Steelworkers of America and the Congress of Industrial Organizations (CIO) in 1948, playing a key role in the merger of the CIO and the American Federation of Labor in 1955. He served as secretary of labor under President John F. Kennedy, who appointed him to fill the "Jewish seat" on the Supreme Court vacated by Felix Frankfurter in 1962.

Breaking sharply with Frankfurter's philosophy of judicial restraint, Goldberg provided the crucial fifth vote to empower and expand the Warren Court's legal revolution, on issues ranging from legislative reapportionment to criminal procedure to privacy rights. But his tenure on the court was brief. Seeking to place his trusted confidant Abe Fortas on the Court, President Lyndon B. Johnson induced Goldberg to leave the Court and succeed Adlai Stevenson as U.S. ambassador to the United Nations in the summer of 1965. The president led Goldberg to believe that he could play a key role in negotiating an end to the escalating war in Vietnam. Johnson may have also held out the prospect that he could become the first Jewish vice presidential candidate or could return to the Court in the future.

Arthur Goldberg, associate justice of the U.S. Supreme Court (1962–1965). (Collection of the Supreme Court of the United States)

None of this came to pass. The Vietnam War continued to escalate; Goldberg's recommendations to the contrary were brushed aside, their only effect being the removal of any chance for a return to the Court under the angry president's auspices. He resigned as UN ambassador in 1968. Nominated as the Democratic candidate for governor of New York in 1970, he was defeated by Nelson Rockefeller. Goldberg spent the balance of his professional career in the private practice of law; in the late 1970s he also served as a roving ambassador in the Carter administration. He died in Washington, D.C., on January 19, 1990.

Abe Fortas (1910–1982)

Born in Memphis, Tennessee, on June 19, 1910, Fortas was educated at that city's Southwestern College and at Yale Law School. In the 1930s, Fortas held legal positions at the Agricultural Adjustment Administration (AAA) and the Securities and Exchange Commission (SEC), forging a reputation as one of the most brilliant of the New Deal lawyers. He joined the Department of the Interior in 1939

Abe Fortas, associate justice of the U.S. Supreme Court (1965–1969). (Library of Congress)

and was named undersecretary in 1942. He entered private practice in Washington after World War II.

While in government service, Fortas became a friend and highly valued counselor to the ambitious Texas congressman Lyndon B. Johnson. Fortas successfully represented him in the court battle over the disputed outcome of the 1948 election that brought Johnson into the Senate. Fortas's law firm (Arnold, Fortas & Porter) combined corporate practice with the representation of targets of congressional investigations and security inquiries during the McCarthy era. The firm's pro bono litigation included Fortas's argument before the Supreme Court of the case (*Gideon v. Wainright*) that established the defendant's right to counsel in state felony cases.

Intent on rewarding Fortas with an appointment to the Supreme Court, President Johnson maneuvered around Fortas's protestations of disinterest, as well as the more pointed objections of Fortas's wife (Carolyn Agger, a noted tax lawyer), to induce Arthur Goldberg to leave the Court, naming Fortas to replace him in the summer of 1965. Fortas followed in Goldberg's path as a key vote for the Warren Court's activist, individual rights–oriented ju-

risprudence and quickly established himself as a highly competent justice in his own right. Despite a tenure of less than four years on the Court, he has been rated a "near great" justice in surveys of scholarly opinion.

However, Fortas's work on the Court did not quell his restless interest in politics and policy—or dissuade Johnson from seeking his private counsel, and this proved to be a grievous misstep. Justice Fortas continued to advise Johnson on a wide range of extrajudicial matters, overstepping generally accepted bounds of proper judicial conduct. President Johnson nominated Fortas to succeed Earl Warren as Chief Justice in 1968. Conservative critics of the Warren Court filibustered the nomination. In a last-ditch effort to overcome the opposition, the justice's supporters highlighted his religious affiliation, attempting to brand Republican opponents as abettors of antisemitism who would face a backlash from Jewish voters. The "anti-antisemitism card" was defused by Jewish Republican senator Jacob Javits's statement that antisemitism was not an issue in the controversy, but after a motion to force an up-or-down vote failed, the nomination was withdrawn.

In spring 1969, charges of an improper financial relationship with a former client led to Fortas's resignation from the Supreme Court. The former justice returned to the private practice of law, but not at the firm he had founded, which refused to take him back. In March 1982 Fortas once again appeared in the Supreme Court, this time as a lawyer arguing a case. He won—but the unanimous decision in his client's favor was not announced until after his death on April 5, 1982.

Ruth Bader Ginsburg (b. 1933)

Ginsburg was born in Brooklyn, New York, on March 15. She attended Cornell University and Harvard and Columbia Law Schools. After clerking for a New York federal judge, she was associated with the Columbia Law School Project on International Procedure and then taught at Rutgers and Columbia Law Schools. In the 1970s, she helped launch the Women's Rights Project of the American Civil Liberties Union and from 1973 to 1980 served as the ACLU's general counsel. In a series of precedent-setting gender equity lawsuits, she pursued an innovative legal strategy that successfully challenged the disparate treatment of men and women under various statutes by suing on behalf of men who claimed that they were being dis-

scope of sexual harassment law, and the separation of church and state.

Stephen G. Breyer (b. 1938)

Breyer was born to a prominent Jewish family in San Francisco on August 15, 1938. Educated at Stanford University and Harvard Law School, he was a law clerk to Supreme Court Justice Goldberg. His subsequent career included a position in the antitrust division of the Justice Department, teaching and writing at Harvard Law School, especially on governmental regulation, and service as a congressional committee counsel, all of which enhanced his reputation as a leading figure in administrative law. He was appointed to the First Circuit Court of Appeals in 1990, where he served as chief judge until his appointment to the Supreme Court in 1994.

President Clinton considered Judge Breyer for his first appointment to the Court in 1993, but passed him over after an unsuccessful interview. When another Court

Ruth Bader Ginsburg, associate justice of the U.S. Supreme Court (1993–). (Corbis)

criminated against on account of *their* sex. In 1980 she was appointed to the United States Court of Appeals for the District of Columbia. In 1993 President Bill Clinton nominated her to the Supreme Court. The second female justice in the Court's history, she was the Court's first Jewish justice since 1969.

On a Court that was often sharply divided, Ginsburg established herself as one of the more liberal justices. Although she had earlier expressed doubts about the legal reasoning of the *Roe v. Wade* abortion rights decision, as a Justice she was stalwart in her defense of a woman's right to choose and staked out liberal positions on civil rights, women's rights (writing the opinion that ordered that women be admitted to Virginia Military Institute), the

Stephen Breyer, associate justice of the U.S. Supreme Court (1994–). (Collection of the Supreme Court of the United States)

vacancy occurred the next year, Breyer was selected, after Clinton abandoned his initial impulse to appoint a political figure with "real-world" experience. With a judicial record that combined a market-based analysis of economic issues with liberal views on social policy, and with service on the United States Sentencing Commission that had established tough guidelines for criminal sentences, Breyer's nomination was calculated to provide the Court with a justice with impeccable academic and professional credentials who could be a "consensus builder," in Clinton's description.

True to expectations, Breyer has compiled a moderately liberal record on the Court. Frequently aligned with fellow Clinton appointee (and fellow former academic) Justice Ginsburg, he resisted the Rehnquist Court's attempt to delimit the reach of federal governmental powers in favor of the states. Justice Breyer has, however, parted company with her on other occasions, most notably in the 2000 presidential election case, in which he, unlike Justice Ginsburg, voted with the majority in finding that the Florida recount process violated the Constitution's equal protection clause, but then (along with Ginsburg and two other justices) dissented from the Court's decision to terminate the recount process entirely.

Jewish Lives

Louis Brandeis, the first Jew on the Supreme Court, came from the least observant background of any of the Jewish justices; yet he is the only one who played a leading role in the American—indeed, the world—Jewish community. If Brandeis's quality and influence as a judge remain unmatched by his Jewish successors on the Court, the same is true of his contributions as a Jewish leader.

Brandeis's parents emigrated to the United States from Prague in 1849 and settled in Louisville, Kentucky, a few years before Louis was born in 1856. Brandeis's mother was a descendant of Jacob Frank, the eighteenth-century follower of the "false messiah" Sabbatai Zvi. She imparted to her son her rationalist worldview that eschewed the ritual aspects of traditional Judaism, while acknowledging that it had, in her words, "a lofty conception of morality" (Gal 1980). The Brandeis family was nonobservant. Brandeis received no religious instruction, did not have a bar mitzvah, and never practiced Jewish rituals. He first set foot inside a synagogue when he appeared at a Zionist con-

vention at the age of sixty. He exchanged Christmas presents with his relatives and did not observe the Jewish holidays. He first publicly affiliated with a Jewish organization in 1905, when he addressed a Jewish group in support of a progressive candidate in a local political campaign.

Thereafter, Brandeis's ties to the Jewish community and to a network of Jewish social and legal reformers increased, drawing him toward the one great Jewish cause of his life: Zionism. His efforts to settle the New York garment workers' strike in 1910 brought him into contact with East European Jewish immigrants, whom he had never before encountered, eliciting in him a newfound sense of kinship with his fellow Jews. In their commitment to collective action in pursuit of a better life, he recognized his own secular vision of a good society. He wrote, "I now saw the true democracy of my people, their idealistic inclinations and their love of liberty and freedom" (Urofsky 1981). Although not a religious nationalist, he found in Zionism the vehicle for creating in Palestine the egalitarian, democratic, cooperative society that could avoid the "curse of bigness" that he was battling in the United States.

In 1912, Brandeis formally joined the Federation of American Zionists. Two years later, he was elected chairman of the Provisional Executive Committee for General Zionist Affairs and assumed the leadership of the American Zionist movement, becoming its most prominent spokesman. After World War I, however, he clashed with world Zionist leader Chaim Weizmann over the stance Zionist organizations should assume toward Great Britain's Palestine mandate. Brandeis argued that the time had come for the movement's "propagandists" to yield to the "builders," who would develop the infrastructure of Palestine in cooperation with the mandatory authority. Weizmann and his allies insisted that the realization of Zionism's goals required continued political and organizational activity among Jews in the Diaspora. Brandeis and his American followers "were not in favour of diaspora nationalism and refused to pay for Zionist activities outside Palestine." Weizmann and the European Zionists scorned Brandeis's approach as "Zionism without Zionists" and claimed that the "American Zionists lacked a 'Jewish heart'" (Laqueur 1972). Weizmann prevailed and Brandeis was ousted from the Zionist leadership.

Nevertheless, Brandeis remained an active elder statesman of American Zionism. He saw his allies recapture the leadership of the American Zionist movement in the 1930s and assisted in the practical efforts required to build a Jewish homeland in Palestine. His last years "were spent reading, writing letters, motoring, talking with friends, and promoting Zionism" (Mason 1946).

The religious background of the Court's second Jewish justice, Benjamin Cardozo, differed radically from that of Brandeis and sets him apart from the Jewish justices who followed him onto the Court as well. The only justice from a Sephardic family, Cardozo's ancestors—allegedly, Portuguese *conversos* (converts) who fled the Inquisition—arrived in the American colonies from London a quarter century before the Revolution. Cardozo's father was a synagogue officer, and Benjamin's upbringing was Orthodox. Shortly after his bar mitzvah, however, Benjamin stopped attending synagogue services and later alluded to "the devastating years" that "obliterated youthful faiths" (Polenberg 1997).

Although he did not attend services, Cardozo remained a member of Shearith Israel—the synagogue of his grandparents—throughout his life (even speaking in favor of maintaining separate seating for men and women in a congregational debate on the issue), and he continued to maintain a kosher home. Indeed, Cardozo's ties to Shearith Israel proved crucial in launching his judicial career. In 1913, the Fusion Party ticket makers nominated Cardozo for a judgeship on the New York Supreme Court. Seeking a religiously balanced slate, they chose Cardozo, a supporter explained, because his rival "is a Felix Adler [the founder of Ethical Culture] Jew, a Modernist. The man you want is a *real* Jew. I'll tell you the man, Cardozo. He is [in] the Portuguese Synagogue" (Kaufman 1998).

Apart from his ties to his family's synagogue, until he became a judge Cardozo had eschewed involvement in Jewish community affairs. In the 1920s, however, he joined the American Jewish Committee (AJCommittee), serving on its executive committee, the board of the American Friends of Hebrew University, and the Jewish Welfare Board, although his participation was limited. Cardozo was not a community leader. Although privately appreciative of the efforts of Jews in the forefront of the struggle against antisemitism, he avoided public comment on antisemitic incidents and joined the Century Club, despite the antisemitism of many of its members. Determined to avoid any appearance of judicial impropriety, he was especially concerned that the actions of a Jewish judge not be construed as placing religious loyalty over legal standards,

and privately he criticized a Jewish magistrate who inserted anti-Nazi political beliefs in an opinion.

Cardozo was notably wary about Zionism, viewing it as a cause with primary appeal to recently arrived East European Jews. In 1916, he rebuffed a plea for support from an American Zionist leader, saying he did not "see how it would help me walking up Fifth Avenue in New York if there were a Jewish state in Palestine" (Kaufman 1998). Within a few years, under the importuning of Justice Brandeis and the prominent rabbi Stephen Wise, Cardozo agreed to affiliate with the Zionist Organization of America, albeit halfheartedly, writing, "I am not yet an enthusiast. But to-day, the line seems to be forming between those who are for the cause and those who are against, with little room for a third camp. I am not willing to join those who are against, so I go over to the others" (Kaufman 1998). But even Cardozo's limited involvement in Jewish communal affairs ended with his appointment to the U.S. Supreme Court in 1932.

Unlike Cardozo, whose family had lived in New York since the eighteenth century, Felix Frankfurter, his successor on the Court, was an immigrant, who arrived in New York at age twelve. Although he "never had heard a word of English spoken," Frankfurter assimilated rapidly. Raised as a practicing Jew, he abandoned religious ritual while a junior at City College, leaving the Yom Kippur service "in the middle of it, never to return" (Burt 1988). Awed at first by the august atmosphere of Harvard Law School—where, the diminutive Frankfurter recalled, "everyone was taller"—he compiled an outstanding academic record and ingratiated himself with leading figures of the legal establishment. Despite this, he found it difficult to gain employment with New York's major law firms, since they generally excluded Jews. Of the firm that finally hired him, he said, "I'd heard that they had never taken a Jew and wouldn't take a Jew. I decided that was the office I wanted to get into," although he rejected the hiring partner's advice that he change his name (Lash 1975).

Frankfurter never denied his Jewishness but associated Jewishness with the immigrant milieu of his childhood. Thus, it was something to move beyond. "To become a full-fledged American," one biographer has argued, "Frankfurter had to separate himself from his immigrant past" (Burt 1988). The once poor boy from the Lower East Side was strongly attracted to the Boston Brahmin lifestyle of a Harvard faculty member. He married the daughter of a

Congregational minister and was proud of her "old Yankee stock" (Burt 1988). His engagement in Jewish causes was rare. Although he did challenge Harvard president A. Lawrence Lowell's imposition of a quota on Jewish enrollment, it was more as an affront to meritocratic values than an expression of religious prejudice. His favorite protégés at Harvard Law School were generally non-Jews. He became involved in Zionist activities in support of Brandeis's efforts, but his interest waned after Brandeis's death, although he did press the Zionist cause in private conversations with British officials during World War II.

Throughout his adult life, Frankfurter did not practice the Jewish faith and was unaffiliated with the Jewish community, but in planning his funeral he took care to include as a speaker a colleague whom he described as "my only close friend who is also a practicing, orthodox Jew. He . . . will know exactly what to say. I came into the world a Jew and although I did not live my life entirely as a Jew, I think it fitting that I should leave as a Jew" (Lash 1975).

The backgrounds of Brandeis, Cardozo, and Frankfurter were, albeit in different ways, unrepresentative of the broader American Jewish community as it coalesced in the first decades of the twentieth century; by contrast, those of Abe Fortas and Arthur Goldberg were entirely characteristic. Unlike their Jewish predecessors, their parents had come to the United States in the great wave of post-1881 immigration from East Europe. Both grew away from the traditional religious practices that characterized their upbringing; both saw their professional choices constrained by antisemitism, and both came to terms with Judaism as adults in representative ways.

Abe Fortas studied Hebrew and was bar mitzvahed, but, although his mother kept a kosher home, the family was not very religious and attended synagogue only on the High Holidays. One biographer concluded that "he always identified himself as a Jew, but he viewed his religion as a handicap to disclose rather than a heritage to claim"; he complained that he had "suffered disadvantages and discrimination" because he was a Jew (Kalman 1990). Conscious of being an outsider as a youth in Memphis, Fortas encountered at Yale Law School an environment where, despite their academic successes, Jews were excluded from social organizations and even a tolerant faculty member assured prospective employers that a Jewish student "had no traces of those characteristics which one associates with Hebrews" (Kalman 1990).

In adult life, Judaism as a religion held little appeal to him, but he became more sensitive to Jewish community concerns after he was appointed to the Court. He stayed home on Yom Kippur, spoke to Jewish groups more frequently, and served as an intermediary between American Jewish organizations and the White House. During the Six Day War, Fortas provided an important "back channel" between the Israeli Embassy and President Johnson, evidencing a concern for the Jewish state that was, arguably, inconsistent with proper standards of judicial behavior.

Arthur Goldberg, the son of a struggling produce peddler who died when Arthur was eight, grew up in the impoverished immigrant milieu of Chicago's Maxwell Street neighborhood, "schooled from childhood in rock-throwing self-defense against Jew-hating Poles and Irish who waylaid him en route to school" (Stebenne 1996). Education was Goldberg's route to a better life. He graduated from Northwestern Law School with the best record in its history and was admitted to practice at the age of twenty-one. Despite his accomplishments, his employment opportunities were limited. Jews were barred from Chicago's most prominent law firms, and Goldberg accepted a job at a less prestigious firm that had been founded by German Jews. Within a few years, he left corporate practice altogether for labor law, where he established the reputation that would carry him to the cabinet and the Supreme Court.

Goldberg made a point of saying, "I'm proud of my Jewish heritage, I don't like any American who's not proud of his heritage" (Lowe 1994). He compiled a strong record of Jewish organizational leadership, including service as president of the AJCommittee, chairman of the board of overseers of Jewish Theological Seminary, and president of the International Association of Jewish Lawyers. As head of the American delegation to the first Helsinki Accords review conference in 1977–1978, he pressed the Soviet Union on the issue of Jewish immigration. A less successful venture was his chairmanship in the early 1980s of the American Jewish Commission on the Holocaust, which, "despite its grandiose title, had no mandate from any responsible institution" and dissolved in an acrimonious controversy over what critics regarded as its draft report's "undocumented charges against the Jewish community" for allegedly failing to assist European Jewry (Kozodoy 1992).

The current Jewish justices exemplify the variegated threads of the contemporary American Jewish experience. If Fortas and Goldberg were the children of the great wave of Jewish immigration to the United States at the turn of the twentieth century, Justices Ruth Bader Ginsburg and Stephen Breyer are its grandchildren. Growing up in more assimilated, although still Jewish, milieus, neither endured the economic hardships or religious discrimination that Fortas and Goldberg overcame in their paths to the bench. Both were educated at elite universities and law schools, and antisemitic prejudices never impeded their careers, inside or outside academia. "Jews in the United States," Justice Ginsburg has said, "face few closed doors and do not fear letting the world know who we are" (Ginsburg 2002). After finishing law school, Breyer served as a law clerk to Arthur Goldberg, but Ginsburg found her clerkship aspirations frustrated by Felix Frankfurter's unwillingness to hire a female law clerk, despite her outstanding law school record—an experience that prefigured her life's work as a pioneering women's rights attorney. Each found inspiration in the example set by the Court's first Jewish justice, but each expressed the sentiment differently. When honored with the University of Louisville's Brandeis Medal, Justice Ginsburg devoted her address to a highly personal appraisal of the status of Jews in the law from the time of Judah Benjamin to the present; Breyer, to an academic exposition of the enduring relevance of Brandeis's mode of jurisprudence (Ginsburg 2002; Breyer 2004).

Justices Ginsburg and Breyer have both lived lives that testify to American Jewry's newly found sense of acceptance. Ginsburg is the most conspicuously Jewish of any justice since Brandeis. She speaks regularly to Jewish audiences and has affixed a mezuzah to the doorpost of her court office, which is adorned with plaques and mementos bearing the biblical quotation "*Tzedek, tzedek tirdof*" ("Justice, justice shall you pursue"). Charting the progress of American Jewry in personal terms, Justice Ginsburg wrote, "what is the difference between a New York City garment district bookkeeper and a Supreme Court Justice? One generation, my life bears witness: the opportunities open to my mother, a bookkeeper, and those open to me" (Ginsburg 2003).

Justice Breyer's life provides an equally telling index of American Jewish adaptation. Breyer married into the British aristocracy, attended the Episcopal Church with his family (a daughter studied for the ministry and became an Episcopal priest), and was unaffiliated with the organized Jewish community, but began holding seders on Passover and attending High Holiday services later in his life.

Jewish Seat, Jewish Justice?

According to a venerable, although perhaps apocryphal, tradition, the first Jew considered for appointment to the Supreme Court was Judah Benjamin of Louisiana, who declined an offer from either President Millard Fillmore or Franklin Pierce in early 1853, and instead entered the U.S. Senate. If an offer was made (there is apparently no contemporary documentation confirming it), it certainly was not made to fill a "Jewish seat" on the court. Nor was Woodrow Wilson filling a Jewish seat when Louis Brandeis became the first Jewish justice six decades later. Brandeis's appointment was due to his standing as the country's most renowned progressive lawyer and the valuable services he had rendered Wilson's administration. That Brandeis was Jewish did not figure significantly in the decision. Similarly, Benjamin Cardozo owed his nomination to his reputation as the country's outstanding jurist, not to his religious affiliation. It was only when Cardozo's tenure ended with his sudden death in 1938 that the concept of a Jewish seat took hold in the high court appointment process.

By then, Jews had become a key constituent of Roosevelt's emerging New Deal coalition, particularly in eastern and midwestern states, where Jewish votes could decide closely contested elections. Jewish lawyers played important roles in the administrative agencies established to combat the Depression. Abe Fortas served his legal apprenticeship in the AAA and SEC; Arthur Goldberg made his mark as counsel to labor unions contending with the new legal structure for labor relations introduced by the Wagner Act. Elite law schools produced a stream of Jewish graduates with impeccable academic credentials, who were beginning to find prestigious places on law school faculties. At a time when a "black seat" or "woman's seat" lay beyond the political imagination, the idea of a Jewish seat took hold, with a supply of highly qualified candidates at hand. It was a way of recognizing the "Jewish" contribution to the New Deal, both as voters and lawyers, and it marked the Depression-era Democratic Party's openness to immigrant communities previously excluded from the councils of state.

Although Cardozo served on the Court while Brandeis was still on the bench, with the subsequent appointments of Frankfurter, Goldberg, and Fortas, one Jewish justice filled a seat vacated by another. When Frankfurter stepped down in 1962, President Kennedy and Attorney General Robert Kennedy expressly discussed the "necessity of replacing Frankfurter with a Jew," and noted that "the various Jewish organizations would be upset if this appointment did not go to a person of the Jewish faith" (Schlesinger 1978). These appointments reflected both the rise of Jews in the larger legal community and the major role they played as legal crafters of the New Deal, at a time when government service provided opportunities not available in the large law firms, which still generally excluded Jews. The bond between Jewish lawyers and the Democratic Party was therefore particularly close, and during the era of the Jewish seat all Jewish court appointees were named by Democratic presidents. That tradition ended in 1969 when Republican president Richard M. Nixon attempted to fill Fortas's seat with a justice from the southern states, which he hoped to meld into an "emerging Republican majority" coalition. After his initial two southern nominees were not confirmed, he named Harry Blackmun to the seat, leaving the Court without a Jewish justice for the first time in over half a century.

In the subsequent two decades, there was one prospective Jewish justice. Federal appeals court judge Douglas Ginsburg was nominated by President Reagan in 1987, but Judge Ginsburg withdrew from consideration after his marijuana use while a law professor was reported. By then, the tradition of a Jewish seat had been eclipsed by new concerns that women and African Americans should be represented on the court. Nor was the tradition restored when President Bill Clinton appointed Ruth Bader Ginsburg and Stephen Breyer to fill the two vacancies that arose during his term. Neither was viewed as a representative of the Jewish community. Their religion apparently did not enter into the nomination decision, nor did the media give it much attention, although it marked the first time that a president had appointed two Jews to the Court. "No one saw us as filling a Jewish seat," Justice Ginsburg has said, contending that "our religion simply was not relevant to President Clinton's appointments" (Ginsburg 2002).

By the time Justices Ginsburg and Breyer were appointed, there had been a shift in the background of lawyers considered for the Court, a transformation reflected in the contrast between their career paths and those of their Jewish predecessors. The time when presidents

looked to Congress (Alabama senator Hugo Black), the statehouse (California governor Earl Warren), or the cabinet (Secretary of State John Marshall) for nominees with independent political standing and prestige had passed. To date, Arthur Goldberg is the last cabinet member named to the high court. With one exception, each justice nominated by all presidents since Nixon has been a sitting judge on a federal appeals court or, in O'Connor's case, a state supreme court. There was no repetition of Lyndon Johnson's selection of his confidant and counselor, Abe Fortas, until Harriet Miers's nomination in 2005.

In the two decades since Fortas left the bench under fire, the Court appointment pool has been professionalized, consisting almost entirely of candidates with proven judicial track records, but without constituencies of their own outside the legal profession. Even as the demographic composition of the Court has become more inclusive, the recruitment path for prospective justices has narrowed. Justices Ginsburg and Breyer fit comfortably within this trend. Both were federal appeals court judges when nominated. Both had compiled distinguished academic records at an elite law school, but neither was a public personality of note. Highly respected legal professionals, neither was the kind of political player who had regularly sat on the Court from its creation through the 1960s. Neither claimed the stature that Brandeis or Frankfurter attained through years of highly publicized legal and political activism before appointment to the high court bench, nor the singular distinction of being the nation's preeminent jurist that had impelled Cardozo's selection. The nomination of a sitting judge, even one as distinguished as Cardozo, was relatively uncommon in his time. Now it is the norm. Justices Ginsburg and Breyer earned their way to the Court as skilled professionals in an age of professionalism.

Given the prominent place that Jews hold in a legal profession shorn of the prejudices that once restricted their opportunities, the demise of the Jewish seat as a political set-aside may actually enhance the prospects for future Jewish appointments to the Court. Reserving *one* seat for a Jewish justice imposed an implicit ceiling on the number of such appointments. President Johnson evidently believed that the appointment of his longtime confidant Abe Fortas to the Court would be more acceptable if Justice Goldberg could be induced to resign. The concurrent service of Justices Ginsburg and Breyer, by contrast, reflects the readiness of a president to make such appointments unconstrained by an implicit quota. In addition, the emergence of a cadre of conservative Jewish lawyers and judges increases the likelihood that future appointments will be by Republican, as well as Democratic, presidents, as President Ronald Reagan's nomination of Douglas Ginsburg suggested.

In assessing the significance of the Jewish presence on the Supreme Court to American Jewish history, it is notable that, unlike Thurgood Marshall, whose route to the Court reflected his status as the leading legal strategist of the civil rights revolution, none of the Jewish justices was appointed as a result of his or her involvement in Jewish causes. Brandeis's recent embrace of Zionism did not play a role in his appointment. Although Ruth Bader Ginsburg is known as the "Thurgood Marshall of gender-equity law," she gained this reputation through her efforts on behalf of women's causes, not Jewish ones. Indeed, apart from Brandeis, who played an important role in the Zionist movement, none of the Jewish justices would merit a place in a history of American Jewry were it not for their service on the Court.

Many have suggested that the Jewish justices brought a particular perspective to the Court, derived from their common heritage and reflected in their commitment to individual rights and the eradication of injustice. Arthur Goldberg explained, "my concern for justice, for peace, for enlightenment, all stem from my heritage" (Lowe 1994). Justice Ginsburg described the "law as protector of the oppressed, the poor, the minority, the loner," a view she found "evident in the life body of work of Justice Brandeis, as it is in the legacies of Justices Cardozo, Frankfurter, Goldberg, and Fortas, the remaining four of the first five Jewish Justices" (Ginsburg 2002). She explained, "I am a judge, born, raised and proud of being a Jew. The demand for justice runs through the entirety of the Jewish history and Jewish tradition. I hope . . . to remain steadfast in the service of that demand" (Ginsburg 2002).

For Goldberg and Ginsburg, these impulses found primary expression in the labor movement (Goldberg) and the women's movement (Ginsburg), not in Jewish causes. Moreover, a sense of Jewish identity and heritage has been reflected in judicial decision-making in more varied and complex ways than these views allow. This can be seen in the best-known, and most passionate, evocation of Jewish heritage by a justice, Frankfurter's dissent in the 1943 flag salute case, *West Virginia State Board of Education v. Bar-*

nette. Here the Court reversed a 1940 decision (written by Frankfurter) that had upheld the mandatory pledge of allegiance and flag salute in public schools. In an extraordinarily emotional preface to his argument in support of the constitutionality of the mandatory pledge, Frankfurter took pains to say that "one who belongs to the most vilified and persecuted minority in history is not likely to be insensible to the freedoms guaranteed by our Constitution." If, as a familiar legal maxim holds, general principles do not decide specific cases, neither does the Jewishness of the judge.

Clearly, the Jewish justices have derived different life lessons from their common Jewish heritage. Robert A. Burt argues that, although Brandeis and Frankfurter shared a perception that as Jews they were "outcasts in a promised land," they "drew diametrically opposed lessons" from that experience. Brandeis "acknowledged a basic identity with outcasts" that he carried into his work on the Court, and "embraced homelessness as his heritage and drew strength from it." By contrast, "to become a full-fledged American . . . Frankfurter had to separate himself from his immigrant past," becoming an "overeager apologist for the existing order." He "struggled against acknowledging his outcast status . . . and he always remained homeless in spite of himself" (Burt 1988).

Still, one must be wary in ascribing too much weight to a Jewish component in the judicial philosophies of the Jewish justices. Justice Brandeis, the embodiment of the judge as prophet—referred to as "Isaiah" by Franklin Roosevelt—and the author of notable free speech opinions, was also a notable exponent of the virtues of judicial "abstention." "The most important thing we do," he wrote, "is not doing." Similarly, he was the architect of the doctrine—reversing a century of practice—that federal courts were bound by state court rulings in cases arising under state law and were not free to fashion "general federal common law" in such cases. And the doctrine of judicial restraint became a hallmark of Frankfurter's increasingly conservative tenure on the court. But his replacements in the "Jewish seat," Goldberg and then Fortas, fully embraced and helped shape the work of the Warren Court toward a more activist role for the courts. Such contrasting views invite caution in drawing sweeping conclusions about the influence of a Jewish heritage on the judicial philosophy of the Jewish justices or on what "the demand for justice" may mean in any particular case.

The extent to which a common religious or ethnic identity influenced the judicial philosophies of the Supreme Court's Jewish justices may be debatable, but the intellectual distinction of their work on the Court is not. Perhaps no one has recognized this more plainly than Nebraska senator Roman Hruska. In a memorable defense of Richard Nixon's unsuccessful nomination of G. Harrold Carswell to the Supreme Court, Senator Hruska pleaded that "there are a lot of mediocre people who deserve some representation. . . . They can't all be Brandeises and Cardozos and that stuff." Whatever else might be said of them, none of the Jewish justices of the Supreme Court have been mediocre.

Henry D. Fetter

References and Further Reading

Abraham, Henry J. 1985. *Justices and Presidents: A Political History of Appointments to the Supreme Court.* 2nd ed. New York: Oxford University Press.

Breyer, Stephen G. 2004. "Justice Brandeis as a Legal Seer." Available at: http://www.supremecourtus.gov/publicinfo/speeches/sp_02–16–04.html. Accessed June 23, 2004.

Burt, Robert A. 1988. *Two Jewish Justices: Outcasts in the Promised Land.* Berkeley: University of California Press.

Elman, Philip. 1987. "The Solicitor General's Office, Justice Frankfurter, and Civil Rights Litigation, 1946–60: An Oral History." *Harvard Law Review* 100 (February): 817–852.

Gal, Allon. 1980. *Brandeis of Boston.* Cambridge, MA: Harvard University Press.

Ginsburg, Ruth Bader. 2002. "From Benjamin to Brandeis to Breyer: Is There a Jewish Seat?" *Brandeis Law Journal* 41 (Winter): 229–236.

Ginsburg, Ruth Bader. 2003. "Justice, Guardian of Liberty." *Forward* (May 30).

Hirsch, H. N. 1981. *The Enigma of Felix Frankfurter.* New York: Basic Books.

Kalman, Laura. 1990. *Abe Fortas.* New Haven, CT: Yale University Press.

Kaufman, Andrew L. 1998. *Cardozo.* Cambridge, MA: Harvard University Press.

Kozodoy, Neal, ed. 1992. *What Is the Use of Jewish History: Essays by Lucy S. Dawidowicz.* New York: Shocken Books.

Laqueur, Walter. 1972. *A History of Zionism.* New York: Holt, Rinehart and Winston.

Lash, Joseph. P., ed. 1975. *From the Diaries of Felix Frankfurter.* New York: W. W. Norton.

Lowe, Jennifer M., ed. 1994. *The Jewish Justices of the Supreme Court Revisited: Brandeis to Fortas.* Washington, DC: Supreme Court Historical Society.

Mason, Alpheus Thomas. 1946. *Brandeis: A Free Man's Life.* New York: Viking.

Murphy, Bruce Allen, 1982. *The Brandeis–Frankfurter Connection: The Secret Political Activities of Two Supreme Court Justices.* New York: Oxford University Press.

Polenberg, Richard. 1997. *The World of Benjamin Cardozo.* Cambridge, MA: Harvard University Press.

Posner, Richard A. 1990. *Cardozo: A Study in Reputation.* Chicago: University of Chicago Press.

Schlesinger, Arthur M., Jr. 1978. *Robert Kennedy and His Times.* Boston: Houghton Mifflin.

Stebenne, David L. 1996. *Arthur J. Goldberg: New Deal Liberal.* New York: Oxford University Press.

Todd, A. L. 1964. *Justice on Trial.* New York: McGraw-Hill.

Urofsky, Melvin I. 1981. *Louis D. Brandeis and the Progressive Tradition.* Boston: Little Brown.

American Jews and Crime

American Jewish Gangsters

Crime and gangsterism form part of the Jewish experience in the United States, and ignoring it presents a distorted and incomplete picture of the American Jewish experience. From their earliest settlement in America, Jews enjoyed the reputation of being among the nation's most law-abiding and least violent citizens. "If we enter a penitentiary or prison of any description," observed one nineteenth-century newspaper editor, "the marked face of an Israelite is rarely to be seen within its walls" (Joselit 1983). By the end of the nineteenth century the situation had changed, and Jewish names increasingly appeared on police blotters in the large urban centers. For the most part, these Jewish criminals worked as confidence men, pickpockets, and thieves, rarely engaging in crimes of violence and murder.

By World War I this, too, had changed. During the period 1881–1914, over 2 million Jews from Eastern Europe entered the United States, most of them crowding into the ethnic enclaves of the great cities of the East Coast and Midwest. Boston's North End, Chicago's West Side, Philadelphia's South Side, and especially New York's Lower East Side were among the better-known. Densely populated, filthy, and disease-ridden, these districts proved to be breeding grounds for Jewish gangs whose members were more vicious and violent than their nineteenth-century predecessors. While Jewish gangs had existed before 1914,

the Prohibition Era (1919–1933) spawned large, powerful crime syndicates, led by Jewish criminals such as Louis "Lepke" Buchalter, Benjamin "Bugsy" Siegel, Meyer "The Little Man" Lansky, Max "Boo Boo" Hoff, Charley "King" Solomon, Moe Dalitz, and Abner "Longy" Zwillman. Between the World Wars, these men, together with their Italian-American associates, organized American crime, making it large, powerful, and deadly. Yet these men had no successors. When they left the scene, the heyday of the Jewish gangster ended.

In 1908, New York police commissioner Theodore Bingham created a sensation when he publicly declared that Jews constituted half of the New York underworld. Until then, Jewish criminality rarely made the newspapers. Jewish criminals may not have been as numerous as Bingham claimed, but Jewish and non-Jewish observers reported that the Jewish neighborhoods of Manhattan's Lower East Side contained hundreds of brothels, saloons, gambling parlors, and gang hangouts.

At the time, the Lower East Side was the most notorious breeding ground for Jewish gangs and gangsters. Over 550,000 Jews lived within its 1.5 square miles, making it one of the most densely populated areas in the world. Immigrant poverty, the trauma of transition from the Old World to the New, and the loss of family and religious structure created conditions that produced men like Joseph "Yoski Nigger" Toblinsky, Dopey Benny Fein, Monk

Eastman, Big Jack Zelig, and hundreds of ruffians, arsonists, thieves, and killers like them. In those days, the major part of the gangsters' incomes came from providing muscle for pimps and gamblers, from their ability to deliver votes to political bosses during elections, and through assorted protection rackets.

Yoski Nigger led a gang that specialized in stealing and poisoning horses. The gang modeled itself on the Italian Black Hand, a loosely run extortion racket practiced in the Little Italy sections of many American cities. Calling themselves the Yiddish Black Hand, Yoski's outfit wrote letters to stablemen or businessmen whose companies used horses. They demanded a certain sum of money to insure the horses from unforeseen "accidents." If the victim refused to comply, his horse would disappear or be poisoned. If he complained to the authorities, he risked bodily harm. Yoski boasted of personally poisoning over two hundred horses.

Benjamin Fein acquired the nickname Dopey because adenoidal and nasal troubles from infancy gave him a sleepy appearance. At the age of sixteen, he commanded one of the toughest gangs of strong-arm men on the Lower East Side. Benny was the first Jewish gangster to make labor racketeering a full-time and profitable business. He institutionalized the practice of supplying gangs of hoodlums to unions in their wars against employers. Using bats, clubs, and blackjacks, but not guns, Dopey Benny's gang protected striking workers from being attacked by management's hired thugs. Throughout his criminal career, Benny remained loyal to the unions and refused to work for the bosses. "My heart," he once explained, "lay with the workers" (Rockaway 2000).

As tough as Yoski and Benny may have been, the most dominant Jewish gangsters of the pre-1914 era were Monk Eastman (born Edward Osterman) and Big Jack Zelig. Monk stood only five feet five inches tall, but he made a ferocious appearance with a bullet-shaped head, broken nose, bull neck, cauliflower ears, heavily veined, sagging jowls, and a face pockmarked with battle scars. Bossing a gang that included as many as a thousand gangsters, Eastman controlled most of the crime on the Lower East Side, engaging in robberies, burglaries, assaults, muggings, and murder for pay. Eastman's supremacy led to his being branded as the first major Jewish gangster in American history.

In 1904 Eastman received a jail sentence of ten years for robbery and assault. In his absence his gang disinte-grated and other mobsters stepped in to take his place. The most successful of these was William Albert, better known as Big Jack Zelig, a master pickpocket turned gunman. He revived the Eastman gang, expanded its operations, and offered clients a fixed rate for services performed. A Zelig associate once gave the police Big Jack's price list:

Slash on cheek with knife	$1 to $10
Shot in leg	$1 to $25
Shot in arm	$5 to $25
Throwing a bomb	$5 to $50
Murder	$10 to $100

New York remained the largest preserve of Jewish criminals and criminal gangs, but Jewish criminality and gang activity also existed in the teeming Jewish quarters of Boston, Philadelphia, Newark, Cleveland, Detroit, and Chicago. In all these places, Jewish criminals engaged in burglary, prostitution, dealing in stolen goods, labor racketeering, and extortion. Jewish criminals also perpetrated rapes, assaults, and murder. However, crimes of violence accounted for a small portion of Jewish criminal activity before World War I. Throughout this period, Jewish criminals remained part of the Jewish community, with their primary victims being Jews.

The Yiddish press, especially in New York, regularly published lurid stories of Jewish criminal activity, while the country's English-Jewish press kept silent. Non-Jews may not have known Yiddish, but they could read English. The editors of the English-language Jewish newspapers worried that publicizing the problem of Jewish criminality would provide ammunition for Jew-haters and lead to increased antisemitism. Consequently they maintained a code of silence. Years later, Philip Slomovitz, a prominent Jewish publisher and editor, regretted their doing so. "We panicked," he admitted. "We worried about what the gentiles would say and submitted to our fears" (Rockaway 2000).

As first- and second-generation Americans who grew up in a Jewish environment, members of the Jewish underworld spoke Yiddish among themselves. Their numbers and prominence in the criminal underworld led to slang criminal expressions in Yiddish entering the lexicon of underworld slang: *schmeer* (bribe), *schmek* (narcotics), *shmeikel* (to swindle), *kosher* (reliable), and *yentzer* (swindler).

Notwithstanding the notoriety of the era's Jewish mobsters, the heyday of the Jewish gangster occurred after World War I. In 1919 three-fourths of the states ratified the Eighteenth Amendment to the Constitution, which forbade the manufacture, sale, or transportation of intoxicating liquors for drinking purposes. Congress then passed the Volstead Act to enforce the amendment, making the federal government responsible for keeping the nation dry. The ban on alcohol went into effect in 1920, and from then on it seemed that every American over the age of twelve had to have a drink. In response to this great national thirst, 200,000 unlicensed saloons, euphemistically called speakeasies and blind pigs, sprung up across the United States. Large bootlegging organizations, led by tough, ruthless, lawbreaking sons of Irish, Italian, and Jewish immigrants, sprang up to service them and made huge amounts of money. Income from the illegal liquor industry ran into the hundreds of millions of dollars annually. In Detroit, the smuggling, manufacturing, and distributing of illegal liquor became the city's second-largest industry, exceeded only by automobile production.

Although Jews made up less than 4 percent of the nation's population, during Prohibition, 50 percent of the nation's leading bootleggers were Jews, and Jews and Jewish gangs bossed the rackets in some of America's largest cities. New York, with some 1.7 million Jews (more than 40 percent of the nation's Jewish population), contained the greatest number of Jewish gangsters. However, the most famous Jewish underworld figure of the 1920s was not a gangster but a professional gambler and New York man about town named Arnold Rothstein. Referred to by the press as "The Czar of the Underworld" and "The Brain," Rothstein achieved nationwide and everlasting notoriety for allegedly fixing the 1919 baseball World Series between the Chicago White Sox and Cincinnati Reds. Rothstein's fame was such that F. Scott Fitzgerald modeled the character Meyer Wolfsheim in *The Great Gatsby* after him.

Historians credit Rothstein with transforming American crime from a poorly organized activity into big business. Rothstein laid the foundation for the enormous profits of Prohibition by creating an organization to buy high-quality liquor by the shipload in England and distribute it to buyers in the United States. To assist him in this enterprise, Rothstein assembled a group of tough young Jewish and Italian hoodlums, including Meyer Lansky, Benjamin "Bugsy" Siegel, Arthur "Dutch Schultz" Flegenheimer, Abner "Longy" Zwillman, Louis "Lepke" Buchalter, Charley "Lucky" Luciano, Vito Genovese, and Carlo Gambino. These men would later have a historic impact on organized crime in the United States. Rothstein next turned his attention to narcotics smuggling, which, until he became involved, had been unorganized. Rothstein converted the racket into a businesslike machine by sending buyers to Europe and the Far East and by controlling the purchasing operation in the United States. By 1926, Rothstein was allegedly the financial overlord of the foreign narcotics traffic in America.

Rothstein's career in crime came to an inglorious end in 1928, when he was shot and killed in a card game. After his death, Rothstein's Jewish protégés took control of a number of his criminal enterprises. Bootlegging became the province of Waxey Gordon, Dutch Schultz, and the Bugsy Siegel and Meyer Lansky combine, known as the Bugs-Meyer Mob, while the labor racketeer Lepke Buchalter continued the narcotics traffic.

Rothstein's legacy persevered in the sense that he had taught his charges that the dollar had one nationality and one religion: profit. His heirs retained the good business sense of forming alliances, regardless of ethnic considerations, not only with underworld accomplices but also with those who could handle the political fix. Consequently, Jewish mobsters cooperated with their Italian counterparts, including Charley "Lucky" Luciano and Frank Costello. Later these same men would create what came to be called the National Crime Syndicate.

Outside of New York, Jewish mobsters and Jewish gangs also dominated the rackets in a number of the nation's largest cities well into the 1930s. Across the river from New York, Abner "Longy" Zwillman, often referred to as the Al Capone of New Jersey, dominated criminal activity in Newark and its suburbs and influenced the city's police, judges, and politicians. Max Hoff and his Jewish syndicate controlled bootlegging, crime, and vice in Philadelphia, and they allegedly bought more machine guns than the city's police force. Charles "King" Solomon, alias Boston Charley, controlled bootlegging in Boston and headed one of the largest liquor, vice, and narcotics smuggling syndicates in New England. The Cleveland Four—Morris "Moe" Dalitz, Morris Kleinman, Sam Tucker, and Louis Rothkopf—bossed bootlegging and gambling in Cleveland. This syndicate coexisted with the Cleveland Mafia, led by Big Al Polizzi and his Mayfield Road gang.

Relations between the Jewish and Italian group remained cordial for many years. Detroit's all-Jewish Purple Gang, reputed to be more violent than Chicago's Capone gang, ruled the Motor City's bootlegging, gambling, prostitution, and extortion rackets. In Minneapolis, Isidore "Kid Cann" Bloomenfeld, identified by the FBI as the overlord of Minnesota, together with his brothers Harry and Yiddy Bloom, managed most of that city's illicit business. Across the river in St. Paul, Leon Gleckman and his syndicate controlled bootlegging and sundry other rackets.

A portrait of the era's Jewish mobster would show that he was descended from immigrant Eastern European Jews, primarily Polish or Russian, who had come to the United States in the great immigration wave of 1881–1914. He was born in the United States or came as a small child. For all intents and purposes, gangsters were second-generation Americans. While some grew up very poor, most of them came from working-class homes where parents provided the basic necessities to their children. A few of the men, such as Monk Eastman, Arnold Rothstein, and Charley Solomon, came from upper-middle-class and even wealthy homes. Most of the boys grew up in traditional rather than strictly Orthodox Jewish homes. That is, the parents observed some religious customs, such as lighting the Sabbath candles, keeping a kosher home, and attending High Holiday services.

Whether out of superstition, to honor their parents, or from habit, a number of the gangsters maintained some attachment to Jewish traditions. They practiced a kind of folk Judaism—going to their parents' home for the Friday evening Sabbath meal or attending synagogue services on the Jewish New Year and Day of Atonement. In one rare case, a gangster was a practicing Orthodox Jew. His name was Sam "Red" Levine, and he had been born in Toledo, Ohio. Red was an accomplished professional killer, a man Lucky Luciano called "the best driver and hit-man I had" (Rockaway 2000). As an Orthodox Jew, Red conscientiously observed the biblical commandment of not working on the Sabbath. He always refused to murder anyone from sundown Friday to sundown Saturday. But if he had no choice and could not avoid doing the job on Saturday, Red would first put a prayer shawl over his shoulders, say his prayers, and then carry out the killing.

Most of the gangsters did not finish high school, and they were generally the only son in the family to pursue a life of crime. Nonetheless, there were exceptions, such as the Amberg and Shapiro brothers in New York, the Bernstein and Fleisher brothers in Detroit, the Bloom brothers in Minneapolis, and the Miller brothers in Chicago.

The activities of these men included bootlegging, extortion, narcotics, prostitution, and murder, especially contract killing. The most famous group of contract killers was a Brooklyn-based gang of Jewish hoodlums led by Abe "Kid Twist" Reles and his friends Harry "Pittsburgh Phil" Strauss, Abraham "Pretty" Levine, Martin "Bugsy" Goldstein, and Irving "Knadles" Nitzberg. These men worked together with an Italian mob led by Harry "Happy" Maione and Frank "Dasher" Abbandando. The New York press dubbed this outfit of killers for hire Murder, Inc. The Jewish members of this gang used as their "office" a candy store located under the elevated tracks at the corner of Saratoga and Livonia Avenues in the Brownsville section of Brooklyn. Owned by a woman named Rose, who kept the place open twenty-four hours a day, the store became known as Midnight Rose's. Local wits claimed that more individual murders were planned in the store than at any other spot on earth.

Lepke Buchalter and other national crime bosses allegedly created this troop of killers during the 1930s as an enforcement arm to maintain order in their ranks and to carry out homicides on assignment. Using ice picks, bludgeons, cleavers, garrotes, knives, and guns, and earning from $125 to $250 per week, these men worked primarily as hired assassins for their initiators. New York police estimated that Murder, Inc. committed from four hundred to five hundred murders at the behest of the bosses. According to the rules, Murder, Inc. killed only for "business" reasons and was never to be used against political figures, prosecutors, or newspaper reporters. The feeling was that killing these "civilians" would create a public stir and a demand for governmental action that would be bad for business.

What motivated these men and other Jewish mobsters to engage in criminal and even murderous activities? Meyer Lansky and Longy Zwillman said they did what they did because they grew up poor and never wanted to endure poverty again. Yet some criminals were raised in comfortable circumstances, and these gangsters were no more deprived than their peers, who grew up in the same crowded slum or overcrowded immigrant quarters and pursued legitimate careers.

Mugshot of gangster Louis "Lepke" Buchalter in 1939. (Library of Congress)

Antisemitism may have been a motive for some, because the United States of the 1920s was not always a pleasant place for Jews. From 1920 to 1927 Henry Ford vilified Jews in the pages of his *Dearborn Independent* newspaper and in pamphlets entitled *The International Jew.* Ford required his automobile dealers to give a pamphlet to everyone who purchased one of his cars, and millions of Americans bought Fords. In the South, the Ku Klux Klan instigated boycotts of Jewish merchants, vandalized Jewish-owned stores, burned crosses outside synagogues, and terrorized prominent Jews. Colleges and professional schools, including Harvard, Dartmouth, Rutgers, Princeton, Penn State, and others, imposed quotas on Jewish enrollment. And Jews encountered economic discrimination in commercial banks, industrial corporations, public utilities, and insurance companies, in addition to widespread social discrimination. Blocked from respectable avenues to success and status, numbers of Jews selected alternate routes to fame and fortune, such as sports and the entertainment industry. And some tough young Jews may have been angry enough at American society to choose crime as a way to strike back.

For the most part, however, Jewish gangsters engaged in crime out of choice. These tough young men selected crime as their vocation because they wanted money, power, recognition, and status, and they wanted it at an early age. Crime attracted them because it offered them the quickest way to realize their dreams. Most of them were uneducated men who rarely finished high school, thus limiting their options for success. Many of them saw hard, legitimate work as something "suckers" did, and they never saw themselves as suckers. They saw crime as more exciting and glamorous than the tedium of studying or the drudgery of working long hours in a shop or factory. In the United States crime has historically served as a ladder of mobility for those who are uneducated, who do not want to work at a legitimate job, and who are willing to use violence to achieve their goal.

West Coast mobster Mickey Cohen exemplifies this. Cohen served as one of Bugsy Siegel's bodyguards and had been involved in numerous rackets. Throughout his career, Cohen displayed a nonchalant attitude toward the use of force and violence in his work. He saw weapons as the tools of his trade and never expressed any remorse or guilt over using them. He claimed that he never killed anyone who did not deserve to be killed, by the standards of his way of life. Cohen also believed that crime provided him with a status and deference he could never have achieved in any other way. Never having finished high school, Cohen asked how an uneducated person like him could have achieved the prominence (or notoriety) he enjoyed and have met the celebrities he had met in his life if he had not been a gangster. As if to validate his analysis, toward the end of his life, Cohen could be found seated on the dais at United Jewish Appeal and Israel Bond rallies in Los Angeles.

As with so many other Jewish men of their generation, the Jewish mobster loved his family and followed a code of never involving his children or close relatives in his criminal activities. Bootlegger Waxey Gordon sent his son to medical school. One of Meyer Lansky's sons graduated from West Point. Lepke Buchalter always set aside money for his stepson's college education. Longy Zwillman kept his family totally separated and uninvolved in his work. And Charley Workman, a Murder, Inc. killer, prevented his brother from entering the criminal world.

In this the Jewish gangsters were different from their Italian counterparts, who frequently brought their offspring and relations into the business. Like the Jews, Italian syndicate leaders were proud and devoted fathers who wanted their children to marry well, to attain success, and to be accepted in the legitimate world. So they sent them to the best schools and paid for their studies in law, medicine, or some other prestigious profession. But they also wanted to keep the control of their criminal enterprise within their biological family. If this was not possible, they made an effort to keep it within their extended family of nephews, cousins, and other relatives. If necessary, they brought in outsiders through marriage and godparentage. Thus, Italian-American criminal syndicates are referred to as "families," because they are tied together by marriage and kinship.

This tradition was totally absent among Jewish gangsters. None of their children married the offspring of other Jewish gangsters, and none of their relatives "inherited" the business. Jewish gangsters knew that what they did was not an honorable occupation, and they did not want to pass it on to their loved ones. That is why the activities of the Zwillmans, Lanskys, Buchalters, and Siegels lasted only a single generation. It lived and died with them.

Jewish gangsters displayed adroitness at compartmentalizing their lives. They could separate what they did to earn a living—their business lives—from how they behaved in their personal lives, even if the result was blatantly inconsistent behavior. Lepke Buchalter's life illustrates this. Lepke commanded an army of gangsters who terrorized the garment industry in New York. His gang's weapons consisted of destructive acids, bludgeons, blackjacks, knives, fire, ice picks, and guns. At his peak, Lepke controlled a wide assortment of businesses and unions in New York, including the bakery and pastry drivers, the fur truckers, the milliners, the garment workers, the shoe trade, the poultry market, the taxicab business, and the motion picture operators. Despite Lepke's murderous brutality in his business affairs, he was a considerate son and a doting husband and father. He described himself as a Jew, contributed to his mother's synagogue, and, according to the FBI, led a quiet home life and was genuinely devoted to his wife and adopted son.

Abe "Kid Twist" Reles, one of Murder, Inc.'s most accomplished killers, exhibited a similar temperament. Reles loved his mother, wife, and child, and he respected certain Jewish traditions, but he felt no compunction about having to kill in his line of work. Reles later turned state's evidence against his associates in Murder, Inc. and against other underworld figures, including Lepke Buchalter. This led to Reles's being killed to stop him from talking.

In an interrogation, Brooklyn district attorney Burton Turkus asked Reles how he could take a human life so casually. "Did your conscience ever bother you? Didn't you feel anything?" queried Turkus. Reles countered by asking Turkus how he felt when he prosecuted his first case. "I was rather nervous," Turkus admitted. "And how about your second case?" asked Reles. "It wasn't so bad, but I was still a little nervous," said Turkus. "And after that?" asked Reles. "Oh, after that I was alright. I was used to it," replied Turkus. "You answered your own question," said Reles. "It's the same with murder. I got used to it" (Turkus and Feder 1951).

Although they kept their families away from their criminal activities, the Jewish mobsters could not always conceal what they did for a living. Once the families discovered that a relative was a gangster, they experienced shame and humiliation. Fathers especially felt betrayed by their son's activities and reacted accordingly. Arnold Rothstein's father, Abraham, cut off all contact with his son and refused to see him. When the father of New York labor racketeer Jacob "Little Augie" Orgen discovered that his son headed a gang of strong-arm men and killers, he declared him dead and sat *shiva* (the seven-day mourning period) for him.

The children of Jewish mobsters often suffered the most because of who their fathers were and what they did. They were often ostracized at school and had difficulties socially. This led them to harbor feelings of anger and resentment toward their fathers. Many of them changed their names, concealed who they were from their acquaintances, and in some instances severed relations with their father. This did not always apply to the third generation. Many grandchildren recalled their gangster grandfather with affection, viewing him as something of a folk hero. Meyer Lansky's granddaughter remembered her grandfather as having compassion for the average man. Jake "Gurrah" Shapiro's granddaughter justified what her grandfather did by saying he only killed people who bothered him.

For its part, the Jewish community was ambivalent to the gangsters in their midst. On the one hand, they evinced shame and horror at the activities and notoriety of these men, because the gangster epitomized the "bad Jew" who would bring onus and hatred down on the entire community. Reacting to a 1928 grand jury investigation exposing the role of Max Hoff and other Jews in the Philadelphia underworld, Rabbi Mortimer J. Cohen of Congregation Beth Shalom bemoaned the shame that these men inflicted on the city's Jewish community. These men, he said, had dragged the Jewish name in the mud and filth of murder, bribery, and corruption. He worried that the whole Jewish community would be blamed and suffer the consequences for the deeds of these men.

This same fear permeated other Jewish communities as well. In Detroit, communal leader Leonard Simon conceded that the community's leaders knew about the Jewish gangsters but were afraid to admit it. Chicago Jewish leader S. M. Melamed warned his coreligionists that the Jewish gangsters brought shame to the community and posed a danger to their position and status in America. Jewish communal leaders in Minneapolis reacted in a similar fashion when the local *Saturday Press* accused Jewish gangsters of committing most of the crimes against the citizens of Minneapolis.

Jewish anxieties increased during the 1930s. The Depression, fears of Communist subversion, and the rise of Hitler exacerbated existing prejudices and fueled a precipitous growth in antisemitic fervor. The era saw the rise of Catholic and Protestant demagogues, such as Father Charles E. Coughlin, the Reverend Gerald Winrod, and William Dudley Pelley, as well as over a hundred antisemitic organizations, including the German-American Bund, the Silver Shirts, the Defenders of the Christian Faith, and the Christian Front. Jewish communal leaders viewed these trends with mounting concern and feared that the activities of the Jewish mobsters would only worsen an already dangerous situation.

Despite their abhorrence of the Jewish gangster, communal leaders utilized his services when it suited their purposes, especially when threats to Jews loomed large. During the late 1930s, Nazi Bund rallies in New York created a terrible dilemma for the city's Jewish establishment. They wanted to stop the meetings but could not do so legally. Nathan Perlman, a New York judge and former Republican congressman, believed that Jews should demonstrate more militancy toward the Nazis. To this end, he surreptitiously contacted Meyer Lansky and asked him to help. Perlman stipulated that the Nazis could be beaten up but not killed. Lansky reluctantly agreed: no killing.

Lansky's crew went around New York disrupting Bund meetings and beating up the participants. They worked very professionally. They broke Nazi arms, legs, and ribs and cracked skulls, but no one died. The attacks continued for more than a year and forced the Bundists to demand police protection. Mayor Fiorello La Guardia, whose mother was Jewish and who spoke Yiddish, complied. He confined the Bundist parades and rallies to Yorkville, and he forbade the Nazis to wear their uniforms or sing their songs. He then sent black and Jewish policemen to guard their meetings.

Nazi sympathizers also demonstrated in Newark, New Jersey. Longy Zwillman, the city's crime boss, had battled antisemites as a youth, and he would not allow the Nazis to congregate with impunity. In 1933 he formed an anti-Nazi group called the Minutemen, made up of former Jewish prizefighters and Jewish gangsters, and he gave the group financial and political support. Beginning in 1933, this group used physical force—iron pipes, clubs, baseball bats, and fists—to beat up the Nazis and break up their rallies. Later, Zwillman allied the Minutemen with the Newark division of the Non-Sectarian Anti-Nazi League (NSANL), made up of young middle-class Jewish men. The Minutemen fought the Nazis in the streets while the Anti-Nazi League boycotted all imports from Germany. The alliance between these two groups lasted from 1934 to 1941, when America entered the war. In Minneapolis, a city with a long history of antisemitism, Davie Berman, a former bootlegger and bank robber, and the city's gambling czar, used his gang to break up local Nazi rallies. Berman and Isidore Blumenfeld paid off the police, and there were never any arrests connected with the raids. Jewish gangsters conducted similar raids in Chicago and Los Angeles.

Jewish mobsters assisted as well in the creation of the State of Israel by providing aid in its war against the Arabs. After the Holocaust, Zionist leaders viewed the establishment of a Jewish state as a matter of life or death. This led them to solicit and accept aid from every quarter, including the Jewish underworld. In 1946 the Haganah, the predecessor of the Israel Defense Forces, sent an emissary, Reuven Dafni, to the United States on a fund-raising mission. One day, when he was in Los Angeles, he received a phone call from a man who identified himself as Smiley and requested a meeting. When they met, Smiley asked Reuven to explain what he was doing in Los Angeles because his boss was interested. The boss turned out to be

Benjamin "Bugsy" Siegel, and Smiley was Allen Smiley, Siegel's right-hand man.

Smiley arranged a meeting between Siegel and Dafni at the LaRue restaurant on LaCienega Boulevard. At the appointed time, Smiley and Reuven went into an empty room at the rear of the restaurant. After a few moments Smiley left, leaving Reuven alone. Soon two tough-looking men entered and searched the premises. When they found it safe, they left. Shortly thereafter, Siegel came in. He sat across the table from Dafni and asked what he was doing in Los Angeles. Reuven explained that he was in the city to raise money for the Haganah and to buy weapons with which to fight. Siegel interrupted him to ask, "You mean to tell me the Jews are fighting?" "Yes," replied Dafni. Siegel then leaned forward until their noses almost touched. "You mean fighting as in killing?" asked Siegel. "Yes," answered Reuven. Siegel looked at him for a moment and said, "I'm with you." "From then on," recalled Dafni, "every week I received a suitcase filled with $5 and $10 bills. The payments continued till I left Los Angeles." Reuven estimates that Siegel gave him a total of $50,000 (Rockaway 2000).

Jewish gangsters also contributed large sums to Jewish charities and were active in raising funds for Jewish causes. Longy Zwillman donated money to the United Jewish Appeal and to Newark's Congregation Beth Torah and Sinai Congregation. Meyer Lansky donated money to the United Jewish Appeal, to Israel-related charities, and to his synagogue, Temple Sinai, in Hollywood, Florida. Moe Dalitz contributed to institutions in Israel and to a variety of Jewish charities. In 1970 he received the City of Peace Award of the State of Israel in recognition of his distinguished service on behalf of the people and the State of Israel. In 1985 the Anti-Defamation League of the B'nai B'rith awarded Dalitz its Torch of Liberty award in appreciation of his financial contributions over the years. Moe Sedway, an associate and close friend of Bugsy Siegel and later an active partner in several Las Vegas casinos, revealed to the Kefauver Committee investigating organized crime that in 1947 he was chairman of the Las Vegas United Jewish Appeal. Jake Guzik, who served as Al Capone's treasurer and who, after Capone's death, continued in this capacity for Capone's successors Tony Accardo and Sam Giancana, contributed substantial sums to Jewish charities and to his synagogue. Lepke Buchalter donated money to his mother's synagogue. Ironically, this was money he earned from beating Jews in New York's garment industry and extorting money from them.

Perhaps these gangsters assisted the Jewish community because, despite their depravity and violent lives, in each of them there burned a *pintele Yid,* a spark of Jewishness. Some may have helped the Jewish community as a way of compensating for the other, less heroic part of their lives. In their later years, some gangsters sought the respect and legitimacy withheld from them in their youth. One way to acquire communal recognition and approbation was through Jewish philanthropy and devotion to Jewish causes. Other mobsters may have sought respectability because of a desire not to embarrass their children and grandchildren and thus jeopardize their chances for success in the legitimate world.

Nevertheless, not every Jewish mobster was altruistic toward the Jewish community or Jewish interests. In 1951 two Detroit Jewish underworld figures, Arthur Leebove and Sam Stein, were convicted in a conspiracy to smuggle twenty-one American warplanes from Newark, New Jersey, to Egypt during the Arab–Israel hostilities in 1948. They schemed to buy surplus military aircraft, load them with British crews in Newark, and fly them to England. Once there, an Egyptian crew would be brought on board, and they would fly the planes to Egypt. The smuggling syndicate purchased twenty AT-6 aircraft and one B-25 bomber. The plot unraveled when bad weather forced the bomber to return to Newark Airport. FBI agents then seized the planes before they could be delivered. For men like these, making money superseded Jewish loyalty.

Bugsy Siegel is reputed to have remarked to Del Webb, the contractor who built the Flamingo Hotel, that people in his profession only kill each other. In a sense he told the truth, because many prominent Jewish mobsters died at the hands of their associates. Thirty-three-year-old Little Augie Orgen was shot and killed by Jacob "Gurrah" Shapiro, Lepke Buchalter's partner. Buchalter then took over Orgen's enterprises. Dutch Schultz was killed at age thirty-three by two Murder, Inc. hit men, Charley "The Bug" Workman and Mendy Weiss, to prevent him from killing Thomas E. Dewey, special district attorney for New York in the 1930s. The forty-two-year-old Bugsy Siegel was slain because his associates suspected he was stealing money from them. Arnold Rothstein was shot and killed in a card game at age forty-six.

The government executed some Jewish mobsters. Forty-seven-year-old Lepke Buchalter died in the electric chair, as did Murder, Inc. killers Harry Strauss and Bugsy Goldstein. Others died in prison. Gurrah Shapiro, Lepke's longtime partner, died in prison at the age of forty-eight. Bootlegger Waxey Gordon died in prison at the age of fifty-four.

A few died by their own hand. Once Prohibition ended, Max Hoff, once "King of Philadelphia's Bootleggers," tried a number of business ventures, each of which ended in failure. He committed suicide in a New York City flophouse at the age of forty-six. Longy Zwillman ostensibly killed himself, but under circumstances that strongly suggest he may have been murdered.

Jewish gangsterism declined after World War II. The urban ghettos that produced these men no longer contained Jews. Jews moved to the suburbs and became part of America's economic, educational, and occupational elite. Third- and fourth-generation American Jews no longer needed crime to "make it." The activities of these men were one-generational. They had no successors.

Robert A. Rockaway

References and Further Reading

Asbury, Herbert. 1927. *The Gangs of New York: An Informal History of the New York Underworld.* New York: Alfred A. Knopf.

Bergreen, Laurence. 1994. *Capone: The Man and the Era.* New York: Simon & Schuster.

Berman, Susan. 1981. *Easy Street.* New York: Dial Press.

Block, Alan. 1983. *East Side–West Side: Organizing Crime in New York, 1930–1950.* New Brunswick, NJ: Transaction Books.

Cohen, Mickey, with John Peer Nugent. 1975. *Mickey Cohen, In My Own Words: The Underworld Autobiography of Michael Mickey Cohen.* Englewood Cliffs, NJ: Prentice Hall, 1975.

Eisenberg, Dennis, Uri Dann, and Eli Landau. 1979. *Meyer Lansky: Mogul of the Mob.* New York: Paddington Press.

Fox, Stephen. 1989. *Blood and Power: Organized Crime in Twentieth-Century America.* New York: William Morrow.

Fried, Albert. 1980. *The Rise and Fall of the Jewish Gangster in America.* New York: Holt, Rinehart, and Winston.

Joselit, Jenna Weissman. 1983. *Our Gang: Jewish Crime and the New York Jewish Community, 1900–1940.* Bloomington: Indiana University Press.

Katcher, Leo. 1959. *The Big Bankroll: The Life and Times of Arnold Rothstein.* New Rochelle, NY: Arlington House.

Lacey, Robert. 1991. *Little Man: Meyer Lansky and the Gangster Life.* Boston: Little, Brown.

O'Kane, James M. 1992. *The Crooked Ladder: Gangsters, Ethnicity, and the American Dream.* New Brunswick, NJ: Transaction Publishers.

Pietrusza, David. 2003. *Rothstein: The Life, Times, and Murder of the Criminal Genius Who Fixed the 1919 World Series.* New York: Carroll and Graf Publishers.

Rockaway, Robert A. 2000. *But He Was Good to His Mother: The Lives and Crimes of Jewish Gangsters.* Jerusalem: Gefen Publishing House.

Ruth, David E. 1996. *Inventing the Public Enemy: The Gangster in American Culture, 1918–1934.* Chicago: University of Chicago Press.

Sann, Paul. 1971. *Kill the Dutchman: The Story of Dutch Schultz.* New Rochelle, NY: Arlington House.

Sifakis, Carl. 1987. *The Mafia Encyclopedia.* New York: Facts on File.

Stuart, Mark. 1985. *Gangster #2: Longy Zwillman, the Man Who Invented Organized Crime.* Secaucus, NJ: Lyle Stuart.

Turkus, Burton B., and Sid Feder. 1951. *Murder, Inc.* New York: Farrar, Straus, and Young.

Zion, Sidney. 1994. *Loyalty and Betrayal: The Story of the American Mob.* San Francisco: Collins Publishers.

American Jews and Labor

Jews and the International Ladies' Garment Workers' Union

The story of Jewish workers in the women's apparel industry and in the International Ladies' Garment Workers' Union (ILGWU) that represented them is that of a people steeped in a tradition of communality engaged in a "class struggle" within their cherished "tribe." The resultant history is the unusual narrative of labor and management engaged in their customary conflict but often conducted in ways that reflected the ancient ties of tradition that bound Jews together.

At the dawn of the twentieth century, on June 3, 1900, eleven men met in New York City to establish the International Ladies' Garment Workers' Union. They represented seven local organizations from New York, Newark, Baltimore, Philadelphia, and Brownsville, a subdivision of Brooklyn. They were all Jewish, conducting their sessions in Yiddish.

It may well be that the number of men who gathered at this founding meeting was no accident. In the Jewish tradition, at least ten persons are required to form a *minyan,* a recognized congregation. Although their desire to form an international organization to embrace workers in Canada as well as the United States was a new idea, the men who gathered at the founding convention were battle-tested veterans of historic struggles in the women's gar-

ment industry. The battleground was the East Coast cities, where sweatshops, inhabited overwhelmingly by Jewish immigrants, had spawned local unions.

The great waves of Jewish immigration, mainly from czarist Russia and its vassals, started in the 1880s on the heels of the assassination of Czar Alexander II. The killing was the result of vast peasant unrest. The czarist regime turned to an old ploy to divert peasant anger: "If the peasants are hungry, feed them Jews." A wave of pogroms descended upon the Jews—tolerated and even instigated by the Russian constabulary. The Jews fled to America.

In 1881, the year of Alexander's assassination, Jewish immigration into the United States was less than 6,000. In 1882, that number had risen to about 18,000. In the six years from 1881 to 1886, Jewish immigrants totaled 77,105. From 1887 to 1892, the number increased to close to a quarter million. To millions of Jews, the United States was "the promised land." They came, as might be expected, to the port cities on the East Coast. And they brought their trades with them—among which the manufacture of clothing was prominent.

That many of the Jewish immigrants were skilled in garment production was a by-product of the limited opportunities that Jews had in the small towns (*shtetlach*) in many parts of Eastern Europe as a result of restrictions on their role in the economy. Often, they were not permitted to own land. They were barred from getting the higher education needed for the professions. To make a living, they turned to trade as peddlers, to baking, or to occupations that required no major capital investment. To produce garments, all a person needed was a needle, thread, and a pair of scissors.

The mass migration of Jews in the decades around the turn of the century also came at a time when America was producing ready-to-wear clothing. In an earlier period, households, usually the women, produced their own clothing. The well-to-do had their fancy clothes produced by professional tailors who fashioned "made-to-order" apparel. In the latter decades of the nineteenth century, with the construction of railroads and the rise of a national market, the apparel industry turned to the mass production of clothing to be sold to an ever-expanding market.

Among the first employers in the manufacture of women's ready-to-wear apparel were German Jews who had come to the United States in the middle of the nineteenth century. Since German and Yiddish are kindred tongues, these employers and their managers could converse with the immigrant Jews.

The immigrant Jews who attended the initial meeting of the eleven were, however, not just sweated workers groping for relief. They generally were members of the Workmen's Circle, a mutual aid society with a socialist orientation and members of *landsmanshaften* (organizations of men who came from the same towns in Europe). They were proletarian ideologues who, to quote a slogan of the Workmen's Circle, wanted a *besere und shenere velt* (a better and more beautiful world).

One of the most powerful informative, ideological, and organizational institutions affecting the members of the ILGWU was a daily Yiddish newspaper, *Der Yidish Forverts* (*The Jewish Daily Forward*). Its orientation was toward the Socialist Party, but it was not the only Jewish daily. There were also *Der Tog* (*The Day*) that leaned toward the Democratic Party, *Der Morgn Zhurnal* (*The Morning Journal*) that leaned toward the Republican Party, and *Der Freier Arbayter Shtimme* (*The Free Workers Voice*) that was anarchist.

New York's Jewish community was politically and ideologically heterogeneous. But the socialist-minded *Forverts* was dominant, with hundreds of thousands of readers. Its relationship with the ILGWU was more than that between a newspaper and its readers. The *Forverts* supplied much of the leadership for the union for many years. For instance,

the ILGWU's second president, Benjamin Schlesinger, elected in 1904, was business manager of the *Forverts*. He was succeeded by a non-Jew, James McCauley, head of the pivotally powerful cutters' local. In 1907, Herman Grossman, the union's first president, was elected for a second time. But in 1914 Schlesinger won another term, and after several others had held the office, he was elected a third time in 1928. When he was not serving as the union's president, he was back at the *Forverts*.

The *Forverts* influence reached beyond its readers and the presence of men like Schlesinger. Abraham Cahan, editor of the *Forverts* and a legendary leader of American Jewry, graced many a mass meeting of the union with his masterful oratory. Although Cahan was not particularly religious, he was keenly aware of how deeply Jewish workers were steeped in biblical tradition. And so he used this circumstance to make his points.

On one occasion when he was urging workers at a union meeting to fight for a five-day workweek, he informed his listeners that God himself had paved the way. The Lord proclaimed that six days shalt thou labor and on the seventh day thou shalt rest. "That," thundered Cahan, "was what God intended as a beginning. It was now up to the workers to carry on the Lord's good intentions and fight for a five-day work week" (Tyler 1995). By evoking Jewish tradition, Cahan converted the struggle for the five-day work week into a holy mission.

Early in the union's history, in 1909, a strike of unprecedented character once more illustrated the profound relationship between the ILGWU and Jewish tradition. It was the Shirtwaist Makers Strike—a militant walkout of some 20,000 workers, almost all young women and girls of immigrant origin. The strike was more than just another walkout. It made history in both the labor and feminist movements in the United States.

The high point of the strike was a meeting held in the Great Hall of Cooper Union, where Lincoln had made one of his memorable addresses. Present was Samuel Gompers, president of the American Federation of Labor. He came because this was no ordinary strike. This was a strike of young women—20,000 of them. It may be also that Gompers was drawn to them because he too was a Jew.

Chairing the meeting was Benjamin Feigenbaum, a Socialist subsequently elected to the New York Assembly and also a Jew. At a climactic moment during a speech by Jacob Panken, a Jewish lawyer and famous Socialist activist later elected to a judgeship, Clara Lemlich, a wisp of a girl, raised her hand and shouted, "I want to say something" (Tyler 1995).

The chair was embarrassed. The esteemed Panken was speaking. The chair wanted to go on. But then came an uproar of enraged voices. "Let her speak." She spoke. Her speech was reported as a philippic in Yiddish. Her words ignited the combustible workers, and a strike was declared.

From the chair, Feigenbaum intoned, "Do you mean faith? Will you take the old Jewish oath?" As they raised their hands, he asked them to repeat after him: "If I turn traitor to the cause I now pledge, may this hand wither from the arm I now raise" (Tyler 1995).

The strike was a landmark. It was the first time that the country had witnessed such a massive strike of women. The uprising inspired the growing feminist movement to embrace the strikers and to let the world know that if women had the right to vote they would not be so maltreated.

In the minds of some of the strikers, the uprising of the women in 1909 was responsible for the revolt of 60,000 almost entirely male cloakmakers (coat and suit workers) in 1910. One of the 1909 women strikers poetized:

Hail the waist makers of 1909
When we fought and bled on the picket line
We showed the world that women could fight
And we rose and won with the women's might
And we gave new courage to the men
Who carried on in Nineteen Ten.

Unlike the shirtwaist-makers' strike, which was largely spontaneous, the strike of the cloakmakers was well organized. The union wanted official recognition of their organization as the industry's collective bargaining instrument. That was primary. But precisely for that reason, they found themselves facing a real although invisible obstacle. The employers were predominantly German Jews who looked down on their East European workers as lesser beings. In the past, the employer might grant the workers a little something after a strike and then would try to take it back later in the slow season. But formal recognition embodied in a contract was unthinkable. The strike dragged on.

Then one day, the chief executive of the employers' association received a message from the Filene brothers, who ran a huge retail outlet headquartered in Boston. Their message advised the employers' association that, unless it settled with the union, Filene would go elsewhere to get women's coats and suits. The association knew it had to do something. It responded that it was prepared to settle with the union but did not really know how to go about it.

The Filenes informed the employers' association that they would send them a bright young lawyer, Louis Brandeis, to guide them. Brandeis mediated an agreement that made labor history, called the Protocol of Peace. It called for a written contract between the employers' association and the union. During the life of the contract there were to be no strikes and no lockouts. If a dispute arose, it would be submitted to the impartial chairman in the industry.

Out of that contract and the spirit behind it emerged many joint ventures between the employers and the union. They set up a Joint Board of Sanitary Control to battle tuberculosis and other industrial diseases that plagued the workers. Unions and employers in other industries copied the model. Ultimately, Brandeis became the first Jewish U.S. Supreme Court justice.

None of this would have happened without the intervention of the Filenes. The Filenes' original family name was Katz. To fit into the American scene, they decided to translate Katz into another language, French. If they decided that the family name would now be Feline, it would give away the real name. So they put a twist on Feline and made it Filene.

After the Bolshevik Revolution in Russia in 1917, there was a tremendous burst of enthusiasm among immigrant Jews who had suffered under the czars. Many enrolled in the Communist Party. In New York, Communists managed to get control of the two largest joint boards: cloaks and dresses. In 1926, they conducted a strike and, in their revolutionary zeal, made unrealistic and impossible demands. The strike dragged on and on. The union went millions of dollars into debt. After the International Office managed to unseat the Communists, the top leadership—President Schlesinger and Secretary Treasurer David Dubinsky— found the ILGWU in a state of near bankruptcy.

What Schlesinger and Dubinsky did is probably without parallel in American or world labor history. They went for a loan to three big Jewish capitalists: bankers Herbert Lehman and Felix Warburg, and the head of Sears Roebuck, Julius Rosenwald. Rosenwald contributed $50,000, and Lehman and Warburg $25,000 each. At that time, that was big money. Once more tradition raised its hoary head to let brotherhood prevail, amid the "class struggle."

As other ethnic groups entered the women's apparel industry labor force in significant numbers in the decades after World War I, the proportion of Jews in the ILGWU diminished. After World War I, there was an influx of Italians. As agricultural mechanization after World War II displaced farm workers in the South, many blacks migrated to the North and entered the garment factories. Then came the Hispanics and the Chinese. In 1995 the ILGWU merged with the Amalgamated Clothing and Textile Workers Union to form the Union of Needletrades, Industrial, and Textile Employees (UNITE). Today UNITE's ethnic composition is strikingly different from that of the ILGWU in the early twentieth century.

An even greater revolution has taken place in the structure of the apparel trade. Increasingly, the great chain stores are their own producers, creating their own styles, promoting their own labels, bypassing American apparel firms, and getting their work done overseas.

What remains constant, however, is the UNITE leadership's deep belief in what was once called social unionism. It holds that a union is and should be far more than just a collective bargaining agency. It should be a socioeconomic-political force in society to achieve a world of freedom and justice for all. That's part of a great and old tradition.

Gus Tyler

References and Further Reading

Tyler, Gus. 1995. *Look for the Union Label: A History of the International Ladies' Garment Workers' Union.* Armonk, NY: M. E. Sharpe.

Jews and the International Fur Workers' Union

"To understand what the fur trade was about," said a retired furrier, "is to know about the people that were in it" (Spingarn 1995). By 1910, Eastern European Jews had replaced Germans as the dominant ethnic group in the fur manufacturing industry in New York City. The fact that both the employers and workers were Jewish, and shared a common culture, shaped labor relations and the develop-

ment of trade unionism in the industry. Many of the Jews entering the garment industry by 1913 were exposed to radicalism in Eastern Europe; some had even been leaders in the radical movement. Others saw the fight for social justice that trade unionism represented as a practical matter; they wanted to improve their working conditions and wages, possibly becoming manufacturers themselves. The struggle between capital and labor in the fur industry was fought within a Jewish milieu, given a Jewish expression, and Jewish culture influenced the outcome.

The prosperity of the fur industry was affected by the weather, politics, and economics. The industry was generally undercapitalized and its financial structure precarious. The labor force was divided into cutters (the most skilled), operators, nailers, and finishers. Wages in the highly skilled fur trade were the highest in the needle trades, but after the short busy season from August to December, the manufacturers laid off more than 30 percent of the workforce. Most shops were small and sanitary conditions poor. In 1911, very few of the hundred largest shops, employing more than twenty workers, adhered to the sanitary code. Workers inhaled hair from the pelts, causing respiratory problems, and the dyes used on the pelts poisoned their fingers.

Despite these maladies, the furriers were slow to form a stable union. It was a story of desperate struggle punctuated by frequent failure. In 1912, the furriers tried to organize. Many of the leaders of the small furriers' union, such as Isadore Cohen, the organizer supported by the United Hebrew Trades, had been organizers for the Bund in Eastern Europe. They agitated for improved sanitary conditions in the shops, a shorter workday, increased wages, and union recognition. As a result, union membership increased from 400 in 1911 to 3,500 by June 1912.

When the manufacturers' associations rejected its demands, the union called a general strike. It was the beginning of the slow season; in 1911 the manufacturers had taken advantage of the low wage-scale to make most of their inventory and were planning the same for 1912. The strike began on June 20, and within two days practically the entire market was at a standstill. The manufacturers' associations generally believed that the strike was good for the industry, since it would allow manufacturers to sell their surpluses.

The furriers took their struggle to the larger immigrant Jewish community, where the conflict between employers and workers, who sometimes belonged to the same organizations, became a community problem. The Jewish labor community supported the furriers. Its financial and moral support were crucial to the success of the strike, which became known as the "people's struggle." The Yiddish daily, *Forverts,* mobilized its resources on behalf of the furriers, collecting over $38,000 in donations for the strikers. The United Hebrew Trades, Socialist Party (SP), Workmen's Circle, Women's Trade Union League, and *landsmanshaftn* all supported the strikers. The Yiddish poet Morris Rosenfeld wrote a poem that was sung with great emotion at mass meetings. The luxurious furs, he wrote, that the furriers toiled over did not keep them warm: "The strong will no longer sleep/Over the damned fur."

Women made up about one-third of the workforce. Some were operators but the majority was concentrated in the finishing branch of the fur industry. Women furriers played a vital role in the success of the strike. They were able picketers, worked hard on committees, and were tenacious fund-raisers. When the strike turned violent, women were also able fighters. Thirty-one percent of strikers arrested were women, and over sixty women were seriously injured. Some heroines, such as Esther Polansky, went on to long and active careers in the furriers' union.

After three months, desperate to open their shops for the busy season, the manufacturers settled the strike. The 1912 agreement provided the possibility of creating an enduring union and establishing stable labor relations. It set up a Conference Committee, with five representatives each from capital and labor and an impartial chairman (a position held by Judah Magnes of the New York Kehillah until 1922), which established a modus operandi for the industry that lasted for many years. The furriers, together with the cloakmakers, pioneered modern industrial relations.

The International Fur Workers' Union of the United States and Canada was born at a convention in Washington, D.C., on June 13, 1913, eight months after the general strike. The new constitution delineated the responsibilities and structure of the union, but the delegates overlooked an inherent weakness that later almost destroyed the union. The problem lay in the relationship of the New York Joint Board, comprising Locals 1, 5, 10, and 15 of the fur manufacturing industry, and the International. The Joint Board included the majority of the workers in the industry and enjoyed considerable autonomy. The International depended on the Joint Board to finance its work elsewhere.

The strength of the International was therefore affected by the strength of the New York locals and their willingness to cooperate with the parent body.

The Conference Committee maintained peace in the industry for the next two years and facilitated a new agreement in 1914. Most important, in the new contract the manufacturers agreed not to discriminate against union members. The agreement endorsed the Conference Committee system of arbitration and created a smaller Committee on Immediate Action to expedite the settlement of disputes within forty-eight hours.

Despite its gains at the bargaining table, the union had difficulty maintaining its membership. The union was born during a time of economic downturn and severe unemployment in the industry. In addition, Jewish workers had a reputation for being tenacious strikers, but poor trade unionists. Many workers refused to pay dues or left the union altogether so that by 1914 less than 10 percent of the workforce belonged to the union. The union generated resentment by insisting that those who had been unemployed become current with their dues and by hiring "gorillas" to "encourage" workers to pay up. The nonpayment of dues was a constant concern, and the union asked the manufacturers to help enforce the agreement. Some manufacturers became so fed up with the problem that they refused to grant the privileges of the agreement to those who refused to bear its burden (by not paying dues).

The fur industry benefited from the general prosperity that accompanied World War I. A labor shortage led to increased wages, and by 1918 two-thirds of the workers were unionized. But the union found it difficult to control workers who acted independently to increase wages. Despite the International's initial denunciation of the war, the manufacturers and workers in New York mobilized behind the war effort. They donated manpower and raised money to support Jewish war relief efforts.

The 1917 contract brought significant gains for the furriers, including a union shop and a minimum wage scale. Tangible benefits and better enforcement of the agreement generated greater confidence in the union, and the Joint Board gained almost 2,000 new members. Yet the negotiations surrounding the 1917 contract saw a new development: the rise of a distinct "left-wing" element in the Joint Board that forced the resignation of manager Isadore Cohen. In 1919, Albert Miller was forced to resign as president of the International. Morris Kaufman, who had succeeded Cohen as manager of the Joint Board, replaced him. During Kaufman's seven-year tenure, the industry experienced a period of rapid growth, which ultimately gave way to an unprecedented level of depression and unemployment.

The union grew and declined, in part due to trade conditions, but also because of the policies of its leadership. The bitter strife following the split in the Socialist Party and formation of the Communist Party (CP) in 1919 also affected the historically radical and socialist furriers' union. This struggle helped to crystallize the dissension within the union and resulted in a bitter struggle for control. Contemporaries characterized the left–right struggle as simply a fight for power or a personality conflict between Morris Kaufman and Ben Gold. It was much more than that. The militants, or left-wingers, objected to the "business" or practical unionism of the old guard, the corruption of business agents and union leaders, and the attempt by the International to gain direct control of the Joint Board.

Born in Bessarabia in 1898, Ben Gold immigrated to America in 1908. He joined the union in 1912 and was active in the strike that year. Socialist friends and the radical political atmosphere at home influenced Gold, and in 1916 he joined the Socialist Party, where he affiliated with the left wing. The furriers were impressed with Gold's dedication to trade union democracy, his championing of workers' rights, his acute mind, his persuasive abilities, and his exceptional oratorical skills. Gold quickly emerged as the leader of the left-wing group.

Despite several attempts at conciliation, the union could not restore harmony between the factions. In 1922, the situation deteriorated further when the Communist-affiliated Trade Union Educational League (TUEL) created a furriers' section. This provided an ideological center, as well as a support group for the left-wing opposition, but it also divided the left-wingers between those who belonged to or sympathized with the CP and those who did not. The TUEL's connection to the CP and the party's alleged subservience to Moscow allowed the right wing to warn against "outside" influences should the left wing gain control of the union. The bitter struggle between the left and right wings was fought in the Jewish press and emotions ran high. In the union, the right wing took steps to prevent the left from gaining control. In 1923, the Joint Board barred left-wing candidates from office and ceased calling local meetings. At the 1924 convention, the International even amended its constitution to allow the General Executive Board to expel any member who participated in protest meetings against the union or who slandered union officers, and it banned Gold from attending sessions of the convention.

The left wing fought back with a huge propaganda campaign among the workers, and its support grew. The left made alliances with other discontented groups, and in 1925 its candidates were elected to office, including Gold as manager of the Joint Board. In a short time, the new manager solved a problem that had long plagued the union: the unorganized Greek workers. Gold used his connections with Greek furrier members of the CP to organize the Greek furriers and then led them in a successful strike. At the acrimonious special convention that year, the right again tried to demolish the left. In an impassioned two-hour speech, Gold countered the accusations against the left. Other New York delegates told of the brutal physical attacks on Gold and other left-wingers. Strengthened, the left ousted Kaufman as president of the International and furthered its agenda through union resolutions.

At the convention, the right produced a telegram containing orders from the Central Executive Committee of the Workers' (Communist) Party to the left-wing delegates. Although Gold denied the telegram's authenticity, the relationship between the CP and the furriers' union was complex. Ben Gold and Aaron Gross, Gold's influential second in command, were party members. Objecting to Stalin's predominance in the party, Gross resigned in 1929, but Gold remained a member until the 1950s. When McCarthyism ravaged the country, Gold was brought before the House Un-American Activities Committee (HUAC), and finally, in the interest of the union, he resigned from the party. The furriers did confer with the party and the party issued directives, but it also criticized the furriers' left wing—and Gold—for placing the practical needs of the union above ideological concerns.

Gold won his reputation through hard work in building the union and fighting tenaciously to improve working conditions. Furriers also supported him because they believed in his personal integrity. One representative of Local 115 who attended conferences with him told of how Gold stood up to the bosses: "He was fearless. He had the guts to talk to them and we always had a good wage. . . . [Gold] was honest. You couldn't buy this man. When he walked down Seventh Avenue everybody wanted to greet him. It was something" (Spingarn 1995).

In 1926, a general strike brought the New York fur manufacturing industry to a standstill. It was part of the continued struggle of the immigrant Jewish furriers for improved material conditions as well as *mentchleke bahandlung* (dignity in the workplace). Violence marked the strike, with each side guilty of attacks. The police were censured for their brutality toward the strikers. The strike had widespread support in the Jewish and labor communities, and after seventeen weeks the furriers won a qualified victory. Most notably, they won a forty-hour week.

Yet it was a hollow victory, for the internecine battle, fought by the left wing under the rubric of "democratic unionism" and by the right wing under the banner of anti-Communism, threatened the very existence of trade unionism in the fur manufacturing industry. The American Federation of Labor joined the attack against the left, using anti-Communism as its rallying cry. Spurious charges against the Joint Board leadership led to their expulsion from the union and the creation of the new Needle Workers' Industrial Union. By 1928 gangsters operated freely in the fur district. The manufacturers took advantage of the chaos to avoid implementing union conditions. In addition, the industry suffered a prolonged depression. By 1930, trade unionism in the fur industry was in retreat, only to be further weakened by the onset of the Great Depression.

At Gold's initiative, the two unions reunited in 1934, and the Needle Workers' Industrial Union disbanded. Two thousand furriers joined the International within three days, and by 1936, the union had 15,000 members. Gold was elected manager of the New York Joint Council in 1935 and president of the International in 1937.

During Gold's tenure, the union became strongly organized and achieved significant improvements in working conditions. In 1936, the fur workers were among the first to join the Committee for Industrial Organization (CIO). In 1939, the furriers led an organizational campaign in the leather industry, and the hitherto unsuccessful leather workers' union joined with the furriers, forming the International Fur and Leather Workers' Union. With the implementation of the Taft-Hartley Act (1947), the union and its leadership became subject to ongoing attacks because of their alleged Communist sympathies. At a time when liberal voices fell silent and anti-Communist hysteria

gripped the nation, Gold intensified the union's struggle against reaction. But ultimately he resigned as president in 1954 to protect the union. Today the fur industry in the United States is but a shadow of what it once was, and most of the production is done overseas.

Sandra Spingarn

References and Further Reading
Epstein, Melech. 1969. *Jewish Labor in the USA*. New York: Ktav Publishing House.
Foner, Philip. 1950. *The Fur and Leather Workers Union*. Newark, NJ: Nordon Press.
Leiter, Robert D. 1950. "The Fur Workers' Union." *Industrial & Labor Relations Review* 3 (January): 163–186.
Spingarn, Sandra. 1995. "Trade Unionism among the Jewish Workers in the Fur Manufacturing Industry in New York City: 1912–1929." PhD dissertation, State University of New York–Binghamton.

David Dubinsky (1892–1982)

Labor Leader

President of the International Ladies' Garment Workers' Union (ILGWU) and a founder of the Committee for Industrial Organization, as well as of the American Labor and Liberal parties, David Dubinsky was a major figure in both labor and politics. A staunch supporter of liberalism, he opposed totalitarianism from the aftermath of the Bolshevik Revolution to the Cold War.

On New Year's Day 1911, the *SS Lapland* brought the young Dubinsky, a fugitive from justice, to New York. He had departed from Lodz, Poland, after escaping from Siberia where czarist justice had sent him for leading a bakers' strike. In Lodz, Dubinsky had belonged to the bakers' union, under the control of the socialist, culturally nationalist Jewish Labor Bund. In New York he became a garment cutter and joined the Socialist Party and the Amalgamated Garment Cutters' Union, Local 10 of the ILGWU, which had been founded in 1900.

Dubinsky entered Local 10 politics, where he rose to prominence by opposing the union's conservative leadership. In 1921 the union elected him general manager, followed the next year by election to an ILGWU vice presidency. There he became embroiled in a civil war that broke out between the International's socialist leaders and

David Dubinsky, president of the International Ladies' Garment Workers' Union and a founder of the American Labor and Liberal parties. (Library of Congress)

Communist-led critics. In 1926 that conflict led to a disastrous strike, during which Dubinsky emerged as a leader of the anti-Communist faction. In 1929 he was elected general secretary-treasurer and served as acting president. The general executive board of the ILGWU elected him president after President Benjamin Schlesinger died in 1932.

Dubinsky projected himself and the ILGWU into the mainstream of American labor and politics. By managing frugally and exploiting the National Industrial Relations Act, which encouraged organized labor, he moved the ILGWU out of debt and dramatically boosted its membership. "Dubinsky's union," as the International was known, would substitute a thirty-five-hour workweek for the sweatshop; enhance security through health, old age, and death benefits; and improve the quality of life through affordable housing and paid vacations. The ILGWU sponsored two housing developments in New York and others in Puerto Rico and Israel. In 1937 the union produced a smash musical revue, *Pins and Needles,* featuring garment

worker performers, and for summer relaxation there was Unity House, an ILGWU-owned "workers' paradise" in Pennsylvania's Pocono Mountains.

In 1934 Dubinsky became a vice president of the American Federation of Labor (AFL). Recognizing that most industrial workers were unorganized, Dubinsky helped found a Committee for Industrial Organization (CIO) within the AFL. As the CIO was unacceptable to the executive council of the AFL, its member unions, including the ILGWU, were suspended. Dubinsky resigned from the executive council. In 1938, when the CIO became a separate Congress of Industrial Organizations, Dubinsky declined to remain with it. He regarded it as a rival federation, which made it guilty of dual unionism. Two years later he led the ILGWU back into the AFL. In 1945 he was reelected to an AFL vice presidency and in that position welcomed the creation of a merged AFL–CIO in 1955.

In 1936 Dubinsky helped found the American Labor Party (ALP), which aided President Franklin D. Roosevelt's reelection by giving him an additional ballot line in New York State. Though the party was an initial success, Dubinsky became increasingly disenchanted with it as it came under leftist influence. Finally, in 1944 he left the ALP and formed the new, more moderate Liberal Party. Along with Alex Rose of the United Hatters, Cap and Millinery Workers International Union, Dubinsky led the Liberals and was a power broker in New York State into the 1970s. The Liberal Party helped elect W. Averell Harriman governor of New York (1954), John F. Kennedy president of the United States (1960), and John V. Lindsay mayor of New York City (1965).

A product of Bundist socialism, Dubinsky fought left- and right-wing totalitarianism within the ILGWU, the American labor movement, and overseas. In 1934 he was a founder of the Jewish Labor Committee (JLC), the anti-Nazi arm of the Jewish labor movement. The JLC supported a boycott of German goods and created a fund to fight Nazism in Germany and fascism in Italy. The next year Dubinsky helped persuade the AFL to organize a central agency to raise funds to combat those evils. In 1936, civil war erupted in Spain and he secured money for anti-fascists there.

Dubinsky faced new challenges in 1939 when Germany invaded Poland and began World War II. He organized efforts to rescue Jewish labor leaders from Nazi-occupied Europe. When Stalin executed two Polish socialists, Henryk Erlich and Victor Alter, he vehemently protested. Anticipating Soviet designs on postwar Europe, in 1944 Dubinsky helped create and served on the Free Trade Union Committee of the AFL, which gave financial support to anti-Communist labor organizations in Western Europe. In 1949 he joined in founding the International Confederation of Free Trade Unions.

At midcentury Dubinsky was America's best-known and most influential leader of a needle-trades union, as well as a prominent, liberal anti-Communist. With other liberals who opposed Soviet policies, in 1947 he helped found Americans for Democratic Action and backed Harry S Truman in the next year's presidential election. Firm but moderate in his anti-Communism, Dubinsky afterward opposed the excesses of Senator Joseph McCarthy of Wisconsin.

Despite his Bundist background, which was anti-Zionist, Dubinsky maintained close ties with the Jewish labor movement in Palestine. After the Holocaust and the Second World War, he had deep concern for the fate of Jewish refugees. In 1948 he became a strong supporter of the new Jewish State of Israel.

In 1957 he achieved success within the AFL–CIO. After nearly two decades of campaigning for action to eliminate racketeering, Dubinsky saw the recently merged labor federation adopt a code of ethics, and he became a member of its Ethical Practices Committee.

A highly visible trade unionist, Dubinsky was vulnerable to criticism. Racketeering was a chronic problem within the ILGWU and the garment industry, one that received much public exposure during hearings conducted by Senator John McClellan of Arkansas. In addition, though the ILGWU had long supported civil rights, complaints arose that the union itself was guilty of racial discrimination, and Dubinsky came under fire. The National Association for the Advancement of Colored People held the ILGWU accountable for the concentration of black and Puerto Rican workers mainly in low-paid, unskilled garment industry trades and accused Dubinsky's own Cutters' Union, Local 10, of denying membership to a black worker on the basis of race. After a bitter dispute, differences were resolved. Traditionally, staff members of the International had been low-paid. In an attempt to improve their working conditions, several formed a union, the Federation of Union Representatives (FOUR), but Dubinsky took personal offense and defeated them after a lengthy battle. As a leader of the Liberal Party, Dubinsky usually went unchallenged. However, in 1965 some senior ILGWU vice presidents questioned his endorsement of Republican John Lindsay as the party's candidate for mayor of New York City. Dubinsky prevailed, but, unaccustomed to such criticism, advancing in age, and failing in health, he retired in 1966. Afterward, the ILGWU made him honorary president and created a Retiree Service Department for him to administer.

Robert D. Parmet

References and Further Reading
Danish, Max D. 1957. *The World of David Dubinsky.* Cleveland, OH: World Publishing Company.
Dubinsky, David, and A. H. Raskin. 1977. *David Dubinsky: A Life with Labor.* New York: Simon & Schuster.
Parmet, Robert D. 2005. *The Master of Seventh Avenue: David Dubinsky and the American Labor Movement.* New York: New York University Press.
Special Supplement. 1968. "David Dubinsky, the I.L.G.W.U., and the American Labor Movement." *Labor History* 9.

Samuel Gompers (1850–1924)

Founder and Longtime President of the American Federation of Labor (AFL)

Samuel Gompers was the nation's leading trade unionist and labor advocate in the late nineteenth and early twentieth centuries. As president of the AFL, the first successful national alliance of trade unions, Gompers championed shorter hours, higher wages, safe and sanitary working conditions, and labor's right to organize, strike, and bargain collectively with employers. Although socialist critics deplored his "pure and simple" strategies, his aversion to independent labor politics, and his willingness to participate in joint labor–management organizations like the National Civic Federation, trade union supporters valued him as a tireless organizer and practical politician who could be trusted to protect their interests in trade negotiations and legislative councils.

As AFL president from 1886 through 1894, and then from 1896 to the end of his life, Gompers successfully campaigned to restrict child, convict, and alien contract labor, to enforce eight-hour laws on government work,

Samuel Gompers, president of the American Federation of Labor, casts his vote, ca. 1920. (Library of Congress)

helped draft a charter of basic labor rights, including the right to organize, work an eight-hour day and a six-day week, and earn living wages and equal pay for equal work. In the process, Gompers also helped organize the International Labor Organization, a permanent board that promised to bring together representatives of governments, employers, and workers to promote and protect those rights. Although his efforts to maintain labor's wartime gains were thwarted in the 1920s, Gompers was nevertheless honored as a patriot and labor statesman when he died in 1924.

The oldest son of Dutch Jewish immigrants, Gompers grew up in poverty in the Spitalfields district of East London. He was a good student at the Jews' Free School, where he learned to read, write, and do arithmetic, but by age ten he had left school to make a living, apprenticing first as a shoemaker and then taking up his father's trade, cigarmaking. After the family immigrated to the United States, settling in New York City's Lower East Side in 1863, he proved to be a skilled cigar roller who was willing and able to defend his shopmates' rights. A member of various fraternal organizations and the Jewish mutual aid association, the Hand-in-Hand Society, Gompers also joined the Cigar Makers' National Union in 1864.

Gompers took no interest in labor reform until 1873, when he went to work at a cigar factory owned by a German socialist, David Hirsch. There he met Ferdinand Laurrell, a Swedish socialist, who persuaded him that trade unions offered wage earners their best hope for change. With Laurrell's help, Gompers began reading socialist tracts, like Karl Marx's *Communist Manifesto* and Carl Hillmann's *Practical Suggestions for Emancipation,* that linked trade unionism and the pursuit of immediate gains to the eventual abolition of the wage system. He also began attending meetings of the International Workingmen's Association (IWA), a Marxist organization, where he joined a group of trade-union socialists who called themselves *Die Zehn Philosophen* (The Ten Philosophers).

Coming of age in an era of ten- and twelve-hour workdays, cyclical economic depressions, and cutthroat wage competition, these workers agreed that strong, well-organized, "pure and simple" unions—with no ties to political parties of any kind—had the best chance of achieving labor solidarity, humanizing industry, and creating opportunities for workers to learn how to think and act for themselves. Although critics would later caricature his

and to establish the U.S. Department of Labor. He was the leading proponent of the Pan-American Federation of Labor (an international forum for Latin American trade unionists) and, until the outbreak of World War I, actively supported the International Federation of Trade Unions (which sought to establish uniform labor laws and to prevent the movement of strikebreakers from country to country).

An avowed pacifist until the United States was on the verge of declaring war against Germany, Gompers was appointed in 1916 to the Advisory Commission of the Council of National Defense, the federal agency established to organize the nation's preparedness program. As chairman of its Committee on Labor, he was instrumental in mobilizing the wartime workforce and shoring up labor's support—both at home and abroad—for the war effort, and he helped develop government labor policies to increase production, reduce industrial conflict, and advance labor's wage and hour standards. At the height of his public popularity early in 1919, Gompers represented the United States on the Commission on International Labor Legislation that met in Paris as part of the peace conference and

trade-union philosophy as a cry for "more, more, more," Gompers believed there was a direct connection between organizing to achieve immediate gains and fundamentally transforming society.

An immigrant surrounded by immigrants, Gompers identified as an American from the start: he spoke English, was used to city living, and feared that "foreigners" who would not, or could not, assimilate—particularly the Chinese—threatened to undermine American standards of living. In his own trade, unskilled Bohemian immigrants were already flooding the industry, thanks to the introduction of a mechanical press, called the mold, that broke down skilled work into component parts. Willing to work for subsistence wages, these "new" immigrants rented tenement apartments from employers and then put the entire family to work at home, a practice that led to long hours, overcrowded and unsanitary conditions, and uneducated children.

Although the Cigar Makers' International Union (CMIU) refused to recognize this branch of the trade, Gompers followed the lead of Adolph Strasser, a Hungarian immigrant he met through the IWA, who had organized an independent cigar makers' union open to skilled and unskilled workers, male and female alike. By 1873 the new union counted almost 2,000 members, and Gompers's hopes were high for "Americanizing" unskilled immigrants and unionizing the entire trade. However, a national economic depression (the Panic of 1873), coupled with an unsuccessful strike, decimated the union.

The experience strengthened his conviction that trade unions had to be financially secure to withstand hard times and employer hostility. So in 1875 Gompers and Strasser organized CMIU Local 144, incorporating a system of high dues, out-of-work and strike benefits, and centralized administration that came to be known as "business unionism." Although critics condemned these policies as elitist, Gompers and Strasser intended to elevate the lowest-paid worker to the standard of the highest, as they put it, in order to secure the means of a satisfying life for every person in the trade.

Other early experiences also shaped his trade union philosophy. After police brutally attacked a crowd of unemployed workers demonstrating in Tompkins Square in 1874, and newspapers applauded the action, Gompers concluded that radical slogans and professions of militancy only invited repression. He would also conclude,

over the next few years, that the state could not be counted on to improve workers' lives. The CMIU's political campaign to outlaw tenement production in the early 1880s, for instance, had resulted in two remedial laws, but both were declared unconstitutional. Yet when union members decided to strike until manufacturers abandoned the tenement system, they got results, a powerful economic lesson that was further confirmed by Gompers's experience with the Federation of Organized Trades and Labor Unions (FOTLU), an annual congress organized in 1881 to prepare and promote labor legislation. Because the FOTLU had neither the funds nor the authority to do more than talk about issues like the eight-hour day or the regulation of child labor, Gompers supported a call, in 1886, to organize the AFL, a voluntary alliance of national trade unions and state and local trade assemblies with the goal of thoroughly organizing the industrial work force.

As the AFL's full-time president (and CMIU vice president since 1886), Gompers was frequently on the road in the 1890s, a practice that would mark his entire career. Whether he was testifying before Congress or state legislatures on the value of organized labor, rallying workers at mass meetings, or negotiating strike settlements, Gompers proved to be a capable, dependable, and unflappable spokesman for the trade union movement, well-known and respected for his integrity, his generosity, and his willingness to speak truth to power. Well aware that wage-earners easily divided along lines of ethnicity, skill, race, gender, and politics, Gompers focused on achieving higher wages and shorter hours as a practical method of raising working-class consciousness. When workers organized and won tangible improvements, they began to expect more out of life than constant drudgery, he believed, and they became more willing to stand together and fight for social justice.

Determined from the start to avoid the factional fights that had destroyed previous national labor organizations, Gompers brooked no interference from outsiders, whether they were middle-class social reformers, radical intellectuals, party politicians, or well-meaning lawyers. As AFL president, he opposed the Knights of Labor, a broad social reform group, when it organized trade assemblies that competed with unions, and he denigrated socialists of all stripes as utopian "rainbow chasers" unless they were willing to put trade union organization first. But, if he spurned the socialist call for industrial unionism, independent labor politics, and cross-class alliances, he did not discount the importance of political action. Instead, Gompers developed a nonpartisan policy of supporting labor's friends in local, state, and federal elections, and defeating labor's enemies, regardless of party. He adhered to this policy throughout his career, save for the 1924 presidential campaign, when the AFL voted to endorse Farmer-Labor candidate Robert La Follette. Supporters of more radical organizations, like the Industrial Workers of the World, regularly complained that Gompers's approach was far too narrow and conservative to serve the needs of the new industrial workforce, especially unskilled black, female, and recent immigrant workers. But under his stewardship, the AFL grew from a "rope of sand" in the 1890s to a permanent organization representing some 4 million members in 1920, far more than any other labor organization could boast at the time (Taft 1957).

Although Gompers was instrumental in helping Jewish immigrants organize the needle trades, and he spoke out against the brutal persecution of Jews during World War I, he never associated his activities with any religious denomination or faith. When David Lubin, an agricultural reformer, attempted to appeal to him on the basis of their shared religion, the AFL president's reply was frank: "You say that your chief glory is that you are a Jew. Mine is that I have a heart, a mind and a conscience, that I have struggled with my fellowmen . . . for a better day when the ridiculous divisions, questions that make man an enemy to man instead of his brother, shall be eliminated" (Kaufman, Albert, and Palladino 1986, 3).

If he took great pride in his family heritage, Gompers had no taste for orthodoxy of any kind, an attitude he attributed to his early experience with the Ethical Culture Society, a group more interested in human behavior and values than ancient religious rites. In the same vein, he firmly believed that Jewish immigrants, like any other immigrant group, had an obligation to become citizens of their new homeland and identify with their future, not their past. Although he eventually agreed that Yiddish-speaking immigrants were most easily organized through the United Hebrew Trades, a New York City central labor organization, he opposed the idea that the Jews should remain a people apart. When the question of supporting the Zionist movement was raised in 1916, for instance, he made it clear that he heartily supported any movement for equality and justice for the Jews, but that he opposed any policy that would perpetuate their isolation.

Although Gompers and his first wife, Sophia Julian Gompers, were both descended from religious families, there is no indication that Gompers was religiously observant or that their children were raised in a religious household. In fact his second wife, Gertrude Gleaves Neuscheler Gompers, whom he married in 1921 after Sophie's death, was Christian. And while Rabbi Stephen S. Wise gave the eulogy at his funeral, it was Gompers's wish that the service be "absolutely non-sectarian" and that it be held under the direction of the local labor movement (President Gompers's File, frame 30).

Grace Palladino

References and Further Reading
Gompers, Samuel. 1925. *Seventy Years of Life and Labor: An Autobiography.* 2 Vols. New York: Dutton.
Kaufman, Stuart B. 1973. *Samuel Gompers and the Origins of the American Federation of Labor, 1848–1896.* Westport, CT: Greenwood Press.
Kaufman, Stuart B., Peter Albert, and Grace Palladino, eds. 1986. *The Samuel Gompers Papers.* 10 Vols. to date. Urbana: University of Illinois Press.
Mandel, Bernard. 1963. *Samuel Gompers: A Biography.* Yellow Springs, OH: Antioch Press.
President Gompers's File. AFL microfilm file, reel 8. Silver Spring, MD: George Meany Memorial Archives.
Reed, Louis S. 1930. *The Labor Philosophy of Samuel Gompers.* New York: Columbia University Press.
Taft, Philip. 1957. *The A. F. of L. in the Time of Gompers.* New York: Harper & Row.

Sidney Hillman (1887–1946)

President of Amalgamated Clothing Workers of America and Leader of Congress of Industrial Organizations

As a young man, Sidney (Simcha) Hillman started on his road to fame by dramatically changing his ideological outlook. While in his teens in Russian Lithuania, he turned quickly from a rigorous Yeshiva student into a Bundist, then into a Menshevik. A few years later, in the United States, he settled into being a practically minded American industrial unionist. Early on, he was well schooled by reform-minded labor leaders and urban progressives. He remained, however, a social democrat who initially served his fellow immigrant workers in the men's clothing industry,

Sidney Hillman, president of the Amalgamated Clothing Workers of America from 1914 to 1946 and a leader of the Congress of Industrial Organizations. (Library of Congress)

and, later, as a leader in the Congress of Industrial Organizations (CIO), served black and white ethnic employees in America's mass-production centers. In the towns and cities of the Northeast, these men and women were mostly first- and second-generation migrants who anchored their collective identities in memories of the American South or East Central and Southern Europe.

Growing numbers of them were mobilizing to promote working-class agendas of political change; some did so with a consciousness of race, ethnicity, and peoplehood. Most, with their industrial unions, wanted the help of the federal government to improve their standard of living and the conditions in their workplace. Within this complex mix of backgrounds and aspirations, Hillman helped to modernize their industrial relations and discipline the capitalist society in which they worked. His accomplishments were remarkable—a testimony, in part, to the comradeship in a large segment of the American labor union movement. His successes occurred in a period riven with ideological conflicts, at home and abroad, and with ever more serious expressions of antisemitism and antiradicalism.

These peaked in the 1930s and 1940s during the years of the New Deal and World War II with its Jewish Catastrophe. But throughout, Hillman remained the union leader searching for ways to widen the scope of organized labor's influence in the American body politic.

Born on March 23, 1887, into a rabbinic family and orthodox household near Kovno, in Zagare, Lithuania, Simcha Hillman rebelled against the ways of his family by joining secular sectarian collectives seeking profound change in the body politic of the czarist empire. In 1904–1905, in Kovno he was jailed twice for short terms, first as a Jewish socialist agitating for the Bund and a second time as an anti-Bundist Menshevik organizer in the Russian Social Democratic Party. In 1906, with his movement forced underground by czarist police, he too went into hiding, and then, as did other endangered revolutionaries, the young Hillman emigrated. Along with large numbers of other Lithuanian Jews, he went westward, first to an uncle and two brothers in Manchester, England, and then, with his brother Harry, via New York to Chicago.

In 1909–1910, during a major strike at Hart Schaffner & Marx, a well-known modern firm manufacturing men's clothing, where Hillman had been hired as an apprentice cutter a few months earlier, both opponents and supporters recognized in him a different kind of union man—one who could lead militant workers toward a new kind of industrial order. Like the militants in the strike, the Yiddish-speaking assistant cutter in Local 39 of the United Garment Workers (UGW) wanted more than union recognition and collective bargaining. He was also eager to become fluent in English and rise above the cacophony of parochial enthusiasms. He wanted to work with shop owners, statistically oriented technical experts, and promoters of arbitration procedures. Together they would be able to reduce wasteful conflict between capital and labor to the benefit of both.

It was the start of a remarkable labor union career, as he and his fellow workers from Yiddish-speaking neighborhoods and workplaces simultaneously fought antisemitic and nativist officers of the UGW, who felt threatened by the immigrants and socialists in the metropolitan centers of the needle trades. In 1914 his Chicago friends asked twenty-seven-year-old Simcha to become president of the Amalgamated Clothing Workers of America (ACW), a new industrial union in the men's clothing industry. He had just been hired as chief clerk of the Joint Board of the International Ladies' Garment Workers' Union (ILGWU) in New

York to administer its new contract. Hillman became the youngest president of any American national union, and he remained president until his death in 1946.

Hillman's organization was born in sin, a dual union competing with the UGW, a craft union that was formally chartered by the American Federation of Labor (AFL). Although freed from the constraints and financial obligations that came with traditional trade union legitimacy, until 1933 Hillman had to cope with institutional opposition from the AFL and its Socialist Party supporters in the Jewish labor movement. He had to focus on the men's clothing industry's cutthroat competitors, on hooligans and Jewish crime gangs—often used in the 1920s in the industrial relations of the needle trades of New York City—on his union's bread-and-butter issues, and on its social welfare reforms. He also had to confront the religious-like fervor of all sorts of ideologues: anarchists and syndicalists, Lenin-inspired Bolsheviks, Zionists, Central European and English-oriented socialists, and the followers of homegrown socialist Eugene V. Debs.

While sympathetic to some of these class-based enthusiasms—in the early years of the Bolshevik Revolution he visited Lenin and some Soviet economic enterprises—Hillman was a practical labor leader. He also followed the trend among national unions that centralized authority in the hands of a strong president whose reelection was never in doubt. He dedicated himself to eliminating market competition harmful to the needle trades and their workers, and established union criteria for applying scientific management to standards of production. During World War I, in his relations with senior administrators of the federal Board of Control of Labor Standards, he learned how to use administrative agencies for his union's needs. These choices put him at odds with fellow unionists whose inclination was for ever more union democracy, spontaneous action, and shop floor control.

Simcha Hillman, after 1917 a naturalized American citizen renamed Sidney, was always the talented foreign-born Jewish labor leader of working men and women, never the leader of their ethnic institutions or politics. In 1920, the ACW—at 177,000 members, most of whom were women—was one of the largest industrial unions in the nation. During World War I and the 1920s, his union's collective bargaining agreements with employers brought a forty-four-hour workweek and such alternatives to disruptive conflict as workshop efficiency, contract discipline, so-

cial welfare benefits, and arbitration procedures. Steven Fraser, his finest biographer, has characterized Hillman as the "true industrial modern: A pioneer of worker participation as a vital component of managerial strategy, he was an architect of a new moral order of work, one based neither on coercion nor on monetary incentives, but on those intangibles of the psyche and the social then being explored by industrial psychology and sociology." Shrewdly, he steered his internally contentious members through competing passions of communism, socialism, and nationalism. By the midtwenties, under Hillman's oversight, including highly controversial tactical arrangements with Communists, the union had avoided the kind of internal sectarian combat that almost destroyed the ILG, the other leading union of the needle trades.

During the Great Depression and World War II, Hillman played major roles in the CIO, the new labor organization formed in 1935, and in three of Franklin Roosevelt's presidential elections; in 1940 and 1941 he was also influential in handling complex labor problems for the administration. One of the founders and leaders of the CIO, he was in many ways as important to the organization as its president, John L. Lewis, the famous leader of the United Mine Workers. In this role, Hillman became a leader in the campaign to organize industrial workers outside of the needle trades. In 1936, in the period of the Soviet-inspired Popular Front, which lasted from 1935 to 1939, he helped to mobilize the antifascist coalition that viewed Roosevelt's Democratic Party as the main bulwark against fascism, at home and abroad. As vice president of the CIO, Hillman, always fighting for FDR and his program, was active in the Labor Non-Partisan League and, beginning in 1936 at its founding, in New York's American Labor Party.

Starting in 1933 he accepted minor appointments in New Deal efforts, and in 1940 Roosevelt appointed him co-director of the Office of Production Management. This was a difficult position for a labor leader such as Hillman, for now, in the days of the Hitler-Stalin Pact, pockets of strong isolationist and Communist sentiment in the workplace opposed Roosevelt's support of the United Kingdom. Hillman also faced aggressive businessmen and contentious unions slowly emerging from the Depression. After Pearl Harbor he lost his position in the war effort, but remained loyal to Roosevelt. In 1943 and 1944 he campaigned for Roosevelt's reelection and helped mobilize organized workers as a liberal force in the Democratic Party.

During the Holocaust years, near the end of the war, he helped the Zionist campaign establish a Jewish Commonwealth in Palestine. After Roosevelt's death Hillman spent his last years working for a World Federation of Labor (WFL) on behalf of a new world order under American–Soviet leadership. That project ended in failure, but the Zionist campaign did not. In 1944–1945, at the founding meetings of the WFL, he worked on a resolution supporting a Jewish Commonwealth. Contrary to his past practices, Hillman, the famous American labor leader and statesman, now publicly identified himself with the Histadruth, the Socialist Zionist labor organization in Palestine, and was instrumental in having its Commonwealth resolution adopted by the WFL.

Hillman had always had a private Jewish life, and in public he had remained engaged with Jewish affairs. He and Bessie Abramowitz, an important ACW leader in her own right, whom he had met in Chicago in the summer of 1909, were married in a synagogue and marked their children's confirmation with religious ceremonies. Together they retained Jewish family connections in Europe and in Palestine.

In his public affairs Hillman was in continuous contact with many Jews and Jewish organizations. Besides his union members, these included businessmen, lawyers, Reform rabbis, settlement house workers, progressive reformers, and all sorts of fellow socialists. Even in union budget matters the Jewish connection made itself felt: there were reports from locals that income had fallen during the months of Passover and the High Holy days.

And always there was the public antisemitism. It came in the form of attacks, and not only from opposing employers and politicians. As did other Jews, so too did Hillman encounter antisemitic outbursts from fellow unionists and from the larger progressive and socialist community. Often expressed during moments of combat, one of the most dramatic outbursts came from John L. Lewis, at a CIO podium in 1940, when he bitterly opposed Hillman and the reelection of Roosevelt. That background of antisemitism was one of the important reasons why, in the 1944 campaign, Republicans and many of their media supporters used the political innuendo "Clear it with Sidney" to mark Hillman as the Jewish immigrant labor leader who, while friendly to Communists and Soviet Russia, controlled the Democratic Party.

Hillman made important decisions that had reverberated in some of the special interest groups in the Jewish world. In the euphoric days of Zionism and the Bolshevik Revolution, the English government's Balfour Declaration, calling for a Jewish homeland in Palestine, did not persuade Hillman to become a socialist Zionist or, for that matter, tolerant of other socialist theories of nationalism. He continued in his socialist assimilationist ways. For a number of years he supported Lenin's economic programs in Russia. Hundreds of thousands of ACW dollars went to the American Industrial Corporation, a product of cooperation between the Soviets and the ACW, though Hillman did not authorize "outside donations" of comparable amounts to Jewish worker groups in Palestine. As late as 1939 the Histadruth was still excluded from the non-American public causes supported directly by Hillman and the Executive Board. To the Labor Zionist Joseph Schlossberg, then on the ACW's board, those were contentious decisions. Still, ten years earlier Hillman had officially declared himself a member of the non-Zionist support group of the Jewish Agency in Palestine. Hillman did not block ACW locals from aiding Jewish causes, including those in Palestine, and he had approved contributions to the Jewish Joint Distribution Committee's work, designed to help Jews in the Soviet Union. And as early as 1933 he had supported efforts of the American Jewish Congress to battle Hitler's antisemitic campaign.

The events of the war years led Hillman to change his mind about the Histadruth. Until jolted by the news of European Jewry's catastrophe, Hillman was locked into his prewar mentality. Influenced by his own history and that of the ACW and the needle trades, he read the future by his strong flickers of socialist enlightenment. He saw Jews as a one-generation proletariat, moving upward and out. Since 1924 restrictive immigration laws had all but ended Jewish migration from Europe to the United States, and the proportion of Jews in the union and in the industry's work force had dramatically declined. In 1940 only about 15 percent of ACW members were Jews. It was clear to him that the Jewish labor movement in the United States was ending. But between 1942 and 1946 he recognized that there would also be no Jewish labor movement in Europe, and that cast the Histadruth in a different light. (Indeed, perhaps he now comprehended that Jewish continuity and survival were at stake.) Now he would work with Socialist Zionists and the Histadruth, because he could do so within an anti-colonialist and anti-imperialist campaign, which corresponded with American foreign policy ideals and with Soviet interests in the Middle East.

What mattered most to Hillman was the wartime alliance between Americans and Russians and the vision of a postwar world under the hegemony of the United States and the Soviet Union. That is why in 1943, when news arrived that the Red Army had murdered two senior leaders of the Bund, he did not join in the public outrage, infuriating anti-Communist Jewish socialists, especially former Bundists like himself. A year earlier, however, Hillman had started to work closely with the representative of the Histadruth in New York. Although no longer part of Roosevelt's inner circle, as always, he moved toward real power on the ground. After November 1942, following the defeat of the German Afrika Corps outside Cairo in Egypt, he believed that the Histadruth would gain increasing power in Palestine. Convinced that the Jewish Labor Movement would exist only there, with Israel Mereminsky, the Histadruth's representative in New York during World War II, he now planned for a physical link between the ACW and the Histadruth. Under its auspices in Palestine, the Amalgamated Clothing Workers would support an Amal vocational school network. "Amal" not only stood for Amalgamated, but also for *amal* (*Ayin, Mem, Lamed*), the Hebrew word used by socialist Zionists to refer to the ideals of pioneering manual labor in the land of Israel.

Following a heart attack in 1942, Hillman lived four more active and influential years. He participated in political election campaigns, was engaged with issues affecting occupied Germany, and was involved in the effort to find a home for 100,000 of the Jewish survivors in Palestine. In May 1946 he publicly linked that campaign to what we now call the Holocaust. In his last address to an ACW convention he said: "[T]here is one group that they decided to destroy completely, so as not even to leave any representatives of this people even to carry water for them. They almost succeeded. They destroyed six million Jews. Those Jews are gone, but there are others in Germany today . . . [who] are required to live in camps with all their memories of the horrors of the past. . . . These people want to get out of Germany and there is only one place they want to go to, and that is Palestine, and I say to you that no one has the moral right to stop them from going there. . . ." Hillman did not live to see the establishment of Israel and the full rapprochement between the leaders of Jewish-led needle trade unions and the socialist Zionists who founded it. But old colleagues and friends on the ACW's Executive Board did, and so did his wife, Bessie.

Sidney Hillman died on July 10, 1946. He had become a different Jew from the Simcha of Zagare. But his Yiddish-speaking comrades remembered his journey into post-Talmudic secular Jewry. At the memorial service in Carnegie Hall, in the presence of thousands of dignitaries, and with tens of thousands of workers milling in the street outside, Jacob Potofsky, Hillman's successor as president of the union, spoke of his old friend as a "great American and a God-fearing man." And when Bessie and the children buried him at the Westchester Hills Cemetery in Mount Hope, New York, another old friend, Rabbi Stephen S. Wise, a major figure in the Zionist wing of the Reform Movement, said Kaddish.

Gerd Korman

References and Further Reading
Brandes, Joseph. 1976. "From Sweatshop to Stability: Jewish Labor between Two World Wars." *YIVO Annual of Jewish Social Science* 16: 1–149.
Brody, David. 1974. "Sidney Hillman." In *Dictionary of American Biography,* Supplement Four, edited by John A. Garraty and Edward T. James. New York: Charles Scribner's Sons.
Carpenter, Jesse. 1972. *Competition and Collective Bargaining in the Needle Trades, 1910–1967.* Ithaca: New York State School of Industrial and Labor Relations.
Foster, James C. 1975. *The Union Politic: The CIO Political Action Committee.* Columbia: University of Missouri Press.
Fraser, Steven. 1993. *Labor Will Rule: Sidney Hillman and the Rise of American Labor.* Ithaca, NY: Cornell University Press.
Josephson, Matthew. 1952. *Sidney Hillman, Statesman of American Labor.* Garden City, NY: Doubleday.
Korman, Gerd. 1986. "Ethnic Democracy and Its Ambiguities: The Case of the Needle Trade Unions." *American Jewish History* 75: 405–426.
Korman, Gerd. 1994. "New Jewish Politics for an American Labor Leader: Sidney Hillman, 1942–1946." *American Jewish History* 82: 195–213.

Pauline M. Newman (1890–1986)

Labor Activist

Pauline Newman was a labor pioneer whose career spanned almost the entire history of the International Ladies' Garment Workers' Union (ILGWU). Associated with that union for more than seventy-five years, Newman nevertheless became, by the end of her long life, a symbol of something much bigger—the militance of early twentieth-century women workers. In 1909, while still in her teens, Newman was appointed general organizer by the ILGWU. She was the first woman to hold such a post. Though she would battle with the men who ran that union over their condescension toward women organizers and their failure to recognize the vital contributions of women workers, Newman stayed on the job for the ILGWU for most of the twentieth century—first as a grassroots organizer, later as a labor journalist and health educator. Newman's other political home was the New York Women's Trade Union League (WTUL), where she served during the 1920s, thirties, and forties as vice president, general organizer, and liaison between labor leaders, captains of industry, and agency chiefs in state and federal government.

Newman referred to the garment unions as "the Jewish movement," because they were so heavily influenced by Jewish immigrant socialists. She was proud of that Jewish movement, which she saw as the primary means through which Jewish progressive thought influenced United States policy during the first half of the twentieth century. She was equally proud of the "women's movement" galvanized by the WTUL. Pauline Newman's influence on labor politics, the emerging welfare state, and the ongoing struggle for women's rights was far greater than any official resume suggests.

A Jewish immigrant from Lithuania, Pauline Newman was an iconoclast even among the Socialist bohemians of the Jewish labor movement. She had a penchant for tweeds, wore her hair slicked back, and was so tough in labor negotiations that she was described admiringly by one male colleague as "one of the boys in many ways. She could smoke a cigar with the best of them" (Orleck 1995). In an era when the idea of unionism was synonymous with notions of brotherhood and masculine bonding, Pauline Newman pushed accepted gender norms in the trade union movement. She was as happy to challenge hard-boiled male union leaders as she was to take on recalcitrant employers. She took pride that union men seemed to accept her as one of their own, even as she longed for the social companionship of women. Newman was one of the key players in the woman-centered trade union network that crystallized around the New York and National Women's Trade Union Leagues because women trade

union activists, like her best friend Rose Schneiderman, sustained her emotionally and intellectually. Throughout her years in the labor movement, Newman was caught between worlds. She pursued a difficult balancing act—negotiating with male unionists, middle- and upper-class women reformers, and government officials for the one goal that mattered most to her—improving the lives of women workers.

Pauline Newman was born into a world that was exploding with change even as she grew up. The exact date of her birth was lost with the family Bible sometime during the family's passage to America. The best estimate is that she was born around 1890. The circumstances of her birth are better known—she was born into a deeply poor and equally religious Jewish family in Kovno, Lithuania, the youngest of four children—three girls and a boy. Newman would later write to her grandchildren that her activist career began when she was still a very small girl—and was told she could not attend *kheydr* (religious day school) with the boys in her village. She demanded to know where in the Torah it said that girls should not receive the same religious education as boys. Her father, a Talmud teacher, couldn't argue with her logic. So he personally taught her to read Hebrew and Yiddish. Years later, Newman claimed that her childhood resentment of the privileges accorded males in Jewish education and worship sparked her life-long commitment to fight sex discrimination along with injustices of class, race, and religion.

Newman, her sisters, and her mother left Kovno for New York after her father died suddenly in 1901. The family was at first put up by Newman's brother, who had emigrated a few years earlier. Now eleven years old, Newman began work at a hairbrush factory, but soon moved to the Triangle Shirtwaist Factory in Greenwich Village. Already a confirmed rebel, Newman felt powerfully drawn to the labor socialism she heard from older workers in her shop. Like so many Jewish immigrants of her generation, Newman also learned the fundamentals of socialism by reading Abraham Cahan's Yiddish language daily, the *Jewish Daily Forward*. Still, Newman knew that reading Russian (which she had taught herself), Yiddish, and Hebrew was not enough. To get by, to thrive in America, she and her fellow workers would need to know English. And so Newman organized reading groups for the teenage girls among whom she worked. By candlelight in the coal-dusty, dimly lit garment shops of Lower Manhattan, Newman and her coworkers taught themselves English by reading literary exposés of nineteenth-century English industry. Newman recalled that the readings only intensified the girls' desire to rise up against the long hours, low pay, and miserable conditions in which they lived and worked. Between 1905 and 1907 Newman and other immigrant Jewish girls engaged in a number of wildcat strikes and walkouts. During the summer of 1907, as a depression and housing shortage hit Lower Manhattan, Newman led 400 girls in building a tent village on the Palisades above the Hudson River. There they lived for the summer and organized a rent strike among Lower East Side Jewish families that became the largest rent strike New York had seen. Involving 10,000 families in all, this strike began decades of tenant activism in New York that ultimately led to the city's first rent control laws.

New York newspapers hailed Newman as the "Lower East Side Joan of Arc." The Socialist Party (SP) nominated the seventeen-year-old activist for New York secretary of state. Campaigning with Eugene Victor Debs, the SP leader, she took the opportunity to promote woman suffrage. Meanwhile, she built support among young women garment workers for a general strike that exploded in the fall of 1909 involving 30,000–40,000 mostly Jewish shirtwaist makers. Besides organizing in advance, Newman helped to sustain the strike in two key ways. Through the long, cold winter, through week after week of intense police brutality, she kept strikers' spirits up with inspiring speeches at union halls and on the picket lines. She also kept strikers fed and housed by raising funds among New York's wealthiest women, quoting liberally from English literary figures to win these educated women's sympathy for the ragged strikers. Newman was even able to persuade some of these women to join picket lines, hoping that their presence would diminish police brutality against the strikers. These "mink brigades" brought the strike its first positive coverage in the city's mainstream newspapers. And the presence of society women on the picket lines made police more cautious about whom they clubbed.

Impressed by her spirit, her bravery, as well as her oratorical and fund-raising skills, the leadership of the ILGWU appointed the eighteen-year-old Newman as the first woman general organizer in the garment trades. The next four years were exhilarating, frustrating, and lonely as Newman traveled the country, living out of suitcases, sleeping in depressingly grim working-class hotels, and organizing garment strikes in Philadelphia, Cleveland, Boston, and Kalamazoo, Michigan. By decade's end, these strikes had resulted in the unionization of more than 40 percent of all women garment workers, a remarkable percentage for workers in any trade and a clear refutation of union leaders' oft-repeated assertions that women could not be organized.

Still, the years on the road were extremely difficult for Newman. She was one of the only women in a male world of labor organizers, still a child in many ways, and vulnerable both to their harassment and their condescension. She felt that the male union leadership undermined and undervalued her work, and wondered if she could somehow find more supportive colleagues. She campaigned for the Socialist Party in the coal-mining camps of southern Illinois and also agitated for women's right to vote, which she considered crucial to the success of the working-class struggle.

Newman was paralyzed by grief when the Triangle Shirtwaist Factory burned on March 25, 1911. One hundred forty-six young workers died, most of them Jewish and Italian women, and many of them cherished friends from Newman's years as a Triangle worker. Newman won a post on the Factory Investigating Commission, which was established by New York State in the aftermath of the fire to improve factory safety. Through this work she met Frances Perkins, eyewitness to the fire and an activist for the Consumers League, later to become Franklin Roosevelt's secretary of labor. Newman also met future New York governor Al Smith and future U.S. senator Robert Wagner, all of whom worked with her in inspecting New York factories to ensure that hazardous conditions were corrected. This experience led Newman to conclude that securing the future of working women required not only organization but also government legislation. For the next thirty years, Newman worked as a lobbyist for the New York WTUL, pushing for passage of wage, hour, and safety legislation for women workers. She never gave up union work, but for the remainder of her career, she divided her energies between organizing, education, and lobbying.

In 1917, Newman left New York again, this time to travel to Philadelphia at the request of the WTUL to organize a new branch of the league in that city. There she met Frieda Miller, a young Bryn Mawr economics instructor. The two hit it off quickly, and the professor jumped at the chance to leave academia to work for "the movement."

Miller fell ill; Newman moved in to nurse her. The two lived together for the next half century. Theirs was a turbulent relationship from beginning to end, but they stayed together until Miller's death in 1974.

In 1923, Newman and Miller returned to New York where Newman had accepted a position as education director for the ILGWU Union Health Center, the first comprehensive medical insurance program created by a union for its members. The couple moved to Greenwich Village where, as part of a community of politically active women couples including Democratic Party activists Molly Dewson and Polly Porter, the two women raised Miller's daughter Elisabeth. This early two-mother family was apparently quite well accepted in the offbeat world of the Village. As Elisabeth Burger later recalled of her childhood in the Village, "conventional ways of living were not stressed." Newman was happy to take a job that would allow her to stay close to New York after more than a decade of traveling. For the next six decades she would use this position to improve the health and education of women workers and to inform the public of their needs and concerns.

Still not content to retreat into education only, Newman continued to organize through the 1930s. Along with her closest friend and WTUL colleague Rose Schneiderman, Newman organized African American and Afro-Caribbean women laundry and hotel workers into unions. She worked with Miller and WTUL activist Maud Swartz, both now officials of New York State, to create employment bureaus for African American domestic workers that would end what were known as "slave markets"—street corners on which southern black migrants bargained with white (often Jewish) housewives for a day's labor. Newman also served as a consultant for New York State on minimum wage and safety issues. As a member of the United Nations Subcommittee on the Status of Women and the International Labor Organization Subcommittee on the Status of Domestic Workers, she worked to improve conditions for labor abroad.

During Franklin and Eleanor Roosevelt's dozen years in Washington, D.C., Newman was invited to the White House with some regularity. She was among several women labor activists whom Eleanor Roosevelt entertained frequently at Val-Kill, the home her husband built for her near the family mansion at Hyde Park. In 1936, when the National WTUL convention was held in Washington, D.C., Newman accompanied a delegation of young

garment and textile workers to sleep in the White House and breakfast with the First Lady during a weeklong stay. It was typical showmanship for the charming president and his equally charismatic wife, but it made front-page headlines in the *New York Times.* "Imagine me," one Jewish garment worker enthused, "Fannia Shapiro sleeping in Lincoln's bed." It was as close as working-class immigrant Jews had yet come to the seat of national power, and it was media moments such as those that cemented the passionate love affair that so many immigrant Jews of that generation had with Franklin Roosevelt.

During World War II, Frieda Miller was appointed director of the U.S. Women's Bureau, a division of the Department of Labor established in 1919. After the war Newman and Miller were asked by President Harry S Truman to investigate workers' conditions in Europe. Newman was invited by Truman to address the White House Conference on the Child, and the U.S. Public Health Service consulted her regularly on labor safety issues. During the early decades of the twentieth century, Newman and her WTUL circle had played a vital role in sparking and sustaining women's labor uprisings. During the 1920s, 1930s, and 1940s, they shaped new government agencies and labor laws that guaranteed a minimum wage and minimum standards of safety for all American workers.

Into the 1980s, Newman lectured, wrote, and advised women trade unionists. Panamanian-born Maida Springer, who became the first black labor unionist appointed to a senior position in the American Federation of Labor, cited Newman as her mentor and called her "one of the giants, determined, articulate, volatile about workers' dignity." Knowing Newman, along with Rose Schneiderman and Fania Cohn, Springer said, "gave you greater strength and support as an activist" (Orleck 1995).

Newman always insisted that male union leaders organize women as well as men, black workers as well as whites, immigrants, and native born. In the 1970s, the Coalition of Labor Union Women recognized her as a foremother of the women's liberation movement. Never comfortable in a role that she felt eclipsed the contributions of thousands who had worked alongside her, Newman still felt it important to serve as a living witness to the sweatshop conditions of the early twentieth century that the union movement had helped to eradicate. (It was a bitter irony for her that, by the end of her life, New York's garment unions were once again fighting the same battle.)

Newman spoke regularly through the 1970s and 1980s to historians, reporters, and groups of young women workers, her heavily wrinkled face, watery eyes, and gravelly voice telling as much as her words about her decades of struggle on behalf of American labor. For eight decades, dancing delicately between worlds, Newman—through her sheer force of will, energy, and heart—made herself into one of the most important women in the history of American labor.

Annelise Orleck

References and Further Reading
Kessler-Harris, Alice. 1976. "Organizing the Unorganizable: Three Jewish Women and Their Union" *Labor History* 17,1 (Winter): 5-23.
Morrison, Joan, and Charlotte Fox Zabrisky, eds. 1982. *American Mosaic*. New York: E. P. Dutton.
Newman, Pauline. Personal Papers. Boston: Schlesinger Library.
Orleck, Annelise. 1995. *Common Sense and a Little Fire: Women and Working-Class Politics in the United States, 1900-1965*. Chapel Hill: University of North Carolina Press.
Schofield, Ann. 1997. *"To Do and To Be": Portraits of Four Women Activists, 1893-1986*. Boston: Northeastern University Press.

Selig Perlman (1888–1959)

Labor Economist

Selig Perlman was a renowned Jewish professor of economics at a leading American university when the species scarcely existed. He specialized in comparative labor history, labor problems, the analytics of Marxian "statics and dynamics," and the evolution of modern capitalism. He published only four books, but his interpretations, based on the Lockean foundation of collective property rights and the experience of worker self-government rather than Marxian class-consciousness, have stood well the test of time. He was famous as a lecturer, even though he spoke with a heavy Yiddish accent and had a considerable stammer. But his command of language, particularly original metaphors, was famous, and he held audiences spellbound.

Perlman was born to Pesha (Blankstein) and Mordecai Perlman in Bialystock, Russia, a center of textile produc-

tion. His father earned a living as a jobber, buying yarn that he distributed to peasant women to weave in their cottages and then immediately selling the title to the woven cloth at a discount to recover his capital—and a bit of profit. He was moderately successful until about 1890 when the mill products seriously undersold the cottage products.

Selig was educated at a Talmud Torah until at about eleven he won a scholarship to the local *Realgymnasium*, an elite state high school specializing in modern languages and science. He graduated in 1905, a day of disappointments, since not only did he fail to get the Gold Medal (the top academic honor), but he had to race home to avoid a pogrom then in progress.

Absent the Gold Medal, treaties rendered Perlman, as a Russian Jew, ineligible to attend universities in Russia, Germany, or Austria-Hungary. Thus he went to study medicine in Italy. There he spent several afternoons explaining Marxian "statics and dynamics" to the American Socialist writer William English Walling and his bride, Anna Strunsky (a quondam co-author with Jack London), whose knowledge of German and thus of Marxism was flawed. The Wallings had contacted Perlman at the urging of Anna Blankstein, Perlman's mother's half-sister, who had made Strunsky's clothes for the couple's European trip and had advised her to look up her "genius nephew, Selig." After their discussions Walling mentioned in passing that were Perlman ever to come to America, he would hire him to produce a competent English translation of Marx.

After Selig returned to his home in Bialystock in 1907, his father told him that Walling had just been imprisoned by the czarist police, charged with sedition. The next day they read that President Theodore Roosevelt had telegrammed the czar, "Send Walling home." As a result of these events Perlman decided to emigrate to America immediately. Anna Walling met him at the pier. Although Walling honored his promise to employ Selig as a translator, he paid little attention to the product, and Perlman felt that his salary was a form of charity. Walling then suggested that he go to the University of Wisconsin and provided him with letters of introduction to Richard T. Ely, John R. Commons, Edward Alsworth Ross, and possibly Frederick Jackson Turner.

He received his baccalaureate degree in 1910, having written a thesis on the history of socialism in Milwaukee. After being offered a research assistantship by Turner, Commons matched the offer, and Perlman remained a

Commons student. His dissertation formed the last part of the two-volume *History of Labour in the United States* (Perlman 1918). While a graduate student, Selig was briefly employed by the United States Commission on Industrial Relations for which he conducted fieldwork. One of his assignments was to interview the Industrial Workers of the World shoe workers in Lawrence, Massachusetts, about their intentions regarding industrial sabotage.

He was told to identify himself as a correspondent of a minor Yiddish newspaper in New York. The workers he contacted agreed to talk, but only if he came to the sixth-floor tenement of one of them. There, accusing him of being a company "fink," they suddenly grabbed him. Going through his pockets they found a personal letter from Walling, which, he reported to Basil Manley, the Commission's Director of Research, literally saved him from defenestration. For the most part, however, his writings were based on reading and analyzing labor union periodicals and similar materials. He was awarded his doctorate in 1915. In the following years he worked on revising Richard T. Ely's earlier work, *The Labor Movement in America* (Ely 1886), an interpretation offering a Christian Socialist theme. Perlman's completed manuscript substituted his own views based on Lockean collective ownership of job opportunity. Thoroughly displeased, Ely told him that his assistantship would not be renewed.

Perlman was then recommended for an appointment at Cornell. Its department of economics chose him, but President Jacob Gould Schurman refused to take a Jewish name to Cornell's trustees. A second effort at employment at the University of Arkansas also failed. Commons's wife, Nell, who had become his partisan, then proposed a "solution." Both Commons and Ross, who had been Ely's students at Johns Hopkins, and whom Ely had chosen as colleagues at Wisconsin, had come to resent his paternalistic attitudes toward them. Mrs. Commons's solution was that Ely retire as chairman of the economics department, that Ross be given his own department of sociology, and that Selig take over Commons's undergraduate teaching.

Although her solution had considerable support, the plan was almost derailed when Commons learned that Perlman planned to vote in the 1920 presidential election for Eugene Debs, the Socialist candidate then serving time in the Atlanta Federal Penitentiary for sedition. After much hesitation, but with a timely reassurance from the Wisconsin Catholic chaplain, the Reverend Francis Kuchera (who

had much influence on the legislature), that a good man could choose Debs, Commons overcame his doubts. One of Perlman's graduate students, Father Aloysius Muench, had taken the initiative to approach Kuchera. Perlman was then appointed assistant professor, became associate professor in 1925, and full professor by 1927. In the early 1920s he took the lead in establishing on the Wisconsin campus a Summer School for Workers. In short courses, union members were taught Robert's Rules of Order (for conducting union meetings), how to negotiate time and motion studies and the pay increases associated with improvements in productivity, union history, and current events of significance to unions.

The volume that Ely rejected was published in 1922 as *A History of Trade Unionism in the United States.* Perlman considered this his most original work, although *A Theory of the Labor Movement* (1928) is usually cited as his chef d'oeuvre. In 1935 he published, with his assistant Philip Taft, the fourth volume of the original Commons & Associates' *History of Labor in the United States.*

He spent the greater part of the academic year 1938–1939 in Cardiff, Wales, where he traded teaching posts and homes with Hilary Marquand, later postmaster-general in the first Clement Atlee government. Although Perlman was the leading critic of Beatrice and Sidney Webb's work on trade unionism, they invited him to spend a day at their home, where Beatrice, in particular, treated him as their academic equal. He was invited to Oxford as the honored guest of G.D.H. Cole and to Cambridge as the honored guest of Maynard Keynes. His year in Britain was cut short by rumors of imminent war, a consequence of the von Ribbentrop–Molotov Pact (1939).

The high tide of union sentiment was in 1936, and, over the following decade, the popularity of unionism in Wisconsin declined, particularly with the regents of the university. In the summer of 1946 Perlman was summoned to appear before the Board of Regents to answer questions about the future of the School for Workers. Perlman wrote of these developments to Father Muench, by now not only bishop of South Dakota but the papal nuncio in postwar Germany. In his reply, Muench stated that his own views had been shaped by two papal encyclicals, *Rerum Novarum* (1891) and *Quadragesimo Anno* (1931), and by Perlman's classroom lectures. The letter was signed "Yours in Christ" with the latter two words struck out (in deference to Perlman's Judaism) and replaced by "ever" and signed Aloysius

Muench. Perlman started his presentation by passing the letter to the chairman of the regents, who read it carefully, showed it to one of his confreres, and suggested that Perlman must have better use for his morning than spending it with them.

Perlman married Eva Shaber (1894–1930) in 1918; they had two sons. She died after a very brief illness in 1930. Later that year he married one of her sisters, Fannie (1897–1981), with whom he had two daughters. His older son, David (1920–1980), a biochemist and the holder of a large number of patents, returned to the University of Wisconsin as dean of the School of Pharmacy. The second son, Mark, is a professor of economics and a pioneering editor of economic journals.

Selig Perlman's Conservative Jewish household was *shomar kosher* (kosher observant), although he and his sons were not *shomar shabbos* (Sabbath observant). He was a quondam corresponding friend of Chaim Weizmann and a Zionist. In the 1950s he was offered a professorship at the Hebrew University, but was forced to decline it for reasons of health.

Perlman retired from the University of Wisconsin in June 1959 after reaching the mandatory retirement age of seventy. He accepted an endowed chair at the University of Pennsylvania for the following academic year (1959–1960). His health had been deteriorating since 1945, and shortly after arriving in Philadelphia in August 1959 he suffered a stroke and died.

Perlman left a great intellectual legacy. As a boy, he had been taught the Jewish theory of historical events, a nonteleological interpretation. At the *Realgymnasium* he learned the Russian Orthodox teleological approach to history, ending with a vivid Day of Judgment. This religious approach was subtly undermined by his teachers, who steered the students to Plekhanov and the Menshevik interpretation of Marxism. By 1905 Perlman was a Marxian, a student member of the Jewish Bund, and an expert on Marx's German writings (and in that sense a teleologist).

At the University of Wisconsin he became aware of Commons's empirical (legal and episodic) approach to the study of worker revolt, an approach conflicting with his previous Marxian interpretation. Thus he was led to form his own interpretation of worker–employer conflict. His doctoral dissertation stressed the differences in approach of the emerging trade unions, each concerned with its own problems of wages and working conditions, and

the more all-for-one/one-for-all approach both of the Knights of Labor and the usual Marxian understanding of labor–class solidarity. The teleological emphasis waned. Commons' earlier work had stressed that pressures on prices led to pressures on wages, with the result that workers often struck to keep prices up so that wages could be maintained. Perlman thought that what the workers more likely had in mind was a kind of collective control of job opportunity—his term was *job-consciousness.* The implication was that wage rates might have to retreat if prices were falling, but the workers' collective Lockean-derived property right was built into the foundations of their working rules.

His *A History of Trade Unionism in the United States* (Perlman 1922) expanded this thesis. Here he also took up the question of why socialism had made so little headway in American unions. His general point was that the American constitutional process, built on tripartite government with specified limited powers, on a large degree of federalism as well as the Fifth and Fourteenth Amendments, and on the political overrepresentation of American farmers in both federal and state upper houses, precluded what the Webbs had preferred, namely statutory reform rather than collective bargaining. Any empirical approach to the history of the American labor movement, he concluded, made the likelihood of socialism and governmentally set standards for wages and working conditions problematic.

A Theory of the Labor Movement (Perlman 1928) can be most easily understood if one recognizes that the title he proposed was *Labor Movements and the Intellectuals.* Examining the British, German, Russian, and American labor movements, he opined that, when workers enjoyed the right to self-organization, they opted for devising their own working rules rather than the more comprehensive social reform blueprints offered by the intelligentsia. In *Labor Union Theories in America* (Perlman 1958), Mark Perlman described Perlman's perception of unionism as part of the democratic process—an interpretation in contrast to socialist paradigms, to the Veblenian-Hoxian theory of factory culture, and to the Webbian approach that saw labor unionism as essentially a political optimization process.

There were many critics of Perlman's 1928 book. Advocates of the various forms of socialism (from Christian Socialism to Leninism) thought his tying of worker interest to an idea of the job as a property right was urging labor to link arms with the devil. Perlman's view that workers suffered individually from a psychological fear of job scarcity contrasted with the Veblen-Hoxie view that the psychological problem was tied to the machine-paced nature of the capitalist system. The overall criticism was that he attributed to workers little or no sense of class solidarity. Indeed, for Perlman the very concept of a working class was a socialist abstraction, and its purported rightful demand for control of industry was but a belief in an abstract mass (labor) in the grip of an abstract force (history).

Mark Perlman

References and Further Reading

Ely, Richard T. 1886. *The Labor Movement in America.* New York: Thomas Y. Crowell & Company.

Perlman, Mark. 1958. *Labor Union Theories in America: Background and Development.* Evanston, IL: Rowe Peterson.

Perlman, Selig. 1918. "Part VI. Upheaval and Reorganization." In *History of Labour in the United States,* edited by John R. Commons & Associates. Volume 2. New York: Macmillan.

Perlman, Selig. 1922. *A History of Trade Unionism in the United States.* New York: Macmillan.

Perlman, Selig. 1928. *A Theory of the Labor Movement.* New York: Macmillan.

Perlman, Selig, and Philip Taft. 1935. *History of Labor in the United States, 1896–1932.* New York: Macmillan.

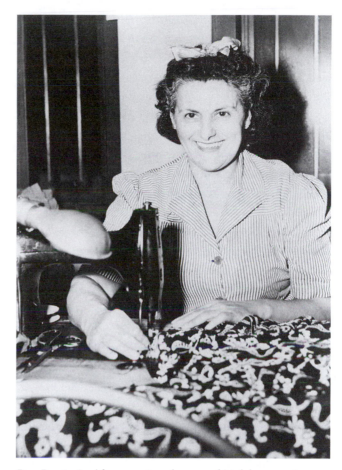

Rose Pesotta, Jewish garment worker, anarchist, labor organizer, and a vice president of the International Ladies' Garment Workers' Union. (Library of Congress)

Rose Pesotta (1896–1965)

Labor Organizer and Anarchist

Nationally known for her firebrand form of organizing, Rose Pesotta (born Rachelle Peisoty) was the third woman vice president of the International Ladies' Garment Workers' Union (ILGWU) and a noted anarchist and author. Pesotta was close friends with Nicola Sacco and Bartolomeo Vanzetti, Emma Goldman, and other anarchist activists in the early twentieth century. She organized women garment workers in New York City, Los Angeles, and Puerto Rico, to name just a few locations, and also organized autoworkers for the Committee for Industrial Organization (CIO). Pesotta was the author of *Bread upon the Waters* and *Days of Our Lives.*

Rose Pesotta was born in Derazhnya, Russia, and attended a private girls' school. Early in her life she learned to speak five languages, which served well in her later work as an organizer. Raised as an Orthodox Jew, when her father was about to arrange a marriage for her, she negotiated immigration to the United States, arriving in New York City on November 24, 1913. She lived with her sister and her family while learning English and becoming a seamstress. After joining the ILGWU as a member of the activist Local 25, she quickly came to the attention of the administration as a firebrand and speaker. She was sponsored to attend the Bryn Mawr Summer School for Women Workers in Industry (1922), Brookwood Labor College (1924–1926), and the Wisconsin School for Workers (1930), where she studied English, public speaking, and other liberal arts subjects.

Pesotta's performance in these schools, as well as her flamboyant personality, led to her nomination as an officer of her local, and in 1933 the ILGWU sent her to Los Angeles to organize seamstresses. In May 1934 she was elected the only woman vice president of the ILGWU, the third woman in the union's history to serve in that capacity. Her charisma, gift of speech, and love and sympathy for the workers won her many ardent followers (Tyler 1965). When she became a vice president, she was not sure this job was right for her. She was afraid that joining the union bureaucracy would compromise her values and that "the voice of a solitary woman among the twenty-four vice presidents would be a voice lost in the wilderness" (Pesotta 1944). Nonetheless, she accepted the challenge.

Soon Pesotta was sent to Puerto Rico to organize seamstresses there. Shocked by their poverty, she dedicated herself to helping low-paid seamstresses change their conditions. Pesotta's colorful organizing style took shape: in later organizing she used seamstresses as models, wearing the garments they sewed as they marched on the picket lines; she had the children of striking workers walk the lines, carrying signs in support of their parents. Anti-union thugs attacked Pesotta in Cleveland in 1937, slashing and beating her. She was known for her leadership style, in which she set up union headquarters, provided food and help for striking workers, as well as parties and musical events. She often brought music to the picket lines, leading songs and chants. She took countless films of union activities, recording action shots of strikes that were useful in gaining union publicity. Over the years she organized workers in Seattle, San Francisco, Milwaukee, Buffalo, Boston, and Montreal.

Pesotta was so effective that in 1936 the ILG lent her to the CIO to organize rubber workers in Akron, Ohio. She also worked with the autoworkers' unions (UAW) in South Bend, Indiana, and then in Flint, Michigan. Often the only woman organizer, she handled herself well in the CIO organizing efforts, becoming one of the "four musketeers," along with organizers from the Amalgamated Clothing Workers and the United Mine Workers. When Pesotta was a CIO organizer in Flint, she was involved in an altercation that left her deaf in one ear. This event did not stop her, and she could be found late into the night running from one picket line to the next, aiding workers in any way possible. Sometimes she worked with the UAW Women's Emergency Brigade, and other times she entered the buildings the autoworkers had seized to offer them advice.

Early in her life in the United States, while working as a seamstress, Pesotta became active in anarchist circles in New York City. She wrote for the anarchist journal *Road to Freedom*, attended meetings, and spoke on behalf of Sacco and Vanzetti in an effort to have their conviction overturned. She considered them close personal friends and mourned their loss. Vanzetti presented her with a hand-carved ivory penholder, with a clenched fist at the tip of the shaft. She traveled around the country speaking in their defense, particularly to union activists. As an anarchist Pesotta believed in decentralization and self-government of workers. She wrote of her ideals and tried to abide by them in her work. It was, however, often difficult for her to be a bureaucrat in the union. Indeed, anarchists often marginalized her because she was in the bureaucracy, while the men on the board of the union marginalized her as a woman.

Nonetheless, Pesotta was practical and knew how to speak to the workers in their own language. She was willing to compromise her principles to reach attainable goals. She learned conciliation, use of careful language, and demure behavior in order to be an effective organizer. Her idea of union leadership was to be egalitarian and to lay the groundwork so that the rank and file would assume positions of authority as they learned how to negotiate and organize themselves.

Pesotta's relationship with Emma Goldman, the anarchist writer, thinker, and activist who served as her role model, was a complex but inspirational one. In 1919 Goldman had been deported along with Pesotta's first American boyfriend, Theodore Kushnarev. The women's relationship resumed when they met again while Pesotta was writing for *Road to Freedom*. Goldman helped Pesotta use anarchist ideology as guiding principles in her organizing work; Goldman led Rose to "believe in anarchism like a rabbi believes in God" (Leibowitz 1984).

The two developed a mentor–student relationship, with Goldman sometimes cheering Rose on for her union activities, while also chastising her for her comfortable lifestyle, as compared to Emma's hardships while she was hounded in the United States and after her deportation. Rose visited Emma in Europe in 1938, and again in Canada in 1939, and, when a stroke incapacitated Goldman, Rose raised money for her upkeep. When Goldman died in May 1940, Pesotta flew to Chicago for the funeral and spoke at a memorial meeting in New York later that month. Allegedly one of Goldman's closest friends at the end of her life, Rose found inspiration from the friendship, which sustained her in the face of hard challenges. Goldman's death left a huge void in Pesotta's personal life.

Pesotta's position as a woman vice president was always problematic for her. At first her relationship with David Dubinsky (the president of the ILG) was that of a father–daughter. However, Dubinsky disapproved of Pesotta's style of leadership, including her spending what he considered vast amounts of money to entertain the workers. Her style was not unlike that of most other women organizers in other fields; she asserted herself and the needs of the workers in a forceful manner. She was also outspoken, often telling the men on the board how she felt about matters, which did not earn her many supporters on the General Executive Board (GEB).

Pesotta's final run-in occurred in Los Angeles, where she was sent in 1942 to cover for an ill vice president. When the vice president returned, he alleged that she had undermined his work and insisted that Dubinsky recall her to New York. He did so, to the ire of the workers who had mobilized around Pesotta. After the recall, Pesotta returned to the sewing machine, an extraordinary act for a vice president. After further misunderstandings with the GEB, she resigned from the board because of her continued marginalization. As a woman and as an anarchist, Pesotta did not fit. Although workers loved her, she had made enemies of those in positions of power, who forced her out.

After leaving the union as a vice president and organizer, Pesotta wrote two books about her experiences. *Bread upon the Waters* (1944), which covered her career as a labor activist, was well received. *Days of Our Lives* (1958), with less glowing reviews, focused mainly on her early life. Pesotta also worked for the Anti-Defamation League (ADL) of the B'nai B'rith, for which she visited labor unions, labor schools, and fraternal organizations to educate them about prejudice and discrimination. Under the auspices of the ADL, she went to Europe in 1945, where she saw the effects of the war and the Holocaust in visits to bombed-out cities and death camps. Upon her return, she spoke widely on what she had seen. The job with the ADL did not last long, however, and Pesotta returned to the sewing machine. She also worked for a short time with the American Trade Union Council of the Histadrut, but once again found her way back to the sewing machine, where she remained until her death.

Pesotta was involved in a number of significant personal relationships. She was married only once, in 1953, to Albert Martin (Frank Lopez), whom she had met much earlier, during the Sacco and Vanzetti case. Before that, she had been deeply in love with Powers Hapgood. Hapgood was a labor organizer for the United Mine Workers, the Amalgamated Clothing Workers, the Textile Workers of Kentucky, the Socialist Party of Massachusetts, and the Southern Tenant Farmers Union in Arkansas. They met while they were organizing for the CIO in the 1930s.

As an anarchist, woman, and organizer, Pesotta has been called a "gentle general" (Tyler 1965), and her legacy has influenced other organizers and women. Many of the sites she organized remain union-affiliated to this day, and, although many of her goals have not been achieved, she served as an inspiration and role model for many.

Elaine Leeder

References and Further Reading

Avrich, Paul. 1991. *Sacco and Vanzetti: The Anarchist Background*. Princeton, NJ: Princeton University Press.

Kessler-Harris, Alice. 1976. "Organizing the Unorganizable: Three Jewish Women and Their Union." *Labor History* (Winter): 5–23.

Leeder, Elaine. 1993. *The Gentle General: Rose Pesotta, Anarchist and Labor Organizer*. Albany: State University of New York Press.

Leibowitz, Esther. 1984. Interview. Workmen's Circle Home, Bronx, NY. January 11.

Marsh, Margaret. 1981. *Anarchist Women: 1870–1920*. Philadelphia: Temple University Press.

Pesotta, Rose. 1944. *Bread upon the Waters.* New York: Dodd Mead.

Tyler, Gus. 1965. "Eulogy on Rose Pesotta." Clara Larsen private papers.

Rose Schneiderman (1882–1972)

Labor Activist

Described as a pint-sized stick of dynamite—just four feet nine inches tall, with flaming red hair—Polish Jewish immigrant Rose Schneiderman changed the course of American labor history, helping to bring shorter hours, higher wages, and safer conditions to millions of U.S. workers. Schneiderman was a brilliant organizer, lobbyist, and legislative strategist. But she was also a visionary. "The woman worker wants bread," Schneiderman famously said in 1911. "But she wants roses too" (Orleck 1995). The phrase Bread

Rose Schneiderman, president of the National Women's Trade Union League, sits between Eleanor Roosevelt and David Dubinsky in 1938. (Library of Congress)

and Roses encapsulated the desire of American working women both for the essentials that sustained life—better wages and job conditions—and for the soul-nourishing extras that made life worth living, among them exposure to literature and drama, and recreational opportunities. Rose Schneiderman insisted that workers should not settle for a grim subsistence. They were entitled to pleasure as well as productivity.

First entering the labor movement as an officer of the United Cloth Hat and Cap Makers' Union in 1904, Schneiderman would serve for decades as president of both the New York and National Women's Trade Union Leagues (WTUL). She became the only woman member of Franklin Roosevelt's National Labor Advisory Board, and one of the few working-class activists to be appointed to

statewide office in New York, where she served as secretary of labor in the late 1930s and early 1940s. In all of those positions, Rose Schneiderman worked tirelessly to improve the lives of working people. She left a lasting imprint on both the labor movement and the welfare state. Pushing both to move beyond simply ensuring worker survival, Rose Schneiderman brought to the labor movement and to government a broader vision of human rights and improved quality of life for all.

Schneiderman made her name as a devastatingly effective orator. Tiny in stature, she could rivet the attention of huge crowds. Beginning in 1904 and continuing through the 1950s, the militant trade unionist and women's rights advocate spoke powerfully from street corner platforms, to union halls, and finally, over the radio, persuading even skeptics of the justice of her positions. In an age when political oratory was a leading form of entertainment, many described her as the most powerful speaker they had ever heard. Some found that power threatening. It's easy to see why. Schneiderman did not mince words. Most famous among her speeches was one made just days after the Triangle Shirtwaist Factory Fire, on March 25, 1911, killed 146 young workers—most of them immigrant Jewish and Italian women. "We have tried you good people and found you wanting," she told an audience that included some of New York's richest and most powerful society matrons. "I can't talk fellowship to you who are gathered here. Too much blood has been spilled. I know from experience it is up to the working people to save themselves" (Orleck 1995). Given such rhetoric, it is perhaps not surprising that Schneiderman was deemed a danger to national security after World War I, when the Bolshevik Revolution sparked a nationwide backlash against foreign-born radicals in the United States. The chair of New York State's investigation of subversive activity dubbed her "the Red Rose of Anarchy."

Still, Schneiderman's warmth and ability to persuade listeners would ultimately provide her entree into the highest circles of political power. One witness to the Triangle Fire, social activist Frances Perkins, introduced her to Franklin and Eleanor Roosevelt. Schneiderman taught them most of what they came to know about working people. Later Roosevelt's labor secretary, Perkins recalled in her memoirs that it was as a result of FDR's long conversations during the 1920s with Rose Schneiderman that he was able to plausibly present himself as someone who understood the dire condition of America's industrial laborers. A trusted FDR advisor, Schneiderman played a key role in shaping the landmark legislation of the New Deal: the National Labor Relations Act, the Social Security Act, and the Fair Labor Standards Act. As president of the New York WTUL from 1917 to 1949, and as New York State secretary of labor from 1937 to 1943, Schneiderman also helped make New York State a laboratory for progressive labor and social welfare legislation.

Schneiderman was active in Jewish organizations and causes throughout her career. In the years before, during, and after World War II she worked tirelessly to help Jews escape from Europe. She made speeches, wrote letters, and solicited the involvement of both labor leaders and such famous refugees from Nazism as Albert Einstein to raise awareness of the persecution and slaughter of European Jewry. Convinced by these events of the importance of establishing a Jewish homeland, Schneiderman also marshaled her considerable rhetorical power and persuasive skills to raise funds to establish the Leon Blum Colony, a Labor-Zionist settlement in Palestine.

Born on April 16, 1882, into an observant Jewish family in Saven, Poland, Rose Schneiderman was the daughter of a tailor (Samuel) and a jane-of-all-trades, her mother Deborah. At a time when one census taker estimated that the vast majority of East European Jews were without obvious means of making a living, Deborah Schneiderman, like many intrepid East European Jewish housewives, did whatever she could to put food on her family table. Rose adored her mother and would later cite her example as modeling strong, independent womanhood. Samuel and Deborah both were unusual among their peers in believing that girls as well as boys deserved an education. They enrolled four-year-old Rose in a previously all-male *kheydr* (religious school). Samuel and Deborah moved the family to the city of Chelm when Rose was six so she could attend public school.

Three years later, in 1890, the family migrated to the United States, settling like so many other East European Jews in New York City. But the family fell on dismal times when Samuel died of meningitis two years later, leaving Deborah pregnant and with three children to support. The bereft mother took in boarders, sewed and washed for neighbors, and did repairs in the building in exchange for a free apartment. In spite of it all, however, she could not earn enough to adequately feed and clothe her children. And so, for a time, Rose and her siblings were forced to live in a home for poor children. Deborah Schneiderman worked round the clock to save enough to bring her children home. And when she did, she insisted that they attend school during the day rather than finding jobs themselves. Still it was not enough, and at thirteen, after Deborah lost her night job, Rose was forced to leave school permanently to help support the family.

Though she was now a single mother, often reduced to feeding her children on charity food baskets, Deborah Schneiderman wanted Rose to find a "respectable" job in a department store, where she could work in clean clothing and hopefully meet a middle-class man to marry. Rose Schneiderman would share her mother's obsession with respectability. Indeed, that preoccupation persisted for the rest of her life, ultimately drawing her away from the socialism of her youth to working with the Democratic Party.

After three years as a salesgirl, Schneiderman asked a friend to train her for a better-paying job as a capmaker. The young girl's wages greatly improved, but she was horrified by the stark inequalities she found among garment workers. Women were consigned to the lowest-paying work, while the best-paying, highest-skill jobs were reserved for men. Schneiderman simply could not remain quiet in the face of such obvious unfairness. When she complained, older women in the shop began to teach her the fundamentals of socialist trade unionism—interpreted through a decidedly feminist lens.

Rose Schneiderman learned fast and, at the tender age of twenty-one, convinced enough of the women in her shop to join the fledgling United Cloth Hat and Cap Makers' Union that the union was able to charter a new local. The East European Jewish immigrant men who made up the bulk of the union leadership were openly skeptical of the ability of young women to organize. Still, they were impressed by Schneiderman. Within a year, they and the shop floor capmakers Schneiderman had organized voted for her to become a union officer. She was the first woman elected to national office in an American labor union.

Schneiderman organized a general strike of New York's capmakers in 1905. The middle-class leaders of the New York WTUL—an organization Progressive-era women reformers established to provide support to women workers attempting to unionize—took notice. The WTUL was still new and had little credibility at that time among the women workers it sought to help. Schneiderman gave the League something essential—a sense of legitimacy among the immigrant working class. The reformers, college students, and settlement house workers who had created the League gave Schneiderman her introduction to organized feminism. They introduced her to the woman suffrage movement. Before long, she had become one of the movement's most electrifying speakers, helping to draw working-class women to a cause they had long viewed with suspicion.

Grateful for her tireless work on behalf of women workers, the members of the New York WTUL elected Schneiderman vice president in 1906. Recognizing the young immigrant's talent, German Jewish philanthropist Irene Lewisohn offered to pay for Schneiderman to attend college. Reluctantly, Schneiderman declined, saying that she could not accept a privilege afforded to so few working

women. She wished, as Socialist Eugene V. Debs put it, to rise with her class, not above it. In 1908, however, Schneiderman did accept Lewisohn's offer to pay her salary when she became chief organizer for the NYWTUL. During the next eleven years, Schneiderman would play a key role in organizing, inspiring, and sustaining a wave of unrest and strikes among women workers that, by 1919, had brought 40 percent of all women garment workers into trade unions. It was a remarkable feat for any industry, especially one dominated by women—still seen by most labor leaders as unorganizable.

Schneiderman's role in sparking the women's labor rebellion of the 1910s began with a furious burst of organizing in Manhattan garment shops that laid the groundwork for the 1909 general strike of New York shirtwaist makers. That strike, the largest by women in the United States to that time, brought 30,000–40,000 young women workers (mostly East European Jews) into the streets of Lower Manhattan and breathed life into the tiny International Ladies' Garment Workers' Union (ILWGU). It also brought the NYWTUL to the attention of the national media. Still, the strike generated tensions between working-class Jews like Schneiderman and her fellow-organizer Pauline Newman, and the middle-class Protestant women who dominated the League. League secretary Helen Marot described Jewish women as too fervent and militant, and urged the League board to devote its resources to "American" girls. Angered by this not-so-subtle stereotyping, Schneiderman resigned from the League. Over the next few years, she would resign and rejoin the League numerous times.

During one of those periods away from the League, from 1914 to 1916, Schneiderman took a job as general organizer for the ILGWU—a position previously held by her close friend, Lithuanian Jewish immigrant Pauline Newman. She encountered many of the same frustrations that Newman had described. The union was run by fellow East European Jews, men who distrusted women organizers and had little taste for organizing women workers. Feeling that the union leadership had time and again undermined her efforts, Schneiderman resigned from that job in 1917 to become chair of the Industrial Section of the New York Woman Suffrage Party.

Schneiderman was an early convert to woman suffrage, at least by the standards of the Jewish working-class in New York. She had begun speaking at suffrage rallies for the Equality League of Self-Supporting Women in 1907.

The members of the Equality League were largely professional women, and Schneiderman hoped to draw industrial workers into the movement. Toward that end, in 1911, she cofounded the Wage Earners League for Woman Suffrage—the first suffrage organization made up primarily of industrial workers. Speaking on behalf of that group, she set out on a tour through the Midwest in 1912, to convince union men to vote for state-based suffrage referenda. In 1917, her whirlwind of speaking engagements and the network of union women she mobilized on behalf of the Industrial Section of the Woman Suffrage Party contributed greatly to the passage of woman suffrage in New York three years before it became federal law.

After that successful campaign, Schneiderman returned to the New York League, whose members elected her their president. It was a post she would hold for thirty-two years. By the time the United States entered World War I, Schneiderman was nationally known in labor, feminist, and socialist politics. In 1920, the Labor Party ran her for the U.S. Senate from New York. The party, which sought to increase the power of the U.S. trade union movement by electing labor leaders to political office, had branches in most industrial states. Though she did not win, nor did she expect to, Schneiderman used the campaign to articulate what WTUL colleague Mildred Moore called an "industrial feminist" agenda. Schneiderman called for the full representation of women in politics and labor, for nonprofit housing for workers, better schools, publicly owned power utilities and staple food markets, and publicly funded health and unemployment insurance for all Americans. Conservative politicians considered her a subversive, and, in the early 1920s, she was investigated by both New York State and federal agencies. But she was viewed much more positively by a pair of rising stars in New York Democratic politics, Franklin and Eleanor Roosevelt.

Newly engaged in urban reform politics, Eleanor Roosevelt joined the New York WTUL in 1922. She took an immediate liking to Schneiderman, and the two launched a friendship that deepened over many years, lasting until Mrs. Roosevelt's death in 1963. Throughout the 1920s, Schneiderman was a regular guest both at Eleanor Roosevelt's New York apartment and at Franklin's Hyde Park estate. Eleanor Roosevelt was there to celebrate in 1926 when Schneiderman was elected president of the National WTUL—a position she held until her retirement in 1950. When Franklin D. Roosevelt was elected governor of New York in 1928, the immigrant labor activist became a close advisor.

In 1933, President Roosevelt brought Schneiderman to Washington to work for the National Recovery Administration. She became secretary of labor for New York State in 1937. These were heady experiences for a Polish Jewish immigrant whose formal schooling had ended at age thirteen. In both posts, Schneiderman fought to gain for blacks the same minimum wages as whites, and to extend Social Security benefits to domestic workers. She also sought to erase the gap in pay between men and women by lobbying for comparable worth and equal pay legislation.

Schneiderman distinguished herself in the 1930s for another reason as well—she was nearly alone both in Washington and among prominent white labor officials in her efforts to reach out to and organize African American women workers. Remaining active in the WTUL, Schneiderman tried to use state legislation to aid union organizing drives among hotel maids, beauty parlor workers, and waitresses. Her long campaign on behalf of New York's laundry workers—almost all of whom were African American—ultimately resulted in mass unionization and dramatically improved wages, hours, and working conditions for one of the most exploited groups of urban workers. Schneiderman also sought to bring domestic workers under the protection of the state and tried to extend New Deal regulations to include exploited women workers in the territory of Puerto Rico.

During those same years, Schneiderman was frenzied in her efforts to rescue European Jews and to resettle them in the United States or Palestine. Albert Einstein wrote, in a letter that became one of her prize possessions, "It must be a source of deep gratification to you to be making so important a contribution to rescuing our persecuted fellow Jews from their calamitous peril and leading them toward a better future" (Orleck 1995). Instead, Schneiderman tormented herself, only able see how few she was ultimately able to rescue.

Schneiderman retired from public life in 1950. She never married, but she did have a twenty-year relationship with Irish immigrant labor activist Maud Swartz, who died suddenly in 1937. Schneiderman never had another long-term relationship. However, she remained on extremely close terms with her lifelong friend and fellow garment organizer Pauline Newman, with Eleanor Roosevelt, and with other League stalwarts, including National League secretary Elisabeth Christman. Schneiderman died on August 11, 1972, at the age of ninety.

Rose Schneiderman passed away at the dawn of the 1970s women's movement, but she was quickly adopted as one of its heroines. Her call for Bread and Roses was taken up by a new generation of women labor activists, and her insistence that workers deserved safety, subsistence, and respect is still being debated in courts, legislatures, and schools. Schneiderman deserves a great share of the credit for the government protections that millions of American workers have enjoyed since the mid-1930s. And just as important, she deserves to be remembered for her vision of Bread and Roses. Every time those words are uttered in contemporary labor struggles—by Central American janitors, Asian garment workers, and African American public service employees—the spirit of Rose Schneiderman lives on.

Annelise Orleck

References and Further Reading
Kessler-Harris, Alice. 1987. "Rose Schneiderman." In *American Labor Leaders,* edited by Warren Van Tine and Melvyn Dubofsky. Urbana: University of Illinois Press.
Orleck, Annelise. 1995. *Common Sense and a Little Fire: Women and Working-Class Politics in the United States, 1900-1965.* Chapel Hill: University of North Carolina Press.
Rose Schneiderman Papers. Papers of the New York Women's Trade Union League and Its Principal Leaders. Ann Arbor, MI: University Microfilms International.
Schneiderman, Rose. 1967. *All for One.* New York: Paul S. Eriksson.

Toni Sender (1888–1964)

Vocal Hitler Opponent

Toni Sender, a Jewish anti-fascist and Reichstag deputy who was forced to flee Germany in 1933 when the Nazis assumed power, became after her arrival in the United States one of the earliest and most prominent public spokespersons against the Hitler regime in this country. After World War II, as representative of the American Federation of Labor (AFL) and the International Confedera-

tion of Free Trade Unions (ICFTU) before the United Nations (UN) Economic and Social Council, Sender repeatedly directed the world's attention to the violation of workers' rights in Communist and fascist dictatorships. In Weimar Germany, Sender was editor of major Social Democratic Party (SPD) and trade union periodicals, as well as a leading women's rights activist. Nazi propaganda minister Josef Goebbels nicknamed her "The Little Woman with the Big Mouth," and the Nazis marked her for death. Sender escaped in disguise to Czechoslovakia and became a permanent resident of the United States in 1936.

Born in the Rhineland town of Biebrich, Germany, to affluent Orthodox Jewish parents, Sender rebelled as a child against their demand for "absolute obedience" (Sender 1939). Although not observant, Sender identified strongly as a Jew throughout her life. As a child and adolescent in Biebrich, she studied Hebrew and Jewish history for eight years. After completing commercial high school in Frankfurt, Sender began work at fifteen in a real estate office, and at eighteen joined the SPD. In 1910, she moved to Paris, where she founded a socialist women's group.

The outbreak of World War I forced Sender to return to Germany, where she immediately adopted an antiwar position. She briefly nursed wounded soldiers, but quit because she did not wish to make men fit for battle again. With other antiwar activists, Sender participated in the formation of the Independent Social Democratic Party (USPD) in 1917. She helped lead the November 1918 revolution in Frankfurt. Heading the USPD's national ticket, Sender was elected to the first postwar Reichstag in 1920, the youngest of forty women chosen. She served in the Reichstag until the Nazis came to power in 1933. Erika and Klaus Mann, Thomas Mann's daughter and son, identified Sender as "one of the few women who have ever played a political part in Germany" (Mann and Mann 1939).

Sender opposed USPD affiliation with the Communist International and rejoined the SPD in 1922, assuming a very active role in both the women's and labor movements. She edited the SPD's women's magazine, *Frauenwelt* (*Women's World*), from 1928 until the Nazis suppressed it in 1933, as well as the shop councils' magazine of the metal workers' union from 1920 to 1933.

When the Nazis first attained significant strength in the Reichstag in 1930, constituting a 107-member bloc, they made Sender—a Jew, a woman, and a Social Democrat—a prime target for abuse. Sender responded to the brownshirted deputies' attempt to disrupt her speaking by "bitterly denounc[ing] them" from the floor, looking "only in their direction" (Sender 1939). During the 1932 election campaign, the Nazis informed her constituents that she was a prostitute. In Dresden the Nazis dropped stench bombs from the balconies around the platform on which Sender was to speak, causing many in the audience to faint. But although the stench bombs badly affected her throat, Sender was determined to thwart the Nazis' efforts and delivered her speech. In early 1933 the Nazis in Dresden plastered Sender's picture over the entire front page of their newspaper *Judenspiegel* (*Jews' Mirror*), which suggested that she should be killed. Sender recalled that during this time the Nazis created a "pogrom atmosphere . . . around [her] name" (Sender 1939).

Driven into exile in Antwerp, Belgium, Sender made extended lecture tours in the United States during 1934 and 1935, providing Americans with one of the first eyewitness descriptions of Germany under Nazi rule. The Nazi government revoked her German citizenship in March 1934. Sender edited a Flemish socialist daily in Antwerp until 1935.

Becoming a permanent resident of the United States in 1936, Sender continued her agitation against Nazi Germany, which she tirelessly warned posed a critical danger to the West. In 1935 she had condemned Nazi oppression of women in the American socialist publication *New Leader* and in an address on New York's Yiddish radio station WEVD. Sender declared that the Nazi regime was forcing women out of the professions and replacing women factory workers with men on a massive scale. She emphasized that the Nazis conceived of only one role for women—to marry and have as many children as they could. From May 1936 until the German invasion of Belgium and France in May 1940, Sender reported on American political developments for publications in Brussels and Paris. In May 1941, Sender formed a picket line with two other exiled SPD Reichstag deputies to protest the screening of the Nazi propaganda film *Sieg im Westen* (*Victory in the West*) at a theater in New York's heavily German American Yorkville section. The film celebrated the German armed forces' conquest of France, the Netherlands, Belgium, and Luxembourg in 1940.

During the early 1940s, Sender held workers' education classes in New York for European anti-fascist refugees, which were designed to prepare them for participation in the American labor movement. She placed many of the exiles, who had extensive experience as labor officials, with union locals across the country, where they assisted in research and organizing work. During World War II, Sender worked for the Office of Strategic Services, and she became a U.S. citizen in 1943.

As AFL (1947–1950) and ICFTU (1950–1956) representative at the UN, Sender demanded an investigation of slave labor in the Soviet Union, which she charged constituted an essential part of the Soviet economy. Testifying before the UN Economic and Social Council in 1949, and again in 1950 and 1951, she provided documentation to support her claim that Soviet labor camp inmates were brutally mistreated. Drawing in part on information supplied by survivors of the camps, Sender demonstrated that scurvy was widespread among inmates because of their meager diet, that prisoners were forced to work in extreme cold in threadbare clothing, that Soviet authorities sent children to toil in the camps and sexually abused female inmates, and that they sometimes tortured prisoners to death. Sender noted that the Soviet government had designated Zionists and members of the Jewish Bund as among the so-called criminals to be deported for forced labor in the camps. In 1955 Sender also called on the UN to take action against Spain's fascist government for abolishing free trade unions and carrying out mass arrests of labor leaders.

During the 1950s, Sender lobbied on behalf of women's issues in international forums. As ICFTU representative at sessions of the UN Commission on the Status of Women, she denounced the denial in many countries of equal access for girls to secondary education and vocational training. She advocated equal pay for equal work as a matter of social justice—not only because without it, women constituted low-wage competition that undermined men's earning power. Sender was also a principal lecturer at an ICFTU workers' education project in France, instructing women trade unionists from twenty-four countries how to organize women workers and on the special problems they confronted in the workplace.

After her retirement as ICFTU representative at the UN, Sender applied for a research fellowship that the Conference on Jewish National Claims against Germany offered to victims of the Nazis. Sender proposed to study the relationship of Jews to the UN, including how that organization addressed the issues of antisemitism, genocide, and displaced persons. During the 1950s, Sender served on the Advisory Committee of the World Jewish Congress.

Sender remained single throughout her life, rejecting one marriage proposal in 1914 because it would be "too severe a strain" upon her "strong sense of independence" (Sender 1939). When she died in 1964, AFL–CIO president George Meany praised her as a "warrior for justice and human dignity all her life" (*AFL–CIO News,* July 4, 1964).

Stephen H. Norwood

References and Further Reading
Mann, Erika, and Klaus Mann. 1939. *Escape to Life.* Cambridge, MA: Riverside Press.

Norwood, Stephen H. 1984. "Toni Sender." In *Biographical Dictionary of American Labor,* edited by Gary M Fink, 512–513. Westport, CT: Greenwood Press.

Sender, Toni. 1939. *The Autobiography of a German Rebel.* New York: Vanguard Press.

Sender, Toni. 1950. "The Fight against Forced Labour before the United Nations." *Free Labour World* (August): 4–6.

"Sender, Toni." 1950. *Current Biography,* 525–527. New York: H. W. Wilson.

Toni Sender Papers. Madison: State Historical Society of Wisconsin.

Albert Shanker (1928–1997)

Educator, Trade Unionist, and Human Rights Advocate

Albert Shanker helped create the modern American teacher union movement in New York City, defended it against attacks from left-wing antisemites and right-wing ideologues, and promoted innovative public school reform as president of the United Federation of Teachers (UFT) in New York and the American Federation of Teachers (AFT) nationally. His combative style, willingness to engage in illegal teacher strikes, and philosophy of "tough liberalism" put him at odds with both traditional liberals and conservatives, prompting Woody Allen to spoof him in the 1973 movie, *Sleeper.* Allen's character awakens two hundred years in the future to learn that civilization was destroyed when "a man by the name of Albert Shanker got hold of a nuclear warhead" (Berger 1997). Over time, however, he became known as a thoughtful statesman on education issues, and he championed a number of leading reforms that

help shape public education today, including education standards, testing, and accountability; teacher professionalism; and public school choice and charter schools.

Albert Shanker was born on September 14, 1928, to Russian Jewish immigrants, Mamie (Burko) Shanker, a seamstress, and Morris Shanker, a newspaper deliverer. One of the only Jewish families in a rough Irish and Italian neighborhood in Queens, the Shankers faced intense antisemitism. An outcast because of his religion, the eight-year-old Al was delighted when a group of neighborhood boys asked him if he wanted to join their club. He was blindfolded for what they said was a club initiation—and then had a noose placed around his neck and was hoisted in a tree. The attempted lynching was only stopped by the intervention of a neighbor.

Public education provided a way out for Shanker, who began school knowing only Yiddish, but soon excelled and was admitted to the selective Stuyvesant High School, where he participated in debate. Shanker attended the University of Illinois in Champaign-Urbana, where he encountered additional discrimination. When he looked for housing, he was faced with signs reading, "No Jews or Negroes wanted." Shanker became a member of the Socialist Club, was active in the Congress of Racial Equality, and participated in sit-ins to integrate the local theaters and restaurants. In 1949, he returned to New York and began study for a doctorate in philosophy at Columbia University in a department that was filled with acolytes of John Dewey. By 1952, however, having completed all the requirements save for his dissertation, Shanker ran out of money, and he took a job as a substitute math teacher in the New York City public schools.

Struck by the low pay and the autocratic powers of the school principal, Shanker soon joined the Teachers Guild, a socialist but anti-Communist teacher trade union affiliated with the AFL–CIO. The Guild was one of 106 teacher unions and social clubs in New York City, divided by teaching level, race, ethnicity, religion, and region. Shanker worked with other Guild members to bring together various factions and create the UFT, affiliated with the AFT and the AFL–CIO. In the early 1960s, the UFT won the first collective bargaining agreement for teachers in the country, defeating forces like the nation's largest teacher organization, the National Education Association (NEA), which held that it was "unprofessional" for teachers to be in unions, to engage in collective bargaining, and to strike.

Albert Shanker, president of the United Federation of Teachers, presents a check to Martin Luther King Jr. for the Alabama voter registration drive. (Library of Congress)

Shanker's talents as a debater, public speaker, and organizer were recognized by his colleagues in 1964, when he was elected president of the UFT. Shanker and the UFT were leading progressive forces in trade unionism and supported the August 1963 March on Washington, despite the AFL–CIO's refusal to do so. Shanker participated in a march for voting rights in Selma, Alabama, and the UFT helped set up Freedom Schools for black children in Mississippi. In 1967, Shanker led a successful fourteen-day walkout of teachers striking for better wages, smaller class sizes, stricter school discipline policies, and a special program for teaching in ghetto schools. He was jailed for fifteen days for violating New York's anti-strike law for public employees. Martin Luther King Jr. sent Shanker a symbolic $10 check for bail.

In 1968, however, Shanker was at the center of a highly controversial teachers strike that split the traditional coalition of blacks, Jews, and labor in New York. Frustrated with

the pace of racial integration, and with the level of black student achievement, some African Americans sought to establish greater "community control" over education. With the help of the Ford Foundation, New York City established three demonstration projects to provide greater community input in schooling, including one experiment in the predominantly minority Brooklyn neighborhood of Ocean Hill–Brownsville. In May 1968, the local governing board, which was predominantly black, attempted to dismiss eighteen white educators (and one black mistakenly included), most of whom were Jewish. When the community board failed to provide an adequate rationale for the dismissals, Shanker engaged in a series of three strikes, lasting a total of fifty-five days, leaving more than 1 million New York City public school students out of school through November 1968.

While Shanker was attacked as a racist for opposing members of the black community on the issue, in fact the controversy revealed a virulent strain of racism and anti-semitism among some extremists in the black community. Crowds of community control activists sought to block white teachers from teaching in ghetto schools, some of them yelling antisemitic epithets. At one point, a black teacher appeared on a radio program and read a poem from a student that was dedicated to Shanker: "Hey, Jew boy, with the yarmulke on your head / You pale faced Jew boy—I wish you were dead" (Podair 2002).

At a time when New York's Mayor John Lindsay was willing to go along with virtually any demand in order to prevent a riot, Shanker stood firm against the notion that teachers could be fired without due process, and against a racial determinism that said black children needed black teachers. In the coming years, Shanker opposed efforts by liberals to provide preferences to minority candidates in education and employment. In doing so, he differed from many conservatives, who offered no alternative to quotas. Shanker championed, among other things, a program of career ladders to help teachers' aides (most of them black and Latino) go back to school and get the training required to become full-fledged teachers.

In December 1970, hoping to improve the public's view of teacher unionism, Shanker decided to purchase advertisement space in the Week in Review Section of the Sunday *New York Times*. He called the column "Where We Stand," and for more than a quarter of a century, until his death, Shanker produced some 1,300 articles on topics involving education, trade unionism, foreign policy, human rights, and politics. The column was widely read among educators and policymakers and was indexed by the *Times* like regular news stories.

In 1974, Shanker was elected president of the national American Federation of Teachers (AFT) and also remained as president of the New York UFT for another decade. In 1975, he played a key role during New York City's fiscal crisis. With the city on the edge of bankruptcy, it was Shanker's decision to purchase city bonds with the UFT's pension funds that kept the city from defaulting.

Shanker was also active in the AFL–CIO, serving on the executive council and, eventually, as chairman of the international affairs committee. A strong anti-Communist, Shanker took a hard line during the 1970s and 1980s, when many liberals were more open to relations with the Soviet Union and China. He joined the board of the National Endowment for Democracy, which was established during Ronald Reagan's presidency, to help build democratic institutions (including trade unions) abroad. During this period, Shanker hired at the UFT and AFT many members of the Social Democrats, USA, a small organization that took a hard-line anti-Communist approach on foreign policy, was skeptical of racial quotas, and favored pro-union economic policies. In a departure from the predictable story line, in which a former Jewish socialist turns neoconservative, Shanker sided with neoconservatives only on foreign policy and certain social policies, but never yielded on his support of trade unionism, progressive health care policy, the minimum wage, and the like. Shanker angered conservatives, for example, in the 1980 Democratic presidential primaries, when his union endorsed Ted Kennedy as its candidate.

During an era when union membership sank nationally, Shanker saw the number of AFT members rise from 71,000 in 1960 to nearly 1 million at the time of his death in 1997, making the AFT one of the largest unions in the AFL–CIO. But as teacher power grew, it provoked a rising chorus of complaints that teacher unions were concerned primarily with parochial interests as opposed to the education of children. Teacher unions were chided for opposing education choice for parents, efforts to fire inadequate teachers, and systems of rewarding high-quality teachers with extra pay.

In the 1980s, Shanker grew concerned that, if teacher unions did not respond to these arguments, public education itself might not ultimately survive, and he began an effort to fashion a new, broader brand of teacher unionism. This new approach stood in sharp contrast to the strategy of the larger teacher union, the NEA, which followed the AFT's lead on collective bargaining in the late 1960s, but which now denied that there were problems in education and resisted reforms.

The pivotal moment came in 1983, when the National Commission on Excellence in Education issued its report, *A Nation at Risk*. The NEA and most of the education establishment blasted the report, which warned of a "rising tide of mediocrity" in American public schools. But Shanker chose to embrace the document, arguing that its critique of public education was basically right, and that reforms were necessary to save public schooling.

In a series of speeches in 1985, Shanker advocated a host of education reforms that were previously unthinkable for the head of a union to embrace. In response to the demand for private school vouchers, Shanker proposed instead that choice be provided to parents within the public school system and through the creation of charter schools, publicly funded schools that are given greater educational flexibility than traditional public schools are allowed. To counter the idea that unions protected bad teachers, Shanker endorsed the practice of "peer review," in which teams of high-quality teachers would evaluate their colleagues, provide counseling and support for struggling teachers, and terminate contracts with those who did not improve. To those who called for "merit pay" for teachers, Shanker proposed the creation of the National Board of Professional Teaching Standards, which set out a system for recognizing outstanding teachers, whom local districts could reward with greater pay. Most important, Shanker pushed hard for the creation of a system of education standards, testing, and accountability, a version of which is now part of federal law.

These reforms were all meant to save a system of public schooling that Shanker believed was absolutely essential in a democracy. He wrote, "Whenever the problems of school reform seem especially tough, I think about this. I think about what public education gave me—a kid who couldn't even speak English when I entered first grade. I think about what it has given me and can give to countless numbers of other kids like me. And I know that keeping public education together is worth whatever it takes" (Shanker 1997).

When he died in 1997, Shanker was eulogized by then-president Bill Clinton and Vice President Al Gore as a giant in the fields of labor, education, and civil rights. He was posthumously awarded the Presidential Medal of Freedom. Journalist Sara Mosle called Shanker "our Dewey, the most important American educator in half a century" (Mosle 1997).

Richard D. Kahlenberg

References and Further Reading
Berger, Joseph. 1997. "Albert Shanker, 68, Combative Leader of Teachers, Dies." *New York Times* (February 23): A1.

Kahlenberg, Richard D. 2002. "Remembering Al Shanker: Five Years after His Death, Shanker's Tough Liberalism Looks Better Than Ever." *Education Week* XXI,24 (February 27): 36, 39.

Kahlenberg, Richard D. 2003. "Philosopher or King? The Ideas and Strategy of Legendary AFT Leader Albert Shanker." *Education Next* 3,3 (Summer): 34–39.

Kahlenberg, Richard D. 2007. *Tough Liberal: Albert Shanker and the Battles over Schools, Unions, Race, and Democracy.* New York: Columbia University Press.

Mosle, Sara. 1997. "Where He Stood." *The New Republic* 216,11 (March 17): 12.

Podair, Jerald E. 2002. *The Strike That Changed New York: Blacks, Whites, and the Ocean Hill–Brownsville Crisis.* New Haven, CT: Yale University Press.

Shanker, Albert. 1997. "Keeping Public Education Together." Where We Stand Column. *American Educator* 21,1 and 2 (Spring/Summer): 112.

Index

Reference